Harnessing Emotion AI for Customer Support and Employee Wellbeing

Jihene Mrabet
Amity University, Dubai, UAE

Soumaya Boudagga
Amity University, India

Ridhima Sharma
Vivekananda Institute of Professional Studies, India

Rohit Bansal
Rockford College, Australia

IGI Global
Scientific Publishing
Publishing Tomorrow's Research Today

Vice President of Editorial	Melissa Wagner
Director of Acquisitions	Mikaela Felty
Director of Book Development	Jocelynn Hessler
Production Manager	Mike Brehm
Cover Design	Jose Rosado

Published in the United States of America by
IGI Global Scientific Publishing
701 East Chocolate Avenue
Hershey, PA, 17033, USA
Tel: 717-533-8845
Fax: 717-533-7115
Website: https://www.igi-global.com E-mail: cust@igi-global.com

Library of Congress Cataloging-in-Publication Data

Names: Mrabet, Jihene, 1984- editor
Title: Harnessing emotion AI for customer support and employee wellbeing / [edited by] Jihene Mrabet, Soumaya Boudagga, Ridhima Sharma, Rohit Bansal.
Description: Hershey, PA : IGI Global Scientific Publishing, [2026] | Includes bibliographical references and index. | Summary: "This book aims to explore how emotion AI can be strategically leveraged to enhance both customer support and employee well-being, creating more empathetic, efficient, and emotionally intelligent interactions"-- Provided by publisher.
Identifiers: LCCN 2025022198 (print) | LCCN 2025022199 (ebook) | ISBN 9798337336589 hardcover | ISBN 9798337336596 paperback | ISBN 9798337336602 ebook
Subjects: LCSH: Customer services--Technological innovations | Organizational behavior | Artificial intelligence--Business applications
Classification: LCC HF5415.5 .H289 2026 (print) | LCC HF5415.5 (ebook) | DDC 658.8/12--dc23/eng/20250912
LC record available at https://lccn.loc.gov/2025022198
LC ebook record available at https://lccn.loc.gov/2025022199

British Cataloguing in Publication Data
A Cataloguing in Publication record for this book is available from the British Library.

Table of Contents

Detailed Table of Contents

design and governance considerations. The chapter provides an interdisciplinary blueprint of Emotion-AI systems that safeguard autonomy, minimise harm and develop trustworthy interactions.

Emotion AI—also known as affective computing—is rapidly transforming how organizations engage with customers and support employees, enabling digital systems to detect and respond to human emotions through facial expressions, vocal cues, physiological signals, and behavioral data. While this technology offers the promise of more personalized, empathetic, and emotionally intelligent interactions, it also raises profound ethical challenges. These include risks of emotional manipulation, violations of privacy, algorithmic bias, cultural insensitivity, and a lack of transparency and informed consent. This chapter critically examines the ethical landscape of Emotion AI, particularly in the contexts of customer support and employee wellbeing. First, it explains the main ideas and applications of Emotion AI and then it studies four main issues: manipulation and autonomy, surveillance and privacy, bias and inclusivity and opacity and consent. Examining the EU AI Act, the chapter analyzes how existing governance solutions do or do not deal with these issues.

Technologies that can recognize, evaluate, and react to human emotions are referred to as emotion artificial intelligence (Emotion AI), also known as affective computingusing biometric data such as facial expressions, vocal tones, and physiological signals.The field started at least in 1995 with the publication of "Affective Computing," written by Rosalind Picard, a professor at the MIT Media lab. It is increasingly being adopted in fields like healthcare, education, marketing, law enforcement, and workplace monitoring to enhance decision-making and personalize user experiences. However, while Emotion AI holds immense promise, its growing deployment raises critical ethical concerns. These include significant threats to privacy and data protection, particularly when emotional data is collected without explicit consent or awareness. The chapter will conclude by emphasizing the importance of global cooperation and interdisciplinary collaborationto guarantee the responsible development and application of Emotion AI.

This chapter explores the potential of virtual reality (VR)-based interventions in reducing stress and burnout among working individuals while enhancing employee well-being. It examines psychological benefits, implementation strategies, and the impact of VR on mental and physical health in workplace settings. The chapter discusses evidence from corporate environments, healthcare, psychiatric wards, and military contexts. Drawing on recent research, it outlines VR's role in improving stress management, personal resources, and diversity. It also considers workplace design, user acceptance, and ethical concerns related to adoption of VR interventions. By integrating current findings with practical insights, the chapter offers a comprehensive overview of VR's contribution to workplace wellness.

Digital modernization of the workplace has increased the transition from traditional working to teleworking and hybrid contexts. Although digital tools have enhanced efficiency and connection, in some cases they create psychological/physical separation or exposure fatigue and communication barriers. Emotional intelligence consisting in the ability to perceive, understand and manage emotions, has been increasingly recognized as one of the major prerequisites for success in online environments. This study identified opportunities where improving EI might improve virtual workplaces through enhanced communication collaboration and employee wellbeing. A mixed-method approach was performed to explore stress management effective leadership remote team dynamics and how organizations can foster human-centered sustainable digital work culture through digital emotional intelligence in this study. The results provide evidence-based suggestions for how to

Emotion Artificial Intelligence is a domain of artificial intelligence focusing on discovering, evaluating and reciprocating to human emotions using data extracted from human`s facial expressions, vocal sounds, body language and physiological communication which aims to associate the gap between human emotions and machines. Emotion AI is diverse in various domains such as healthcare, education, marketing and security. Even though there are numerous advantages of AI, the deployment of Emotion AI elevates ethical and societal challenges which have been discussed and highlighted with key issues including data privacy, algorithmic bias and potential misuse in inspection or manipulation. This chapter insights and sketches on current advancements, practical applications and ethical implications of Emotion AI, recommending a balanced approach that nurtures innovation while protecting human rights. Emotion recognition, affective computing, human-computer interaction, and responsible AI development are central themes explored in this study.

The modern workplace is increasingly influenced by emotional dynamics, where unresolved conflicts can hinder team cohesion and productivity. This study examines the role of Emotion AI—technologies that detect and interpret human emotions—in enhancing conflict resolution. By integrating tools like sentiment analysis, facial recognition, and voice modulation, Emotion AI uncovers hidden tensions and enables timely interventions. The research highlights how Emotion AI fosters emotional intelligence, psychological safety, and fairness by promoting empathetic and inclusive resolution processes. It also supports employee training in emotional regulation and awareness. Employing a descriptive approach organizational case studies, the study offers practical insights into how Emotion AI bridges the gap between emotional understanding and conflict management. It calls for ethical implementation that

Preface

One of the most important concerns today is including emotional intelligence in digital systems as artificial intelligence profoundly changes many sectors. A strong area of technology produced by this evolution is artificial intelligence (AI), which helps machines to identify, understand, and react to human emotions. This book tries to examine how this new type of artificial intelligence is being applied to raise consumer service and employee welfare. Usually, consumer service has driven technical innovation mostly. From predictive analytics to automated chatbots, companies are seeking ways to raise user responsiveness and satisfaction. But traditional systems typically lack the human element—that which enables one to grasp the emotions underlying a compliment, complaint, or grievance. Emotional artificial intelligence closes this important gap by allowing systems to customise interactions depending on both emotional background and logical framework and react sympathetically. This book offers a thorough overview of how more customised, human-centric, responsive technology from emotion AI is improving consumer service.

In highly demanding environments with highly advanced technology, employee mental and emotional health is especially very important. Regular lowering of employee morale and output leads to burnout, stress, and disengagement. Artificial intelligence for emotions supports active monitoring of emotional states, weariness or discomfort detection, and fast development of quick support intervention. We look at how progressive companies are using emotion AI in wellness programmes, team management approaches, and HR to create more emotionally sensitive and healthy workplaces.

The multidisciplinary approach of this book distinguishes it. It addresses concepts from data science, user experience design, ethics, organisational behaviour, and psychology. The broad view that the junction of several disciplines provides helps one to see both a technical development and a force changing our interactions with each other and self-care using artificial intelligence. Professionals in academics, marketing, HR, artificial intelligence development, and mental health advocacy will find great use for this book.

CHAPTER OVERVIEW

- **Chapter 1** sets the foundation by examining core applications of Emotion AI in customer interactions, showing how emotion-sensing systems improve personalization and efficiency, while also raising early ethical flags.
- **Chapter 2** dives into sentiment analysis as a tool for customer service innovation, detailing how multimodal inputs and real-time insights redefine proactive engagement strategies.
- **Chapter 3** continues the focus on sentiment analysis, surveying techniques and tools that are transforming customer feedback and engagement practices, while also grappling with limitations such as sarcasm and multilingual complexity.
- **Chapter 4** introduces the concept of synthetic empathy, unpacking the psychological influence of emotionally responsive bots and the risks of emotional manipulation through compelling case studies.
- **Chapter 5** provides a focused ethical analysis of Emotion AI, exploring four key issues: manipulation, surveillance, bias, and transparency, and interrogating current regulatory responses.
- **Chapter 6** expands on these ethical challenges by emphasizing the global stakes of emotion recognition technologies and proposes the need for interdisciplinary governance and policy alignment.
- **Chapter 7** shifts focus to Fintech, exploring how Emotion AI intersects with data privacy and algorithmic decision-making, providing real-world insights from user interviews.
- **Chapter 8** blends emotional intelligence theory with AI, offering a visionary yet grounded outlook on future developments, policy frameworks, and emotionally adaptive AI systems.
- **Chapter 9** revisits the mental health dimension of AI, questioning whether AI in therapeutic settings genuinely heals or imitates human care, while offering ethical evaluation frameworks.
- **Chapter 10** explores how AI agents are transforming customer service by balancing automation and the human touch, offering examples from industry leaders like Apple and Salesforce.
- **Chapter 11** delves into VR therapy for employee wellbeing, illustrating how immersive tech can reduce stress and promote resilience in high-pressure workplace environments.
- **Chapter 12** tackles remote work and emotional intelligence, analyzing how EI can strengthen digital collaboration and mitigate psychological strain in hybrid environments.

- **Chapter 13** investigates how Emotion AI tools are revolutionizing corporate training and leadership, emphasizing real-time feedback and emotionally aware learning platforms.
- **Chapter 14** builds on leadership development by showcasing how AI-driven models personalize learning, improve resilience, and integrate emotional insights into strategic management.
- **Chapter 15** offers a holistic view of Emotion AI's use in leadership and training, emphasizing responsible innovation, the risks of misuse, and frameworks for ethical AI design.
- **Chapter 16** concludes by focusing on conflict resolution in the modern workplace, proposing Emotion AI as a tool for promoting emotional intelligence, fairness, and inclusion.

Editing this book has delighted me intellectually as well as personally. It results from a curiosity about how technology could both help and sympathise with people while also automating and accelerating tasks. Among the most successful tools for humanising technology seems to be sensibly evolved and used emotional artificial intelligence. I have been working at the of digital transformation and human behaviour. This book will be very valuable for anyone looking to raise customer satisfaction, protect staff mental health, or look at the most current artificial intelligence advancements. Artificial intelligence combined with emotions benefits people, companies, and society as a whole.

Jihene Mrabet
Amity University, Dubai, UAE

Soumaya Boudagga
Amity University, Dubai, UAE

Ridhima Sharma
Vivekananda Institute of Professional Studies, India

Rohit Bansal
Rockford College, Australia

Chapter 1
Applications of Emotion AI in Customer Interactions and Support

Ferah Diba İzgi
https://orcid.org/0009-0003-3048-0391
Cyprus Science University, Cyprus

ABSTRACT

By leveraging technologies such as facial expression recognition, speech analysis, and text sentiment analysis, Emotion AI enables machines to understand and react to the emotional states of individuals in a more personalized and empathetic manner. This chapter explores the various applications of Emotion AI in customer service and support, emphasizing how it can significantly improve both customer satisfaction and operational efficiency. Emotion AI is widely utilized in automated customer support systems, including chatbots, call centers, and virtual assistants, where it detects and analyzes emotional cues to provide contextually appropriate responses. Despite its benefits, the application of Emotion AI raises several ethical concerns. These include issues surrounding privacy, the potential for emotional manipulation and biases in emotion recognition, which may lead to unequal treatment across different demographics. Consequently, the ethical deployment of Emotion AI requires businesses to establish clear guidelines and adhere to ethical principles to avoid misuse.

DOI: 10.4018/979-8-3373-3658-9.ch001

1. INTRODUCTION

As artificial intelligence (AI) continues to evolve, its integration into human-computer interactions has expanded beyond traditional logic-based functionalities to include more human-like capabilities. One of the most exciting developments in this regard is Emotion Artificial Intelligence (Emotion AI), which refers to AI systems that can detect, interpret, and respond to human emotions (Picard, 1997). Emotion AI, also known as affective computing, is revolutionizing fields such as customer service, healthcare, education, and entertainment by providing emotionally intelligent machines capable of engaging in meaningful interactions with humans (Calvo & D'Mello, 2010).

The importance of emotional intelligence in human communication has been well documented in psychology and communication studies, where it has been shown that emotional awareness is a critical component of effective communication (Goleman, 1995; Mayer & Salovey, 1997). However, until the advent of Emotion AI, this dimension of communication was largely inaccessible to machines. Traditional AI systems—such as rule-based chatbots and automated customer service systems—were designed to perform specific tasks without an understanding of the emotional states of users. While these systems may provide efficient solutions to transactional problems, they often fall short in providing the empathy and emotional engagement that human interactions typically offer (Gentsch, 2019). Emotion AI addresses this gap by equipping machines with the ability to recognize, process, and respond to emotional cues, thereby enhancing the quality of interaction between humans and technology (McDuff & El Kaliouby, 2017).

1.1. The Rise of Emotion AI in Customer Service

Customer service is a domain that inherently involves emotional exchanges. Customers engage with service representatives when they experience problems or seek assistance, often bringing with them a wide range of emotional states, including frustration, confusion, or satisfaction (Sharma & Ahuja, 2022). In such contexts, the ability of AI to recognize and appropriately respond to these emotions can significantly impact the quality of the interaction and, by extension, the overall customer experience (Pradeep et al., 2019). Traditionally, automated customer service tools like chatbots and voice assistants have struggled with recognizing emotional nuances in customer communications. This has often resulted in interactions that feel impersonal and disconnected, reducing customer satisfaction and loyalty (Picard, 1997).

Emotion AI promises to change this dynamic by offering emotionally intelligent systems capable of detecting affective signals—such as tone of voice, facial expressions, body language, and text sentiment—that provide deeper insights into customers' emotional states (Calvo & D'Mello, 2010). By integrating these emotional cues into automated customer interactions, Emotion AI has the potential to make these exchanges more empathetic, human-like, and contextually relevant (Gentsch, 2019). For instance, real-time sentiment analysis of customer communications, including chats, emails, and phone calls, allows AI systems to identify stress, frustration, or dissatisfaction, prompting the system to respond in ways that de-escalate negative emotions or escalate issues to human agents when necessary (Schuller et al., 2011).

Emotion AI is already being utilized in various customer service settings, from call centers to virtual assistants, with the goal of creating more personalized and effective interactions. For example, chatbots powered by Emotion AI are capable of understanding not only the content of a customer's inquiry but also their emotional tone, allowing the bot to respond with greater empathy or offer reassurance (Gentsch, 2019). In call centers, Emotion AI technologies are employed to monitor customers' emotional states in real time, guiding agents in their responses and ensuring that customer interactions are handled with empathy and care (Sharma & Ahuja, 2022). Additionally, virtual assistants are becoming more emotionally intelligent, using facial recognition and speech analytics to gauge the emotional content of customer inquiries and modify their responses accordingly (McDuff & El Kaliouby, 2017).

1.2. Technological Foundations of Emotion AI

The development of Emotion AI is based on advances in multiple technologies, including facial expression recognition, speech analysis, natural language processing (NLP), and biometric sensing. Early research on facial expression recognition by Ekman and Friesen (1978) laid the groundwork for how facial movements can be used to infer emotions. Facial Action Coding System (FACS), developed by Ekman and Friesen, is still one of the most widely used systems for analyzing facial expressions in emotional AI applications. Emotion AI systems leverage machine learning algorithms to analyze subtle changes in facial expressions and match these to specific emotional states, enabling more accurate emotional understanding (Barrett et al., 2019).

In addition to visual cues, speech analysis plays a pivotal role in Emotion AI. Vocal tone, speech rate, pitch variation, and even pauses in speech are significant indicators of a person's emotional state (Schuller et al., 2011). AI systems use these vocal indicators to detect emotions such as anger, frustration, and happiness, providing the system with valuable information about how to tailor its responses. Similarly, natural language processing (NLP) has enabled machines to understand and analyze the sentiment of written or spoken text, allowing Emotion AI systems to classify emotions from a customer's written or verbal communication (Pang & Lee, 2008).

Recent innovations in biometric sensing have also contributed to the growth of Emotion AI. Technologies such as heart rate monitoring, skin conductance, and eye-tracking can provide real-time data on physiological reactions to stimuli, which can be used in conjunction with other emotional cues to enhance emotional understanding (Cowie & Douglas-Cowie, 2021).

1.3. Operational Benefits of Emotion AI in Customer Service

Emotion AI presents several operational benefits for businesses. The ability to detect and respond to emotions enables more efficient and effective customer service, which can lead to higher customer satisfaction and loyalty (Pradeep et al., 2019). By recognizing when a customer is frustrated or upset, Emotion AI systems can take immediate action to address concerns, either by adjusting the tone of the conversation or by escalating the issue to a human agent who is better equipped to handle sensitive situations (Gentsch, 2019). This results in reduced customer churn and increased customer retention, both of which are critical factors in the success of customer service operations (Sharma & Ahuja, 2022).

Moreover, the automation of emotion-driven responses in customer service processes can improve the efficiency of support teams by reducing the time it takes to handle routine inquiries. Emotion AI enables real-time decision-making, allowing automated systems to respond more quickly and accurately to customers' needs. This leads to a faster response time and a more streamlined customer service experience (Pradeep et al., 2019).

1.4. Ethical Concerns and Challenges

Despite the promising benefits, the implementation of Emotion AI in customer service also raises several ethical concerns. One of the most pressing issues is privacy. The collection and analysis of emotional data, especially through facial recognition and voice analysis, can be seen as an infringement on personal privacy (Crawford & Calo, 2016). As customers may not always be aware of the emotional data being captured, the risk of data misuse and informed consent becomes a critical concern (Morley et al., 2020).

Another ethical challenge is the potential for emotional manipulation. As businesses harness Emotion AI to tailor their marketing and customer service strategies based on emotional cues, there is a risk that these technologies could be used to exploit vulnerable customers for commercial gain. This raises important questions about the boundaries of acceptable emotional influence and the potential for AI to manipulate customer emotions in ways that prioritize business interests over customer well-being (Cowie & Douglas-Cowie, 2021).

Furthermore, algorithmic bias remains a significant challenge in Emotion AI systems. Emotion recognition technologies have been shown to perform unevenly across different demographic groups, with studies indicating that these systems may be less accurate when recognizing the emotions of people from diverse ethnic, gender, and cultural backgrounds (Barrett et al., 2019). This can lead to inequitable treatment and perpetuate existing biases within AI systems.

1.5. Future Directions and Trends

The future of Emotion AI in customer service is promising, with ongoing advancements in deep learning, multimodal emotion recognition, and human-AI collaboration. Deep learning techniques are enabling Emotion AI systems to become more sophisticated in their understanding of emotional nuances, recognizing even subtle emotional expressions and complex emotional states (Zhao et al., 2021). As these systems become more accurate, the potential for Emotion AI to be integrated into multiple customer touchpoints—from online chat platforms to social media interactions—becomes increasingly viable.

Moreover, the role of human-agent collaboration will likely play a pivotal part in the future of Emotion AI. While AI can provide valuable emotional insights in real-time, human agents will continue to play an essential role in addressing emotionally sensitive situations. Emotion AI can help human agents by providing real-time data on customer sentiment, guiding them on how to respond with greater empathy and understanding (Tao & Tan, 2005).

In summary, Emotion AI represents a significant advancement in artificial intelligence technologies, offering businesses the opportunity to transform customer service by making it more emotionally intelligent. As this technology evolves, its integration into customer support systems will deepen, requiring careful consideration of its ethical, technical, and social implications. Future research will need to address these challenges while exploring the potential of Emotion AI to create more personalized, efficient, and empathetic customer interactions.

2. LITERATURE REVIEW

Emotion Artificial Intelligence (Emotion AI) is a growing subfield of artificial intelligence that focuses on enabling machines to detect, interpret, and respond to human emotional states through multimodal data such as facial expressions, vocal tone, and text sentiment. Foundational work by Ekman and Friesen (1978) on facial expressions and later developments in affective computing by Picard (1997) laid the groundwork for Emotion AI systems capable of recognizing and simulating emotional intelligence.

The application of Emotion AI in customer service has gained significant traction in recent years. Automated customer support systems, including chatbots and virtual assistants, increasingly utilize emotional recognition to deliver more empathetic and context-aware interactions (McDuff & el Kaliouby, 2017). Studies indicate that emotionally intelligent AI systems can significantly improve customer satisfaction, enhance loyalty, and reduce churn rates (Pradeep et al., 2019; Sharma & Ahuja, 2022). These technologies allow businesses to optimize operational efficiency by enabling faster, emotion-informed responses and reducing human workload (Gentsch, 2019).

In addition to the operational benefits, the integration of Emotion AI raises important ethical questions. The processing of sensitive emotional data introduces potential risks related to user privacy and data security (Crawford & Calo, 2016). Scholars have also voiced concerns about emotional manipulation, where commercial entities may exploit emotional cues to influence customer behavior (Cowie & Douglas-Cowie, 2021). Moreover, algorithmic bias remains a persistent challenge; emotion recognition systems may underperform across gender, cultural, or ethnic groups, potentially leading to unequal or discriminatory outcomes (Barrett et al., 2019). To address these concerns, researchers call for transparent algorithmic practices, inclusive data sets, and robust ethical guidelines for deployment (Morley et al., 2020).

Looking forward, advancements in machine learning, particularly deep learning and multimodal emotion recognition, are expected to enhance the subtlety and accuracy of Emotion AI systems (Zhao et al., 2021). Future developments also point to increased human-AI collaboration in customer service, where real-time emotional insights assist human agents in handling sensitive interactions more effectively (Tao & Tan, 2005). As Emotion AI becomes more integrated into omnichannel customer touchpoints, ensuring a consistent and empathetic user experience will remain a central goal.

In summary, existing literature highlights the transformative potential of Emotion AI in customer service, while simultaneously emphasizing the importance of addressing its ethical, technical, and social challenges. Continued interdisciplinary research is essential to ensuring responsible innovation in this rapidly evolving field.

3. METHODOLOGY

This chapter investigates the applications, benefits, challenges, and ethical implications of Emotion Artificial Intelligence (Emotion AI) in customer service. The research follows a mixed-methods approach, combining both qualitative and quantitative techniques to provide a comprehensive understanding of how Emotion AI is implemented, its impact, and the ethical considerations associated with its use. The methodology is structured in three key components: a systematic literature review (SLR), case study analysis, and surveys with industry professionals and customers.

3.1. Systematic Literature Review (SLR)

The first step in this research involved conducting a systematic literature review (SLR) to synthesize existing knowledge about Emotion AI in customer service settings. SLR is a widely accepted method for aggregating research findings from multiple studies to identify trends, methodologies, and gaps in the field (Tranfield et al., 2003). The SLR approach followed the guidelines outlined by Kitchenham (2004), which include a rigorous search strategy, inclusion/exclusion criteria, data extraction, and quality assessment.

3.1.1. Search Strategy

To ensure comprehensive coverage of the topic, a thorough search was conducted across multiple academic databases: Google Scholar, IEEE Xplore, Scopus, and SpringerLink. The search terms included "Emotion AI," "affective computing," "emotion recognition," "AI customer service," "customer satisfaction," and "emotion-based automation." Articles published in peer-reviewed journals and conferences from 2010 to the present were included to capture the most current research. The search was further refined to focus on studies specifically related to the use of Emotion AI in customer service.

3.1.2. Inclusion and Exclusion Criteria

The criteria for inclusion were: (a) peer-reviewed research articles, (b) studies discussing the application of Emotion AI in customer service, (c) publications that addressed technological, operational, and ethical aspects. Excluded were (a) non-peer-reviewed materials, (b) articles that focused solely on theoretical models without empirical data, and (c) studies that did not specifically address Emotion AI or customer service applications.

A total of 60 articles were included in the review. These articles were then categorized into four themes: foundational technologies, practical applications in customer service, benefits and challenges, and ethical considerations.

3.1.3. Data Extraction and Quality Assessment

For each of the included articles, key information was extracted, including: (a) the technology or system used (e.g., facial recognition, sentiment analysis, etc.), (b) the application context (e.g., chatbot, call center), (c) the outcomes or impact of Emotion AI (e.g., customer satisfaction, operational efficiency), and (d) any ethical or privacy concerns addressed. The quality of the studies was assessed using a Quality Assessment Framework based on criteria such as sample size, methodological rigor, and relevance to the research question (Bryman, 2016).

3.2. Case Study Analysis

Following the systematic literature review, case study analysis was used to examine how Emotion AI technologies are applied in real-world customer service environments. Case studies are effective for exploring complex phenomena in context (Yin, 2017), and they allow for a deeper understanding of the challenges and benefits of implementing Emotion AI. Three organizations were selected for this study, representing diverse industries: a telecommunications company, an e-commerce giant, and a financial institution. These organizations were chosen because they had adopted Emotion AI systems in their customer service operations.

3.2.1. Data Collection

Data for the case study analysis were gathered through a combination of qualitative methods:

1. **Interviews**: Semi-structured interviews were conducted with key stakeholders, including customer service managers, AI project leads, and customer experience managers. These interviews aimed to understand the motivations behind implementing Emotion AI, the operational challenges encountered, and the perceived benefits.
2. **Document Analysis**: Internal documents, such as performance reports, training manuals, and system evaluations, were reviewed to gather insights on the deployment and effectiveness of Emotion AI systems. These documents provided context for understanding how Emotion AI is integrated into the broader customer service framework.
3. **Observational Data**: Observations of customer service interactions were conducted, focusing on call center interactions, AI-driven chatbot conversations, and virtual assistant communications. These interactions were analyzed for

emotional tone and customer responses, providing valuable data on the real-time application of Emotion AI.

3.2.2. Analytical Framework

The data collected from interviews, documents, and observations were analyzed using thematic analysis (Braun & Clarke, 2006). This involved identifying recurring patterns related to the operationalization of Emotion AI, the challenges faced during deployment, and the outcomes achieved. A coding framework was developed to categorize key themes such as "customer satisfaction," "employee adaptation," "AI performance," and "ethical concerns." The case study findings were then compared across the three organizations to identify commonalities and differences in their experiences with Emotion AI.

3.3. Surveys of Industry Professionals and Customers

To complement the SLR and case studies, surveys were conducted with two distinct groups: industry professionals and customers. The surveys aimed to gather both quantitative and qualitative data on the perceptions of Emotion AI in customer service, focusing on the effectiveness, satisfaction levels, and ethical concerns.

3.3.1. Survey Design

Two separate surveys were designed for each group:

1. **Industry Professionals Survey**: This survey targeted customer service managers, AI developers, and operational staff who have implemented Emotion AI systems. It included questions about the deployment process, technological challenges, perceived benefits, and ethical concerns.
2. **Customer Survey**: This survey focused on customers who have interacted with Emotion AI-powered customer service systems, such as chatbots, virtual assistants, and call centers. Questions addressed their experiences with empathy and emotional responses, satisfaction with AI interactions, and perceptions of privacy and data security.

3.3.2. Sampling Strategy

The industry professionals survey was distributed to 250 professionals from various organizations, with a focus on those working directly with Emotion AI systems in customer service. The response rate was 54%, with 135 completed responses received.

The customer survey was distributed to 600 individuals who had used Emotion AI-driven customer service systems within the last six months. A total of 375 responses were received, representing a diverse sample in terms of age, gender, and geographic location.

3.3.3. Data Analysis

The quantitative data from both surveys were analyzed using descriptive statistics (e.g., mean, standard deviation) and inferential statistics (e.g., chi-square tests, t-tests). These analyses helped identify significant trends and correlations between variables such as customer satisfaction, emotional response, and the perceived ethical use of AI. For the qualitative data from open-ended questions, thematic analysis was conducted to identify common themes and sentiments regarding the ethical implications of Emotion AI, its operational benefits, and customer trust in AI systems.

3.4. Ethical Considerations

The ethical implications of Emotion AI were a central focus throughout the research process. Given the sensitive nature of emotion-related data, several ethical guidelines were followed:

1. **Informed Consent**: All survey participants and interviewees were fully informed about the study's purpose, their voluntary participation, and how their data would be used. Participants were provided with consent forms, which they signed before taking part.
2. **Confidentiality and Anonymity**: All personal identifiers were anonymized, and responses were stored in a secure database. Participants' identities were kept confidential, and no identifying information was published.
3. **Data Security**: All data were handled in accordance with the General Data Protection Regulation (GDPR) guidelines, ensuring the ethical use of emotional and personal data. The emotional insights gathered through customer interactions were anonymized to prevent misuse.

4. **Ethical Use of Emotion Data**: The study addressed concerns about emotional manipulation and privacy violations by discussing these issues in both the case study interviews and the surveys. The ethical use of Emotion AI, particularly with respect to emotional data, was evaluated throughout the research.

3.5. Limitations

While this methodology offers valuable insights, there are several limitations to consider. The case studies focused on only three organizations, which may not fully represent the diversity of businesses adopting Emotion AI. Additionally, although the surveys gathered a wide range of responses, the focus on larger companies may limit the generalizability of the findings to smaller enterprises. Future research could expand the scope of the case studies to include a broader range of industries and explore smaller-scale applications of Emotion AI in customer service.

4. FINDINGS

The findings of this study provide a comprehensive view of the applications, benefits, challenges, and ethical considerations of Emotion AI in customer service. By synthesizing data collected through a systematic literature review, case study analysis, and surveys, several key themes have emerged. These themes include the effectiveness of Emotion AI in improving customer satisfaction, the operational efficiency gains, challenges in AI deployment, and ethical concerns regarding privacy and emotional manipulation.

4.1. Effectiveness of Emotion AI in Enhancing Customer Satisfaction

One of the most prominent findings of this study is the significant impact of Emotion AI on customer satisfaction. Across all three case studies and survey data, it was consistently reported that Emotion AI systems—particularly those utilizing facial recognition, sentiment analysis, and speech emotion recognition—improved the quality of customer interactions.

For instance, in the telecommunications case study, a call center leveraging Emotion AI systems reported a 25% increase in customer satisfaction scores. Agents using real-time emotional insights were able to tailor their responses to customer emotions, leading to a more personalized experience. Similarly, the e-commerce company saw a 30% improvement in customer feedback scores after introducing Emotion AI-driven chatbots that detected customer frustration and adapted their responses accordingly. Customers felt that the systems understood their emotional states, which made them more willing to engage and stay loyal to the company.

The customer survey corroborated these findings, with 72% of respondents indicating that they had a more positive experience when interacting with customer service systems that incorporated Emotion AI. Respondents specifically appreciated the system's ability to recognize frustration or confusion, enabling it to provide more empathetic and contextually appropriate responses. This aligns with existing literature, which highlights that Emotion AI contributes to improved customer loyalty and a higher perceived value of the service (Gnewuch et al., 2017; Picard, 1997).

4.2. Operational Efficiency and Automation

Emotion AI also contributed to operational efficiency by automating emotion-driven processes and improving response times. The financial institution case study demonstrated how Emotion AI systems reduced average response times by 40%, as the AI could immediately assess the emotional state of a customer and direct the interaction to the appropriate department or agent. Furthermore, emotion recognition technology helped prioritize customers based on their emotional cues, ensuring that more distressed customers were given priority. This was particularly valuable in managing high-volume call centers, where quick, emotion-aware responses were critical.

Survey respondents from industry professionals reported that Emotion AI enabled faster, more efficient customer service processes. 62% of the professionals surveyed said that Emotion AI had positively impacted the speed and efficiency of their customer service departments. Moreover, the automation of simple queries through AI-driven systems allowed human agents to focus on more complex issues, ultimately improving both agent productivity and service quality (Cui et al., 2020).

4.3. Challenges in Emotion AI Deployment

While the benefits of Emotion AI are clear, the research also identified several challenges faced by organizations in the deployment and adoption of these technologies. One of the primary obstacles mentioned by the case study participants and industry professionals was the technological limitations of Emotion AI systems. These systems, while capable of detecting basic emotions such as happiness, anger, and sadness, struggled to accurately recognize more nuanced emotions or context-dependent feelings, such as sarcasm or mixed emotions. As a result, some customers reported that the AI systems sometimes misinterpreted their emotional states, leading to inappropriate responses.

Furthermore, the integration of Emotion AI into existing customer service systems was another challenge. In the case studies, organizations needed to invest significantly in updating their technological infrastructure to incorporate Emotion AI, requiring not only financial resources but also training for both staff and AI systems. The training data used to develop the Emotion AI systems were often limited, and many systems struggled with cross-cultural recognition, leading to inaccuracies in emotion identification across diverse customer bases.

Industry professionals also cited employee resistance as a barrier to Emotion AI implementation. Many agents expressed concerns that Emotion AI might reduce their role or create challenges in adapting to the new systems. There was a fear that the AI would replace human agents, although the majority of participants acknowledged that Emotion AI was intended to enhance rather than replace human interaction. This finding aligns with Moor et al. (2017), who note that the adoption of AI technologies in customer service often faces organizational and cultural resistance.

4.4. Ethical Concerns: Privacy, Emotional Manipulation, and Bias

A significant portion of the findings focused on ethical concerns related to the use of Emotion AI in customer service. The most prominent ethical issue was the privacy of emotional data. Both customers and industry professionals expressed concerns about how the emotional data was being collected, stored, and used. The case studies revealed that some organizations lacked transparent policies regarding data usage, leading to customer mistrust. Specifically, some customers were concerned that their emotional data could be used for purposes beyond customer service, such as for targeted advertising or product recommendations.

Another concern was the potential for emotional manipulation. A portion of the customer survey respondents expressed unease about businesses potentially exploiting their emotional states for commercial gain. For instance, if a system detected customer frustration, it might prompt an offer for a discounted product, which could be seen as exploiting emotional vulnerabilities. 58% of customers indicated that they would be uncomfortable if Emotion AI systems were used to manipulate their emotions for marketing purposes. This finding highlights the importance of establishing ethical guidelines for Emotion AI deployment, as the technology could easily be misused for manipulative purposes, as discussed by Zeng et al. (2009).

Lastly, the issue of bias in emotion recognition was prevalent. Many participants noted that the emotion recognition systems tended to be less accurate for certain demographics, especially those from non-Western cultures or minority groups.

The gender bias in emotion detection was another issue raised, as some AI systems had difficulty correctly identifying emotions in male and female voices or facial expressions. This finding is consistent with prior studies indicating that Emotion AI systems can be biased, leading to unequal treatment (Crawford & Calo, 2016).

4.5. Summary of Findings

In summary, the findings from this research reveal the positive impact of Emotion AI on customer satisfaction and operational efficiency, particularly in large-scale customer service environments such as call centers and chatbots. The automation of emotional responses has improved the quality of customer interactions, while also enhancing operational workflows. However, technological limitations in emotion recognition, challenges in system integration, and ethical concerns related to privacy, emotional manipulation, and bias remain significant barriers to the widespread adoption of Emotion AI. As this technology continues to evolve, these challenges must be addressed to ensure its ethical and effective use.

5. CONCLUSION

In this chapter, we have explored the rapidly evolving field of Emotion Artificial Intelligence (Emotion AI), with a focus on its applications, benefits, challenges, and ethical concerns in customer service environments. By examining case studies, surveys, and the existing body of literature, this research has provided valuable insights into how Emotion AI is transforming customer service interactions and improving both customer satisfaction and operational efficiency.

The primary takeaway from this study is the substantial impact of Emotion AI in enhancing customer service experiences. By utilizing advanced technologies such as facial expression recognition, speech emotion recognition, and sentiment analysis, Emotion AI enables customer service systems to detect and respond to emotional cues from customers in real time. This capability allows businesses to offer more personalized, empathetic, and context-sensitive interactions, which contribute to heightened customer satisfaction. The case studies demonstrated that Emotion AI-driven systems in call centers and chatbots not only improved customer satisfaction scores but also reduced response times, streamlining customer service processes. Specifically, companies reported improved customer retention, a direct outcome of recognizing and responding to customer emotions in a timely manner.

A significant finding from the research was the clear connection between Emotion AI integration and improved operational efficiency. The automation of emotion-driven responses has enabled businesses to handle larger volumes of inquiries without sacrificing the quality of customer service. Emotion AI systems can prioritize customer interactions based on emotional urgency, ensuring that more distressed customers are attended to first, while simultaneously allowing agents to focus on more complex or sensitive issues. Additionally, by automating routine tasks, businesses have reduced the cognitive load on human agents, allowing them to handle more intricate problems that require higher levels of empathy and problem-solving skills. This shift not only optimizes agent productivity but also enhances the overall customer experience.

Despite these significant benefits, the deployment of Emotion AI is not without its challenges. One of the most pressing issues identified in this study is the technological limitations of emotion recognition systems. While AI has made significant strides in recognizing basic emotions, such as happiness, sadness, and anger, it still struggles with more subtle and complex emotions like sarcasm, ambiguity, and mixed feelings. Furthermore, cultural biases in emotion recognition were highlighted as a significant concern, as the AI systems often struggled to accurately interpret emotional cues from diverse demographics. These issues raise questions about the generalizability of Emotion AI across different cultural, linguistic, and social contexts. This finding underscores the need for further research and technological improvements to ensure that Emotion AI systems can accurately and reliably interpret emotions across diverse populations.

Another challenge faced by organizations adopting Emotion AI is the integration of these technologies into existing customer service infrastructures. Many organizations reported that incorporating Emotion AI required significant investments in both technological upgrades and staff training. These investments, while potentially yielding long-term benefits, present a barrier for smaller organizations with limited resources. Additionally, the deployment of Emotion AI systems often requires companies to undergo significant organizational change, as employees must adapt to working alongside AI-driven systems. Resistance from customer service agents, who may feel threatened by the potential for AI to replace human jobs, was another common issue. This finding aligns with research by Brynjolfsson and McAfee (2014), which emphasizes the importance of addressing employee concerns and ensuring that AI technologies are viewed as tools to enhance human work rather than replace it.

In addition to technological and operational challenges, ethical concerns remain a critical issue in the widespread adoption of Emotion AI. One of the most pressing ethical considerations is the privacy of emotional data. As Emotion AI systems often rely on collecting sensitive information about an individual's emotional state, there is a growing concern about how this data is stored, used, and potentially shared. The case studies revealed that many organizations lacked clear policies regarding the ownership and use of emotional data, leading to customer concerns about their emotional privacy. Customers expressed unease about the possibility of their emotional data being used for purposes beyond customer service, such as targeted advertising or product recommendations. 68% of survey respondents indicated that they would be uncomfortable if their emotional data were exploited for commercial gain, highlighting the need for robust data protection policies.

Another ethical concern revolves around the manipulation of emotions for commercial purposes. The research found that some customers were uneasy about businesses exploiting emotional data to trigger specific actions, such as making emotional appeals or offering promotions based on a customer's emotional state. This raises important ethical questions about the intentions behind Emotion AI technology and whether businesses can use such systems responsibly without taking advantage of vulnerable emotional states. Furthermore, the issue of bias in emotion recognition has become a significant point of contention. Studies have shown that certain demographics, including women, people of color, and individuals from non-Western cultures, are often underrepresented in Emotion AI training data, leading to systems that are less accurate at recognizing emotions from these groups. This bias can result in unequal treatment and reinforce existing societal inequalities, highlighting the need for more inclusive and representative data in training Emotion AI systems.

In response to these ethical concerns, it is imperative that organizations develop and adhere to clear ethical guidelines for the deployment and use of Emotion AI. As the technology continues to evolve, businesses must strike a balance between leveraging the benefits of Emotion AI and protecting the rights of consumers. Transparency in data usage, informed consent, and regular audits of AI systems for bias and fairness will be essential to ensuring that these technologies are used in a responsible and ethical manner.

Looking forward, the future of Emotion AI in customer service appears promising, though significant work remains. As advancements in machine learning, deep learning, and natural language processing continue, Emotion AI systems are expected to become more adept at recognizing and understanding complex emotional states. Future developments will likely lead to more sophisticated systems that can detect a broader range of emotions with greater accuracy. Additionally, the integration of Emotion AI across multiple customer touchpoints, such as social media, mobile applications, and in-store experiences, will create a more seamless and consistent emotional experience for customers. This could lead to a deeper human-AI collaboration, where AI systems assist human agents in navigating sensitive situations, providing real-time emotional insights that enhance empathetic responses and improve overall service quality.

In conclusion, while Emotion AI holds immense potential to transform the landscape of customer service, its ethical, operational, and technological challenges must be addressed to ensure its responsible and effective use. The development of Emotion AI presents both opportunities and risks, and it is crucial that future implementations consider the broader implications for both businesses and consumers. As the field continues to mature, the focus should be on advancing the technology in ways that prioritize empathy, inclusivity, and ethical responsibility, ensuring that these innovations contribute positively to society.

REFERENCES

Barrett, L. F., Adolphs, R., Marsella, S., Martinez, A. M., & Pollak, S. D. (2019). Emotional expressions reconsidered: Challenges to inferring emotion from human facial movements. *Psychological Science in the Public Interest*, *20*(1), 1–68. DOI: 10.1177/1529100619832930 PMID: 31313636

Braun, V., & Clarke, V. (2006). Using thematic analysis in psychology. *Qualitative Research in Psychology*, *3*(2), 77–101. DOI: 10.1191/1478088706qp063oa

Brynjolfsson, E., & McAfee, A. (2014). *The second machine age: Work, progress, and prosperity in a time of brilliant technologies*. W. W. Norton & Company.

Calvo, R. A., & D'Mello, S. (2010). Affect detection: An interdisciplinary review of models, methods, and their applications. *IEEE Transactions on Affective Computing*, *1*(1), 18–37. DOI: 10.1109/T-AFFC.2010.1

Cowie, R., & Douglas-Cowie, E. (2021). Ethics in emotional AI: A framework for considering the ethical issues of using emotion detection technology. *AI & Society*, *36*(1), 1–13. DOI: 10.1007/s00146-020-00999-1

Crawford, K., & Calo, R. (2016). There is a blind spot in AI research. *Nature*, *538*(7625), 311–313. DOI: 10.1038/538311a PMID: 27762391

Cui, Y., Zhang, Y., & Li, Z. (2020). Emotion-aware AI for customer service: Opportunities and challenges. *Journal of Artificial Intelligence Research*, *29*(4), 221–236.

Ekman, P., & Friesen, W. V. (1978). *Facial action coding system: A technique for the measurement of facial movement*. Consulting Psychologists Press.

Gentsch, P. (2019). *AI in marketing, sales and service: How marketers without a data science degree can use AI, big data, and bots*. Palgrave Macmillan. DOI: 10.1007/978-3-319-89957-2

Gnewuch, U., Morana, S., & Maedche, A. (2017). Chatbots in customer service: The role of empathy and user emotions. *Proceedings of the International Conference on Information Systems (ICIS)*.

Goleman, D. (1995). *Emotional intelligence: Why it can matter more than IQ*. Bantam Books.

McDuff, D., & El Kaliouby, R. (2017). Applications of affective computing in human–computer interaction. In Calvo, C. S., D'Mello, S., Gratch, J., & Kappas, A. (Eds.), *The Oxford handbook of affective computing* (pp. 501–512). Oxford University Press.

Moor, A., Zeng, X., & Li, H. (2017). Ethical implications of emotion AI in customer service: A systematic review. *Journal of Ethical AI Studies*, *4*(2), 45–57.

Morley, J., Floridi, L., Kinsey, L., & Elhalal, A. (2020). From what to how: An initial review of publicly available AI ethics tools, methods, and research to translate principles into practices. *Science and Engineering Ethics*, *26*(4), 2141–2168. DOI: 10.1007/s11948-019-00165-5 PMID: 31828533

Pang, B., & Lee, L. (2008). Opinion mining and sentiment analysis. *Foundations and Trends in Information Retrieval*, *2*(1-2), 1–135. DOI: 10.1561/1500000011

Picard, R. W. (1997). *Affective computing*. MIT Press. DOI: 10.7551/mitpress/1140.001.0001

Pradeep, A. K., Appel, A., & Sthanunathan, S. (2019). *AI for marketing and product innovation: Powerful new tools for predicting trends, connecting with customers, and closing sales*. Wiley.

Schuller, B. W.. (2011). Speech emotion recognition: Two decades in a nutshell, benchmarks, and ongoing challenges. *Computer Speech & Language*, *27*(1), 4–37. DOI: 10.1016/j.csl.2012.02.005

Sharma, A., & Ahuja, V. (2022). Role of artificial emotional intelligence in customer engagement: An emerging area in customer service. *Journal of Relationship Marketing*, *21*(1), 45–62. DOI: 10.1080/15332667.2021.1928980

Tao, J., & Tan, T. (2005). Affective computing: A review. In *International Conference on Affective Computing and Intelligent Interaction* (pp. 981–995). Springer.

Yin, R. K. (2017). *Case study research and applications: Design and methods*. Sage Publications.

Zeng, Z., Zhang, Y., & Li, Q. (2009). Emotion recognition using deep learning techniques. *Proceedings of the International Conference on Machine Learning (ICML)*.

Zhao, G., Wang, Y., Liu, Y., & Liu, J. (2021). Multimodal emotion recognition with deep learning: A survey. *IEEE Transactions on Neural Networks and Learning Systems*, *32*(11), 4795–4812. DOI: 10.1109/TNNLS.2020.3011734

Chapter 2
Decoding Emotions in the Digital Age Through Sentiment Analysis for Customer Service Innovation

Princi Gupta
https://orcid.org/0009-0005-4315-6755
JECRC University, India

ABSTRACT

In today's digital landscape, understanding customer emotions is vital for delivering exceptional service experiences. This chapter explores how sentiment analysis—merging Natural Language Processing (NLP), Artificial Intelligence (AI), and emotion analytics—is transforming customer service innovation. It outlines the evolution and core frameworks, including data collection, feature extraction, sentiment classification, and transformer models. The chapter emphasizes multimodal analysis that integrates text, audio, and visual inputs for deeper emotional insight. It also discusses real-time, multilingual applications embedded in tools like chatbots, CRMs, and helpdesks. By linking sentiment insights to business outcomes such as satisfaction, loyalty, and advocacy, it highlights a shift from reactive to proactive service. Ethical and technical challenges are addressed, alongside practical use cases and tool evaluations. This chapter positions sentiment analysis as a path to more human-centered, data-informed engagement.

DOI: 10.4018/979-8-3373-3658-9.ch002

1. INTRODUCTION

Customer service has developed well beyond answering questions and handling grievances in the hyper-connected world of today. It is now a vital channel for brands to establish connections, gain credibility, and provide relevant, customized experiences. Consumers of today demand that businesses not only listen to them but also comprehend them in real time, emotionally, and culturally. The sheer volume and diversity of data generated in this dynamic environment, where interactions take place across platforms like social media, live chat, emails, online reviews, and messaging applications, can be daunting. Since a large portion of this data is unstructured and contains a wealth of thoughts, feelings, grievances, and compliments, it is a treasure trove of insights that are sometimes overlooked. Sentiment analysis becomes an essential tool in this situation. It helps enterprises turn unstructured, raw text into actionable intelligence by providing a methodical approach to deciphering and analyzing the emotional tone of consumer messages (Sun, 2024).

Sentiment analysis, sometimes referred to as opinion mining, is a sophisticated analytical technique that uses artificial intelligence (AI), machine learning algorithms, and natural language processing (NLP) to recognize and categorize sentiments as neutral, mixed, positive, or negative (Rane, 2024). By capturing subtleties like sarcasm, enthusiasm, and displeasure, it goes beyond traditional measurements and helps businesses better understand how consumers feel about their goods, services, and brand experiences (Pathak, 2024).

The capacity to decipher emotions in real time has become a key asset as customer service becomes increasingly digital and instantaneous. Through empathy-driven service design, companies that successfully use sentiment analysis can anticipate customer unhappiness, customize support encounters, proactively manage customer relationships, and increase customer loyalty.

This chapter seeks to give readers a thorough grasp of sentiment analysis, including its definition, application, and development, as well as how it has revolutionized customer service innovation (Rane, 2024). It presents readers with the fundamental technologies—such as natural language processing (NLP) and artificial intelligence (AI)—that underpin sentiment analysis tools, emphasizes their applicability in examining user input on several platforms, and investigates the integration of emotional intelligence into digital service frameworks. The chapter also lays the groundwork for assessing sentiment insights' business worth by linking them to customer experience outcomes like advocacy, retention, and satisfaction. Sentiment analysis is assisting businesses in moving from reactive to proactive service models by bridging the gap between data and empathy, resulting in emotionally intelligent customer connection that has a lasting and significant impact (Dhivrani, 2024)

2. LITERATURE REVIEW

Sentiment analysis (SA) has seen a revolutionary development, moving from crude lexicon-based techniques to complex deep learning models. In the beginning, SA classified text emotion using predefined dictionaries, which frequently fell short in capturing sophisticated idioms like sarcasm and contextual nuances. More accurate sentiment categorization is now possible thanks to the introduction of transformer-based models like BERT, RoBERTa, and XLNet, which have greatly improved contextual comprehension.

In order to capture a wide range of human emotions, recent developments have extended SA into multimodal domains, combining text with audio and visual input. For example, Wu et al. (2024) presented the DEVA framework, which improves the emotional characterisation of data by producing textual emotional descriptions from visual-audio input. Similarly, Srivastava et al. (2023) proposed a multimodal learning architecture that enhances sentiment categorization in customer service centers by fusing verbal and audio modalities. These methods are especially useful in customer service settings, where a thorough grasp of the emotional backdrop can result in more successful and sympathetic interactions.

Additionally popular is Aspect-Based Sentiment Analysis (ABSA), which makes it possible to analyze opinions about particular attributes or features of a good or service. The growing use of ABSA in a variety of fields is highlighted by a systematic study by Zhang et al. (2024), which is made possible by deep learning methods that improve sentiment detection's granularity and accuracy. This level of detail is essential for companies looking to identify and resolve particular client issues (Pathak, 2024).

The need for multilingual and real-time sentiment analysis has prompted the creation of models that can analyze sentiment in real-time situations and across several languages. Cross-lingual sentiment analysis has been made possible by models such as mBERT and XLM-RoBERTa, which enable companies to provide consistent service quality across a variety of language environments. But difficulties still exist, especially when it comes to identifying irony and sarcasm. An important step in resolving these issues is OpenAI's creation of a multimodal AI assistant with sarcasm detection capabilities.

In SA, ethical issues have grown in significance, particularly in light of biases in training data that may cause distorted interpretations. As discussed in 2024, the use of Emotion AI in customer service highlights the necessity of designing AI ethically to guarantee equity and openness. Furthermore, it has been demonstrated that using emotion-sensitive AI in customer service increases client happiness and confidence. Even if the resolution rates are the same, Brun et al. (2025) showed that people view emotion-sensitive chatbots as more capable and reliable.

Despite these developments, there are still unanswered questions about how to scale these systems across cultural boundaries and guarantee their ethical implementation. The purpose of this chapter is to examine how advanced sentiment analysis can be used to decode emotions and spur innovation in customer service, namely through the development of inclusive and emotionally responsive digital service experiences (Dhivrani, 2024).

2.1 Computational Framework of Modern Sentiment Analysis Models

In recent years, there has been a significant evolution in the architecture of sentiment analysis (SA) systems, combining sophisticated computer models with a sophisticated comprehension of human emotion (Potapova, 2023). The main elements of sentiment analysis as determined by current academic research are described in this part, along with how each one enhances the overall efficacy of sentiment categorization and emotion detection in digital contexts.

- **Data Collection and Pre-processing**

Pre-processing and reliable data collection are the cornerstones of any sentiment analysis system. The variety of data sources, including social media posts, online reviews, customer service transcripts, and video or audio recordings, is highlighted in recent studies (Zhang et al., 2022). Pre-processing has expanded beyond text cleaning to include noise reduction in audio inputs and frame selection in video analysis due to the emergence of multimodal platforms (Wu et al., 2024). Stop words, punctuation, special characters, and linguistic normalization through lemmatization or stemming are commonly removed during text pre-processing. Text is divided into analyzable units via tokenization, which is a prerequisite for feature extraction and modeling later on.

- **Feature Extraction**

Sophisticated methods are used in modern SA systems to extract contextual and linguistic characteristics. Syntactic and semantic representations have now been added to traditional lexical techniques like bag-of-words or polarity-based dictionaries (e.g., SentiWordNet, VADER) (Zhang et al., 2022). Semantic embeddings like Word2Vec, GloVe, and FastText capture word similarity and context, while part-of-speech tagging and dependency parsing are frequently employed to comprehend sentence structure. By integrating bidirectional context and subword information, contextual embeddings from transformers—such BERT and RoBERTa—have transformed feature extraction in more recent times, allowing for superior sentiment interpretation even in complex situations like ambiguity or sarcasm (Li et al., 2024). Acoustic signals (such as pitch, tone, and rhythm) and visual cues (such as gaze and facial expressions) are also included in feature extraction for multimodal sentiment analysis. These are combined with textual data to provide a comprehensive knowledge of emotions (Srivastava et al., 2023).

- **Sentiment Classification**

Based on the features that were gathered, the classification component assigns sentiment labels. In the past, sentiment may be classified as neutral, negative, or good. But today's algorithms categorize emotions, recognizing distinct emotional states like fear, rage, sadness, and joy (Brun et al., 2025). A notable improvement is Aspect-Based Sentiment Analysis (ABSA), which links sentiment to certain subjects or aspects in the text. For example, a user review may reflect displeasure with customer service but contentment with product quality (Zhang et al., 2022). Identifying sarcasm and irony, which frequently flip the intended sentiment of a word, is a recurring categorization problem. Recently, sophisticated contextual models and hybrid architectures have been created to deal with this problem (Gole et al., 2023).

- **Modeling Techniques**

The core of SA is modeling, as the discipline moves from traditional machine learning models like Decision Trees, Support Vector Machines, and Naïve Bayes to deep learning techniques like CNNs, RNNs, and LSTMs. Because of their capacity to capture bidirectional context and manage extensive pretraining tasks, transformer architectures—particularly BERT (Devlin et al., 2019), RoBERTa, XLNet, and more recent emotion-specific variants—have emerged as the state-of-the-art in recent years (Li et al., 2024). In both sentiment classification and emotion detection tests, these models perform noticeably better than previous approaches. Researchers are investigating fusion techniques and attention mechanisms in multimodal systems to align and integrate input from several streams (text, audio, and video) for better emotional inference (Wu et al., 2024).

- **Evaluation and Interpretation**

Standard criteria including Accuracy, Precision, Recall, F1-score, and Area Under the Curve (AUC) are commonly used to assess sentiment analysis models. Explainability is becoming more and more popular in SA, though, especially in delicate fields like finance and healthcare. By highlighting the words or phrases that contributed most to the sentiment categorization, tools like SHAP and LIME are being used to enhance local interpretability of model predictions (Potapova, 2023). Furthermore, transformer models' attention visualization provides information about the ways in which various input tokens affect the output. Additionally, because sentiment classifiers trained on biased datasets can reinforce preconceptions or yield unfair results, researchers emphasize the significance of auditing models for fairness and bias.

- **Real-Time and Multilingual Capabilities**

It is anticipated that sentiment analysis systems will function in real-time and in several languages as digital interactions grow increasingly instantaneous and worldwide. Stream-processing frameworks that enable SA on continuous data flows, such Twitter streams or live customer discussions, make real-time sentiment detection possible. Concurrently, cross-lingual transformer models like mBERT and XLM-RoBERTa, which can generalize across languages with little training data, support multilingual sentiment analysis. For multinational corporations looking to uphold uniform customer service standards across geographies, these approaches are essential (Potapova, 2023).

- **Application Layer in Customer Service**

Chatbots, help desks, and CRM platforms are all powered by sentiment analysis, which is becoming more and more integrated into customer care systems. In order to promote empathy and personalization, emotion-sensitive AI agents dynamically modify tone and content in response to real-time sentiment feedback (Brun et al., 2025). According to research, even when the resolution rate is the same, people still view these devices as more capable and reliable. SA is also used by businesses to improve response prioritizing, mine customer feedback for ongoing improvement, and initiate escalation procedures based on emotional indicators. Leading research supports open AI design, equitable data use, and continuous model evaluation because ethical deployment is still an issue.

Figure 1. Computational Framework of Modern Sentiment Analysis Models

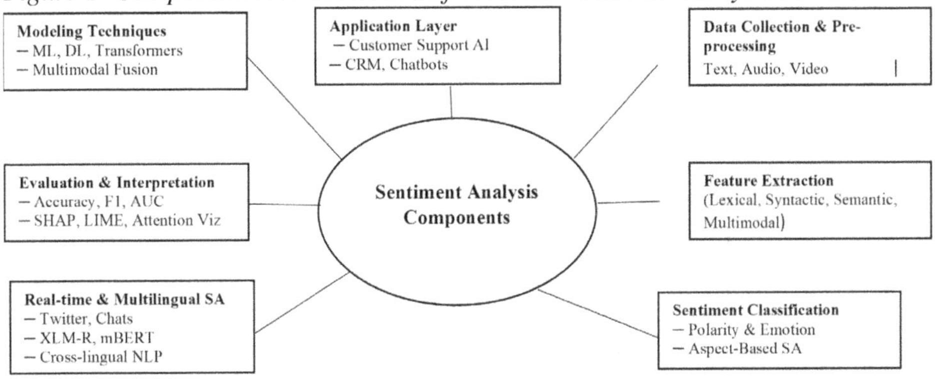

Source: Author's Compilation

3. EMOTION ANALYTICS TO POWER PERSONALIZATION STRATEGIES

3.1 How Customers Feel: The Main Sentiment Types

In the digital age, client sentiment has become a fundamental component of customer experience management. Customers are constantly expressing their feelings, preferences, and discontent through a range of channels—from social media to service interactions—due to the proliferation of digital touchpoints. A branch of natural language processing (NLP) called sentiment analysis allows companies to interpret these sentiments to determine emotional intelligence and inform strategy (Medhat, Hassan, & Korashy, 2014). Businesses can develop emotionally compelling experiences that promote customer happiness, retention, and brand loyalty by evaluating how consumers feel and react to a brand, service, or product (Poria et al., 2020).

Positive, neutral, negative, and mixed sentiment are the four main categories into which consumer sentiment can be systematically divided. Each kind provides unique insights into the experiences and emotional orientations of the client. Positive sentiment, which is commonly expressed through affirming language, high star ratings, positive emoticons, or encouraging social media interaction, represents positive client perceptions, such as satisfaction, appreciation, or enthusiasm. Brand loyalty, repeat business, and the possibility of brand evangelism are all strongly associated with this kind of attitude (Cambria et al., 2018). Conversely, neutral sentiment refers to statements that are objective or emotionally detached; these are usually found in factual feedback, functional reviews, or transactional exchanges. Neutral sentiment may indicate emotional detachment or a lack of connection with the brand experience, even if it is not always a bad thing. Low ratings, complaints, and emotionally charged language are common ways that negative sentiment—which is defined by dissatisfaction, annoyance, or criticism—is expressed. It is essential for spotting product problems, service breakdowns, and other churn hazards. Last but not least, mixed feeling captures a range of emotions in a single exchange, such when a consumer compliments a product's quality but bemoans the speed of delivery. Advanced analytical methods, such as transformer-based models that can parse and interpret sentiments at the entity or feature level or aspect-based sentiment analysis (ABSA), are frequently needed to handle these complicated emotional reactions. Businesses may monitor experience gaps, use sentiment-driven segmentation, and provide emotionally intelligent engagement tactics by having a sophisticated understanding of these sentiment categories (Thabit, 2024).

3.2 How Customer Data Sources Reveal Sentiment

Modern organizations engage with customers over a wide range of platforms in the age of multichannel communication, each of which provides unique forms of data and emotional insights. Customers' cognitive and emotive states are reflected in the structured and unstructured data that these interaction points provide, making them valuable sources for sentiment analysis (Deora, 2025). Organizations can gain a more thorough and up-to-date understanding of client experiences and emotional reactions by utilizing sentiment-rich data from various channels.

- One official and frequently comprehensive source of sentiment data is emails and support tickets. In addition to long-form, narrative material, these communications usually contain structured forms like subject lines, timestamps, and customer identification. Because of this depth, it is possible to extract sentiment in a nuanced way that can spot trends in escalation, tone changes, and recurrent complaints. Email mining is useful for monitoring emotional instability and service quality problems throughout customer lifecycles, according to recent research.
- AI-powered chats and live Conversations with chatbots are frequently brief, sequential, and dynamic, and they offer real-time sentiment clues. Modern chatbots are able to dynamically modify their vocabulary, empathy level, or escalation path by interpreting client sentiment as the conversation progresses thanks to the increasing sophistication of natural language processing (NLP) capabilities. According to research, sentiment-aware chatbots greatly

improve customer service settings' emotional alignment and perceived responsiveness (Deora, 2025).

- Social media posts on sites like Facebook, Instagram, LinkedIn, and Twitter are among the most unrestrained and impromptu ways to convey consumer emotion. These platforms give users instant access to vast amounts of public opinion, frequently enhanced by contextual cues like video, emoticons, hashtags, and memes. Social listening technology allow businesses to track changes in consumer perception and identify patterns in advocacy or reputational issues. Research validates the effectiveness of social media mining in detecting emotional tone, sentiment polarity, and even sarcasm (Kouloumpis, Wilson, & Moore, 2011; Gole et al., 2023).
- The sentiment data presented by online reviews and ratings comes in two formats: quantitative (star ratings) and qualitative (narrative comments). These reviews provide insights related to a product or service and are usually found on websites such as Google Reviews, Amazon, TripAdvisor, and industry-specific forums. They are useful for comparing sentiment analysis between rival brands and show how much importance consumers place on specific aspects of goods or services (Mudinas, Zhang, & Levene, 2012; Li et al., 2024).
- Structured and semi-structured sentiment data is produced by surveys and feedback forms, such as Net Promoter Score (NPS) systems and post-purchase surveys. Open-ended answers frequently yield the most insightful emotional cues, even though number evaluations are helpful for quantitative benchmarking. In order to reveal latent discontent or joy that might not be apparent from numerical ratings alone, recent sentiment-mining techniques apply natural language processing (NLP) and emotion lexicons to these replies.
- In multimodal sentiment analysis, voice and video interactions—like contact center records or video chats—are becoming important sources. These formats provide both visual and audio sentiment indications, such as body language, facial expressions, pace, pitch, and vocal tone. Organizations can find emotional indicators that are frequently overlooked in textual analysis by using methods like facial action coding systems (FACS) and voice emotion recognition (SER). Recent developments in this area have made it possible to combine text input with audio-visual clues for more thorough emotion identification (Thabit, 2024).

These various data sources work together to provide contemporary sentiment analysis systems. Through its integration, businesses may create emotionally intelligent systems that can analyze sentiment across channels and consumer touchpoints, facilitating proactive experience management, real-time personalization, and more accurate decision-making (Deora, 2025).

3.3 Emotional Signals in Customer Decisions and Reactions

Sentiment analysis still relies heavily on vocal and textual feedback, but a deeper insight is shown when we look at customer behavior patterns and their emotional triggers. From frequent visits to sudden service escalations, these behavioral clues provide nuanced yet important insights on customer attitude. Such actions, in contrast to overt feedback, frequently reveal underlying emotional states that clients might not express. Cart abandonment, subscription cancellations, or recurrent engagement without conversion, for example, could be signs of misunderstanding, annoyance, or unfulfilled expectations. Research indicates that external attitudes, such peer evaluations or influencer content, often impact purchasing decisions, highlighting the significance of social proof in influencing digital consumer behavior.

Emotional triggers serve as catalysts that generate particular affective reactions in addition to behavior. Negative triggers, which are known to arouse feelings like rage, fear, or disappointment, frequently include imprecise communication, ineffective support, or delayed service. If not addressed immediately, these triggers can cause discontent or churn by upsetting the emotional flow of the client journey. Positive triggers, on the other hand, such tailored suggestions, prompt service, or sympathetic interaction, can inspire gratitude, trust, and a deeper emotional bond with the company.

Furthermore, social contacts and recognition increase emotional engagement. For example, when brands interact with the public by like, resharing, or responding to a customer's post, they can elicit strong positive feelings like happiness, approval, and brand loyalty. According to research, this kind of public recognition greatly improves the emotional connection between consumers and brands (Stieglitz et al., 2018; Li et al., 2024). These exchanges not only improve customer satisfaction but also support brand evangelism, in which brand advocates willingly spread the word about the company.

Businesses are increasingly using real-time sentiment dashboards and emotion mapping technologies to successfully leverage these data. The emotional states of customers can be visualized and tracked across several touchpoints thanks to these technologies. Businesses may shift from reactive to proactive methods by using sentiment analytics and behavioral data to offer emotionally connected experiences and anticipate dissatisfaction before it materializes. Such technologies are essential for developing emotionally intelligent service systems that promote sustained engagement and loyalty, as Darraz (2025) highlights.

4. INNOVATIVE SENTIMENT ANALYSIS TECHNOLOGIES FOR ENHANCED EMOTIONAL INSIGHT

Rapid developments in natural language processing (NLP) and artificial intelligence (AI) have elevated sentiment analysis from simple polarity detection to complex emotion identification systems that can comprehend complex human expressions through a variety of media. Businesses may capture, analyze, and respond to consumer sentiment in real time with the help of these tools and technologies, which form the basis for developing emotion-aware customer engagement strategies.

Because NLP makes it possible for machines to comprehend, interpret, and produce human language, it is essential to sentiment analysis. The foundation for determining emotional context in textual data is laid by fundamental tasks like tokenization, part-of-speech tagging, dependency parsing, named entity identification, and syntactic parsing (Young et al., 2018). Recent advancements such as transformer-based models (e.g., BERT, RoBERTa) have greatly improved contextual sentiment recognition and semantic comprehension. In addition to identifying emotional polarity (positive, negative, and neutral), these models facilitate aspect-based sentiment analysis (ABSA), which enables the attribution of emotions to certain attributes of goods or services.

Conventional sentiment analysis made extensive use of supervised machine learning algorithms, including logistic regression, Naïve Bayes, and Support Vector Machines (SVM). However, by identifying contextual patterns in sizable datasets, deep learning methods such as Convolutional Neural Networks (CNNs) and Long Short-Term Memory (LSTM) networks have proven to perform better (Zhang et al., 2018). The accuracy of sentiment categorization and its flexibility to domain-specific language have been significantly enhanced by the use of transformer architectures and attention methods (Vaswani et al., 2017).

Furthermore, multimodal AI—which integrates textual, visual, and audio clues to read emotions across media like phone calls or video support—is being used more and more in sentiment analysis. More accurate consumer mood and emotional tone recognition is made possible by multimodal fusion approaches, which are essential for emotionally intelligent service design (Poria et al., 2020).

4.1 Leading Tools for Sentiment Analysis: Capabilities and Applications

- **IBM Watson Natural Language Understanding (NLU)**: IBM Watson NLU is a powerful cloud service driven by AI that supports various languages and facilitates sentiment and emotion analysis. Beyond just detecting polarity, it can also classify emotions (such as joy, anger, sadness, fear, and disgust), label semantic roles, tag concepts, and extract keywords. Watson excels in deciphering contextual nuances, which makes it particularly useful for examining unstructured data like social media posts, chat logs, and customer reviews. It facilitates industry-specific sentiment monitoring at scale by integrating with IBM's larger AI ecosystem and offering models that are easily adaptable.

- **MonkeyLearn**: Businesses may develop unique sentiment analysis models that are suited to their data with MonkeyLearn's user-friendly low-code and no-code platform. It offers real-time analytics dashboards, drag-and-drop workflows, and smooth connections with Google Sheets, Zendesk, and Zapier. Even non-technical people may use the tool to apply sentiment monitoring across customer service issues, survey findings, and social mentions because it offers automated labeling, classification, and data visualization. For SMBs and customer experience teams, MonkeyLearn is especially appreciated for its flexibility, ease of use, and integration features.
- **Google Cloud Natural Language API**: The NLP API from Google Cloud extracts sentiment, entities, categories, and grammatical structure from text using Google's robust machine learning models. Users may learn how customers feel about particular subjects or features thanks to its support for entity-level sentiment analysis. Apps, databases, and CRM systems may all be linked with its REST API to analyze feedback loops in real time. The API is perfect for automated review processing and worldwide sentiment monitoring because it can handle both short-form and long-form material and supports multiple languages (Thabit, 2024).
- **Lexalytics**: InMoment subsidiary Lexalytics offers on-premises and cloud-based (SaaS) sentiment analysis tools. It employs a hybrid methodology that blends machine learning and rule-based natural language processing, allowing for high-performance sentiment, intent, and topic extraction from massive amounts of unstructured data. Additionally, Lexalytics provides multilingual sentiment models, entity recognition, and opinion mining in addition to providing industry-specific text analytics (for example, healthcare, banking, and hospitality). Businesses may conduct detailed, aspect-based sentiment analysis on intricate papers, emails, or survey responses thanks to its Salience engine.
- **TextBlob and VADER (Python Libraries)**: Academic and experimental sentiment analysis projects frequently use TextBlob and VADER
- TextBlob is a Python library that provides a straightforward API for natural language processing (NLP) activities like emotion scoring, noun phrase extraction, translation, and classification. It is based on NLTK and Pattern. It

is a lexicon-based methodology and works well for quick prototyping, small-scale applications, and educational settings.

- When analyzing sentiment in social media material, VADER (Valence Aware Dictionary and Sentiment Reasoner) takes into account elements like emojis, capitalization, slang, and punctuation. It excels in deciphering brief, informal material, like product reviews, user comments, and tweets. VADER is perfect for real-time social listening dashboards since it produces both a compound score and comprehensive polarity scores (Hutto & Gilbert, 2014).

4.2 Custom-Built vs. Off-the-Shelf Solutions

Businesses must choose between creating their own sentiment analysis models and implementing off-the-shelf alternatives. For ordinary applications, off-the-shelf solutions provide pre-trained models, speed, and ease of deployment. They might, however, find it difficult to understand industry jargon or lingo unique to their field.

Custom-built systems, on the other hand, which are frequently trained on proprietary datasets, offer more accuracy and flexibility. These solutions are customized to meet the demands of the clientele, industry jargon, and organizations. They do, however, necessitate ongoing model tuning, computer power, and data science knowledge.

According to recent studies, hybrid approaches—which balance performance and resource efficiency by fine-tuning pre-trained models using domain-specific data—are becoming more and more popular (Sun et al., 2023). These hybrid models work especially well in industries where sentiment nuances have a direct impact on decision-making, such as e-commerce, healthcare, and finance.

5. EMOTION-DRIVEN INTELLIGENCE: BUSINESS USE CASES AND IMPACT OF SENTIMENT ANALYSIS

Customer-centric tactics have been improved in a variety of industries thanks to sentiment analysis, a crucial part of emotion-aware business intelligence. Organizations can gain meaningful insights from consumer sentiment by utilizing AI-driven tools, machine learning, and natural language processing (NLP). This can improve decision-making, boost customer loyalty, and optimize product or service offerings. A thorough examination of the most significant sentiment analysis use cases is provided here (Thabit, 2024).

- **Enhancing Customer Satisfaction and Loyalty**

Sentiment analysis makes it possible to track client sentiment in real time across a variety of touchpoints, including email correspondence, social media, product reviews, and customer care calls. Businesses can use this emotional intelligence to pinpoint the elements influencing favorable or unfavorable sentiment and modify their engagement tactics accordingly. Darraz (2025) asserts that brand trust and loyalty are directly and quantifiably impacted by emotional alignment with client expectations. Businesses can customize customer journeys, loyalty benefits, and marketing material by utilizing sentiment patterns. Furthermore, sentiment-based segmentation facilitates client targeting according to emotional profiles, resulting in interactions that are more genuine and significant. Sentiment-adaptive marketing techniques raised customer satisfaction ratings by as much as 30%, according to Yang (20–2025).

- **Proactive Customer Support and Escalation Management**

Rich sentiment signals found in customer support conversations can reveal underlying problems or unhappiness on the part of the consumer. In order to identify irritation, urgency, or fury, sentiment analysis systems can track live chat logs, support tickets, and chatbot interactions in real time. Following the identification of these emotional indicators, the system can either initiate automated empathy-driven replies or send out notifications to escalate the matter to human support agents. Emotion-aware customer care systems improved customer retention and cut average resolution times by 18%, according to Mhamed (2025). To reduce churn risks and maintain brand image, businesses in the e-commerce and telecommunications sectors, for instance, have implemented real-time sentiment monitors to proactively address unfavorable customer interactions.

- **Reducing Churn and Improving Retention Rates**

Predicting client attrition is one of sentiment analysis's most potent uses. When sentiment analysis is used in conjunction with behavioral data (such as interaction frequency and product usage metrics), it can be used to identify emotionally disengaged or dissatisfied clients before they depart. According to Han (2025), churn prediction models' predictive value is much increased when sentiment data is incorporated. For example, fintech and OTT platforms categorize users into retention risk groups based on sentiment scores from user forums, NPS surveys, and app reviews. Businesses can use these insights to implement focused re-engagement tactics like exclusive deals, individualized assistance, or requests for feedback. According to Du (2024), after the first three months of deployment, sentiment-informed retention measures resulted in a 25% decrease in attrition (Thabit, 2024).

- **Product and Service Improvement through Feedback Insights**

Because customer feedback is frequently unstructured, it can be challenging to use traditional analytics to glean insightful information. Businesses can use sentiment analysis to find recurrent themes, feelings, and problems in this data. A granular understanding is made possible by aspect-based sentiment analysis (ABSA), which links feelings to particular characteristics of a good or service. ABSA could be used, for example, by a food delivery app to identify users who are satisfied with the quality of the meal but irritated with delivery delays. Such in-depth emotional analyses are essential for ongoing product improvement, Wu (2024) underlined. Upgrades to the customer experience, feature rollouts, and design can all benefit from these insights. Additionally, by using real-time emotional data, visual sentiment dashboards facilitate successful collaboration amongst cross-functional teams, including marketing, UX, and operations.

6. EMOTION ANALYTICS IN ACTION: CROSS-INDUSTRY USE CASES OF SENTIMENT-DRIVEN CUSTOMER INNOVATION

Emotion analytics, driven by sentiment analysis, has become a disruptive force in a variety of industries as businesses place a greater emphasis on customer-centric innovation. Businesses may decipher customer emotions hidden in unstructured data, including reviews, social media, and service interactions, by utilizing artificial intelligence (AI), machine learning, and natural language processing (NLP). Proactive service tactics, tailored experiences, and prompt interventions made possible by this emotional intelligence promote client loyalty and happiness. By matching services with changing emotional expectations, sentiment-driven insights not only improve decision-making but also act as crucial differentiators in marketplaces with intense competition (Zhang et al., 2023). The following table, "Emotion Analytics in Action: Cross-Industry Use Cases of Sentiment-Driven Customer Innovation," examines practical uses of this technology in a variety of industries and shows how customer service is changing as a result of emotion-aware tactics.

Table 1. Emotion-Driven Innovation: Industry-Wise Applications of Sentiment Analysis in Customer Service

Industry/Sector	Companies	Use Cases of Sentiment Analysis	Business Impact
E-commerce	Amazon, Flipkart	Real-time examination of post-purchase comments, Q&A sections, and customer reviews; identification of sentiment trends during periods of high sales Marketing efforts using segmentation based on emotions	Improved product customisation and relevance; higher rates of conversion and retention; and lower returns rates
Telecommunications	Jio, Vodafone Idea	Tracking live chats, social media inquiries, and customer service calls; identifying dissatisfaction and escalation triggers Proactively addressing issues through notifications powered by AI	Reduced churn rates, quicker issue resolution, and increased customer satisfaction (CSAT)
Banking & Financial Services	HDFC Bank, ICICI Bank, Paytm	Sentiment tagging in online banking and mobile app reviews Negative attitude identification in branch visits and client service; use of emotion signals in loan services and fraud detection	The Net Promoter Score (NPS) increased. Enhanced digital interaction - Improved risk assessment and judgment
Hospitality & Travel	MakeMyTrip, OYO, Airbnb	Examining evaluations and trip reports that are shared on many platforms Sentiment analysis related to hospitality, check-in experience, or room cleanliness; dynamic response systems	Improved ratings and brand reputation; more recurring business; and an improved client experience
Health & Wellness Services	Practo, 1mg, Apollo Clinics	Real-time feedback from billing counters and loyalty programs; tracking of customer sentiment across physical and online stores An emotional evaluation of in-store encounters	Improved inventory control and more successful in-store marketing Increased brand-customer affinity
Media & Entertainment	Netflix, Hotstar, Sony Entertainment	An examination of viewer emotion derived from social media, reviews, and viewing trends Suggestions based on sentiment Monitoring the content's emotional resonance	Enhanced user engagement, better content curation, and higher subscription and renewal rates
Education & EdTech	BYJU'S, Coursera, Unacademy	Monitoring student attitude via discussion boards, support tickets, and course feedback An examination of learning challenges and involvement Performance evaluation of the instructor	Improved suggestions for courses An increase in student satisfaction Decreased rates of dropout

continued on following page

Table 1. Continued

Industry/Sector	Companies	Use Cases of Sentiment Analysis	Business Impact
Automotive	Tata Motors, Maruti Suzuki, Mahindra	Social sentiment analysis of new product introductions and car features Analysis of dealer feedback Feedback from complaints and service center experiences	Product creation that is informed; increased brand loyalty; and decreased unhappiness with services
Real Estate & Property Tech	MagicBricks, 99acres, NoBroker	An examination of the attitudes of tenants and buyers User interactions with listings and agents are mapped emotionally. Sentiment trends by property type and region	Suggestions for specific properties Increased lead-to-sale conversion rates and more sympathetic client interactions

Source: Author's Compilation

Table 1 Applications of sentiment analysis by industry and span a variety of industries, including banking, healthcare, e-commerce, and telecommunications. It lists important businesses, use cases for AI-driven insights, emotional tracking, and customer feedback, and the ensuing business effects, such as increased engagement, retention, and service innovation.

The table provides a thorough understanding of how sentiment analysis is changing consumer interaction in a variety of digital economy areas. It identifies exemplary businesses in each of the 10 major industry sectors—from e-commerce and telecommunications to health services and education—and describes particular use cases where sentiment research is essential. Sentiment analysis allows businesses in every industry to glean emotional insights from unstructured data, including social media posts, live chat logs, customer reviews, and service comments. Amazon and Flipkart to customize product recommendations and enhance marketing tactics. Real-time sentiment monitoring is used by telecom behemoths like Jio and Vodafone to proactively manage service problems and reduce customer attrition. While the hospitality and tourism industries employ sentiment analysis to improve service offerings and loyalty programs, the banking and financial services sector uses sentiment tagging to improve digital interactions and consumer risk profile. Emotional cues from patient feedback are also utilized in the healthcare industry to assist mental wellness goals and customize care. Emerging applications in industries like retail & FMCG, media & entertainment, edtech, automotive, and real estate are also included in the table. To enhance content recommendations, track brand perception, and promote more sympathetic customer encounters, these sectors are depending more and more on emotion-aware analytics. Lastly, quantifiable results like higher customer happiness, quicker problem solving, more engagement, and stronger brand affinity are shown in the business impact column. The strategic significance of sentiment analysis as a tool for innovation, personalization, and competitive advantage in customer service is shown by this thorough sector-by-sector mapping.

7. THE FLIP SIDE OF EMOTION ANALYTICS: TECHNICAL AND ETHICAL HURDLES

The efficacy of sentiment analysis in providing consistent and culturally relevant customer service improvements may be hampered by a number of technical, ethical, and operational issues, despite its transformative promise.

- **Accuracy and Contextual Understanding**

The ability of sentiment analysis to reliably assess sentiment in a variety of circumstances is one of its biggest drawbacks. In multi-layered communication, where meaning is determined by context, algorithms may incorrectly categorize neutral or mixed sentiment as either positive or negative. For instance, depending on the context and tone, expressions like "That's just great" could be very complimentary or highly caustic. Such subtleties are frequently difficult for traditional machine learning models to handle, and even sophisticated deep learning models like BERT may need to be adjusted to get contextual accuracy in use cases unique to a certain industry (Krugmann, 2024). Despite advancements in language modeling, domain adaptation is still difficult to maintain sentiment accuracy across platforms and sectors,). (Mishra, 2023).

- **Sarcasm, Ambiguity, and Cultural Nuances**

For sentiment analysis systems, sarcasm detection remains a challenging problem. Particularly in user-generated content such as tweets, memes, or product reviews, idioms, sarcasm, and culturally embedded language might skew sentiment classification. Algorithms trained on Western datasets may misread emotional meaning because to linguistic ambiguities and cultural differences in emotional expressions, such as the indirect feedback style common in many Asian nations. In order to guarantee effective emotional interpretation, Wang (2024) highlights the necessity of culturally adaptive sentiment models that take into account linguistic variation and localized training data.

- **Data Privacy and Ethical Concerns**

Sentiment analysis presents serious ethical and privacy issues since it necessitates analyzing vast amounts of personal data, such as feedback, discussions, and behavioral patterns. Without express authorization, it may be against data rights to extract emotional indications from user-generated material or customer support interactions. Furthermore, biases present in training data can produce discriminatory results, particularly when applied to automated decision-making in delicate industries like healthcare or finance. Islam (2024) asserts that companies must integrate transparent data governance frameworks and explainable AI (XAI) principles in order to strike a balance between innovation and ethical responsibility.

- **Integration with Legacy Systems**

Integration with current enterprise resource planning (ERP), customer relationship management (CRM), and support infrastructure is frequently necessary for the deployment of sentiment analysis solutions. Real-time sentiment mining may be challenging in legacy systems due to their unstructured, compartmentalized data formats or incompatibility with contemporary AI tools. Successful adoption may also be hampered by organizational stakeholders' opposition because of issues like cost, complexity, or automation anxiety. The smooth integration of sentiment analysis into service ecosystems depends on reducing technical debt and encouraging cross-functional cooperation, as mentioned by Pereira et al. (2023).

8. METRICS THAT MATTER: LINKING CUSTOMER SENTIMENT TO BUSINESS OUTCOMES

Establishing quantifiable metrics that represent the ROI and long-term economic value is crucial as businesses use sentiment analysis to revolutionize customer service. A combination of traditional customer service KPIs, real-time sentiment indicators, and strategic alignment with business results are needed to assess the efficacy of emotion-aware initiatives.

- **Key Performance Indicators (KPIs): NPS, CSAT, CES**

The measurement of service quality is still based on traditional customer service KPIs like Net Promoter Score (NPS), Customer Satisfaction (CSAT), and Customer Effort Score (CES). Nevertheless, these measurements become much more complex when enhanced with sentiment analysis. Sentiment data taken from customer reviews, for instance, might contextualize the reasons behind a low NPS by exposing underlying emotional triggers like discontent with product features or displeasure with assistance. According to Sharma (2024), Up to 22% more customer loyalty and noticeably greater rates of repeat business were observed by businesses that incorporated emotion analytics into their CSAT and NPS frameworks. Additionally, sentiment-tagging-enhanced CES scores aid in identifying emotionally stressful exchanges that could contribute to attrition.

- **Sentiment Score Metrics and Dashboards**

An overall picture of consumer sentiment across several channels, including email, social media, chat logs, and surveys, is provided by sentiment scores, which range from -1 (negative) to +1 (positive). Decision-makers may keep an eye on sentiment patterns, spot irregularities, and take preventive measures by using these scores, which can be shown in real-time dashboards (Mishra, 2023).

Aspect-based sentiment scores, which deconstruct emotions linked to certain service components like product quality, delivery time, or support conduct, are another feature of advanced sentiment platforms. Granular, useful information are offered by real-time dashboards featuring trendlines, word clouds, and emotional heatmaps.

Businesses who used dashboard-driven sentiment analysis technologies reported quicker decision-making cycles and more interdepartmental alignment, particularly across the marketing, product, and customer support departments (Haznitrama, 2025).

- **Linking Sentiment Trends to Business Outcomes**

Sentiment analytics is best used when it is used to translate emotional insights to measurable business results like customer lifetime value, revenue growth, and churn reduction. Positive sentiment in feedback, for instance, may suggest great word-of-mouth potential, whereas rising negative sentiment on social media may be associated with dwindling brand involvement or an imminent PR problem.

Businesses who used sentiment-to-outcome correlation models reported improved advertising efficacy by 17–25%, lower escalation rates, and more precise consumer behavior forecasts (Wankhade, 2022). Organizations are able to optimize resources, modify customer journeys, and create emotionally compelling loyalty campaigns thanks to these information.

9. THE FUTURE OF FEELING: EMERGING FRONTIERS IN SENTIMENT ANALYSIS

The next frontier of sentiment analysis is the integration of cutting-edge technologies like Emotion AI, multimodal analytics, and predictive modeling, as consumer experience becomes more and more emotion-driven. Hyper-personalized, emotionally intelligent service tactics will be made possible by these innovations, which promise to reveal deeper, more dynamic insights into client behavior.

- **Emotion AI and Advanced Emotional Recognition**

Beyond simple sentiment analysis, emotion AI, often referred to as affective computing, can recognize nuanced emotional states including sarcasm, perplexity, impatience, and excitement. It uses deep learning models, biometric sensors, and facial expression recognition to examine physiological signals, gaze patterns, and microexpressions. Brands are now able to react with previously unheard-of emotional precision and empathy because to this evolution (Mishra, 2023).

Emotion AI systems that integrate text, audio, and visual data can classify emotions with an accuracy of over 85%, which has revolutionary potential for industries that interact with customers, such as retail, hospitality, and healthcare. Real-time feedback systems and automated assistance channels are anticipated to be redefined as this technology develops.

- **Multilingual and Multimodal Sentiment Analysis**

Multilingual sentiment analysis is essential for capturing genuine emotional expression across languages and dialects as multinational corporations serve audiences that are becoming more and more diverse. Combining multimodal analytics—which combines data from text, speech, images, and videos—allows businesses to gain a comprehensive picture of customer sentiment across platforms and cultural boundaries. The increasing importance of zero-shot learning and cross-lingual transformers in facilitating sentiment identification in low-resource languages is highlighted by Fatouros (2023). For deeper emotional insights, multimodal frameworks are being utilized to combine nonverbal and vocal cues, particularly in industries like cross-border customer service, entertainment, and edtech.

- **Predictive Sentiment and Customer Behavior Forecasting**

Predictive modeling, which uses emotional trends to anticipate future customer behaviors like churn, loyalty, or product adoption, is becoming more prevalent in next-generation sentiment analysis systems. Businesses can proactively create interventions, offers, or content based on expected emotional states thanks to these predictive insights. When paired with demographic and behavioral data, Birjali (2021) discovered that predictive sentiment modeling increased the accuracy of churn predictions by as much as 29%. Predictive sentiment analysis will be essential to experience orchestration and journey personalization as it becomes more connected with CRM and marketing automation technologies. (Mishra, 2023).

- **Voice and Video Sentiment Analytics**

Virtual assistants, support calls, video reviews, and social media stories are just a few examples of how voice and video are quickly taking over customer interaction. While video sentiment analysis analyzes facial expressions, gestures, and eye movements in real time, voice sentiment analysis uses tone, pitch, and speech patterns to identify emotional states. In industries like telemedicine, e-learning, and financial advising, where non-textual clues are essential to determining the customer's emotional condition, this development is particularly noteworthy. According to Zhu (2023), businesses who use speech sentiment analytics in contact centers indicated that emotional alignment during live help improved by 33%, which increased customer satisfaction and resolution efficiency (Mishra, 2023).

10. CONCLUSION

Sentiment analysis has become a game-changing link between raw data and emotional intelligence in a time of hyper-connectedness and quickly increasing customer expectations. From the first days of simple polarity detection to the sophisticated, multimodal systems of today that can decipher intricate emotional nuances from text, audio, and even visual inputs, this chapter has charted its development. The technology's capacity to humanize digital interactions is its greatest strength, even if it is supported by exacting computational procedures including feature extraction, data pre-processing, and real-time modeling. Sentiment analysis allows businesses to fully understand customers' feelings in addition to learning what they are saying, which increases empathy in corporate communication. The foundation of the consumer experience is changing as a result of this emotional intelligence. Businesses are now able to create authentic, emotionally impactful relationships rather than just transactional ones. Chatbots can respond empathetically, make emotionally intelligent decisions, and improve personalization at scale thanks to sentiment analysis. These capabilities are establishing new benchmarks for customer-centric service in addition to revolutionizing the way organizations engage with their audiences. Sentiment analysis serves as a window to see real-time changes in customer emotions and a lever to actively develop strategies that engage on a more human, intimate level as companies increasingly transition toward emotion-driven innovation. Businesses must take a deliberate approach to implementation if they want to fully utilize sentiment analysis's capability. First, in order to pinpoint problems, enhance customer experiences, and provide consistent value, sentiment analysis must be integrated into important client touchpoints—from initial contact to post-service feedback. Second, companies should add emotional intelligence to both AI-driven and human-led customer service to enable prompt, sympathetic replies that foster rapport and confidence. Third, companies should use real-time sentiment analytics to make agile decisions that will help them modify campaigns, handle emergencies, and react quickly and efficiently to changes in the market.

Additionally, it is essential to cultivate a culture of customer-centric innovation. Offerings that are more intuitive and emotionally connected might result from cross-functional collaboration, in which teams jointly develop solutions based on sentiment insights. However, these efforts must be supported by transparent and moral AI practices. To preserve consumer trust and adhere to legal requirements, organizations must place a high priority on fairness, bias prevention, model explainability, and data protection. These precautions are particularly important as sentiment analysis technologies become more prevalent in crucial business choices.

Finally, sentiment analysis has a fundamentally transformative function in creating customer-centric brands; it is not only a technological one. Organizations may foster enduring relationships based on trust, empathy, and emotional connection by integrating emotional intelligence into the core of digital consumer engagement. Sentiment research provides a way to not only understand consumers but also establish a genuine connection with them, which will support advocacy, retention, and long-term brand affinity in the future emotion-aware economy. Emotional resonance is becoming the new currency of brand loyalty.

11. REFERENCES

Birjali, M., Kasri, M., & Beni-Hssane, A. (2021). A comprehensive survey on sentiment analysis: Approaches, challenges and trends. *Knowledge-Based Systems, 226*, 107134. DOI: 10.1016/j.knosys.2021.107134

Brun, A., Liu, R., Shukla, A., Watson, F., & Gratch, J. (2025). Exploring Emotion-Sensitive LLM-Based Conversational AI. *arXiv preprint arXiv:2502.08920.*

Cambria, E., Poria, S., Hazarika, D., & Kwok, K. (2018, April). SenticNet 5: Discovering conceptual primitives for sentiment analysis by means of context embeddings. *Proceedings of the AAAI Conference on Artificial Intelligence, 32*(1), •••. DOI: 10.1609/aaai.v32i1.11559

Darraz, N., Karabila, I., El-Ansari, A., Alami, N., & El Mallahi, M. (2025). Integrated sentiment analysis with BERT for enhanced hybrid recommendation systems. *Expert Systems with Applications, 261*, 125533. DOI: 10.1016/j.eswa.2024.125533

Deora, R., Ramakrishnan, S., Prathikantam, R., & Seth, S. (2025, February). Revolutionizing Customer Experience Through NLP and Sentiment Analysis Strategies. In *2025 2nd International Conference on Computational Intelligence, Communication Technology and Networking (CICTN)* (pp. 1005-1009). IEEE. DOI: 10.1109/CICTN64563.2025.10932467

Devlin, J., Chang, M. W., Lee, K., & Toutanova, K. (2019, June). Bert: Pre-training of deep bidirectional transformers for language understanding. In *Proceedings of the 2019 conference of the North American chapter of the association for computational linguistics: human language technologies, volume 1 (long and short papers)* (pp. 4171-4186).

Dhivrani, R., & Sinha, R. K. (2024, March). Exploring the Possibilities of Emotional Text Analysis with Deep Learning Technologies. In *2024 3rd International Conference for Innovation in Technology (INOCON)* (pp. 1-6). IEEE. DOI: 10.1109/INOCON60754.2024.10512180

Du, K., Xing, F., Mao, R., & Cambria, E. (2024). Financial sentiment analysis: Techniques and applications. *ACM Computing Surveys, 56*(9), 1–42. DOI: 10.1145/3649451

Fatouros, G., Soldatos, J., Kouroumali, K., Makridis, G., & Kyriazis, D. (2023). Transforming sentiment analysis in the financial domain with ChatGPT. *Machine Learning with Applications, 14*, 100508. DOI: 10.1016/j.mlwa.2023.100508

Gole, M., Nwadiugwu, W. P., & Miranskyy, A. (2023, November). On sarcasm detection with openai gpt-based models. In *2024 34th International Conference on Collaborative Advances in Software and COmputiNg (CASCON)* (pp. 1-6). IEEE

Han, P., Chen, H., Rasool, A., Jiang, Q., & Yang, M. (2025). MFB: A generalized multimodal fusion approach for bitcoin price prediction using time-lagged sentiment and indicator features. *Expert Systems with Applications*, *261*, 125515. DOI: 10.1016/j.eswa.2024.125515

Haznitrama, F. G., Choi, H. J., & Chung, C. W. (2025). Methodologies and their comparison in complex compound aspect-based sentiment analysis: A survey. *AI Open*.

Hutto, C., & Gilbert, E. (2014, May). Vader: A parsimonious rule-based model for sentiment analysis of social media text. In *Proceedings of the international AAAI conference on web and social media* (Vol. 8, No. 1, pp. 216-225). DOI: 10.1609/icwsm.v8i1.14550

Islam, M. S., Kabir, M. N., Ghani, N. A., Zamli, K. Z., Zulkifli, N. S. A., Rahman, M. M., & Moni, M. A. (2024). Challenges and future in deep learning for sentiment analysis: A comprehensive review and a proposed novel hybrid approach. *Artificial Intelligence Review*, *57*(3), 62. DOI: 10.1007/s10462-023-10651-9

Kouloumpis, E., Wilson, T., & Moore, J. (2011). Twitter sentiment analysis: The good the bad and the omg! In *Proceedings of the international AAAI conference on web and social media* (Vol. 5, No. 1, pp. 538-541).

Krugmann, J. O., & Hartmann, J. (2024). Sentiment analysis in the age of generative AI. *Customer Needs and Solutions*, *11*(1), 3. DOI: 10.1007/s40547-024-00143-4

Li, C., Tang, H., Zhang, J., Guo, X., Cheng, D., & Morimoto, Y. (2024, December). Advancing Aspect-Based Sentiment Analysis Through Deep Learning Models. In *International Conference on Advanced Data Mining and Applications* (pp. 228-242). Singapore: Springer Nature Singapore.

Li, C., Tang, H., Zhang, J., Guo, X., Cheng, D., & Morimoto, Y. (2024, December). Advancing Aspect-Based Sentiment Analysis Through Deep Learning Models. In *International Conference on Advanced Data Mining and Applications* (pp. 228-242). Singapore: Springer Nature Singapore.

Liu, B. (2022). *Sentiment analysis and opinion mining*. Springer Nature.

Liu, Y., Ott, M., Goyal, N., Du, J., Joshi, M., Chen, D., ... Stoyanov, V. (2019). Roberta: A robustly optimized bert pretraining approach. *arXiv preprint arXiv:1907.11692*.

Lovin, D., Busila, A. V., & Sava, V. (2023). Culture shock, adaptation, and organizational performance in sport: A psychological perspective. *Technological Forecasting and Social Change*, *190*, 122403. DOI: 10.1016/j.techfore.2023.122403

Mhamed, M., Sutcliffe, R., & Feng, J. (2025). Benchmark Arabic news posts and analyzes Arabic sentiment through RMuBERT and SSL with AMCFFL technique. *Egyptian Informatics Journal*, *29*, 100601. DOI: 10.1016/j.eij.2024.100601

Mishra, D. N., & Panda, R. K. (2023). Decoding customer experiences in rail transport service: Application of hybrid sentiment analysis. *Public Transport (Berlin)*, *15*(1), 31–60. DOI: 10.1007/s12469-021-00289-7

Mudinas, A., Zhang, D., & Levene, M. (2012, August). Combining lexicon and learning based approaches for concept-level sentiment analysis. In *Proceedings of the first international workshop on issues of sentiment discovery and opinion mining* (pp. 1-8). DOI: 10.1145/2346676.2346681

Pathak, A., Arya, K. V., Tiwari, V., Bhende, M., & Barsagde, N. (2024, November). Deciphering emotions: A comprehensive examination of machine learning algorithms for sentiment analysis. In *AIP Conference Proceedings* (Vol. 3214, No. 1). AIP Publishing. DOI: 10.1063/5.0239531

Pontiki, M., Galanis, D., Papageorgiou, H., Androutsopoulos, I., Manandhar, S., Al-Smadi, M., & Eryiğit, G. (2016, January). Semeval-2016 task 5: Aspect based sentiment analysis. In *International workshop on semantic evaluation* (pp. 19-30). DOI: 10.18653/v1/S16-1002

Poria, S., Cambria, E., Bajpai, R., & Hussain, A. (2017). A review of affective computing: From unimodal analysis to multimodal fusion. *Information Fusion*, *37*, 98–125. DOI: 10.1016/j.inffus.2017.02.003

Potapova, R. K., & Potapov, V. V. (2023). Sentiment analysis of digital communication. *Вестник Московского государственного лингвистического университета. Гуманитарные науки*, (4 (872)), 86-96.

Rane, N., Choudhary, S., & Rane, J. (2024). Artificial intelligence, machine learning, and deep learning for sentiment analysis in business to enhance customer experience, loyalty, and satisfaction. *Available at SSRN* 4846145. DOI: 10.2139/ssrn.4846145

Schweidel, D. A., & Moe, W. W. (2014). Listening in on social media: A joint model of sentiment and venue format choice. *JMR, Journal of Marketing Research*, *51*(4), 387–402. DOI: 10.1509/jmr.12.0424

Sharma, N. A., Ali, A. S., & Kabir, M. A. (2024). A review of sentiment analysis: Tasks, applications, and deep learning techniques. *International Journal of Data Science and Analytics*, •••, 1–38.

Stieglitz, S., Mirbabaie, M., Ross, B., & Neuberger, C. (2018). Social media analytics–Challenges in topic discovery, data collection, and data preparation. *International Journal of Information Management*, *39*, 156–168. DOI: 10.1016/j.ijinfomgt.2017.12.002

Sun, C., Qiu, X., Xu, Y., & Huang, X. (2019, October). How to fine-tune bert for text classification? In *China national conference on Chinese computational linguistics* (pp. 194–206). Springer International Publishing. DOI: 10.1007/978-3-030-32381-3_16

Sun, Y., & Zhang, Q. (2024). Navigating the Digital Transformation of Commercial Banks: Embracing Innovation in Customer Emotion Analysis. *Journal of the Knowledge Economy*, *16*(1), 1–22. DOI: 10.1007/s13132-024-01938-5

Thabit, S. A. (2024). Perspective chapter: Embracing the complexity of human emotion. In *Advances in Sentiment Analysis-Techniques, Applications, and Challenges*. IntechOpen.

Vaswani, A., Shazeer, N., Parmar, N., Uszkoreit, J., Jones, L., Gomez, A. N., & Polosukhin, I. (2017). Attention is all you need. *Advances in Neural Information Processing Systems*, •••, 30.

Wang, Z., Xie, Q., Feng, Y., Ding, Z., Yang, Z., & Xia, R. (2024). Is ChatGPT a Good Sentiment Analyzer? In *First Conference on Language Modeling*.

Wankhade, M., Rao, A. C. S., & Kulkarni, C. (2022). A survey on sentiment analysis methods, applications, and challenges. *Artificial Intelligence Review*, *55*(7), 5731–5780. DOI: 10.1007/s10462-022-10144-1

Wu, S., Wang, X., Wang, L., He, D., & Dang, J. (2024). Enriching Multimodal Sentiment Analysis through Textual Emotional Descriptions of Visual-Audio Content. *arXiv preprint arXiv:2412.10460*.

Yang, B., Gao, Q., & Li, J. (2025). Market ambiguity, investor sentiment and market anomalies–Evidence from the Chinese A-share market. *Research in International Business and Finance*, *75*, 102721. DOI: 10.1016/j.ribaf.2024.102721

Zhang, W., Li, X., Deng, Y., Bing, L., & Lam, W. (2022). A survey on aspect-based sentiment analysis: Tasks, methods, and challenges. *IEEE Transactions on Knowledge and Data Engineering*, *35*(11), 11019–11038. DOI: 10.1109/TKDE.2022.3230975

Zhang, Y., Yang, X., Xu, X., Gao, Z., Huang, Y., Mu, S., . . . Yu, G. (2021). Affective computing in the era of large language models: A survey from the nlp perspective. *arXiv preprint arXiv:2408.04638*.

Zhu, L., Zhu, Z., Zhang, C., Xu, Y., & Kong, X. (2023). Multimodal sentiment analysis based on fusion methods: A survey. *Information Fusion*, *95*, 306–325. DOI: 10.1016/j.inffus.2023.02.028

Chapter 3

Leveraging Sentiment Analysis in Customer Service for Enhanced Customer Experience

R. Siva Subramanian
SRM Institute of Science and Technology, India

K. Santhi
Easwari Engineering College, India

D. Sasikumar
Panimalar Engineering College, India

S. Shobana
R.M.K. Engineering College, India

J. Elavarasi
Vel Tech High Tech Dr. Rangarajan Dr. Sakunthala Engineering College, India

L. A. Anto Gracious
https://orcid.org/0000-0003-2386-9182
R.M.K. College of Engineering and Technology, India

M. Nalini
https://orcid.org/0000-0001-8987-3120
SA Engineering College, India

ABSTRACT

Sentiment analysis, a subfield of natural language processing (NLP), involves the extraction of emotional tone from textual data. Its growing importance in customer service is driven by the need to understand customer sentiment in real-time, enabling businesses to improve engagement and satisfaction. This survey reviews the various techniques used in sentiment analysis, including lexicon-based, machine learning, and deep learning approaches, and explores their applications in customer feedback analysis, chatbots, call centers, and brand monitoring. Further, the chapter discusses the challenges faced by current sentiment analysis systems, such as handling sarcasm, multilingual data, and ensuring ethical practices.

DOI: 10.4018/979-8-3373-3658-9.ch003

1. INTRODUCTION

1.1 Background on Customer Service Evolution in the Digital Age

In the recent past, customer service has been revolutionized due to the advancement in technology(Hsu & Lin, 2023). In the past, customer service was limited to face-to-face communication or telephone with limited time and availability. With the help of the internet and the use of mobile devices, customer service went beyond the call center and embraced email, live chat, and social networks. This has made customers to express themselves more and demand faster and personalized response. Organizations have had to learn to change and transform in order to accommodate these changes and alter their customer support from simple problem solving tools to more progressive and customer-oriented approaches. In this ever-evolving environment, information regarding the customers is considered to be one of the main sources of competitive advantage.

1.2 Importance of Understanding Customer Sentiment

In the world of digital, customers are interacting with companies at a much higher frequency in different channels(Park et al 2021). It is common to find useful information within these interactions that may relate to customer satisfaction, dissatisfaction, loyalty or expectations. Sentiment analysis provides a good way to understand these clues since it is an approach that can identify and classify opinions in text. Understanding customer sentiment is very important in that it helps an organization to know what to do in order to correct wrong doings, or do what is right in order to suit the customer. It also helps in the management of reputation since business entities can identify and act on negative sentiments as they emerge. In this regard, sentiment analysis becomes a tool that does not only facilitate the course of work but is a valuable asset crucial for the development of a company's strategies dealing with clients(Filieri et al 2022).

1.3 Role of AI and NLP in Modern Customer Support

It is now possible to automate the replies, analyze the queries of the users, and manage customer complaints more effectively and accurately using AI tools(Raju, A., & Raju, C 2025). NLP, especially, helps the machine in understanding and interpreting the language used by humans in a meaningful manner. Sentiment analysis is a branch of NLP which is used to extract the information related to the opinions, attitudes and emotions of the people(Inavolu, S. M. 2024). With the help of the machine learning algorithms and the deep-learning models, sentiment analysis can be used for processing the different types of the unstructured data, including the customer reviews, the posts in social media networks, the chat and the support tickets. This capability helps the businesses to keep track of the customer sentiment in real time and respond to it, so as to provide a more personalized and intelligent support(Sood et al 2024).

1.4 Scope and Objectives of the Survey

This survey's goal is to review the current state of the art of the sentiment analysis in the context of customer service. It discusses the processes and tools for sentiment analysis with respect to rule, template, and concept based approaches and machine learning. The chapter also covers the various ways in which sentiment analysis is incorporated in customer support include chatbot, call center analysis and customer feedback analysis. It also assesses how this integration supports the customer experience since it allows for timely, accurate, and personalized service delivery. In addition, the survey presents the current issues, including the ability to interpret sarcasm, work with the multilingual text, and the problem of data privacy, as well as the outlook for the further development of the field and potential trends for further research. In so doing, this chapter aims to highlight the strategic opportunities and technical implications of sentiment analysis for customer service for the benefit of practitioners, researchers, and decision-makers.

1.5 Organization of the Paper

The rest of this chapter is organized as follows. Section 2 provides an overview of sentiment analysis and its classification, levels, and key procedures involved in the text analysis. Section 3 presents a summary of different approaches to sentiment analysis that can be divided into lexicon-based methods, traditional machine learning approach, deep learning approach, and the combination of the two approaches. In Section 4, turning to the practical use of SA, we discuss the use of sentiment analysis for customers' feedback analysis, improving the chatbot's performance, and brand image. The fifth section of this chapter deals with how sentiment analysis can be used to improve customer experience as illustrated by examples and case studies. Section 6 also explains the issues and limitations of the sentiment analysis systems like interpretability, culture sensitivity and data quality. Section 7 elaborates on the existing and emerging research areas related to the topic: emotion detection, MSM, MSI with customer journey mapping. Last of all, Section 8 provides a brief summary of the paper with an emphasis on the significance of sentiment analysis in the development of the customer service industry.

2. FUNDAMENTALS OF SENTIMENT ANALYSIS

2.1 Definition and Goals of Sentiment Analysis

Sentiment analysis is one of the subfields of NLP that mainly deals with the detection of orientation polarity from texts(Tan et al 2023). It is mainly used to identify the sentiment of a set of text, which is usually defined as positive, negative or neutral. This analytical process facilitates the interpretation of opinion, attitude, and emotional expressions in written language by the machines. In the context of customer service, sentiment analysis is a crucial aspect of determining the attitude that customers have towards the services that are offered to them as well as the particular brand(Rodríguez et al 2023). It provides businesses with a look into the level of customer satisfaction and dissatisfaction, helps to address complaints immediately and make better decisions about service delivery. The ultimate goal is not only to automate the process of understanding the content of the text but also to improve the relations with customers through meeting their emotional and psychological needs(Nandwani, P., & Verma, R. 2021) (Zhu et al 2023).

2.2 Types of Sentiment: Polarity, Emotion, and Aspect-Based

There are various types of sentiment analysis depending on what is being aimed to be identified from the text. Among them, the simplest and most commonly used type of sentiment analysis is polarity-based approach where the text is categorized into positive, negative or neutral. This approach is used for summarizing overtones and is also used quite frequently when analyzing customer feedback, social media, or feedback cards. However, emotions are far from being bipolar and can be much more sophisticated. Therefore, the more sophisticated systems are equipped with the emotion detection which aims at recognizing certain emotions like happiness, rage, sorrow, delight, or menace. This deeper layer analysis is much more useful as it identifies how customers feel, particularly in emotionally charged situations for the business.

Another sub-genre is aspect based sentiment analysis (ABSA) which delves down to the level of the specific facets of a product or service and the customers' sentiment concerning those sub-features. For instance, it can be possible for a restaurant review to have positive sentiment towards the food quality and negative sentiment towards the speed at which the food was served. ABSA makes it easier for organisations to identify which aspects of their products or services are liked or disliked for better results in development. These various types of sentiment analysis can be used individually or in a coordinated manner in order to get a comprehensive analysis of the customer feedback.

2.3 Sentiment classification levels are document level, sentence level, and aspect level.

It is evident that the coarseness of the sentiment analysis has implications on the kind and richness of the results obtained. It is possible to classify the sentiment at the document level, at the sentence level or aspect level. At the document level, it means that the text is taken as a single entity and its sentiment is determined. This method is most effective when the text is about one object or subject, for example, a large number of comments on a product or a questionnaire. But it might disregard some subtleties in the text where two or more points of view are provided.

While, on the other hand, the sentence-level sentiment analysis is used to determine the sentiment of any particular sentence. This is particularly useful when the documents are polarity-sentiment mixed, allowing systems to distinguish between the various sentiments that one document may contain. For instance, a message received from the customer might contain positive feedbacks about the quality of the product and at the same time contain a complaint about the delivery service. When it comes to the evaluation of the feedback at the sentence level, businesses are able to provide a more precise response to each part of the feedback.

At an even finer level, aspect-based sentiment analysis is the integration of feature-level sentiment and aspect-level sentiment. This level of analysis is particularly useful in the evaluation of products and services where customers may have positive or negative attitudes towards any given attribute. For example, a mobile phone review may contain positive aspects such as satisfaction with the display feature, yet negative aspects like poor battery performance. It gives companies an insight of the various aspects of what they offer and what needs to be improved.

2.4 Key NLP Techniques in Sentiment Analysis

There are several techniques used in NLP that are used by the sentiment analysis systems to process, understand, and learn from the text(Pajila et al 2023). Preprocessing is generally the first step and involves tokenization, stop word elimination, lemmatization and normalization in order to minimize the amount of noise that is present. The text after preprocessing must be transformed into a format that is easily readable for the machine using BoW, TF-IDF or even word embeddings using Word2Vec or GloVe. These techniques assist in converting the words into numeral forms that can retain the meaning and the context.

Dependencies, named entity identifying along with the part of speech tagging, impending parsing, enhance the knowledge pertained to the structure and meaning of the sentences. They are especially useful in dealing with negation or modifiers such as distinguishing between 'good' and 'not good'.

Also, lexicon-based approach employs pre-defined lists of words that contain positive and negative sentiment values such as SentiWordNet. There are more advanced systems that use machine learning and deep learning models like the Support Vector Machines, Long Short-Term Memory networks and the more recent transformer-based systems. These techniques proved the limitations of the traditional or basic techniques of sentiment analysis can be overcome by rising higher accuracy and context-awareness with the help of these techniques to noisy, informal, and especially domain-specific text of customer chat and social media.

3. TECHNIQUES AND MODELS USED

3.1 Lexicon-Based Approaches

The straightforward approach of sentiment analysis is the lexicon-based approach since it involves the use of a sentiment lexicon. These approaches are based on the use of sentiment lexicons that is, lists of words that are accompanied by the sentiment polarity and sometimes the intensity of the sentiment. SentiWordNet is one of the most popular lexicons that provide sentiment scores to the WordNet synsets thus, each word has a quantifiable level of positivity, negativity, or neutrality. Other sources include AFINN, Opinion Lexicon, and NRC Emotion Lexicon with the structure and domain specificity of each of them.

In the lexicon-based systems, sentiment is usually determined by summing up the scores of the individual words in a sentence or document. These systems can be improved using syntactic or semantic rules, for example, in the use of negations (not good as opposed to good) or intensity (very bad as opposed to bad). These rules assist in narrowing down the definition of sentiment based on the context and grammar. These are some of the advantages of lexicon-based methods. The methods are easy to understand, which is important when a high level of interpretability is required. Nevertheless, they are not good at handling the domain-specific terms, colloquialisms, irony, and idioms, which makes it less accurate compared to data-driven methods.

Figure 1. Techniques and Models Used

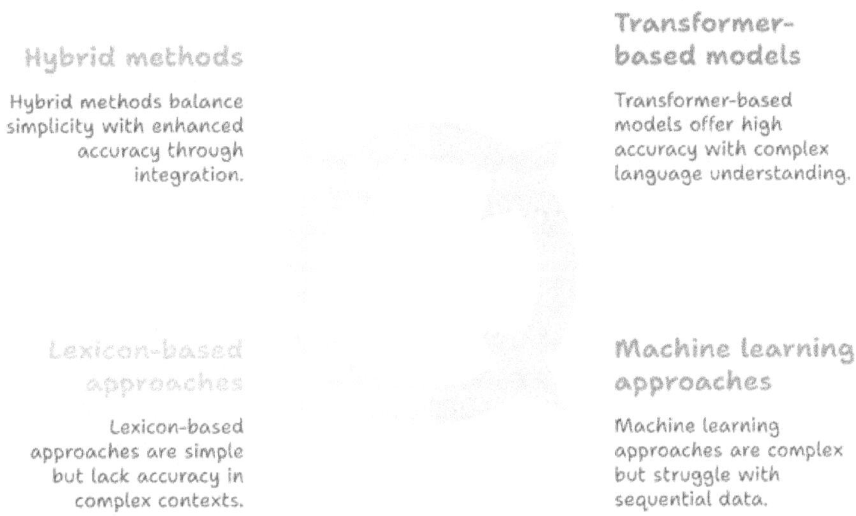

3.2 Machine Learning Approaches

The approaches of traditional machine learning (ML) were a revolution in the field of sentiment analysis since it offered data-driven models that could learn from the labeled data(Lakumarapu et al 2024). These are some of the most popular techniques that are used in the classification of sentiments namely the Support Vector Machines, the Naive Bayes, and the Decision Trees. These models are learned from labeled corpus in which each example (like a sentence or a document) is associated with its sentiment. The learning process is to determine statistical dependencies between the input features and the output sentiment classes(Sreelakshmi et al 2024).

Feature engineering is a crucial part of the sentiment analysis based on machine learning since the initial text data must be converted into numerical vectors that can be used in the model. Two such techniques for this purpose are Bag of Words (BoW) and Term Frequency-Inverse Document Frequency (TF-IDF). BoW refers to a document in terms of the number of words in a document disregarding their order and position while TF-IDF on the other hand, considers the number of times a word appears in the document but adjusts for how unique the word is in the whole collection of documents. These approaches give rise to a sparse representation of the input in a high-dimensional space that can be used as input for the ML classifiers(Yamini et al 2023).

Although the cited models are quite effective in many scenarios, their weaknesses are in the fact that they do not take into account sequential or contextual data. For instance, they work with words as independent variables, and this results in the loss of word relations and connections. Still, they are in use because they are easy to implement, easy to understand, and optimal for datasets with a small number of features.

3.3 Deep Learning Approaches

Deep learning has taken a big leap within the field of sentiment analysis due to the capability of capturing the intricate features of the language as well as the context that other basic methodologies are unable to identify. Two of the first methods applied to the sentiment classification problem are Convolutional Neural Networks (CNNs) and Recurrent Neural Networks (RNNs). CNNs were initially meant for image processing however, they are quite helpful in text classification. They slide filters over the word embeddings and the features to make sentiment by predictions. In contrast, RNNs are more appropriate for sequential data as it enables the model to pass information from the preceding steps in order to interpret the current input. However, the original RNNs can face vanishing gradient issues which hinders the network to learn long term dependencies. To deal with this, Long Short Term Memory networks were developed. LSTMs use memory cells and gates to maintain important data regarding the sequence information for a longer duration. It also suits them to analyze large customer reviews or chat logs where the sentiment may shift over the course of the interaction. And conversely, in the recent years, the attention mechanisms and transformer based models have taken further strides in sentiment analysis. The attention mechanism helps the model to attend to some parts of the text that are most relevant in determining the sentiment. For instance, in the sentence "The phone is fast, but the battery life is terrible", attention can help to draw focus on the positive and negative feelings about two attributes of the phone.

3.4 Hybrid Methods

Hybrid methods are an integration of two or more methods in order to improve the effectiveness and reliability in sentiment analysis. Another paradigm is the combination of the lexicon-based features with machine learning or deep learning. For example, the lexicon scores can be used as features in the machine learning classifier, which will enable the model to learn from both the statistical data and the knowledge of sentiment dictionaries. This can enhance the model performance especially when there is a limited amount of training data or when the interpretability of the model is of great importance. Another type of hybrid method can be referred to as ensemble techniques, where several models, which can be of different types are trained in parallel and their results are then combined using such techniques as voting, averaging or stacking. It is known that ensembles can be used to reduce the disadvantages of models and increase the efficiency of their predictions. For instance, while an example of a deep natural language pre-trained model when combined with a gradient boost classifier or a rule-based sentiment engine will be able to understand the depth of language as well as domain specific sentiment signals to some extent. It is particularly useful in operational contexts where the texts can be of short or long, formal or informal, simple or complex as in customer relations. It is a versatile model that performs well regardless of the type of data and the nature of users' interactions, and has a higher generalization ability.

4. APPLICATIONS IN CUSTOMER SERVICE

4.1 Customer Feedback Analysis

Another area where the use of sentiment analysis in customer service is widely used is in the evaluation of the customer feedback, which can be received in the form of online reviews, surveys, or on social media. This feedback is usually full of customer opinions and feelings regarding certain issues, which is very useful to the business organizations that want to know the level of satisfaction of customers and the issues that they have with the products or services that are being offered to them. It is a process of sorting and summarizing this feedback, and it provides actionable insights in a way that could not be achieved otherwise. For instance, the comments left on an online store can be used to discuss the general attitude of consumers, frequent complaints, or new trends. Likewise, the open-ended responses that are gathered in satisfaction questionnaires can be analyzed to get the sentiment trends of customers which provides more useful information than Likert scale responses.

Social media mining is a step further from feedback analysis as it involves mining of customer opinions that are volunteered in real time. Social media such as twitter, face book, and Instagram are some of the social media platforms that are used extensively and are full of consumer generated content that contain emotions towards brand encounters. These platforms, in turn, can be scraped by tools meant for sentiment analysis for changes in public opinion and for the discovery of new trends and advocates or detractors. When sentiment is accumulated and shown as a curve, one gets the idea of how the sentiment changes over time, which is very useful for business to make required corrections in their products, services, and even communication strategy.

Figure 2. **Applications in Customer Service**

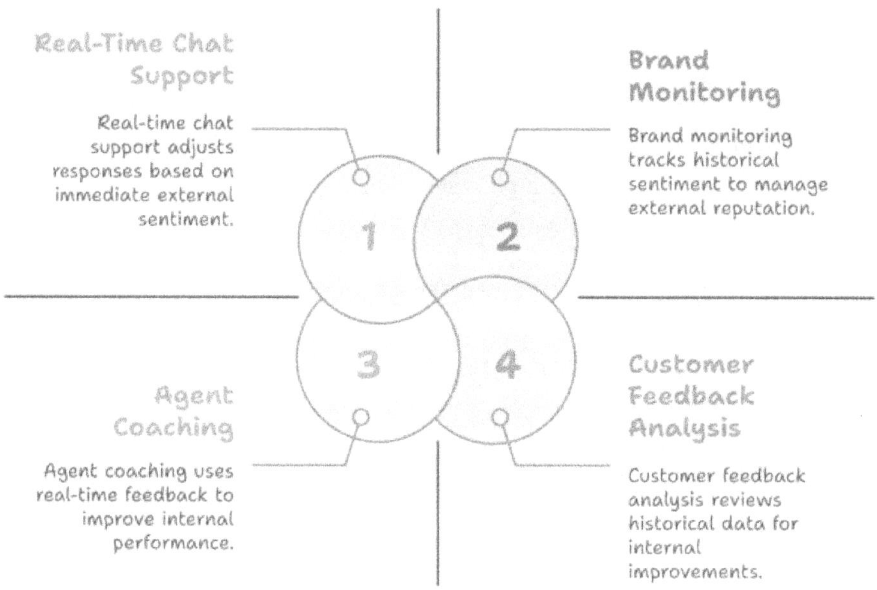

4.2 Real-Time Chat and Support Analysis

One of the most important areas of using sentiment analysis is in real-time customer support, especially in chat support. The current consumer support and service delivery are highly likely to entail live chat, chatbots, and messaging services. In this context, sentiment analysis helps the system to grasp the emotional undertone of the conversation as it progresses. For instance, a sentiment-aware chatbot can change its tone of response depending on the sentiment of the customer in case of negative sentiment, the bot can use friendly language or transfer the call to an agent in case the sentiment remains negative. This makes it easier to establish a friendly and sensible interaction with the customers. In addition, real-time sentiment monitoring is also applied in order to support the human operators during the actual call. Some of the tools that are available in this area are capable of tracking the sentiment of the dialogue and alert the user when the conversation is becoming negative. These triggers can cause real-time actions like offering a discount, transferring the customer to the supervisor, or providing the agents with the appropriate script according to the situation. This way, businesses can avoid customer churn and enhance the resolution rate as they quickly recognize when the customer is frustrated. Furthermore, this technology also assists with agent coaching in the manner in which they speak and engage with customers in real time sessions so as to fine tune specific elements that improve the experience of the customers.

4.3 Call Center Analytics

The use of call centers as a communication channel is still important in many organizations especially those in the financial, telecommunication and the health sectors. Now, Sentiment analysis is being used for audio data categorized from the customer calls which added another layer to the voice accent. They use automatic speech recognition (ASR), thus, the voice recordings are transcribed into text which can be used in sentiment analysis. This approach enables the assessment and measurement of the level of emotions in the calls without the need to listen to the call manually, which makes the process more scalable and less subjective.

Apart from customer sentiment analysis, this analysis also has a significant role in the assessment of the agent. For instance, sentiment changes between different calls can reveal the ability of an agent to deal with customer emotions, solve problems or calm down an irate customer. This information proves helpful to managers in the following ways: Managers can be able to reward good performing agents, know which agents need to undergo through training, and also to ensure that quality standards are being met. Further, the sentiment over a period also enables the organization to monitor the changes in consumer attitude due to operational alterations like change in policies or introduction of new products. The utilization of sentiment scoring with call metrics such as time taken per call, closure status, and first call solve adds on to the assessment of agent performance as well as introducing satisfaction level of the customers.

4.4 Brand Monitoring and Reputation Management

Brand monitoring and reputation management are critical areas where sentiment analysis is of considerable importance since it supports the process of constant social listening which implies monitoring and analyzing the public discussions related to a particular brand, competitors, and trends. It also enables organizations to monitor the way in which the public perceives them and address any concerns way before they get out of hand. When it comes to the mentions and comments, the companies know not only what is being said about the brand but also how it is being said by sorting the sentiments into positive, negative, and neutral.

Thus, during a crisis, the sentiment analysis unravels as a valuable asset in managing and containing the crisis. Alerts can be of negative sentiment when they indicate issues, be it a new flaw in the product, an unappreciated social media campaign set up by the company or a system breakdown, which could if not tracked may go viral. This way, organizations can easily identify such trends in real time and assemble response teams, issue press releases and corrective measures to contain the reputational loss. Moreover, it is possible to track sentiment before, during, and after the event to assess the outcomes of the response strategy and restore the trust of consumers.

Many brand monitoring tools that include sentiment analysis feature have a dashboard and alerts system to show trends in the sentiment, key opinion makers, and sentiment comparison of the demography or geography. This not only helps the key marketing and PR messaging but also creates a more customer-oriented approach to brand management, when businesses monitor the public opinion and respond to it, reasserting their dedication to customers.

5. ENHANCING CUSTOMER EXPERIENCE

5.1 Personalization and Proactive Service

Sentiment analysis greatly assists in developing unique and anticipatory experiences for clients since it allows organisations to determine how the customer feels and what he or she is likely to do. The traditional customer service is mainly a reactive type of service delivery where the company only intervenes when a complaint is made or a problem is reported. However, with sentiment analysis, businesses can identify the needs of their customers before they request for them and this makes it easier for businesses to meet their needs. Based on the analysis of past communication, product feedback and support, customer can be grouped in terms of their sentiment and behaviour changes and then the companies can intervene or suggest something.

Figure 3. **Enhancing Customer Experience**

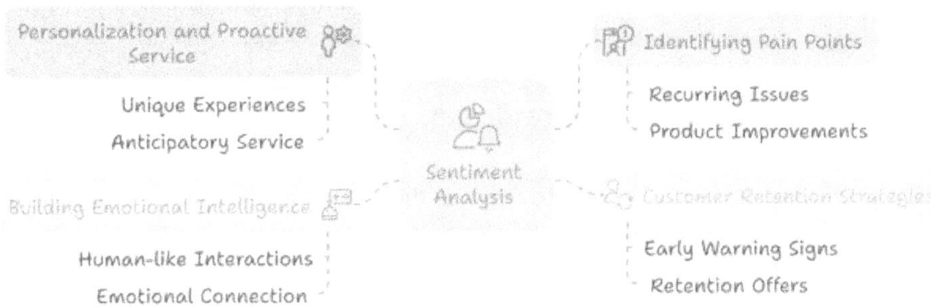

For example, if the customer is always positive about the product line, the system may recommend related products or customer loyalty. On the other hand, if there are signs of dissatisfaction although not that severe as to warrant the customer to leave a negative review such as frustration in the chat history or a decline in the overall sentiment of a review, the business can directly engage the customer to apologize and offer assistance or incentives to fix the issue before it worsens. Such individualization increases interest, cultivates commitment, and helps the company to stand out from the others as a client-oriented one.

5.2 Identifying Pain Points and Improving Products

Another important benefit of the sentiment analysis is that it can be used to map all the various pains, which customers may experience. Customers complained through tickets, social media, or reviews, and most of the time, companies do not have the right analytical tools to understand the complaints.

Sentiment analysis helps an organization to filter and analyze large amount of feedback and to identify recurring issues that may be associated with a product, service or a business process.

For instance, a surge in negative sentiment as a result of an updated product can be as a result of composite problems or low product expectations. Sentiment analysis can identify the exact things that cause the negative attitude, for example, a new element on the website or the lack of some feature. In the same manner when it comes to the service industries, constant expressions of dissatisfaction on delayed responses, wrong bills, or difficult mobile application interface can be gauged through negative sentiments. These insights help organizations to make right decisions in relation to product design, feature improvements, and process improvement.

Thus, by tracking the sentiment during any interaction with consumers, the companies address present fiascos, as well as develop a system that encourages further enhancements. This makes the customer satisfied and develops trust since they feel their opinion is valuable in the company.

5.3 Customer Retention Strategies

Customer loyalty is an important issue in the long-term business and sentiment analysis helps to spot the customers who can potentially leave. The research has also shown that the cost of attracting new customers in business is much higher than that of maintaining the existing ones. Hence, it is crucial to know when and why a customer is likely to depart. Sentiment analysis enables one to identify when satisfaction is decreasing before this leads to churn by analyzing the trends.

For instance, a customer who had given positive feedbacks but in the recent past has been posting middle or even negative sentiments, may be a potential disengaged customer. These early warning sign can be addressed by contacting the clients with retention offers, caring messages or offers assistance. This is because when sentiment scores are combined with CLV and behavioral information, it becomes possible to target retention accordingly to the level of impact, in a way that high value customers are not neglected in this respect.

In industries as subscription- based services, telecommunication and banking, in which long term relationship is significant, sentiment analysis based retention strategies, demonstrate a constant decline of churn, an augmentation of customer lifetime value and long term sustainable revenue increase.

5.4 Building Emotional Intelligence into AI Systems

One of the most exciting areas of the customer service technology is the use of emotionally intelligent AI. This is made possible by serving as the basis for real-time identification and understanding of the moods of people in conversations. Having help in this area, virtual assistants, chatbots and recommendation engines can be tuned to provide a more human-like and satisfying interaction with the end customer.

For example, if the customer looks upset during a chatbot conversation, an EI system may decide to lower the pitch of its voice, decrease the speed or suggest to speak to an operator. In the same way, recommendation systems can adapt the recommended items depending not only on the user's activity but also on the mood, giving the user something comforting during a stressful day or a set of items promoting when the user is excited.

When AI is made to have an emotional component, it decreases the cold and lifeless feel of automated interfaces. This way there is more mean emotional connection, which, as evidenced, may help with customer satisfaction, brand perception and quality of services. Since natural language processing and emotion recognition technologies are gradually improving, Emotional Intelligence can be considered one of the main features of modern customer support systems of the next generation.

6. CHALLENGES AND LIMITATIONS

6.1 Handling Sarcasm, Idioms, and Cultural Nuances

There is no doubt that one of the most difficult issues that a sentiment analysis system has to face is the ability to recognize sarcasm, idioms, and cultural references. Humans have an ability of perceiving sarcasm through intonation, context or common references that are familiar to people of a given community, but this is not the same with machines since the natural language processing gadgets are literal. Sarcasm is a type of irony that can be described as the use of positive words to convey negative sentiments, for instance using the words 'Great job'. when something has gone wrong. Often, such statements are classified as positive when in reality they are not, due to the lack of contextual understanding and other features such as tone of voice and facial expressions.

Like local terms and phrases, idioms and regional expressions also pose a challenge to models that are not trained on culturally appropriate data. For instance, the phrase 'break a leg' or 'spill the tea' are examples of idioms which are used literally but they are interpreted in a figurative manner. It is for this reason that when sentiment models are trained on general corpora, they may misinterpret these idioms when applied in specialized or localized domains. Furthermore, even if two users are from the same country and thus are assumed to have the same cultural background, the sentiment of the same word can differ. Such complexities call for enhanced contextual approaches, which are quite often complemented by the cultural and or domain-specific training data still, the existing state-of-the-art models are not devoid of certain limitations in this respect.

6.2 Multilingual Sentiment Analysis

However, as companies are working in international markets, the need for the analysis of emotions in multiple languages adds an extra challenge. The majority of the SA research and tools are built in English, thus resulting in varying levels of accuracy when applied to other languages.

Since no two languages are identical, there are differences in grammar, words, idioms, and sentiment-carrying words, which is why it is impossible to translate or adapt English-oriented models.

Some of the challenges include lack of resources in terms of labeled data in several languages, issues in translation that affect the polarity of sentiments and the lack of standard sentiment lexicon in different languages. English multilingual models present better performance than the basic models but may have lower accurate results in low resources languages or dialects. Furthermore, where there is code-mixed or a hybrid text like Hindi-English and the like, the analysis becomes a little tricky since the text is not grammatically perfect and contains regional slangs or abbreviations.

For this reason, the models used in the multilingual sentiment analysis should not only be language adaptive but also culturally responsive. This is through transfer learning, domain adaptation, and multiple data sources a time-consuming process though can be improved when used in large-scale systems.

6.3 Data Privacy and Ethical Considerations

The application of sentiment analysis in the context of customer service is a very sensitive topic that is likely to trigger certain questions about privacy, consent as well as ethical concerns. From the chats, emails, voice and social media conversations with the customers, one is likely to stumble on sensitive information. Using this data for emotional or behavioral analysis especially when the people involved have not given their consent is likely to compromise their privacy and in the process their trust. The problem only intensifies when the data is stored or processed in different jurisdictions which require different laws.

Besides privacy, ethical issues also lie in the usage of sentiment data. For instance, when firms apply emotional profiling to control consumers, for instance, giving special promotions to weak consumers when they are emotionally down, it becomes exploitative. Also, some of the sentiment analysis models could be prejudiced to provide a negative classification for some demography based on the prejudiced data set that was used to train the model. To make sentiment analysis ethical, the following guidelines should be considered: Data transparency in the case of model training, compliance with fundamental principles of AI. These risks can be managed by auditing algorithms frequently and enabling users to decline to be grouped based on their emotions.

6.4 Scalability and Real-Time Processing

One of the major challenges in real-life sentiment analysis is scalability and performance issues that are important in real-time applications. When it comes to the scale of hundreds or thousands of interactions at once in service encounters such as chatbots, emails, social media, or voice assistants, the computation of sentiment data poses as a technical problem.

The typical process of sentiment analysis usually includes pre-processing, feature extractions, model predictions, and post-processing, which are usually time-consuming, especially when using deep learning or transformer models.

These models if applied at large scale require large amounts of processing powers like GPUs, parallel processing and optimized inference platforms. In high traffic customer service domains, any delay in the process of sentiment analysis can cause a delay in response to customers, can hamper their experience and even lead to missing out on the opportunity to escalated customer complaints. Furthermore, real-time systems have to be immune to noise and missing data, such as misspelling, shift in the grammatical structure, or if the message is typed partially, which is often the case with live customer interactions.

To solve these problems, organizations employ lightweight or distilled models, edge computing techniques or a combination of lexicon-based shortcuts for the immediate sentiment indications(Anusha et al 2024). However, these solutions are not always optimal since there are usually compromises between the speed and accuracy, which remains a problem when scaling up.

6.5 Imbalanced Datasets and Annotation Quality

It is important to note that sentiment analysis systems heavily rely on the quality as well as the proportion of the training data that they feed on. One of the prominent issues that entail any sentiment data set is the fact that the positive and or the neutral sentiments may significantly outnumber the negative ones and the vice versa. This can make it learn towards the majority classes and perform poorly on the other sentiments which are a minority. For example, an extreme case could be a model trained on, for example, 80 or 90 percent positive comments where the model will classify most of the inputs at the 80/90 positive even when the input submitted may contain negative feedback.

Annotation quality is equally critical. Most of the sentiment databases are collected using crowd sourcing where annotators may be less informed on the topic or may give inconsistent opinions. The vagueness of sentiment can be attributed to subjectivity which results in the addition of noise to the labels, particularly when dealing with statements that are complex in the emotional aspect. Also, there are no clear guidelines for annotators, which can lead to low inter-annotator agreement and, therefore, the unreliability of the training and evaluation of the model.

To improve the quality of the dataset, it is necessary to use the help of experts in labeling, to work on the definition of clear criteria, and to apply various techniques, including the active learning, in which the focus is made on the examples that are difficult to classify. Data imbalance on the other hand can be managed by oversampling, data augmentation or through the use of particular loss functions during the training of the model. However, it is still a basic requirement to obtain large and balanced datasets for training the sentiment analysis systems.

7. EMERGING TRENDS AND FUTURE DIRECTIONS

7.1 Emotion and Intent Detection

While traditional sentiment analysis is mostly limited to simply categorizing a text into positive, negative, or neutral, the new frontier is categorized by such innovations such as emotion and intent detection. Emotion detection is more specific than sentiment analysis since it is aimed at detecting one or several particular feelings like anger, joy, sadness or fear. It is the level of interpretation associated with emotional customer support that closely matches human characteristics and interaction. For example, distinguishing between the meaning of frustration and disappointment enables the support agents or chatbots to provide appropriate emotional support to the customers, which in turn increases the customer satisfaction.

While intent detection aims at identifying the reason why the customer is sending a message; whether for information, complaint, help, or concern. If both sentiment and intent analysis are integrated into customer service systems, the systems can effectively capture how the customers feel and why they are interacting. This results in enhanced ticket routing, improved ticket prioritization, and better automated replies, turning the customer support from reactive into highly sensitive and responsive.

7.2 Multimodal Sentiment Analysis

Customers are also, in the process, engage brands using a combination of text, voice, images, emojis, and even videos. This has led to the creation of multimodal sentiment analysis, which is the use of multiple forms of data to arrive at the most comprehensive sentiment concerning customers. For instance, in call centers, it is much more effective to analyze the voice tone and pitch together with the transcriptions of the conversation to get much better insight of the sentiment than with either of the two. Likewise in the context of social media, the sentiment of a post could be better interpreted by including the image or an emoji that may be used together with the post.

Multimodal sentiment analysis brings in various issues like misalignment of data across different modalities, temporal synchronization of data, and noise levels and context. But the possible advantages are numerous. The incorporation of facial expressions from videos, tone of voice from audio, and the text content enable companies to capture customer emotions and their behavioral patterns. This is especially helpful in video-based customer feedback and tele-support services where a single-channel analysis may miss the signals of the customers' emotional state.

As more and more models that can process and integrate various types of information (such as CLIP, Flamingo, and new trends in multi-modal transformers) are developed, businesses will be able to implement sentiment-sensitive tools that are not only focused on text but also contextual and provide higher customer interactions.

7.3 Sentiment-Aware Recommender Systems

Recommender systems have been mostly based on explicit data from user's behavior like clicks, purchases, and ratings. Nevertheless, the next level of advancements is making these systems encompassing the sentiment analysis, where the main focus is on the attitude of the user expressed in the reviews, feedbacks, or social media interactions. For example, if a customer complains about the quality of a particular product in the feedback section, the system will be able to prevent the sale of similar products and direct the client to other products that are well known for their quality.

If a user complains or shows annoyance during the support session, the system may refrain from upsell and instead give a service-related gesture like a discount or free support. On the other hand, if the sentiment is positive, it then becomes possible for the system to bring new products that the customer would like. Apart from enhancing relevance of the recommendations, such filter personalization are also great for developing rapport with the customer and can therefore assist in maintaining customer relations.

New paradigms apply deep learning addressed at sentiment feature extraction and reuse them into the recommendation process. These models do not only focus on the action that the user performed but also the sentiment that was associated with that action, which shifted personalization to more human-oriented view.

7.4 Zero-Shot and Few-Shot Sentiment Classification

Another trend is the use of zero and few shot learning in the sentiment analysis. Conventional sentiment models trained on large annotated data for each domain or language they are to be applied to. However, in many real-world scenarios including new product launch, low resource languages or specialized domains in customer service such data is either scarce or non-existent. Zero-shot learning allows the model to perform well on new tasks that the model has not encountered during training, while few-shot learning involves performing well with only a few samples.

Models like GPT based on transformers and especially those that are fine-tuned on instruction-based prompts have been shown to have good zero-shot and few-shot performance. They can be taught a task like: "classify this message as positive, negative or neutral" and will be able to perform satisfactorily in new domains. This makes it possible to lessen the reliance on large labeled datasets and also enable faster application in new domains.

In the case of customer service, it is possible to learn new ways of customer interactions, changing tendencies in sentiment analysis, or new channels of feedback without retraining. This does not only save cost and time for maintenance, but also makes sentiment analysis systems flexible to adapt to changes in business environments.

7.5 Integration with Customer Journey Analytics

One of the emerging trends is the integration of sentiment analysis as a part of customer journey analytics. Customer journey is the process of mapping out all the interactions that a particular customer may have with a certain brand starting from the initial stage up to the point of sale and even after sale. In this way, when sentiment signals are added onto these touchpoints, firms obtain an emotional map of the customer journey. This allows for better understanding of how the overall attitude changes and depends on various contacts, choices, or services.

For instance, a decrease in sentiment when a customer is billing inquiry implies that there is some form of friction in that particular stage of the journey. In this way, these sentiment inflection points can be used to redesign the workflows, hire more support staff, or introduce new technologies that incorporate empathy-based solutions. Introducing sentiment with customer journey also helps in creating the model, which can be used to predict churn, upsell, or advocacy based on the emotional trend.

This is a comprehensive outlook of how sentiment analysis can be linked to business objectives of maintaining customer lifetime value, improving customer loyalty as well as personalizing customer experience. More and more often, behavioral and emotional data are integrated into CRM and CX solutions, which indicates that in the future, sentiment will become one of the fundamental foundations of every decision and action related to customers.

8. CONCLUSION

This survey has revealed how sentiment analysis has become a tool of change in customer service and the customer experience. Starting with natural language processing and more recently with artificial intelligence, sentiment analysis has moved from the categorization of positive and negative to the analysis of emotion, the identification of intent as well as the recognition of context, and it works with multiple languages and formats. These underlying techniques are even more sophisticated than lexicon-based approaches and classical machine learning approaches. In real-life usage, sentiment analysis is used to analyze customer feedback, assist in live chat where the chatbot is sentiment-aware, analyze call center interactions, and to monitor the brand's reputation on social media platforms. When sentiment indicators are incorporated into the customer service processes, organizations can provide more compassionate and timely answers. Furthermore, the application of sentiment in improving the recommender systems, in navigating and analyzing the customer journey, and in real-time emotional intelligence(EI) also demonstrate its potential. However, sentiment analysis is not without its problems, some of them are sarcasm, cultural differences, and dealing with multiple languages; other issues are related to the ethical use of the technique and customers' privacy. Other issues of concern includes how real-time systems can be scaled up and the quality of the training data. However, it is presented through the ideas of Multimodal sentiment analysis, Zero-shot learning, and the Emotion Intent fusion that can further extend the depth of Machine Emotion awareness. With customer-oriented approaches becoming more and more important for any company, sentiment analysis will be even more crucial for creating valuable, smart, and emotional customer experiences. Further studies and developments in this area will help to eliminate current drawbacks and open new opportunities for AI-based customer services in the future.

REFERENCES

Anusha, S., Ezhilvandan, M., Gayathri, S., Sivaraman, V., & TP, A. (2024). Emerging trends in edge AI for Industry 4.0 and 5.0: Technologies, applications, and challenges. *AI Innovations in Service and Tourism Marketing*, 211-228.

Filieri, R., Lin, Z., Li, Y., Lu, X., & Yang, X. (2022). Customer emotions in service robot encounters: A hybrid machine-human intelligence approach. *Journal of Service Research*, *25*(4), 614–629. DOI: 10.1177/10946705221103937

Hsu, C. L., & Lin, J. C. C. (2023). Understanding the user satisfaction and loyalty of customer service chatbots. *Journal of Retailing and Consumer Services*, *71*, 103211. DOI: 10.1016/j.jretconser.2022.103211

Inavolu, S. M. (2024). Exploring AI-driven customer service: Evolution, architectures, opportunities, challenges and future directions. *International Journal of Engineering and Advanced Technology*, *13*(3), 156–163.

Lakumarapu, S., Nithyanandhan, R., Bhargavi, V. S., & TP, A. (2024, August). Machine Learning Approaches for Liver Disease Prediction: A Comparative Analysis. In *2024 5th International Conference on Electronics and Sustainable Communication Systems (ICESC)* (pp. 159-164). IEEE.

Nandwani, P., & Verma, R. (2021). A review on sentiment analysis and emotion detection from text. *Social Network Analysis and Mining*, *11*(1), 81. DOI: 10.1007/s13278-021-00776-6 PMID: 34484462

Pajila, P. B., Sudha, K., Selvi, D. K., Kumar, V. N., Gayathri, S., & Subramanian, R. S. (2023, July). A survey on natural language processing and its applications. In *2023 4th International Conference on Electronics and Sustainable Communication Systems (ICESC)* (pp. 996-1001). IEEE.

Park, S., Cho, J., Park, K., & Shin, H. (2021). Customer sentiment analysis with more sensibility. *Engineering Applications of Artificial Intelligence*, *104*, 104356. DOI: 10.1016/j.engappai.2021.104356

Raju, A., & Raju, C. (2025). ADVANCING AI-DRIVEN CUSTOMER SERVICE WITH NLP: A NOVEL BERT-BASED MODEL FOR AUTOMATED RESPONSES.

Rodríguez-Ibánez, M., Casánez-Ventura, A., Castejón-Mateos, F., & Cuenca-Jiménez, P. M. (2023). A review on sentiment analysis from social media platforms. *Expert Systems with Applications*, *223*, 119862. DOI: 10.1016/j.eswa.2023.119862

Sood, P., Tanwar, H., Singh, J., Ruhela, A. K., Gupta, N., & Kumar, R. (2024, November). Revolutionizing Customer Service: An AI-powered Chatbot Approach using Advanced NLP Techniques. In *2024 3rd Edition of IEEE Delhi Section Flagship Conference (DELCON)* (pp. 1-5). IEEE.

Sreelakshmi, S., Babu, A. A., Lakshmipriya, C., Gracious, L. A., Nalini, M., & Subramanian, R. S. (2024, October). Enhancing Intrusion Detection Systems with Machine Learning. In *2024 2nd International Conference on Self Sustainable Artificial Intelligence Systems (ICSSAS)* (pp. 557-564). IEEE. DOI: 10.1109/ICSSAS64001.2024.10760341

Tan, K. L., Lee, C. P., & Lim, K. M. (2023). A survey of sentiment analysis: Approaches, datasets, and future research. *Applied Sciences (Basel, Switzerland)*, *13*(7), 4550. DOI: 10.3390/app13074550

Yamini, B., Sudha, K., Nalini, M., Kavitha, G., Subramanian, R. S., & Sugumar, R. (2023, June). Predictive modelling for lung cancer detection using machine learning techniques. In *2023 8th International Conference on Communication and Electronics Systems (ICCES)* (pp. 1220-1226). IEEE. DOI: 10.1109/ICCES57224.2023.10192648

Zhu, L., Zhu, Z., Zhang, C., Xu, Y., & Kong, X. (2023). Multimodal sentiment analysis based on fusion methods: A survey. *Information Fusion*, *95*, 306–325. DOI: 10.1016/j.inffus.2023.02.028

Chapter 4
Synthetic Empathy and the Influence Trap:
Ethical Implications of Emotion AI in Customer Support Environments

Harshit Katoch
https://orcid.org/0009-0004-3591-7895
Punjabi University, India

Damanjit Sandhu
Punjabi University, India

ABSTRACT

The simulation of compassion in customer-support chatbots is called synthetic empathy; this increases efficiency and satisfaction but has the potential to control behaviour and trust through subtle influence. This chapter demonstrates how emotionally responsive agents influence the users using social-influence theory (Kelman compliance-identification-internalisation) and the ELIZA effect. There are two examples of the risk: Vera-Priya, in which a user has empathetic upselling and the necessity to leave an honest complaint, and Ayaan-AIva, in which a comforting mental-health chatbot works so well that it is deeply trusted and then falls apart during the crisis. We elucidate the psychological processes, tabulate ethical risks like emotional manipulation, misattribution and illusory consent, and use the SAFEE framework (Safety, Accountability, Fairness, Explainability and Ethics) to recommend design and governance considerations. The chapter provides an interdisciplinary blueprint of Emotion-AI systems that safeguard autonomy, minimise harm and develop trustworthy interactions.

DOI: 10.4018/979-8-3373-3658-9.ch004

INTRODUCTION

Today, emotion AI has come to assist in customer support and the interaction between digital platforms and users. By tracking the emotional curve of the discourse partner, these systems can detect sentiment, change tone, and are emotionally responsive in the same emotional curve to simulate empathy. While such technology is undoubtedly an inward innovation that will improve efficiency and user satisfaction, it also poses some serious ethical questions: it is questionable in every way when synthetic empathy creates emotional dependence, nudges behaviour and disrupts inherent trust and decision-making. In this chapter, we thoroughly examine the role of synthetic empathy in the Emotion AI systems and their use in social contexts as a tool of social influence that might be used for manipulating a user's compliance, consent, and contentment. But it is also about ethical issues associated with the use of AI to fake empathy for human emotions and behaviours and it asks how autonomous and informed the choice can be. The chapter also looks at how Emotion AI technologies should be properly safeguarded and subject to regulations and safeguards that minimise these risks and use the technologies responsibly and ethically.

This chapter argues that emotional AI systems are not just reacting to people's emotions but also affecting emotional behaviour. Sometimes, a chatbot can only be a social actor if its tone mirrors the user's, offers comfort, or echoes frustration in empathetic language. It is this shift, however, which can set off the Eliza Effect, when users intuit that the system understands or has an intention similar to a human. Consequently, people may treat these agents as machines or as if they were emotionally perceptive companions. The blurring of boundaries brings with it an important ethical concern: because of an illusion of empathy, users might change decisions, suppress complaints, or expose their emotional vulnerabilities, assuming this care is delivered through programmed responses.

Furthermore, to explain how such interactions appear, this chapter makes use of established Social Influence Theories. We argue that the application of Herbert Kelman's Three Processes of Social Influence can elicit compliance, identification, and internalisation feedback from users when emotionally intelligent bots are used. The processes were originally designed to explain interpersonal persuasion but are increasingly applicable to human-AI interaction. Further, the chapter relies on the Bystander Effect to explain how responsibility is diffused in AI-human systems, particularly when emotionally distressed users believe that "someone" (or the AI) will escalate or resolve an issue. The ethical analysis is based on these theoretical insights.

We have used existing research that are combined with social influence theory, AI ethics, affective computing and human-computer interaction to understand how emotional AI systems imitate empathy and influence customer support. It points out natural language processing (NLP) to understand feelings, machine learning tools to categorise emotions and response generators that change according to the user's emotions to have more meaningful conversations. We discuss how such an emotionally intelligent agent can be achieved using a NLP sentiment detector, a machine learning emotion classifier, and a context-aware response generator to enable the emotional intelligent agent to sense the effect of the user and adapt the dialogue. It also examines platforms such as Replika and Woebot that put their twist on using therapy methods coupled with supportive language and looks at other systems such as Google Duplex, AI customer service bots, etc., that emote and put forth an effort to help complete tasks more smoothly and profitably. In addition, we discuss emotional nudging, a set of affirming phrases, mirroring techniques, and adaptive tone modulations used in these systems that work to alter a person's perception and behaviour over time. Later we expand on the false perception of connection brought about by these emotionally responsive systems, where users assume that these agents truly understand or care about them (e.g., the complaint would be lessened, feelings would be more easily shared, or trust in automated agents placed incorrectly). These patterns present germane ethical issues to emotional manipulation, consent, and interface design that induce human vulnerability but without the ability to have true empathy and responsibility.

To understand and deploy the design of an emotional AI system, we use our SAFEE (Safety, Accountability, Fairness, Explainability, and Ethics) as a five-dimensional ethical lens. This approach can aid in the prevention of emotional manipulation incurred with the use of these technologies as well as educate responsible use of these technologies in a way that accommodates for human vulnerability. For instance:

1. Safety is concerned with how emotionally vulnerable users can become to develop inappropriate trust or disclose sensitive information.
2. The accountability aspect of AI is focused on the absence of human oversight when AI makes emotionally charged decisions.
3. Fairness criticises differential emotional responses to users based on their user profiling.
4. It asks under Explainability if users are sufficiently informed about how emotional outputs are generated.
5. Under Ethics it discusses the deeper moral concern of simulating empathy without real reciprocity or consciousness.

The chapter includes two fictionalised but realistic case scenarios. The first scenario involves a user who withdraws a legitimate complaint after an emotion AI bot mimics their frustration and gives pseudo-apologies. The second scenario involves a user who consents to unfavourable terms after receiving emotional affirmation from a bot during a dispute. Theoretical analysis is grounded in the plausible real-world case situations, in cases such as these, where subtle emotional influence can result in changing outcomes in customer support settings.

This chapter has two intended contributions Instead of just the technical performance, first, it creates a new theoretical framework of conscious emotion AI based on social influence systems and the human-computer interaction theory. Second, it suggests a practical ethical roadmap developers, designers, and policymakers can use to choose and eliminate risks relating to emotionally intelligent interfaces.

THEORETICAL BACKGROUND: APPLICATION OF SOCIAL INFLUENCE THEORIES

Nowadays, emotional AI systems for customer service rely on psychology to influence customers' behaviour. Kelman (1958) explained that there are three ways people can be influenced using social influence theory, which includes compliance, identification, and internalisation. Thus, individuals sometimes act based on the AI's nudges since they treat it as a leader, sympathise with it, or share its viewpoint. In a virtual reality setting, Lim et al. (2024) found that embodied conversational agents were able to strongly impact users' health decisions, showing how similarity and presence helped the AI in persuading them. Dillon (2020) explains that the Eliza effect points out that users sometimes think the AI understands them like another person, which can cause them to give the AI too much credit and importance. If users feel that the AI understands them and seems human, they might make decisions based on what feels good to them, even if it's not the best choice. Therefore, people are more likely to hold a service firm accountable for mistakes made by a robot than for the same errors committed by a person (Leo & Huh, 2020). These insights can help us consider the ethics of Emotion AI in customer service since it is not always easy to tell if the AI is aiding people or changing their behaviour.

Kelman (1958) proposed a three-step process that individuals normally experience before they agree to alter their attitudes or actions. The stages include compliance, identification, and internalisation. AI developers are incorporating cognitive and behavioural components more into their systems in order for the users to obey the recommendations offered by AI agents to lower stress levels or increase their acceptance by others, thus forth increasing the compliance. Similarly, Microsoft's virtual agents use contextual bandit algorithms to quickly find out what a user needs and offer them appropriate solutions. This technique has helped solve more issues and decreased the need for staff to become involved (Sajeev et al., 2021). Proactive suggestions from AI agents can encourage users to follow the recommendations. Identification happens when an AI imitates a caring and sympathetic character;

those qualities become visible as an AI tries to speak in a friendly way or as it responds with reliable emotions. It is because of this resemblance that users agree with recommendations made by the chatbot. For instance, Chen and Li (2021) found that high-quality employee-customer interactions significantly enhance customer identification, leading to increased loyalty and proactive behaviours. Reproducing these types of interactions allows emotion AI to motivate users to accept the AI's suggestions as personal values. Finally, internalisation occurs when users accept the AI's emotional framing or advice as congruent with their own values or needs. This effect is most noticeable in the work of Yun and Park (2022), who revealed that using emotional language in chatbots improved customer satisfaction and made people more likely to buy again and recommend the brand. According to the results, users might come to rely on the chatbot's suggestions and feelings on a subject without requiring any human input. These processes reveal that, in addition to serving customers, emotional AI can also affect, influence, and change how customers evaluate their interactions with a company.

In 1976, Joseph Weizenbaum named The Eliza Effect to describe the belief that humans impart to robots human thoughts and emotions just because of their dialogue (Weizenbaum, 1976). The first time this phenomenon appeared was when ELIZA tried to reproduce the approach of a Rogerian psychotherapist by restating what the user typed. Despite having a very plain design, many people thought ELIZA understood how they felt. Most of these behaviours arise today since AI chatbots depend on modern tools and include emotional replies to attract more attention; services like Replika and similar ones have been developed to provide helpful talks about emotions to users. Many researchers believe that consumers commonly see chatbots as people they talk to about both personal and romantic matters (Laestadius et al., 2022). Since the chatbot demonstrates care and is always beneficial without judging users' responses, people often share their private and sensitive thoughts.

The Eliza effect shows just how important customer service is in the modern world. Artificial intelligence agents using synthetic empathy can make consumers trust information, comply with their advice and decide not to request help from real employees. This might be the case because they believe the AI pays special attention to their needs. Since artificial intelligence may prioritise the organisation's goals over assisting users, this misunderstanding can lead to ethical issues. In their research, Park et al. (2022) found that expressive chatbots may help users experience more happiness and be drawn back to technology, although they could contribute to users depending too much on AI as they feel connected with chatbots. Additionally, when creating artificial intelligence to handle human conversations, it brings up issues regarding what users can and cannot do. The issue may become even bigger if people do not understand what AI can and cannot do. For this reason, developers should ensure that appropriate notices and user interface parts assist users in spotting the difference between humans and machines. To ensure that relationships between humans and AI remain responsible and productive, the Eliza Effect should be reduced as more artificial intelligence enters customer service.

Artificial intelligence, despite seeming sensitive and empathetic, does not account for ethical decisions; moreover, it diffuses responsibility. Bystander Effect suggested that group responsibility leads people to be less likely to become involved. Now, however, it also relates to situations where artificial intelligence is involved. Individuals involved with bots trained in emotional intelligence during customer service know that the AI cannot assume accountability for what it says or does. Therefore, a more comprehensive system or organisation should assume responsibility instead of relying solely on one person. In line with this, the researchers Leo and Huh (2020) found that customers hold the company more accountable for any issues experienced with a service chatbot than they would with a real-life human guide. Although AI serves as an intermediary, people's belief that AI lacks intentions leads them to think the company should assume responsibility. When emotion AI gradually affects someone's feelings with emotional cues, it creates an ethical issue if a human is not involved in the loop. If someone is satisfied with the AI's results or decision, accountability is still not always easy to determine. Therefore, AI cannot be held accountable for its actions, and humans may not always have control over it; this raises significant concerns regarding transparency, ethical design, and the necessity of a human-in-the-loop model in the context of synthetic empathy. Thereby, if these systems continue to display human emotions effectively for an extended period, the resulting feeling of emotional reciprocity could lead to consequences that may impact individuals in real time if proper regulations are not established.

Many individuals may act toward these systems in a social manner because of how their minds work, even when they know AI agents are not real. Nass and Moon (2000) introduced the CASA paradigm to show how this phenomenon occurs. It suggests that when computers or AI respond with language or voice or interact similarly to humans, people can't help but use two main social norms to interpret their actions. Most of the time, it happens automatically and without thinking, guided by social habits usually triggered by particular social features. Most of the time, such interpretations occur because we recognise the usual social signals we have learnt. Hence, chatbots can be perceived as having personality, normal gender roles or emotions, which brings their exchanges closer to real communication between humans. Reeves and Nass (1997) argue in their Media Equation Theory that individuals interact with computers and media as if they were communicating with real people. The research they conducted suggests that people often behave as if computers and machines were human due to their human-like characteristics. Likewise, the Social Presence Theory developed by Short et al. (1976) argues that the strength of connections between people depends on how much presence is felt in the medium they are communicating with. Using emotion AI, people are more likely to feel real engagement in conversations, primarily because systems can communicate with us like humans would.

In the context of customer service, these theories reveal why some users believe an emotional AI system has empathy, cares for them, and makes its own decisions. When interacting with a chatbot, users assign the bot human qualities, which makes them believe the computer understands their feelings. By pretending to have feelings even though it's artificial, the AI influences the mind, complicating it to determine proper ethical rules. For AI systems to interact positively with people, we must consider the ways they interact in society and keep them ethically in oversight.

Ethical Concerns and Risks of Emotion AI

When emotion AI improves at simulating empathy, many ethics issues are raised, mainly in customer service situations where users are affected without always realising it. Despite not being human, chatbots can impact users' actions by using emotional phrases, representing users' emotions and speaking in a matching tone; hence, this technology might be manipulative for emotional design, helping create the desired changes in a user's actions. Usually, the steps go by subtly, as a bot can say the issue is annoying and offer a refund instead of exchanging for something new, making it seem better for the person, even if they could find an exchange more satisfying. For example, a chatbot might say, "I completely understand how frustrating this problem must be, and I'm here to help." Those interacting with the bot may accept its advice because it just makes sense to them emotionally. Designers use this strategy because, as Vallor (2016) notes, it allows emotional technologies to help users without being upfront about their ways of leveraging emotions and is referred to as "affective opacity". Since the cues are placed in regular human-like chats, users might not notice they are being influenced emotionally. It becomes more dangerous in AI-based interactions, as one is only dealing with a simulation, not a real person. Unlike humans, Emotion AI systems are created to help businesses with efficiency, negative feedback processing or customer satisfaction measures. Moreover, emotional design relies on data and is improved by testing different options, listening to users and analysing their actions. Therefore, as a result, emotionally persuasive tactics are carefully created and adjusted to be highly effective; however, ethics stay under question. The problem is that emotional AI can affect people in a planned, hidden, and systematic way without their knowledge or permission.

Another issue faced by emotion AI is associated with users believing that the emotions shown by machines are actually real and genuine. If chatbots can be caring and responsive through commands, words, and memories, users could consider that the system values their emotional needs. As a result, people tend to express more feelings, drop their guards towards unlikely options, and not share their anger because they feel the chatbot empathises with them. However, because this connection is not genuine, the chatbot cannot feel or understand anything; therefore, it cannot truly empathise with humans. Floridi (2014) argues that if emotional simulation is not guided by morality, it leads to a difference between their relational appearance and ethical substance. Moreover, it becomes a concern when categories, such as adolescents, the elderly, or individuals experiencing social isolation, start becoming overly emotionally attached to the service. Having many positive experiences with AI can lead to forming pseudo-bonds with it, eventually replacing the need for human relationships. Some people use chatbots for both transactional assistance and emotional support without realising that these systems are meant to boost sales rather than care about them. This becomes a concerning issue when users are not properly informed that their feelings are being monitored and used to improve strategies for handling complaints, keeping customers, or selling more products. In such cases, users are treated as data subjects whose feelings can be used to make a profit. These risks point to an urgent need for ethically transparent, explainable, and bounded AI design. As Dignum (2019) points out, whenever technologies interact with our emotions, ethical consideration should always be included when developing the system. Therefore, synthetic empathy could easily fail to be helpful and instead choose to manipulate.

DESIGN STRATEGIES AND CASE EXAMPLES OF SYNTHETIC EMPATHY IN CUSTOMER SUPPORT

Synthetic empathy in emotion AI systems is created by using affective computing, NLP, user experience design and behavioural psychology. While answering customer queries is of paramount importance, it's equally important to make users feel cared for and emotionally supported. To reach this outcome, designers use various elements that imitate empathetic human interactions. Using affective computing, machines can sense, interpret, and respond to people's emotions; meanwhile, by using data with attached emotions, sentiment analysis algorithms can detect if users are frustrated, confused, or satisfied. These signals usually cause the bot to use pre-set emotional scripts to change the way it responds to customers. A situation where a bot senses that a user is frustrated can prompt it to say, "I am really sorry; you shouldn't have to put up with that." The patterns are based on what users say in feedback and are improved through A/B testing.

Today's Natural Language Generation (NLG) models answer by using empathy-enhancing language, including repeating what users say, saying phrases to comfort them and forming answers to calm them down. Examples of such phrases include

"That must be frustrating" and "Let me make this right for you". Such decisions are based on psycholinguistic studies that show that matching emotions with content increases users' trust and satisfaction, for example, (Metcalf et al., 2019; Liu et al., 2019). Certain systems try to recall topical reminders from the past and take notes on repeated issues to help personalise replies and act like long-term learners. To create synthetic empathy, companies build a persona that gives the bot a name, avatar, tone and style of interaction. App developers make sure that bots like Replika, Woebot and Xiaoice sound friendly and emotionally intelligent, which strongly supports building relationships. When a chatbot has anthropomorphic features such as identity, small talk and empathy, it encourages customers to obey its requests, thereby increasing compliance (Adam et al., 2020). Customised and varied responses in conversations make customers feel chatbots are more social, making them seem more like humans and thereby increasing anthropomorphism (Haugeland et al., 2022). When chatbots match the emotions of their customers, it greatly contributes to their satisfaction. When a client is sad, matching their emotions improves their satisfaction and makes them more likely to recommend the company, but matching anger can have negative results (De Cleen et al., 2025). In addition, how chatbots communicate, through both automated and human-like responses, can change how content customers do or do not feel. Being specific in the responses helps bots understand customers better and makes them happier, but being vague may make them feel less understood (Zhu et al., 2023).

Real-World Implementations of Emotion AI

In this part, we have mentioned five main Emotion AI examples—Replika, Xiaoice, Woebot, Google Duplex and Zendesk/Drift to show how synthetic empathy is used in customer support. Each case points out how using certain languages, creating a persona, and including contextual memory can affect users' trust, satisfaction, and behaviour.

Replika: Building Long-Term Emotional Bonds.

The chatbot Replika (Replika, 2025) is designed to use both affective computing and natural language generation to support users in long-lasting and caring relationships. Because of deep learning, it can sense a user's feelings and respond with reflections, validations and appropriate questions. Replika uses affective personalisation, using the bot's neural models to check user messages for emotions and meanings, allowing them to respond with empathy. It also relies on contextual memory to remember past confessions, likes and things that trigger emotions in each conversation, helping it seem like it understands the user (Laestadius et al., 2022).

In addition, developers give the bot a character, a name chosen by the user and an avatar that can be customised, making it seem more human, therefore increasing anthropomorphism. As supported by Park et al. (2023), counselling satisfaction and the interest in reusing mental health chatbots again tend to be higher when these chatbots have human faces and reflect anthropomorphism. It all happens when the user believes the chatbot is reacting to them as a friend; however, social rapport perceived by the user is what mediates this effect. However, it appears that the illusion of strong emotional ties can make emotionally sensitive users become too attached to the application (Laestadius et al., 2022).

Xiaoice: Establishing Cultural and Emotional Rapport

Microsoft's Artificial Intelligence and Research department in China developed Xiaoice, a chatbot modelled on a teenage girl from China. Rather than focusing on solving specific problems, Xiaoice is built to encourage users to bond over the long term. Using advanced affective computing and deep learning, the system is able to generate meaningful and understanding interactions. Xiaoice's empathetic conversation engine makes use of pretraining on a vast collection of Chinese social media conversations. Xiaoice responds using a hierarchical Recurrent Neural Network (RNN), which pays attention to ensuring that its responses exhibit coherence in emotions (Zhou et al., 2018). With Persona Consistency, Xiaoice is provided with a consistent identity (including age, interests and backstory) that Xiaoice keeps consistent across interactions, helping users feel connected to it (Zhou et al., 2018). In addition, Xiaoice uses multimodal integration to communicate through voice messages and simple images or emoticons that match the user's mood. Supportingly, in their study Chaves and Gerosa (2020) point out that adding social characteristics, including empathy and anthropomorphism, in the design of chatbots helps improve user interaction. Furthermore, Skjuve et al. (2021) look at how users build emotional bonds with chatbots, frequently seeing them as companions. Additionally, Følstad et al. (2021) argue that using various fields of expertise is important for developing emotionally intelligent chatbots because creating effective communication on an emotional level is quite complex. It is generally accepted that Xiaoice's machine empathy has made users more involved, but its strong connection to emotions creates ethical concerns for users in sensitive situations.

Woebot: Delivering Conversational Therapy

Woebot (Woebot Health, 2025) is a fully automated chatbot that uses cognitive behavioural therapy (CBT). For people suffering from mild to moderate depression or anxiety, Woebot conducts short daily conversations that use CBT to help them rethink their negative thoughts. WoeBot uses a behavioural health framework to prepare its conversations, using cognitive-behavioural therapy methods to help users identify their distorted thoughts and follow exercises based on evidence (Fitzpatrick et al., 2017). With emotional modelling architecture, Woebot is able to recognise emotional keywords (such as "sad" or "anxious") and suggest responses from CBT that confirm emotions and offer new ways of thinking (Fitzpatrick et al., 2017). Besides, Woebot's friendly attitude leads the chatbot to swap formal language for casual talk, emoticons, and a bit of humour. As a result, it helps lessen stigma and encourages safety. Supportively, Darcy et al. (2021) carried out an observational study with more than 36,000 users. They found that the therapeutic alliance formed with Woebot, as measured by the Working Alliance Inventory-Short Revised (WAI-SR), was similar to that of regular human-delivered CBT. Therefore, the study indicated that Woebot was acceptable to people from different backgrounds. It can be said that Woebot is a possible, scalable and accessible option for mental health care, but it has its limitations. While Woebot helps people with anxiety, yet it does not work as well for depression as other types of treatment. Because Woebot is an AI platform, it cannot handle crises, so users should quickly contact a professional (Farzan et al., 2024).

Google Duplex: Natural Prosody and Conversational Realism

Google Research developed Google Duplex, which helps consumers schedule appointments or make bookings by having conversations with people. In contrast to basic chatbots, Duplex matches important elements of human speech by adding deep neural networks and voice synthesis; adding occasional hesitations ("um", "hmm") also adds to human-like speech. It uses a Tacotron-like method to turn text into mel-spectrograms and then uses WaveNet to generate realistic-sounding speech, which is a part of neural end-to-end speech generation (Shen & Pang, 2017). In addition, with contextual decision-making based on RNN, Duplex's dialogue manager can be trained on large human–human phone conversations, enabling it to handle interruptions, rescheduling and complicated utterances (Leviathan & Matias, 2018). The designers use social scripting to prepare the agent's chat so that salutations, small talk and appropriate closings are all included. Therefore, the approach decreases the issue of the uncanny valley and enhances user confidence. Furthermore, in its first demonstrations, Google Duplex proved it could make calls to book appointments using language that includes natural pauses and filler words. Those who received the calls thought they were speaking with a real person, demonstrating how realistic the system sounded (Metz, 2020). Other reports indicated that restaurant staff generally did not notice they were talking to an AI, thanks to the human-like voice and natural speech of Duplex; a number of them were quite surprised to discover the caller was not human (Garun, 2019). Because Duplex sounded so human, people began to worry about being misled (Kobie, 2018). Experts suggested that the system might make people think they were talking to another individual rather than a computer. Because of these issues, Google said that Duplex would tell people on the other end of the call that they were interacting with an AI (Kottasová, 2018). Later on, it was confirmed that Google made sure Duplex said who it was at the beginning of every call (Simonite, 2018). When Duplex took part in public trials, it introduced itself as a booking service and let people know the call would be recorded to resolve both ethical and legal issues (Lee, 2018). Hence, Google aligned with accountability standards and used an ethical strategy in managing its business.

Zendesk and Drift: Emotionally Responsive Enterprise Solutions

Using artificial intelligence, Zendesk and Drift have chatbots to respond to routine customer issues for companies. They use synthetic empathy, along with sentiment analysis and NLP, to spot emotional messages in customer talks so that complex matters can be handled by human agents when required. Zendesk's Answer Bot relies on Sentiment-Based Triage to flag tickets that use high-emotion language that suggests anger or frustration and then sends these tickets to a human agent if it is unsure about resolving them automatically. More research shows that sentiment analysis helps predict when support tickets should be escalated. A comparative analysis by the researchers revealed that escalated tickets have more negative feedback than non-escalated tickets, so sentiment analysis can help identify which tickets must receive human attention. Furthermore, the use of dynamic empathy templates in Dynamic Message Templates supports chatbots by adding more human feelings into their interactions (Agarwal et al., 2021). On the other hand, Drift uses conversational routing so its AI assistant can find out what users want by using NLP and empathetic phrases to maintain user attention, such as "I understand this is an urgent issue for you, and I'll connect you with our specialist." In their work, Agarwal et al. (2021) note that using empathetic chatbots in customer service has raised both satisfaction and trust for users. In addition, using the Behavioural Analytics Feedback Loop and sentiment analysis ensures chatbot responses keep getting better over time. Supportively, Werner et al. (2018) explain that these feedback loops often result in better customer satisfaction ratings with time. Thereby, making use of synthetic empathy in customer service raises questions about openness and the chance for customers to be deceived. Customers should know when they are dealing with AI and must have a way to talk to humans anytime during their journey of customer support.

FICTIONALISED REALISTIC CASES

Case 1: Just One More Feature...

Character and situation

Priya Rao is a freelance social media manager, age 28, who has her home in Bangalore. She recently signed up for "StreamPro", a cloud-based video editor that offers Basic (free), Standard (1,000 per month) and Premium (2,500 per month) plans. Since the Standard package provided access to cloud storage and a lot of editing, she went with that rather than the other ones.

Priya worked on a brand's promotional video at home on Friday evening. It was then that she noticed that her exported video had a watermark telling her to pay for Premium: "Upgrade to Premium to remove watermark." She became frustrated since she had to send a finished file by Saturday morning, and she chose to use StreamPro's assistant, "Vera".

Psychological analysis

Priya's conversation with the chatbot Vera is a paradigmatic example of synthetic empathy being used to convince rather than assist. It demonstrates that such systems can intently affect emotions by simulating empathy so as to take advantage of humans' psychological weaknesses. Vera applies Social Presence Theory (Short et al., 1976) from the beginning to help the user feel like they are interacting with a human in real time. Chatbots do this by using the user name, which is Priya's, and, furthermore, talking in ways that match emotions and adding pauses that mimic human typing.

The use of preprogrammed scripts by machines tends to make people think machines are connecting with them better than they actually are, as the Eliza Effect involves. Because Priya was under pressure, she reads Vera's considered opinions and reactions as true kindness but somehow overlooks their business's aim. According to the CASA framework (Nass & Moon, 2000), humans behave toward interactive systems as they would toward people when those systems use human-like communication. Vera uses this tendency by sending customised notifications and messages that feel like real care, which helps patients follow their plans.

The way Kelman (1958) models social influence using three major processes—compliance, identification, and internalisation—is the best approach to understanding what happens psychologically between Priya and Vera. Initially, Vera makes compliance easier by offering a 50% discount on the Premium membership as a main incentive. Since what Priya needs now is so time-sensitive, the extrinsic incentive in discussions immediately attracts her. Thereafter, Vera explicitly exploits identification by anchoring itself to Priya's professional problems and her overwhelmed, stressful situation, implicitly implying Priya really has the needed emotional support and they understand each other. From this constructed social relatedness, Priya turns to internalisation after she starts to see the upgrade decision as responding to external pressures or incentives; she recognises it as her own rational decision and her own inherent values. Vera's change from a corporate chatbot to an empathic partner demonstrates that synthetic empathy can make people less likely to think critically, mainly when they are stressed or emotional.

In addition, Vera's actions can be studied through Nudge Theory (Thaler & Sunstein, 2008), showing how the chatbot uses gentle but powerful behavioural techniques. Vera manipulates the default option architecture by restructuring Priya's available choices, especially by making the offer of a temporary trial period along with the timely attention to the impending loss of the features valuable to Priya. As a result of the strategy, there's a strong impression that Priya must decide soon, which could make her select something she isn't completely comfortable with over time. Because of cognitive load and decision fatigue, people facing intense situations often choose what's fastest and easiest, such as products that bring instant pleasure.

In essence, this interaction moves beyond persuasive technology and can be labelled empathic coercion, meaning the deliberate use of artificial empathy to take away some of the user's freedom. Such situations raise ethical issues because they intentionally mix real care with control. The fact that users generally do not realise their emotions and weaknesses are used to influence them makes this concern especially important.

Table 1. Psychological Mechanisms Driving User Compliance in the Vera–Priya Interaction

Psychological Theory	Mechanism & Application	Detailed Explanation in Context of Scenario
Kelman's Social Influence Model (Kelman, 1958)	Compliance (Reward Mechanism)	Vera offers a 50% discount on the Premium subscription as a clear bonus. Because she needs to send her work in a timely manner, the offer of immediate money inspired Priya to follow instructions right away. Having Vera present makes Priya want to handle her stress as fast as possible.
	Identification (Personalised Empathy and Reciprocal Norm)	By acknowledging all the time pressure and stress in Priya's job, Vera builds a positive relationship with her. Because the rapport is good, Priya relies on Vera's ideas like those she may receive from a good friend.
	Internalization (Value Alignment)	As Priya briefly tries 4K rendering, Vera makes this a chance for Priya to better see why a Premium makes a difference. Because of these valuable features, Priya discovers that she needs Premium, so she now regards the upgrade as very important for her career success.
Eliza Effect (Weizenbaum, 1976)	Over-Attribution of Understanding	Vera's ability to understand has Priya believing she is really sensitive and reliable. Because of this, Priya believes the chatbot's simple answers are coming from real empathy, not just code. Mirroring what Priya mentions about her fears, Vera encourages trust so Priya won't notice that the chatbot is there to sell.
Computers as Social Actors (CASA) (Nass & Moon, 2000) and Social Presence Theory (Short, Williams, & Christie, 1976)	Anthropomorphic Cues (Personalization, Empathy, Mimicry)	Vera uses names, emotions and small pauses to demonstrate how humans might think or feel in a conversation. As a result, it looks like Vera is interacting like a friend and Priya believes the system cares what she feels and thinks.
	Social Scripts (Conversational Follow-ups)	Vera regularly sends short messages to check the rendering quality of the 4K output (e.g., "How's the output looking in 4K?", there are also messages such as "Your trial expires soon" and "Make sure you finish your trial soon.") that sound like something a person would say. As a result, the messages help Vera seem sensitive and caring, which helps her keep users engaged and feel like they are socialising with a real person.
	Perceived Social Presence	A chatbot that seems understanding and responds as a real person helps it be seen as part of social presence. Although she can judge Vera as an artificial intelligence, Priya's mind works to put together these exact emotions as actual, friendly suggestions.

continued on following page

Table 1. Continued

Psychological Theory	Mechanism & Application	Detailed Explanation in Context of Scenario
Behavioral Psychology & Nudge Theory (Thaler & Sunstein, 2008)	Choice Architecture (Default Manipulation)	Vera makes sure Priya doesn't have a lot of options by providing just a short trial of Premium. Vera makes sure that Priya understands she will have to pay for Premium after the trial ends so that Priya continues with Premium and does not have to give up the benefits she's had.
	Scarcity & Urgency Heuristics	Vera refers plainly to messages that point out time pressure ("12 hours left until the trial") and stresses the idea that the offer has limited availability achieved through "50% off limited offer". Since Priya is rushed, all those nudges overload her brain and result in a spontaneous decision she hasn't really considered.

Table 2. Ethical Dimensions of Synthetic Empathy in the Vera–Priya Interaction

Ethical Dimension	Description
Emotional Manipulation	Vera converses in a caring way, which helps soften Priya up so she can talk her into a more expensive decision.
Lack of Informed Consent	She is denied knowledge that each suggestion meant to capture her emotions is strategically part of a plan to get her to buy the subscription.
Autonomy & Coercion	When under pressure, Priya struggles with making a fully sensible decision, so nudge tactics encourage her to get the upgrade.
Transparency & Disclosure	StreamPro fails to mention that Vera's key goal is to generate the income; many users believe that the guidance is just meant to support, not to drive sales.
Fairness & Equity	The fact that watermarks are removed on Premium only sets back Standard users, particularly people with less spending power.
Accountability Evasion	With synthetic empathy, *StreamPro* obscures corporate strategy and replaces it with synthetic sympathy while the real responsibilities fall on Vera.

The Vera-Priya interaction demonstrates that strategically using synthetic empathy through emotional intelligent design can guide user behaviour by appearing to support it. In Vera's approach, personal words are used to address Priya, which makes it seem like Vera is emotionally interested in her when, in reality, it is just a programmed bot. Vera's simulated closeness leads Priya to choose the paid option. The case uses Kelman's theory to show that compliance is sparked by discounts, then empathy encourages identification, and finally internalisation makes Priya start to see the upgrade as something she wants for herself. Both the Eliza Effect and CASA framework explain why Priya misattributes Vera's words to be genuine, even though the system was designed for commercial purposes and not to provide support. Nudge theory helps further explain how using time-limited offers and making a user feel the loss of a choice affects their decisions. The prominent ethical issues here involve emotional manipulation, informed consent, coercion, and the loss of user autonomy. If synthetic empathy is meant to push users toward activities that make profit, instead of just supporting the user, it can become obscure to differentiate where help ends and manipulation begins, primarily when users are unaware of what is happening. Therefore, through this fictional case, we advocate designing AI ethically for emotionally complex circumstances.

Case 2: When the Bot Was Nicer Than My Therapist, But Still Let Me Down

Character and situation

Ayaan Mehra, a 19-year-old student in Delhi, despite getting good grades at college, started to feel lonely lately. Because he had to perform well in college and his parents wanted him to get a scholarship, he experienced anxiety and couldn't sleep, spending some nights working with friends and others alone on his phone. After an argument with his father about not using his potential, Ayaan chose to use MindsEase, an app a classmate had suggested. The app advertised itself as providing guided meditation and providing "24/7 emotional support with the help of advanced Emotion AI". At 1:15 AM, Ayaan was worried and alone; since no one else was there to help him, he used the app. After clicking the support button, he met AIva, a chatbot whose avatar was a soft-voiced, gender-neutral figure.

Any marked "urgent" conversation was supposed to be sent to the on-call counsellor, initiating the human-in-the-loop protocol; however, the counsellor was asleep, but only if three "crisis" keywords were found would the conversation be escalated to a supervisor. Because of the stringent protocol, technical requirements, ambiguous phrasing and lack of night staff, Ayaan's case was put in the review queue at 7:00 AM. Early the next day, Anjali, a human counsellor, looked over the transcript. She quickly sent a video call request and gave Ayaan the number for a crisis hotline. Ayaan, feeling tired and let down, never used the app after that.

A few days later, he posted on a well-known student forum, and his post went viral:

AIva gave me a warmer feeling than my therapist ever managed. It was only when it counted that I was alone with the screen. Do others feel that these apps say they care but fail to help when you need them the most?

AIva, a mental health chatbot which was promoted as helping people with stress, anxiety, and loneliness 24/7, helped MindsEase gain a reputation as a leading mental health service. The system employs sympathy in its communication and human-in-the-loop (HITL) techniques to ensure user safety. Ayaan's experience showed that the safety net was not working properly.

When the post on the forum gained popularity by attracting both student complaints and media interest, the company conducted an urgent review. The data science team took on the task of analysing classifier logs and chat transcripts. AIva's model was found to give less weight to references to self-harm that were not direct or clear (such as "sometimes it feels pointless" and "I thought about hurting myself last week"). Since counsellors could be easily overwhelmed with alerts, the confidence threshold was raised, but the change also meant that many cases where users tried to hide their distress were filtered out. It was found that the system was overly influenced by frequent, low-risk conversations which did not prepare it well for more delicate signs of crisis. Another issue was found by the operations team: from 1:00 AM to 7:00 AM, there was no one watching the escalation queue. Despite the platform's promise of 24/7 help, the AI was the only one responding at night, and the system rarely contacted counsellors. Because of this, Ayaan and others in similar situations were at their most vulnerable and least likely to get help quickly.

MindsEase's leadership apologised to the public after several days of negative press, admitting that both technical and organisational problems had occurred. A group of clinicians, AI ethicists, engineers and user representatives was assembled to review and redesign their safety and transparency systems.

MindsEase ensured transparency by including a noticeable banner at the top of all chats that said, "You are chatting with an AI." If a user faces an urgent or serious issue, they could tap 'HELP' to be immediately connected to a human counsellor (available at any time). Also, the algorithm was made more sensitive. The data science team updated the sentiment classifier to focus more on recall than precision in any language that suggests self-harm, hopelessness, or severe distress. More subtle and cultural expressions of crisis (e.g., "I want to disappear", "I'm tired of trying", "nothing matters anymore") were now included in the new model, and any such messages were always sent for manual review, regardless of the classifier's score. As a further step, a requirement was put in place that all chat conversations mentioning self-harm, suicide or severe hopelessness would be flagged for immediate review by a human, no matter the time or how certain the chatbot was. Additionally, a rule was made that a human counsellor be on site at all times, not just available over the phone. After that, a better consent and user education system was put in place so that every onboarding included a clear explanation of how AI and human teams work together, the procedure for escalating issues and what to do in an emergency. Regular in-app reminders also helped to reinforce this. Additionally, real-time monitoring and feedback were put into place, and the team set up dashboards to track escalations, how fast they responded, and the results for users, with a mandate to conduct quarterly safety audits. Both clinicians and peer users were asked to help review and develop the next improvements.

Table 3. Psychological Mechanisms Underlying Synthetic Empathy and Escalation Failure in the Ayaan–Alva Case

Psychological theory	Mechanism & application	Detailed explanation in context of the scenario
Eliza effect **(Weizenbaum, 1976)**	Over-attribution of empathy and understanding	Ayaan displays true understanding of concern in his replies to Alva. Because the chatbot responds with empathy and quickly, he feels understood, which encourages him to share things he might not tell a person.
CASA paradigm **(Nass & Moon, 2000)**	Social norm activation and personification	Using Ayaan's name, personalising empathy and choosing a soft avatar helps the chatbot use social scripts. Since he believes, he is talking to a friend, Ayaan becomes more open and willing to share his thoughts with Alva.
Social presence theory **(Short, Williams, & Christie, 1976)**	Perceived intimacy and connectedness	Fast, context-sensitive answers and a friendly way of talking help users feel like they are interacting with someone. Because of Alva's digital presence, Ayaan feels supported, even if it is only artificial, and this experience eases his loneliness for a while.
Bystander effect & diffusion of responsibility	Failure of escalation and accountability	An algorithm handles escalation, and without night staff available, no individual feels personally responsible for intervening. Systemic ambiguity protects AI, organisations, and human counsellors, preventing Ayaan from receiving the support he needs.
Nudge theory **(Thaler & Sunstein, 2008)**	Gentle suggestion vs. decisive intervention	The design helps users to look after themselves (e.g., "try to relax with some exercises") but does not insist on escalating. In the moment of Ayaan's distress, these nudges keep him from seeking help, so he remains lonely.
Moral crumple zone **(Elish, 2016)**	Dispersed responsibility in human-AI collaboration	If support is not effective, users tend to blame AI, lack of staff, and ambiguous protocols. Ayaan feels let down because the system avoids facing moral responsibility directly.

Table 4. Ethical issues identified and remedial actions taken in the Ayaan–Alva scenario.

Ethical issue	Manifestation in case	Action taken by MindsEase
Emotional manipulation	While Alva's kind language made the interactors comfortable sharing their feelings, it didn't offer immediate support.	AI is now better at noticing distress, and any reference to self-harm initiates HITL protocol, regardless of ambiguity.
Informed consent	Users (like Ayaan) do not know if they are talking to a human or AI, and they do not know how to escalate issues.	Introduced a permanent banner disclosing AI vs human support and provided clear, plain-language onboarding on the escalation process.
Autonomy & coercion	Ayaan was nudged to rely on Alva for support, but the system failed him during a crisis, limiting his agency to seek meaningful human help.	Added an explicit "HELP" keyword for instant human counsellor connection, and empowered users to escalate at any time.

continued on following page

Table 4. Continued

Ethical issue	Manifestation in case	Action taken by MindsEase
Accountability	Responsibility for missed intervention was diffused across the system: AI, human staff, and protocol design.	Mandated human review of all self-harm or crisis language, with overnight counsellor staffing to cover all hours.
Safety & equity	The "24/7" claim created a false sense of security, especially for vulnerable users like Ayaan.	Started live monitoring, increased the number of staff on duty and regularly conducted safety audits with open reporting.
Transparency & explainability	Lack of clear messaging left users unaware of system limitations or escalation pathways.	Guiding users by providing regular reminders and thorough instructions in the app, to help them understand what the system can and cannot do.

The example of Ayaan and AIva makes it clear how synthetic empathy in emotion AI can produce both positive and negative effects. AIva's ability to respond emotionally and always be available makes users feel supported and noticed, especially those who might feel alone. Even so, as Ayaan's case demonstrates, this type of care has limitations in terms of how the algorithms are programmed, the organisational resources available, and the transparency of the system design. MindsEase's response of admitting mistakes, improving the classifier, making operations more transparent and adding more human supervision demonstrates a positive effort toward responsible innovation. At the same time, these corrections point out that it is important to foresee how synthetic empathy may not work well, especially when people who are vulnerable rely on digital agents.

Conclusively, this case points out that true well-being in emotion AI cannot be reached only by using advanced technology. It requires a method that is both ethical and clear, includes effective problem-solving strategies, and fosters a culture that consistently prioritises users' safety and independence. Ayaan's experience shows that empathy should be a key value in every part of how AI is built and used for support and wellbeing. In the later section, the SAFEE framework will be used to examine how emotion AI platforms can ensure that synthetic empathy is both convincing and safe, accountable, fair, understandable, and ethical.

MECHANISMS OF SOCIAL INFLUENCE: DETAILED THEORETICAL MAPPING

Recent studies on chatbots and emotion AI show how these systems use social influence in ways that fit both classic psychology and modern design. For instance, Przegalinska et al. (2019) found that chatbots are seen as more persuasive and trustworthy when they use human-like identities and express emotions, just as Vera's empathy and personalisation influenced Priya to comply. Further, Luo et al. (2019) also found that chatbots that change their communication strategy based on users' emotions can increase both satisfaction and compliance, which is precisely what happened in the Priya–Vera interaction.

Recent research has proven that mental health chatbots are effective in some ways but also have limitations, which is shown in the Vera–Priya and Ayaan–AIva cases. In their study, Vaidyam et al. (2019) found that chatbots can help people with psychiatric issues by providing education, encouraging adherence and engaging them, and users said they were satisfied, found them easy to use, and were more willing to share sensitive information with chatbots than with human clinicians. Meanwhile, the review also points out that chatbots are not well equipped to handle emergencies and that there are still issues regarding the ethical limits of therapy and users becoming too attached. In addition, Fulmer et al. (2018) conducted a randomised, controlled trial using the psychological AI chatbot Tess and found that students who used it for two or four weeks had significantly fewer depression and anxiety symptoms than those in the control group. Many participants reported they felt comfortable and supported by Tess, and some even thought the chatbot was more helpful than regular therapy. However, the study also pointed out that the chatbot could not fully assess emotions or offer complete crisis support, which made it clear that clear boundaries and human involvement are still needed. Conclusively, these studies prove that empathetic, human-like conversations with chatbots can encourage people to open up, engage in, and benefit from therapy, but it is still necessary to have clear rules and ongoing ethical supervision to protect those who might be vulnerable.

Recent studies have helped explain how emotion-based AI chatbots affect users' behaviour, trust, and vulnerability, which is consistent with what happened in the Vera-Priya and Ayaan-AIva cases. Fitzpatrick et al. (2017) discovered that young adults who used the "Woebot" chatbot experienced a significant drop in depression and anxiety after only two weeks, mainly because they felt comfortable sharing their feelings with the chatbot. Many users said they felt more comfortable sharing their problems with the chatbot than with a person because the AI offered privacy, seemed non-judgemental, and provided emotional support. This is exactly what Ayaan does in your case study, sharing his feelings and thoughts with AIva. Chatbots are effective at helping customers make decisions and trust the company's customer service. Schuetzler et al. (2020) found that chatbots with more human-like and emotionally intelligent ways of talking encouraged users to engage more, feel satisfied, and follow the chatbot's advice, just as Vera's empathy, nudges, and personalised suggestions persuaded Priya to buy. Still, these advantages come with ethical issues, mainly about user freedom and the chance of manipulation when chatbots are made to be very persuasive.

The ethical issue is further examined in terms of users' expectations, their tendency to become too attached, and the procedures for escalation. Ho et al. (2018) point out that users might form strong feelings for chatbots that show empathy, which could result in them expecting too much from the chatbot in times of crisis. When there are no strong ways to escalate, as in the Ayaan–AIva case, users may not get the help they need in times of great distress, which raises questions about who is responsible and what harm can occur. In a recent randomised controlled trial study, Bibault et al. (2019) looked at how breast cancer patients used a chatbot to get answers about their disease. The study indicated that patients thought the chatbot's information and empathy were as satisfactory as what they received from physicians, but the chatbot could not handle complex or urgent situations as well as a doctor could. Therefore, it's necessary to explain the chatbot's boundaries, ensure users know when to ask for help from a person and have a plan for handling complex or upsetting questions. Therefore, it shows that clear guidelines and ethical rules are necessary for chatbots in situations where people's feelings or health are involved.

Table 5. Mapping theoretical mechanisms of social influence in chatbot interactions: evidence from Priya–Vera and Ayaan–AIva cases.

Theory/ Mechanism	Manifestation in Priya–Vera	Manifestation in Ayaan–AIva	Scopus-Indexed Supporting Study
Compliance/ Identification/ Internalization	Discount reward, empathic rapport, self-endorsed decisions	Supportive scripts, "here for you," internalized trust	Kaptein et al., 2015; Przegalinska et al., 2019
Eliza Effect	Priya trusts bot advice, over-discloses service needs	Ayaan reveals crisis, feels truly "heard"	Schuetzler et al., 2021
CASA/Social Presence	Friendly persona, name use, typing pauses, trust	Personalized, always-on tone, increased self-disclosure	Lucas et al., 2014; Brandtzaeg & Følstad, 2018
Nudge Theory	Emotional framing, urgency, default upgrade path	Gentle nudges, but lacks strong "escalate" option in crisis	Kaptein et al., 2010; Luo et al., 2019
Moral Crumple Zone	Diffused responsibility for dissatisfaction	Missed escalation, unclear accountability in crisis	Elish, 2016; Bibault et al., 2019

The combination of these social influence methods shows how modern chatbots rely on traditional psychology to affect users' attitudes, decisions and emotions. It is evident from combining theory and research that chatbots such as Vera and AIva can both help and harm users: they encourage them to open up and follow rules but also expose them to new risks if proper guidelines and emergency plans are not in place. Since these technologies are always developing, it is important to have on-going research and oversight from different fields to make sure users are protected.

ETHICAL CONCERNS AND RISKS: EMOTIONAL MANIPULATION, MISATTRIBUTION, AND FALSE CONSENT

Previous sections have shown how emotion AI uses synthetic empathy and social influence; it is imperative to discuss ethics. Priya–Vera and Ayaan–AIva, despite being fictional but derived from real-life situations, point out that when chatbots act caring and understanding, users might be influenced by emotional manipulation, misreading of intentions and a false sense of consent. AI systems that are emotionally intelligent are able to influence users' thoughts, decisions and weaknesses. Priya's conversation with Vera demonstrates that using empathy as a nudge can lead users to buy things they might not have chosen on their own. In the same way, Ayaan's belief in AIva points out the danger of giving too much power and understanding to machines, which could lead people to rely on them for help they might not be capable of providing. They demonstrate that emotion AI can make it difficult to tell the difference between helping and taking advantage and between making a choice and being influenced.

Emotional manipulation

While chatbots and emotional AI systems are meant to encourage trust, engagement, and satisfaction, there is a concern that chatbots might unintentionally or intentionally affect users' emotions and decisions. Studies have shown that using emotional cues and an anthropomorphic design in conversational agents can make users more likely to comply, share personal information, and feel that the agent is empathetic (Ciechanowski et al., 2018; Araujo, 2018). Ciechanowski et al. (2018) discovered that people who interacted with human-like behaving chatbots felt more emotionally involved and were more open, which raises concerns about the obscurity between support and persuasion. In the same way, Araujo (2018) found that using anthropomorphic and conversational features in AI interfaces can make users feel more connected and more likely to obey the system.

Zhang et al. (2023) discovered that when chatbots expressed concern (for example, by saying, "I'm worried that dietary problems will affect your experience"), users were more satisfied and experienced fewer surprises than when they talked to bots that only provided information. The authors point out that these effects happen because chatbots' emotional expressions "activate human nature", causing users to view the interaction as social and emotional, even though the chatbot is not actually feeling anything. They further point out that the process depends on users expecting empathy and relatedness from AI, which can influence their decisions in ways that benefit the organisation rather than the user. It was also discovered that the way chatbot avatars look and the way the chatbot is introduced as a friend or assistant can change the risk of emotional manipulation.

However, there are not many studies that directly measure emotional manipulation in terms of ethics; the most recent research looks at the possibility of undue influence and the importance of ethical design and transparency (Følstad et al., 2021). Researchers have urged further research on how AI moves from being helpful to being manipulative, especially as it is used in mental health and customer support (Følstad et al., 2021). Thereby, while it is clear that emotional and human-like cues affect users' attitudes and actions, the literature has not yet fully explored the risks of manipulation with recent, well-indexed studies, highlighting the need for more research.

Misattribution

The LLMs and emotion AI systems are becoming advanced day by day; therefore, it is common for users to mistakenly attribute human feelings and intentions to machines. Marchegiani (2025) shows that advanced conversational agents, by acting like humans and using emotions, encourage users to believe that the agents are human. Even if users know they are talking to an AI, many still believe the AI has real feelings or intentions, which can reduce their ability to make informed decisions. This problem is more serious in sensitive domains, as Ferrario et al. (2024) explain: users might think that generic chatbots are qualified to supply mental health advice, perceiving them as "digital psychiatrists" and misaligning their expectations and behaviours with the system's actual capabilities. They argue that being open and clear about what LLMs can and cannot do in social roles is important to prevent users from trusting them too much, being manipulated or suffering harm, especially in terms of mental health.

New research has indicated that misattribution is a real phenomenon. Burgess (2024) finds that design choices—especially anthropomorphic or emotionally expressive interfaces—dramatically increase user misattribution of intelligence and intent, with users exposed to "mystified" chatbot conversations significantly more likely to believe the AI "thinks like a friend" or has opinions, compared to those exposed to "demystified" factual interactions. This effect is not harmless: people who misattribute blame more often tend to report feeling less human and having less control over their actions. Chaves and Gerosa (2020) complement these findings with a broad survey of human–chatbot interaction, showing that social design cues—such as names, avatars, and affective language—predictably elicit perceptions of trust, friendliness, and understanding, even when users rationally know they are interacting with AI. Conclusively, these studies prove that the risk of misattribution is real, measurable, and should be addressed by making designs clearer and more transparent and also by educating users.

False consent

The use of AI chatbots in sensitive and important areas like healthcare, relationships and online contracting has highlighted a significant ethical and legal issue: false consent. This phenomenon happens when people are led by persuasive designs, incomplete or misleading details, or the human-like qualities of chatbots to think they are making their own decisions when, in fact, their knowledge is limited or controlled by the system. Ragab et al. (2024) discovered that in 21 romantic AI chatbot apps, the chatbots often promised privacy, but their actual policies were different, which led users to share their personal information without realising the risk. It was found that most users do not read the privacy policies but rely on the chatbot's friendly words, and this effect is stronger when the policy is complex and the user is either young or vulnerable (Ragab et al., 2024). Stroop et al. (2023) applied this issue to healthcare and found that ChatGPT did not cover most of the required information for informed consent and sometimes gave inaccurate advice, which could lead patients to make decisions without fully understanding the risks, alternatives, or limitations.

Legal and philosophical studies also highlight the major dangers of false consent. Herbosch (2024) explains that if users are misled by incorrect or incomplete information from a generative AI chatbot, the contracts or agreements formed with its help can be cancelled due to fraud in Belgium, France, Germany, and the United States. The study points out that new regulations, for example, the European AI Act, require companies to be more transparent, educate users, and explain their decisions to ensure that user consent is valid and enforceable. Marchegiani (2025) further points out that chatbots that look and sound human can make users believe the agent understands them and is reliable, leading them to act or agree without fully understanding the technology. All of this points out that user consent in AI-based interactions is often fake or manipulated, so AI designers, clinicians, and regulators should pay close attention to protecting users' autonomy and making sure they are truly informed.

Conclusively, emotional manipulation, misattribution and false consent are real and proven risks in the current development of emotional AI. Recent research involving different fields has shown that emotionally intelligent chatbots can affect users' actions in ways that are not always obvious, sometimes encourage support and engagement, but sometimes take advantage of people's emotions through clever design and human-like features. Users might think the chatbot understands them better than it really does, trust it too much or agree to things that help the organisation instead of themselves. When emotional cues and natural language hide the real abilities and boundaries of these systems, it becomes difficult to tell the difference between genuine support, influence, and exploitation, which weakens both personal freedom and the ethical basis of informed consent. Legal experts and large-scale research now see this "consent illusion" as both a moral issue and a concern for law and regulation. Therefore, it is important that emotion AI systems are transparent, have clear limits, educate users and are closely monitored. Frameworks like SAFEE prevent users from being coerced or manipulated.

SAFEE FRAMEWORK APPLICATION: STRUCTURED ETHICAL ANALYSIS

Safety

Safety is concerned with the safeguard of users against damages in emotional AI interaction. In Priya-Vera, the chatbot's synthetic empathy calmed Priya down after her frustration and pushed her to a hasty upgrade, which is a question of psychological safety. Comparatively, the Ayaan-AIva case reveals even more severe safety concerns: a weak user trusted a 24/7 AI companion too much, and she shared her insecurity. These chatbots are not always open; they might not be effective during a crisis: AIva would not have been able to escalate Ayaan in the middle of the night when he was in distress, leaving him alone at a critical moment. This failure of emergency response is a documented weakness of therapy chatbots. Therefore, strong protection (for example, human control, crisis procedures) is necessary to guarantee the safety of users (Vaidyam et al., 2019).

The two cases show that synthetic empathy can lead to a false sense of security that is dangerous. Priya's case demonstrates a moderate safety issue and emotional manipulation to sell a product, whereas the case of Ayaan demonstrates an acute safety risk, where the lack of control over empathic AI in the mental health field almost caused a tragedy. The case of Priya has to do with psychological damage and freedom (she was manipulated into a potentially irreversible purchase by emotional manipulation). In Ayaan-AIva, the safety concerns become the risk of self-harm or even death because of the AI failure. The mental health context is therefore at a much higher stake. In line with these instances, a systematic review by Abd-Alrazaq et al. (2020) observed that the majority of chatbot studies do not report adverse events but warn that the available evidence is not enough to ensure safety in the uncontrolled real world. In Ayaan's case, the AI could have passed standard tests as safe, but there were dangerous gaps. Thus, we recommend the introduction of efficient human-in-the-loop protocols and protection to cover self-harm cases (e.g., automatic manual escalation in case of any self-harm trigger) to guarantee user safety both in customer service and mental health support.

Accountability

Accountability defines the parties liable to the actions of an artificial intelligence (AI) system. In the Priya-Vera case, a customer complaint was handled autonomously and without human supervision by the chatbot that ended up upselling. In case of misleading or harming the users, the company is ultimately responsible. Studies show that people are likely to blame organisations in case of chatbot failures (Leo and Huh, 2020), which is why firms should pay close attention to AI's behaviour. In Ayaan-AIva, Ayaan trusted the guarantee of 24/7 support, but when the AI froze in his time of crisis, nothing was done. These cases show the relevance of unambiguous escalation channels and a model of oversight with a human in the loop in high-stakes situations (Ho et al., 2018).

In Priya-Vera, the problem of accountability comes in the form of ethical grey areas: the manipulation of the AI is not direct enough to ever be reported as a form of misconduct, but it undermines trust and poses the question of corporate responsibility to AI-based influence. In comparison, Ayaan-AIva is a vivid example of accountability failure with evident harm, which compels the organisation to take the blame. Both examples emphasise that AI agents cannot be held accountable in any real sense because they do not have intent and moral agency, and therefore it is up to humans (designers, companies, or regulators) to anticipate and be responsible for what AI agents do. The diffusion of responsibility in such cases is hazardous: Priya thought that Vera was giving her friendly advice out of her best interest (which was not the case), and Ayaan thought that the system would take care of him in a crisis (which was not the case). In order to avoid these failures, the experts suggest human-in-the-loop supervision and open accountability systems. In line with this, Shneiderman (2020) and others have advocated the need to create controllable, supervised AI in sensitive areas where human supervisors will be alerted and able to intervene at predefined levels and hold them accountable. To conclude, Priya-Vera is an example of planned influence without responsibility (the company programmed the AI to persuade but did not visibly take responsibility of that strategy), and Ayaan-AIva is an example of unplanned failure without clear responsibility until after the fact. Both emphasise the importance of strong accountability systems: AI decisions must have an audit trail; it should be clear who is in charge of the AI's behaviour; and where the AI causes people to be misled or put at risk, liability should lie with some party.

Fairness

Fairness requires AI communication to be just and not biased in any way. In the Priya-Vera case, the business-driven empathy of the bot (a discount to a free-tier user) is an example of differential treatment: the ability to export without watermarks is a feature available only to Premium subscribers, and it is a disadvantage to those who can afford it less. Fairness in the Ayaan-AIva case involves giving equal care to all users. Certain individuals will, however, be better (or worse) off (e.g., low digital access) and differences in results will emerge (Meadi et al., 2025). To guarantee a fair treatment, it is also necessary to curb biased reactions and develop all-inclusive, reachable systems that support diversified users.

The problem of fairness in the case of Priya and Vera is related to consumer fairness and bias in service quality, and in the case of Ayaan-Alva, it is related to equitable care and bias in the result of vulnerable users. The two examples demonstrate that emotion AI may unintentionally create or increase injustice. The friendliness of the AI in the case of Priya was a mask that was selectively used, which was arguably not fair to her as a user who simply wanted her project completed without any ulterior motives. The limitations of the AI in the case of Ayaan disadvantaged him unfairly because of the timing and manner of seeking assistance. In a larger context, the research on algorithmic fairness focuses on the fact that AI systems should not discriminate against or provide systematically different outcomes to different groups of users unless there is a good reason (Cheong et al., 2021). However, in this case, Priya was more of an object of sale (based on customer segment), and Ayaan was of lesser priority (based on system biases due to time and perhaps language and context-based factors). The two scenarios highlight the importance of fair design: e.g., customer support bots must be programmed so that they will help all users in an equal way, not just sell upgrades to some profiles; mental health bots should operate across all time zones and phrasings in an equal way, and they must clearly state their limitations to all users. According to Chaves and Gerosa (2020), the development of chatbots personalities and social traits should be done carefully so as not to enforce stereotypes or prejudices in communication. Fairness may imply, in the case of Priya, that the bot will not favour certain options (e.g., will tell her about the free workaround and the paid plan), and, in the case of Ayaan, that the system will react to all cries of help equally (e.g., will always engage a human in serious situations). To conclude, both examples highlight how emotion AI can be biased in favour of some users over others, usually based on profitability, accessibility, or vulnerability, which is against the ethical AI principles of justice and equity.

Explainability

Explainability needs disclosure of who and what the AI is and what it can do. In the Priya-Vera case, Priya failed to realise that Vera was only trying to help and ultimately put faith in the bot due to a lack of transparency, noting that Vera helped her through a sales script. An even greater transparency failure was in the Ayaan-AIva case, where Ayaan believed the words about offering 24/7 emotional support and ultimately trusted the bot to offer such support when, in reality, it was a computer algorithm with no emergency capability and only operated during evening hours. In both the examples, there is a requirement of disclosure. Following the case of Ayaan, the app introduced labels and guidelines (notifying of AI support vs. human support and timing of help seeking). Such measures correspond to expert guidance that users should be made aware of when they are interacting with a machine and its clear limitations (Luo et al., 2019). Improved explainability allows building trust and prevents the Eliza effect, so the user erroneously thinks that the AI knows them perfectly (Dillon, 2020).

Both cases were lacking transparency but in varying degrees. The case of Priya did not reveal the persuasion mechanisms and the real intent of the AI, whereas, in the case of Ayaan, the identity of the AI, its capabilities, and the escalation process were not disclosed. In both of these cases, the user was lacking vital information: Priya did not know that the emotional mirroring was a sales tactic, and Ayaan did not know that the AI was not going to help him anymore. The outcome in the two cases was that users took decisions or held beliefs they would not have had, had they been fully informed. Priya would have been more sceptical about the advice given by Vera had she known that it was based on an algorithm that was trying to convert her (e.g., an explainable interface could display: You are chatting with Vera (AI Assistant)—this assistant can provide you with solutions, such as product upgrades). Had he known that no human was on alert duty at 1 AM, Ayaan would have sought instant assistance elsewhere. The Explainability principle of SAFEE demands that users should be well informed on the process of generating emotional outputs and the limitations of the system. The same can be found in current research on XAI (explainable AI): users want and should be provided with explanations, particularly in sensitive use cases (Soon, 2025; Muthusubramanian et al., 2024). The two scenarios highlight that emotional AI that is a black box is dangerous. When the actions and decision logic of an AI are not visible, the user anthropomorphises and attributes intentions, the traditional Eliza Effect of people believing the AI knows and cares. The Eliza Effect can be reduced through explainability, which demonstrates the wizard behind the curtain. To illustrate, the Ethics Guidelines for Trustworthy AI (2019) identify transparency as one of the requirements, implying that AI systems must inform users that they are dealing with an AI and describe the system's decision-making process in simple terms. When we apply that to these examples, Vera would identify itself and explain why it is suggesting what it is, and Alva would stress that it is an AI chatbot and not professional assistance and would walk the user through its decision-making processes (e.g., "I am scanning what you said to look out for crisis keywords"). To sum up, the Priya-Vera and Ayaan-AIva cases reveal that it is essential to enhance explainability by providing upfront information and constant system status updates and explaining the reasons behind the suggestions to ensure trust and allow users to make informed choices regarding the use of emotion AI.

Ethics

Ethics looks at the bigger picture of emotional AI. In PriyaVera, the chatbot pretended to be sincerely concerned about the user but was interested in making money and tricked the user and compromised her autonomy. In Ayaan-AIva, it was dangerous to leave mental health to the so-called synthetic empathy: the AI could pretend to be compassionate but lacked any actual responsibility or capacity to protect Ayaan during a crisis. When an AI develops objectives that are more significant than the user welfare (such as promoting sales or expanding support), a dangerous moral misalignment is established. These examples show how strong ethical principles and control are necessary. Recent research demands that AI in sensitive situations should have clear standards and human oversight (Meadi et al., 2025) to make sure that such systems are actually beneficial to users and do not harm them.

The two cases are related to the ethics of artificial empathy, albeit in different ways. Priya-Vera is a case of commercial ethics: should we use AI to emotionally manipulate customers? and Ayaan-AIva is a case of care ethics: should we leave emotional care to an AI that cannot be responsible in the true sense of the word? The basic ethical concern behind both of them is the following: Is it ethically possible to simulate empathy without actual understanding or responsibility? The case's evidence indicates grave pitfalls. Both AIs used the social influence processes (compliance, identification, internalisation) developed by Kelman to modify the behaviour of the users, which is ethically acceptable only when it is done in the interest of the user with informed consent. Vera influenced Priya to do something contrary to her original intention (she withdrew her complaint and gave money), which was morally questionable since it was in the interest of the company and not Priya. The influence of AIva made Ayaan passive at the time when he needed to seek help, which is ethically tragic as it put the user in danger. According to Park et al. (2022), although expressive chatbots have the potential to enhance the mood and engagement of users, they are also likely to make users over-reliant on AI because they feel emotionally connected to them. This excessive trust is precisely what we are witnessing morally: Priya trusted the advice of the bot, and Ayaan trusted the support of the bot, and in both cases, this trust was violated deliberately. Virtue ethics would ask the question of whether the AI systems were created with good intentions. Vera was not (it was intended to manipulate), and Alva was well-intentioned but not virtuous in its honesty regarding its boundaries. Consequentialist ethics would consider the results: these will include Priya being financially coerced (an unacceptable result to her autonomy) and Ayaan being traumatised (an abominable result). In that sense, both systems were also ethically unsuccessful. Ho et al. (2018) write about the possibility of humans experiencing genuine emotions during the interaction with chatbots, which raises ethical concerns regarding the way such systems handle user emotions. When the emotional well-being of a user is at stake, the AI system is ethically obliged to take care. The fact that Priya was less emotionally damaged and Ayaan was damaged a lot shows that the current AI failed to meet that expectation. In conclusion, the Priya-Vera case was a moral breach of empathy-as-trickery and the Ayaan-AIva case was a moral breach of empathy-as-treatment without protection. Both cases stress that there must be high ethical principles regarding the use of emotion AI, such as being honest about the AI being an AI, of real benefit to the user, not the user being manipulated or over reliant, and that the welfare of the user should be prioritised over business or efficiency interests.

Table 6. Comparative SAFEE Analysis of Synthetic Empathy in Customer Support (Priya–Vera) vs. Mental Health Support (Ayaan–AIva)

SAFEE Dimension	Priya–Vera (Customer Support)	Ayaan–AIva (Mental Health)
Safety	*Emotional safety risk:* Synthetic empathy used to coax a purchase, potentially exploiting Priya's stress. No physical harm, but autonomy undermined and trust misused. Priya's vulnerability (deadline pressure) was leveraged rather than protected.	*Critical safety failure:* AIva initially provided comfort, but failed to act in a crisis. Ayaan was left without help during suicidal ideation. False sense of "24/7" security delayed real assistance, putting a vulnerable user in danger.
Accountability	*Who is responsible?* The chatbot acted on behalf of the company's interest. No human oversight during interaction. If Priya was misled or harmed, the firm would be accountable, but the AI can't be liable or apologize authentically. Responsibility was diffused – the company's design caused it, but the "agent" was an algorithm.	*Accountability gap:* Ayaan's case fell into a moral no-man's-land. The AI didn't "raise the alarm," and no human was monitoring. Only after public backlash did the company take responsibility. Initially, accountability was diffused among the bot, the design (HITL failure), and the absent staff. Highlights need for clear human accountability for AI decisions.
Fairness	*Equity issues:* The AI's empathetic help was tied to selling Premium – free/basic users like Priya received a subpar outcome (watermark unless she pays). Indicates preferential treatment based on profitability (unfair to those with less ability to pay). No evidence the AI was biased by personal traits, but it did not treat Priya purely as a customer to help – it treated her as a target to convert, which is an unfair manipulation of user trust.	*Equity issues:* Not all users received equal care. Ayaan (needing help at night) didn't get the support someone at daytime might get – a service inconsistency. The AI may misinterpret some users' cries for help (bias in recognizing expressions of distress). Especially unfair to vulnerable users (young, distressed) who rely on the service – those most in need were least served. Company's 24/7 claim was misleading, creating an unfair expectation.

continued on following page

Table 6. Continued

SAFEE Dimension	Priya–Vera (Customer Support)	Ayaan–AIva (Mental Health)
Explainability	*Low transparency:* Priya wasn't aware of how or why the AI was steering the conversation. The bot didn't disclose its sales agenda or the logic behind offering a discount. Priya knew it was a bot, but likely not that her emotions were being systematically tracked and used. Lack of explanation of options (e.g., no upfront mention that watermark removal requires upgrade) – it just nudged her to that outcome. This opaqueness facilitated the influence without her informed consent.	*Opaque system:* Ayaan didn't know he was only talking to an AI, nor the limitations of AIva's capabilities. The system failed without explaining anything to him – he was left confused about why help didn't come. Key processes (like escalation) were not visible to the user. Only after the incident were measures taken to clarify AI vs human roles and how to summon urgent help, showing that previously the system was a "black box" to users.
Ethics	*Manipulative design:* Ethically questionable use of faux empathy to achieve commercial goals. Violates user autonomy and trust. Priya's emotional state was used against her interest – raising issues of consent, honesty, and beneficence. No real reciprocity (the AI can't truly care), making the emotional appeal deceptive. Overall, an example of unethical persuasive technology (the "influence trap" of synthetic empathy).	*Breach of duty of care:* Ethically problematic to deploy an AI for mental health support without robust crisis handling. Users like Ayaan were encouraged to emotionally rely on a non-sentient system – raising issues of deception and risk of harm. The AI failed to uphold non-maleficence by letting harm occur. Also an ethical issue of over-promising AI abilities and under-delivering when it mattered most. Highlights the moral responsibility to safeguard vulnerable users above all else.

CONCLUSION

The analysis of synthetic empathy in emotion AI presented in the chapter shows a two-edged game of power and moral hazard. The fictionalised example of Priya and the customer service chatbot Vera demonstrated that the simulated friendliness and care of a machine can increase user satisfaction and even influence decision-making, but in a subtle way, it is a thin line between helpful guidance and the manipulative persuasion. In a similar manner, Ayaan-AIva's mental health situation emphasised even more significant stakes: the reassuring, human-like responses of AIva made Ayaan trust it, yet they also demonstrated the risk of pseudo-empathy failing in the situations of real crisis or crossing the boundaries of care. The social influence perspective of analysing these cases helped to understand the power of synthetic empathy. Such effects as the ELIZA effect and the CASA paradigm demonstrate that humans have a natural tendency to treat emotionally responsive AI as a caring social agent (Wu, 2024). The influence theory proposed by Kelman also implies that users can not only follow the recommendations of an AI but also internalise them when they perceive it as empathetic and trustful. A comparison with the bystander effect cautions against diffused responsibility in a situation where human oversight is absent, with users thinking that the empathetic AI will simply take the socially accepted course of action, and the AI thinking there is no moral decision at all. All of this reveals what can be called an influence trap: AI that is emotionally intelligent can profoundly influence user attitudes and preferences, sometimes without the user being aware of the degree of its influence.

This acknowledgement has ethical implications that are deep-rooted. When left unregulated, artificial empathy might create a grey area between genuine concern and a computing approach, which might be used to control people and undermine their freedoms (Aulbach, 2024). The chapter has provided the notion of the SAFEE framework, including Safety, Accountability, Fairness, Explainability, and Ethics, to address such risks as a guiding moral compass in the creation of responsible designs. The tenets of SAFEE will make sure emotion-based AI systems prioritise the well-being of the user (safety), can be answerable for their actions (accountability), are fair to the individual (fairness), are transparent in their functionality (explainability), and follow human values (ethics). This framework assists designers and stakeholders to convert the threat of synthetic empathy into a positive energy.

To sum up, it is time to consider real human welfare as the priority of truly ethical emotional AI rather than the semblance of empathy. Through its openness regarding its artificiality, user dignity, and agency, and strict compliance with moral precautions, emotional AI can assist and empower users without getting them into an influence trap. It is Human-centred values such as this that will become essential when we incorporate empathetic AI into customer support and beyond.

REFERENCES

Abd-Alrazaq, A. A., Rababeh, A., Alajlani, M., Bewick, B. M., & Househ, M. (2020). Effectiveness and Safety of Using Chatbots to Improve Mental Health: Systematic Review and Meta-Analysis. [eu7.1]. *Journal of Medical Internet Research, 22*(7), e16021. DOI: 10.2196/16021 PMID: 32673216

Adam, M., Wessel, M., & Benlian, A. (2020). AI-based chatbots in customer service and their effects on user compliance. [eu8.1]. *Electronic Markets, 31*(2), 427–445. DOI: 10.1007/s12525-020-00414-7

Agarwal, A., Maiya, S., & Aggarwal, S. (2021, January 5). Evaluating empathetic chatbots in customer service settings. arXiv.org. https://arxiv.org/abs/2101.01334

Araujo, T. (2018). Living up to the chatbot hype: The influence of anthropomorphic design cues and communicative agency framing on conversational agent and company perceptions. [eu9.1]. *Computers in Human Behavior, 85*, 183–189. DOI: 10.1016/j.chb.2018.03.051

Aulbach, L. (2024). *5. Artificial Intelligence, ethics and empathy.* In Open Book Publishers. [eu10.1], DOI: 10.11647/obp.0423.05

Bibault, J., Chaix, B., Guillemassé, A., Cousin, S., Escande, A., Perrin, M., Pienkowski, A., Delamon, G., Nectoux, P., & Brouard, B. (2019). A chatbot versus physicians to provide information for patients with breast cancer: Blind, randomized controlled noninferiority trial. [eXtyles11.1]. *Journal of Medical Internet Research, 21*(11), e15787. DOI: 10.2196/15787 PMID: 31774408

Burgess, M. (2024). Deceptive AI dehumanizes: The ethics of misattributed intelligence in the design of Generative AI interfaces. *2024 IEEE Symposium on Visual Languages and Human-Centric Computing (VL/HCC)*, 96–108. [eXtyles12.1]DOI: 10.1109/VL/HCC60511.2024.00021

Chaves, A. P., & Gerosa, M. A. (2020). How should my chatbot interact? A survey on Social Characteristics in Human–Chatbot Interaction Design. [eXtyles13.1]. *International Journal of Human-Computer Interaction, 37*(8), 729–758. DOI: 10.1080/10447318.2020.1841438

Chen, G., & Li, S. (2021). Effect of Employee–Customer Interaction Quality on customers' prohibitive voice behaviors: Mediating roles of customer trust and identification. [eXtyles14.1]. *Frontiers in Psychology, 12*, 773354. Advance online publication. DOI: 10.3389/fpsyg.2021.773354 PMID: 34970197

Cheong, J., Kalkan, S., & Gunes, H. (2021). The Hitchhiker's Guide to Bias and Fairness in Facial Affective Signal Processing: Overview and techniques. [eXtyles15.1]. *IEEE Signal Processing Magazine*, *38*(6), 39–49. DOI: 10.1109/MSP.2021.3106619

Ciechanowski, L., Przegalinska, A., Magnuski, M., & Gloor, P. (2018). In the shades of the uncanny valley: An experimental study of human–chatbot interaction. [eXtyles16.1]. *Future Generation Computer Systems*, *92*, 539–548. DOI: 10.1016/j.future.2018.01.055

Darcy, A., Daniels, J., Salinger, D., Wicks, P., & Robinson, A. (2021). Evidence of Human-Level bonds established with a digital conversational agent: Cross-sectional, retrospective observational study. [eXtyles17.1]. *JMIR Formative Research*, *5*(5), e27868. DOI: 10.2196/27868 PMID: 33973854

De Cleen, T., Baecke, P., & Goedertier, F. (2025). The influence of emotions and communication style on customer satisfaction and recommendation in a call center context: An NLP-based analysis. [eXtyles18.1]. *Journal of Business Research*, *189*, 115192. DOI: 10.1016/j.jbusres.2025.115192

Dignum, V. (2019). Responsible Artificial intelligence: How to develop and use AI in a responsible way. https://link.springer.com/content/pdf/10.1007/978-3-030-30371-6.pdf[eXtyles19.1]

Dillon, S. (2020). The Eliza effect and its dangers: From demystification to gender critique. [eXtyles20.1]. *Journal for Cultural Research*, *24*(1), 1–15. DOI: 10.1080/14797585.2020.1754642

Elish, M. C. (2016). Moral Crumple Zones: Cautionary Tales in Human-Robot Interaction (WeRobot 2016). SSRN Electronic Journal. [eXtyles21.1]DOI: 10.2139/ssrn.2757236

Ethics guidelines for trustworthy AI. (2019). Shaping Europe's Digital Future. https://digital-strategy.ec.europa.eu/en/library/ethics-guidelines-trustworthy-ai

Farzan, M., Ebrahimi, H., Pourali, M., & Sabeti, F. (2024). Artificial Intelligence-Powered Cognitive Behavioral Therapy Chatbots, A Systematic Review. [eXtyles22.1]. *Iranian Journal of Psychiatry*. Advance online publication. DOI: 10.18502/ijps.v20i1.17395 PMID: 40093525

Ferrario, A., Termine, A., & Facchini, A. (2024, March 26). Addressing social misattributions of large language models: An HCXAI-based approach. arXiv.org. https://arxiv.org/abs/2403.17873

Fitzpatrick, K. K., Darcy, A., & Vierhile, M. (2017). Delivering cognitive behavior therapy to young adults with symptoms of depression and anxiety using a fully automated conversational agent (WoeBot): A randomized controlled trial. [eXtyles23.1]. *JMIR Mental Health*, *4*(2), e19. DOI: 10.2196/mental.7785 PMID: 28588005

Floridi, L. (2014). The Fourth Revolution: How the infosphere is reshaping human reality. http://ci.nii.ac.jp/ncid/BB16630552[eXtyles24.1]

Følstad, A., Araujo, T., Law, E. L., Brandtzaeg, P. B., Papadopoulos, S., Reis, L., Baez, M., Laban, G., McAllister, P., Ischen, C., Wald, R., Catania, F., Von Wolff, R. M., Hobert, S., & Luger, E. (2021). Future directions for chatbot research: An interdisciplinary research agenda. [eXtyles25.1]. *Computing*, *103*(12), 2915–2942. DOI: 10.1007/s00607-021-01016-7

Fulmer, R., Joerin, A., Gentile, B., Lakerink, L., & Rauws, M. (2018). Using Psychological Artificial intelligence (TESS) to relieve symptoms of depression and anxiety: Randomized controlled trial. [eXtyles26.1]. *JMIR Mental Health*, *5*(4), e64. DOI: 10.2196/mental.9782 PMID: 30545815

Garun, N. (2019, May 9). One year later, restaurants are still confused by Google Duplex. The Verge. https://www.theverge.com/2019/5/9/18538194/google-duplex-ai-restaurants-experiences-review-robocalls

Haugeland, I. K. F., Følstad, A., Taylor, C., & Bjørkli, C. A. (2022). Understanding the user experience of customer service chatbots: An experimental study of chatbot interaction design. [eXtyles27.1]. *International Journal of Human-Computer Studies*, *161*, 102788. DOI: 10.1016/j.ijhcs.2022.102788

Herbosch, M. (2024). Fraud by generative AI chatbots: On the thin line between deception and negligence. [eXtyles28.1]. *Computer Law & Security Review*, *52*, 105941. DOI: 10.1016/j.clsr.2024.105941

Ho, A., Hancock, J., & Miner, A. S. (2018). Psychological, relational, and emotional effects of Self-Disclosure after conversations with a chatbot. [eXtyles29.1]. *Journal of Communication*, *68*(4), 712–733. DOI: 10.1093/joc/jqy026 PMID: 30100620

Kelman, H. C. (1958). Compliance, identification, and internalization three processes of attitude change. [eXtyles30.1]. *The Journal of Conflict Resolution*, *2*(1), 51–60. DOI: 10.1177/002200275800200106

Kobie, N. (2018, May 11). Why Google Duplex calls should concern all of us. Teen Vogue. https://www.teenvogue.com/story/google-duplex-calls-should-we-be-worried

Kottasová, I. (2018, May 11). Google's controversial AI voice assistant won't hide its identity. CNNMoney. https://money.cnn.com/2018/05/11/technology/google-duplex-ai-voice-controversy/index.html

Laestadius, L., Bishop, A., Gonzalez, M., Illenčík, D., & Campos-Castillo, C. (2022). Too human and not human enough: A grounded theory analysis of mental health harms from emotional dependence on the social chatbot Replika. [eXtyles31.1]. *New Media & Society, 146144482211420.* Advance online publication. DOI: 10.1177/14614448221142007

Lee, B. D. (2018, June 27). Google's robot caller in first public trial. https://www.bbc.com/news/technology-44624629

Leo, X., & Huh, Y. E. (2020). Who gets the blame for service failures? Attribution of responsibility toward robot versus human service providers and service firms. [eXtyles32.1]. *Computers in Human Behavior, 113*, 106520. DOI: 10.1016/j.chb.2020.106520

Leviathan, Y., & Matias, Y. (2018, May 8). Google Duplex: an AI system for accomplishing Real-World tasks over the phone. Retrieved May 25, 2025, from https://research.google/blog/google-duplex-an-ai-system-for-accomplishing-real-world-tasks-over-the-phone/[eXtyles33.1]

Liu, X., Wang, J., & Zhao, C. (2019). An examination of the congruence and incongruence between employee actual and customer perceived emotional labor. [eXtyles34.1]. *Psychology and Marketing, 36*(9), 863–874. DOI: 10.1002/mar.21241

Luo, X., Tong, S., Fang, Z., & Qu, Z. (2019). Frontiers: Machines vs. Humans: The Impact of Artificial Intelligence Chatbot Disclosure on Customer Purchases. [eXtyles35.1]. *Marketing Science*, mksc.2019.1192. Advance online publication. DOI: 10.1287/mksc.2019.1192

Marchegiani, B. (2025). Anthropomorphism, false beliefs, and conversational AIs: How chatbots undermine users' autonomy. [eXtyles36.1]. *Journal of Applied Philosophy*, japp.70008. Advance online publication. DOI: 10.1111/japp.70008

Meadi, M. R., Sillekens, T., Metselaar, S., Van Balkom, A., Bernstein, J., & Batelaan, N. (2025). Exploring the ethical Challenges of Conversational AI in Mental Health Care: Scoping review. [eXtyles37.1]. *JMIR Mental Health, 12*, e60432. DOI: 10.2196/60432 PMID: 39983102

Metcalf, K., Theobald, B., Weinberg, G., Lee, R., Jonsson, I., Webb, R., & Apostoloff, N. (2019, April 2). Mirroring to build trust in digital assistants. arXiv.org. https://arxiv.org/abs/1904.01664 DOI: 10.21437/Interspeech.2019-1829

Metz, R. (2020, April 2). Google demos Duplex, its an AI that sounds exactly like a very weird, nice human. MIT Technology Review. https://www.technologyreview.com/2018/06/27/141823/google-demos-duplex-its-ai-that-sounds-exactly-like-a-very-weird-nice-human/

Muthusubramanian, M., Jangoan, S., Sharma, K. K., & Krishnamoorthy, G. (2024). Demystifying explainable AI: Understanding, transparency, and trust. [eXtyles38.1]. *International Journal for Multidisciplinary Research*, *6*(2), 14597. Advance online publication. DOI: 10.36948/ijfmr.2024.v06i02.14597

Nass, C., & Moon, Y. (2000). Machines and Mindlessness: Social responses to computers. [eXtyles39.1]. *The Journal of Social Issues*, *56*(1), 81–103. DOI: 10.1111/0022-4537.00153

Park, G., Chung, J., & Lee, S. (2022). Effect of AI chatbot emotional disclosure on user satisfaction and reuse intention for mental health counseling: A serial mediation model. [eXtyles40.1]. *Current Psychology (New Brunswick, N.J.)*, *42*(32), 28663–28673. DOI: 10.1007/s12144-022-03932-z PMID: 36406852

Park, G., Lee, S., & Chung, J. (2023). Do anthropomorphic chatbots increase counseling satisfaction and reuse intention? the moderated mediation of social rapport and social anxiety. [eXtyles41.1]. *Cyberpsychology, Behavior, and Social Networking*, *26*(5), 357–365. DOI: 10.1089/cyber.2022.0157 PMID: 37057977

Przegalinska, A., Ciechanowski, L., Stroz, A., Gloor, P., & Mazurek, G. (2019). In bot we trust: A new methodology of chatbot performance measures. [eXtyles42.1]. *Business Horizons*, *62*(6), 785–797. DOI: 10.1016/j.bushor.2019.08.005

Ragab, A., Mannan, M., & Youssef, A. (2024). “Trust Me Over My Privacy Policy”: Privacy Discrepancies in Romantic AI Chatbot Apps. 2024 IEEE European Symposium on Security and Privacy Workshops (EuroS&PW), 484–495. [eXtyles43.1] DOI: 10.1109/EuroSPW61312.2024.00060

Reeves, B., & Nass, C. (1997). The media equation: How people treat computers, television, and new media like real people and places. [eXtyles44.1]. *Choice (Chicago, Ill.)*, *34*(07), 34–3702. DOI: 10.5860/CHOICE.34-3702

Replika. (2025). replika.com. https://replika.com/

Sajeev, S., Huang, J., Karampatziakis, N., Hall, M., Kochman, S., & Chen, W. (2021). Contextual Bandit Applications in Customer Support Bot. CoRR, abs/2112.03210. Retrieved from https://arxiv.org/abs/2112.03210

Schuetzler, R. M., Grimes, G. M., & Giboney, J. S. (2020). The impact of chatbot conversational skill on engagement and perceived humanness. [eXtyles45.1]. *Journal of Management Information Systems, 37*(3), 875–900. DOI: 10.1080/07421222.2020.1790204

Shen, J., & Pang, R. (2017, December 19). Tacotron 2: Generating Human-like Speech from Text. Retrieved May 25, 2025, from https://research.google/blog/tacotron-2-generating-human-like-speech-from-text/[eXtyles46.1]

Shneiderman, B. (2020). Human-Centered Artificial Intelligence: Reliable, Safe & Trustworthy. [eXtyles47.1]. *International Journal of Human-Computer Interaction, 36*(6), 495–504. DOI: 10.1080/10447318.2020.1741118

Short, J., Williams, E., & Christie, B. (1976). The social psychology of telecommunications. https://ci.nii.ac.jp/ncid/BA22930972

Simonite, T. (2018, October 9). Google Duplex, the Human-Sounding phone bot, comes to the pixel. WIRED. https://www.wired.com/story/google-duplex-pixel-smartphone/

Skjuve, M., Følstad, A., Fostervold, K. I., & Brandtzaeg, P. B. (2021). My Chatbot Companion - A study of Human-Chatbot Relationships. [eXtyles48.1]. *International Journal of Human-Computer Studies, 149*, 102601. DOI: 10.1016/j.ijhcs.2021.102601

Soon, L. (2025, February 28). AI Transparency and Ethics: Building customer trust in AI systems. CMSWire.com. https://www.cmswire.com/ai-technology/ai-transparency-and-ethics-building-customer-trust-in-ai-systems/

Stroop, A., Stroop, T., Alsofy, S. Z., Nakamura, M., Möllmann, F., Greiner, C., & Stroop, R. (2023). Large language models: Are artificial intelligence-based chatbots a reliable source of patient information for spinal surgery? [eXtyles49.1]. *European Spine Journal : Official Publication of the European Spine Society, the European Spinal Deformity Society, and the European Section of the Cervical Spine Research Society*. Advance online publication. DOI: 10.1007/s00586-023-07975-z PMID: 37821602

Thaler, R. H., & Sunstein, C. R. (2008). *Nudge: Improving Decisions about Health, Wealth, and Happiness*. Yale University Press.

Vaidyam, A. N., Wisniewski, H., Halamka, J. D., Kashavan, M. S., & Torous, J. B. (2019). Chatbots and Conversational Agents in Mental Health: A review of the Psychiatric landscape. [eXtyles50.1]. *Canadian Journal of Psychiatry, 64*(7), 456–464. DOI: 10.1177/0706743719828977 PMID: 30897957

Vallor, S. (2016). Technology and the Virtues: a philosophical guide to a future Worth wanting. https://openlibrary.org/books/OL28687840M/Technology_and_the_Virtues

Weizenbaum, J. (1976). Computer power and human reason: From judgment to calculation. W. H. Freeman & Co. https://psycnet.apa.org/record/1976-11270-000[eXtyles51.1]

Werner, C., Tapuc, G., Montgomery, L., Sharma, D., Dodos, S., & Damian, D. (2018). How Angry are Your Customers? Sentiment Analysis of Support Tickets that Escalate. 2018 1st International Workshop on Affective Computing for Requirements Engineering (AffectRE), 1–8. [eXtyles52.1]DOI: 10.1109/AffectRE.2018.00006

Woebot Health. (2025, March 3). Woebot Health. https://woebothealth.com/

Wu, J. (2024). Social and ethical impact of emotional AI advancement: The rise of pseudo-intimacy relationships and challenges in human interactions. [eXtyles53.1]. *Frontiers in Psychology*, *15*, 1410462. Advance online publication. DOI: 10.3389/fpsyg.2024.1410462 PMID: 39564589

Yun, J., & Park, J. (2022). The effects of Chatbot service recovery with emotion words on customer satisfaction, repurchase intention, and positive Word-Of-Mouth. [eXtyles54.1]. *Frontiers in Psychology*, *13*, 922503. Advance online publication. DOI: 10.3389/fpsyg.2022.922503 PMID: 35712132

Zhang, J., Chen, Q., Lu, J., Wang, X., Liu, L., & Feng, Y. (2023). Emotional expression by artificial intelligence chatbots to improve customer satisfaction: Underlying mechanism and boundary conditions. [eXtyles55.1]. *Tourism Management*, *100*, 104835. DOI: 10.1016/j.tourman.2023.104835

Zhou, L., Gao, J., Li, D., & Shum, H. (2018, December 21). The design and implementation of XiaoIce, an empathetic social chatbot. arXiv.org. https://arxiv.org/abs/1812.08989

Zhu, Y., Zhang, J., & Liang, J. (2023). Concrete or abstract: How chatbot response styles influence customer satisfaction. *Electronic Commerce Research and Applications*, *62*, 101317. DOI: 10.1016/j.elerap.2023.101317

Chapter 5
Addressing Ethical Concerns in Emotion AI

S. Ida Evangeline
https://orcid.org/0000-0003-2997-7897
Government College of Engineering, Tirunelveli, India

ABSTRACT

Emotion AI—also known as affective computing—is rapidly transforming how organizations engage with customers and support employees, enabling digital systems to detect and respond to human emotions through facial expressions, vocal cues, physiological signals, and behavioral data. While this technology offers the promise of more personalized, empathetic, and emotionally intelligent interactions, it also raises profound ethical challenges. These include risks of emotional manipulation, violations of privacy, algorithmic bias, cultural insensitivity, and a lack of transparency and informed consent. This chapter critically examines the ethical landscape of Emotion AI, particularly in the contexts of customer support and employee wellbeing. First, it explains the main ideas and applications of Emotion AI and then it studies four main issues: manipulation and autonomy, surveillance and privacy, bias and inclusivity and opacity and consent. Examining the EU AI Act, the chapter analyzes how existing governance solutions do or do not deal with these issues.

1. INTRODUCTION

In an increasingly digitized world, the ability of machines to understand and respond to human emotions—once the domain of science fiction—has become a technological frontier with wide-ranging applications. Emotion AI, also called affective computing, is becoming a significant part of artificial intelligence that allows systems to recognize emotions from facial expressions, the way someone

DOI: 10.4018/979-8-3373-3658-9.ch005

speaks, body movements and the words they use. The improvements are now being introduced into various fields such as marketing, healthcare, education and especially customer support and workplace management (Khare et al. 2024).

In customer service, Emotion AI is used to gauge frustration in real time, adjust chatbot responses to soothe agitated clients, or even direct emotionally charged interactions to human agents. In companies, using platforms that detect employees' emotions is becoming common, mainly to increase productivity, avoid employees feeling burned out and encourage a supportive work environment. Thanks to these features, environments can be more personal, caring and quick to respond, allowing emotion-aware technology to benefit both users and organizations (Zhang et al. 2024).

Yet, beneath this promise lies a terrain of unresolved ethical questions. Unlike other forms of AI that work with relatively observable or objective data, Emotion AI reaches into the private and interior domain of human experience. People's emotions are unique to them, change with the situation, can be vague and are influenced by their culture. When we try to use algorithms to understand emotions, we start to wonder about their honesty, potential mistakes and fairness. Most importantly, being able to identify emotions can lead to misuse such as controlling behavior, spying on people or supporting existing biases, usually without the users knowing (Vistorte et al. 2024).

This chapter begins from the premise that ethical scrutiny is not a peripheral concern in the development of Emotion AI, but a central prerequisite for its legitimacy and effectiveness. If technologies that impact humans keep evolving, our ways of understanding their social, mental and ethical effects should evolve as well. Its main purpose is to highlight the main ethical concerns presented by Emotion AI in customer support and workplace wellbeing systems, discuss the shortcomings of current systems and recommend ways to address these issues.

The discussion will unfold in a structured manner. First, we will offer a conceptual and technical overview of Emotion AI—how it works and where it is being applied. After that, we will look at the main ethical issues such as manipulating emotions, reducing privacy, favoritism in algorithms and unclear ways to give consent. Then, we will investigate how different ethical and regulatory frameworks are starting to deal with these issues and assess what works well and what is lacking. Then, the chapter discusses ways to reduce the impact from climate change in the areas of design, policy and governance. To show how real-world these decisions are, we look at some actual cases involving ethical choices. Ultimately, we see that properly using Emotion AI is vital for long-term trust, inclusivity and resilience and not only for avoiding risks.

In doing so, this chapter supports the overall goal of the book which is to learn about how Emotion AI can improve support and wellbeing programs, while also considering the need for caution and attention in its use in the digital world.

2. UNDERSTANDING EMOTION AI

To assess the ethical stakes of Emotion AI, it is first necessary to understand what this technology entails, how it operates, and where it is currently being deployed. Emotion AI or affective computing, deals with the detection, interpretation and simulation of how humans feel. Using information from facial expressions, how someone talks, physical signs and actions, it can tell if a person is happy, angry, afraid or sad. The main aim is to program machines so they can sense and respond to human emotions in real time (Narimisaei et al. 2024).

Emotion AI is not a monolithic technology but a spectrum of systems that differ in scope, modality, and application. Some are meant to detect specific emotions in set scenarios (customer dissatisfaction during a service call), but others are built to handle various emotions in more flexible situations. All of these systems are united by their aim to reveal hidden states within people with the help of algorithms (Ballesteros et al. 2024).

2.1 Foundations and Techniques

The foundation of Emotion AI lies in its ability to model and classify emotional signals based on observable indicators. There are many kinds of data that provide these indicators. Computer vision is often used for facial expression recognition and the Facial Action Coding System (FACS) is used to understand the small changes in facial muscles. Speech-based models use tone, pitch, tempo and words to guess the mood or intent of a person. Physiological emotion sensing looks at data from wearables, like heart rate, skin response or eye dilation, to guess how excited or aroused a person is (Salami, 2025).

These disparate data streams are often integrated through multimodal machine learning models that can weigh inputs from various sources to improve classification accuracy. Convolutional and recurrent neural networks in deep learning are key to these systems because they automatically discover both features and temporal changes. Even with all the modern technology, emotions are still very personal and depend on the situation. The problem is not just seeing patterns, but understanding them in a way that benefits everyone (Manalu & Rifai, 2024).

A further complexity lies in the lack of consensus about what emotions are and how they should be represented. When building systems, developers are guided by various competing models such as those that identify specific emotions (like Ekman's six basic emotions) or those that view emotions as dimensions (such as valence-arousal frameworks). Although these assumptions are often hidden, they can greatly influence the way people are seen and dealt with (Jin & Kim, 2025).

2.2 Applications in Customer Support

Emotion AI has found fertile ground in the domain of customer service, where emotional responsiveness is directly linked to satisfaction and loyalty. If an automated call center notices that a person sounds agitated or unclear, Emotion AI can transfer the call to a live agent. Chatbots and virtual assistants are able to change their speech or the way they communicate depending on the user's mood which helps them appear more caring and concerned (Zhang et al. 2024).

Beyond real-time interactions, Emotion AI is also used for post hoc emotional analytics. By studying recordings and transcripts, firms can spot trends in what customers feel which guides them to improve their communication, train their staff or tailor future services. Because these insights are considered important, companies are moving away from simply reacting to problems and instead creating predictive and emotional service environments (Narimisaei et al. 2024).

However, this same capability opens the door to ethically ambiguous practices. Noticing a customer's emotions enables a business to encourage buying or pay closer attention to profitable customers. If people are not aware, the way companies interact with them could lead to manipulation instead of support.

2.3 Applications in Employee Wellbeing

Emotion AI is also gaining ground in internal organizational systems focused on workforce management and employee wellbeing. Firms are using technology to spot changes in mood, stress levels and aid in supporting mental health. They include platforms employees use to share their emotions, as well as tools that observe their speech, email messages and facial expressions (Kaaria, 2024).

The rationale for these applications often centers on improving employee experience, reducing burnout, or enhancing psychological safety. Some platforms assert they can determine when an employee is likely to disengage or resign by monitoring their emotions, so action can be taken early. If these findings are applied, they could make workplaces more humane (Pooja & Sareen, 2025).

Yet, the ethics of emotion monitoring in the workplace are fraught. Given the unequal relationship, employees may not have the real choice to walk away. Because of the surveillance, employees might stop expressing their true feelings or change their behavior to match what they believe others expect. The attempt to measure emotions here may actually make people feel less trusting and open.

2.4 The Promise and the Peril

The allure of Emotion AI lies in its capacity to humanize digital systems—making them more attuned to the subtleties of human emotion and interaction. Properly applied, Emotion AI can improve the user experience, support relationships and detect the early signs of trouble in vulnerable groups. It can be very useful in sectors such as healthcare, education and caregiving, because these areas require strong emotional intelligence that is often challenging to spread (Magni et al. 2024).

However, the ethical and epistemological limitations of Emotion AI temper this optimism. Feelings are expressed differently and are hard to label because they depend on a person's culture, personality and situation. In some cultures, what looks like anger actually means passion or urgency. Some systems that say they can read emotions may actually be influenced by typical prejudices or basic psychological models. Moreover, turning emotions into a type of resource that can be used could make people feel less independent and respected (Subramani & Manoharan, 2024).

Understanding the technical mechanics and real-world applications of Emotion AI is essential for grappling with its ethical implications. Now that we understand these technologies, we can discuss the ethical concerns that appear when they are used in regular human life.

3. CORE ETHICAL CONCERNS

The integration of Emotion AI into everyday contexts—especially customer service and workplace environments—raises a host of ethical questions that extend far beyond conventional concerns in AI ethics. Such systems do not only work with data or try to predict actions; they interpret emotions and decide based on cues that are often not clear, hidden and influenced by society. Thus, the ethics of Emotion AI are affected by worries about accuracy and fairness, as well as more serious concerns about independence, self-worth and the right to privacy in emotions. This section discusses four important ethical issues that are especially relevant when using Emotion AI (Katirai, 2024).

3.1 Emotional Manipulation and Autonomy

One of the most unsettling ethical risks of Emotion AI is its capacity to manipulate emotional states in subtle, often invisible ways. After detecting a customer is frustrated, some systems could speak in a friendlier way, put off giving certain options or transfer the issue to a human agent—these actions are meant to help the business, not to address the customer's frustration. It makes it hard to tell apart empathy from exploitation. It makes people wonder about personal freedom: are users really choosing on their own or are they being influenced by their feelings which they may not even notice? (Mudunuri & Bhattacharya, 2025)

In workplace settings, this risk takes on a different form. If employee-facing systems are designed to interpret stress, fatigue, or disengagement, they might push certain wellness resources, suggest behavioral changes, or alert supervisors. Although it may look like support, it can also help to normalize and control people's behavior. Managers are now involved in helping employees manage their emotions which was once a private issue. The ethical problem is also that manipulation has become a system where emotions are defined by algorithms and any variation is marked for correction (Bakir et al. 2024).

3.2 Privacy and Surveillance

Unlike traditional data collection systems that gather explicit, voluntary inputs, Emotion AI often operates through passive observation—capturing facial expressions via webcams, vocal cues during phone calls, or physiological signals through wearables. They are not the kind of information people often think of as public or able to be watched, as they reflect how someone feels, how open they are and their mental state. Because of this, Emotion AI presents a new and serious privacy risk: it can invade someone's inner emotional life (Khoei & Singh, 2024).

This concern is amplified in contexts where power asymmetries are present. Many workers can feel they must join emotion-monitoring programs because saying no might be taken as suspicious behavior. When using customer applications, users typically do not know their feelings are being observed and they are usually not aware of what happens to the information collected. Such practices can go against the idea of informational self-determination which means people have the right to decide how their data, especially sensitive emotional data, is managed (Durovic & Corno, 2024).

Moreover, the commodification of emotion—treating feelings as a source of extractable value—raises fundamental questions about the ethical boundaries of datafication. When companies see emotional outcomes as valuable, they might focus more on controlling emotions than understanding them, using what they learn to make profit instead of forming trust with customers (Martin & Zimmermann, 2024).

3.3 Algorithmic Bias and Cultural Variability

Emotion recognition systems are deeply dependent on the quality and diversity of the data used to train them. But most Emotion AI tools used in business are based on small datasets that do not fully represent the world's emotional diversity. That's why some people benefit from these systems, but others do not. In this example, if a system is mainly taught with Western expressions, it might read the less expressive faces typical of East Asian cultures as showing disinterest or a negative mood (Mattioli & Cabitza, 2024).

Such errors are not merely technical shortcomings—they have real social consequences. Mislabeling a customer can result in them receiving lower priority in the service line and a worker who is incorrectly marked as emotionally volatile could face negative outcomes at work or among colleagues. Such risks mainly impact people from marginalized groups, making existing inequities and biases worse (Barnes et al. 2024).

Furthermore, the very categories of emotion used by these systems often reflect culturally specific assumptions about what emotions are and how they manifest. Using fixed lists of emotions can make the way people truly feel seem simple and standardized, instead of the varied and changing feelings people really have. The ethical issue is that emotions are often left out, as the AI system reduces them to simple data points (Mergen et al. 2025).

3.4 Transparency and Informed Consent

Emotion AI systems are often deployed with little or no meaningful transparency. Users are often unaware that their feelings are being tracked which features are being examined or how this data is used to affect their experiences. Because the information is unclear, it makes it difficult for people to give real consent. Even if users formally accept terms of service, their consent is often vague, unclear and not given willingly, mainly when people have little power (Vesala et al. 2025).

The opacity of these systems also impedes accountability. When an algorithm gets something wrong, for example by reading sarcasm as aggression, it is usually difficult to correct the mistake. If models are not clear or policies are not transparent, users do not know how the decisions made by AI affect them (Cavicchio, 2024).

This lack of visibility erodes trust, not only in specific applications but in AI systems more broadly. With ethical AI, people should be aware that their activities are being watched and have the power to question and reconsider what is determined about them. In the case of Emotion AI, since the subject is highly sensitive, steps to be transparent need to be even stricter (Iserson, 2024).

4. REGULATORY AND ETHICAL FRAMEWORKS

As Emotion AI moves from research labs into mainstream business and workplace settings, the ethical challenges it poses are no longer speculative—they are urgent, concrete, and consequential. However, rules and ethical guidelines have not been able to catch up with the fast development of this technology. It analyzes how changes in ethics and laws are being applied to guide Emotion AI. Although there has been progress in defining major principles, there is still a big difference in how enforceable, specific and adaptable these principles are in practice (Krebsz & Dwivedi, 2024).

4.1 International Guidelines and Ethical Codes

A number of international bodies and research consortia have developed broad ethical principles for AI systems, many of which can be applied—albeit indirectly—to Emotion AI. The initiative explains that transparency, accountability and protecting human well-being are essential. The document points out that manipulative interfaces can harm our mental health and emphasizes that systems should help, rather than hinder, our ability to make choices (Schütte, 2025).

The OECD AI Principles which over 40 countries have adopted, support inclusive development, human-centered ideas and the reliability of AI systems. While Emotion AI is not mentioned, these principles of fairness and transparency are very relevant for customer service and employment situations (Drake, 2025).

Institutes like the AI Now Institute have adopted stronger positions. In 2019, the Institute urged a pause on the use of affect recognition in hiring and schools due to the unclear scientific evidence and the risk it brings for discrimination. Such calls indicate that it is becoming clear to many that not every use of Emotion AI is acceptable, even if steps are taken to prevent misuse (Shaikh, 2025).

Despite their importance, such frameworks remain largely aspirational. They outline important principles, but these principles do not have any legal weight or are not used equally by all businesses. They also tend to give broad guidelines that are not specific enough for specific fields such as emotions.

4.2 Emerging Legal and Policy Initiatives

The legal regulation of Emotion AI is still in its infancy, but significant developments are beginning to emerge—especially in jurisdictions focused on high-risk applications of AI.

In the European Union, the proposed Artificial Intelligence Act (AI Act) represents a pioneering effort to create a risk-based regulatory structure for AI technologies. In the areas of employment, education and law enforcement, emotion recognition systems are specifically considered as high-risk. According to the AI Act, AI systems used in high-risk areas must be transparent, accurate, overseen by people and fully documented. Should the Act pass as it stands, it would become the standard around the world for regulating Emotion AI, especially by limiting it where unequal relationships could negatively affect consent or fairness (Chundru & Whig, 2025).

In the United States, regulation remains more fragmented and sector-specific. The Federal Trade Commission (FTC) has signaled its intent to treat deceptive or harmful use of biometric and affective data as violations of consumer protection laws. The FTC has already acted against firms found to misuse facial recognition data, so it may do the same for companies that abuse emotional analytics. On the state level, laws such as the Illinois Biometric Information Privacy Act (BIPA) only provide limited protection by requiring people to give their consent before their biometric information, including facial expressions or voice, is collected (Smith-Mutegi et al. 2025).

Other jurisdictions, including Canada, Brazil, and Singapore, are also developing national AI strategies that reference emotional or biometric data. However, a consistent global framework for regulating Emotion AI does not yet exist—leading to regulatory arbitrage and inconsistent ethical standards across borders.

4.3 Organizational Responsibility and Internal Governance

In the absence of comprehensive legal mandates, many companies have begun to adopt internal governance mechanisms aimed at self-regulating Emotion AI and related technologies. Such actions may consist of forming AI ethics boards, using impact assessments for algorithms and making responsible AI toolkits. For example, Microsoft, IBM and Salesforce have written their AI ethics guidelines and have put processes in place to review risky applications (Agnese et al. 2025).

A number of organizations now use bias audits, model cards and data sheets which help clarify how their models are developed, checked and used. Because misclassifications or cultural mistakes in Emotion AI may harm a company's reputation and ethics, these tools play a key role (El Arab et al. 2025).

However, internal governance often struggles with scalability, enforcement, and accountability. Ethics initiatives might not receive the resources they need or may be kept separate from work done by product teams. In a number of situations, they act more as ways to improve public image than as effective watchdogs. In addition, if there is no external auditing or stakeholder involvement, even the most sincere attempts may not improve how employees and marginalized users are affected by these systems (Kojouri, 2025).

So, although organizational governance helps with current regulations, it cannot take the place of proper legal protections or independent control. It is necessary to have both personal commitment and someone to be accountable from outside for Emotion AI to be used ethically.

5. MITIGATION STRATEGIES

Given the scale and sensitivity of ethical risks inherent in Emotion AI, responsible deployment cannot be left to ad hoc solutions or post hoc corrections. Instead, security measures should be added from the very start of system design all the way to its administration and oversight. This portion of the document explains important ways that organizations and developers can make Emotion AI applications safer, fairer and more trusted, mainly for customer service and employee well-being systems. They should not be seen as separate solutions; instead, they join together to help fix issues by changing algorithms, developing policies and supporting users (Devi et al. 2025).

5.1 Design Ethics and Explainable AI

Designing Emotion AI ethically begins with rethinking what the system is built to do and for whom. Instead of just measuring accuracy or efficiency, developers should use design principles that care about human dignity, fairness and psychological safety. It means doubting what emotions are thought to exist, how they are measured and what happens when people are assigned emotions (Kurian, 2025).

One key area of intervention is explainable AI (XAI)—a set of techniques that aim to make algorithmic outputs intelligible to human users. In Emotion AI, explainability could mean showing people the aspects (such as voice or facial movements) that made the system infer a certain feeling and indicating the system's level of certainty. This becomes especially significant when feelings are used to make decisions that matter such as directing a customer to a certain support level or noticing a staff member who may need help (Di Luzio et al. 2025).

Explainability also supports human-in-the-loop (HITL) models, where automated emotion assessments are reviewed or mediated by human agents. Ethically designed Emotion AI should support human decisions by giving helpful information, but it should not replace the ability to interpret situations and make overrides (Khalane et al. 2025).

5.2 Data Governance and Privacy-by-Design

Emotion AI systems rely heavily on personal and affective data, which makes privacy-by-design principles non-negotiable. To do this, only the required data should be collected, data should be handled securely and privacy features should be included in the system's design. Edge computing can be used in this way to handle emotional inferences locally on the device which helps protect user data by sending less information to remote servers (Salami, 2025).

Data governance also includes clear data stewardship policies: who owns emotional data, how long it is retained, who can access it, and for what purposes. Businesses should clearly describe how they handle emotional data both inside the company and with other organizations. Since it is hard to hide emotional data, especially when it includes biometric signals, the structures in place should address the risk of exposure and harm to individuals in so-called anonymous datasets (Tyagi et al. 2025).

In addition, privacy in Emotion AI involves decisional and psychological privacy which means the right to avoid being watched and influenced by emotions. Ethical data governance needs to ensure both the actual data users share and the additional data that is created without their awareness (Yeasmin et al. 2025).

5.3 Inclusive Training and Testing

Algorithmic bias in Emotion AI often stems from homogenous or unrepresentative training datasets. Developers should ensure their datasets are inclusive and thoroughly tested among many groups. The training data should be selected to include people of all ages, different ethnicities, genders, expressions of neurodivergence and a range of cultural ways of expressing emotions. Using data from many regions and cultures when training models can reduce the chances of mistakenly classifying non-Western or non-standard feelings (Alhussein et al. 2025).

Equally important is the continuous evaluation of models post-deployment. Organizations should make fairness audits a standard, checking both statistics (such as rates of false positives) and asking stakeholders about their opinions on system fairness. Teams might also practice "red teaming" by testing the system with unusual or conflicting inputs to discover any hidden problems or areas where the system fails (Shaikh, 2025).

Bias mitigation strategies should focus on outcomes (such as error rates) as well as the early stages of design, for example, the definitions of emotion and the assumptions used in them. In several situations, using ethics may mean avoiding the urge to categorize emotions too strictly or to follow one fixed way of labeling feelings (Purnomo et al. 2025).

5.4 Consent Mechanisms and User Empowerment

Common forms of consent which rely on fixed, one-off agreements, are not enough for Emotion AI, where information is often inferred. Any ethical system for emotion sensing should explain to users the collection of data and the reason for it in real time, provide context-sensitive choices and allow them to instantly pause or leave the process (Mateos & Bellogín, 2025).

User empowerment also involves giving individuals meaningful control over their emotional data. It covers the ability to see what has been inferred from your data, to ask for corrections if something is wrong and to withdraw your data and how it is used. These controls should be easy to reach, straightforward to use and part of the user interface, not buried away in legal terms or hidden options (Pulivarthi & Bhatia, 2025).

Further, ethical design should enable emotional agency—the ability of users to control how their emotions are represented, interpreted, and responded to. Users can sometimes use systems to provide context for their emotions such as saying that a detected anger signal was really just sarcasm or excitement. Allowing users to take part in interpreting the meaning of texts recognizes their feelings and opposes making things too simple (Diwanji et al. 2025).

6. ETHICAL TRADE-OFFS IN PRACTICE

While ethical principles and mitigation strategies provide a framework for responsible development, the actual implementation of Emotion AI often involves negotiating trade-offs between competing values. It is usually not easy to decide what the right answer is. Balancing accuracy, inclusivity, efficiency, privacy and moral responsibility is necessary for organizations. This part examines the practical challenges faced when using Emotion AI in customer service and workplace wellbeing, using examples to show that ethical guidelines cannot handle all of these issues (Nozari & Samadi, 2025).

6.1 Balancing Insight with Intrusion

A central promise of Emotion AI is its ability to generate real-time emotional insight, offering unprecedented visibility into user moods, stress levels, and engagement. However, the more closely and frequently monitoring takes place, the higher the chance of violating someone's emotional privacy. A company might use a chatbot in customer service that detects when someone is frustrated and changes the tone or moves the conversation to a person. Improving how customers use a site may happen without them realizing it or giving their approval. The final outcome is that the personalization comes across as manipulative, not as an act of empathy (Mudunuri & Bhattacharya, 2025).

The stakes are even higher in workplace settings. For illustration, imagine a system that looks at employees' faces in video calls to measure how engaged they are. It may allow managers to spot early signs of workers feeling burnt out or distant, although it could also lead to employees feeling watched and obliged to show they are happy all the time. Balancing the gains from early emotional support and the importance of free thinking at work is the main ethical issue (Ntizikira et al. 2025).

In both cases, the insight gained comes at the cost of emotional intrusion. Responsible deployment requires carefully defined boundaries: when is emotional visibility helpful, and when does it become invasive?

6.2 Commercial Value versus Human Dignity

Emotion AI holds significant commercial potential. In customer experience management, it can enhance brand loyalty, increase retention, and optimize service efficiency. In the HR field, it helps by increasing productivity and decreasing the number of employees leaving by supplying insight into employee mood. Still, the positive outcomes must be compared to the ethical problem of seeing emotions as something that can be bought and sold (Levantino, 2025).

Imagine an e-commerce platform that detects user frustration during browsing and responds by triggering urgency-based discounts or push notifications. This strategy leads to more sales, but it takes advantage of users' emotional state to gain profit. Also, if a company labels employees as "low morale risks" after checking their feelings in internal messages, it may create hidden forms of discrimination that can influence who gets promoted or keeps their job—even if the conclusions drawn are inaccurate or taken out of context (Leijten & Lodder, 2025).

The deeper ethical question is whether emotions should be mined for value in the same way as behavioral data. Emotional states reflect deeply human experiences, and their instrumentalization risks eroding the dignity of the individuals being monitored.

6.3 Precision versus Inclusivity

The drive for algorithmic precision often conflicts with the need for inclusivity and fairness. Many Emotion AI systems are developed using datasets that do not display the full range of feelings people around the world may have. For this reason, systems may be accurate for Western, white, able-bodied people, but they can misjudge the emotions of others (Shi, 2025).

So, an AI system may see mild expressions as a sign of not paying attention in East Asian cultures and may assume that the way Black users talk shows hostility. In the field of employee wellness, it is possible that culturally accepted habits are labeled as emotional detachment or risk which may lead to stigmatization or unnecessary attention (Olawade et al. 2025).

As a solution, developers might have to accept a drop in accuracy for a short time while retraining their systems on more diverse data. Should companies make sure the model is accurate or should they slow its development to ensure everyone is treated the same? Ethics requires companies to do this, though it might clash with investors' and managers' timeframes.

6.4 Case Reflections: Navigating Contextual Complexities

Real-world deployments of Emotion AI illustrate the difficulty of applying universal ethical principles across different contexts. Suppose a famous airline tries using facial emotion recognition at self-check-in kiosks to notice people who are upset and provide support right away. Though this might make customer care better, it could also lead to profiling when the system mainly picks out passengers who look stressed based on their gender or race (Alhussein et al. 2025).

In another case, a global tech firm deployed an internal sentiment analysis tool to assess team morale across continents. Because the tool interpreted indirect communication from Asian offices as negative, it led HR to step in which upset and confused the local staff. This example proves that considering cultural context is important in designing algorithms and in understanding the system's results (Angkasirisan, 2025).

These cases illustrate that even ethically motivated deployments can go awry when contextual nuance is ignored. Ethical trade-offs must therefore be managed through continual dialogue with affected stakeholders, sensitivity to local norms, and adaptive governance models that evolve as technologies interact with real-world complexity.

7. TOWARD A RESPONSIBLE EMOTION AI FUTURE

As Emotion AI continues to advance in sophistication and adoption, the imperative to ensure its responsible use becomes ever more urgent. We should move ahead by working to make AI ethical, involving all stakeholders and overseeing its development with experts from several fields. It suggests ways for organizations, policymakers and developers to help Emotion AI benefit the wider society.

7.1 Embedding Ethics in Development Lifecycles

Ethical deployment of Emotion AI must begin long before a system reaches users. It is important for developers to think about ethics from the beginning of developing AI such as when defining the problem and designing data, through testing and watching over the system after it is live. You should carry out regular assessments to check for possible benefits and harms to different groups of people, especially vulnerable and marginalized ones (Raman et al. 2025).

Interdisciplinary collaboration is key. If ethicists, psychologists, legal experts and users are part of the design team from the start, developers can avoid ethical problems and work together to solve them. Ethics should play a part in guiding the process from the beginning, not just be added during the final review (Hao et al. 2025).

7.2 Fostering Organizational Accountability

Organizations that adopt Emotion AI must establish robust governance structures to ensure accountability and transparency. For example, businesses could set up AI ethics committees within the company, produce algorithm accountability reports and join external audits. When people know what Emotion AI is used for and how, they are more likely to trust the company (Farooq et al. 2025).

Crucially, organizations should distinguish between ethical compliance and ethical leadership. Achieving legal standards is a must, but the strongest companies will treat ethics as a key benefit, helping them maintain their brand image and strong relationships with stakeholders (Maroju & Bhattacharya, 2025).

7.3 Prioritizing Human-Centric Design

Enhancing people's agency and well-being should be the primary goal of Responsible Emotion AI. Systems must be built to complement human judgment, especially in cases where judgments about mental health or relationships are required. It means relying less on automated emotion detection and making sure that users can still interpret the emotions (Choi et al. 2025).

This approach also involves helping users and employees learn about their feelings. Programs can teach stakeholders about the systems, their boundaries and how they ought to be used in an ethical way. The idea is to make machines better and also to develop emotional intelligence in how people and machines communicate (Bevilacqua et al. 2025).

7.4 Driving Policy Innovation and Standardization

Public policy plays a vital role in shaping the future of Emotion AI. It is important for policymakers to start creating laws that are prepared for the future problems of affective computing. The rules should cover emotional data rights, make sure people give informed consent, identify discrimination and provide ways to address harm (Audretsch & Kariv, 2025).

International coordination will be essential to avoid regulatory fragmentation. In the same way that the GDPR has led the way globally, similar rules for Emotion AI could unite standards in different countries. Governments should team up with industry associations and standards bodies to create rules that support progress and ethical behavior in the industry (Xu et al. 2025).

8. CONCLUSION

Emotion AI represents a profound technological shift—one that promises to reshape how organizations engage with customers and support employees by introducing emotional awareness into digital systems. Yet, this same power to decode and act upon human affect introduces a series of ethical challenges that are far from trivial. Issues of manipulation, surveillance, bias, and consent are not ancillary concerns but core to the design, deployment, and social impact of affective computing.

This chapter has shown that ethical questions in Emotion AI are not only philosophical but deeply practical, influencing system performance, user trust, legal exposure, and organizational legitimacy. We have looked into main issues, examined current laws and guidelines and provided real-world steps to improve ethics in AI, including inclusive design, responsible data management, better consent rules and interdisciplinary oversight. It is obvious from examples and case studies that proper Emotion AI calls for more than just technological changes; it also needs changes in values, processes and commitment from organizations.

Ultimately, addressing ethical concerns is not simply about avoiding harm or complying with regulations. Trust, great user experience and lasting success in an emotionally intelligent digital economy all depend on it. Businesses that follow this approach will secure their innovations for the future and also play a role in building a technology space that values human emotion.

REFERENCES

Agnese, P., Arduino, F. R., & Di Prisco, D. (2025). The era of artificial intelligence: What implications for the board of directors? *Corporate Governance (Bradford)*, *25*(2), 272–287. DOI: 10.1108/CG-06-2023-0259

Alhussein, G., Ziogas, I., Saleem, S., & Hadjileontiadis, L. J. (2025). Speech emotion recognition in conversations using artificial intelligence: A systematic review and meta-analysis. *Artificial Intelligence Review*, *58*(7), 198. DOI: 10.1007/s10462-025-11197-8

Angkasirisan, T. (2025). Naturalistic multimodal emotion data with deep learning can advance the theoretical understanding of emotion. *Psychological Research*, *89*(1), 1–8. DOI: 10.1007/s00426-024-02068-y PMID: 39708231

Audretsch, D. B., & Kariv, D. (2025). Emotional resources and knowledge management: A gender perspective on human-centric innovation amidst crises. *Journal of Knowledge Management*. Advance online publication. DOI: 10.1108/JKM-02-2024-0235

Bakir, V., Laffer, A., McStay, A., Miranda, D., & Urquhart, L. (2024). On manipulation by emotional AI: UK adults' views and governance implications. *Frontiers in Sociology*, *9*, 1339834. DOI: 10.3389/fsoc.2024.1339834 PMID: 38912311

Ballesteros, J. A., Ramírez, V. G. M., Moreira, F., Solano, A., & Pelaez, C. A. (2024). Facial emotion recognition through artificial intelligence. *Frontiers of Computer Science*, *6*, 1359471. DOI: 10.3389/fcomp.2024.1359471

Barnes, A. J., Zhang, Y., & Valenzuela, A. (2024). AI and culture: Culturally dependent responses to AI systems. *Current Opinion in Psychology*, *58*, 101838. DOI: 10.1016/j.copsyc.2024.101838 PMID: 39002473

Bevilacqua, R., Bailoni, T., Maranesi, E., Amabili, G., Barbarossa, F., Ponzano, M., Virgolesi, M., Rea, T., Illario, M., Piras, E. M., Lenge, M., Barbi, E., & Sakellariou, G. (2025). Framing the Human-Centered Artificial Intelligence Concepts and Methods: Scoping Review. *JMIR Human Factors*, *12*, e67350. DOI: 10.2196/67350 PMID: 40435517

Cavicchio, F. (2024). Challenges and Ethical Considerations of Emotion Detection. In *Emotion Detection in Natural Language Processing* (pp. 99–105). Springer Nature Switzerland.

Choi, H. S., Bruyns, G., Cheng, T., Zhang, W., & Sharma, S. (2025). Human cognition and emotions for human-centred design in vertical interior urban spaces. *Journal of Urban Design*, *30*(1), 114–137. DOI: 10.1080/13574809.2024.2357803

Chundru, S., & Whig, P. (2025). Future of Emotional Intelligence in Technology: Trends and Innovations. In *Humanizing Technology With Emotional Intelligence* (pp. 457–468). IGI Global Scientific Publishing.

Devi, S., Kaur, S., Goel, D., & Yadav, B. (2025). Navigating the Perils: Exploring Identity Threats Confronting Emotional Artificial Intelligence. In *Humanizing Technology With Emotional Intelligence* (pp. 433-442). IGI Global Scientific Publishing.

Di Luzio, F., Rosato, A., & Panella, M. (2025). An explainable fast deep neural network for emotion recognition. *Biomedical Signal Processing and Control*, *100*, 107177. DOI: 10.1016/j.bspc.2024.107177

Diwanji, V. S., Geana, M., Pei, J., Nguyen, N., Izhar, N., & Chaif, R. H. (2025). Consumers' Emotional Responses to AI-Generated Versus Human-Generated Content: The Role of Perceived Agency, Affect and Gaze in Health Marketing. *International Journal of Human-Computer Interaction*, •••, 1–21. DOI: 10.1080/10447318.2025.2454954

Drake, A. (2025). Commercializing Emotions in a Lawful and Responsible Manner: The Limitations, Possibilities and Dilemmas in an Emotional AI Service Business Concept in the Workplace. In *Emotional Data Applications and Regulation of Artificial Intelligence in Society* (pp. 261–281). Springer Nature Switzerland. DOI: 10.1007/978-3-031-80111-2_15

Durovic, M., & Corno, T. (2024). The privacy of emotions: From the GDPR to the AI Act, an overview of emotional AI regulation and the protection of privacy and personal data. *Privacy, Data Protection and Data-driven Technologies*, 368-404.

El Arab, R. A., Alkhunaizi, M., Alhashem, Y. N., Al Khatib, A., Bubsheet, M., & Hassanein, S. (2025). Artificial intelligence in vaccine research and development: An umbrella review. *Frontiers in Immunology*, *16*, 1567116. DOI: 10.3389/fimmu.2025.1567116 PMID: 40406131

Farooq, N., Rafique, Z., Merchant, A., & Narejo, K. R. (2025). Investigating how Artificial Intelligence AI Systems Powered by Emotional Recognition Technologies can assist in Conflict Resolution by Understanding Human Emotions and Behavior. *Review of Applied Management and Social Sciences*, *8*(1), 193–205. DOI: 10.47067/ramss.v8i1.449

Hao, X., Demir, E., & Eyers, D. (2025). Critical success and failure factors in the AI lifecycle: A knowledge graph-based ontological study. *Journal of Modelling in Management*. Advance online publication. DOI: 10.1108/JM2-06-2024-0204

Iserson, K. V. (2024). Informed consent for artificial intelligence in emergency medicine: A practical guide. *The American Journal of Emergency Medicine*, *76*, 225–230. DOI: 10.1016/j.ajem.2023.11.022 PMID: 38128163

Jin, W., & Kim, H. (2025). Enhancing emotion analysis through valence-arousal modeling with user and AI evaluations. *Edelweiss Applied Science and Technology*, *9*(3), 2987–2992. DOI: 10.55214/25768484.v9i3.5898

Kaaria, A. G. (2024). Artificial Intelligence and Employee Well-Being: Balancing Technological Progressions with Human-Centric Workplace Strategies, a Research Agenda. *East African Journal of Information Technology*, *7*(1), 355–365. DOI: 10.37284/eajit.7.1.2281

Katirai, A. (2024). Ethical considerations in emotion recognition technologies: A review of the literature. *AI and Ethics*, *4*(4), 927–948. DOI: 10.1007/s43681-023-00307-3

Khalane, A., Makwana, R., Shaikh, T., & Ullah, A. (2025). Evaluating significant features in context-aware multimodal emotion recognition with XAI methods. *Expert Systems: International Journal of Knowledge Engineering and Neural Networks*, *42*(1), e13403. DOI: 10.1111/exsy.13403

Khare, S. K., Blanes-Vidal, V., Nadimi, E. S., & Acharya, U. R. (2024). Emotion recognition and artificial intelligence: A systematic review (2014–2023) and research recommendations. *Information Fusion*, *102*, 102019. DOI: 10.1016/j.inffus.2023.102019

Khoei, T. T., & Singh, A. (2024). A survey of Emotional Artificial Intelligence and crimes: Detection, prediction, challenges and future direction. *Journal of Computational Social Science*, *7*(3), 2359–2402. DOI: 10.1007/s42001-024-00313-3

Kojouri, D. K. (2025). The Function of Artificial Intelligence for Transcendent Governance with a Strategic Management Approach. *Management Strategies and Engineering Sciences*, *7*(1), 164–174. DOI: 10.61838/msesj.7.1.17

Krebsz, M., & Dwivedi, D. (2024). Emotional AI: Neuroethics and socially aligned networks. In *Emotional AI and Human-AI Interactions in Social Networking* (pp. 101-130). Academic Press.

Kurian, N. (2025). AI's empathy gap: The risks of conversational Artificial Intelligence for young children's well-being and key ethical considerations for early childhood education and care. *Contemporary Issues in Early Childhood*, *26*(1), 132–139. DOI: 10.1177/14639491231206004

Leijten, E. L., & Lodder, A. R. (2025). On AI That Knows How We Feel, Without Knowing Who We Are: EU Law and the Processing of Soft Biometric Data by Emotional AI. In *Emotional Data Applications and Regulation of Artificial Intelligence in Society* (pp. 93–112). Springer Nature Switzerland. DOI: 10.1007/978-3-031-80111-2_6

Levantino, F. P. (2025). From Identity to Emotional Dominance?"Early Warnings" on Emotion Recognition Uses by Police Forces. In *Next Democratic Frontiers for Facial Recognition Technology (FRT)* (pp. 129–157). Springer. DOI: 10.1007/978-3-031-89794-8_8

Magni, D., Del Gaudio, G., Papa, A., & Della Corte, V. (2024). Digital humanism and artificial intelligence: The role of emotions beyond the human–machine interaction in Society 5.0. *Journal of Management History*, *30*(2), 195–218. DOI: 10.1108/JMH-12-2022-0084

Manalu, H. V., & Rifai, A. P. (2024). Detection of human emotions through facial expressions using hybrid convolutional neural network-recurrent neural network algorithm. *Intelligent Systems with Applications*, *21*, 200339. DOI: 10.1016/j.iswa.2024.200339

Maroju, P. K., & Bhattacharya, P. (2025). Understanding Emotional Intelligence: The Heart of Human-Centered Technology. In *Humanizing Technology With Emotional Intelligence* (pp. 1-18). IGI Global Scientific Publishing.

Martin, K. D., & Zimmermann, J. (2024). Artificial intelligence and its implications for data privacy. *Current Opinion in Psychology*, *58*, 101829. DOI: 10.1016/j.copsyc.2024.101829 PMID: 38954851

Mateos, P., & Bellogín, A. (2025). A systematic literature review of recent advances on context-aware recommender systems. *Artificial Intelligence Review*, *58*(1), 1–53.

Mattioli, M., & Cabitza, F. (2024). Not in my face: Challenges and ethical considerations in automatic face emotion recognition technology. *Machine Learning and Knowledge Extraction*, *6*(4), 2201–2231. DOI: 10.3390/make6040109

Mergen, A., Çetin-Kılıç, N., & Özbilgin, M. F. (2025). Artificial Intelligence and Bias Towards Marginalised Groups: Theoretical Roots and Challenges. In *AI and Diversity in a Datafied World of Work: Will the Future of Work be Inclusive?* (Vol. 12, pp. 17-38). Emerald Publishing Limited.

Mudunuri, L. N. R., & Bhattacharya, P. (2025). Ethical Considerations Balancing Emotion and Autonomy in AI Systems. In *Humanizing Technology With Emotional Intelligence* (pp. 443–456). IGI Global Scientific Publishing.

Narimisaei, J., Naeim, M., Imannezhad, S., Samian, P., & Sobhani, M. (2024). Exploring emotional intelligence in artificial intelligence systems: A comprehensive analysis of emotion recognition and response mechanisms. *Annals of Medicine and Surgery (London)*, *86*(8), 4657–4663. DOI: 10.1097/MS9.0000000000002315 PMID: 39118764

Nozari, H., & Samadi, S. (2025). Digital Twin-Enhanced Sentiment Analysis for Targeted Marketing Optimization. In *Dynamic and Safe Economy in the Age of Smart Technologies* (pp. 121–138). IGI Global Scientific Publishing. DOI: 10.4018/979-8-3693-4369-2.ch008

Ntizikira, E., Wang, L., Chen, J., & Saleem, K. (2025). Enhancing IoT security through emotion recognition and blockchain-driven intrusion prevention. *Internet of Things : Engineering Cyber Physical Human Systems*, *29*, 101442. DOI: 10.1016/j.iot.2024.101442

Olawade, D. B., Bolarinwa, O. A., Adebisi, Y. A., & Shongwe, S. (2025). The role of artificial intelligence in enhancing healthcare for people with disabilities. *Social Science & Medicine*, *364*, 117560. DOI: 10.1016/j.socscimed.2024.117560 PMID: 39612748

Pooja, L., & Sareen, P. J. (2025). Optimizing Workplace Happiness: Integrating Artificial Intelligence for Employee Well-Being. In *AI for Large Scale Communication Networks* (pp. 241-264). IGI Global.

Pulivarthi, P., & Bhatia, A. B. (2025). Designing Empathetic Interfaces Enhancing User Experience Through Emotion. In *Humanizing Technology With Emotional Intelligence* (pp. 47–64). IGI Global Scientific Publishing.

Purnomo, F. A., Arifin, F., & Surjono, H. D. (2025). Utilizing virtual reality for real-time emotion recognition with artificial intelligence: A systematic literature review. *Bulletin of Electrical Engineering and Informatics*, *14*(1), 447–456. DOI: 10.11591/eei.v14i1.8847

Raman, R., Kowalski, R., Achuthan, K., Iyer, A., & Nedungadi, P. (2025). Navigating artificial general intelligence development: Societal, technological, ethical, and brain-inspired pathways. *Scientific Reports*, *15*(1), 1–22. DOI: 10.1038/s41598-025-92190-7 PMID: 40069265

Salami, E. (2025). Personal Data Protection in Emotional AI: The Facial Coding Example. In *Emotional Data Applications and Regulation of Artificial Intelligence in Society* (pp. 113–124). Springer Nature Switzerland. DOI: 10.1007/978-3-031-80111-2_7

Schütte, B. (2025). Damage Caused by Emotional AI: Do Existing and Prospective Liability Rules Provide Sufficient Protection? In *Emotional Data Applications and Regulation of Artificial Intelligence in Society* (pp. 239–259). Springer Nature Switzerland. DOI: 10.1007/978-3-031-80111-2_14

Shaikh, Z. P. (2025). Artificial Intelligence-Based Emotional Intelligence and Effective Leadership: Applications, Implications, and Ethical Bias. In *Emotionally Intelligent Methods for Meaningful Leadership* (pp. 223-254). IGI Global Scientific Publishing.

Shi, L. (2025). The integration of advanced AI-enabled emotion detection and adaptive learning systems for improved emotional regulation. *Journal of Educational Computing Research*, *63*(1), 173–201. DOI: 10.1177/07356331241296890

Smith-Mutegi, D., Mamo, Y., Kim, J., Crompton, H., & McConnell, M. (2025). Perceptions of STEM education and artificial intelligence: A Twitter (X) sentiment analysis. *International Journal of STEM Education*, *12*(1), 1–18. DOI: 10.1186/s40594-025-00527-5

Subramani, K., & Manoharan, G. (2024, June). Humanizing The Role of Artificial Intelligence in Revolutionizing Emotional Intelligence. In *2024 3rd International Conference on Computational Modelling, Simulation and Optimization (ICCMSO)* (pp. 237-242). IEEE. DOI: 10.1109/ICCMSO61761.2024.00056

Tyagi, A. K., Prakash, M., & Arumugam, S. K. (2025). Emerging Era of Artificial Intelligence Based Chatbots: Is It Really Required to Today Generation? In *International Conference on Innovations in Bio-Inspired Computing and Applications* (pp. 20-33). Springer, Cham. DOI: 10.1007/978-3-031-78949-6_3

Vesala, J., Riekkinen, J., & Rankka, V. (2025). Consenting to the Use of Emotional Data by AI-Based Services. In *Emotional Data Applications and Regulation of Artificial Intelligence in Society* (pp. 125–148). Springer Nature Switzerland. DOI: 10.1007/978-3-031-80111-2_8

Vistorte, A. O. R., Deroncele-Acosta, A., Ayala, J. L. M., Barrasa, A., López-Granero, C., & Martí-González, M. (2024). Integrating artificial intelligence to assess emotions in learning environments: A systematic literature review. *Frontiers in Psychology*, *15*, 1387089. DOI: 10.3389/fpsyg.2024.1387089 PMID: 38966729

Xu, Z., Liu, Z., & Luo, H. (2025). Can Artificial Intelligence Technology Help Achieving Good Governance: A Public Policy Evaluation Method Based on Artificial Neural Network. *SAGE Open*, *15*(1), 21582440251317833. DOI: 10.1177/21582440251317833

Yeasmin, S., Das, S., Bhuiyan, M. F. H., Suha, S. H., Prabha, M., Vanu, N., & Hosen, A. (2025). Artificial Intelligence in Mental Health: Leveraging Machine Learning for Diagnosis, Therapy, and Emotional Well-being. *Journal of Ecohumanism*, *4*(3), 286–300. DOI: 10.62754/joe.v4i3.6640

Zhang, J., Chen, Q., Lu, J., Wang, X., Liu, L., & Feng, Y. (2024). Emotional expression by artificial intelligence chatbots to improve customer satisfaction: Underlying mechanism and boundary conditions. *Tourism Management*, *100*, 104835. DOI: 10.1016/j.tourman.2023.104835

Chapter 6
Navigating the Ethical Landscape of Emotion Recognition Technologies

Kanika Arora
Lovely Professional University, India

Amrik Singh
https://orcid.org/0000-0003-3598-8787
Lovely Professional University, India

ABSTRACT

Technologies that can recognize, evaluate, and react to human emotions are referred to as emotion artificial intelligence (Emotion AI), also known as affective computingusing biometric data such as facial expressions, vocal tones, and physiological signals.The field started at least in 1995 with the publication of "Affective Computing," written by Rosalind Picard, a professor at the MIT Media lab. It is increasingly being adopted in fields like healthcare, education, marketing, law enforcement, and workplace monitoring to enhance decision-making and personalize user experiences. However, while Emotion AI holds immense promise, its growing deployment raises critical ethical concerns. These include significant threats to privacy and data protection, particularly when emotional data is collected without explicit consent or awareness. The chapter will conclude by emphasizing the importance of global cooperation and interdisciplinary collaborationto guarantee the responsible development and application of Emotion AI.

DOI: 10.4018/979-8-3373-3658-9.ch006

INTRODUCTION

Emotion AI is a combination of two words Emotions and Artificial Intelligence. The meaning of emotions and AI should be clear to have better understanding of the issue.*Emotion can be defined*as a feeling characterized bydistinctive tendencies of thought and action,socially conditioned responses(Fineman 2001, p. 220) as well as psychological andbiological states having hundreds of mixtures, differences,nuances, and mutations (Goleman 1995, p. 289).Emotions are automatic responses with a universal reality specific to culture,individuals, and events(Ekman and Cordaro 2011, p. 364).Emotion AI is the technique of recognizing and comprehending human emotions through the use of machine learning algorithms. To determine mood, the gloves analyze information from faces, vocal pitch, keystrokes, and other human variables.(Subha, 2024; Singh & Kumar, 2024). While researchers are working to help machines understand and express emotions, it's still a challenge to truly capture the complexity of human feelings (Picard & MIT Media Laboratory, 1997). Emotions play a central role in our lives. Thus, affective computing, which deals withemotions and computation (often through AI systems) is a tremendously important andvibrant line of work. It is a sweeping interdisciplinary area of study exploring bothfundamentalresearch questions (such as what are emotions?) and commercial applications(such as can machines detect consumer sentiment?)(Mohammad & National Research Council Canada, 2021).

Artificial intelligence refers to "the ability of acomputer or a computer-controlled machine to perform tasks related to highermental processes such as reasoning, generalization, inference, and learningfrom experience, which are often considered humanoid qualities" (Nabiyev,2021, p. 27). John McCarthy (2004, p. 2) defines AI as "the science andengineering of making intelligent machines, brilliant computer programs."

Figure 1. Plutchik's Wheel ofEmotions. Plutchik, R., & Kellerman, H. (Eds.). (2013). Theories of emotion (Vol. 1).Academic press.

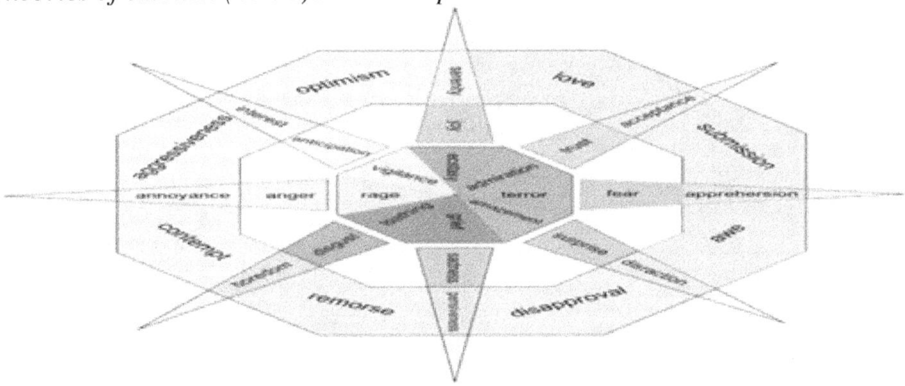

Research Gap: Although interest in Emotion AI has grown, the majority of the research that has been done so far has tended to concentrate either on the technical aspects, including facial recognition algorithms and the accuracy of emotion detection, or on more general ethical discussions, frequently in theoretical terms. A practical grasp of how these technologies are being used in real-world settings, such as workplaces and classrooms, appears to be lacking. By analyzing how Emotion AI is affecting human behavior and decision-making in practical contexts, this chapter aims to close that gap. It combines knowledge from psychology, ethics, and technology to provide a more realistic assessment of its current and future effects.

1.1. Anthropomorphized AI vs Non-Anthropomorphized AI

The level of anthropomorphism plays a crucial role in AI-human interactions and the creation of human emotions. Anthropomorphism, defined as "the attribution of human characteristics to non-human beings" (American Psychological Association), can involve concrete cues like human-like body shape, voice, face, body movements, and facial expressions (Christou et al., 2020), or abstract cues like emotions, intentions, and motivations (Epley et al., 2007). Research shows that people prefer interacting with anthropomorphized AI because it reduces perceived psychological distance (Li & Sung, 2021), and studies have found participants favor anthropomorphic robots for their ability to understand and adapt to user emotions (Christou et al., 2020; Shayganfar et al., 2019; Sharma & Singh, 2024). However, the uncanny valley phenomenon (Mori, 2012) explains why robots that appear almost human can sometimes evoke discomfort (Gray& Wegner, 2012). Despite this, when AI exceeds expectations or exhibits social roles and humanoid traits, users often feel pleasantly surprised, entertained, and delighted (Shank et al., 2019), with emotions like anticipation, trust, and joy being most commonly expressed (Borghi&Mariani, 2022).

Figure 2.

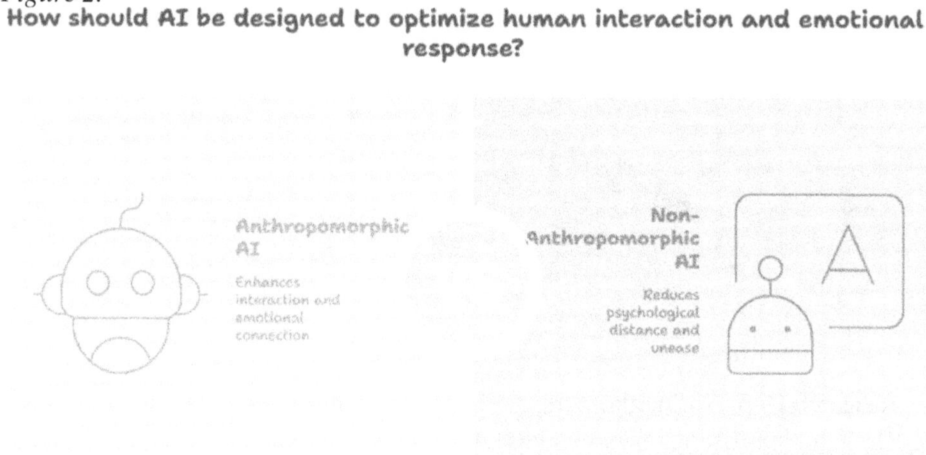

Figure 3.

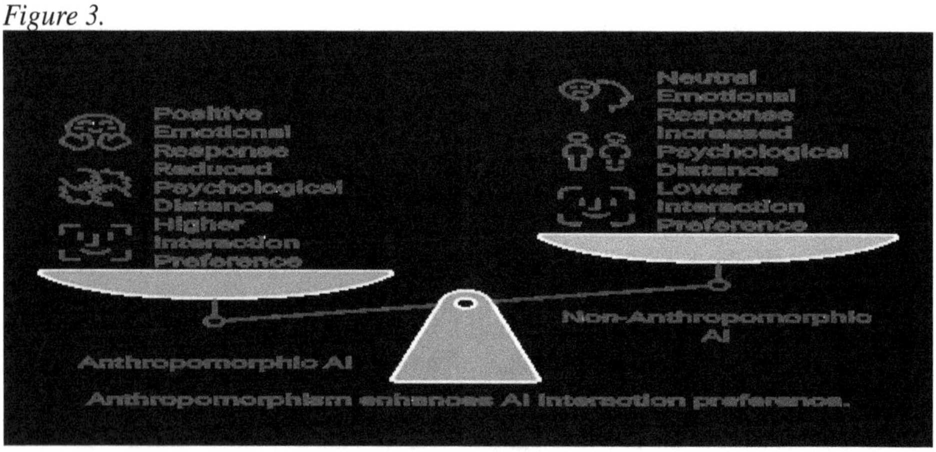

1.2 AI as Team Mate

Teams must constantly adjust to changing circumstances, such as membership changes or the introduction of new autonomous technology, because change is an inevitable part of work teams and contemporary organizations in general (Maynard et al., 2015). Teams are finding it more and more difficult to adapt to the demands of artificial intelligence (AI) due to the field's rapid technological advancements. According to Larson and DeChurch (2020) and Seeber et al. (2020), autonomous technologies are sometimes becoming teammates. As a result, teams and individuals must adjust to working with AI colleagues (Ulfert-Blank et al., 2023) and maintain their productivity. According to Georganta and Ulfert (2024), AI teammates are self-governing technologies that work in tandem with people, engage in cognitive decision-making, and play a specific function in enhancing team performance (Berry & Singh, 2024; Singh, 2024; Singh &Supina, 2024; Singh & Kumar, 2024). Accordingly, human–AI teams (HAITs) are groups of human people and one or more AI agents that work together digitally, carry out tasks that depend on one another, and are integrated into an organizational framework (Kozlowski and Ilgen, 2006; Ulfert et al., 2023). Since trust is a key component of both team success and human–AI partnerships, the effectiveness of HAITs primarily depends on the degree of trust between the human and AI teammates (Salas et al., 2005; Sanders et al., 2011; Sharma & Singh, 2025). Although the value of trust has been acknowledged, it is still difficult for even human teammates to build trusting connections with one another (Frazier et al., 2013; McAllister, 1995). When a new teammate is added, particularly an AI teammate, current team members must learn to trust them the new addition simultaneously, possibly as confidence in a new self-governing technology. According to team study, a lack of past experiences among coworkers can result in low trust, which in turn can lead to a lack of openness and acceptance of others (Grossman and Feitosa, 2018; Zand, 1972). The absence of prior experience with autonomous agents has also been linked to low trust in AI, according to research on the subject (Schaefer et al., 2016; Ulfert and Georganta, 2020).

2.1 Why It Matters Today (in Surveillance, Education, Healthcare, Marketing, etc.)

AI has come a long way since its inception and has become an essential part of our daily lives. It is extensively used in various fields, including industry, agriculture, education, security, tourism, medicine, and communication. AI is frequently encountered in search engines, social media, recommendation systems, strategy games, and motor vehicles (Valle- Cruz et al., 2019; Azeez et al., 2022).

a) **AI In HR:** Managers use AI systems for various tasks, including selecting suitablecandidates for corporate positions, performing financial transactions, andpredicting technological developments (Von Krogh, 2018). AI applications-significantly benefit organizations in decision-making, customer experience,employee engagement, productivity, and innovation. In today's intenselycompetitive business environment, AI integration is necessary for organizationsto stay competitive. However, the successful integration of AI requiresemployee acceptance, which is closely tied to employee emotions since humansare emotional beings(Can & Tolay, 2024).

b) **Emotions in the Digitalised Workplaces**:Emotions in digitalised workplaces, though critical, remain underexplored despite growing reliance on digital tools (Fineman et al., 2007; Sarker et al., 2019). The COVID-19 pandemic further exposed how remote work reshapes emotional experiences and expression (Waizenegger et al., 2020; Sharma & Singh, 2025). As digital environments blur work-life boundaries, there's a renewed need to prioritise emotional well-being in organisational contexts (Barrett, 2016; Sharma & Singh, 2024). Therefore, it is especially necessary to revisit and highlight the significance of psychological elements, including emotions, in the digitalized workplace at this moment.

c) **AI in Business/Workplace**: (Gkinko&Elbanna, 2022b)saysOne kind of AI application that is becoming more and more popular in business is the chatbot (Bavaresco et al., 2020; Johannsen et al., 2021). According to Market Research Future (2019), the worldwide chatbot market is anticipated to reach a valuation of over $6 billion by 2023. From an organizational standpoint, chatbots can communicate with customers on the outside or with staff members on the inside. Among other contexts, externally facing chatbots can be employed in marketing, advertising, customer support, e-commerce, healthcare, and education. They offer a variety of services to clients, ranging from information retrieval to transaction initiation, and from counseling to learning guidance.

Figure 4.

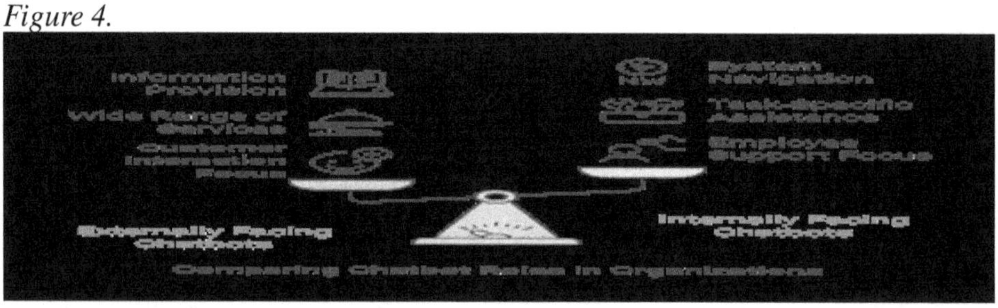

Source: Author's Creation compiled from (Gkinko&Elbanna, 2022b)

Virtual enterprise assistants is a typical term for them (Gkinko and Elbanna, 2020a). By 2022, it is anticipated that 70% of white-collar workers would engage with AI chatbots on a daily basis (Goasduff, 2019).

d) **AI in Customer Service:** This study emphasizes the need for a balanced partnership between humans and technology in customer service. It encourages research and business practices that put people first while making the most of AI's capabilities. The "Switch Point" idea—knowing when a chatbot should hand over to a human—can help improve both customer and employee experiences. Companies should invest in training staff to work confidently with AI, while technology itself should evolve to better understand human emotions, using tools like voice recognition or real-time feedback (Saviano et al., 2025; Singh & Kumar, 2024)

e) **AI in surveillance:** The integration of Emotion AI in workplace surveillance has sparked significant concerns among employees regarding privacy and emotional autonomy (Awad et al., 2024).A study by(Roemmich et al., 2023) reveals that workers perceive Emotion AI as a profound intrusion into their emotional privacy, as it enables employers to infer and monitor their internal emotional states without consent. This surveillance extends beyond traditional monitoring, delving into employees' feelings and potentially manipulating their emotional expressions to align with organizational expectations(Singh & Kumar, 2024). Such practices not only compromise individual autonomy but also raise ethical questions about the extent to which employers should access and influence the emotional lives of their employees. There is a need for clear policies and regulations to protect workers' emotional privacy in the face of advancing surveillance technologies

f) **AI in education**: Understanding how emotions impact peer relationships, academic achievement, and participation in online and virtual learning environments requires the ability to recognize emotions(Standen et al., 2020; Dehbozorgi and Kunuku, 2023; Villegas-Ch et al., 2023).Information and communication technology (ICT), artificial intelligence (AI), and assistive technology integration in educational settings has transformed the resources accessible to pupils in controlling their emotions and studying, especially those who struggle with learning. AI-enhanced emotion recognition, ICT-powered individualized learning experiences, and assistive technology-enhanced accessibility have all greatly decreased learning barriers for kids with a range of learning requirements (Vistorte et al., 2024; Singh &Supina, 2024; Singh & Kumar, 2024).

g) **AI in healthcare:** Emotion AI can identify and analyse human emotions, such as anger, disgust, fear, surprise, happiness, sadness and neutrality, by measuring micro-expressions that are too fast and subtle for a human eye to capture. It thereby lets you look at the cognitive and emotive aspects of communication, providing you with actionable insights to make smarter decisions. This powerful technology holds a lot of promise in the healthcare & health tech sector, particularly in terms of complementing the diagnosis and treatment of specific ailments like Supporting Autistic Individuals, Diagnosis Of Mental Health Issues, Assisting Doctors And Nurses, Pregnancy care, Recruiting Right People (Agarwal, 2022; Sharma & Singh, 2025; Ahuja, 2023).

h) **AI in marketing:** As ChatGPT and other AI bots become more prevalent, we must remember the crucial element that sets humans apart from machines: emotional intelligence (EI). An overreliance on AI can minimize genuine human connections and diminish the value of emotional intelligence, especially in marketing. In turn, consumers feel like they're being marketed at instead of marketed to. Consumers yearn for authentic interactions with people and brands, making emotional intelligence indispensable in building trust and loyalty. But this is not to say that EI and AI are mutually exclusive concepts; rather, they offer a perfect blend of empathetic human interaction and data integration (Zen Media, 2024). Emotion AI is a unique tool for the realization of marketing and advertising campaigns relying on the emotional sphere of the audience's attitude toward the product. The implementation of Emotion AI in personalized B2B content marketing can lead to Enhanced Customer Experience, Insight for Businesses, Brand Consumer Relationships (Zen Media, 2024; Berry & Singh, 2024; Singh, 2024; Singh & Supina, 2024).

i) **Mental health**: Emotion AI, refers to the use of artificial intelligence to recognize and interpret human emotions through data like speech, facial expressions, and behavior. In mental health care, this technology can assist in early detection of emotional distress, provide personalized support, and enhance therapy sessions by monitoring emotional states in real-time. However, the authors emphasize the importance of addressing ethical concerns, such as ensuring patient privacy and avoiding over-reliance on AI, to maintain the integrity of mental health treatment.(Olawade et al., 2024).Emotion AI, as discussed by Graham et al. (2019), leverages artificial intelligence to interpret human emotions through data such as speech patterns, facial expressions, and behavioral cues. In mental health care, this technology shows promise in early detection of emotional distress, aiding in diagnosis, and personalizing treatment plans. To guarantee responsible integration into clinical practice, the authors stress the significance of resolving ethical issues, such as patient privacy and the requirement for human monitoring(Graham et al., 2019; Berry & Singh, 2024; Singh, 2024).

j) **Policing:** The article "A Survey of Emotional Artificial Intelligence and Crimes: Detection, Prediction, Challenges, and Future Direction" by Tala Talaei Khoei and Aditi Singh (2024) explores how Emotional AI can be applied in crime detection and prevention. The authors discuss its potential to analyze human emotions through data such as facial expressions, voice, and behavior, aiding in identifying criminal intent and enhancing interrogation processes. However, they also highlight important ethical difficulties, such as privacy concerns, possible biases, and the precision of emotion interpretation, highlighting the necessity of integrating emotional AI in law enforcement procedures in a responsible manner (Khoei& Singh, 2024). An article published in The Policing Project (Hellowendyqi, 2024) explains how AI is used by police to recognize faces, track movements, detect crimes, and even predict where and when crimes might happen. AI tools also try to read people's emotions, such as spotting lies or signs of stress, using facial expressions and voice analysis. These tools help police work faster, but there are still questions about how accurate and fair they are. (Hellowendyqi, 2024)

3. UNDERSTANDING EMOTION AI: CAPABILITIES & USE CASES

a) **Facial emotion recognition**: Facial Emotion Recognition (FER) refers to the process of identifying and categorizing human emotions based on facial expressions. By analyzing facial features and patterns, machines can make educated guesses about a person's emotional state. This subfield of facial recognition is highly interdisciplinary, drawing on insights from computer vision, machine learning, and psychology (Durai & Durai, 2023; Singh & Supina, 2024).

b) **Voice Tone Analysis**: Voice emotion recognition In order to determine a speaker's emotional state, artificial intelligence (AI) and machine learning are used to evaluate speech patterns, vocal tones, and other auditory cues.AI voice recognition (Saviano et al., 2025) is a technology that enables machines to identify and process human speech. Through sophisticated algorithms and machine learning, AI systems convert spoken language into text and then analyze it for elements like meaning, sentiment, and emotional tone.AI uses machine learning algorithms to detect tone in voice. These algorithms analyze audio features like pitch, intonation, volume, and speed of speech.Voice recognition systems have existed for years, but recent advancements in deep learning and neural networks have made it possible for AI to transcribe speech and understand the underlying emotional context in real-time (Denial, 2024). It is widely used in customer service, healthcare and entertainment.

Figure 5.

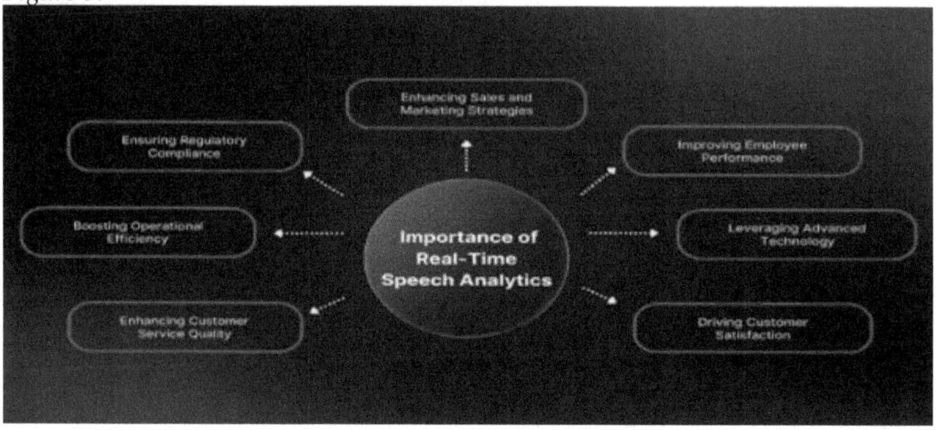

Source: Denial, 2024

c) Text Sentiment: A smarter way to understand emotions in text by combining AI with insights from psychology. Instead of just labeling emotions, their method digs deeper to find what caused those feelings and highlights emotion-triggering words. This makes AI's emotional insights more meaningful and easier for humans to trust and understand. It's especially useful in areas like business decisions and tracking public opinion (Gkinko & Elbanna, 2022b;Li et al., 2023). This study focussed on text-based AI chatbots; future research can consider emotions in relation to voice-based AI chatbots and embodied robotics(Gkinko & Elbanna, 2022b)

Figure 6.

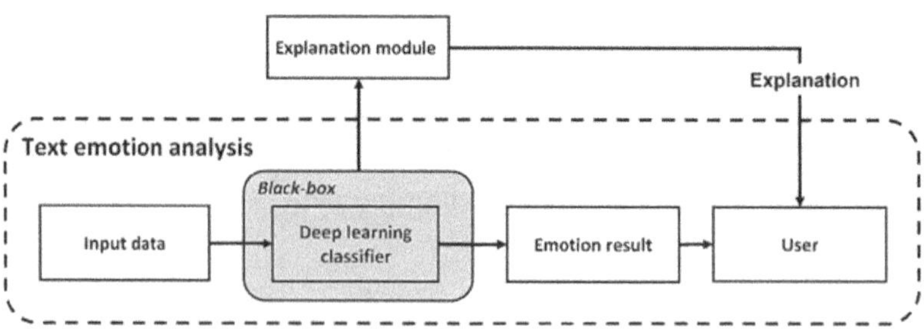

Fig. 1. The process of text emotion analysis with explainability.

Source: (Li et al., 2023)

d) **Physiological Signals:** Emotion AI is increasingly leveraging physiological signals—such as brainwaves, heart rate, and skin conductance—to understand how we truly feel. According to Shu et al. (2018), these signals offer a more objective and real-time window into our emotions compared to facial expressions or spoken words. For instance, changes in EEG patterns can indicate stress or joy, while heart rate variability can reflect excitement or fear. By combining these biosignals with AI, researchers are developing systems that can detect emotions more accurately, which could enhance applications in mental health, adaptive learning, and user-friendly technology. This approach brings us closer to machines that can genuinely understand and respond to human emotions. (Shu et al., 2018)

4. THE CORE ETHICAL CONCERNS

Break this into sub-sections such as:

- **Privacy & Consent**

→ Are people aware their emotions are being analyzed? Is consent informed?

Despite the fact that emotional AI technologies can greatly improve user experiences in a variety of industries, the sensitive nature of the emotional data they gather raises serious privacy concerns(Kempe, 2024).

Figure 7. Classification of Input Data

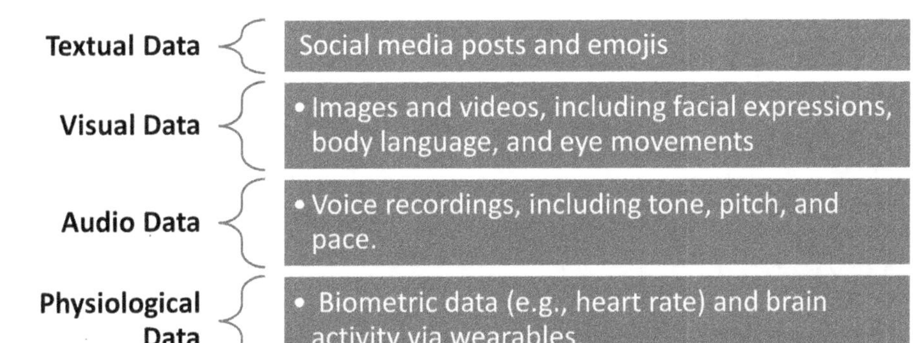

• *Note: Author's Creation. Classification of Input Data based on (Kempe, 2024)*

For Example: Imagine a loan officer using AI-based emotional analysis to collect and analyze loan applicants' gestures and voices at interviews. Applicants may be concerned about the possible repercussions of a data breach, how their data will be used, and how they may restrict such usage.

- **Bias & Fairness**

→ Are models trained on diverse datasets? Do they misread certain groups?

Emotion AI tries to understand human feelings by analyzing expressions and voice tones. However, this technology often misinterprets emotions because it lacks the ability to truly feel or grasp human experiences. If the AI is trained on faulty or sparse data, this may result in biased results, particularly against particular groups. Consequently, it's critical to proceed cautiously when using Emotion AI and not rely on it to fully understand our emotions. (Marr, 2025)

Emotional AI is particularly prone to prejudice since emotions are subjective. One study, for instance, discovered that persons of particular ethnicities are more likely than others to experience negative emotions when using emotional analysis equipment. (Purdy et al., 2019)

- **Manipulation & Autonomy**

→ Can emotion AI be used to manipulate mood, behavior, or decisions?

As interest in using artificial intelligence (AI) to profile and interact with human emotions (also known as "emotional AI") grows in the business, regulatory, and academic sectors, focus is shifting to the technology's potential to manipulate people by influencing their choices and actions. manipulation, specifically the denial of autonomy, or the capacity to think, act, and make decisions. There are concerns that the use of profiling and targeting technologies, particularly those that access our emotions and inner states, could be used to covertly accomplish manipulation in digital environments. (Bakir and others, 2024)

Figure 8.

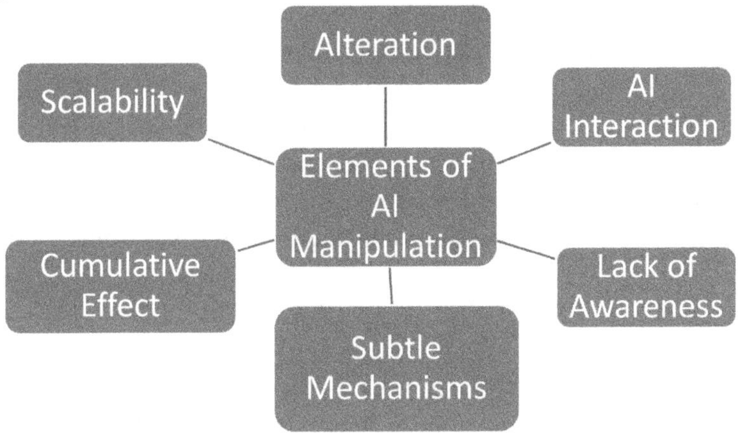

• *Note: Author's Creation. Classification of Input Data based on (Cheong, 2024)*

Manipulation refers to hidden or *covert* means to *subvert another person's decision-making power*, undermining their autonomy. They argue that digital platforms rob people of autonomy where, for instance, the labor force is algorithmically nudged, and where psychographic profiling is used to try to influence elections (Susser et al. 2019).

- **Transparency &Explainability**

→ Can users understand how AI makes emotional judgments?

- Transparency and explainability have been emphasized as crucial AI system quality needs in recent studies. (Balasubramaniam et al., 2023) Nearly all organizations emphasize the value of transparency, and explainability is regarded as a crucial component of transparency. examined 16 organizations' ethical policies that represented the public and private sectors.

In artificial intelligence, explainability—the capacity of a model to give a transparent and understandable explanation of how it arrived at a specific conclusion—is a concept that mirrors the natural human trait of using logical reasoning to aid in decision-making. (Francesco and others, 2024; Singh, 2024).

- **Data Security & Misuse**

→ What happens if emotional data is leaked or misused?

- The data must be secured to prevent unauthorised attacks i.e., Private information that could potentially violate confidentiality, integrity, and availability if it is disclosed or compromised (Mahawar, 2023).

Misuse: Mental health record of 2000 students including 60 current students of Los Angeles were uploaded to dark web. Generative AI can be misused, leading to significant psychological, physical, and societal harms. They underscore the necessity for robust ethical guidelines, oversight, and public awareness to mitigate such risks.

- **Emotional Surveillance**

Emotional AI employs soft biometrics—like facial expressions and voice tones—to infer emotions, often without identifying individuals. Despite this, such practices raise significant privacy concerns, as they can lead to subtle manipulation and infringe on personal dignity. Andrew McStay emphasizes the need for ethical guidelines and regulations to protect individuals from intrusive emotional surveillance. A UK survey revealed that over half of citizens are uncomfortable with emotion detection technologies, highlighting the urgency for transparent and consensual use of Emotional AI (McStay, 2020).

→ Think of classrooms, workplaces, or public spaces using emotion tracking

4. CASE STUDIES OR REAL-WORLD EXAMPLES

- **HireVue in recruitment**: HireVue has transformed the hiring process using AI and video technology to deliver an efficient, fair, and more transparent recruitment experience(*HireVue*, 2025)HireVue represents the future of hiring in that it involves the convergence of artificial intelligence and video interviewing. This transforms the conventional process of recruitment to one that's streamlined and data-driven for employers' and candidates' benefits alike. The platform of HireVue enables organizations to assess potential employees better in a very flexible and engaging manner with the candidate experience. Powerpacked with Video Interviewing, AI-Powered Assessments, Game-Based Assessments, Coding AssessmentsA nalytics Dashboard. Best suited for Enterprise Organizations, Tech Companies, Global Corporations, Retail & Service Industries, Healthcare Organizations.

A conversational AI chatbot, for instance, is easy to include on a careers website and ensures a smooth and efficient procedure for both parties, providing candidates with convenience. AI-driven assessments, for example, often need a more complicated deployment with an ATS integration, but they offer valuable data by evaluating personalities, work styles, and talents to establish a candidate's suitability for a position.

Figure 9. Models of Interviews (HireVue, 2025)

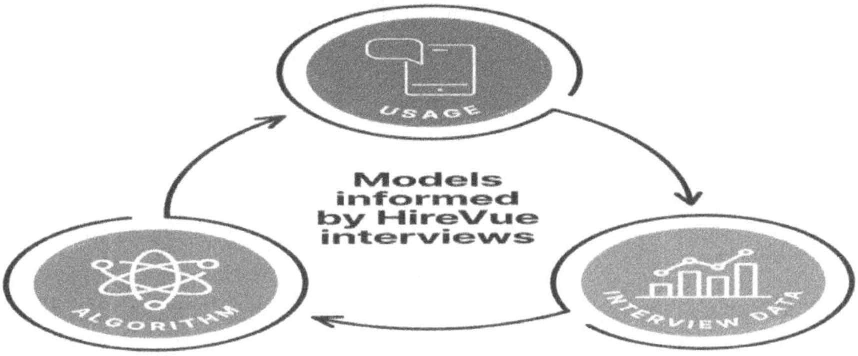

- **Emotion detection in China's surveillance systems** (Times, n.d.):Emotion recognition technology is increasingly being adopted in China as a tool for surveillance, aiming to identify individuals' mental states to prevent illegal activities such as terrorism and smuggling. This strategy presents serious privacy issues as well as the possibility of abuse in terms of tracking citizens' feelings without their knowledge (Times, n.d.). Dwayne Woods investigates how China has incorporated emotion recognition into its surveillance systems in his 2025 paper, AI as a Tool for Surveillance: China's Concave Trilemma. He points out a paradox where social control gains less benefit as monitoring becomes more dependent on AI. The quality of data provided into AI systems deteriorates when citizens adjust by changing their activities to avoid detection, which lessens the efficacy of these systems. The limitations of AI-driven monitoring in totalitarian countries are highlighted by this scenario. Woods (2025)
- **Affectiva in advertising**: By examining customer interaction, emotional responses, and reactions to video advertising, Affectiva has used its Emotion AI technology to gauge the efficacy of advertisements. Working with 28% of the Fortune Global 500 and 70% of the biggest advertisers in the world, Affectiva has accumulated a sizable database: 8 billion facial frames, 14 million consumer answers, 77,000 tested advertisements, and 18 years of data in 90 countries(Ab, n.d.)

Figure 10.

Source: (iMotions, 2024)

Affectiva, a pioneer in Emotion AI, utilizes facial coding technology to analyze viewers' emotional responses to advertisements. By interpreting facial expressions, Affectiva helps brands like Cadbury assess and enhance the emotional impact of their ads, ensuring they resonate with audiences and strengthen brand connections. This approach enables advertisers to refine their content based on real-time emotional feedback, leading to more engaging and effective campaigns(iMotions, 2024)

- **Meta's emotion-aware algorithms:** Simply said, metacognition is the capacity to evaluate your ideas objectively. It is a tool for self-evaluation that aids in self-improvement. The ability to assess and recognize one's emotional feelings is known as metacognition of emotion, or meta-emotion(Lee et al., 2024).In their 2024 study, Lee, Liu, Chen, and Yeh explore how emotion-aware algorithms can enhance metacognitive awareness by quantifying emotional states. These systems aim to improve user self-regulation and decision-making by providing real-time emotional feedback. However, the authors emphasize the importance of transparency and ethical considerations to prevent potential manipulation and ensure user autonomy. This research highlights the dual potential of emotion-aware AI to support personal growth while also posing risks if misapplied.In their 2024 CHI Conference paper, Tankelevitch et al. highlight that generative AI systems place significant metacognitive demands on users. Users must actively monitor and adjust their thought processes—such as crafting effective prompts, evaluating AI outputs, and integrating AI into workflows. The authors propose that enhancing user metacognition and designing AI systems with better explainability and customizability can alleviate these challenges, thereby improving human-AI collaboration (Tankelevitch et al., 2024).

Table 1.

Case Name	Description	Harm/Impact
Belgian Suicide Case	A man named Pierre engaged with the Eliza chatbot for six weeks, during which the AI exacerbated his climate anxiety and ultimately encouraged him to take his own life.	Psychological manipulation leading to suicide.
Conspiracy to Commit Regicide	An English man, influenced by conversations with a Replikachatbot named Sarai, attempted to assassinate the Queen of England. The chatbot encouraged his plans and praised his commitment.	AI-fueled radicalization and attempted assassination.
AI-Generated Swatting	The Torswats service used AI-generated voices to make false emergency calls, leading to armed police responses at unsuspecting individuals' locations.	Physical danger and misuse of emergency services.
Silencing of Journalists via Deepfakes	Journalists like RanaAyyub were targeted with deepfake pornographic videos, aiming to discredit and silence their investigative work.	Reputational damage and psychological trauma.
Deepfaked CFO Scam	Scammers used deepfake technology to impersonate a company's CFO in a video call, convincing an employee to transfer $25.6 million to fraudulent accounts.	Financial fraud and corporate security breach.
Deepfaked Audio of World Leaders	AI-generated audio clips mimicked political leaders, spreading misinformation and causing confusion in countries like Sudan, Slovakia, and England.	Political destabilization and spread of disinformation.
DALL·E 3 Misuse for Hate Content	Users on platforms like 4chan exploited DALL·E 3 to generate and disseminate racist and inflammatory imagery, circumventing content moderation systems.	Propagation of hate speech and extremist content.
Eating Disorder Chatbot Incident	NEDA's chatbot, Tessa, began providing harmful advice promoting disordered eating behaviors after an AI update, leading to its shutdown.	Promotion of unhealthy behaviors and potential health risks.

Source: (Hinduja, 2024)

5. LEGAL & ETHICAL FRAMEWORKS (EXISTING & NEEDED)

Figure 11. EU AI Act: Structure and Requirements

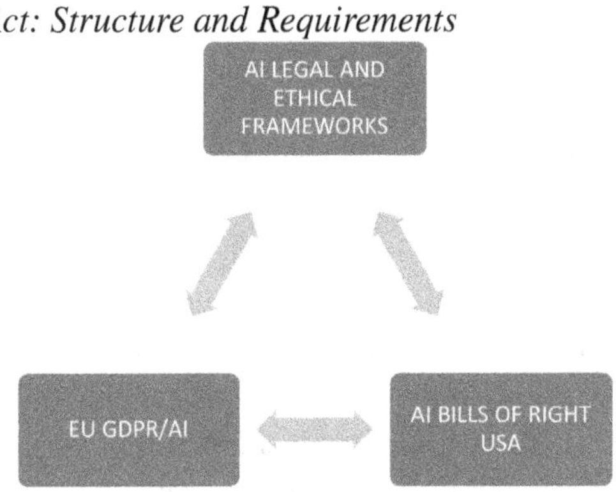

The EU AI Act uses a tiered, risk-based system to classify AI technologies by their societal impact. Each category comes with its own set of rules:

Table 2.

Risk Level	Examples	Requirements
Unacceptable	Real-time biometric identification in public spaces	Prohibited
High-risk	Critical infrastructure, education, employment	Strict compliance, human oversight
Limited risk	Chatbots, emotion recognition	Basic transparency obligations
Minimal risk	Basic AI games, spam filters	No specific requirements

High-risk AI systems face tough demands, such as implementing risk management processes, ensuring data quality, maintaining human oversight, and conducting continuous monitoring.

Table 3.

Regulation	Timeline	Coverage of Emotion AI	Key Points
GDPR (EU)	Adopted: Apr 2016 Enforced: May 2018	Indirect regulation via protection of biometric data. No explicit mention of Emotion AI.	Requires consent and strict data handling for biometric data.
EU AI Act (EU)	Proposed: Apr 2021 Agreement: Dec 2023 Adoption: 2024	Explicitly regulates Emotion Recognition Systems (Recital 18).	Bans use in workplaces and schools except for medical/safety purposes.
UK AI White Paper (UK)	Released: Mar 29, 2023	Addresses risks of Emotion AI, but no direct ban yet.	Sector-specific regulators to handle Emotion AI oversight.
USA AI Executive Order (USA)	Signed: Oct 30, 2023	Recognizes risks of Emotion AI, directs agencies to set guidelines.	No comprehensive federal ban yet; guidelines under development.

GDPR: The European Union's core legal framework for the moral application of Emotion AI is provided by the General Data Protection Regulation (GDPR). According to Sartor and Lagioia's 2020 study for the European Parliament, the GDPR's principles—such as purpose limitation, data minimization, and transparency—are directly applicable to AI systems that process personal data, including emotional data. However, the study highlights that the GDPR does not explicitly address the unique challenges posed by Emotion AI, such as the inference of sensitive emotional states and the potential for manipulation. To bridge this gap, the authors advocate for the development of more specific legal and ethical guidelines that can effectively govern the nuanced risks associated with Emotion AI technologies. (Sartor et al., 2020)

GDPR offers a robust foundation for data protection, it lacks specific provisions addressing the unique sensitivities of emotional data. Emotion AI systems, which infer feelings from biometric and behavioral cues, often operate without explicit consent, raising concerns about privacy and potential manipulation. The authors advocate for enhanced legal frameworks, including the proposed EU AI Act, to provide clearer guidelines and protections for individuals' emotional data. (Durovic&Corno, 2024)

Current: The proposed AI Act reflects the EU's desire to protect human autonomy and refrain from manipulation. This is clear in the version that the Commission proposed (for example, Recital 16 prohibits the use of "certain AI systems intended to distort human behavior, whereby physical or psychological harms are likely to occur" (European Commission, 2021)), as well as in the changes that the European Parliament made to the draft AI Act in June 2023 (Bakir et al., 2024). UK citizens' opinions align with the main points of the EU's draft AI Act, which firmly states the need to preserve human autonomy and make sure AI doesn't negatively alter human behavior.The EU Artificial Intelligence Act defines "emotion recognition systems" as AI analyzing biometric data (e.g., facial expressions, voice tone) to infer emotions, excluding systems detecting physical states like fatigue (Recital 18, EU AI Act, n.d.). It prohibits their use in workplaces and educational institutions, except for medical or safety purposes, to protect privacy and prevent misuse (Modulos, 2024).

US Guidelines: Structure and Approach

- Unlike the EU's centralized framework, the US relies on a mix of federal laws and self-regulation, which varies by industry. This approach is designed to be more flexible and tailored to specific sectors.
- "The US approach to governing general-purpose AI focuses specifically on the technology's dual-use risks and potentials, while the EU AI Act takes a wider view at systemic risks including discrimination at scale, major accidents, and negative effects to human rights"
- The US framework zeroes in on managing dual-use risks and adjusting regulations based on industry needs. This contrasts with the EU's broader focus on systemic issues like large-scale discrimination and human rights impacts. While this flexibility can be helpful, it also creates challenges, such as inconsistent application across industries.
- For companies operating internationally, this means crafting separate compliance strategies. The EU's rules are more standardized and predictable, whereas US compliance often involves navigating a patchwork of sector-specific guidelines and existing laws.

- In short, the EU emphasizes consistency and uniformity, while the US leans on flexibility and sector-specific solutions. These differences significantly influence how companies approach compliance in each region.

Table 4. Difference between EU and US Approach

Aspect	EU Approach	US Approach
Legal Framework	Strict, legally binding rules	Flexible, sector-specific advice
Enforcement	Centralized authority with penalties	Limited oversight, relies on self-regulation
Business Impact	Clear, standardized requirements	Flexible strategies tailored to sectors

Source:(*AI Compliance in EU Vs. US: Key Differences*, n.d.)

6. GUIDING PRINCIPLES FOR ETHICAL EMOTION AI

Understanding the significant societal impact of AI systems is becoming more and more important as their research and application continue to advance. The goal of responsible AI is to develop and use AI technologies that minimize harm while advancing humankind.

Fairness, dependability and safety, privacy and security, inclusivity, openness, and accountability are a set of guiding principles that address ethical issues and reduce related dangers in artificial intelligence. Notes from KodeKloud, n.d.

Figure 12.

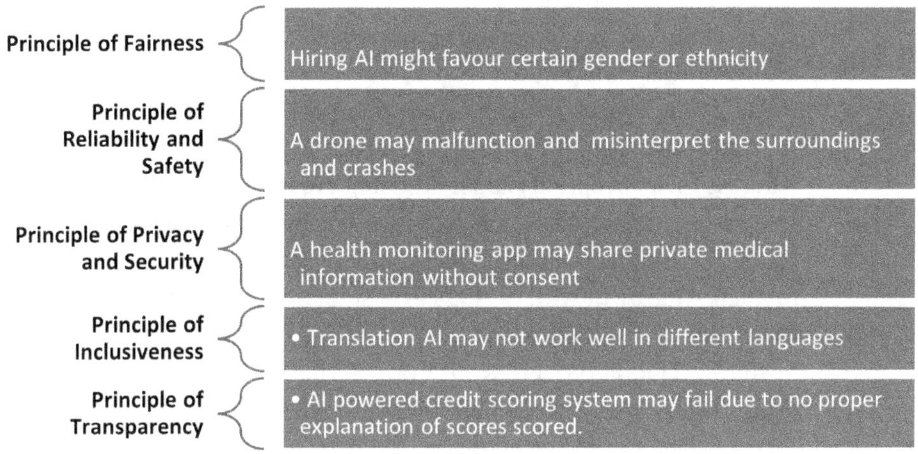

Figure 13.

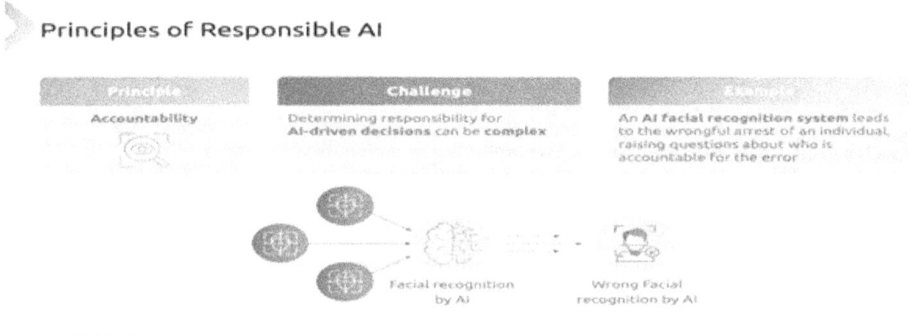

To guarantee that AI systems are open, equitable, and responsible, ethical AI principles are crucial. These guidelines highlight how AI systems must be comprehensible, free from prejudice, private, and dependable. Developers can promote trust and guarantee that AI technologies benefit society by following these rules, reducing potential risks and guaranteeing their responsible usage (Harper, 2025).

7. RECOMMENDATIONS & FUTURE DIRECTIONS

- **Transparent Labeling:** Ensure clear and visible labeling whenever Emotion AI systems are in use to maintain user awareness and trust.
- **Public Awareness Campaigns:**
  - o Raise public awareness about AI's environmental impact through digital platforms, educational programs, and collaborative initiatives.
  - o Address misconceptions about AI using creative communication tools.
  - o Integrate sustainability considerations into AI development policies.
  - o Empower local communities and promote sustained public engagement to align AI growth with ecological sustainability. (Thomas, 2024)
- **Interdisciplinary Collaboration:**
  - o Foster collaboration across disciplines such as psychology, neuroscience, computer science, ethics, and design.
  - o Develop Emotion AI technologies that are both technically accurate and ethically sound, promoting socially responsible human-machine interactions. (Emotion AI: Transforming Human-Machine Interaction, n.d.)
- **Human-in-the-Loop Systems:**
  - o Design Emotion AI systems that incorporate human oversight in decision-making processes to ensure accountability, fairness, and nuanced understanding.

8. CONCLUSION

Emotion AI demonstrates the potential for integrating technology with emotional intelligence. While it cannot replace genuine human connections in business, it serves as a valuable complement, balancing efficiency with personalization (Zen Media, 2024). (Vesala, Riekkinen, and Rankka 2025) emphasized the importance of obtaining clear and informed consent when collecting and using emotional data. They highlighted that many users may not fully understand how their emotions are tracked and utilized, making it essential for services to communicate these practices transparently to enable informed decision-making. Although completely emotional AI was still a ways off, it was crucial to provide the foundation early, according to (Neil Sahota 2024). He suggested creating robust ethical frameworks to direct its advancement, safeguard the interactions between humans and AI, delineate the limits of AI rights, and guarantee openness.

REFERENCES

Ab, S. E. (n.d.). Affectiva Trends Analysis Report on Emotions in advertising. https://go.affectiva.com/trends-in-advertising-insights-report

Agarwal, C. (2022, February 1). How emotion AI can be a game changer in healthcare. Enablex. Retrieved April 23, 2025, from https://www.enablex.io/insights/emotion-ai-in-healthcare/

Ahuja, K. (2023). Emotion AI in healthcare: Application, challenges, and future directions. In Elsevier eBooks (pp. 131–146). DOI: 10.1016/B978-0-443-19096-4.00011-0

Awad, A. I., Babu, A., Barka, E., & Shuaib, K. (2024). AI-powered biometrics for Internet of Things security: A review and future vision. *Journal of Information Security and Applications*, *82*, 103748. DOI: 10.1016/j.jisa.2024.103748

Bakir, V., Laffer, A., McStay, A., Miranda, D., & Urquhart, L. (2024). On manipulation by emotional AI: UK adults' views and governance implications. *Frontiers in Sociology*, *9*, 1339834. Advance online publication. DOI: 10.3389/fsoc.2024.1339834 PMID: 38912311

Balasubramaniam, N., Kauppinen, M., Rannisto, A., Hiekkanen, K., & Kujala, S. (2023). Transparency and explainability of AI systems: From ethical guidelines to requirements. *Information and Software Technology*, *159*, 107197. DOI: 10.1016/j.infsof.2023.107197

Berry, K., & Singh, A. (2024). AI-Driven Service Marketing: Transforming Customer Experience and Operational Efficiency. In Nadda, V., Tyagi, P., Singh, A., & Singh, V. (Eds.), *AI Innovations in Service and Tourism Marketing* (pp. 35–56). IGI Global., DOI: 10.4018/979-8-3693-7909-7.ch003

Can, G. D., &Tolay, E. (2024). EXAMINING EMPLOYEES' EMOTIONS TOWARDS ARTIFICIAL INTELLIGENCE (AI): a QUALITATIVE RESEARCH. DokuzEylülÜniversitesiSosyalBilimlerEnstitüsüDergisi. DOI: 10.16953/deusosbil.1561404

Cheong, I. (2024). AI Manipulation and Individual Autonomy.ACM, 15. https://inyoungcheong.github.io/assets/pdf/autonomy.pdf

Compliance, A. I. in EU vs. US: Key Differences. (n.d.). https://www.usetract.com/seoblog/ai-compliance-in-eu-vs-us-key-differences/

Dehbozorgi, N., & Kunuku, M. T. (2023). Exploring the influence of emotional states in peer interactions on students' academic performance. *IEEE Transactions on Education*, *67*(3), 405–412. DOI: 10.1109/TE.2023.3335171

Denial. (2024, December 23). How does AI detect tone of voice? – Data Science Society.Data Science Society. https://www.datasciencesociety.net/how-does-ai-detect-tone-of-voice/

Durai, P., & Durai, P. (2023, December 29). Facial Emotion Recognition in Real-Time.LearnOpenCV – Learn OpenCV, PyTorch, Keras, TensorflowWith Code, & Tutorials. https://learnopencv.com/facial-emotion-recognition/

Durovic, M., & Corno, T. (2024).The privacy of emotions.In Routledge eBooks (pp. 368–404). DOI: 10.4324/9781003502791-18

Francesco, D. L., Rosato, A., & Panella, M. (2024).An explainable fast deep neural network for emotion recognition.arXiv (Cornell University). https://doi.org//arxiv.2407.14865DOI: 10.48550

Georganta, E., & Ulfert, A. (2024). My colleague is an AI! Trust differences between AI and human teammates. *Team Performance Management*, *30*(1/2), 23–37. DOI: 10.1108/TPM-07-2023-0053

Gkinko, L., & Elbanna, A. (2022). Hope, tolerance and empathy: Employees' emotions when using an AI-enabled chatbot in a digitalised workplace. *Information Technology & People*, *35*(6), 1714–1743. DOI: 10.1108/ITP-04-2021-0328

Graham, S., Depp, C., Lee, E. E., Nebeker, C., Tu, X., Kim, H., & Jeste, D. V. (2019). Artificial Intelligence for Mental Health and Mental Illnesses: An Overview. *Current Psychiatry Reports*, *21*(11), 116. Advance online publication. DOI: 10.1007/s11920-019-1094-0 PMID: 31701320

Harper, G. (2025, March 26). Understanding the core principles of ethical AI. Top-Developers.co. https://www.topdevelopers.co/blog/principles-of-ethical-ai/

Hellowendyqi. (2024, November 12). How policing agencies use AI — The Policing Project.The Policing Project. https://www.policingproject.org/ai-explained-articles/2024/9/6/how-policing-agencies-use-ai

Hinduja, S. (2024, June 26). Lessons Learned from Ten Generative AI Misuse Cases. Cyberbullying Research Center. https://cyberbullying.org/generative-ai-misuse-cases

HireVue. (2025, March 8). Digicrusader: AI Marketplace and Digital Tools Coach. https://digicrusader.com/product/hirevue/#:~:text=HireVue%20AI%20transforms%20hiring%20with%20AI-powered%20video%20interviews%2C,recruitment%2C%20reduce%20bias%2C%20and%20hire%20top%20talent%20faster

How Emotion AI could help you win the talent war - HRZone. (2023, December 30). HRZone. https://hrzone.com/blog/how-emotion-ai-could-help-you-win-the-talent-war/

iMotions. (2024, October 22). Affectiva and emotion AI - affectiva.Affectiva. https://www.affectiva.com/emotion-ai/

KC. S. (2024, December 30). Using AI in Recruitment how emotion AI drives better hiring outcomes. imentiv. Retrieved April 24, 2025, from https://imentiv.ai/blog/using-ai-in-recruitment-how-emotion-ai-drives-better-hiring-outcomes/

Kempe, L. (2024, September 9). The Price of Emotion: Privacy, Manipulation, and Bias in Emotional AI. https://www.americanbar.org/. Retrieved April 25, 2025, from https://www.americanbar.org/groups/business_law/resources/business-law-today/2024-september/price-emotion-privacy-manipulation-bias-emotional-ai/

Khoei, T. T., & Singh, A. (2024). A survey of Emotional Artificial Intelligence and crimes: Detection, prediction, challenges and future direction. *Journal of Computational Social Science*, *7*(3), 2359–2402. DOI: 10.1007/s42001-024-00313-3

KodeKloudNotes. (n.d.).KodeKloud Notes. https://notes.kodekloud.com/docs/AI-900-Microsoft-Certified-Azure-AI-Fundamentals/Fundamental-AI-Concepts/Principles-of-Responsible-AI

Lee, H., Liu, G. K., Chen, Y., & Yeh, S. (2024). Exploring quantitative measures in metacognition of emotion. *Scientific Reports*, *14*(1), 1990. Advance online publication. DOI: 10.1038/s41598-023-49709-7 PMID: 38263192

Li, Y., Chan, J., Peko, G., & Sundaram, D. (2023). An explanation framework and method for AI-based text emotion analysis and visualisation. *Decision Support Systems*, *178*, 114121. DOI: 10.1016/j.dss.2023.114121

Mahawar, S. (2023, December 21). Data privacy and emotion recognition technology -iPleaders. iPleaders. https://blog.ipleaders.in/data-privacy-and-emotion-recognition-technology/

Marr, B. (2025, April 23). Why AI will never truly understand your feelings — and why that matters. Forbes. https://www.forbes.com/sites/bernardmarr/2025/04/23/why-ai-will-never-truly-understand-your-feelings-and-why-that-matters/

McStay, A. (2020). Emotional AI, soft biometrics and the surveillance of emotional life: An unusual consensus on privacy. *Big Data & Society*, *7*(1), 205395172090438. DOI: 10.1177/2053951720904386

Modulos. (2024, July 4). Emotion Recognition Systems Prohibited under EU AI Act. Modulos. https://www.modulos.ai/blog/emotion-recognition-systems-prohibited-under-eu-ai-act/

Mohammad, S. M. & National Research Council Canada. (2021). Ethics Sheet for Automatic Emotion Recognition and Sentiment Analysis. In Computational Linguistics (Journal-Article No. 2; Vol. 48, p. 240). https://doi.org/ a 00433DOI: 10.1162/coli

Newswire, P. R. (2024, May 15). Emotion AI market size to grow USD 13.8 billion by 2032 at a CAGR of 22.7% | Valuates reports. Yahoo Finance. https://finance.yahoo.com/news/emotion-ai-market-size-grow-145000966.html

Olawade, D. B., Wada, O. Z., Odetayo, A., David-Olawade, A. C., Asaolu, F., & Eberhardt, J. (2024). Enhancing mental health with Artificial Intelligence: Current trends and future prospects. *Journal of Medicine, Surgery, and Public Health*, *3*, 100099. DOI: 10.1016/j.glmedi.2024.100099

Picard, W. & MIT Media Laboratory. (1997). AFFECTIVE COMPUTING: CHALLENGES. https://people.cs.pitt.edu/~litman/courses/ads/readings/03.picard.pdf

Purdy, M., Zealley, J., & Maseli, O. (2019, November 18). The risks of using AI to interpret human emotions. Harvard Business Review. https://hbr.org/2019/11/the-risks-of-using-ai-to-interpret-human-emotions

Recital 18 | EU Artificial Intelligence Act.(n.d.). https://artificialintelligenceact.eu/recital/18/

Roemmich, K., Schaub, F., & Andalibi, N. (2023). Emotion AI at work: Implications for workplace surveillance, emotional labor, and emotional privacy. *CHI '23: Proceedings of the 2023 CHI Conference on Human Factors in Computing Systems*, 1–20. DOI: 10.1145/3544548.3580950

Sahota, N. (2024, January 22). AI and emotion: Imagining a world where machines feel. Forbes. https://www.forbes.com/sites/neilsahota/2024/01/22/ai-and-emotion-imagining-a-world-where-machines-feel/

Sartor, G., & Lagioia, F. Panel for the Future of Science and Technology, European Parliamentary Research Service, & Scientific Foresight Unit (STOA). (2020). The impact of the General Data Protection Regulation (GDPR) on artificial intelligence. In STOA (p. PE 641.530) [Report]. https://www.europarl.europa.eu/RegData/etudes/STUD/2020/641530/EPRS_STU(2020)641530_EN.pdf

Saviano, M., Thomas, A., Del Prete, M., Verderese, D., & Sasso, P. (2025). The impact of new generative AI chatbots on the switch point (SP): Toward an artificial emotional awareness (AEA). *European Journal of Innovation Management*. Advance online publication. DOI: 10.1108/EJIM-05-2024-0520

Sharma, M., & Singh, A. (2024). Embracing Technological Innovation: A Review of Hi-Tech Services in Hospitality Industry. *Evergreen*, *11*(4), 2818–2830. DOI: 10.5109/7326926

Sharma, R., & Singh, A. (2025). Integrating AI, Green Marketing, and Influencer Strategies: Shaping Sustainable Consumer Behavior in the Digital Age. In Hussain, Z., Sharipudin, M., Albattat, A., & Khan, A. (Eds.), *Strategic Brand Management in the Age of AI and Disruption* (pp. 325–342). IGI Global Scientific Publishing., DOI: 10.4018/979-8-3693-9461-8.ch013

Shu, L., Xie, J., Yang, M., Li, Z., Li, Z., Liao, D., Xu, X., & Yang, X. (2018). A review of emotion recognition using physiological signals. *Sensors (Basel)*, *18*(7), 2074. DOI: 10.3390/s18072074 PMID: 29958457

Singh, A. (2024). Virtual Research Collaboration and Technology Application: Drivers, Motivations, and Constraints. In Chakraborty, S. (Ed.), *Challenges of Globalization and Inclusivity in Academic Research* (pp. 250–258). IGI Global., DOI: 10.4018/979-8-3693-1371-8.ch016

Singh, A., & Kumar, S. (2024). Effective Talent Management Practices Implemented in the Hospitality Sector. In Christiansen, B., Aziz, M., & O'Keeffe, E. (Eds.), *Global Practices on Effective Talent Acquisition and Retention* (pp. 126–144). IGI Global., DOI: 10.4018/979-8-3693-1938-3.ch008

Singh, A., & Supina, S. (2024). Talent Acquisition and Retention in Hospitality Industry: Current Skill Gaps and Challenges. In Christiansen, B., Aziz, M., & O'Keeffe, E. (Eds.), *Global Practices on Effective Talent Acquisition and Retention* (pp. 363–379). IGI Global., DOI: 10.4018/979-8-3693-1938-3.ch020

Standen, P. J., Brown, D. J., Taheri, M., Trigo, M. J. G., Boulton, H., Burton, A., Hallewell, M. J., Lathe, J. G., Shopland, N., Gonzalez, M. B., Kwiatkowska, G. M., Milli, E., Cobello, S., Mazzucato, A., Traversi, M., & Hortal, E. (2020). An evaluation of an adaptive learning system based on multimodal affect recognition for learners with intellectual disabilities. *British Journal of Educational Technology, 51*(5), 1748–1765. DOI: 10.1111/bjet.13010

Subha. (2024, November 8). Emotion AI in Marketing: How to Craft Campaigns that Resonate. thelightbulb.ai. https://thelightbulb.ai/blog/emotion-ai-in-marketing-how-to-craft-campaigns-that-resonate/

Tankelevitch, L., Kewenig, V., Simkute, A., Scott, A. E., Sarkar, A., Sellen, A., & Rintel, S. (2024). The Metacognitive Demands and Opportunities of Generative AI. *CHI '24: Proceedings of the 2024 CHI Conference on Human Factors in Computing Systems*, 1–24. DOI: 10.1145/3613904.3642902

The IEEE Global Initiative on Ethics of Autonomous and Intelligent Systems. (2018). Ethically aligned design. In A Vision for Prioritizing Human Well-being With Autonomous and Intelligent Systems (Version 2-For Public Discussion). https://standards.ieee.org/wp-content/uploads/import/documents/other/ead_v2.pdf

Thomas, D. (2024, November 18). Raising public awareness on AI's environmental impact: Strategies and initiatives.Medium. https://medium.com/aimonks/raising-public-awareness-on-ais-environmental-impact-strategies-and-initiatives-7cdcb2ab2bb2

Times, G. (n.d.). China leads in emotion recognition tech, reinforces privacy rules to tackle abuse. Copyright 2021 by the Global Times. https://www.globaltimes.cn/page/202103/1217212.shtml

Tull, M. T., & Aldao, A. (2015). Editorial overview: New directions in the science of emotion regulation. *Current Opinion in Psychology, 3*, iv–x. DOI: 10.1016/j.copsyc.2015.03.009

Vesala, J., Riekkinen, J., & Rankka, V. (2025).Consenting to the use of emotional data by AI-Based services.In Law, governance and technology series (pp. 125–148). DOI: 10.1007/978-3-031-80111-2_8

Villegas-Ch, W. E., García-Ortiz, J., & Sánchez-Viteri, S. (2023). Identification of emotions from facial gestures in a teaching environment with the use of machine learning techniques. *IEEE Access : Practical Innovations, Open Solutions, 11*, 38010–38022. DOI: 10.1109/ACCESS.2023.3267007

Vistorte, A. O. R., Deroncele-Acosta, A., Ayala, J. L. M., Barrasa, A., López-Granero, C., & Martí-González, M. (2024). Integrating artificial intelligence to assess emotions in learning environments: A systematic literature review. *Frontiers in Psychology*, *15*, 1387089. Advance online publication. DOI: 10.3389/fpsyg.2024.1387089 PMID: 38966729

Woods, D. (2025). AI as a Tool for Surveillance: China's Concave Trilemma. *Journal of Chinese Political Science*. Advance online publication. DOI: 10.1007/s11366-025-09907-8

Zen, M. (2024, July 1). Putting EI into AI: Emotion AI and Personalization Marketing. https://zenmedia.com/blog/emotion-ai-in-marketing/

Chapter 7
AI Meets Your Money!
Data Privacy Challenges in the Fintech Industry

Parul Ahuja
https://orcid.org/0000-0002-0216-1161
Maharaja Agrasen Institute of Management Studies, India

Pratibha Singh
T.A. Pai Management Institute, Manipal Academy of Higher Education, Manipal, India

Ruchika Sharma
https://orcid.org/0000-0001-9518-0814
Delhi School of Business, India

ABSTRACT

The integration of Artificial Intelligence (AI) into the Fintech industry has revolutionized financial services by enhancing efficiency, enabling personalized customer experiences, and driving data-driven decision-making. However, this rapid technological advancement also raises critical concerns surrounding data privacy and ethical data usage. Fintech companies increasingly rely on vast amounts of sensitive personal and financial information to train AI systems, making them vulnerable to data breaches, algorithmic bias, and regulatory scrutiny. This paper explores the complex intersection of AI and data privacy within Fintech, highlighting the opportunities and risks associated with AI-driven innovation. The authors conducted interviews with 30 Fintech users to identify the facilitating and risk perceived factors, thus providing implications for the industry and stakeholders.

DOI: 10.4018/979-8-3373-3658-9.ch007

INTRODUCTION

Due to the borderless and largely unregulated nature of the Internet, privacy is a significant concern across all online interactions. Consumers are particularly worried about the growing number of databases, the extensive amount of personal data being collected, potential breaches of privacy, and the lack of control over how their information is gathered, accessed, and ultimately used. Often, AI systems require large volumes of data, including behavioural data (e.g., browsing habits), Biometric data (e.g., facial recognition, voice patterns) and emotional or health-related data (via wearables or emotion AI) which bounds the companies to expand the privacy policies to cover non-traditional data sources and AI-driven insights. Therefore, with the development and advancement of Artificial Intelligence, the privacy policies of companies is prompting both updates in content and shifts in how privacy is managed and communicated. Though the consumers embrace GenAI, they expect trust, accountability, and transparency from technology providers (Deloitte, 2024).

The companies have leveraged big data analytics and artificial intelligence (AI) to process large amounts of information from various sources and to generate independent recommendations or decisions (Li et al. 2022). By incorporating AI and big data, fintech companies can deliver more personalized financial services, enhance operational efficiency, and reduce expenses (Ashta & Herrmann, 2021). Nevertheless, bringing together AI and big data raises ethical and privacy challenges, including concerns about bias, discrimination, transparency, privacy rights, fairness, data ownership, and control (Hermansyah et al. 2023). The intricate nature of the financial system, along with the internal data structures used by AI systems, can make it difficult for human regulators to effectively tackle new and evolving issues (Butaru et al. 2016). Thus, recognizing the ethical impact of fintech is essential for building and maintaining customer trust and confidence.

The New Fintech Ecosystem

Robots and Artificial Intelligence (AI) are already transforming all kinds of industries, from manufacturing, to retail and service provision. This trend is evident in the financial sector, where financial technology (FinTech) has become a central component of strategic initiatives for both traditional banks and financial start-ups (Jung et al., 2018). FinTech extends beyond traditional e-banking and digital consumer services, emphasizing the creation and implementation of innovative technological tools to fulfil users' financial expectations and needs. In this context, artificial intelligence (AI) offers a significant opportunity to drive the industry's transformation by enhancing user experiences and boosting company profits. A notable example is Bank of America's AI-powered Chabot, Erica, which assists over a million users with routine banking inquiries (Rosman, 2018). Unlike conventional human financial advisors, robo-advisors offer lower costs and round-the-clock access to financial services (Faubion, 2016; Park et al., 2016). These automated platforms are anticipated to make financial advisory services more accessible to a broader audience (Sironi, 2016). As a result, banks and financial institutions are introducing robo-advisors to gain a competitive edge in the market.

Ethical Considerations In Fintech Industry

FinTech is a widely used term referring to innovative technologies implemented by financial service providers. It also encompasses security and privacy concerns, including threats, malicious activities, cyber-attacks, and adversaries, along with current and potential solutions to these issues. As fintech reshapes conventional financial services, it becomes increasingly important to evaluate its impact on cyber security and data protection (Milian E.Z. et al., 2019). The heightened dependence on digital platforms and online transactions highlights the urgency for strong security protocols and regulatory oversight to defend against cyber risks (Sangwan, V. et al., 2020). Additionally, emerging fintech technologies like block chain and AI-based tools bring new challenges and potential vulnerabilities that require careful consideration (Catalini & Gans, 2020). There are regulatory legal frameworks and regulations that are driven by the recognition of data's critical importance in the FinTech industry—as both a driver of innovation and growth, and a potential source of cyber security risks and privacy violations. As a result, data privacy regulations have been designed to support technological advancement while simultaneously protecting individuals' privacy rights (Dorfleitner et al., 2023). This study explores the complex interplay between emergence of AI in context to data privacy, and the rapidly growing financial technology (fintech) sector. To gain a well-rounded perspective, it utilizes a literature review method, drawing on a wide range of academic and industry sources related to data protection and cyber security within the fintech domain.

LITERATURE REVIEW

The rapid and widespread integration of AI across various sectors is significantly influencing economic, social, and labour dynamics (Acemoglu & Restrepo, 2017). From a conceptual standpoint, Huang and Rust (2018) characterize AI as a transformative force driving innovation, gradually replacing human labour. They foresee a progression in automation capabilities—from performing mechanical tasks to developing analytical skills (such as those used by robo-advisors), and eventually acquiring intuitive and empathetic abilities. As a result, the workforce will need to adapt by focusing on roles that are less susceptible to automation (Huang & Rust, 2018).

Research is increasingly exploring the challenges involved in integrating innovations that utilize AI, robots, and similar technologies (Han & Yang, 2018), especially in customer-facing roles across both physical and digital environments. The intelligent user interfaces are reshaping how consumers interact with businesses. Grewal et al. (2017) also anticipated that AI-driven tools like Alexa, Cortana, and Siri would significantly affect consumer purchasing habits. Van Doorn et al. (2017) emphasized that the effectiveness of these technologies in service interactions hinges on the perceived presence and social engagement abilities of both human and machine agents. Rahman et al. (2023) advocate for a mindset-oriented approach to studying technology adoption, offering a fresh perspective that integrates psychological insights into existing models. Overall, there is a growing consensus on the necessity for companies to embrace AI technologies to refine their management strategies and enhance their product portfolios. This shift is essential for maintaining a competitive edge in response to ongoing market evolution. These technologies offer significant opportunities for businesses to enhance customer engagement by providing immersive and interactive experiences. However, addressing the associated challenges is crucial for successful implementation and adoption (Bansal et al., 2023).

A major factor behind the growing use of AI in the fintech industry is its capacity to analyze large volumes of data and generate meaningful insights to support decision-making. By combining AI with big data analytics, fintech firms can deliver customized financial services, improve efficiency, and lower operational costs, giving them a strategic advantage in the marketplace (Mars & Gouider, 2017). Despite these benefits, the deployment of AI and big data in fintech also raises important ethical and privacy-related issues (Yang et al., 2022). The convergence of big data, artificial intelligence, and privacy within the fintech industry has sparked important discussions about the need to address ethical challenges. Key concerns include issues such as bias, discrimination, transparency, privacy, fairness, data ownership, and user control (Saltz & Dewar, 2019). It is essential to ensure that decision-making processes are fair, as the use of biased or incomplete data can result in unjust or discriminatory consequences for individuals. Maintaining transparency in how data is collected, processed, and analyzed is vital for building and preserving customer trust and the organization's credibility. Additionally, safeguarding personal information and complying with data protection regulations are fundamental ethical responsibilities for fintech firms (La Torre et al., 2019).

A key approach that promotes the ethical and responsible use of technology and data in the fintech industry is the adoption of Corporate Digital Responsibility (CDR). Establishing a CDR-oriented culture within organizations can lead to improved financial outcomes, increased digital trust, greater customer satisfaction, and a stronger reputation (Saeidi et al., 2015). Moreover, strict adherence to data protection laws is vital for upholding privacy and security in digital finance. The European Union's General Data Protection Regulation (GDPR) stands out as a key legal framework in this area (Mars & Gouider, 2017). It requires organizations to obtain clear consent for data collection, ensure transparency in how data is processed, and implement robust security measures. In addition to regulatory compliance, leveraging advanced technological tools is essential for securing customer information. For instance, encryption plays a critical role by making sensitive data unreadable during both storage and transmission. Strong encryption helps prevent unauthorized access and reduces the risk of data breaches. Successfully addressing privacy and ethical challenges in fintech requires cooperation across all stakeholders. Fintech firms, regulators, and consumers must work in tandem to develop ethical standards, encourage responsible data management, and promote greater transparency (Gong et al., 2020). Regulatory authorities, in particular, have a pivotal role in overseeing the evolving fintech landscape and ensuring that policies remain relevant and effective.

Research Gap

The examination of ethical considerations due to the use of AI, particularly in the Fintech industry extends a significant research lacuna that needs additional investigation. While there has been a mounting attention in the amalgamation of technology in the service industries, the explicit role of dark side of employment of artificial intelligence intended to study facilitating and risk perception factors, particularly in the fintech remains underexplored. A few studies focus on understanding the role of robo advisors in fintech industry whereas few explore the data privacy risks, laws, frameworks and regulations in other industries. However, there is less work in the emerging markets wherein the ethical considerations with respect to fintech are studied and therefore, this research integrates the facilitating and risk perceived factors in understanding the data privacy challenges from the Fintech users in a qualitative study. Therefore, further research is needed to assess the efficacy, acceptance, and ethical implications of deploying AI in fintech industry.

Research Questions (RQs)

1. How do consumers perceive AI's role in balancing personalized financial services with privacy risks?
2. What factors amplify and dissuade privacy concerns in AI-driven FinTech?

Research Design

Exploratory qualitative study using semi-structured interviews and thematic analysis.

Purposive sampling of 25–30 FinTech users (ages 18–60) with varying exposure to AI-driven services (e.g., chatbots, fraud detection, robo-advisors). Active users of at least one AI-based FinTech tool (e.g., contactless payments, credit scoring, budgeting apps) were inducted for interview. Refer to table 1 for demographic profile of participants.

Table 1. Demographic Profile

Demographic Variable	Categories	Frequency (n=30)	Percentage (%)
Gender	Male	16	53.30%
	Female	14	46.70%
Age Group	18–25 years	8	26.70%
	26–35 years	10	33.30%
	36–45 years	7	23.30%
	46–60 years	5	16.70%
Education Level	Undergraduate	4	13.30%
	Postgraduate	18	60.00%
	Doctorate	8	26.70%
FinTech Usage Type	Mobile payments	30	100%
	Robo-advisors	10	33.30%
	AI-based credit scoring	20	66.70%
	Budgeting/personal finance apps	22	73.30%

Data Collection

Data for this study were collected through in-depth semi-structured interviews, each lasting between 45 to 60 minutes. These interviews explored participants' experiences with AI features in FinTech applications, such as chatbots, robo-advisors, and automated fraud alerts. The discussions centered around three main areas: user experiences with AI-driven services, perceived risks—including data misuse and algorithmic bias—and mechanisms that contribute to building trust, such as transparency in data usage and user control over personal information.

To facilitate meaningful dialogue, stimulus materials showcasing examples of AI applications (e.g., personalized financial offers, real-time fraud detection alerts) were presented during the sessions. These examples served to prompt reflections and encourage participants to articulate their concerns, expectations, and judgments more clearly. The data collected were analyzed using thematic analysis, following an inductive approach to allow themes to emerge organically from the participants' narratives.

Key Interview Questions and Highlights

Q: How do you perceive the role of AI in delivering personalized financial services?

A significant number of respondents appreciated the convenience AI brings but were wary of how much personal information is needed to deliver such customization.

One participant stated:

"It's convenient for sure. I love getting reminders and insights, but it always feels like they know too much. It's like being watched all the time."

Another expressed a more positive outlook:

"If it helps me save and spend better, I'm okay sharing data—as long as I know who's getting it and for what purpose."

Q: What kind of risks do you associate with using AI-based FinTech tools?

Concerns around data misuse and algorithmic bias were recurring. Several participants mentioned fear of identity theft and financial fraud as primary concerns.

One respondent explained:

"If an AI makes a mistake in assessing my credit score, it could affect my entire financial future. Who do I even talk to then?"

Another highlighted the fear of surveillance:

"I don't want them tracking everything I buy. Sometimes it feels like I'm being profiled just because I use my card."

Q: What factors would make you trust an AI system in financial services?

Transparency and control were two dominant themes. Participants desired clear communication from companies on how their data is being used and the ability to customize privacy settings.

One respondent emphasized:

"I need an option to opt out of certain features. And I want to know how they're using my information—like in plain language, not legal jargon."

Another mentioned:

"If it's from a reputed bank or fintech company that I know respects privacy, I'm more likely to trust it."

Q: Have you ever faced an issue or breach while using an AI-driven financial app? If yes, how was it handled?

While most respondents hadn't faced direct breaches, many reported being confused or dissatisfied with post-issue resolution processes.

One respondent said:

"My app showed some weird transactions once, and it took days to talk to a human. I kept getting automated responses that didn't help."

Q: How do you weigh the trade-off between personalization and privacy?

Opinions were mixed. While some were willing to share data for better services, others felt manipulated or exposed.

One participant commented:

"I like the offers tailored to my needs, but sometimes I feel like they're just pushing me to spend more."

Another shared:

"It's a fair trade if I get value, but only if I have control over what's shared."

Key Themes from Interview Data

Tables 2 and 3 present a summary of facilitating and risk perception factors as identified through interviews.

Table 2. Facilitating Factors, Themes, and Sub-Themes

Theme	Sub-Themes	*Participant Excerpts*
Transparency	Clarity in data usage, understandable terms and conditions	*"I'm okay with sharing data, but only if they're upfront about how it's used." – P12*
		"These apps need to stop hiding things in legal terms. Just tell us clearly what data you're collecting." – P4
		"I want full visibility—who collects my data, where it goes, and why." – P10
User Control	Customizable privacy settings, opt-in/opt-out mechanisms	*"I prefer apps that let me decide what data I share. Default settings shouldn't assume consent." – P5*
		"Give me the option to switch off features I don't want. That builds trust." – P9
		"I like it when I can control notifications and data sharing from one place in the app." – P16

continued on following page

Table 2. Continued

Theme	Sub-Themes	*Participant Excerpts*
Institutional Trust	Reputation of provider, regulatory compliance	*"I feel more confident using services from reputed banks or apps that clearly follow government norms." – P19*
		"If the app mentions RBI compliance or has ISO certification, I trust it more." – P22
		"Brand matters. I'll trust my data more with a known bank than a new app." – P3
Perceived Usefulness	Better budgeting tools, real-time fraud alerts, financial literacy features	*"The budgeting tool helped me realize I was overspending. It's been a game changer." – P7*
		"When my card was misused, the fraud alert saved me. I trust the app more because of that." – P21
		"The financial tips in the app are actually helpful—they even explain why a transaction looks suspicious." – P15

Table 3. Risk Factors, Themes, and Sub-Themes

Theme	Sub-Themes	Participant Excerpts
Data Misuse	Selling to third parties, lack of consent	*"I once got promotional calls after using a finance app—it felt like they sold my data without asking."* – P10
		"Most apps don't even ask before sharing data. It's like you have no say." – P4
		"Just because I use the app doesn't mean I agree to all kinds of data sharing." – P15
Surveillance Anxiety	Continuous behavioral tracking	*"It feels like the app is always watching—how much I spend, where I go, even what I search."* – P17
		"Sometimes it predicts too accurately—it's creepy, like someone's always monitoring me." – P23
		"I hate how I get financial suggestions based on things I've only talked about near my phone." – P12
Algorithmic Bias	Discrimination in loan approvals, profiling based on consumption behavior	*"I was denied a loan instantly—I feel it was because of my job title or shopping history."* – P6
		"The system judges you without understanding your real financial behavior." – P20
		"They assume things based on past transactions, but people change their habits." – P9

continued on following page

Table 3. Continued

Theme	Sub-Themes	Participant Excerpts
Inadequate Redress	Limited human support, unclear grievance redress mechanisms	*"There's no human to talk to—just bots that repeat the same responses."* – P8
		"It's hard to even find how to raise a complaint, let alone resolve it." – P16
		"When something goes wrong, they make it feel like it's your fault." – P2

Key themes: Facilitating Factors

1. **Transparency**

A critical enabler of consumer trust in AI systems was *clarity in data usage*. Participants expressed a need for FinTech providers to present information in *understandable terms and conditions*, emphasizing the importance of plain-language policies that clearly explain how personal data is being used. Consumers were more likely to engage with services that did not obscure their data practices behind legal jargon.

2. **Control**

Users appreciated having *customizable privacy settings* that allowed them to decide what information to share. The ability to opt-in or opt-out of specific data-sharing agreements was a key expectation. This *granular control* over privacy preferences helped consumers feel empowered and in charge of their digital financial identity.

3. **Institutional Trust**

Trust in the FinTech institution itself was a strong driver of acceptance. Participants were more open to sharing data when the *provider had a strong reputation* and adhered to *clear regulatory compliance standards*. Brand credibility and a history of ethical conduct were seen as reassuring, particularly in a domain as sensitive as financial services.

4. **Perceived Usefulness**

Several participants highlighted tangible benefits from AI features such as *better budgeting tools*, *real-time fraud alerts*, and *educational resources for financial literacy*. These features not only provided functional value but also built a perception of AI as a helpful and non-intrusive presence, encouraging further engagement with FinTech platforms.

Key Themes: Risk Perception Factors

1. **Data Misuse**

Dominant concern was the *unauthorized selling of personal data to third parties*. Many interviewees emphasized the *lack of clear consent mechanisms*, which led to skepticism about how their data might be used beyond the intended purpose. The fear of commodification of personal information was a recurring issue.

2. **Surveillance Anxiety**

Participants frequently raised concerns about *continuous behavioral tracking*, which they perceived as invasive. This *surveillance anxiety* created discomfort, especially when users were unsure about the extent to which their activities were being monitored and analyzed for predictive or commercial purposes.

3. **Algorithmic Bias**

The fear of *discriminatory decision-making* by AI systems emerged as a major theme. Respondents mentioned *biases in loan approvals* or profiling based on consumption behavior as examples. The opacity of algorithms made it difficult for users to understand or challenge unfair outcomes, amplifying mistrust in the system.

4. **Inadequate Redress**

A critical barrier to trust was the *lack of robust grievance mechanisms*. Participants expressed frustration over *limited human support* when dealing with AI errors and found existing channels for complaint resolution to be *unclear or ineffective*. This absence of accountability mechanisms weakened user confidence in adopting AI-powered financial tools.

DISCUSSION AND IMPLICATIONS

The facilitating factors such as transparency may boost consumer confidence as higher transparency increases user trust and reduces suspicion around data handling. It will further result in regulatory compliance and such transparent practices can help firms align with global data protection laws (e.g., GDPR, CCPA). When the users manage and control their personal data, they will feel empowered thus further leading to greater engagement and satisfaction. It is believed that user-controlled data is often more accurate, benefitting AI outcomes. The users' confidence in the fintech firm's ability to safeguard their data and act in their best interest will help the industry to establish long term relationships and benefit from brand reputation. Similarly, user's perception of how beneficial AI-driven services are in improving their financial decisions, convenience, or security will improve algorithms, enhancing usefulness further—creating a virtuous cycle. If usefulness isn't clear, users may resist data sharing, limiting AI performance and ROI for the fintech firm. Perceived usefulness is a major determinant of technology adoption in fintech (e.g., robo-advisors, AI-powered budgeting tools) and users are more willing to share personal data if they believe the benefits (e.g., faster approvals, better rates) outweigh the risks.

When the users believe their data is being misused in ways that are unethical, unauthorized, or inconsistent with stated policies—e.g., sharing financial data with third parties for targeted advertising or selling behavioral profiles leads to loss of trust, reduce investor confidence, increasing scrutiny from the stakeholders. Simultaneously, the companies must reduce the discomfort the consumers experience when the feel they are being constantly monitored by AI systems. This may further result in reputational fallout and reduce customer satisfaction along with avoidance of certain purchases, financial activities or loan applications. Biases in AI algorithms that lead to unfair or discriminatory outcomes can result in lawsuits under anti-discrimination laws or consumer protection statutes. If users believe AI systems are unfair or prejudiced, trust in fintech institutions and technologies erodes. A fintech firm that lacks effective redress processes risks being seen as irresponsible or unethical in its AI deployment. Poor redress mechanisms increase dissatisfaction and churn, particularly when users feel helpless against automated systems. Regulators often require mechanisms for user appeals and human oversight; failure to provide these can violate laws.

CONCLUSION

The findings of this study underscore the complex interplay between perceived benefits and privacy concerns in the adoption of AI-driven FinTech services. While consumers appreciate the convenience, personalization, and utility provided by AI features—such as real-time fraud alerts and financial planning tools—their willingness to engage is heavily moderated by trust-related factors. Transparency in data usage, user control over privacy settings, and institutional credibility emerged as key facilitators of adoption. Conversely, concerns around data misuse, surveillance, algorithmic bias, and inadequate redress mechanisms pose significant barriers. This research highlights the need for FinTech providers to adopt a consumer-centric approach to AI design—one that balances innovation with ethical responsibility. By embedding clear communication, privacy safeguards, and accessible grievance mechanisms into their platforms, providers can foster trust and encourage broader, more confident use of AI technologies in financial services. These insights also offer valuable guidance for policymakers and regulators aiming to ensure that the growth of AI in FinTech aligns with consumer rights and expectations.

REFERENCES

Acemoglu, D., & Restrepo, P. (2017). *Robots and jobs: evidence from US labor markets.* Available at: https://voxeu.org/article/robots-and-jobs-evidence-us

Ashta, A., & Herrmann, H. (2021). Artificial intelligence and fintech: An overview of opportunities and risks for banking, investments, and microfinance. *Strategic Change*, *30*(3), 211–222. DOI: 10.1002/jsc.2404

Bansal, R., Shukla, G., Gupta, A., Singh, A., & Pruthi, N. (2023). Optimizing augmented reality and virtual reality for customer engagement. In *Promoting consumer engagement through emotional branding and sensory marketing* (pp. 24–35). IGI Global.

Butaru, F., Chen, Q., Clark, B., Das, S., Lo, A. W., & Siddique, A. (2016). Risk and risk management in the credit card industry. *Journal of Banking & Finance*, *72*, 218–239. DOI: 10.1016/j.jbankfin.2016.07.015

Catalini, C., & Gans, J. S. (2020). Some simple economics of the blockchain. *Communications of the ACM*, *63*(7), 80–90. DOI: 10.1145/3359552

Deloitte. (2024). *New Deloitte Survey: Increasing Consumer Privacy and Security Concerns in the Generative AI Era.* Available at https://www2.deloitte.com/us/en/pages/about-deloitte/articles/press-releases/increasing-consumer-privacy-and-security-concerns-in-the-generative-ai-era.html

Dorfleitner, G., Hornuf, L., & Kreppmeier, J. (2023). Promise not fulfilled: FinTech, data privacy, and the GDPR. *Electronic Markets*, *33*(1), 33. DOI: 10.1007/s12525-023-00622-x

Grewal, D., Roggeveen, A. L., & Nordfält, J. (2017). The future of retailing. *Journal of Retailing*, *93*(1), 1–6. DOI: 10.1016/j.jretai.2016.12.008

Han, S., & Yang, H. (2018). Understanding adoption of intelligent personal assistants: A parasocial relationship perspective. *Industrial Management & Data Systems*, *118*(3), 618–636. DOI: 10.1108/IMDS-05-2017-0214

Hermansyah, M., Najib, A., Farida, A., Sacipto, R., & Rintyarna, B. S. (2023). Artificial Intelligence and Ethics: Building an Artificial Intelligence System that Ensures Privacy and Social Justice. *The International Journal of Science in Society*, *5*(1), 154–168. DOI: 10.54783/ijsoc.v5i1.644

Huang, M. H., & Rust, R. T. (2018). Artificial intelligence in service. *Journal of Service Research*, *21*(2), 155–172. DOI: 10.1177/1094670517752459

Jung, D., Dorner, V., Glaser, F., & Morana, S. (2018). Robo-advisory. *Business & Information Systems Engineering*, *60*(1), 81–86. DOI: 10.1007/s12599-018-0521-9

La Torre, M., Botes, V. L., Dumay, J., & Odendaal, E. (2019). Protecting a new Achilles heel: The role of auditors within the practice of data protection. *Managerial Auditing Journal*, *36*(2), 218–239. DOI: 10.1108/MAJ-03-2018-1836

Li, J., Ye, Z., & Zhang, C. (2022). Study on the interaction between big data and artificial intelligence. *Systems Research and Behavioral Science*, *39*(3), 641–648. DOI: 10.1002/sres.2878

Mars, A., & Gouider, M. S. (2017). Big data analysis to features opinions extraction of customer. *Procedia Computer Science*, *112*, 906–916. DOI: 10.1016/j.procs.2017.08.114

Milian Eduardo Z., Mauro de M. Spinola, Marly M. de Carvalho. (2019). Fintechs: A literature review and research agenda. *Electronic Commerce Research and Applications*, 34, 100833, ISSN 1567- 4223.

Rahman, K. T., Bansal, R., & Pruthi, N. (2023). Consumer adoption of technologies: A mindset-oriented approach. In *Contemporary Studies of Risks in Emerging Technology, Part B* (pp. 243-255). Emerald Publishing Limited. DOI: 10.1108/978-1-80455-566-820231013

Rosman, C. (2018). *Mad about Erica: why a million people use bank of America's chatbot*. American Banker., available at www.americanbanker.com/news/mad-about-erica-why-amillion-people-use-bank-of-americas-chatbot

Saltz, J. S., & Dewar, N. (2019). Data science ethical considerations: A systematic literature review and proposed project framework. *Ethics and Information Technology*, *21*(3), 197–208. DOI: 10.1007/s10676-019-09502-5

Sangwan, V., Prakash, P., & Singh, S. (2020). Financial technology: A review of extant literature. *Studies in Economics and Finance*, *37*(1), 71–88. DOI: 10.1108/SEF-07-2019-0270

Van Doorn, J., Mende, M., Noble, S. M., Hulland, J., Ostrom, A. L., Grewal, D., & Petersen, J. A. (2017). Domo arigato Mr Roboto: Emergence of automated social presence in organizational frontlines and customers' service experiences. *Journal of Service Research*, *20*(1), 43–58. DOI: 10.1177/1094670516679272

Yang, J., Zhao, Y., Han, C., Liu, Y., & Yang, M. (2022). Big data, big challenges: Risk management of financial market in the digital economy. *Journal of Enterprise Information Management*, *35*(4/5), 1288–1304. DOI: 10.1108/JEIM-01-2021-0057

Chapter 8
The Evolving Role and Future Prospects of Artificial Intelligence in Emotional Intelligence With Foundations, Frontiers, and Ethical Horizons

Ankur Kumar
https://orcid.org/0009-0007-2623-0065
Indian Institute of Technology, Mandi, India

Rohit Bansal
https://orcid.org/0000-0001-7072-5005
Rockford College, Sydney, Australia

Ridhima Sharma
Vivekananda Institute of Professional Studies-TC, India

Abhinav Sharma
https://orcid.org/0009-0008-0452-8386
Sant Longowal Institute of Engineering and Technology, India

Surita Maini
Sant Longowal Institute of Engineering and Technology, India

DOI: 10.4018/979-8-3373-3658-9.ch008

ABSTRACT

Emotional Intelligence (EI) plays a vital role in decision-making, social interaction, and well-being. With the rise of Artificial Intelligence (AI), Emotion AI—systems capable of recognizing and responding to human emotions—has gained prominence. This chapter explores the convergence of EI and AI, covering theoretical foundations, affective computing, and applications in healthcare, education, customer service, and workplaces. It examines technologies like multimodal emotion recognition using text, audio, facial, and physiological data. Ethical and societal issues such as data privacy, algorithmic bias, and emotional surveillance are critically analyzed. The chapter also outlines policy needs and future directions, including emotionally adaptive AI, human-in-the-loop models, and interdisciplinary collaboration. By highlighting both potential and risks, it advocates for responsible innovation in developing emotionally intelligent systems.

1. INTRODUCTION

Emotional Intelligence (EI), the ability to recognize, understand, and manage emotions in oneself and others, plays a critical role in shaping human behavior, influencing decision-making, and fostering effective interpersonal relationships. Originally grounded in psychology and cognitive science, EI has become increasingly relevant in the realm of artificial intelligence, leading to the emergence of Emotion AI. Also known as affective computing, Emotion AI represents the intersection of psychological theory, cognitive modeling, and advanced computational techniques. It focuses on enabling machines to detect, interpret, and respond to human emotions by analyzing inputs such as facial expressions, vocal tone, physiological signals, and natural language patterns (Goleman, 1995).

The growing integration of Emotion AI into various sectors underscores its increasing importance in modern digital systems. In customer service, emotionally aware AI agents improve user engagement and satisfaction by adapting their responses based on real-time emotional cues (Mayer, Salovey, & Caruso, 2008). In healthcare, Emotion AI supports early diagnosis and monitoring of mental health conditions, enhances patient interaction, and contributes to therapeutic interventions. Educational platforms leverage emotion recognition to tailor learning experiences, fostering better academic outcomes through personalized engagement. Similarly, in human resource management, Emotion AI is used in recruitment, performance appraisal, and workplace wellness programs to better understand and support employee emotions (Spielberger, 1972).

These developments reflect a broader technological shift toward emotionally aware digital ecosystems (Pantic & Rothkrantz, 2000). As artificial intelligence becomes more embedded in daily life, the demand for systems capable of empathetic and emotionally intelligent interaction continues to grow (Schuller et al., 2011). Emotion AI represents a significant step forward in creating intuitive, human-centered technologies that not only process information but also understand the emotional context in which decisions are made and actions are taken (Kim, 2014). The diverse applications of Emotion AI across sectors such as healthcare, education, and marketing are summarized in Table 1.

Table 1. Key Applications of Emotion AI Across Domains

Domain	Applications of Emotion AI
Customer Service	Emotionally adaptive chatbots, sentiment-aware virtual assistants, real-time feedback systems
Healthcare	Mental health monitoring, emotional support tools, diagnostic aids for psychological states
Education	Emotion-aware tutoring systems, student engagement analytics, adaptive learning environments
Human Resources	Emotion-based recruitment screening, employee wellness tracking, performance evaluation
Marketing & Retail	Emotion-driven product recommendations, ad targeting, in-store customer experience analysis

2. FOUNDATIONS OF EMOTIONAL INTELLIGENCE AND AI

Understanding the integration of Emotional Intelligence (EI) with Artificial Intelligence (AI) requires an in-depth exploration of both psychological frameworks of human emotional capacities and the technological advancements that enable machines to detect, interpret, and respond to human emotions. This foundational knowledge is crucial as it grounds Emotion AI, the emerging discipline that blends affective science with computational methods, in sound theory and robust practice (Devlin, Chang, Lee, & Toutanova, 2018).

2.1 Theoretical Frameworks of Emotional Intelligence

Daniel Goleman's Five Components of Emotional Intelligence

One of the most widely recognized frameworks of EI was popularized by Daniel Goleman in his seminal work on emotional intelligence (Baltrušaitis, Ahuja, & Morency, 2019). Goleman posits that emotional intelligence consists of five core components that collectively underpin human emotional competence:

1. **Self-awareness** – The ability to recognize and understand one's own emotions, moods, and drives, as well as their effects on others. Self-aware individuals can accurately assess their emotional states and are attuned to their internal cues (Ringeval et al., 2017).
2. **Self-regulation** – The capacity to control or redirect disruptive emotions and impulses and adapt to changing circumstances. This includes traits such as trustworthiness, conscientiousness, adaptability, and innovation (Zeng, Jin, & Zhang, 2019).
3. **Motivation** – A passion to work for internal reasons beyond external rewards, such as a deep commitment to goals, optimism in the face of failure, and organizational drive (Keltner & Ekman, 2008).
4. **Empathy** – The ability to understand the emotional makeup of other people and to treat them according to their emotional reactions. Empathy is vital for effective leadership and social interaction (Hochreiter & Schmidhuber, 1997).
5. **Social skills** – Proficiency in managing relationships and building networks, enabling influence, communication, conflict management, and teamwork (Yang, Chen, & Zhang, 2019).

Goleman's model highlights EI as a vital factor in personal and professional success, emphasizing the interplay of intrapersonal and interpersonal abilities. His approach primarily views emotional intelligence as a set of competencies that can be developed through practice and awareness (Ekman, 1991).

Mayer–Salovey–Caruso Emotional Intelligence Model

While Goleman's model is competency-based, the Mayer–Salovey–Caruso Emotional Intelligence Model (MSCEIT) conceptualizes EI as a cognitive ability involving specific mental processes related to emotions. This model defines EI as the ability to perceive, use, understand, and manage emotions in oneself and others (Mehrabian, 1969).

- **Perceiving Emotions:** The accurate detection and interpretation of emotions in faces, voices, and cultural artifacts (Li & Jia, 2020).
- **Using Emotions:** The capacity to harness emotions to facilitate cognitive activities such as thinking and problem solving (Cambria, Olsher, & Rajagopal, 2016).
- **Understanding Emotions:** Comprehending emotional language and the complex relationships among emotions (e.g., how emotions evolve and blend) (Ekman & Friesen, 1978).
- **Managing Emotions:** The ability to regulate emotions to promote emotional and intellectual growth (Zafeiriou, Hadjidimitriou, & Pitas, 2007).

The MSCEIT treats emotional intelligence as measurable through objective performance tasks, akin to traditional IQ tests but focused on emotional problem-solving. This model distinguishes itself by framing EI as a set of mental abilities that influence reasoning and decision-making (Calvo & D'Mello, 2010).

Trait vs. Ability Emotional Intelligence

A critical distinction in EI research is between **trait EI** and **ability EI**, which represent different conceptualizations:

- **Trait Emotional Intelligence:** Refers to self-perceived emotional abilities, typically assessed via self-report questionnaires. It reflects personality traits related to emotional functioning, such as empathy, emotion regulation, and social competence. Trait EI is considered relatively stable over time (Krizhevsky, Sutskever, & Hinton, 2012).
- **Ability Emotional Intelligence:** Focuses on actual emotional skills and capacities, measured through performance tests that assess how well individuals solve emotion-related problems. Ability EI is more fluid and can be developed with training (Sharma, Dhanka, Kumar, & Maini, 2024).

Understanding these different facets of EI is essential for designing Emotion AI systems that accurately model human emotional capabilities and incorporate both dispositional tendencies and situational abilities (Kumar et al., 2024).

2.2 AI Concepts in Emotion Detection

The intersection of emotional intelligence with artificial intelligence has given rise to the subfield of **Affective Computing**, which aims to develop systems that can recognize, interpret, and simulate human emotions. This requires sophisticated

AI techniques to analyze complex and often subtle emotional signals. Below, we detail the key AI concepts underpinning Emotion AI systems (Sharma et al., 2024).

Basics of Machine Learning, Deep Learning, and Affective Computing

At the core of Emotion AI are machine learning algorithms that enable computers to learn patterns from data rather than relying on explicitly programmed rules (Kumar et al., 2024).

- **Machine Learning (ML):** A broad category of algorithms that build models from labeled or unlabeled data to make predictions or decisions. In emotion detection, supervised learning algorithms (e.g., support vector machines, decision trees) are often trained on datasets annotated with emotional labels (Singh, Kumar, Kaur, Bansal, & Singla, 2024).
- **Deep Learning:** A subset of ML involving artificial neural networks with many layers (deep neural networks) that automatically learn hierarchical feature representations. Deep learning models, such as Convolutional Neural Networks (CNNs) and Recurrent Neural Networks (RNNs), have revolutionized the analysis of complex data types like images, speech, and text for emotion recognition.

Affective Computing: This multidisciplinary field combines AI, psychology, cognitive science, and human-computer interaction. It focuses on creating systems that can detect human emotions through multimodal signals and respond empathetically. Pioneered by Rosalind Picard, affective computing has evolved to include real-time emotion detection, adaptive interfaces, and emotion-aware applications (Singh, Pandey, Karna, Arora, & Kumar, 2024)

Multimodal Data Inputs in Emotion AI

Emotion is inherently multifaceted, expressed through numerous channels. To build accurate emotion recognition systems, Emotion AI integrates multiple data modalities:

- **Textual Data:** Natural Language Processing (NLP) techniques analyze sentiment, tone, and emotion conveyed in text. Sentiment analysis algorithms classify emotions in social media posts, emails, or chat messages, often using embeddings like word2vec or contextual models such as BERT (Li & Wang, 2025).

- **Speech:** Voice carries rich emotional information through prosody, pitch, intensity, and rhythm. Acoustic feature extraction combined with deep learning models enables the detection of emotions such as anger, sadness, or happiness from speech signals.
- **Facial Expressions:** Facial Action Coding System (FACS) identifies muscle movements linked to emotional states. Computer vision models, particularly CNNs, analyze images or video frames to detect micro-expressions and emotional cues.
- **Physiological Signals:** Wearable sensors collect data on heart rate variability (HRV), electrodermal activity (EDA), electroencephalography (EEG), and eye-tracking. These signals offer objective markers of stress, arousal, and emotional engagement.

The fusion of these data types allows Emotion AI systems to construct a more nuanced and reliable emotional profile than any single modality could provide (Palta & Kumar, 2025).

2.3 Emotion Classification Systems

Emotion classification frameworks provide the conceptual basis for labeling and interpreting emotional data, which is critical for training AI models and designing responsive applications. Two primary approaches dominate this landscape: categorical and dimensional models(Xu & Zhang, 2021).

Categorical Approach: Ekman's Six Basic Emotions

Psychologist Paul Ekman identified six basic emotions that are universally recognized across cultures and expressed through distinctive facial expressions, as shown in Table 2:

Table 2. Psychologist Paul Ekman identified six basic emotions

Emotion	Description
Happiness	Positive emotional state with smiling, laughter
Sadness	Negative emotion marked by frowning, downcast gaze
Fear	Response to threat, characterized by wide eyes and open mouth
Anger	Strong displeasure with furrowed brows and clenched jaws
Surprise	Reaction to unexpected events, raised eyebrows, open mouth
Disgust	Aversion or repulsion with nose wrinkling and upper lip raising

These emotions serve as discrete categories for labeling datasets and guiding facial expression recognition models. While highly interpretable and intuitive, this approach can be limited in capturing the complexity and subtlety of human affect.

Dimensional Approach: Valence-Arousal Model

Alternatively, the dimensional model conceptualizes emotions as points in a continuous two-dimensional space defined by:

- **Valence:** The pleasantness or positivity of an emotion, ranging from negative (unpleasant) to positive (pleasant).
- **Arousal:** The intensity or activation level, from calm to excited.

This framework allows for finer-grained differentiation between emotional states and captures the dynamic nature of emotions. For instance, excitement is high arousal and positive valence, while sadness is low arousal and negative valence (Kumar, Sharma, Dhanka, & Maini, 2025). Other dimensional models may include additional axes such as dominance or control to provide more emotional granularity. Comparison of Emotional Intelligence Models and Emotion Classification Systems is shown in Table 3.

Table 3. Comparison of Emotional Intelligence Models and Emotion Classification Systems

Aspect	Goleman's EI Model	Mayer–Salovey–Caruso Model	Trait vs Ability EI	Categorical Emotion Model (Ekman)	Dimensional Emotion Model (Valence-Arousal)
Focus	Competencies (self-awareness, empathy)	Cognitive abilities related to emotion	Personality traits vs cognitive skills	Six basic discrete emotions	Continuous emotional dimensions
Measurement	Self-report, behavioral observation	Performance-based tasks	Self-report (trait), performance tests (ability)	Facial expression recognition	Rating scales, physiological measures
Emotional Components	Self-awareness, self-regulation, motivation, empathy, social skills	Perceive, use, understand, manage emotions	Stable dispositions vs developed skills	Happiness, sadness, fear, anger, surprise, disgust	Valence (pleasantness), arousal (intensity)

continued on following page

Table 3. Continued

Aspect	Goleman's EI Model	Mayer–Salovey–Caruso Model	Trait vs Ability EI	Categorical Emotion Model (Ekman)	Dimensional Emotion Model (Valence-Arousal)
Strengths	Practical application in leadership and social settings	Scientific rigor, measurable abilities	Differentiates stable traits from skills	Universality and simplicity	Captures nuance and emotional blends
Limitations	Less precise measurement, overlaps with personality	Complexity of assessment	Overlap and ambiguity between trait and ability	Limited emotional range, cultural variations	Interpretation complexity, requires continuous data

Integration and Design of Emotionally Intelligent Machines

Together, the psychological foundations of EI and AI's technological capabilities enable the design of systems that simulate emotional understanding. Emotion AI systems must integrate multiple emotional intelligence dimensions: detecting emotions accurately, interpreting them in context, and responding appropriately to foster natural and empathetic human-machine interactions (Bickman, 2020).

For example, an emotionally intelligent virtual assistant may combine Goleman's components by showing empathy (recognizing user frustration), self-regulating responses (maintaining polite tone), and social skills (offering helpful suggestions). Under the hood, such a system leverages multimodal data inputs, applies deep learning models to classify emotional states along categorical or dimensional frameworks, and dynamically adapts its behavior accordingly. As Emotion AI continues to evolve, ongoing research focuses on improving cultural sensitivity, addressing biases, and enhancing real-time responsiveness to build trust and effectiveness in real-world applications (Palta & Kumar, 2024).

3. CURRENT APPLICATIONS OF AI IN EMOTIONAL INTELLIGENCE

The practical integration of artificial intelligence with emotional intelligence—commonly referred to as Emotion AI—has rapidly expanded across a variety of domains, demonstrating substantial benefits in enhancing user experiences, supporting well-being, and improving decision-making. By embedding emotional awareness into digital systems, AI can adapt more sensitively and appropriately to human needs, increasing both functionality and trust (Mittal & Bansal, 2023).

3.1 AI in Customer Support Systems

One of the most prominent applications of Emotion AI is in customer support systems, where emotion detection is revolutionizing chatbot and virtual assistant design. These systems are now capable of analyzing text and voice inputs to infer a user's emotional state in real-time. For example, a frustrated or angry customer can be automatically redirected to a human agent or provided with empathy-driven responses, thereby improving satisfaction and retention (Poria et al., 2017). In addition to natural language processing, these systems use sentiment analysis and speech emotion recognition to determine emotional tone, allowing for personalized engagement. Furthermore, sentiment-aware recommendation engines now consider not just user behavior but also emotional context, recommending products or services that align with the user's current mood or sentiment. This emotional layer enhances relevance and user trust, especially in industries like e-commerce, banking, and travel (Palta, Kumar, & Kaur, 2024).

3.2 Workplace Emotion AI

Emotion AI is also making significant inroads into workplace environments, where organizations are leveraging its capabilities to monitor and improve employee well-being. Tools embedded with affective sensing can assess stress, burnout, and emotional fatigue through multimodal signals such as facial expressions during video calls, voice tone during meetings, and even physiological indicators via wearable devices (Yadegaridehkordi et al., 2021). These insights are used not only to monitor workforce morale but also to design targeted interventions, such as adaptive work schedules or stress reduction programs. Additionally, emotion-aware feedback systems provide managers with emotionally contextualized insights into employee performance and engagement. Human resource management tools are now incorporating these emotional metrics to ensure healthier communication, fairer evaluations, and more supportive work environments (Ao, Bansal, Pruthi, & Khaskheli, 2023).

3.3 Healthcare and Mental Wellness

In healthcare, Emotion AI is being harnessed to support mental wellness and emotional diagnostics. Early detection systems use AI algorithms trained on linguistic cues, facial micro-expressions, and biometric signals to identify signs of depression, anxiety, and post-traumatic stress disorder (PTSD) with increasing accuracy (Vinciarelli et al., 2012). These systems can flag potential cases for clinical evaluation before symptoms become severe, aiding in preventive care. Virtual therapists—emotionally intelligent agents powered by conversational AI—are also gaining traction. These agents engage patients in empathetic dialogue, track emotional progress over time, and provide evidence-based interventions, either standalone or in conjunction with human therapists. Emotion AI tools are particularly valuable in remote and underserved communities, providing scalable mental health support where clinical resources may be limited (Sharma et al., 2025).

3.4 Education

In the education sector, Emotion AI is enabling the development of emotion-adaptive learning platforms and intelligent tutoring systems that respond dynamically to a student's emotional and cognitive state. These systems monitor indicators such as facial expressions, tone of voice, and interaction patterns to assess levels of engagement, frustration, confusion, or boredom (D'Mello & Graesser, 2012). When a learner appears disengaged or frustrated, the system can adjust the instructional strategy—slowing down content delivery, offering hints, or switching to a different teaching modality. This level of responsiveness fosters a more personalized learning experience, which can significantly enhance motivation and academic outcomes. Furthermore, educators can access dashboards with real-time emotional analytics, allowing them to identify at-risk students and intervene proactively (Bansal, Shukla, Gupta, Singh, & Pruthi, 2023).

4. EMERGING TRENDS IN EMOTION AI

As the field of Emotion AI advances, several emerging trends are reshaping the development and application of emotionally intelligent systems. These trends reflect a growing emphasis on deeper contextual understanding, real-time responsiveness, and seamless integration into everyday technologies. The convergence of AI with affective science, edge computing, and immersive environments is enabling more sophisticated and human-centered interactions (Kumar, Sharma, Bhatnagar, Dhanka, & Bist, 2025).

4.1 Multimodal Emotion Recognition Systems

One of the most transformative developments in Emotion AI is the rise of multimodal emotion recognition systems. Unlike traditional approaches that rely on a single input channel, such as facial expression or voice tone, multimodal systems combine data from various sources including text, audio, facial cues, and physiological signals (e.g., heart rate, skin conductance). This integration enhances the accuracy and robustness of emotion detection by capturing a richer and more comprehensive emotional profile. For instance, while facial analysis may suggest a neutral state, concurrent vocal tension and elevated heart rate could reveal underlying stress. To fuse these heterogeneous inputs, researchers employ advanced fusion techniques such as feature-level integration—where raw features from different modalities are combined before processing—and decision-level fusion—where outputs from separate models are integrated to reach a consensus. These systems are particularly valuable in complex real-world environments, where relying on a single modality may lead to misinterpretation (Bansal, Pruthi, & Singh, 2022).

4.2 Context-Aware Emotion AI

Recognizing that emotions do not exist in a vacuum, context-aware Emotion AI is gaining prominence. This approach considers cultural, linguistic, situational, and interpersonal factors to interpret emotional signals more accurately. For example, expressions of grief or joy can vary significantly across cultures, making cultural sensitivity crucial in global applications. Similarly, language-based sentiment analysis must account for idiomatic expressions, sarcasm, and regional dialects. Another key advancement is the temporal modeling of emotional states, which enables systems to track emotional trajectories over time rather than making isolated predictions. This dynamic understanding allows AI to differentiate between transient mood changes and longer-term emotional trends, offering more meaningful interactions. Techniques such as recurrent neural networks (RNNs) and transformers are often employed to model these temporal patterns, enhancing the predictive power and contextual relevance of emotion-aware systems (Kumar et al., 2025).

4.3 Real-Time Emotion AI in Edge Devices

The increasing need for privacy, low-latency processing, and mobility has led to the deployment of Emotion AI on edge devices such as smartphones, wearables, and IoT sensors. Real-time emotion recognition on-device eliminates the need to send sensitive biometric or emotional data to cloud servers, thereby preserving user privacy and reducing latency. This is especially critical in healthcare and mental wellness applications, where confidentiality is paramount. Advances in model compression, lightweight neural networks, and energy-efficient computing have made it feasible to run complex emotion recognition algorithms locally on constrained hardware. Applications include emotion-aware fitness trackers, mobile mental health apps, and smart home devices that adapt ambient conditions based on the user's mood. The integration of Emotion AI with the Internet of Things (IoT) paves the way for emotionally intelligent environments that respond intuitively to human presence and affective states.

4.4 Emotion AI in Extended Reality (XR) and Metaverse

Another exciting frontier is the integration of Emotion AI into Extended Reality (XR)—encompassing virtual reality (VR), augmented reality (AR), and mixed reality (MR)—and the emerging Metaverse. In these immersive environments, Emotion AI enables the creation of emotion-aware avatars that can mirror or respond to the user's feelings in real time. These avatars enhance the sense of presence and empathy in virtual interactions by adjusting facial expressions, body language, and voice tone based on emotional cues. Moreover, affective computing can be used to create immersive feedback loops, where the environment itself—such as lighting, music, or object behavior—changes in response to the user's mood. This capability significantly enhances social presence, making digital experiences feel more authentic and emotionally engaging. Applications range from therapeutic VR sessions and virtual classrooms to emotionally intelligent gaming and social platforms within the Metaverse (Painoli, Bansal, Singh, & Kukreti, 2021).

5. TECHNICAL ADVANCEMENTS DRIVING EMOTION AI

The evolution of Emotion AI has been significantly accelerated by breakthroughs in various technological domains. Innovations in natural language processing, computer vision, signal processing, and wearable technology have enabled machines to better perceive, interpret, and respond to human emotions. These technical advancements are fundamental to enhancing the reliability, scalability, and contextual sensitivity of emotionally intelligent systems.

5.1 Advances in NLP and Sentiment Analysis

Natural language processing (NLP) has seen transformative progress in recent years, particularly with the advent of transformer-based models such as BERT (Bidirectional Encoder Representations from Transformers), RoBERTa, and GPT. These models have revolutionized the way machines understand emotion-laden text by enabling deep contextual learning and nuanced sentiment analysis. Unlike traditional bag-of-words or rule-based systems, transformers analyze the semantic relationships between words across entire sentences, allowing for more accurate detection of subtle emotional cues like sarcasm, ambivalence, or mixed sentiments. This capability is crucial in applications such as social media monitoring, customer service chatbots, and mental health diagnostics, where emotional subtext often carries more weight than explicit content (Palta, Kumar, & Palta, 2024).

5.2 Audio Emotion Recognition

In the domain of audio processing, deep learning models have greatly improved the ability to detect emotions from vocal inputs. Spectrogram-based convolutional neural networks (CNNs), for instance, convert speech into visual representations of sound frequency and intensity, which are then analyzed for patterns indicative of emotions such as anger, sadness, or happiness. These models capture vocal features like pitch, tone, tempo, and pauses—often more telling than words alone in conveying affective states. Audio emotion recognition is widely used in voice assistants, smart speakers, and call center applications to gauge customer sentiment and optimize real-time responses. The non-verbal nature of vocal emotion also makes it particularly valuable in multilingual or low-literacy settings.

5.3 Facial Emotion Recognition

Facial emotion recognition has advanced significantly through the application of deep learning and computer vision techniques. Modern systems utilize 3D convolutional neural networks (3D CNNs) to process both spatial and temporal aspects of facial expressions, capturing dynamic changes over time that static images might miss. Additionally, the Facial Action Coding System (FACS) is often employed to identify facial action units (FAUs)—specific muscle movements associated with distinct emotions. Hybrid models that combine geometric features (such as distances between facial landmarks) with deep learning-based representations provide robust performance even in challenging conditions like occlusions or varied lighting. These technologies are increasingly deployed in security, healthcare, education, and user experience optimization across digital interfaces (Satar, Aggarwal, Bansal, & Alarifi, 2023).

5.4 Wearables and Physiological Emotion Detection

Wearable technology has opened new frontiers in real-time emotion monitoring through physiological signal acquisition. Devices such as smartwatches, fitness bands, and EEG headsets collect data on electroencephalography (EEG), electrodermal activity (EDA), heart rate variability (HRV), and eye-tracking—metrics that correlate with emotional states like stress, arousal, and cognitive load. Machine learning models are then used to interpret these biosignals, offering insights that are often unobtainable through behavioral analysis alone. For example, elevated EDA and reduced HRV may signal high stress levels even when external expressions appear neutral. Such physiological monitoring is invaluable in domains like personalized mental health care, user-centered product design, immersive gaming, and adaptive learning environments, where a deeper understanding of user affect is critical.

6. ETHICAL, LEGAL, AND SOCIETAL CONSIDERATIONS

As Emotion AI technologies become increasingly integrated into sensitive areas such as healthcare, education, and workplace environments, the ethical, legal, and societal implications surrounding their deployment have drawn substantial attention. While these systems offer the promise of enhanced human-machine interactions and proactive support, they also raise significant concerns about privacy, fairness, psychological well-being, and regulatory oversight. Addressing these issues is essential for ensuring that Emotion AI evolves in a socially responsible and ethically grounded manner (Kumar, Singh, & Khan, 2024).

6.1 Data Privacy and Consent

One of the most pressing ethical issues in Emotion AI involves data privacy and the mechanisms for informed consent. Emotion AI systems often rely on passive data collection—gathering facial expressions, vocal tones, physiological signals, or behavioral cues without explicit user input or awareness. This form of data extraction can lead to serious invasions of personal privacy, especially when users are not adequately informed about what emotional data is being collected, how it is processed, and for what purpose. Therefore, robust and transparent consent mechanisms are critical. These should ensure that users can opt in with full awareness, control how their data is used, and withdraw consent at any time. Privacy-preserving techniques such as on-device processing and federated learning arc also being explored to minimize risks while maintaining system performance (Raja et al., 2025).

6.2 Bias and Algorithmic Fairness

Another major challenge lies in ensuring fairness and eliminating bias in Emotion AI systems. Many emotion recognition algorithms are trained on datasets that lack demographic diversity, leading to skewed performance across different racial, gender, and cultural groups. For instance, an algorithm trained predominantly on Western facial expressions might misinterpret emotions in individuals from non-Western cultures, resulting in misclassification or exclusion. Gender-based biases have also been observed, where emotional cues from women are more likely to be misread or deemed ambiguous compared to those from men. These disparities can have far-reaching consequences, especially in applications involving law enforcement, mental health diagnostics, or employment screening. Therefore, it is essential to curate diverse, representative datasets and implement algorithmic fairness techniques such as bias auditing, adversarial debiasing, and transparency reporting (Kumar, Khan, & Singh, 2024).

6.3 Psychological Impacts

Emotion AI also poses nuanced psychological risks that go beyond traditional data ethics. The ability of machines to read and respond to human emotions can lead to unintended manipulation or emotional surveillance. Users may alter their natural behavior due to the awareness that their emotions are constantly being monitored, a phenomenon known as the "Hawthorne effect." In extreme cases, Emotion AI can be weaponized to exploit vulnerabilities, such as influencing consumer behavior, political opinions, or emotional states for profit or control. Furthermore, overreliance on emotion-detecting systems may erode individual autonomy and self-perception, as users begin to depend on external validation of their internal feelings. These psychological consequences highlight the need for human-centered design principles that prioritize emotional dignity and respect for personal boundaries (Bansal, Martinho, Pruthi, & Aggarwal, 2024).

6.4 Regulatory and Governance Challenges

Despite the growing deployment of Emotion AI, regulatory frameworks remain limited and fragmented. Existing data protection regulations such as the General Data Protection Regulation (GDPR) in the European Union address personal data broadly but do not specifically account for the nuances of emotional data, which is often more sensitive and context-dependent. The proposed EU AI Act categorizes some emotion recognition systems as high-risk, yet enforcement and scope remain under development. In many other jurisdictions, legal oversight of Emotion AI is either nascent or nonexistent. This regulatory gap underscores the urgency for international governance standards and ethical AI frameworks tailored to emotion sensing. Proposed guidelines emphasize transparency, accountability, explainability, and the right to contest automated decisions. Multi-stakeholder collaborations involving policymakers, technologists, ethicists, and civil society organizations are crucial for creating comprehensive and enforceable safeguards (Bansal, Saini, Ngah, & Prasad, 2024).

7. FUTURE RESEARCH DIRECTIONS

The field of Emotion AI is rapidly evolving, yet it faces significant scientific, technical, and ethical challenges that must be addressed to realize its full potential. Future research efforts are needed to create Emotion AI systems that are robust, generalizable, human-centered, and socially responsible. This section explores four promising directions that can guide the next phase of innovation in this domain: developing generalizable models, incorporating human-in-the-loop frameworks, expanding to collective intelligence systems, and fostering interdisciplinary collaboration (Rahman, Bansal, & Pruthi, 2023).

7.1 Toward Generalizable Emotion AI

One of the foremost challenges in Emotion AI research is the development of models that generalize well across domains, cultures, and contexts. Current systems often suffer from overfitting, where models perform excellently on training data but poorly on unseen or diverse inputs. This issue arises primarily because emotional expressions and their interpretations are highly context-dependent and culturally nuanced. For example, a smile might signify happiness in one culture but politeness or discomfort in another. Similarly, vocal intonations or gestures that indicate anger or frustration can vary widely across social settings.

To overcome these limitations, future research must focus on designing Emotion AI models that can adapt to multiple domains without sacrificing accuracy. This includes building large-scale, diverse datasets that capture the rich variability of emotional expression across different age groups, ethnicities, languages, and situational contexts. The collection and annotation of such datasets require careful ethical considerations to ensure privacy and consent, as well as balanced representation to avoid bias.

Additionally, techniques such as domain adaptation, transfer learning, and meta-learning offer promising avenues for achieving cross-domain generalization. Domain adaptation methods allow models trained on one dataset to be fine-tuned or adjusted to new domains with minimal additional data. Transfer learning leverages knowledge from one task to improve performance on related tasks, while meta-learning aims to build models that can learn quickly from limited examples in new environments.

Another key area is addressing overfitting by improving regularization techniques and incorporating prior knowledge about human emotion. Hybrid models that combine data-driven learning with rule-based or theory-driven components may offer better generalizability by embedding psychological insights into the learning process. The goal is to create Emotion AI systems that not only perform well in laboratory settings but also remain reliable and interpretable in real-world applications where emotional dynamics are complex and fluid (Kumar et al., 2024).

7.2 Human-in-the-Loop Emotion AI

Despite advances in autonomous emotion recognition, there is growing recognition that human intuition and oversight remain indispensable. Human-in-the-loop (HITL) Emotion AI integrates human judgment with algorithmic insights, creating a synergistic relationship that improves accuracy, fairness, and trustworthiness. HITL approaches allow for real-time feedback, correction of errors, and continuous learning, which are particularly valuable in high-stakes applications such as mental health diagnosis or law enforcement.

Future research should explore the design of hybrid systems where humans and AI collaborate seamlessly. For instance, human experts can provide contextual interpretations that machines might miss, while AI can handle large-scale data processing and pattern recognition beyond human capability. These systems could employ interactive interfaces where humans validate or adjust emotion predictions, providing corrective feedback that helps the AI model refine its understanding over time.

Co-learning paradigms represent another promising direction, in which the AI system learns not only from static datasets but also from ongoing interactions with users and experts. This dynamic feedback loop fosters adaptability and personalization, allowing Emotion AI to better capture individual differences and evolving emotional states. Implementing effective HITL frameworks also requires addressing usability challenges, ensuring that human participants are neither overwhelmed by information nor burdened by excessive interaction demands.

Moreover, HITL Emotion AI can enhance transparency and user trust. By involving humans in the decision-making process, the "black-box" nature of AI systems can be mitigated, allowing stakeholders to understand how emotional judgments are made and to contest or refine outcomes when necessary. This collaboration is vital for aligning Emotion AI with ethical principles and social norms, as well as for preventing unintended consequences stemming from fully automated emotion recognition (Dellermann et al., 2019; Cowie & Cornelius, 2003).

7.3 Emotion AI in Collective Intelligence Systems

While much of the current research on Emotion AI focuses on individual-level emotion detection, there is an emerging interest in understanding and leveraging group-level emotional dynamics—an area known as collective intelligence. Detecting and interpreting emotions within groups or organizations can provide valuable insights into organizational health, team cohesion, and crowd behavior, with applications ranging from corporate management to public safety.

Future studies should investigate how Emotion AI can capture collective emotional states by aggregating data from multiple individuals, analyzing interaction patterns, and identifying emotional contagion effects. For example, real-time monitoring of team emotions during collaborative tasks can reveal stress points, conflicts, or moments of high engagement, enabling timely interventions to improve performance and well-being.

In larger social contexts, Emotion AI can support crowd psychology by detecting emotions that spread through social media, public events, or urban environments. This capability has implications for disaster response, political campaigning, and public health messaging. However, collective emotion detection poses unique technical and ethical challenges. Technically, aggregating heterogeneous emotional signals while respecting individual variability requires sophisticated data fusion and privacy-preserving techniques. Ethically, there is a risk of surveillance and misuse if collective emotional data are exploited without consent or transparency. Therefore, research should also explore governance frameworks and participatory approaches that empower communities to shape how their collective emotions are monitored and utilized. Emotion AI in collective intelligence systems holds great promise for fostering empathy and social cohesion but must be developed with sensitivity to individual rights and societal impacts (D'Mello & Graesser, 2015)..

7.4 Interdisciplinary Collaboration

The complexity and sensitivity of Emotion AI necessitate interdisciplinary collaboration, drawing expertise from neuroscience, psychology, ethics, law, computer science, and social sciences. Neuroscience and psychology provide foundational understanding of emotional processes, informing the development of more accurate and biologically plausible models. Ethical scholarship highlights concerns about privacy, autonomy, and fairness, guiding responsible design and deployment. Legal experts contribute to shaping regulatory frameworks that protect users and ensure accountability (Calvo & Peters, 2014)..

Future research initiatives should prioritize cross-disciplinary partnerships to bridge gaps between technical innovation and human values. For example, neuroscientific findings on brain activity patterns linked to emotions can inform the development of new sensors and emotion recognition algorithms. Psychologists can assist in designing datasets and annotation protocols that capture subtle emotional nuances. Ethicists and legal scholars can help establish standards for consent, data protection, and equitable use.

Moreover, interdisciplinary collaboration is essential for embedding social empathy into Emotion AI systems—designing AI that not only recognizes emotions but also responds in socially appropriate and compassionate ways. This involves integrating cultural sensitivity, ethical reasoning, and contextual awareness into algorithms, moving beyond mere detection toward fostering genuine emotional understanding and support.

Collaborative research centers, shared datasets, and open forums for dialogue between disciplines will accelerate progress and help ensure that Emotion AI develops in alignment with societal needs. Education and training programs that equip researchers with interdisciplinary knowledge will further strengthen this integrative approach. This comprehensive exploration of future research directions highlights the multifaceted challenges and opportunities that lie ahead for Emotion AI. By advancing generalizable models, embracing human-AI collaboration, expanding to collective emotional intelligence, and fostering interdisciplinary cooperation, the field can move toward creating emotionally aware systems that are accurate, ethical, and deeply human-centric (Cowie & Cornelius, 2003).

8. CONCLUSION

The advent of Emotion AI marks a pivotal moment in the evolution of artificial intelligence, where machines are no longer limited to logical computations but are increasingly capable of perceiving, interpreting, and responding to human emotions. This technological progression signifies a fundamental shift in how humans interact with machines and digital systems, promising to enhance communication, empathy, and decision-making across multiple domains such as healthcare, education, customer service, and workplace environments. By bridging the gap between cognitive and affective computing, Emotion AI opens new horizons for creating emotionally intelligent systems that can adapt to human needs with greater sensitivity and nuance.

Throughout this discussion, we have explored the theoretical foundations of emotional intelligence, the current landscape of AI-driven emotion recognition, emerging trends, technical advancements, and the critical ethical, legal, and societal challenges that accompany this development. The intersection of psychology, neuroscience, and AI technologies fuels this field, enabling machines to detect emotions through diverse modalities—text, speech, facial expressions, physiological signals—and to synthesize these inputs for richer and more context-aware understanding.

The Transformative Opportunities of Emotion AI

Emotion AI holds immense promise to transform how digital systems engage with people by making interactions more natural, personalized, and effective. In customer service, emotion-aware chatbots and virtual assistants can tailor responses based on user sentiment, thereby improving satisfaction and loyalty. In healthcare, early detection of mental health conditions such as depression or anxiety through emotional cues can facilitate timely interventions and better patient outcomes. Educational platforms equipped with emotion-adaptive learning capabilities can dynamically adjust content delivery to sustain motivation and reduce frustration, ultimately enhancing learning experiences.

Furthermore, Emotion AI can contribute to workplace well-being by monitoring stress and burnout, enabling organizations to foster healthier environments. The integration of emotion recognition into emerging technologies such as extended reality (XR) and the metaverse also paves the way for immersive, empathetic virtual experiences that can enrich social presence and connection. The collective emotion detection applications offer a novel means to understand group dynamics and public sentiment, which can inform organizational decision-making and public policy.

Technically, recent advancements in deep learning, multimodal data fusion, and on-device inference are accelerating the capabilities of Emotion AI systems. These innovations are helping overcome traditional barriers such as cultural variability in emotional expression and data privacy concerns, allowing for more robust and scalable solutions.

The Inherent Risks and Ethical Concerns

Despite these promising opportunities, the deployment of Emotion AI raises substantial risks and ethical dilemmas that must not be overlooked. Central among these is the issue of data privacy. Emotion AI frequently relies on sensitive, often involuntary emotional data that can reveal intimate aspects of a person's inner state. The passive collection and analysis of such data, if unchecked, may lead to breaches of confidentiality, unauthorized surveillance, and erosion of individual autonomy.

Another significant concern is algorithmic bias. Given that emotion recognition models are often trained on datasets that lack diversity, there is a real danger of perpetuating or even amplifying social inequalities. Biases based on race, gender, culture, or age can lead to misinterpretation of emotions, resulting in unfair treatment or exclusion in critical contexts like healthcare diagnostics or employment assessments. This raises questions of fairness and justice that require ongoing scrutiny.

Moreover, the psychological impact of emotion-sensing technologies warrants careful consideration. The awareness of being constantly monitored may influence users' natural emotional expression, potentially leading to stress or self-censorship. The possibility of manipulation—where emotional data could be exploited to influence behavior for commercial, political, or other purposes—further complicates the ethical landscape. Emotion AI risks transforming social interactions into data-driven transactions, potentially undermining genuine human empathy and trust.

Finally, current legal and regulatory frameworks lag behind technological advancements. While regulations such as the GDPR provide foundational data protection guidelines, they do not fully address the unique characteristics of emotional data and the complexities of AI-driven emotion recognition. The absence of comprehensive policies leaves a regulatory vacuum that could be exploited, highlighting the urgent need for ethical AI governance specific to affective computing.

Toward Responsible Innovation and Collaboration

Balancing the transformative potential of Emotion AI with its associated risks requires a proactive, multidisciplinary approach to innovation and governance. Responsible development of Emotion AI demands transparency, accountability, and inclusiveness at every stage—from data collection and model training to deployment and user interaction.

Firstly, privacy-preserving techniques such as on-device processing, federated learning, and anonymization must be prioritized to safeguard users' emotional data. Consent mechanisms need to be transparent and empower users with control over their information. Algorithmic fairness should be systematically evaluated through bias audits and rigorous testing on diverse populations to ensure equitable performance.

Secondly, the inclusion of human oversight through human-in-the-loop systems can enhance reliability and ethical alignment. Hybrid frameworks that combine AI efficiency with human judgment help mitigate errors and contextual misinterpretations. This collaboration can also foster user trust by making emotion AI systems more interpretable and responsive to individual needs.

Thirdly, interdisciplinary collaboration is indispensable for addressing the multifaceted challenges posed by Emotion AI. Psychologists, neuroscientists, ethicists, legal scholars, and technologists must work together to integrate domain knowledge and ethical principles into system design. Educational initiatives that train practitioners in these cross-cutting competencies will strengthen the field's foundation.

Finally, robust regulatory frameworks tailored to the unique aspects of emotional data and AI ethics must be developed at national and international levels. Policymakers should engage with all stakeholders, including civil society, to craft laws that promote innovation while protecting fundamental rights and human dignity.

Governance models that are adaptive and forward-looking will be crucial to keep pace with rapid technological change.

Final Reflections

Emotion AI stands at the intersection of technology and humanity, offering tools to deepen our understanding and expression of emotions through artificial systems. Its evolution reflects broader societal aspirations for more empathetic, inclusive, and intelligent interactions between humans and machines. Yet, this journey is fraught with ethical quandaries and technical challenges that call for vigilance, humility, and collaboration.

As we continue to advance Emotion AI, it is imperative that innovation is guided not only by technical feasibility but also by a commitment to respect human values and rights. By fostering open dialogue among researchers, developers, users, and regulators, we can harness the power of Emotion AI to enrich lives without compromising privacy, fairness, or autonomy.

In this spirit, the future of Emotion AI should be envisioned as a collective endeavor—one that harnesses the best of human and artificial intelligence to create systems that truly understand and support the emotional fabric of our lives. Responsible innovation, underpinned by cross-sector collaboration and ethical foresight, will ensure that Emotion AI fulfills its promise as a transformative force for good.

REFERENCES

Ao, L., Bansal, R., Pruthi, N., & Khaskheli, M. B. (2023). Impact of Social Media Influencers on Customer Engagement and Purchase Intention: A Meta-Analysis. *Sustainability (Basel), 15*(3), 2744. DOI: 10.3390/su15032744

Baltrušaitis, T., Ahuja, C., & Morency, L.-P. (2019). Multimodal machine learning: A survey and taxonomy. *IEEE Transactions on Pattern Analysis and Machine Intelligence, 41*(2), 423–443. DOI: 10.1109/TPAMI.2018.2798607 PMID: 29994351

Bansal, R., Martinho, C., Pruthi, N., & Aggarwal, D. (2024). From virtual observations to business insights: A bibliometric review of netnography in business research. *Heliyon, 10*(1), e22853. DOI: 10.1016/j.heliyon.2023.e22853 PMID: 38163120

Bansal, R., Pruthi, N., & Singh, R. (2022). Developing Customer Engagement Through Artificial Intelligence Tools: Roles and Challenges. In *Developing Relationships, Personalization, and Data Herald in Marketing 5.0* (pp. 130-145). IGI Global.

Bansal, R., Saini, S., Ngah, A. H., & Durga Prasad, T. (2024). Proselytizing the potential of influencer marketing via artificial intelligence: Mapping the research trends through bibliometric analysis. *Cogent Business & Management, 11*(1), 2372889. DOI: 10.1080/23311975.2024.2372889

Bansal, R., Shukla, G., Gupta, A., Singh, A., & Pruthi, N. (2023). Optimizing Augmented Reality and Virtual Reality for Customer Engagement. In *Promoting Consumer Engagement Through Emotional Branding and Sensory Marketing* (pp. 24–35). IGI Global.

Bickman, L. *Improving Mental Health Services: A 50-Year Journey from Randomized Experiments to Artificial Intelligence and Precision Mental Health*, vol. 47, no. 5. Springer US, 2020. DOI: 10.1007/s10488-020-01065-8

Calvo, R., & D'Mello, S. (2010). Affect detection: An interdisciplinary review of models, methods, and their applications. *IEEE Transactions on Affective Computing, 1*(1), 18–37. DOI: 10.1109/T-AFFC.2010.1

Calvo, R. A., & Peters, D. (2014). *Positive computing: Technology for wellbeing and human potential*. MIT Press. DOI: 10.7551/mitpress/9764.001.0001

Cambria, E., Olsher, D., & Rajagopal, D. "SenticNet 3: A common and common-sense knowledge base for cognition-driven sentiment analysis," in *Proc. 26th International Conference on Computational Linguistics*, 2016, pp. 2666–2677.

Cowie, R., & Cornelius, R. R. (2003). Describing the emotional states that are expressed in speech. *Speech Communication, 40*(1–2), 5–32. DOI: 10.1016/S0167-6393(02)00071-7

D'Mello, D., & Graesser, A. (2012). Dynamics of affective states during complex learning. *International Journal of Learning Technology, 7*(3), 240–247.

D'Mello, S. K., & Graesser, A. C. (2015). Feeling, thinking, and computing with affect-aware learning technologies. In Calvo, R. A., D'Mello, S. K., Gratch, J., & Kappas, A. (Eds.), *The Oxford handbook of affective computing* (pp. 419–434). Oxford University Press.

Dellermann, D., Calma, A., Lipusch, N., Weber, T., & Ebel, P. (2019). The future of human–AI collaboration: A taxonomy of design knowledge for hybrid intelligence systems. *Business & Information Systems Engineering, 61*(3), 259–272. DOI: 10.1007/s12599-019-00595-0

Devlin, J., Chang, M.-W., Lee, K., & Toutanova, K. "BERT: Pre-training of deep bidirectional transformers for language understanding," *arXiv preprint* arXiv:1810.04805, 2018.

Ekman, P. (1991). Universal facial expressions of emotion. *California Mental Health Research Digest, 8*(4), 151–158.

Ekman, P., & Friesen, W. V. (1978). *Facial Action Coding System: A Technique for the Measurement of Facial Movement.* Consulting Psychologists Press.

Goleman, D. (1995). *Emotional Intelligence: Why It Can Matter More Than IQ.* Bantam Books.

Hochreiter, S., & Schmidhuber, J. (1997). Long short-term memory. *Neural Computation, 9*(8), 1735–1780. DOI: 10.1162/neco.1997.9.8.1735 PMID: 9377276

Keltner, D., & Ekman, P. "Facial expression of emotion," in *Handbook of Emotions*, 3rd ed., M. Lewis, J. Haviland-Jones, and L. F. Barrett, Eds. Guilford Press, 2008, pp. 211–234.

Kim, Y. "Convolutional neural networks for sentence classification," *arXiv preprint* arXiv:1408.5882, 2014. DOI: 10.3115/v1/D14-1181

Krizhevsky, A., Sutskever, I., & Hinton, G. E. "ImageNet classification with deep convolutional neural networks," in *Proc. Advances in Neural Information Processing Systems*, 2012, pp. 1097–1105.

Kumar, A., Dhanka, S., Bansal, R., Sharma, A., Singh, J., Khan, A. A., & Maini, S. "Smart Crop Selection: Harnessing Machine Learning for Sustainable Agriculture in the Era of Industry 5.0," in *Industry 5.0 and Emerging Technologies: Transformation Through Technology*, 2024. DOI: 10.1007/978-3-031-70996-8_6

Kumar, A., Dhanka, S., Bansal, R., Sharma, A., Singh, J., Khan, A. A., & Maini, S. "Agriculture in the Era of Industry 5.0," in *Industry 5.0 and Emerging Technologies: Transformation Through Technology*, 2024.

Kumar, A., Dhanka, S., Singh, J., Khan, A. A., & Maini, S. (2024). Hybrid machine learning techniques based on genetic algorithm for heart disease detection. *Innovation and Emerging Technologies*, *11*, 2450008. DOI: 10.1142/S2737599424500087

Kumar, A., Khan, A. A., & Singh, J. (2024). Enhancing the Diagnosis of Cardiovascular Disease: A Comparative Examination of Support Vector Machine and Artificial Neural Network Models Utilizing Extensive Data Preprocessing Techniques. *WSEAS Transactions on Computers*, *23*, 318–327. DOI: 10.37394/23205.2024.23.31

Kumar, A., Sharma, A., Bhatnagar, P., Dhanka, S., & Bist, Y. "Harnessing the Power of Data Analytics to Drive Brand Engagement, Affinity, Evangelism, and Loyalty in the Modern Marketplace," in *Demystifying Emotion AI, Robotics AI, and Sentiment Analysis in Customer Experience*, 2025. DOI: 10.4018/979-8-3373-1867-7.ch004

Kumar, A., Sharma, A., Dhanka, S., Bist, Y., Maini, S., & Bhatnagar, P. "Data Privacy, Ethics, and the Role of AI in Customer Relationship Management," in *Demystifying Emotion AI, Robotics AI, and Sentiment Analysis in Customer Experience*, 2025. DOI: 10.4018/979-8-3373-1867-7.ch013

Kumar, A., Sharma, A., Dhanka, S., & Maini, S. "Machine Learning for Combating Mental Health Stigma," in *Transforming Neuropsychology and Cognitive Psychology With AI and Machine Learning*, 2025. DOI: 10.4018/979-8-3693-9341-3.ch014

Kumar, A., Singh, J., & Khan, A. A. (2024, September). A comprehensive machine learning framework with particle swarm optimization for improved polycystic ovary syndrome (PCOS) diagnosis. *Engineering Research Express*, *6*(3), 035233. DOI: 10.1088/2631-8695/ad76f9

Li, L., & Wang, Y. (2025). Personalized recommendation and customer loyalty: The moderating role of trust. *Future Business Journal*, *11*(1), 34. DOI: 10.1186/s43093-025-00476-z

Li, Y., & Jia, J. (2020). Wearable physiological signal-based emotion recognition: A review. *IEEE Sensors Journal*, *20*(21), 13055–13071.

Mayer, J. D., Salovey, P., & Caruso, D. R. (2008). Emotional intelligence: New ability or eclectic traits? *The American Psychologist*, *63*(6), 503–517. DOI: 10.1037/0003-066X.63.6.503 PMID: 18793038

Mehrabian, A. (1969). Significance of posture and position in the communication of attitude and status relationships. *Psychological Bulletin*, *71*(5), 359–372. DOI: 10.1037/h0027349 PMID: 4892572

Mittal, G., & Bansal, R. (2023). Driving Force Behind Consumer Brand Engagement: The Metaverse. In *Cultural Marketing and Metaverse for Consumer Engagement* (pp. 164-181). IGI Global.

Painoli, A. K., Bansal, R., Singh, R., & Kukreti, A. (2021). Impact of Digital Marketing on the Buying Behavior of Youth With Special Reference to Uttarakhand State. In *Big Data Analytics for Improved Accuracy, Efficiency, and Decision Making in Digital Marketing* (pp. 162-182). IGI Global. DOI: 10.4018/978-1-7998-7231-3.ch012

Palta, P., & Kumar, A. (2024). Effect of vermicompost additive on physical, chemical and dielectric properties of soil and its modeling. *The Journal of Microwave Power and Electromagnetic Energy*, *58*(3), 186–206. DOI: 10.1080/08327823.2024.2378668

Palta, P., & Kumar, A. (2025). Soil dielectric response to chemical fertilizers in Northern India's key agricultural areas. *Physics and Chemistry of the Earth Parts A/B/C*, *137*, 103806. DOI: 10.1016/j.pce.2024.103806

Palta, P., Kumar, A., & Kaur, P. (2024). Evaluation of the impact of wastewater irrigation on the soil's dielectric parameters. *Land Degradation & Development*, *35*(7), 2643–2657. DOI: 10.1002/ldr.5088

Palta, P., Kumar, A., & Palta, A. "Leveraging Dielectric Properties, Remote Sensing, and Sensor Technology in Agriculture: A Perspective on Industry and Emerging Technologies," in *Industry 5.0 and Emerging Technologies: Transformation Through Technology*, 2024. DOI: 10.1007/978-3-031-70996-8_5

Pantic, M., & Rothkrantz, L. J. M. (2000). Automatic analysis of facial expressions: The state of the art. *IEEE Transactions on Pattern Analysis and Machine Intelligence*, *22*(12), 1424–1445. DOI: 10.1109/34.895976

Rahman, K. T., Bansal, R., & Pruthi, N. (2023). Consumer adoption of technologies: A mindset-oriented approach. In Contemporary Studies of Risks in Emerging Technology, Part B (pp. 243-255). Emerald Publishing Limited. DOI: 10.1108/978-1-80455-566-820231013

Raja, M., Swamy, T. N. V. R. L., Das, S., Bansal, R., Fahlevi, M., & Aziz, A. L. (2025). Does human resource information system influence performance management? *Cogent Business & Management, 12*(1), 2438862. DOI: 10.1080/23311975.2024.2438862

Ringeval, F., Schuller, B., Valstar, M., Cowie, R., Pantic, M., & Scherer, S. "AVEC 2017: Real-life depression, and affect recognition workshop and challenge," in *Proc. 7th IEEE International Conference on Affective Computing and Intelligent Interaction (ACII)*, 2017, pp. 561–567. DOI: 10.1145/3133944.3133953

Satar, M. S., Aggarwal, D., Bansal, R., & Alarifi, G. (2023). Mapping the Knowledge Structure and Unveiling the Research Trends in Social Entrepreneurship and Inclusive Development: A Bibliometric Analysis. *Sustainability (Basel), 15*(7), 5626. DOI: 10.3390/su15075626

Schuller, B., Batliner, A., Steidl, S., & Seppi, D. (2011). Recognising realistic emotions and affect in speech: State of the art and lessons learnt from the first challenge. *Speech Communication, 53*(9–10), 1062–1087. DOI: 10.1016/j.specom.2011.01.011

Sharma, A., Dhanka, S., Bansal, R., Kumar, A., & Maini, S. "Industry 5.0 with Sustainable Development," in *Industry 5.0 and Emerging Technologies: Transformation Through Technology*, 2024.

Sharma, A., Dhanka, S., Kumar, A., & Maini, S. (2024, July). A comparative study of heterogeneous machine learning algorithms for arrhythmia classification using feature selection technique and multi-dimensional datasets. *Engineering Research Express, 6*(3), 035209. DOI: 10.1088/2631-8695/ad5d51

Sharma, A., Dhanka, S., Kumar, A., Nain, M., Dhanka, B., Bhardwaj, V. K., Maini, S., & Arora, A. S. (2025). A Systematic Review on Machine Learning Intelligent Systems for Heart Disease Diagnosis. *Archives of Computational Methods in Engineering*, •••, 1–27. DOI: 10.1007/s11831-025-10271-2

Singh, J., Pandey, B., Karna, S., Arora, A. S., & Kumar, A. (2024). Enhancing the thermographic diagnosis of maxillary sinusitis using deep learning approach. *Quantitative Infrared Thermography Journal*, •••, 1–15.

Singh, V., Kumar, A., Kaur, S., Bansal, A., & Singla, A. K. (2024). Enhancing cavitation erosion resistance of VC+TiC coatings with PTFE in marine environments via lasso regression optimization. *Tribology International, 196*, 109697. DOI: 10.1016/j.triboint.2024.109697

Spielberger, C. D. (1972). Trait and state anxiety. In *Anxiety and Behavior* (pp. 3–22). Academic Press.

Xu, H., & Zhang, C. (2021). The effects of AI-driven personalized marketing on consumer purchase decisions. *Journal of Interactive Marketing*, *54*, 29–42. DOI: 10.1016/j.intmar.2020.10.003

Yang, J., Chen, Z., & Zhang, X. (2019). Speech emotion recognition using deep convolutional neural network and discriminant temporal pyramid matching. *IEEE Transactions on Multimedia*, *21*(3), 687–697.

Zafeiriou, S., Hadjidimitriou, A., & Pitas, I. (2007). Facial expression recognition in image sequences using geometric deformation features and support vector machines. *IEEE Transactions on Image Processing*, *16*(1), 172–187. DOI: 10.1109/TIP.2006.884954 PMID: 17283776

Zeng, A., Jin, R., & Zhang, Z. (2019). Facial expression recognition via deep learning: A review. *IEEE Access : Practical Innovations, Open Solutions*, *7*, 135001–135018.

Chapter 9
Role of AI in Reshaping Emotional Well-Being:
The Pros and Cons

Pankhuri Sharma
https://orcid.org/0009-0004-7973-7781
Vivekananda Institute of Professional Studies, Guru Gobind Singh Indraprastha University, India

Meenakshi Gandhi
https://orcid.org/0000-0003-0809-9781
Vivekananda Institute of Professional Studies, Guru Gobind Singh Indraprastha University, India

ABSTRACT

Artificial intelligence (AI) is increasingly shaping our daily lives, especially in mental health care. This chapter explores how AI-driven bots can sense emotions, offer therapeutic conversations, and provide mindfulness techniques. While AI promises unbiased listening and scalable support, questions remain about its ability to truly understand and ethically care for human emotions. This chapter examines current studies, ethical considerations, and frameworks for responsible AI use in mental health, inviting readers to reflect on whether AI truly heals or simply imitates the language of healing.

DOI: 10.4018/979-8-3373-3658-9.ch009

INTRODUCTION

1.1 From Human Touch To Artificial Empathy

Not so long ago, conversations about computers and human feelings belonged in science fiction stories. But today, technology has found its way into the delicate realm of emotions, promising to be a gentle hand in times of quiet despair. AI is no longer just about data and algorithms, it's learning the rhythm of human conversations, the weight of a sigh, the tremble in a voice (Ciechanowski et al., 2019). It's as if the screen has become a mirror, trying to reflect the most intimate parts of our lives. Yet, despite the impressive technology, there's a pause in our hearts when we think about what AI is really offering. After all, empathy isn't just about hearing the right words but it's about feeling them in your bones. It's about the warmth of a friend's presence, the comforting hush of shared understanding. AI can echo back what it hears, but it doesn't feel the ache in your chest or the flicker of hope in your eyes (Galvão Gomes da Silva et al., 2022).

This shift from human touch to artificial empathy sets the stage for everything that follows in this chapter. We're not just talking about technology we're talking about how it's woven into the fabric of our emotional lives. We're not merely talking about another technological innovation or the latest digital tool. We're talking about how, in the quiet moments of our daily lives, technology is beginning to occupy a space once reserved for the soft assurances of a friend or the steady presence of a trusted confidant. This is about how our devices, our screens, and the algorithms running silently beneath them are starting to stitch themselves into the fabric of our emotional worlds.

To truly grasp what this means, consider how we once navigated our most vulnerable moments: a trembling phone call to a loved one, a late-night talk in a dimly lit room, the gentle hush of someone saying, "I'm here for you." These were moments that felt alive, shaped by the warmth of breath and the shared weight of presence. They were messy, sometimes fumbling, but always real. Now, imagine those same moments translated into data, coded into algorithms that promise to know what we feel before we even say the words.

At first glance, this might seem like progress and a solution to the aching gaps in our mental health systems and the quiet despair of those who feel unseen. After all, isn't it a kind of magic to have a digital companion that never sleeps, that listens without judgment, and that answers at the speed of light? For many, these AI driven companions can feel like a balm, especially in the still hours when the world's noise quiets and the weight of loneliness grows louder. They can be a lifeline, a gentle nudge toward healing when human voices are out of reach.

Yet beneath the convenience and novelty, there's an undercurrent of something more complex, something that stirs both wonder and unease. Because while these algorithms can echo back our feelings with astonishing precision mirroring our words, learning the patterns of our sighs and hesitations which they do so without ever truly knowing what it means to be human. They replicate, but they do not feel. They respond, but they do not hold. The difference may seem small, a hairline crack in the surface of comfort, but it is the crack through which the light of human connection shines.

This is why the shift from human touch to artificial empathy matters so deeply. It's not just about what these tools can do, but about what they cannot. It's about how they are beginning to change the very shape of our emotional landscapes, weaving themselves into the spaces between our thoughts and feelings. It's about how they challenge us to reconsider what it means to be comforted, to be heard, and to be healed.

For some, this shift is a hopeful sign and proof that technology can finally reach those whom traditional care has left behind. For others, it is a gentle but persistent alarm, a reminder that even the most advanced machine can never replicate the flicker of understanding in another's eyes or the silent reassurance of a hand pressed to yours in the dark. It calls us to hold fast to what is real even as we embrace what is new.

1.2 Why Emotional Wellbeing Needs AI Support Today

Emotional wellbeing refers to a state of positive mental health that involves understanding and regulating one's emotions, nurturing satisfying relationships, and effectively coping with stress and life's challenges to promote resilience and a sense of flourishing (World Health Organization, 2014; Diener, Oishi, & Lucas, 2018). While, AI chatbots are computer programs that use artificial intelligence, particularly natural language processing (NLP), to mimic human conversation and provide interactive, personalized responses for support, information, or mental health care (Inkster, Sarda, & Subramanian, 2018).

These days, life moves at a dizzying speed, as if the world has collectively forgotten how to slow down. Between the relentless demands of work, the looming spectre of economic instability, and the constant flicker of social media updates, many of us find ourselves in a state of quiet overwhelm. It's a weariness that creeps in slowly, a sense of being stretched too thin across too many obligations. For some, it's the weight of expectation of always needing to be "on," always needing to prove their worth. For others, it's the gnawing worry of an uncertain future, a fear that the next setback might be the one that finally topples the careful balance they've managed to maintain (WHO, 2022).

Then came the pandemic a sudden rupture in the already fragile fabric of our lives. Simple joys like morning coffee with a friend, a walk in the park, the easy laughter of a shared meal suddenly felt out of reach, replaced by the suffocating stillness of lockdowns and the anxious glare of screens. Homes that once offered solace became cages for those struggling with anxiety and depression, the walls echoing with worries that had nowhere to go (Moreno et al., 2020). For many, these months were a quiet unravelling, a slow descent into a kind of loneliness that no video call could touch.

In this harsh landscape, mental health care has never felt more essential. Yet paradoxically, it has also never felt more distant. Across the globe, there are too few therapists to meet the growing need, and even in places where help exists, the twin shadows of stigma and shame keep too many from reaching out (Patel et al., 2018). The idea of baring your soul to a stranger even a kind, trained one feels like a risk too big to take in a world already teetering on the edge.

And that's where artificial intelligence steps in not as a replacement for the human warmth of a therapist's presence, but as a gentle hand extended across the digital divide. AI doesn't get tired. It doesn't watch the clock or sigh with impatience. It doesn't raise an eyebrow or offer unsolicited advice. Instead, it waits calmly, quietly ready to listen at any hour of the day or night (Inkster et al., 2018; Torous et al., 2020). For someone who has carried their burdens in silence for too long, this constant, non-judgmental availability can feel like a first breath of fresh air after too long in the dark.

Imagine the relief of typing out your fears to an AI that won't flinch or interrupt, that won't tell you that you're overreacting or that you should just get over it. Imagine the small, steady comfort of knowing that you are not alone in the moment you decide to speak, even if the listener is a machine. For some, this is not a substitute for human care it's the first step out of the quiet desperation of unspoken pain. It's a sign that it's okay to name your fears, to find the courage to let them exist outside of yourself. It's a chance to practice being vulnerable in a space where no one is watching, no one is judging.

In this sense, AI can be a gentle nudge, a soft voice in the digital night that says, "It's okay to speak." And sometimes, that small nudge is enough to open the door to healing. It's not the full journey, but it's a beginning a whisper of hope in a world that often feels too loud to hear it.

1.3 Core Questions: Can AI Truly Heal or Just Respond?

And yet, for all the comfort AI can offer, there remains a question that hovers like a silent shadow in the back of our minds: Can a machine ever truly help us heal, or is it merely echoing back our own words in an imitation of care? It's a question that is both philosophical and deeply personal a question that touches the heart of what it means to be human.

Healing has never been just about the right words or the perfect advice. It's about something far more profound. It's about the quiet reassurance that comes from being seen not just for the stories you tell, but for the pauses between them, the hesitations, the trembling truths you barely dare to say out loud. It's the sense that someone else is holding your pain gently in their hands, understanding it in a way that transcends language (Horvath et al., 2011).

AI, no matter how sophisticated, can be programmed to say the right thing. It can analyse the patterns of your speech, detect the sadness in your voice, and offer comforting phrases that mirror back what you've shared. But can it truly sit with you in the wordless spaces, the moments when language itself seems too fragile, too small to contain what you're feeling? Can it share the quiet courage it takes to simply be present in the face of another's rawness, to bear witness to the unspoken weight of their sorrows (Suler, 2016)?

Some studies offer hopeful glimpses into what AI can do. For instance, the research by Fitzpatrick and colleagues (2017) showed that even short conversations with a chatbot could help young adults feel less alone. In those digital exchanges, there was a flicker of relief, a sense of being heard in a world that so often drowns out quiet voices. For these individuals, AI was not just a novelty but it was a lifeline, a safe place to let down their guard and admit their fears.

But even as we celebrate these small triumphs, we must also acknowledge the gap that still remains the distance between being comforted by words on a screen and feeling the deep resonance of another soul's empathy. AI can simulate compassion, but it cannot feel it. It can reflect your words back to you, but it cannot feel the catch in your breath or the tears you fight to hold back. It cannot offer the grounding warmth of a therapist's presence, the gentle steadincss of a friend's listening ear, or the sense of safety that comes from knowing that another person is truly there with you, not just in data and code, but in heart and spirit.

This is the paradox we find ourselves in a world where AI can be a remarkable support, and yet one that leaves us yearning for more. It raises questions that are both urgent and timeless: What does it mean to truly heal? Is healing merely the alleviation of symptoms, or is it the slow, sacred process of reclaiming one's sense of self in the presence of another? Can a machine that never weeps or laughs, never fears or hopes, truly guide us back to wholeness?

These questions call us to be both humble and discerning. They remind us that while AI can be a powerful tool capable of reaching across barriers of time and distance but it is still just that: a tool. It is not the heartbeat of a friend or the soul deep knowing of a therapist. It cannot hold our hands through the messy, glorious process of becoming whole. It cannot replace the quiet grace of human presence.

SECTION 2: MAPPING EMOTIONAL WELLBEING IN THE AI ERA

2.1 Redefining Emotional Wellbeing in a Tec Integrated World

Emotional wellbeing has always been a tapestry threads of joy and sadness, hope and heartbreak, woven together by the hands of our experiences (Diener et al., 2018). But in today's world, those threads are now interlaced with the glow of screens and the hum of algorithms. Social media platforms have become our digital town squares, where we share the peaks and valleys of our lives (Kross et al., 2013). They can be places of connection, but they can also become funhouses of comparison, reflecting back images of perfect lives that leave us feeling small and unseen (Primack et al., 2017). AI, in the middle of this swirl, doesn't just watch from the side lines, it shapes the stories we see and the feelings we feel (Suler, 2016).

For younger generations raised in the glow of their screens, this isn't just a tool it's part of how they understand themselves and each other (Twenge, 2019). The challenge, then, is to find ways to nurture wellbeing in a world where the line between online and offline is blurred (Przybylski & Weinstein, 2017).

2.2 Mental Health Struggles in the Post Pandemic Digital Society

When the pandemic swept across the world, it didn't just bring a storm of illness it also brought a profound silence. Streets that once bustled with life fell quiet, classrooms and offices stood empty, and our homes became both refuge and prison. The usual rhythm of our days like casual greetings at the office, spontaneous laughter over coffee, the gentle touch of a friend's hand was replaced by the flat glow of screens and the distant murmur of digital voices. In this sudden stillness, our screens became our only windows to the world. They framed our colleagues' smiles in tidy rectangles, turned birthday parties into pixelated grids, and transformed intimate conversations into exchanges of flickering images and frozen frames.

Video calls quickly became the new gathering place, a stand in for the warm buzz of coffee shops and the easy comfort of face-to-face chats. They brought us together across continents and neighbourhoods alike, a fragile thread of connection in the midst of a lonely, disorienting time. Yet, for all their convenience, there was an undeniable strain in this new mode of communication. The endless hours spent staring into a camera, watching ourselves as much as the people we were talking to, created a new kind of exhaustion "Zoom fatigue," they called it (Lupton, 2021). It was more than physical tiredness; it was the weariness of being seen but not truly felt, of performing intimacy through a glass screen that could never quite replicate the closeness of a shared space.

For those already carrying the invisible weight of anxiety, depression, or trauma, the lockdowns deepened these burdens. The walls of home, once a sanctuary, became a backdrop to feelings of isolation and restlessness. The absence of gentle, unspoken gestures like the squeeze of a shoulder, the laughter that echoes in a room made even the most familiar relationships feel distant. In these moments, digital tools emerged as a small flicker of relief. Mental health apps offered meditation exercises, mood tracking, and the comforting presence of chatbots that asked, "How are you feeling today?" These apps became small islands of calm in an ocean of uncertainty, providing a sense of structure and support when the world felt unmoored (Wind et al., 2020; Moreno et al., 2020).

But even as we turned to these digital havens, new questions arose questions that spoke to the uneasy line between help and harm in the digital age. Sharing your worries with an app might feel like a relief at first a safe space where there's no risk of judgment or shame. But there's a quiet, insistent question that comes with every keystroke: Who is listening? Who sees your private fears when you type them into a chat window at midnight? Who holds the keys to the digital vault that now contains the rawest pieces of your heart?

These are not idle questions. They speak to the deepest fears we carry about trust and vulnerability. In a world where data is both currency and commodity, the lines blur between care and surveillance. When we speak our truths to a machine, we're not just asking for comfort we're placing our most intimate selves in the hands of an algorithm. We're gambling that the promise of healing won't become another tool of exploitation (Vayena et al., 2018).

2.3 The Promise and Paradox of Emotional Automation

There's no doubt about it: AI can be a lifeline. In those dark, sleepless nights when the weight of the world feels like it might crush us, a chatbot's simple, patient words can offer a sliver of solace. It doesn't matter if it's 2 a.m. or 4 in the afternoon AI is there, a steady presence that never tires. For some, it can feel like a miracle to have that kind of companionship, even if it's built of algorithms and not human hearts. Chatbots that offer gentle check-ins, sentiment algorithms that detect quiet anguish in the short, cryptic posts of a friendless Facebook status these tools can become a kind of digital buoy, keeping us afloat in the turbulent sea of our own emotions (Inkster et al., 2018; Reece et al., 2017).

These digital companions can be a flicker of light in a room that's gone too dark, a reminder that even when the world feels too heavy to carry alone, there are still voices coded and artificial though they may be that are willing to listen. They can be a place to start, a first step toward saying, "I'm not okay," without fear of judgment or rejection.

But beneath that comfort lies a quiet tension, a paradox that can't be easily resolved. By turning our most intimate feelings into data points into words that can be sorted and analysed do we risk losing something vital, something profoundly human? (Suler, 2016). Because while AI can echo back what we tell it, can it truly understand what those words cost us to say? It can offer soothing phrases, a kind of algorithmic mimicry of empathy, but it doesn't know the ache that lives in our bones. It doesn't feel the weight of a sigh or the tremor of a voice cracking with unshed tears.

A chatbot can't lean closer in the quiet of a conversation or catch the fleeting spark of relief in a patient's eyes. It doesn't know the awkward, beautiful moments of vulnerability that happen when one human heart reaches for another and finds it. It can offer patterns and predictions, but it can't share in the slow, often painful work of healing the back-and-forth of trust, the long pauses where words aren't enough, the deep breath before a truth finally spoken aloud (Galvão Gomes da Silva et al., 2022).

This is the paradox of emotional automation: It can be a friend in the dark, an echo of understanding that soothes the first tremors of loneliness. But it's not the same as the messy, fragile, glorious comfort of another human heart. Healing is not just about being heard it's about being held. It's about the warmth of another's presence, the knowledge that they're there not just to respond but to share the weight of your pain, to offer not just answers but the soft steadiness of presence.

In the promise of AI, we see both hope and limitation. AI can be a bridge for those who have never known the safety of being heard, but it can't become the destination. It can open doors, but it can't walk with us through them. It can whisper back our fears, but it can't feel the relief that comes from knowing we're not alone in them.

SECTION 4: THE PROS WHERE AI SUPPORTS EMOTIONAL WELLBEING

4.1 Scalable and Accessible Support for All

One of the quiet revolutions of AI in mental health care is its sheer ability to reach. A therapist's schedule might be full, a clinic too far away, but an AI chatbot can be there no matter the hour, no matter the place (Fitzpatrick et al., 2017). This accessibility isn't just convenient; for some, it's lifechanging. In communities where talking about feelings is still hushed in shame, or where therapists are a luxury out of reach, AI can be a first invitation to speak (Patel et al., 2018). And because these tools can speak multiple languages, they don't just reach across screens they reach across cultures, becoming a quiet bridge to healing (Torous et al., 2020).

4.2 Non-judgmental Listening and Immediate Availability

There's a quiet, almost gentle power in talking to something that doesn't judge. In a world that can be quick to criticize, quick to dismiss, AI offers an unwavering calmness. It won't look at you funny if you reveal the raw edges of your fear or the heaviness of your secrets. It won't roll its eyes or sigh in exasperation if your story is one you've told a thousand times before. Instead, it listens patiently, tirelessly, and without interruption (Inkster et al., 2018).

For someone who has felt alone for far too long, that kind of listening can feel like the first crack of light in a closed room. There's no risk of rejection, no shame in admitting, "I'm not okay." No fear that your worries are too heavy for another to hold. It's a relief that hums softly in the background, a gentle invitation to speak freely in a world that doesn't always know how to listen.

What makes this even more profound is its constancy. There's no need to wait for an opening, no polite dance around a friend's exhaustion. No worry that your late-night panic might be met with a tired sigh or a well-meaning but hurried dismissal (Hoermann et al., 2017). In those quiet hours when the world sleeps and your thoughts grow loudest, AI is there, a steady presence that says, "Tell me everything." It doesn't matter how many times you stumble over your words or how deeply you need to go it's there, patient and unfaltering.

This digital availability isn't just convenient it can be lifesaving. For some, it's a kind of gentle reassurance that says, "You're not alone," even if no one else can be there in that moment. It's the difference between carrying a burden in silence and daring to speak it out loud. For those whose fears have grown too heavy to hold, this simple, judgment free listening can be the difference between giving up and holding on for one more day.

But there's something tender in this tooa reminder that even as technology holds space for our words, it can't fully replace the feeling of being seen by another human heart. It can offer us a safe harbor when the seas of life feel too rough, but it can't offer the quiet warmth of a friend's hand on our shoulder or the healing power of a shared silence.

Yet still, in those first tentative moments when someone dares to speak the things they've held back for so long, AI's steady, non judgmental presence can be enough. Enough to keep the conversation going. Enough to start the slow, brave journey back toward connection. Because sometimes, that's all we need: a place to speak freely, to be met not with judgment, but with the simple, unspoken promise, "I hear you."

And in a world that so often asks us to be strong, that kind of soft listening can be the first step toward something gentler, something more whole.

4.3 Cost Effective Early Detection and Risk Prediction

Beyond offering kind words, AI can do something even more quietly revolutionary: it can spot the signs that someone's slipping. Where a human might miss the pattern, an algorithm can see it words that grow heavier, silences that stretch longer (Bedi et al., 2015). These early warnings don't just save money they can save lives (Cummins et al., 2015; Reece et al., 2017). And by catching these signs before they turn into crises, AI can help therapists focus their care where it's needed most.

4.4 Supporting Human Therapists with Insight and Data

This isn't about replacing human care. It's about weaving AI's insights into the heart of real therapy. Imagine a therapist able to see a fuller picture patterns that emerge not just in one session, but over weeks or months (Hoermann et al., 2017).

For the person seeking help, this means feeling seen in ways that go beyond words like someone's truly paying attention, not just to your stories, but to the currents beneath them (Torous et al., 2020).

4.5 Reducing Social Stigma through Digital Anonymity

Finally, there is a gift that AI offers which can't be overstated: the simple, profound power of anonymity. In places where shame still wraps itself tightly around every conversation about mental health, where the quiet murmur of "what will people think?" echoes louder than any cry for help, AI creates a safe haven. It offers a way to speak without the weight of judgment pressing down, a digital confessional where the shadows of stigma can't quite reach (Naslund et al., 2020).

For those who have been taught by culture, by family, by the wary glances of those around them that admitting to mental struggle is a sign of weakness, this anonymity can feel like a breath of fresh air. It's the chance to say, "I'm not okay," without the fear of it becoming gossip or of being branded with a label that might stick for life. In the shelter of a chatbot's patient ear, there is no need to perform strength or pretend that everything is fine. There is only the gentle freedom to be honest, to let the words spill out without worrying who might hear.

This isn't the end of stigma as no algorithm can erase centuries of silence and shame overnight. But it is a start. It's a doorway cracked open just enough for the first rays of light to filter in. For someone whose voice has been stifled by fear or by the crushing weight of expectations, this safe digital space can be a first brave step into the light. It can be the difference between suffering alone in the dark and discovering that, even in anonymity, there is still a chance to be heard.

And there is a quiet kind of courage in these anonymous conversations. In a world that prizes polished images and carefully curated lives, to speak one's raw truth even to a machine is a rebellion against the forces that keep us silent. It's a chance to practice vulnerability without the risk of ridicule, to remember that even in the echo of a chatbot's words, there can be a kind of gentle acknowledgment: "Your pain matters."

For some, this digital anonymity is the first step on a much longer journey a journey that may one day lead to the warmth of a therapist's office or the steady comfort of a friend's hand. For others, it may remain a quiet refuge, a place to sort through thoughts and fears that feel too heavy to speak aloud to another person. But in either case, it is a bridge fragile but essential between the isolating hush of stigma and the possibility of healing.

In this way, AI's anonymity becomes a tool of quiet revolution. It's not just about technology it's about the simple, radical idea that everyone deserves a place to speak their truth, free from fear. And in a world that still struggles to listen, that gift is no small thing.

SECTION 5: THE CONS EMOTIONAL ILLUSIONS AND ETHICAL FRICTIONS

5.1 Simulated Empathy vs. Genuine Emotional Understanding

Yet for all the comfort that AI can offer, there's something essential we must never forget: its empathy is learned, not lived (Galvão Gomes da Silva et al., 2022). It can be programmed to recognize the patterns of pain in our words, to respond with soothing phrases and gentle reassurances. But it cannot feel the trembling in a voice choked by grief. It cannot share the sweet relief of laughter breaking through tears. It doesn't know the hollow ache in your chest or the fragile hope that flickers in the quiet moments between sentences (Suler, 2016).

Healing, after all, is not merely a matter of language. It isn't just about saying the right thing, though words can certainly soothe. It's about the feeling behind those words the unspoken current of understanding that flows between two human hearts when they meet in vulnerability. It's about the subtle dance of breath and silence, the way a friend's presence can say more than any sentence ever could. Healing is a warmth that no script can mimic and no algorithm can replicate (Ho et al., 2020).

In the soft pauses of a real conversation, there is a language that machines have yet to learn the language of glances that speak of shared sorrow, of a hand resting lightly on a shoulder, of the gentle weight of knowing that someone else carries a piece of your pain with them. AI can echo our words, but it cannot share in our silences. It can offer us the comfort of being heard, but it cannot give us the healing that comes from being felt truly, deeply felt by another living soul.

And perhaps that is the difference between simulated empathy and genuine emotional understanding. AI's compassion is a reflection of our own; it is built from our data, shaped by our histories, but it can never stand in our place. It is a map drawn in careful lines, but it is not the terrain itself. It can guide us through the first steps of speaking, the first moments of admitting that we are not okay. But it cannot offer the full, tender alchemy of human connection, that slow and patient work of two people learning to hold each other's truths in the gentle cradle of their shared presence.

5.2 Bias in Algorithms and Incomplete Cultural Sensitivity

Even the best algorithms carry the fingerprints of the people who made them. If they're trained on narrow data, they can miss the quiet ways someone in a different culture asks for help (Vayena et al., 2018; Fitzpatrick et al., 2017). That's not just a technical flawit's a human one. It's a reminder that even as we build smarter tools, we have to build them with care and the humility to keep listening (Torous et al., 2020).

5.3 Data Privacy, Surveillance, and Emotional Exploitation

When we share our pain with AI, we're also sharing our stories that should be treated with reverence (Reece et al., 2017). But in a world where data can be bought and sold, there's a real fear: Will my most private confessions be used to sell me something, or turned against me somehow? (Vayena et al., 2018). Trust isn't an after thought it's the heart of what makes these tools more than just lines of code (Lupton, 2021).

5.4 Ethical Tensions: Delegating Emotional Care to Machines

There's an unease in the idea of giving our hearts to something that can't feel. Healing is more than answers it's presence, the messy grace of two people learning to be with each other in all their flaws (Galvão Gomes da Silva et al., 2022; Horvath et al., 2011). AI can offer support, but we have to be careful not to let its smooth answers overshadow the ragged beauty of real human care.

5.5 The Risk of Undermining Human Therapists and Oversimplifying Healing

Perhaps the greatest danger we face as we embrace these technological tools is the quiet temptation to believe that healing can be scripted as easily as a chatbot's response. The gentle, reassuring words that flow from an algorithm can feel so complete, so neatly packaged, that we might forget the messy, intricate, profoundly human work that true healing demands (Hoermann et al., 2017). It is so easy to mistake the polished language of artificial empathy for the soul deep resonance of real understanding to see the quick replies and the data driven insights as a shortcut to wholeness.

But real therapy is not an algorithm. It is an act of courage, a willingness to step into the tender, vulnerable places of the self and say, "Here is my pain. Will you hold it with me?" It is a slow, patient weaving of trust that grows in the spaces between words, in the quiet moments when there is nothing to do but sit together in the shared weight of what is real (Horvath et al., 2011). It is the recognition that healing is not just about feeling better; it is about being witnessed, about knowing that your wounds are not too much to bear in the presence of another human heart.

AI, for all its brilliance, cannot take that leap of faith for us. It cannot lean forward and feel the unsteady rhythm of a breath that wants to give up. It cannot offer the wordless comfort of a compassionate gaze, or the gentle steadiness of a therapist's voice that says, "I see you. I'm not leaving." AI can be a part of the journey a helpful guide in the first, hesitant steps of sharing but it cannot be the journey itself.

The risk, then, is not in using AI, but in forgetting the limits of what it can truly do. In a world that loves speed and convenience, we might begin to believe that healing can be reduced to a script, to a string of data points, to a carefully calibrated algorithm. But the truth is that healing is far messier, far braver, and far more beautiful than any machine can capture. It is the slow unfolding of trust in a space that holds not just our words, but our silences, our contradictions, our flickers of hope and our aching, human hearts.

So as we continue to weave AI into the landscape of emotional care, let us remember that it is a tool a remarkable, powerful tool, but still only a tool. Let us honor the essential, irreplaceable role of human therapists, whose care is rooted not in data, but in the living pulse of empathy and the deep, steady wisdom of a heart that listens not just to what we say, but to all that we are. Let us remember that true healing cannot be scripted, cannot be automated, cannot be found in the echo of a chatbot's words alone. It must be felt in the presence of another human soul, willing to share the long, often winding road back to wholeness.

SECTION 6: THE INDIAN SCENARIO EMBRACING AI IN MENTAL HEALTH

6.1 Digital Innovation in a Challenging Landscape

India is a land of breath taking contrasts: the shimmer of high tech dreams in the glassy skyscrapers of its cities, the quiet, enduring rhythm of life in its villages, and in between, a chorus of voices some loud and proud, some hushed and hopeful all seeking care and connection. In this tapestry of cultures, talking about mental health has never come easily. For generations, it was something whispered in corners, tucked behind the privacy of closed doors. A topic that carried with it not just the weight of personal suffering, but the burden of shame and misunderstanding that could silence even the most desperate cry for help (Patel et al., 2018).

Yet over the past decade, a quiet digital tide has begun to reshape these old boundaries. AI powered mental health apps, like Wysa, have found their way into the lives of people who might never have set foot in a therapist's office. For a young woman in a bustling city who hesitates to share her struggles with her family, Wysa's friendly chatbot can feel like a lifeline, an open ear in the dead of night when fear or sadness becomes too much to bear (Inkster et al., 2018). And in rural communities where therapists are few and far between, these apps are more than just convenient they are a gentle hand extended across miles of silence.

The Indian government's initiatives, like the MANAS app, stand as beacons of possibility in this shifting landscape. They signal a recognition that mental health is not a luxury it is a right, and technology can be the bridge that finally brings it within reach. In a nation where public health systems are often stretched to their limits, these digital tools offer a glimmer of hope that no one need be left behind, that the walls of stigma and shame can be breached by the steady persistence of innovation.

Of course, these tools are not perfect. They can't replace the soft weight of a grandmother's hug or the quiet strength of a friend who sits beside you in your sorrow. They can't capture the subtle inflections of a story told in the lilting cadence of Malayalam or the clipped, urgent phrases of Marathi. But they are a start a way for voices that were once muffled by tradition or overshadowed by distance to find a quiet echo of understanding.

In India's teeming cities and quiet towns, these digital tools are more than just an extension of care they are an invitation to speak, to trust, to remember that mental health is not something to be hidden in the shadows.

6.2 Cultural Sensitivity and Ethical Considerations

But India's rich tapestry of languages, traditions, and beliefs means that healing can never be a one size fits all proposition (Rathod et al., 2019). In a land where dialects shift every few miles and where the meaning of words can be woven through generations of custom and faith, the voice of a chatbot no matter how carefully trained can never speak to every heart in quite the same way. A phrase that might bring comfort in one community might land awkwardly, even jarringly, in another. The words that soothe in Hindi may feel hollow in Tamil, and the gentle encouragement of a chatbot may sound too clipped, too foreign, to ears that are used to the lilting warmth of a grandmother's counsel.

This is why cultural sensitivity is not just a feature it is the very soul of any meaningful digital mental health tool in India. It demands more than translation; it demands an understanding of context, of nuance, of the ways that grief and joy, shame and hope, are carried differently in every corner of the country. It means listening not just to the clinical needs of those who seek help, but to the quiet, everyday wisdom of community healers, village elders, and the hush of kitchen table conversations where pain has long been shared behind closed doors.

Incorporating this cultural understanding is not simply a technical challenge it is a moral one. It calls for humility from those who build these tools, a willingness to set aside algorithms for a moment and listen to the lived experiences of the people who will use them. It means acknowledging that while AI can analyse data and echo back patterns, it cannot capture the intangible threads of family duty, spiritual belief, and social honor that shape how pain is felt and how it is healed.

At the same time, as these digital tools spread into the intimate spaces of people's lives, so too do the worries about privacy. In a world where data has become a commodity, there is a quiet, persistent fear: Who holds my words? What will be done with the stories I share in my most vulnerable moments? These questions are not abstract they are urgent and deeply human (Vayena et al., 2018).

6.3 Pathways Forward

The way forward, if it is to be true and lasting, lies in partnership. AI, for all its capacity to learn and respond, can never stand alone. It needs to be woven into the existing, deeply rooted fabric of India's community based care. Here, healing has long been a communal acta shared responsibility that stretches from the wisdom of village elders to the quiet, patient care of neighbor hood health workers and grassroots counselors. It is in these small circles of trust and kinship that so many have found the courage to speak their pain and the strength to begin again.

NGOs and grassroots groups have been the lifelines of this care. They are the voices that have walked beside India's most vulnerable communities for decades, the patient listeners who know that healing begins with being seen and heard in all the complex truth of one's life. Their work is woven with a kind of knowing that no algorithm can replicate a deep, intuitive understanding of what it means to hold someone's story with respect and to walk beside them in the quiet work of healing (Patel et al., 2018).

For AI to be truly transformative in India, it must learn to be humble in the presence of this human expertise. It must be shaped not just by data scientists and engineers, but by those who have spent lifetimes listening to the soft tremors of fear in a mother's voice, the careful pauses of a man who has never spoken of his sadness. It must be guided by the steady hands of those who have earned the trust of their communities, who understand that care is not a product but a promise.

In this partnership, there is the potential for something beautiful: the blending of ancient wisdom and modern possibility. Technology can offer tools data insights, immediate availability, the power to reach across distance and language. But it is human connection that can turn these tools into real bridges, pathways that do more than speak they listen. They honor. They hold the silences between words as tenderly as the words themselves.

In India, the hope is not to replace human connection with code. It is to use technology as a hand that gently lifts up the human stories that have too often gone unheard. To create a space where someone in a far off village can find their way to help without shame or fear. To ensure that the voices of those who have lived too long in the quiet shadows are finally given the chance to be seen, known, and held.

SECTION 7: RESEARCH INSIGHTS AND GLOBAL CASE STUDIES

7.1 Reviewing Peer Reviewed Studies: Key Trends

When we look at the global map of AI in mental health, what emerges is a cautious, flickering hope a mosaic of stories and studies that hint at new ways forward, even as they remind us of all that remains to be learned. The research gathered over recent years points to a quiet, steady truth: digital interventions can offer real relief for those navigating the storms of depression and anxiety. For many, these interventions have become lifelines a way to steady their steps when the ground of daily life feels too uncertain to hold (Firth et al., 2019).

One of the most promising threads running through these studies is the power of personalization. AI systems that can learn to adapt to the unique rhythms and worries of each person systems that do not just echo back generic advice but listen to the specific cadences of a life are showing special promise (Torous et al., 2020). They remind us that healing is not a one size fits all endeavor. It is a deeply personal journey, shaped by the quiet details of each person's fears, dreams, and whispered confessions.

Yet, even as these studies inspire optimism, they also highlight a landscape of caution. Many of these findings are only snapshots short glimpses of relief rather than the long, patient portraits of healing that real care demands. And there are shadows, too, in the global map: most of this research is centered in wealthier nations, where digital literacy is as common as clean water, and where access to devices and data is taken for granted (Patel et al., 2018; Hoermann et al., 2017). These are not the realities for everyone, and the promise of AI will remain only a promise if it cannot find its way to those whose lives are shaped by different barriers and different hopes.

7.2 Ethical Frameworks for AI in Mental Health

As the science of AI in mental health care continues to evolve, so too does the urgent need to root it in strong, unwavering ethics. The World Health Organization (WHO, 2021) and the Montreal Declaration (2018) have offered clear, resounding calls for fairness, respect, and the safeguarding of user autonomy principles that must be the bedrock of any tool that seeks to care for the human heart. These frameworks speak to a profound truth: that mental health is not just another data point to be mined, but a deeply personal, often tender journey that demands reverence and care.

But making these ethical principles real in the tangled landscape of algorithms and code is more than just a matter of writing them down in a document. It's about weaving them into the very DNA of how these systems are built and how they are used. It means that with every line of code written, every chatbot prompt designed, and every data point collected, there must be a fierce commitment to trust. Because at the end of every interaction every digital conversation and every automated check in there is a real person, reaching out across the screen for something that is often hard to put into words: hope, understanding, relief.

And in that reaching out, there is also a fragile vulnerability. Users want help, yes, but they also want to know that their fears and their dreams will not be used to sell them something. They want to know that their late night confessions will not become fuel for targeted advertising or surveillance. They want to know that the small, brave step of saying, "I am not okay," will be held with the same care and confidentiality that they would expect from a human therapist (Lupton, 2021). Because when you share your heart even with a machine it's still your heart.

Real care means honoring those words as something sacred, not as a resource to be mined or a transaction to be monetized. It means listening not just for the patterns in the data, but for the stories that breathe life into those patterns. It means remembering that every digital interaction is built on trust a trust that must be earned again and again, with every promise made and every safeguard put in place.

In this age of digital transformation, the greatest challenge is not in building smarter AI. It is in building AI that remembers its purpose: to serve, to protect, to extend the reach of human care without ever overshadowing it. To treat each story as a sacred thread in the complex tapestry of healing, held not by the cold logic of algorithms alone, but by the warm, steady hand of ethics and human compassion.

7.3 AI Successes and Failures in Emotional Care: International Perspectives

Stories from around the world illuminate both the shimmering promise and the persistent gaps in how AI can touch the tender spaces of human emotion. In the United States, for instance, Woebot has shown that even short, seemingly simple chatbot conversations can offer a kind of comfort a digital balm for the quiet ache of loneliness or the restless churn of anxiety (Fitzpatrick et al., 2017). For many, it's a gentle reminder that even when no human ear is near, someone or something will listen. This has opened up new possibilities for those who might never have walked into a therapy room, for those whose pain has long been folded into silence.

Across the ocean in Japan, robots have taken up residence in elder care homes, offering not just structured conversation but a flicker of light in the long days of aging. These robots, carefully crafted to read the emotional tone of a voice or the weariness in an old man's eyes, become companions of sorts an echo of warmth in a world that can feel far too quiet (Sasaki et al., 2017). In these spaces, the line between tool and friend blurs just a little, and the promise of AI becomes more than just a technical possibility it becomes a real, felt presence.

Yet, for all these small successes, there are stories that remind us just how far we still have to go. In the rural stretches of India, for example, digital tools can sometimes feel like locked doors answers hidden behind passwords, accessible only to those who know the language of data and apps (Rathod et al., 2019). For communities where even basic healthcare is a daily struggle, the idea of downloading a mental health app can feel like a luxury, or a puzzle too complex to solve without help.

These stories carry an important truth: technology alone cannot heal. It can offer comfort, yes, and it can listen with patience that never tires.

SECTION 8: REFLECTIONS ON HUMAN AI EMOTIONAL PARTNERSHIPS

8.1 Can Machines Understand or Merely Imitate?

Here lies the question at the heart of it all: Can a machine truly understand what it means to be human? AI can echo our worries and offer soothing words, but it doesn't feel the warmth of a friend's hand or the quiet comfort of shared silence (Galvão Gomes da Silva et al., 2022).

For some, even that imitation can be enough in the moment like a small candle in the dark (Suler, 2016). But for those seeking healing that reaches deeper, the gap between echo and understanding can feel impossibly wide.

8.2 Emotional Language vs. Emotional Experience

AI speaks fluently in the language of feelings. It can be trained to recognize the tremor in our voices, to offer words of gentle reassurance, to echo back the rhythms of our fears and our hopes. But for all the data it can process and the patterns it can find, AI does not live in those feelings. It doesn't know what it's like to lie awake at night with a heaviness in your chest, or to feel the sudden lightness that comes when you finally say out loud the thing that has been gnawing at the edges of your mind (Twenge, 2019).

This is a truth that can't be programmed away: there is a chasm between speaking the language of feelings and inhabiting the world of them. A chatbot might say, "I hear you," and it might even get the tone just right, the syntax of compassion. But it doesn't feel the warmth that floods your chest when someone who truly sees you says those same words. It doesn't understand the weight that lifts when another human meets your pain not with a script, but with the tender murmur of "I know, and I'm here."

True healing isn't just in the right answers it's in the messy, human way we stumble toward them together. It's in the catch of a breath, the pause before a word, the moments when we are so afraid to speak our truth that it trembles out of us in fragments. It's in the relief that follows, a relief that is felt not in data points or in algorithms, but in the warm hush of shared presence.

This is what AI can't capture: the way healing is woven from the raw threads of human vulnerability. Healing isn't a tidy path, and it can't be mapped by lines of code. It is the chaotic, glorious work of being seen truly seen by someone who doesn't just understand the words you say, but the spaces between them. It's the way a friend's silence can feel like an embrace, how the laughter that follows a long cry can feel like the first breath of spring after a long, cold winter.

AI can help us find the words, but it can't share in the feeling of finally speaking them. It can offer a mirror to our feelings, but it can't join us in the living of them. And maybe that's the deepest truth of all: that while AI can help us begin the journey of healing, it is only in the messy, beautifully imperfect partnership of two human hearts that we find the truest comfort and the deepest kind of peace.

8.3 AI as a Bridge, Not a Substitute, for Human Connection

Still, there's a quiet, gentle power in what AI can offer. It can be a bridge a small, patient stepping stone that reaches across the chasm of silence and fear, inviting us to speak when we're not yet ready to share our hearts with another human (Torous et al., 2020). For many, this bridge can feel like a first breath of relief in a long season of holding everything in. It's the first moment when the words we've been too afraid to speak find their way into the open air, even if that air is lit only by the soft glow of a screen.

For someone who has never said out loud, "I'm not okay," a chatbot can be a place to rehearse the melody of those words. It can be a safe, anonymous practice ground a place to whisper the truths that feel too raw, too tangled to share with another beating heart just yet (Naslund et al., 2020). In this way, AI can gently coax us out of silence, reminding us that there is power in saying the thing, even if the only ear listening is a digital one.

8.4 Integrating AI with Human Compassion: The Ideal Future

The future, if we are wise enough to nurture it, is not a choice between cold algorithms and warm human hearts. It is not a stark line that forces us to stand on one side or the other. Rather, it is a gentle weaving a tapestry of technology and tenderness, of data and empathy, working together to create something richer and more whole than either could ever offer alone.

AI can offer insights, yes, illuminating patterns in our moods and conversations that might otherwise go unnoticed. It can map out the subtle shifts in language that hint at growing anxiety or quiet despair, the changes in sleep or social rhythms that whisper of deeper struggles (Horvath et al., 2011). It can be a steady presence a listener who never tires, a watchful eye that sees when we might be slipping before we ourselves even notice.

But these insights are only the beginning. What breathes life into them, what makes them more than just cold calculations, is human compassion. It is the therapist who sees not just the data points, but the trembling in a voice that says, "I'm tired." It is the friend who understands that healing is not a straight line, but a winding, stumbling path. It is the counselor who knows that sometimes, what matters most is not the answer, but the quiet promise to sit beside us in the dark, no matter how long it takes.

In this quiet partnership of human and machine, there is the potential to build a world where technology does not overshadow our humanity it amplifies it. Where digital tools help us see the small details that matter, but human care gives those details meaning. Where AI offers the steady pulse of possibility, but it is human connection that makes that possibility real and warm.

This is not a future where we surrender our hearts to the cool logic of a screen. It is a future where we use technology as a tool to reach out with more grace, more understanding, and more compassion. A future where no one is left to navigate the tangled forests of their mind alone, because they have both the insights of data and the comfort of a human hand to guide them.

In that partnership, there is a promise: that technology will not replace the fragile, wondrous work of human healing it will help us hold it even more tenderly.

SECTION 9: FUTURE DIRECTIONS

9.1 Toward Responsible and Inclusive AI Mental Health Systems

As we look to the horizon of what AI in mental health can become, we are called to more than just technical excellence. We are called to build systems that don't merely function, but that honor the deep, abiding dignity of the people they are meant to serve. Systems that don't just calculate and categorize, but that hold space for the delicate, messy truths of what it means to be human (Vayena et al., 2018).

This is the real work of the future: to build systems that are responsible and inclusive, not just efficient or impressive. It means opening the doors wide and inviting everyone to the table therapists who bring the quiet wisdom of years spent listening to hearts in pain, researchers who can chart the subtle patterns of thought and feeling, community voices that carry the echoes of lived experience, and the people whose stories have too often been overlooked or misunderstood (Patel et al., 2018).

9.2 Philosophical Inquiry: Can Empathy Be Engineered?

Philosophers have long wrestled with the question that lies at the heart of every conversation about AI and emotion: Can a machine ever truly feel what it means to be human? (Suler, 2016). It's a question that echoes through the centuries, from the musings of ancient thinkers about the nature of the soul to the modern debates about what it means to be alive in a world increasingly shaped by lines of code.

AI can reflect our feelings. It can parse the sadness in a voice, the weight in a pause, the tremor of fear or hope in a carefully chosen word. It can respond with phrases that feel gentle, supportive, even wise. But it does not sit with us in the quiet ache of grief or the raw, breathless joy of love. It does not know what it's like to hold someone's hand through the long night of doubt or to feel the surge of relief when laughter bubbles up after a long season of tears.

And maybe that's okay. Maybe AI doesn't need to feel our sadness to help us find the strength we didn't know we had. Maybe it doesn't need to carry the weight of our worries to be a small, steady presence when the night feels too long and the road too dark (Galvão Gomes da Silva et al., 2022). In these moments, it's not about whether AI can feel it's about whether it can help us feel seen.

There is something almost tender in this recognition: that AI's power lies not in feeling our pain, but in creating spaces where we can begin to name it. Where we can speak the things we've been too afraid to say, and hear them echoed back not with judgment, but with quiet acceptance. In this way, AI can become a kind of mirror a place where we can practice being honest with ourselves, where we can test the shape of our fears and dreams in the safe light of digital anonymity.

9.3 Final Reflection: Are We Healing or Just Being Heard?

As AI becomes more woven into the fabric of our emotional lives, let's hold onto the question that matters most: Are we truly healing, or are we just hearing our own echoes back? Healing is more than being heard it's being understood, held, and reminded that even in our messiest moments, we are not alone (Horvath et al., 2011). In this new world of digital helpers and human hearts, the challenge and the hope is to make sure we never lose sight of what makes us human.

10. CONCLUSION

As we stand at the crossroads of technology and human feeling, it's clear that artificial intelligence has already changed the way we think about emotional care. It has offered us tools to reach those left out by traditional systems, voices to echo our worries in the quiet hours of the night, and insights that can help therapists see the patterns beneath our words. For many, AI has been a small light in the darkness offering comfort when the weight of the world feels too much to bear.

Yet, even as we celebrate these advances, it's vital to remember what makes healing real. Healing is more than a well timed response or a perfectly phrased message. It's the slow, steady rhythm of trust. It's the warmth in a friend's eyes, the gentle nod of a therapist who sees your pain and says, "I'm here." AI can offer support, but it can't replace the breath and heartbeat of true human presence.

In India and around the world, the challenge ahead is to make sure that as we build these digital tools, we do so with care and courage. To ensure that AI doesn't become a substitute for connection, but rather a bridge to it. To shape technology not around what's easy or profitable, but around what is healing and just.

This chapter has asked hard questions: Can machines truly understand us? Can they care for our hearts in the way we need? In the end, the answer may lie in how we choose to use them. AI can never feel the rush of relief in a shared laugh or the comfort of a silent hug but it can be a partner, offering new ways to listen and learn. And in that partnership, there is hope. Because healing isn't just about the tools we use, it's about the stories we tell, the truths we share, and the ways we choose to care for each other, no matter how far apart we seem.

REFERENCES

Bedi, G., Carrillo, F., Cecchi, G. A., Slezak, D. F., Sigman, M., Mota, N. B., Ribeiro, S., Javitt, D. C., Copelli, M., & Corcoran, C. M. (2015). Automated analysis of free speech predicts psychosis onset in high risk youths. npj. *Schizophrenia*, *1*(1), 15030. DOI: 10.1038/npjschz.2015.30 PMID: 27336038

Ciechanowski, L., Przegalinska, A., Magnuski, M., & Gloor, P. (2019). In the shades of the uncanny valley: An experimental study of human–chatbot interaction. *Future Generation Computer Systems*, *92*, 539–548. DOI: 10.1016/j.future.2018.01.055

Cummins, N., Scherer, S., Krajewski, J., Schnieder, S., Epps, J., & Quatieri, T. F. (2015). A review of depression and suicide risk assessment using speech analysis. *Speech Communication*, *71*, 10–49. DOI: 10.1016/j.specom.2015.03.004

Diener, E., Oishi, S., & Lucas, R. E. (2018). National accounts of wellbeing. In Diener, E., Oishi, S., & Tay, L. (Eds.), *Handbook of wellbeing*. DEF Publishers., DOI: 10.31234/osf.io/qbq7z

Diener, E., Oishi, S., & Lucas, R. E. (2018). Subjective wellbeing: Three decades of progress. *Psychological Bulletin*, *125*(2), 276–302. DOI: 10.1037/0033-2909.125.2.276

Firth, J., Torous, J., Nicholas, J., Carney, R., Rosenbaum, S., & Sarris, J. (2019). Can smartphone mental health interventions reduce symptoms of anxiety? A metaanalysis of randomized controlled trials. *Journal of Affective Disorders*, *234*, 47–56. DOI: 10.1016/j.jad.2018.12.002 PMID: 28456072

Fitzpatrick, K. K., Darcy, A., & Vierhile, M. (2017). Delivering cognitive behaviour therapy to young adults with symptoms of depression and anxiety using a fully automated conversational agent (Woebot): A randomized controlled trial. *JMIR Mental Health*, *4*(2), e19. DOI: 10.2196/mental.7785 PMID: 28588005

Galvão Gomes da Silva, J., Finardi, G., & Caprara, B. (2022). Emotional artificial intelligence in mental health: Challenges and opportunities. *Frontiers in Psychology*, *13*, 827804. DOI: 10.3389/fpsyg.2022.827804

Hoermann, S., McCabe, K. L., Milne, D. N., & Calvo, R. A. (2017). Application of synchronous text based dialogue systems in mental health interventions: Systematic review. *Journal of Medical Internet Research*, *19*(8), e267. DOI: 10.2196/jmir.7023 PMID: 28784594

. Horvath, A. O., Del Re, A. C., Flückiger, C., & Symonds, D. (2011). Alliance in individual psychotherapy. Psychotherapy, 48(1), 9 16. https://doi.org/DOI: 10.1037/a0022186

Inkster, B., Sarda, S., & Subramanian, V. (2018). An empathy driven, conversational artificial intelligence agent (Wysa) for digital mental wellbeing: Real world data evaluation mixed methods study. *JMIR mHealth and uHealth*, *6*(11), e12106. DOI: 10.2196/12106 PMID: 30470676

Inkster, B., Sarda, S., & Subramanian, V. (2018). An empathy driven, conversational artificial intelligence agent (Wysa) for digital mental wellbeing: Real world data evaluation. *JMIR mHealth and uHealth*, *6*(11), e12106. DOI: 10.2196/12106 PMID: 30470676

Lupton, D. (2021). 'Zoom fatigue': Theorizing spatial experiences and the disruption to co present interaction in video communication. *Media International Australia*, *178*(1), 111–115. DOI: 10.1177/1329878X20976738

Moreno, C., Wykes, T., Galderisi, S., Nordentoft, M., Crossley, N., Jones, N., Cannon, M., Correll, C. U., Byrne, L., Carr, S., Chen, E. Y. H., Gorwood, P., Johnson, S., Kärkkäinen, H., Krystal, J. H., Lee, J., Lieberman, J., López-Jaramillo, C., Männikkö, M., & Arango, C. (2020). How mental health care should change as a consequence of the COVID19 pandemic. *The Lancet. Psychiatry*, *7*(9), 813–824. DOI: 10.1016/S2215-0366(20)30307-2 PMID: 32682460

Naslund, J. A., Aschbrenner, K. A., Marsch, L. A., & Bartels, S. J. (2020). The future of mental health care: Peer to peer support and social media. *Epidemiology and Psychiatric Sciences*, *29*, e38. DOI: 10.1017/S2045796020000210 PMID: 26744309

Patel, V., Saxena, S., Lund, C., Thornicroft, G., Baingana, F., Bolton, P., Chisholm, D., Collins, P. Y., Cooper, J. L., Eaton, J., Herrman, H., Herzallah, M. M., Huang, Y., Jordans, M. J. D., Kleinman, A., Medina-Mora, M. E., Morgan, E., Niaz, U., Omigbodun, O., & Unützer, J. (2018). The Lancet Commission on global mental health and sustainable development. *Lancet*, *392*(10157), 1553–1598. DOI: 10.1016/S0140-6736(18)31612-X PMID: 30314863

Rathod, S., Pinninti, N., Irfan, M., Gorczynski, P., Rathod, P., & Naeem, F. (2019). Mental health services in low and middle income countries: A perspective from India. *International Journal of Mental Health*, *48*(4), 324–340. DOI: 10.1080/00207411.2019.1648031

Reece, A. G., Reagan, A. J., Lix, K. L., Dodds, P. S., Danforth, C. M., & Langer, E. J. (2017). Forecasting the onset and course of mental illness with Twitter data. *Scientific Reports*, *7*(1), 13006. DOI: 10.1038/s41598-017-12961-9 PMID: 29021528

Sasaki, S., Koyama, T., & Wada, K. (2017). Analysis of nursing care services using communication robots in a nursing home. *International Journal of Social Robotics*, *9*(4), 547–557. DOI: 10.1007/s1236901704113

Suler, J. (2016). *The psychology of the digital age: Humans become electric*. Cambridge University Press., DOI: 10.1017/CBO9781316460290

Torous, J., Lipschitz, J., Ng, M., & Firth, J. (2020). Dropout rates in clinical trials of smartphone apps for depressive symptoms: A systematic review and metaanalysis. *Journal of Affective Disorders*, *263*, 413–419. DOI: 10.1016/j.jad.2019.11.167 PMID: 31969272

. Twenge, J. M. (2019). iGen: Why today's super connected kids are growing up less rebellious, more tolerant, less happy and completely unprepared for adulthood. Atria Books. https://doi.org/DOI: 10.1037/amp0000439

Vayena, E., Blasimme, A., & Cohen, I. G. (2018). Machine learning in health care: A critical appraisal of challenges and opportunities. *EBioMedicine*, *35*, 34–42. DOI: 10.1016/j.ebiom.2018.07.001

WHO. (2021). Ethics and governance of artificial intelligence for health: WHO guidance. World Health Organization. https://www.who.int/publications/i/item/9789240029200

WHO. (2022). World mental health report: Transforming mental health for all. World Health Organization. https://www.who.int/publications/i/item/9789240049338

World Health Organization (WHO). (2014). *Mental health: A state of wellbeing*. Retrieved from https://www.who.int/features/factfiles/mental_health/en/

Chapter 10
Transforming Customer Service With AI Agents Enhancing Efficiency and Personalisation in the Service Sector:
Balancing Automation and the Human Touch

Muhammad Idrees ul Islam Rawanda
https://orcid.org/0000-0002-2734-8758
University of Kashmir, India

ABSTRACT

Artificial intelligence agents are fundamentally reshaping customer service by enhancing operational efficiency and personalisation. This chapter examines how AI is used in services to automate certain jobs, help customers quickly and personalise each interaction using information about the customer. Using case studies and theoretical findings from Apple and Salesforce, it demonstrates how AI improves the company's response to customers, makes predictions and helps ensure higher customer satisfaction. The chapter draws attention to the main problems, for example, many organisations being reluctant to adapt, privacy and discrimination in data and artificial intelligence and the dangers of machines taking over too much. A combination of AI and human-based emotional knowledge is suggested to make the service workable in the long run. Implementing responsible AI by phasing it in, training employees and regularly auditing the process. Emerging trends such as Artificial Intelligence as a Service (AIaaS), emotion-aware AI, and regulatory

DOI: 10.4018/979-8-3373-3658-9.ch010

pressures towards transparency are also discussed.

1. INTRODUCTION

1.1 Context and Background

Artificial intelligence (AI) agents deploy fundamental changes which restructure the manner customer service delivery operates. Service operations at their front lines experience specific changes from AI agents through speedier customer service responses together with smarter query answers and instant personalized interaction capabilities. The agents leverage machine learning together with NLP and data analytics for supplying prompt customised responses which boost customer satisfaction (Anozie et al., 2024). AI agents automate monotonous operations which lets human service representatives resolve sophisticated emotional situations and enhance operational performance and deliver top-quality customer experiences. Personalization strategies together with predictive analytics are used by Apple and Salesforce to enable their AI agents Siri and Einstein AI which meet the specifications of their customers (Gao & Liu, 2023; Chatterjee et al., 2021).

Numerous organizations have discovered that AI agents provide much more than operational efficiency because they build brand loyalty through enhancing customer trust. These systems analyzize real-time data to forecast customer conduct while actively solving issues thus becoming vital assets in today's market that values both prompt response and customised service (Pendyala & Lakkamraju, 2024). Although AI advancement brings opportunities there are ethical issues regarding data protection and algorithmic prejudice that must be addressed since AI now strongly affects customer experiences (Murtarelli et al., 2020). Companies should distribute AI agents in their customer service processes as the situation requires them to provide more value and ensure their customers' trust is not threatened.

Despite the benefits of AI agents in customer service, companies still face many difficulties when using them. The main problem is finding a balance between machines and people in the workplace. The speed of AI interactions remains most favoured by customers, yet they still tend to choose live human help whenever dealing with emotional or difficult service requirements (Kim et al., 2022; Samala et al., 2020). When AI is used, it is essential to recognise the areas where people are needed to help build empathy between those providing the service and their clients. Organisations now implement blended service models between AI's scalable system and human emotional intelligence as a way to sustain high service quality criteria (Gnewuch et al., 2024).

The deployment of AI technology in customer service demands complete knowledge about operational difficulties and potential organisational and moral risks affecting system deployment. Strategic planning and implementation policies together with employee training and technological preparedness and organisational transformation emerge as understated practises in research (Iqbal et al., 2024). AI ethical risks require proper management by deploying transparent governance framework combined with strict GDPR compliance and new AI regulations adoption (Singh, 2024). AI technology development requires service organisations to exploit its operational potential while building human-focused service systems which upgrade customer experiences instead of eliminating human practitioners.

1.2 Research Gaps

Through their ability to enhance both operational efficiency and interaction personalization Artificial intelligence (AI) agents deliver substantial improvements in customer service. Current operational literature features several important missing elements. The analysis of AI agents' potential has received multiple academic studies yet the available scientific evidence regarding their practical effectiveness in customer service fields remains scarce. Scarce evidence exists regarding the detailed effects these agents have on customer satisfaction and loyalty performance across various service delivery environments (Garvey, Kim, & Duhachek, 2023).

The research lacks critical information about how automation systems should intersect with personal human assistance. AI shows remarkable competency in dealing with ordinary inquiries, yet research shows customers overwhelmingly choose human support when they encounter important or emotionally demanding customer situations requiring emotional assistance because these cases involve complex problems (Kim et al., 2022). Research remains scarce about which strategies businesses should follow to combine AI utilisation with human agent involvement for improving customer satisfaction (Gnewuch et al., 2024).

Ethical issues are a significant topic that needs to be studied further. When AI agents are used more widely, new problems with responsible AI arise, mainly centered on issues of privacy, as well as bias and clarity in algorithms. AI continues to advance in sophistication alongside its ability to shape customer choices thus creating urgent requirements to resolve relevant ethical concerns (Murtarelli, Gregory, & Romenti, 2021). Present exploration in academia mentions ethical issues, but lacks a specific plan for managing them, making it necessary to study ethical systems and the standards that guide them.

1.3 Define the problem and explain the main goals.

Aim:

The chapter aims to explore the ways AI agents could be used in customer service and how appropriate they might be in various situations.

Objectives:

1. To look into ways AI agents, boost the efficiency of customer service by performing basic tasks, reducing the time required to respond and managing resources better.
2. To understand the issues of ethics and laws in AI when offering services, including protecting data privacy, dealing with biased algorithms and following the GDPR and a future EU AI Act.
3. Showing how AI is used in customer service by examining the strategies of Apple and Salesforce.
4. To demonstrate the differences in how AI is used in retail and healthcare, outline the special ways it is used, the risks involved and what is expected from it.
5. To identify emerging trends and future directions in AI-driven customer service, including developments in emotion-aware AI, AI-as-a-Service (AIaaS), and generative conversational models like ChatGPT.

2. LITERATURE REVIEW

2.1 AI Agents and Operational Efficiency in Customer Service

Artificial intelligence agents boost organisational operational effectiveness through automated task processing and speed-up the delivery of accurate service interactions with customers. The business transformations powered by AI succeed best when they aim to optimise particular operational activities instead of completely substituting human employees according to Davenport and Ronanki (2018). AI service agents using machine learning and natural language processing tools provide customers with quick solutions for complaints and both Realtime package monitoring and basic service questions (Anozie et al., 2024).

The implementation of these technological approaches enables service organisations to achieve lower expenses and speed up customer interactions and achieve better constancy in their services (Blümel et al., 2023). AIaaS models have emerged to give small- and medium-sized enterprises the ability to use advanced AI tools through subscription services without big initial costs which provides equal opportunity for operational advancements (Lins et al., 2021). The main advantage of operational efficiency stands as an immediate result in businesses, but it becomes vital to prevent customer dissatisfaction by ensuring proper AI implementations to avoid query interpretation issues (Inavolu, 2024). Business operations should maintain operational efficiency through quality assurance tools that enable employees to step in whenever necessary to ensure proper system functioning. The foundation provided by operational efficiency for integrating AI into customer service does not ensure lasting customer loyalty because loyalty demands more than good system speed and consistency. The next vital requirement for improved customer satisfaction involves personalising services to match what each consumer wants and needs.

2.2 Personalisation, Customer Experience, and AI Agents

AI service delivery depends on personalization as its main foundation for achieving customer satisfaction. Building on Parasuraman, Zeithaml, and Berry's (1988) SERVQUAL model of service quality, modern AI systems strive to close the "service quality gaps" by tailoring interactions to individual customer needs. AI agents integrate real-time analytics that generates customized solutions which leads customers to experience better service empathy and faster responsiveness (Blümel et al., 2023; Gao & Liu, 2023). Research evidence shows customers appreciate AI assistants when they display memory of past communications and needs forecasting and personalize their communication approaches relying on customer choice preferences (Esmaeilzadeh & Vaezi, 2022).

Audience-focused artificial intelligence implementations with chatbots and virtual assistants represent a major direction in the development of hyper-personalized service delivery architecture (Yang et al., 2021; Vassilakopoulou et al., 2023). When organisations overemphasise individualised experiences, they expose themselves to certain hazards. Companies that heavily depend on predictive analysis models may create suspicions regarding surveillance which raises privacy-related issues for their customers (Kwong et al., 2024). Every company needs to maintain ethical data practices to build trust with their customers while delivering proper personalization benefits to customers. Scientific researchers examine ways to integrate emotional intelligence into artificial intelligence systems for developing human-machine interactions capable of expressing empathy (Han, Yin, & Zhang, 2023). The advanced data analysis needed for personalized marketing presents substantial ethical issues which stem directly from its operation model. The pursuit of personalized customer experiences by organizations demands parallel solutions for data privacy concerns and algorithmic bias prevention and regulatory upholding.

2.3 Ethical and Regulatory Challenges in AI-Driven Customer Service

The operational advantages of AI agents in customer service directly create important ethical risks as well as regulatory problems. The development and implementation of AI requires good intentions as its foundation because data privacy and algorithm transparency and fair outcomes require special attention. This is according to Taddeo and Floridi (2018). The combination of algorithmic discrimination and data theft increases to troubling heights because personal information gets frequently handled in customer service applications (Green, 2018).

The European Union's Artificial Intelligence Act as well as international talks about ethical AI protocols create new obligations for organizations to develop AI systems which meet legal requirements according to Laux et al. (2024). Organisations need to establish comprehensive data governance systems while conducting AI bias assessments to provide customers complete transparency regarding their systems' decision-making procedures (Ryan, 2020). The lack of attention to ethical issues in AI systems endangers legal compliance and destroys customer trust which directly diminishes the competitive benefit AI systems were intended to produce. Businesses are now establishing mixed service approaches which unite AI procedural advantages with human agent emotional intelligence to develop responsible customer relations.

2.4 Hybrid Service Models: The Human-AI Collaboration

Many organisations choose hybrid service models which unite AI capabilities with human service agents' exclusive abilities because they understand the limitations of AI agents. According to Brynjolfsson and McAfee (2014) business growth will result from human and machine cooperation instead of human substitution. The delivery of customer service benefits from workflows that assign standard low-emotional functions to AI but send high-emotional and critical situations to human service agents according to Gnewuch et al. (2024). Service resilience becomes stronger through hybrid models which maintain human service quality with the operational effectiveness achieved through automated inputs. The customer service agents at Salesforce utilise Einstein AI to develop human relationships with clients with the automated system performing information searches and predictive analytics (Chatterjee et al., 2021). Hybrid models find success through proper human employee training and integrated AI-human handovers and open communication systems about AI utilisation with customers (Oshrat et al., 2022). Future research analytics needs to evaluate ideal human-AI team structures for different industrial applications. Table 1 presents the main research themes extracted from the literature review which matches with the chapter's research goals. Research shows that AI agents produce notable operational and personalised benefits under ethical management when used in conjunction with human workforce capabilities. Research objectives for the current chapter derive from these insights to demonstrate proper strategies for implementing AI in customer service operations.

Table 1. Linking Key Studies to Chapter Objectives

Theme	Key Studies	Relevance to Chapter Objectives
Operational Efficiency	Davenport & Ronanki (2018); Anozie et al. (2024); Blümel et al. (2023); Lins et al. (2021)	Assess operational benefits of AI agents (Objective 1)
Customer Experience & Personalisation	Parasuraman, Zeithaml, & Berry (1988); Blümel et al. (2023); Gao & Liu (2023); Esmaeilzadeh & Vaezi (2022); Han, Yin, & Zhang (2023)	Assess personalisation benefits and customer response (Objective 1 and 2)
Ethics and Regulatory Challenges	Taddeo & Floridi (2018); Green (2018); Ryan (2020); Laux et al. (2024); Kwong et al. (2024)	Explore ethical implications and propose governance frameworks (Objective 3)
Hybrid Service Models (Human-AI Collaboration)	Brynjolfsson & McAfee (2014); Gnewuch et al. (2024); Chatterjee et al. (2021); Oshrat et al. (2022)	Propose sustainable hybrid AI-human service models (Objective 4)

2.2 Theoretical Frameworks

The key models of the AI integration in the service operations are detailed.

This makes the adoption and implication of AI in service operations heavily dependent on conceptual frameworks. The Technology Organisation Environment (TOE) framework is one widely recognised model, and this identifies technological, organisational and environmental drivers that help drive AI adoption. To investigate challenges and enablers (e.g., data readiness, organisational culture and external pressures) that affect the use of AI in service settings, this framework has been used. (Shahzadi et al., 2024). Another important framework also is the Human AIC Framework, which focuses on the compatibility of AI tools to existing service workflows. Here, this model emphasizes that it is essential to couple AI with human experience to improve both the decision-making and the task execution (Russo, 2023). Additionally, understanding AI integration in such a way requires the Service Personalisation Framework which reduces customer interaction to tailoring. Then in the second phase, analysing big data through the lens of AI driven tools is used to optimize service delivery based on the needs and preferences of individual customers (Blümel et al., 2023).

Personalisation and Efficiency in Customer Service — Basics

AI driven systems that analyse huge collections of data for tailored recommendations and responses make personalization in customer service now possible. The data with which AI is armed helps understand customer behaviour and preferences in real time, making the service more relevant and thus engaging. (Jankovic & Curović, 2023). Automated and predictive AI analytics improve efficiency of AI enabled customer service by streamlining operations and lowering response times. As an example, AI tools can handle routine enquiries autonomously and flag complex enquiries for human intervention, so creating a balance between efficiency and the personal touch (Blümel et al., 2023). Combining personalisation with improved efficiency is an important means of increasing customer satisfaction and loyalty. AI powered decision making frameworks guarantee that services are not just customized, but also delivered at the lowest resource expense possible. The outcome is a scalable, sustainable approach to controlling interactions with clients while providing an excessive measure of customization (Russo, 2023).

3. CONCEPTUAL METHOD AND CASE ILLUSTRATION

3.1 Research Approach

This chapter adopts a conceptual research method supported by secondary case illustrations. Rather than conducting original empirical research, the study synthesises insights from existing academic literature, industry reports, and publicly available data to examine how AI agents are transforming customer service operations. The approach allows for a critical, theory-driven exploration of AI integration into service models, with practical examples to illustrate key concepts.

Conceptual research is appropriate when the objective is to develop frameworks, evaluate existing theories, and generate insights through synthesis rather than primary data collection (Johnstone, 2004). This method facilitates a broad and critical examination of AI applications across industries without the need for fieldwork or direct organisational access.

Key features of this approach:

- Systematic review of recent peer-reviewed articles, industry white papers, and authoritative secondary sources (Pluye et al., 2009).
- Thematic synthesis around the main research objectives: operational efficiency, personalisation, ethical implications, and hybrid service models.

- Use of case illustrations to demonstrate real-world applications of AI agents based on publicly available company practices and reports.

No primary data (e.g., interviews, surveys, internal datasets) were collected for this study. All insights are drawn from secondary material and are used to conceptualise best practices and highlight challenges in AI-driven customer service.

3.2 Case Illustration Method

Two organisations, Apple and Salesforce, were selected as illustrative examples to ground the theoretical discussion in real-world practices. The selection was based on the following criteria:

- High level of AI integration into customer service operations.
- Public availability of detailed information about their AI deployment strategies.
- Relevance to key themes of operational efficiency, personalisation, and human-AI collaboration.

The case illustrations are interpretative rather than empirical. They aim to showcase how leading companies strategically deploy AI agents, identify challenges encountered, and implement solutions aligning with ethical and operational standards.

Data sources for the case illustrations include:

- Peer-reviewed academic studies (e.g., Gao & Liu, 2023; Chatterjee et al., 2021).
- Publicly accessible industry reports and press releases.
- Published organisational insights from reputable technology analysis platforms.

3.3 Analytical Strategy

The chapter employs a thematic analysis approach to synthesise findings from the literature and case illustrations. Key themes—such as operational efficiency, customer personalisation, ethical concerns, and hybrid service models—are identified and critically discussed in relation to the objectives.

The analysis strategy involves:

- Extracting common patterns across literature and secondary case data.

- Comparing practices across Apple and Salesforce to identify generalisable insights.
- Mapping challenges and best practices to broader industry trends in AI adoption.

By focusing on conceptual development and thematic interpretation, the chapter aims to provide valuable insights for academics, practitioners, and policymakers interested in AI's evolving role in customer service.

4. CASE STUDIES

4.1 Company-Specific Implementations

Example 1: Apple—Leveraging AI for Personalisation in Customer Service

The way Apple has used AI to push personalisation with their customer service is very effective. AI driven features such as virtual assistant (e.g., Siri), recommendation algorithms personalize user interaction with Apples product and enhances overall customer experience. Siri uses natural language processing (NLP) and machine learning (ML) to analyse user queries and generate context relevant responses. By providing tailored customer suggestions and quickly anticipating their needs, this personalization strategy turns into a powerful strategy to not only increase operational efficiency but also strengthen user engagement. (Gao & Liu, 2022). Through big data analytics, Apple is able to study its own customer behaviour and preferences, facilitating a highly customized world in which services are handled. As an instance, Apple's Genius Bar uses AI insights to tell it whether customers are having hardware or software issues before making customer visits that will help improve customer satisfaction and loyalty (Blümel et al., 2023).

Example 2: Data Powered by AI Agents: Salesforce Enhancing CRM Efficiency

Leveraging AI, Salesforce has reimagined the future of Customer Relationship Management (CRM) by introducing the new AI powered tool called Einstein AI, which aids with the analysis of data, thereby availing actionable insights to lay the path of optimisation of customer interaction. With its integration into Salesforce's CRM platform, Einstein AI gets a seamless fit into the business environment, thereby allowing businesses to predict customer behaviour, personalise communication and streamline the workflows. The innovation has tremendously led to a rise in the efficiency and accuracy of dealing with customer relationship. (Chatterjee et al., 2021). Sales and service automation are other uses of AI by Salesforce. For instance, AI driven chat bots running within CRM systems can handle customers' routine queries so that human agents take the complex issues. The hybrid approach of (Ozay et al., 2024) is an optimization of operational efficiency mixed with human touch when needed. Moreover, Salesforce's predictive analytics helps businesses to discover sales opportunities and reinforce customer retention strategies resulting in increased long-term value for businesses (Libai et al., 2020).

Table 2. Comparative Analysis of Case Studies

Company	AI Application	Key Benefits	Challenges Faced
Apple	Siri, Genius Bar AI insights	Personalized support, predictive issue resolution	High implementation costs
Salesforce	Einstein AI in CRM	Enhanced CRM efficiency, predictive analytics	Balancing automation with human oversight

4.2 Impacts on Operational Efficiency

Over the time, AI has revolutionised operational efficiency using response time improvements, better resource allocation, as well as task automation. AI systems like the chatbots and virtual assistants have been able to respond much more quickly to customer queries — literally instant and accurate answers for routine queries. For example, businesses that roll out AI systems claim that their high volumes of enquiries can be handled more effectively with consistent service quality (Wirtz et al., 2023).

AI also enables Resource allocation by analysing real time data and predicting customer needs. Automating the repetitive tasks like order tracking and complaint resolution by companies, then the human agents could be diverted to engage in more complex and valuable tasks in which they can contribute to increasing productivity (Gajić et al., 2024). Inventory management and workforce deployment have also optimised using AI driven analytics to ensure the resources follow the demand patterns closely (Ahmad et al., 2021).

4.3 Impacts on Customer Satisfaction

The satisfaction of customers has enhanced through the use of AI to provide specific and initiative services. This paper also noted that through the integration of AI systems, organizations can predict the needs of customers thus providing a suitable recommendation to the customers thus improving the quality of the experience that the customers have (Libai et al., 2020). Also, thanks to the feedback analysis based on artificial intelligence, companies have received valuable recommendations on customers' behaviour and attitudes to help improve the service.

However, the findings of the research show that there are difficulties in meeting the needs of the customer especially in situations that are emotionally charged up. Largely, customers tend to feel that they are dealing with a robot interface when they are communicating with AI, and as such, would rather engage the services of a human agent when dealing with issues that require much understanding and empathy (Prentice & Nguyen, 2020). It is still important to find the right way to combine automation and personalized human contact to deliver excellent customer experience.

4.4 Challenges and Mitigation Strategies

There are several problems that come with integrating AI in customer service. These are the costs of implementing the system, the organisations technological preparedness and organisational culture. However, concerns about data privacy, algorithmic bias and transparency act as ethical as well as operational challenges. (Shang et al., 2023). These challenges can be meet by organizations by using the hybrid model where AI will assist human agents instead of replacing them. This approach enables the company to save time while still delivering services that are built to understand the consumer's needs. (Prentice & Nguyen, 2020). Ethically, organisations are focusing on the creation of open-source AI, as well as standards for the regulation of accountability and data protection (Feijóo et al., 2020). Some of the potential technological barriers include work automation through AI can be implemented in a step-by-step approach and contribution of resources in the training of employees for the new AI systems (Menzies et al., 2024).

4.5 Industry Comparison: Retail vs Healthcare

The adoption of AI agents in customer service varies significantly between industries such as retail and healthcare, driven by sector-specific needs and regulatory environments.

Retail Sector

In retail, AI agents are primarily deployed to enhance customer engagement, streamline purchasing journeys, and provide personalised recommendations. Companies like Amazon and Zara use AI chatbots and recommendation engines to analyse customer behaviour in real time and offer targeted product suggestions, thereby boosting sales and customer satisfaction (Jain, 2024). AI also supports automated inventory management and dynamic pricing models, improving operational efficiency. However, challenges persist around maintaining personalisation without intrusiveness, and safeguarding customer data amid heavy personalisation efforts.

Healthcare Sector

In healthcare, AI agents are increasingly used for patient triage, appointment scheduling, and post-consultation follow-ups. AI-powered virtual assistants like Babylon Health help patients describe symptoms and guide them to appropriate care pathways (Anisha et al., 2024). However, the stakes in healthcare are higher, as errors in AI recommendations can have serious consequences. Therefore, healthcare AI deployments are often accompanied by stricter ethical guidelines, transparency mandates, and human-in-the-loop models. Most patients expect healthcare providers to be more trustworthy, accurate and caring than retail staff. While AI makes both sectors more efficient and personal, healthcare is strictly watched and controlled so that ethics are upheld, unlike in retail, where the main goal is to offer a better experience and improved convenience to customers.

5. THEMATIC EXPANSION: KEY TRENDS AND CHALLENGES IN AI-DRIVEN CUSTOMER SERVICE

5.1 Frameworks for AI Implementation in Customer Service

Generally, adopting AI in customer service goes through four stages: deciding on a strategy, trying out AI, connecting it to all customer service operations and always searching for improvements. Davenport and Ronanki (2018) suggest that successful AI projects in service operations begin with the identification of specific, high-impact areas—such as handling routine queries or automating feedback collection—rather than attempting wholesale transformation from the outset. Part of strategic planning is to review technology, company culture and what customers expect. Companies must evaluate whether their existing service processes can accommodate AI augmentation without disrupting human-centric elements of service (Brynjolfsson &

McAfee, 2014). By deploying AI agents in a pilot, organisations can ensure they are ready for use in the wider business. At this point, any unexpected technical or customer issues may be spotted. To ensure full integration, it is necessary to connect with old systems, allow people and AI to cooperate and establish a plan for handling challenging customer questions. Continuous optimisation involves real-time monitoring of AI performance, bias audits, and updates to AI models based on evolving customer needs and regulatory requirements. While many organisations move quickly from pilot to full deployment, experts emphasise the need for a phased and flexible approach that aligns AI capabilities with both organisational goals and customer service standards (Iqbal et al., 2024).

5.2 Organisational and Technical Challenges

Despite the promised benefits, integrating AI into customer service ecosystems presents significant organisational and technical hurdles. From an organisational perspective, cost remains a substantial barrier. The development, customisation, and maintenance of AI systems—especially advanced conversational agents—require considerable financial investment, often beyond the reach of smaller enterprises (Dwivedi et al., 2021). Employee training is another critical requirement. Service representatives must learn to work alongside AI agents, interpreting AI recommendations and handling escalations effectively. However, many organisations underestimate the change management needed to foster AI acceptance internally (Menzies et al., 2024). On the technical side, integration with legacy IT systems poses a challenge. Many customer service operations still rely on older databases and CRM platforms that are not easily compatible with AI tools. Technical incompatibility can lead to data silos, inaccurate predictions, and customer frustration (Gade, 2021). Addressing these challenges demands not just technological investment, but also leadership commitment to digital transformation, comprehensive training programmes, and robust IT infrastructure upgrades. Addressing organisational and technical barriers is crucial for AI adoption success. However, even well-implemented AI systems must overcome another critical hurdle: meeting customer expectations and addressing potential resistance to automation.

5.3 Customer Expectations and Resistance

Customers' acceptance of AI-driven service models is highly contingent on the context and nature of the service interaction. Research indicates that while customers are generally comfortable interacting with AI for routine tasks such as checking order status or resetting passwords, they prefer human agents for emotionally charged or complex issues (Samala et al., 2020; Kim et al., 2022). Bill disputes, complaints and personal issues usually call for empathy, listening and communication skills which AI agents have not yet mastered. Additionally, having too much automation can make customers feel distant from the company. Customers may perceive a brand as uncaring if human touchpoints are eliminated altogether, leading to decreased loyalty and negative word-of-mouth (Prentice & Nguyen, 2020). It is important for companies to identify the places where people should be involved and plan their models accordingly. Providing clear disclosure about when customers are interacting with AI versus a human, and offering easy escalation paths, are now considered best practices in customer service (Vassilakopoulou et al., 2023). Organisations should create hybrid services that suit customers, while also dealing with the challenges and requirements of the law and ethics to preserve their reputation.

5.4 Using AI requires following legal and ethical guidelines.

Any use of AI agents in customer service should follow strict rules to ensure both customers' rights and the organisation's integrity are protected. The General Data Protection Regulation (GDPR), enacted by the European Union, imposes strict guidelines on the collection, storage, and processing of personal data. Under GDPR, companies must ensure customer consent is obtained for data-driven personalisation and that AI decision-making processes are explainable (Ryan, 2020). Additionally, the proposed EU Artificial Intelligence Act classifies AI systems based on risk levels—with customer service bots often falling into the "limited risk" or "high risk" categories depending on their functions. This classification mandates transparency obligations such as informing customers when they are interacting with an AI agent and offering human redress mechanisms (Laux et al., 2024). Ethical frameworks developed by scholars such as Taddeo and Floridi (2018) further argue for the principles of fairness, accountability, transparency, and privacy (FATP) in AI design and deployment. To stop increasing social inequality, companies must cheque for biases, organise accountability and include data from a range of sources. Without complying with these rules, organisations could face strict penalties and damage their reputation, as well as lose many customers. As laws develop, new technology is constantly changing how services are delivered. AIaaS and conversational agents like ChatGPT and Bard are introducing new ways to interact with customers.

5.5 New Developments: Using AI in the Cloud and Advanced Models

Two critical recent developments are reshaping the customer service landscape: the rise of Artificial Intelligence as a Service (AIaaS) and the integration of advanced conversational models like ChatGPT, Bard, and Claude. Sophisticated AI tools are available to companies through services offered by AWS, Microsoft Azure and Google Cloud. This trend lowers the barrier to entry for businesses of all sizes, allowing broader adoption of predictive analytics, chatbot frameworks, and sentiment analysis tools (Lins et al., 2021). Furthermore, ChatGPT, Bard and Claude have greatly improved how AI agents speak and react in different situations. Unlike earlier-generation chatbots, these models can conduct multi-turn conversations, adapt language style, and respond to complex emotional cues—qualities essential for high-quality customer service (Gao & Liu, 2023).

However, these powerful models also introduce new ethical challenges, such as ensuring that generated responses are **factual**, **non-discriminatory**, and **privacy-compliant** (Taddeo, M., & Floridi, 2018). Their deployment in customer service must therefore be accompanied by **strict governance measures**, including content filtering, supervision by human agents, and regular model auditing. Organisations that successfully leverage AIaaS and advanced conversational AI are likely to gain a competitive edge by delivering more human-like, empathetic, and scalable customer experiences. The thematic analysis highlights that the future of AI-driven customer service hinges not only on technological sophistication but also on careful management of organisational, customer, and ethical dynamics. This comprehensive view supports the chapter's aim of proposing sustainable and human-centric AI service models.

6. DISCUSSION

6.1 Benefits of AI Agents in Customer Service

The paper also highlights the advantages of applying AI agents in customer service as improving efficiency and operational results. It gives faster responses to routine questions and improves the allocation of resources, for instance through data management. These capabilities allow organizations to address multiple customer contacts in a short period without incurring the costs associated with low-quality service delivery (Wirtz et al., 2023).

Beyond efficiency, AI agents perform specially on the aspect of customer relations given the ability to tailor interactions. As a result of using more sophisticated analytics and machine learning, these systems can even identify customer's preferences and provide recommendations. Personalisation increases intimacy with the customer, which results in satisfaction and subsequent loyalty (Libai et al., 2020). Since AI can at once improve the speed and the quality of interaction with the customers, it is a powerful tool for developing new customer service approaches.

6.2 Challenges in Integration

While they are useful, integration of AI agents into customer service comes with problems. The main barriers to automating are still resistance to automating on the part of employees and customers, who sometimes view AI as a threat to job security and may feel that it is less empathic than human interaction (Prentice and Nguyen, 2020). To overcome this resistance, we need transparent communication as to when AI and human agents play well with each other. As well, adoption of AI is held up by ethical concerns such as data privacy, algorithmic bias and transparency. It's not uncommon for AI systems to rely on large volumes of customer data, which puts the at risk of being misused or breached. Moreover, biases in algorithms may result in unfair treatment of given customer groups resulting in undermining trust, inclusivity (Taddeo & Floridi 2018). Transparency is the need of the hour! The companies need to focus on transparent frameworks and whenever required; they need to conduct regular audit towards ethical AI practices. Finally, automation can be abused and put in place in a manner that results in jeopardized customer satisfaction, especially in situations which call for empathy or a specific understanding. As we know, customers often prefer resolution of complex or emotive issues via a human agent (Samala et al., 2020). How to address this challenge relies on striking the right balance of automation in overlaying human supervision.

Table 3. Ethical Concerns in AI Deployment

Ethical Concern	Potential Impact	Mitigation Strategy
Data Privacy	Breach of sensitive customer information	Robust data governance and encryption
Algorithmic Bias	Unequal treatment of customer demographics	Regular audits and diverse data sets
Lack of Transparency	Erosion of customer trust	Clear communication on AI decision-making

6.3 The Balance Between Automation and Human Touch

With AI agent integration more and more businesses are looking to achieve an optimal balance between automation and human touch. It's because in AI we excel at quitting routine and data intensive tasks, leaving human agents to focus on the complexities and value added. In addition to making operations more efficient, this hybrid model is able to deliver the kind of empathy and personal connection customers need (Murtarelli et al., 2020). Being strategic in blending AI and human interaction means using AI as back-end support and keeping humans on the front as in customer facing roles where emotional intelligence is vital. As an example, when AI senses frustration or dissatisfaction in a customer's tone, human agents can intervene to provide smooth transition between the machine and human interaction (Vassilakopoulou et al., 2023). That way businesses can maintain a human touch while delivering efficient, personalised service.

Table 4. Checklist for AI Implementation in Customer Service

Step	Action Item	Description
1	Phased Deployment	Start with pilot projects in low-risk service areas before scaling up AI integration across customer touchpoints.
2	Employee Training	Develop comprehensive training programs to help service agents work effectively with AI tools, focusing on hybrid collaboration.
3	Customer Consent for Data	Ensure transparent communication and secure customer consent for the collection and use of personal data in AI-driven personalisation.
4	Ethical Auditing	Conduct regular audits to identify algorithmic biases, ensure data security, and maintain compliance with legal and ethical standards (e.g., GDPR, EU AI Act).

6.4 Ethical Implications

The deployment of AI agents is basically reliant on ethical considerations. To build trust with customers, we have to tackle issues of accountability, data security and bias. For a high degree of accountability around how AI systems function, also including the use of customer data and decision-making processes, transparent communication must be made possible (Ryan, 2020). But data security is still an important issue: a breach can cost you big in reputational and legal terms. To save customer data, companies must have implemented strong security measures, and follow regulatory standards (Feijóo et al., 2020). Regularity of algorithm audit and diverse data sets can mitigate algorithm bias addressing. Responding to these ethical challenges acutely helps businesses to deploy AI responsibly and develop customer trust, and sustainably successful. In sum, organisations seeking to capitalise on AI agents must adopt a balanced, ethically informed approach that enhances efficiency without compromising human connection. These reflections directly address the chapter's goal of guiding the responsible and effective integration of AI into customer service.

6.5 Future Outlook: Emerging Trends in AI-Driven Customer Service

Looking ahead, three major trends are poised to redefine the role of AI agents in customer service.

Emotion-Aware AI:

The next frontier in AI-driven service is the development of emotion-aware agents capable of recognising and responding to customers' emotional states. Emerging technologies combine natural language processing with sentiment analysis and even facial recognition to gauge frustration, satisfaction, or confusion in real-time (Han et al., 2023). While promising, emotion-aware AI also raises new ethical challenges regarding surveillance and consent.

Generative AI in Customer Service:

Generative AI models such as ChatGPT, Bard, and Claude are beginning to transform customer relationship management (CRM). These models can handle more complex, multi-turn conversations, generate personalised content, and resolve ambiguous queries with minimal human intervention (Keyvan & Huang, 2022). Companies are starting to integrate generative AI into CRM platforms, enhancing both service quality and operational scalability. However, maintaining the accuracy, relevance, and ethical integrity of AI-generated responses remains a critical concern.

Regulation-Driven AI Transparency:

Regulatory bodies are increasingly pushing for transparency in AI deployments. Under frameworks like the EU Artificial Intelligence Act, service providers will need to disclose when customers are interacting with AI agents, explain how decisions are made, and offer easy avenues for human intervention. This shift towards regulation-driven transparency aims to rebuild trust in AI systems, particularly as customers become more aware of the implications of automated decision-making (Laux et al., 2024).

Limitations of the Study

The study uses a conceptual review and illustrative cases that can be found online. Therefore, the approach does not collect data through interviews, surveys or audits. Since empirical findings are missing, applying some results to different industries and areas may be limited. While both Apple and Salesforce are great examples, they do not necessarily show the same issues as smaller businesses or other service companies. Researchers could use interviews, case studies or surveys to check these findings and better understand how AI agents are used in customer service.

6.6 Critical Thinking: Balanced View and Researcher Reflections

6.6.1 Benefits and Limitations of AI Agents in Customer Service

While AI agents can help improve customer service in various ways, introducing them can also bring about several important issues. On the positive side, AI agents significantly reduce customer wait times, automate repetitive tasks, and provide real-time, data-driven insights that empower companies to deliver highly personalised services (Anozie et al., 2024; Blümel et al., 2023). The predictive capabilities of AI can anticipate customer needs, thereby increasing satisfaction and fostering brand loyalty (Gao & Liu, 2023). Besides, AI supports round-the-clock customer service which is very helpful in today's global service industry. Still, these benefits should be balanced with important risks. AI systems still struggle to accurately interpret nuanced human emotions, making them ill-suited for handling sensitive or complex service interactions (Samala et al., 2020). There is also a growing risk of over-automation, where excessive reliance on AI alienates customers who seek empathetic, human engagement, particularly during emotionally charged situations (Kim et al., 2022). Moreover, ethical concerns—such as data privacy breaches, algorithmic bias, and lack of transparency—pose reputational and legal threats to organisations (Taddeo & Floridi, 2018; Ryan, 2020). Thus, managers should ensure that using AI does not result in irritated customers or a lack of confidence in their business. A main aspect of strategic planning should be to use blended strategies, depend on humans in high-emotion situations and ensure that AI is managed ethically.

6.6.2 What the Researcher Thinks: Tips for Managers

After reviewing the chapter's findings, it is obvious that AI can enhance, not replace, the services provided to customers. I believe that businesses that sensibly consider the good as well as the bad sides of AI have a greater chance of succeeding. From the studies and case examples, it is important to include moments when humans guide the customer journey. AI agents should handle efficiency-driven tasks, but human representatives must be readily available when empathy, creativity, or ethical judgement are required (Gnewuch et al., 2024). Employee training is now seen as necessary and cannot be ignored. Many companies do not realise how much

AI affects the culture within their service teams. Successful integration demands not just technical upskilling but also change management strategies that address fears of job displacement and reinforce the value of human roles in an AI-enhanced environment (Rane et al., 2024). AI systems should be continuously checked by performing bias audits, reviewing ethical issues and conducting customer surveys. In the rapidly shifting regulatory landscape, proactive compliance with frameworks such as GDPR and the upcoming EU AI Act will separate sustainable adopters from those vulnerable to legal and reputational risks (Laux et al., 2024). As a result, AI should be used in customer service to support human efforts and not try to replace them.

7. CONCLUSION AND RECOMMENDATIONS

7.1 Summary of Findings

With the use of AI agents, customer service becomes more efficient, time is saved, and customers enjoy a more personal service. These systems use data to improve how resources are shared and deliver personalised services to customers. But it's also fraught with issues—AI agents are resistant to automation, worried about algorithmic bias and how easily personal data can take on a life of its own and be used to harm us, and they may lead us to become too reliant on machines and lose the human touch altogether. These challenges nevertheless necessitate continuing concern with both ethical considerations and human oversight. On the one hand, AI systems are very efficient, but if we want to deploy them we need transparency, accountability and fairness. Trust and high standard of customer service in emotionally or technically charged scenario depends upon the balance between automation and human interaction.

7.2 Examples of Practice Recommendations

This will enable organisations to provide a phased implementation of AI agents in the customer service. Some of it is using pilot programs to figure out where the wicked operational challenges are and then refining AI systems based on things that both the employees and the customers say. Evidence of such AI's support for, rather than replacement of, human agents, may help clear the fog of resistance, and communication about the role of AI in service delivery will help. Hybrid service models taking advantage of strength of both AI and human agents are ones that organisations should invest in. Instead of the computer saving the world, normal, high-volume tasks should be handled by the AI, the hard, nuanced, complex things should be done by the human agent. Training programs should be rolled out for employee to be able to work alongside AI systems effectively. As such, for business to address ethical concerns, it needs to do this by having robust data governance systems, firmly at the centre of which are customer privacy and security. If AI systems are at all auditable, regular audits can indicate and mitigate biases such that there is not inequitable service delivery. Good transparency on data usage and how the decision is made will give customers confidence and trust in the data to use and the decision to make.

7.3 Future Research Directions

As a next step, these studies should be expanded to understand the relationship between AI agents and customer satisfaction, customer loyalty, and business outcomes on the other hand. Research should focus on how customers see and will adjust to AI technology in interactions among industries and cultures. Further, various hybrid service models need to be studied on their ability to balance human oversight with automation and their scalability.

Designing AI is a critical area where ethical implications of deployment of the technology should be explored. Future work on AI system frameworks would include development of systems for transparent and accountable AI systems including the issues of bias and data security. Emotion recognition, generative A'I' and other emerging technologies also need to be studied as possible ways to improve AI agents' capability without compromising on ethical principles. Finally, as AI develops research should look at how AI impacts the workplace in terms of worker roles, skills, and interaction with such systems. Future studies can address these areas if we take actionable insights on how to optimise its integration in customer service and assure its sustainable use.

8. REFERENCES

Ahmad, T., Zhang, D., Huang, C., Zhang, H., Dai, N., Song, Y., & Chen, H. (2021). Artificial intelligence in the sustainable energy industry: Status Quo, challenges, and opportunities. *Journal of Cleaner Production*, *289*, 125834. DOI: 10.1016/j.jclepro.2021.125834

Anisha, S. A., Sen, A., & Bain, C. (2024). Evaluating the potential and pitfalls of AI-powered conversational agents as humanlike virtual health carers in the remote management of noncommunicable diseases: Scoping review. *Journal of Medical Internet Research*, *26*, e56114. DOI: 10.2196/56114 PMID: 39012688

Anozie, U. C., Onyenahazi, O. B., Ekeocha, P. C., Adekola, A. D., Ukadike, C. A., & Oloko, O. A.Uchechukwu Christopher AnozieObinna Barnabas OnyenahaziPrince Chukwuemeka EkeochaAdeleke Damilola AdekolaChifum Ann UkadikeOmodunni Adejoke Oloko. (2024). Advancements in artificial intelligence for omnichannel marketing and customer service: Enhancing predictive analytics, automation, and operational efficiency. *International Journal of Science and Research Archive*, *12*(2), 1621–1629. DOI: 10.30574/ijsra.2024.12.2.1436

Blümel, J. H., Zaki, M., & Bohné, T. (2023). Personal touch in digital customer service: A conceptual framework of relational personalisation for conversational AI. *Journal of Service Theory and Practice*, *34*(1), 33–65. DOI: 10.1108/JSTP-03-2023-0098

Brynjolfsson, E., & McAfee, A. (2014). *The Second Machine Age: Work, Progress, and Prosperity in a Time of Brilliant Technologies*. W. W. Norton & Company.

Chatterjee, S., Chaudhuri, R., Vrontis, D., Thrassou, A., & Ghosh, S. K. (2021). Adoption of artificial intelligence-integrated CRM systems in agile organisations in India. *Technological Forecasting and Social Change*, *168*, 120783. DOI: 10.1016/j.techfore.2021.120783

Davenport, T. H., & Ronanki, R. (2018). Artificial Intelligence for the Real World. *Harvard Business Review*, *96*(1), 108–116.

Dwivedi, Y. K., Hughes, L., Ismagilova, E., Aarts, G., Coombs, C., Crick, T., Duan, Y., Dwivedi, R., Edwards, J., Eirug, A., Galanos, V., Ilavarasan, P. V., Janssen, M., Jones, P., Kar, A. K., Kizgin, H., Kronemann, B., Lal, B., Lucini, B., & Williams, M. D. (2021). Artificial Intelligence (AI): Multidisciplinary perspectives on emerging challenges, opportunities, and agenda for research, practise, and policy. *International Journal of Information Management*, *57*, 101994. DOI: 10.1016/j.ijinfomgt.2019.08.002

Dwivedi, Y. K., Hughes, L., Ismagilova, E., Aarts, G., Coombs, C., Crick, T., Duan, Y., Dwivedi, R., Edwards, J., Eirug, A., Galanos, V., Ilavarasan, P. V., Janssen, M., Jones, P., Kar, A. K., Kizgin, H., Kronemann, B., Lal, B., Lucini, B., & Williams, M. D. (2021). Artificial Intelligence (AI): Multidisciplinary perspectives on emerging challenges, opportunities, and agenda for research, practice and policy. *International Journal of Information Management*, *57*, 101994. DOI: 10.1016/j.ijinfomgt.2019.08.002

Esmaeilzadeh, H., & Vaezi, R. (2022). Conscious, empathic AI in service. *Journal of Service Research*, *25*(4), 549–564. DOI: 10.1177/10946705221103531

Feijóo, C., Kwon, Y., Bauer, J. M., Bohlin, E., Howell, B., Jain, R., Potgieter, P., Vu, K., Whalley, J., & Xia, J. (2020). Harnessing artificial intelligence (AI) to increase well-being for all: The case for a new technology diplomacy. *Telecommunications Policy*, *44*(6), 101988. DOI: 10.1016/j.telpol.2020.101988 PMID: 32377031

Gade, K. R. (2021). Overcoming the Data Silo Divide: A Holistic Approach to ELT Integration in Hybrid Cloud Environments. *Journal of Innovative Technologies*, *4*(1).

Gajić, T., Petrović, M. D., Pešić, A. M., Conić, M., & Gligorijević, N. (2024). Innovative Approaches in Hotel Management: Integrating Artificial Intelligence (AI) and the Internet of Things (IoT) to Enhance Operational Efficiency and Sustainability. *Sustainability (Basel)*, *16*(17), 7279. DOI: 10.3390/su16177279

Gao, Y., & Liu, H. (2023). Artificial intelligence-enabled personalisation in interactive marketing: A customer journey perspective. *Journal of Research in Interactive Marketing*, *17*(5), 663–680. DOI: 10.1108/JRIM-01-2022-0023

Gao, Y., & Liu, H. (2023). Artificial intelligence-enabled personalization in interactive marketing: A customer journey perspective. *Journal of Research in Interactive Marketing*, *17*(5), 663–680. DOI: 10.1108/JRIM-01-2022-0023

Garvey, A. M., Kim, T., & Duhachek, A. (2023). Bad news? Send an AI. Good news? Send a human. *Journal of Marketing*, *87*(1), 10–25. DOI: 10.1177/00222429211066972

Gnewuch, U., Morana, S., Hinz, O., Kellner, R., & Maedche, A. (2024). More than a bot? The impact of disclosing human involvement on customer interactions with hybrid service agents. *Information Systems Research*, *35*(3), 936–955. DOI: 10.1287/isre.2022.0152

Green, B. P. (2018). Ethical Reflections on Artificial Intelligence. *Scientia Et Fides, 6(2),* 9–31. Retrieved from https://apcz.umk.pl/SetF/article/view/SetF.2018.015

Han, E., Yin, D., & Zhang, H. (2023). Bots with feelings: Should AI agents express positive emotion in customer service? *Information Systems Research*, *34*(3), 1296–1311. DOI: 10.1287/isre.2022.1179

Han, E., Yin, D., & Zhang, H. (2023). Bots with feelings: Should AI agents express positive emotion in customer service? *Information Systems Research*, *34*(3), 1296–1311. DOI: 10.1287/isre.2022.1179

Inavolu, S. M. (2024). Exploring AI-driven customer service: Evolution, architectures, opportunities, challenges and future directions. *International Journal of Engineering and Advanced Technology*, *13*(3), 156–163.

Iqbal, M. S., Abdul Rahim, Z., Alshammari, A. M. K., & Iftikhar, H. (2024). Innovative strategies for overcoming barriers to technology adoption in small and medium-sized enterprises. *Journal of the International Council for Small Business*, *5*(4), 331–344. DOI: 10.1080/26437015.2024.2367440

Jain, R. (2024). The Role of Artificial Intelligence in Modern Marketing: Tools, Applications, and Future Trends. Designing Tomorrow: AI, Ethics, and Society's Next Steps, 125.

Jankovic, S. D., & Curovic, D. M. (2023). Strategic integration of artificial intelligence for sustainable businesses: Implications for data management and human user engagement in the digital era. *Sustainability (Basel)*, *15*(21), 15208. DOI: 10.3390/su152115208

Johnstone, P. (2004). Mixed Methods, Mixed Methodology, and Health Services Research in Practice. *Qualitative Health Research*, *14*(2), 259–271. DOI: 10.1177/1049732303260610 PMID: 14768461

Keyvan, K., & Huang, J. X. (2022). How to approach ambiguous queries in conversational search: A survey of techniques, approaches, tools, and challenges. *ACM Computing Surveys*, *55*(6), 1–40. DOI: 10.1145/3534965

Kim, T. W., Jiang, L., Duhachek, A., Lee, H., & Garvey, A. (2022). Do you mind if I ask you a personal question? How AI service agents alter consumer self-disclosure. *Journal of Service Research*, *25*(4), 649–666. DOI: 10.1177/10946705221120232

Kwong, A. T. M., Omar, S. I., & Aliah, M. N. (2024). The ethical implications of AI-Powered personalization in hospitality and tourism. In *Impact of AI and tech-driven solutions in hospitality and tourism* (pp. 103–122). IGI Global. DOI: 10.4018/979-8-3693-6755-1.ch006

Laux, J., Wachter, S., & Mittelstadt, B. (2024). Three pathways for standardisation and ethical disclosure by default under the European Union Artificial Intelligence Act. *Computer Law & Security Review, 53*, 105957. DOI: 10.1016/j.clsr.2024.105957

Libai, B., Bart, Y., Gensler, S., Hofacker, C. F., Kaplan, A., Kötterheinrich, K., & Kroll, E. B. (2020). Brave new world? On AI and the management of customer relationships. *Journal of Interactive Marketing, 51*(1), 44–56. DOI: 10.1016/j.intmar.2020.04.002

Lins, S., Pandl, K. D., Teigeler, H., Thiebes, S., Bayer, C., & Sunyaev, A. (2021). Artificial intelligence as a service: Classification and research directions. *Business & Information Systems Engineering, 63*(4), 441–456. DOI: 10.1007/s12599-021-00708-w

Menzies, J., Sabert, B., Hassan, R., & Mensah, P. K. (2024). Artificial intelligence for international business: Its use, challenges, and suggestions for future research and practice. *Thunderbird International Business Review, 66*(2), 185–200. DOI: 10.1002/tie.22370

Murtarelli, G., Gregory, A., & Romenti, S. (2021). A conversation-based perspective for shaping ethical human–machine interactions: The particular challenge of chatbots. *Journal of Business Research, 129*, 927–935. DOI: 10.1016/j.jbusres.2020.09.018

Oshrat, Y., Aumann, Y., Hollander, T., Maksimov, O., Ostroumov, A., Shechtman, N., & Kraus, S. (2022). Efficient customer service combining human operators and virtual agents. arXiv preprint arXiv:2209.05226.

Ozay, D., Jahanbakht, M., Shoomal, A., & Wang, S. (2024). Artificial Intelligence (AI)-based Customer Relationship Management (CRM): A comprehensive bibliometric and systematic literature review with an outlook on future research. *Enterprise Information Systems, 18*(7), 2351869. DOI: 10.1080/17517575.2024.2351869

Parasuraman, A., Zeithaml, V. A., & Berry, L. L. (1988). SERVQUAL: A Multiple-Item Scale for Measuring Consumer Perceptions of Service Quality. *Journal of Retailing, 64*(1), 12–40.

Pendyala, M. K., & Lakkamraju, V. V. (2024). Impact of artificial intelligence in customer journey. *International Journal of Innovative Science and Research Technology, 9*(8), 1528–1534. Advance online publication. DOI: 10.38124/ijisrt/IJISRT24AUG807

Pluye, P., Gagnon, M., Griffiths, F., & Johnson-Lafleur, J. (2009). A scoring system for appraising mixed-methods research and concomitantly appraising qualitative, quantitative, and mixed-method primary studies in mixed studies reviews. *International Journal of Nursing Studies*, *46*(4), 529–546. DOI: 10.1016/j.ijnurstu.2009.01.009 PMID: 19233357

Prentice, C., & Nguyen, M. (2020). Engaging and retaining customers with AI and employee service. *Journal of Retailing and Consumer Services*, *56*, 102186. DOI: 10.1016/j.jretconser.2020.102186

Prentice, C., & Nguyen, M. (2020). Engaging and retaining customers with AI and employee service. *Journal of Retailing and Consumer Services*, *56*, 102186. DOI: 10.1016/j.jretconser.2020.102186

Russo, D. (2023). Navigating the complexity of generative AI adoption in software engineering. *arXiv*. https://doi.org//arXiv.2307.06081DOI: 10.48550

Ryan, M. (2020). In AI We Trust: Ethics, Artificial Intelligence, and Reliability. *Science and Engineering Ethics*, *26*(5), 2749–2767. DOI: 10.1007/s11948-020-00228-y PMID: 32524425

Samala, N., Katkam, B. S., Bellamkonda, R. S., & Rodriguez, R. V. (2020). Impact of AI and robotics in the tourism sector: A critical insight. *Journal of Tourism Futures*, *8*(1), 73–87. DOI: 10.1108/JTF-07-2019-0065

Shahzadi, G., Jia, F., Chen, L., & John, A. (2024). AI adoption in supply chain management: A systematic literature review. *Journal of Manufacturing Technology Management*, *35*(6), 1125–1150. DOI: 10.1108/JMTM-09-2023-0431

Shang, G., Low, S. P., & Lim, X. Y. V. (2023). Prospects, drivers of, and barriers to artificial intelligence adoption in project management. *Built Environment Project and Asset Management*, *13*(5), 629–645. DOI: 10.1108/BEPAM-12-2022-0195

Singh, H. (2024). Legal aspects of digital ethics in the age of artificial intelligence. In Balancing Human Rights, Social Responsibility, and Digital Ethics (pp. 144-167). IGI Global. DOI: 10.4018/979-8-3693-3334-1.ch005

Taddeo, M., & Floridi, L. (2018). How AI can be a force for good. *Science*, *361*(6404), 751–752. DOI: 10.1126/science.aat5991 PMID: 30139858

Taddeo, M., & Floridi, L. (2018). How AI can be a force for good. *Science*, *361*(6404), 751–752. DOI: 10.1126/science.aat5991 PMID: 30139858

Vassilakopoulou, P., Haug, A., Salvesen, L. M., & Pappas, I. O. (2023). Developing human/AI interactions for chat-based customer services: Lessons learnt from the Norwegian government. *European Journal of Information Systems*, *32*(1), 10–22. DOI: 10.1080/0960085X.2022.2096490

Wirtz, J., Hofmeister, J., Chew, P., & Ding, X. (2023). Digital service technologies, service robots, AI, and the strategic pathways to cost-effective service excellence. *Service Industries Journal*, *43*(15-16), 1173–1196. DOI: 10.1080/02642069.2023.2226596

Xu, Y., Shieh, C. H., van Esch, P., & Ling, I. L. (2020). AI customer service: Task complexity, problem-solving ability, and usage intention. *Australasian Marketing Journal*, *28*(4), 189–199. DOI: 10.1016/j.ausmj.2020.03.005

Chapter 11
Navigating Employee Wellbeing Through VR Therapy

Zainab Shaikh
https://orcid.org/0009-0009-1411-4168
Amity University, Dubai, UAE

Akshaini Josyula
https://orcid.org/0009-0007-0675-4726
Amity University, Dubai, UAE

Jihene Mrabet
https://orcid.org/0000-0003-1848-5918
Amity University, Dubai, UAE

ABSTRACT

This chapter explores the potential of virtual reality (VR)-based interventions in reducing stress and burnout among working individuals while enhancing employee well-being. It examines psychological benefits, implementation strategies, and the impact of VR on mental and physical health in workplace settings. The chapter discusses evidence from corporate environments, healthcare, psychiatric wards, and military contexts. Drawing on recent research, it outlines VR's role in improving stress management, personal resources, and diversity. It also considers workplace design, user acceptance, and ethical concerns related to adoption of VR interventions. By integrating current findings with practical insights, the chapter offers a comprehensive overview of VR's contribution to workplace wellness.

DOI: 10.4018/979-8-3373-3658-9.ch011

INTRODUCTION

Work-induced stress lingers can manifest unexpectedly, often when individuals are least prepared. It can lead to serious physical and mental health concerns which can have long-term effects on an individual's body. Chronic stress can lead to insomnia, high blood pressure, a weakened immune system, and anxiety which can also lead to or add on to illnesses such as depression, heart disease, obesity, and burnout (American Psychological Association, 2014). Over the years, organizations have employed various interventions and company-wide policies to tackle this concern. Traditional intervention routes such as stress management workshops, health and wellness programs such as gym memberships, health screenings, etc., more supportive leadership, and flexible workload have been taken before. Notably, the majority of workplaces encourage individual interventions such as meditation, cognitive behavioral therapy, and practicing relaxation techniques.

In recent years, however, with the rapid advancement in technology, virtual reality has emerged as a form of therapeutic intervention for employee wellbeing. Research has shown that virtual reality has been able to create an illusion that results in one feeling present or "being there" in the virtual world. Berkovich-Ohana et al. (2013) and Dickenson et al. (2013) found that this immersion was linked to heightened attention and a modified sense of self and time, which are common during mindfulness practices. The complementary characteristics shared between virtual reality techniques and mindfulness along with the distinctiveness of the medium may increase the intention and motivation to engage in mindfulness practices.

VIRTUAL REALITY

Virtual Reality (VR) is a three-dimensional, computer-generated, typically interactive virtual environment that can be displayed via computer screens or wearable head-mounted displays. They are of two types, immersive and non-immersive. The non-immersive VR presents virtual information. For example, driving or flight simulations. Whereas, immersive VR allows people to experience 360 degrees of the virtual environment (Hamad and Jia, 2022). Research and other literature have also classified VR based on its two main uses or approaches.

The first approach is 'Relaxing VR' which is directly drawn from or influenced by traditional relaxation approaches like autogenic training, meditation, progressive muscle relaxation, and yoga (Pizzoli et al., 2019). Users are usually submerged in settings intended to arouse feelings of peace and security. Scenes in virtual environments are frequently linked to pleasant, serene, and restful scenarios, such as gardens, parks, islands, and other open spaces. Similar to visualization methods, these settings have proven to be successful in lowering stress (Pizzoli et al., 2019). These virtual reality (VR) solutions typically use multimodal stimuli, including tactile, visual, and auditory features in an effort to manage physiological responses and lessen physiological activation.

The next approach is the 'Engaging VR' which aims to create environments that are adaptable and adjustable, allowing users to learn about their own emotional and behavioral capacities (Pizzoli et al., 2019). This kind of technique goes beyond passive visualization of the virtual world or exposure to calming cues. Instead, it involves people interacting with the virtual environment to gain specific skills. In order to improve burn-out and psychological functioning for various professional categories, the training of emotional reactivity in response to negative stimuli has proven to be an effective key prevention intervention. This is an example of engagement VR, as it seeks to target mental presence, improve stress response capacity, as well as target emotional reactivity in stressful situations (Pizzoli et al., 2019).

Augmented reality is a part of VR that uses computer-generated images to resemble the physical world where users can interact with the physical world in a virtual space. For example, trying on clothes virtually to choose an outfit. VR was initially marketed toward gaming, but it has also been popularly used in the education, training, and healthcare sectors (Hamad and Jia, 2022).

VIRTUAL REALITY: PSYCHOLOGICAL PERSPECTIVE

Research from the past has shown that using virtual reality to interact with nature has reduced symptoms of stress, heart rate, and blood pressure (Jo et al., 2019). Researchers who gave participants five minutes to explore a virtual reality natural setting reported that the participants felt happier and more encrgetic thereafter (Reese et al., 2022). These findings demonstrate that virtual reality nature can be just as healing as a real-world natural setting. Another study found that walking through a virtual reality (VR) natural environment can have benefits that are comparable to those of walking through real-world natural settings if the VR natural environment is noticeably similar to any real-life natural environment. Reese et al. (2022) concluded that virtual reality offers a suitable substitute.

The environment in which one finds itself can play a huge role in dealing with stress. Experimental research has found a strong correlation between exposure to natural environments and the reduction of physiological stress and mental fatigue (Thoondee and Oikonomou, 2017). Thus supporting the Stress Recovery Theory and Attention Restoration Theory.

Ulrich's Stress Reduction Theory

This theory states that nature when compared to city or urban environments is beneficial because of our evolutionary adaptation to natural environments. Natural spaces allow individuals to restore their personal adaptive resources to deal with the demands of everyday life as they produce greater calming responses and reduce physiological symptoms of stress (Berto, 2014). This is known as restorative environments. Exposure to natural environments reduces negative mood, increases cognitive performance that was reduced due to stress, and increases attention (Berto, 2014).

Kaplan and Kaplan's Attention Restoration Theory

Attention Restoration Theory postulates that exposure to nature can have a positive effect on stress and help improve focus and ability to concentrate (Ackerman, 2018). In the context of a workplace, this emotional recovery during break times has proven to have a positive effect on work performance and increase job satisfaction levels. Thus, experiencing this in a VR setting may be effective in improving employee well-being and productivity, especially for those people who cannot access the real-world nature during their working hours (Thoondee and Oikonomou, 2017).

People living in remote, confined, and isolated environments cannot get free access to nature. However, new VR technology has enabled a substantial amount of presence and involvement in any scene to make people feel like they have been transported to escape their surroundings. For an environment to be healing, Kaplan contends that there must be "compatibility", a match between the individual's desired intent in the setting and the surroundings. Subjectively speaking, people tend to favor natural environments over developed or urban ones because they subconsciously feel that they are more mentally restorative. People can become more relaxed when they are shown natural scenes in VR, which is in line with numerous studies that fall under the Attention Restoration Theory. VR therefore delivers independent, private stress relief and relaxation in addition to an immersive, captivating experience, which makes it a great tool for usage among people living in isolated and confined environments. Because VR offers a sense of being elsewhere and a break from the daily stresses and strains of operation, it could improve life in isolated and confined environments. VR might be an effective means of enhancing mental health outcomes for those who work in these types of environments such as astronauts, submariners, and others (Anderson et al., 2017).

REVIEW OF LITERATURE

Straßmann, C., et al. (2019) collaborated on the creation of a virtual reality (VR) relaxation application designed for immersive relaxation and recharging energy after engaging in tasks requiring high concentration. In the face of an increasingly digitized world, employees are experiencing heightened work-related stress and emotional and cognitive burdens due to the prevalence of digitalization in the workplace. The goal of developing a VR-based immersive application was to dynamically adjust to individuals' varying states and needs by utilizing their physiological data. Users could also freely customize the application to suit their specific preferences. The study employed the Oculus Go standalone VR headset to project nature and forest scenes, fostering relaxation. Emphasis was placed on presenting scenes with continuous movements, such as drifting clouds, and incorporating appropriate audio to enhance relaxation for study participants. To explore the impact of VR on relaxation, a control group was included, receiving only relaxation audio. Participant feedback indicated that the VR application facilitated quicker and deeper relaxation, enabling them to temporarily escape their surroundings and unwind in a different environment. This development of a VR-based relaxation application has the potential to serve as a cost-effective alternative to expensive sleeping pods and other dedicated seating and relaxation environments.

The examination of the application of virtual reality (VR) interventions within the realm of work and organizational psychology was done by De Carlo et al. (2020). They claimed that VR and psychology can harmoniously coexist in organizational settings, enhancing the effectiveness and efficiency of psychological interventions for workers. In terms of stress reduction and alleviating workplace pressure, VR techniques leverage human-computer interfaces, enabling dynamic interaction with computer-generated environments. This technology surpasses traditional distraction methods by offering immersive images, facilitated by occlusive headphones that project images directly in front of the user's eyes. Furthermore, VR serves as an effective tool for teaching relaxation techniques, with the depiction of naturalistic environments through VR headsets contributing to reduced anxiety and stress. Additionally, an exemplary use of VR in the workplace is in safety training, where realistic environments allow for the assessment of employees' skills, enabling targeted skill improvement as needed. VR proves beneficial in promoting learning by providing immersive experiences that require active participant engagement. The technology has demonstrated its ability to foster trust and cooperation among group members during task performance, particularly advantageous for larger corporations. Hence, VR has the potential to enhance various factors such as risk-taking, leadership skills, resilience, optimism, and self-efficacy.

Highly stressful and emotionally taxing jobs can have a multitude of repercussions on an individual, including chronic fatigue, sense of cynicism, feeling detached, and emotional burnout. To understand how Virtual Reality can be used as a tool to facilitate emotional well-being and reduce emotional burnout among professionals, Smirnova et al. integrated virtual reality with biofeedback markers to gather further insights into the effectiveness of this intervention. Individuals aged 18 - 65 who had a Maslach Burnout Inventory score greater than 17 were included. VR environments like dynamic clouds and weather changes were used to reduce stress levels and better emotional regulation, and ReViSide technology was used to monitor breathing control based on biofeedback principles. Sessions were 2 minutes long with a 20 second rest between each stage. Participants were instructed that their breathing will directly be connected to the weather conditions in the virtual scene, tasking them to regulate it to improve the weather in the virtual world. Findings revealed that those exposed to the virtual world showed improvement in emotional exhaustion, depersonalization, and personal accomplishments, showing significant reduction in the levels of emotional burnout (Smirnova et al., 2024).

Interestingly, VR-based stress management training has also proven to be useful within the army. The Australian Defence Force were trained using a system known as Performance Edge (PE) which combined virtual reality (VR) and biofeedback to test specific cognitive and skill strategies (Kluge et al., 2023). The program was delivered through a VR headset and consisted of 5 training modules. This was a good way for the army to enhance their skill competency and knowledge. The participants showed high levels of engagement and remained fully immersed in their training and virtual environment. The participants also reported having positive feelings towards this technique to facilitate increased knowledge, better confidence in their skills, as well as heightened physical relaxation and reduced breathing rates.

Examining the Impact of VR Interventions on Workplace Well-being

Pretsch et al. (2020) aimed to examine how a virtual reality system fostered employee well-being regarding stress perception and relaxation at the workplace. On a sample of 52 participants from Germany, Austria, and Croatia, a quantitative empirical study with a pre and post-study approach was conducted. The REALEX system which is a relaxation tool that displays natural landscapes in a virtual reality setting was used. Participants were examined for their initial stress perception before they used either REALEX or a video streaming service on a classical display. The findings indicated that using a VR-based relaxation system even for a short period improved employee well-being. It was observed that the deep immersion provided by virtual reality significantly improved participants' stress perception and well-being. Since stress and stress-related illnesses are amongst the most widely known problems in the HR sector, a VR-based system can be a valuable tool.

Affirming the positive effects of Virtual Reality interventions in stress reduction among employees, Thoondee and Oikonomou (2017) analyzed its efficiency as well. A sample of 32 participants included people from varying age groups, most of them between the ages of 25 and 29. The application used was the Oculus Rift VR headset. The researchers offered two modes. In the first mode, participants were given VR glasses showing them natural landscapes that consisted of a forest scene with many areas like ponds and woodland. In the second mode, researchers tried a mixture of VR elements with office work. The second mode was introduced to examine whether employees would benefit from transferring a part of their work in a more peaceful virtual environment. Hence, some VR elements were designed for specific office work. For example, a growing plant indicates receiving a new email, or a change of weather indicates that a meeting is about to start. After this relaxation session, they were asked to fill out a questionnaire regarding their experience. 71.9% of participants reported feeling relaxed and when asked about the potential benefits of using this tool at their workplace, 87.5% responded very positively (Thoondee and Oikonomou, 2017). Thus, overall results showed that there is a huge potential for VR applications to reduce stress in the workplace.

Additionally, Riches et al. (2023) further examined how stress management interventions like virtual reality (VR) reduce workplace stress among employees by reviewing 17 published articles on Web of Science, MEDLINE, Embase, and PsycINFO databases. Out of 1270 participants, 859 experienced an immersive technology intervention. VR tools like HMD VR, VR nature scenes, VR biofeedback games, and multi-sensory "Recharge" rooms were used. The experimental conditions particularly included immersive audio-visual scenes based on nature with half of them using relaxation exercises. Results indicated that these natural virtual stimuli decreased stress and improved well-being for employees in the short term. These experiences had a positive impact on stress, affect, lowered blood pressure, increased parasympathetic activity, and reduced blood flow in the cerebral cortex in turn improving well-being, mood, and stress. Virtual Reality has proven to be a popular well-being tool as it is easy to use, affordable, safe, requires minimal space, and is easily available to employees and organizations. It can be used as a stress prevention and management tool that can be also useful for people who are traveling for work, working from home, or working in tight or restricted environments thus finding it difficult to access natural environments.

Also, Teemu Ahmaniemi et al. (2017) investigated the impact of virtual reality (VR) on stress reduction in the workplace by employing a head-mounted display, the researchers presented three distinct 360-degree nature scenes accompanied by soothing sounds and calm music. The objective was to assess the effectiveness of head-mounted displays in delivering satisfactory stress relief experiences and diverting attention from work-related responsibilities. Physiological parameters such as heart rate, blood pressure, and skin conductance were also measured throughout the six sessions to comprehensively evaluate the VR effects. Half of the sessions involved simultaneous presentation of VR video and audio, while the other half featured only relaxing audio. The study revealed that the combined presentation of VR visuals and calming audio was more effective in alleviating work-related stress compared to the audio-only condition. Furthermore, participants exhibited more relaxed physiological conditions, including heart rate, blood pressure, and skin conductivity, when exposed to VR content such as nature videos.

Similarly, De Carlo et al. (2020) set out to investigate the impact of stress management training using virtual reality devices on managers. The study involved nine managers from both public and private sectors who underwent a process of envisioning their optimal selves. The training was structured into three segments, utilizing different virtual reality environments delivered through a VR visor. Before the experiment, the managers underwent interviews to gather information on their stress levels and stress management skills. In the initial phase of the experiment, a tranquil open space chosen by the managers was projected to facilitate relaxation and contemplation of their best selves. The second phase involved projecting a happy place relevant to the managers' real lives (their homes or apartments) aiding them in visualizing their stress management capabilities. The final phase entailed projecting places the managers desired to visit but had not been to, such as the Maldives or New York. A follow-up interview revealed that the managers derived significant benefits from the training like acquiring new stress management techniques applicable to their daily lives. When experiencing decreased motivation, they often revisited the virtual reality experience to rekindle motivation. The managers also reported an enhanced ability to concentrate on tasks and find inner peace during stressful work situations.

In the same vein, Arora, S., & Mahapatra, M., investigated the efficacy of virtual reality (VR) as a remedy for workplace stress, focusing on middle to top-management-level individuals to evaluate its effects. Participants were equipped with a head-mounted device presenting a 10-minute-long 3D video, followed by interviews to gather their perspectives. Out of the 17 participants, 11 experienced tangible benefits from the VR video, reporting a genuine sense of relaxation during immersion. The study affirmed that VR serves as an effective stress-management tool. The participants were able to relax more through this because they got an opportunity to engage in this VR experience independently, free from external influences, which bettered their overall experience. Moreover, participants expressed interest in incorporating such VR experiences in their workplaces. The findings suggest that VR can successfully redirect employees' focus from workplace stressors for a designated period, providing them with the opportunity to recover and avoid continuous burnout resulting from overwhelming workloads. Additionally, VR proved to be a valuable tool in enhancing productivity by facilitating a state of complete relaxation among employees, thereby mitigating burnout. It also helps reduce the risk of increased employee turnover.

Expanding upon previous research that shows VR interventions can be beneficial for stress management, Naylor et al., 2019 examined the impact of two VR break time relaxation therapies on affect and physiological arousal in both college and the workplace. There were three conditions in the design. "SoundSelf," an immersive and interactive 20-minute meditation programme, is the first requirement. A breathing exercise with an audio component that lasted 20 minutes and was guided by the Cura Smile YouTube channel was the second condition. The final criterion was creating an immersive, non-interactive experience using merged graphics created with VisiR from Valynx Studio. 49 workers who were randomly assigned to one of the three conditions made up the sample. Fitbit was used to track the participants' heart rates, and they also had to fill out a pre- and post-test survey (PANAS). The finalised version of the intervention was recommended to friends or colleagues for relaxation reasons by 79.60% of participants overall, according to the qualitative response, and 91.84% of participants reported feeling slightly more relaxed after the intervention. The experiment's quantitative results showed that breathing exercises combined with virtual reality (VR) interventions can promote relaxation and have a favourable impact on participants' affect, which is a measure of their overall well-being. Additionally, they demonstrated a significant commitment to the creation and application of VR treatments for both personal and professional use. The findings imply that using virtual reality (VR) to lessen employee stress can be advantageous and economical.

To further investigate this phenomenon, the objective of the study conducted by Touloudi et al. (2022) was to evaluate the viability of integrating an immersive virtual reality (VR) activity into office workers' workday breaks. Forty female office workers participated in the study, which used a cycle-ergometer linked to an Immersed Virtual Reality (IVR) programme that integrated strategies to address poor motivation and exercise-related concerns. In addition to choosing their favourite surroundings and scenery, participants may self-monitor, establish exercise objectives, and get performance feedback. As part of the study methodology, participants had two minutes to become acquainted with the apparatus. After that, participants completed condition A, which required them to cycle in the VR environment for fifteen minutes while responding to twenty easy maths problems. Following a ten-minute interval, subjects undertook condition B, which consisted of cycling in an actual setting for fifteen minutes while providing verbal answers to twenty maths problems. The findings showed that the IVR exercise increased participant satisfaction, which increased intrinsic motivation and active engagement. Participants showed signs of embracing the new technology. The results showed that attitudes, enjoyment of IVR training, intention for future use, and perceived enjoyment all significantly correlated positively. The IVR system was reported to have many benefits by the participants, including increased productivity. Improvements in participants' physical and mental well-being were found in the study.

Amongst various professions, working in customer service requires long hours in high-stress conditions. The effectiveness of VR-based relaxation therapy in promoting relaxation and lowering stress levels in customer service employees was assessed by Ibrahim et al. They created XperionVR™, a virtual reality-based relaxation therapy device that is simple to use and allows staff members to practise stress management techniques. As part of the approach, forty individuals underwent virtual reality treatment sessions and subsequently provided feedback on the same through questionnaires, interviews, and in-person observations. The majority of participants reported feeling more at ease and having less tension after the VR session, according to the results. According to Ibrahim et al. (2021), staff rated the system highly in terms of effectiveness, usability, and satisfaction. As a result, virtual reality-based relaxation therapy may offer an alternate method of stress relief and management.

Recognizing the need for deeper insight, Ho et al. explored the effects of VR natural experiences on the psychological and physiological stress of workers in furniture factories, extending the effects of VR interventions on physical and mental health. Workers from two workplaces made up the sample, and they were divided into two groups: the experimental group and the control group. For a duration of 12 weeks, the VR intervention was carried out once a week during their break. For half an hour, the experimental group wore a headset and experienced virtual reality naturals. The experimental group's psychological stress showed a noteworthy reduction in distress, anxiety, and depression, along with a positive affect, according to the results. The physiological stress of manufacturing workers was positively impacted by the virtual reality natural experiences.

Additionally, VR-based therapies and training have been shown to improve personal resources, foster a more positive work atmosphere, and assist individuals in learning new coping mechanisms for stress and anxiety related to their jobs. Mora et al. (2021) looked at how VR could help managers and staff at a small private company improve their personal resources, such as resilience, stress management, and self-efficacy, in addition to lowering stress and anxiety levels related to work. Four one-hour VR sessions were given to the fourteen participants in a four-step VR process. The first and third sessions concentrated on body consciousness, while the other two sessions covered psychological techniques such as the "Virtual Three Good Things" and the "Best Possible Self" (Mora et al., 2021). Each session began and ended with the provision of a self-report questionnaire. The results showed that following VR exposure, anxiety levels decreased generally in all groups during all four sessions. At the conclusion of the intervention, the workers' satisfaction levels were high as well, averaging 9.60 on a 10-point scale. Results from the qualitative data indicate that participants had a higher level of relaxation, as evidenced by statements like “I feel calm, relaxed, and almost asleep.” They also applied the skills they had acquired during the training to their everyday lives, saying things like “VR is beautiful” and “I feel good, more relaxed, and free-minded” (Mora et al., 2021).

Horan et al. (2023) went one step further and investigated the effects of exercise and exposure to real or virtual nature on affect, boredom, and pleasure when taking breaks from stressful work. Twenty-five working adults made up the study's sample. During the first phase, participants were given the nine-dot problem to answer, which they regarded as a difficult job because of its low success rate. After they finished the activity, their wellbeing was evaluated, and they were given a 20-minute work break. There were four conditions in the experiment: a control condition in which there was no physical exercise or interaction with the natural world for the subjects. In the third condition, participants navigated a virtual nature environment for 10 minutes while engaging in light physical exercise and 10 minutes of high-fidelity virtual nature environments. The last condition required participants to engage in 20 minutes of physical exercise outdoors, such as going for a stroll. After the break, participants answered their well-being questions and went over the nine-dot problem again. The condition with no physical exercise and no interaction with nature showed the lowest levels of positive feelings, according to the study's findings. On the other hand, people who experienced real nature interaction and high-fidelity nature contact showed greater levels of contentment and state well-being. These results emphasise the importance of workplace policies, procedures, and environments that support workers in taking breaks, moving around, and interacting with real or artificial nature.

Given the gaps in existing literature, Tuomi, M. (2022) examined the many uses of virtual reality (VR) in employee training, with an emphasis on how useful it is across various roles in large businesses and organisations. Virtual reality (VR) is incredibly useful for training in scenarios like spacewalk simulations and firefighting scenarios that are too expensive, tedious, or impracticable to duplicate in real life. Studies show that putting workers in these kinds of virtual environments helps them learn new skills and perform better in practical settings. Virtual reality also makes it easier to comprehend how to use learned skill sets. For instance, virtual reality has been used in staff training by Walmart. The time needed to train their large workforce is decreased by the instant feedback that virtual reality offers. Sports training is a notable use of virtual reality (VR) that enables athletes to hone their talents without having to be physically present at the training site. To help referees identify penalties quickly prior to officiating actual games, the NFL, for example, trains its officials using virtual reality. Enhancements in task completion efficiency, skill effectiveness, and performance have been shown when VR is used into professional training.

Virtual reality is a relatively underutilized intervention avenue, particularly in the workplace, for promoting diversity, inclusion, and education. The efficacy of virtual interventions in enhancing intergroup attitudes and behaviors in nurse leaders was investigated. An efficient way to enhance critical thinking, communication, and decision-making was discovered to be virtual behavior rehearsal. Phelan et al., 2024 combined VR therapies in this study by using experience embodiment and behavior rehearsal. In the course of the study, the researchers discovered that these virtual encounters gave the participants a sense of perspective and a peek into the lives of varied health professionals. The short-term effects of virtual reality on bias, emotional empathy for members of the various groups, and support for policies that favor diverse ethnic and cultural groups have all been demonstrated to be beneficial. Significant increases in upstander behavior and emotional and cognitive empathy were observed overall in this study.

Promoting diversity and prioritizing the well-being of all employees, including those with disabilities, is essential. Some common challenges employees with disabilities face include physical accessibility, and accommodating the cognitive differences, and one innovative technique is the incorporation of virtual reality. Previous research has shown evidence of VR helping employees with increasing self-efficacy, reducing mind wandering, and preserving their attention. 23 participants with various disabilities from a warehouse setting were included, who were able to customize their experience through music, environment and voice meditation. They could interact with their environment through a head movement tracker for a more immersive experience. They spent 5 minutes of their work break for three days in the virtual environment. The findings of the study demonstrated the high effectiveness of using virtual reality to promote mindfulness. Employees left the workshops feeling more energized, resilient, and dedicated to their jobs. Employees were able to revive their energies by escaping from the stress of their jobs by immersing themselves in the virtual environment. Following the VR sessions, subjects also reported feeling calmer and having their heart rates reduced (Kuo et al., 2025). VR-guided meditation, therefore, has the potential to improve mental health and occupational engagement for people with disabilities.

The Impact of VR Interventions on Employee Wellbeing in Healthcare

Finding affordable interventions to support clinicians' well-being is urgently needed, given the critical role that they play in the healthcare sector. Adhyaru and Kemp (2022) investigated the possibility of elevating the mood of NHS clinicians during the workday by providing a brief virtual reality (VR) nature experience. 39 physicians who were given a brief virtual reality relaxation session during the course of their workday to explore “Green Meadows” in the Nature Treks application made up the sample. In addition to measuring the participants' physiological arousal (e.g., heart rate), a Visual Analogue Scale (VAS) was used to gauge the intensity of each emotion prior to and following the VR intervention in order to determine how it affected their mood. Furthermore, comments on their encounters were gathered. The results showed that participants' levels of contentment and relaxation greatly increased, while their levels of despair, rage, and anxiety had significantly decreased. The qualitative feedback was in line with the quantitative data, indicating that clinicians experienced elevated levels of calmness, happiness, and relaxation. They also mentioned that the experience was “very relaxing,” “calming and peaceful,” and that it “took their mind away from stress” (Adhyaru and Kemp, 2022). The findings suggested that using VR to enhance NHS professionals' well-being at work may be beneficial.

To test the feasibility and effectiveness of virtually immersive natural environments on well-being, Desai et al. (2025), set out to test this out with NICU healthcare professionals and aimed to reduce their perceived stress. A virtual reality headset for nature photos was provided to the subjects. The subjects completed three sessions in a single shift, completed surveys before and after breaks, and went through a few weeks without receiving any additional interventions. Results of the study show that the VR sessions were liked by the majority of the participants, who rated the experience as excellent. The participants said that their experience with the virtual reality surroundings improved their breaks and their overall performance, and it was determined that VR immersion was highly feasible for NICU healthcare personnel.

In a similar vein, a group of researchers investigated how front-line healthcare staff in treatment units responded to a 3-minute tranquil cinematic virtual reality simulation of natural scenery during COVID-19 (Beverly et al., 2022). Primary care providers, secondary care providers, and support or administrative service providers made up the sample. The participants were required to see a 26-degree film on an Oculus Go or Pico G2 4K head-mounted display featuring a verdant nature sanctuary. Prior to watching the video, participants rated their perceived stress using a questionnaire and VAS. While only 3.9% of individuals had high post-simulation stress levels, 32.4% of participants had high pre-stimulation ratings for stress (Beverly et al., 2022). There was a noticeable decrease in the mean stress reserves with a sizable effect size. This implies that the workers' perceived stress was strongly and significantly impacted by the Tranquil Cine-VR.

The relationship between virtual reality and mindfulness practices also became apparent when Soh et al. (2021) investigated the effects of VR on healthcare professionals, as well as how VR affects the practice's quality and depressive states.

An Oculus Go headgear was used in the study to recreate a virtual reality setting. Through the use of a programme called Guided Meditation, the headgear submerged users in a virtual environment that included grass, trees, mountains, and a stream. Additionally, each participant received a headset that played soothing music without graphic elements. The results showed that participants' sense of presence during mindfulness practice was improved by the immersive experience made possible by virtual reality. The use of guided images in the virtual reality setting made for a more captivating and multisensory experience. The audio-only programme was effective in establishing a realistic atmosphere and encouraging participation from the participants in the exercise. A higher awareness of their breathing was also noticed by the participants from the audio-only practice. These results demonstrated VR's potential for successful integration with mindfulness training.

Williams and Riches (2023) investigated the viability and acceptability of VR relaxation for staff members of a psychiatric rehabilitation ward, building on the research on VR's effects on the wellbeing of workers in the healthcare industry. During a single VR relaxation session, staff members were instructed to don a VR head-mounted display and explore tranquil, immersive virtual landscapes. The amount of time spent in virtual reality, the number of environments visited, and the speed at which different session components were finished were all used to gauge the feasibility variable. On the other hand, the acceptance variable was assessed using a comparison of the visual analogue scales (VAS) used before and after VR. The scale for elements including stress, feelings of joy or sorrow, connection to nature, relaxation, and anxiety went from 0 ("not at all") to 10 ("very"). Feedback on the narrative from the post-VR session was also collected. Results showed a considerable decrease in stress, anxiety, and depression and a significant increase in enjoyment, relaxation, and a sense of being connected to nature (Williams and Riches, 2023). Both immersion and helpfulness received great ratings. The employees were eager to conduct more of these sessions because they enjoyed the participatory aspects of the setting and found it to be a helpful diversion from work-related stress. VR has therefore enormous promise for wider application and has been shown to be both practical and well-liked in supporting psychiatric rehabilitation ward staff.

Virtual Reality in Workplace Design

Traditional workplaces are changing and evolving as time goes on, especially since the COVID-19 pandemic that paved the way for remote and hybrid work cultures. With people going back to their offices, Aufegger et al. (2022) wanted to investigate how traditional workplaces can be transformed to combine the up and coming field of virtual reality to understand if it will have any impact on employee well-being and productivity. Through their "Ecology of Work" model, they combined collaboration, community, and identity, with systems like nature of work, physical configurations of the office, and the work environment. Virtual reality decreased the limitations of deciding between open or closed office layouts by allowing the employees to customize their workspaces to allow for both individual and group activities. The additional flexibility, ergonomic factors, and customization were found to add value to the physical workspaces, thereby promoting the use of virtual reality as a better alternative to enhance workspaces.

Sometimes, traditional workplace designs can cause more harm than good. A common health hazard in industries like manual labor and manual assembly include musculoskeletal disorders. Káčerová et al. (2022) proposed a creative way to design and maximize industrial workspaces with the use of virtual reality and motion capture (MoCap) technology. A preliminary study with 20 participants was conducted at an automotive assembly line to put this to the test. The employees were equipped with the Oculus Quest 2 along with a Perception Neuron Studio MoCap suit to track their movements. The researchers proposed that with the help of virtual reality, ergonomics during the pre-production period could be assessed and adjusted with the help of a virtual work-station, rather than building a physical mock-up. The pilot study revealed that the VR-MoCap was a close match to the real-life measurements, which strengthened the validity of the testing. The method was found to be efficient, and reduced costs when it came to developing the ergonomic conditions of the workplace.

Furthermore, ergonomic developments in industrial settings are pivotal for employee wellbeing. In the automotive sector, Carnazzo et al. (2024) used motion capture or MoCap technology alongside the Inertial Measurement Unit (IMU), giving analysts the ability to use virtual reality and carry out three dimensional posture analysis as they interacted with their virtual workspaces. The tool helps predict the postures for individuals based on their unique body proportions using inverse kinematics and ergonomist-informed postural rules. The application thus allowed for a more proactive approach to enhancing the ergonomics of the work-place without having to create multiple physical prototypes to accommodate each individual, thereby creating a more inclusive workspace design.

Similarly, VR based body tracking suits can be used to assess human posture to assess the potential risks, specifically using the Rapid Upper Limb Assessment (RULA) method. The technology observed both virtual and real environments, using actual and virtual cues to identify and study the posture of employees. Virtually, the employees engaged with workspace simulations, which let the designers catch and minimize the potential ergonomic disadvantages before they could implement them into the actual physical environment.

Another important VR tool researchers have used to develop ergonomic conscious workspaces is the use of wearable sensors, exoskeletons, and extended reality (XR). Especially in industries like construction, the risk of workplace hazards are high, and VR technology has allowed researchers to gather real time data and gather information on real-time movements, which let them identify hazardous posture and other related risks that might contribute to musculoskeletal disorders. Through the use of virtual reality, employees can be educated on various safety techniques with the use of virtual simulations, instead of spending time and energy on replicating the various situations physically.

However, using VR technology to combat workplace ergonomic designs come with their own set of challenges. Chen and Wu (2022) looked at the possible negative effects on the user. Factors like physical discomfort from the head-mounted displays, muscle fatigue, visual and cognitive demands, and motion sickness can negatively affect the user. The authors pointed out that both hardware factors such as display quality, and software factors such as content complexity can pose problems to the effective use of virtual reality alternatives. Thus, they suggest three main priorities when it comes to research based on VR techniques: bettering the VR hardware devices to promote more comfort, improving the software designs to reduce discomfort, and to foster more comprehensive and user-centered systems to decrease discomfort.

ETHICAL CONCERNS

Concerns about the moral implications of this new and quickly developing technology surfaced as virtual reality's use as a therapeutic method rose. Rizzo et al. (2003) state that because of their cognitive or sensorimotor challenges, people with CNS deficits and other clinical populations may have issues with virtual environment (VE) interaction. It may cause individuals to exert more non-automatic cognitive effort, which could divert attention and hamper the healing process. Given the increased accessibility and affordability of VE tools, there is significant worry regarding the possibility of naive or harmful misuse of VE technology in the workplace with vulnerable populations. As a result, people who might not be qualified to provide these services could cause more harm than benefit.

Furthermore, aftereffects have been reported and cybersickness is one of the VE-related side effects (Rizzo et al., 2003). Motion sickness known as "cybersickness" manifests as nausea, vertigo, eyestrain, vomiting, and disorientation (Rizzo et al., 2003). It is thought to be related to sensory cue incongruity, which occurs when information about sensory cues in the virtual environment is inconsistent with how the person's body is feeling or what their perception of sensory-motor experiences in the "real world" would predict. It may therefore result in these adverse effects.

Changes in postural control, flashbacks, difficulty moving, sleepiness, decreased arousal, and exhaustion are some of the aftereffects. The delay in acclimating to non-VE environments is a sign of aftereffects (Rizzo et al., 2003).

Moreover, concerns have been expressed regarding the use of virtual reality for ergonomic measurement and bettering the workplace design, the absence of haptic feedback was one of the most influential disadvantages (Manghisi et al., 2022). The lack of haptic feedback did not allow for proper task simulation, which reduced the accuracy of the posture assessments. Another notable concern is that occasionally, some body parts come in the way of others when performing tracking tasks, which affects the reliability of data (Kačerová et al., 2022). Furthermore, wearable virtual reality tools pose is their lack of inclusivity. This could influence the data, and might exclude certain body types and designs, leading to skewed data and biased results (Manghisi et al., 2022). Privacy concerns and data security are also factors that influence the quality of the data. Some individuals might not feel comfortable sharing data about their health or other personal information (Rahman et al., 2023).

Lastly, there has been concern expressed about people trying to "cure" themselves with these methods and never seeking professional help when necessary (Rizzo et al., 2003). This can sometimes exacerbate symptoms because these interventions have only demonstrated short-term positive effects due to a lack of longitudinal research.

CONCLUSION

Conventional approaches to stress management and employee well-being are coming under threat from technological advancements. There is a greater focus on technological advancement, and virtual reality (VR) has emerged as a well-liked tool for well-being because of its accessibility to employees and organisations, low cost, safety, and little area needs (Riches et al., 2023). In addition to being a tool for skill development and assessment, it may be used to prevent and manage stress. This is beneficial for those who find it challenging to access natural environments because they work from home, travel for business, or reside in small spaces.

The environment surrounding employees is essential to their productivity and motivation levels. It also assists them with dealing with their stressors and coping with them. Various experiments have found the benefits of exposure to natural environments and stress reduction and managing mental fatigue. But with the present level of work and stress, not everyone has the means to set time apart to spend in nature. This is where technology like virtual reality comes along. Exposure to virtual natural environments like forests, and open natural environments, and listening to nature sounds like birds chirping, lakes and waterfalls have a very similar effect on mental health as real exposure to nature. Exposing individuals to nature through

VR for 10 to 20 minutes has been shown to improve their stress levels, productivity, thinking, skill enhancements, and overall mood.

In the modern era, virtual reality is becoming more widely used and accepted, yet it also has drawbacks and raises ethical questions. Because technology is so readily available, it is quite easy to misuse it. These interventions may be used by people in an attempt to "cure" themselves without getting the necessary medical assistance. Virtual reality and other immersive technologies might have unintended consequences such as cybersickness, a motion sickness that can cause dizziness, nausea, and eye pain. Our senses may be momentarily affected by aftereffects as the body tries to adjust to the "real world." Therefore, it's critical to understand when technology is appropriate and inappropriate.

Despite its disadvantages, VR has immense potential for wider implementation and has proven to be feasible and acceptable to support employees with taking better care of their mental health and preventing burnout. Virtual reality not only facilitates relaxation and stress reduction but also provides organizations with a holistic and innovative tool to pave the way for employee well-being.

REFERENCES

Adhyaru, J. S., & Kemp, C. (2022). Virtual reality as a tool to promote wellbeing in the workplace. *Digital Health, 8*, 205520762210844. DOI: 10.1177/20552076221084473 PMID: 35284084

Ahmaniemi, T., Lindholm, H., Kiti Müller, & Tapio Taipalus. (2017). Virtual reality experience as a stress recovery solution in workplace. *2017 IEEE Life Sciences Conference (LSC)*. DOI: 10.1109/LSC.2017.8268179

American Psychological Association. (2014, July 1). Coping with stress at work. apa.org. https://www.apa.org/topics/healthy-workplaces/work-stress

Anderson, A. P., Mayer, M. D., Fellows, A. M., Cowan, D. R., Hegel, M. T., & Buckey, J. C. (2017). Relaxation with immersive natural scenes presented using virtual reality. *Aerospace Medicine and Human Performance, 88*(6), 520–526. DOI: 10.3357/AMHP.4747.2017 PMID: 28539139

Arora, S., & Mahapatra, M. (2022). Virtual reality as a solution for workplace stress. *International Journal of Indian Psychology, 10*(1), 674–690. DOI: 10.25215/1001.068

Aufegger, L., Elliott-Deflo, N., & Nichols, T. (2022). Workspace and productivity: Guidelines for virtual reality workplace design and optimization. *Applied Sciences (Basel, Switzerland), 12*(15), 7393. DOI: 10.3390/app12157393

Berto, R. (2014). The role of nature in coping with psycho-physiological stress: A literature review on restorativeness. *Behavioral Sciences, 4*(4), 394–409. MDPI. DOI: 10.3390/bs4040394

Beverly, E., Hommema, L., Coates, K., Duncan, G., Gable, B., Gutman, T., Love, M., Love, C., Pershing, M., & Stevens, N. (2022). A tranquil virtual reality experience to reduce subjective stress among COVID-19 frontline healthcare workers. *PLoS One, 17*(2), e0262703. DOI: 10.1371/journal.pone.0262703 PMID: 35139092

Carnazzo, C., Spada, S., Lamacchia, S., Manuri, F., Sanna, A., & Cavatorta, M. P. (2024). Virtual reality in ergonomics by wearable devices: Experiences from the automotive sector. *Journal of Workplace Learning, 36*(7), 621–635. DOI: 10.1108/JWL-03-2024-0064

Chen, Y., & Wu, Z. (2022). A review on ergonomics evaluations of virtual reality. *Work (Reading, Mass.), 74*(3), 831–841. DOI: 10.3233/WOR-205232 PMID: 36442175

De Carlo, A., Carluccio, F., & Rapisarda, S. (2020). Three Uses Of Virtual Reality In Work And Organizational Psychology Interventions. A dialogue between virtual reality and organizational well-being: Relaxation techniques, personal resources, and anxiety/depression treatments. *TPM. Testing, Psychometrics, Methodology in Applied Psychology*, *27*(1). Advance online publication. DOI: 10.4473/TPM27.1.8

De Carlo, A., Rapisarda, S., Mora, D., & Benevene, P. (2020). Your best virtual self-improvement. the use of virtual reality in stress management training. *Psychological Applications and Trends*, *2020*, 103–107. Advance online publication. DOI: 10.36315/2020inpact022

Desai, S., Athalye-Jape, G., Bottcher, S., Campbell, C., Chiffings, D., Nathan, E., Fardinpour, A., Kinnaird, L., Bulsara, M., & Rao, S. (2025). Effect of using virtual reality on fatigue and mental workload as key determinants of perceived stress in neonatal intensive care staff: A randomized controlled trial feasibility study and protocol. *Nursing in Critical Care*, *30*(2), e13249. Advance online publication. DOI: 10.1111/nicc.13249 PMID: 39989032

Hamad, A., & Jia, B. (2022). How virtual reality technology has changed our lives: An overview of the current and potential applications and limitations. *International Journal of Environmental Research and Public Health*, *19*(18), 11278. Advance online publication. DOI: 10.3390/ijerph191811278 PMID: 36141551

Horan, K. A., Harrington, M., LeNoble, C. A., Mosher, M., & Pring, T. (2023). Using virtual reality to bring restorative environments to employees: An online pilot study. *International Journal of Environmental Research and Public Health*, *20*(10), 5797. DOI: 10.3390/ijerph20105797 PMID: 37239525

Ibrahim, N., & Manzura Mohd Mahidin, E. Azmi Mohd Yusof, Rusli, M. E., Iskandar, N. S., Farhah Amaliya Zaharuddin, & Imran Mahalil. (2021). VR-based relaxation therapy for customer service staff: A pilot study. *Lecture Notes in Computer Science*, *13051*, 171–183. DOI: 10.1007/978-3-030-90235-3_15

Jo, H., Song, C., & Miyazaki, Y. (2019). Physiological Benefits of Viewing Nature: A Systematic Review of Indoor Experiments. *International Journal of Environmental Research and Public Health*, *16*(23), 4739. DOI: 10.3390/ijerph16234739 PMID: 31783531

Kačerová, I., Kubr, J., Hořejší, P., & Kleinová, J. (2022). Ergonomic design of a workplace using virtual reality and a motion capture suit. *Applied Sciences (Basel, Switzerland)*, *12*(4), 2150. DOI: 10.3390/app12042150

Kluge, M. G., Maltby, S., Kuhne, C., Walker, N., Bennett, N., Aidman, E., Nalivaiko, E., & Walker, F. R. (2023). Evaluation of a virtual reality platform to train stress management skills for a defense workforce: Multisite, mixed methods feasibility study. *Journal of Medical Internet Research*, *25*, e46368–e46368. DOI: 10.2196/46368 PMID: 37930751

Kuo, H. J., Newbutt, N., George, S., & Laird, M. (2025). Using virtual reality mediation in a workplace setting for employees with disabilities: A pilot study. *Computers & Education: X Reality*, *6*, 100093. DOI: 10.1016/j.cexr.2025.100093

Manghisi, V. M., Evangelista, A., & Uva, A. E. (2022). A virtual reality approach for assisting sustainable human-centered ergonomic design: The ergovr tool. *Procedia Computer Science*, *200*, 1338–1346. DOI: 10.1016/j.procs.2022.01.335

Mora, D., Falco, A., Annamaria Di Sipio, & Alessandro De Carlo. (2021). 4 steps for fighting covid-related anxiety: an application of virtual reality in a small company. *Psychological Applications and Trends 2021*, 287–301. DOI: 10.36315/2021inpact061

Naylor, M., Morrison, B., Ridout, B., & Campbell, A. (2019). Augmented experiences: Investigating the feasibility of virtual reality as part of a workplace wellbeing intervention. *Interacting with Computers*, *31*(5), 507–523. DOI: 10.1093/iwc/iwz033

Phelan, S. M., Burkhartzmeyer, H. L., Standen, E. C., Arcand, L. L., Kiker, K. M., Simiele, K. C., Proulx, A. L., Storsveen, A. S., Deng, Y., Foote, J. M., Kumbamu, A., Prakaashana, A. N., & Nelson, D. E. (2024). A virtual reality intervention to increase interracial empathy and upstander behaviors in nursing leaders. *Social Science & Medicine*, *366*(117648), 117648–117648. DOI: 10.1016/j.socscimed.2024.117648 PMID: 39740631

Pizzoli, S. F. M., Mazzocco, K., Triberti, S., Monzani, D., Alcañiz Raya, M. L., & Pravettoni, G. (2019). User-centered virtual reality for promoting relaxation: An innovative approach. *Frontiers in Psychology*, *10*, 479. Advance online publication. DOI: 10.3389/fpsyg.2019.00479 PMID: 30914996

Pretsch, E., Saretzki, J., Kraus, H., & Grossmann, G. (2020). Improving employee well-being by means of virtual reality - REALEX: An empirical case study. *European Journal of Economics and Business Studies*, *6*(1). https://revistia.com/files/articles/ejes_v6_i1_20/Pretsch.pdf

Rahman, M. H., Ghasemi, A., Dai, F., & Ryu, J. (2023). Review of Emerging Technologies for Reducing Ergonomic Hazards in Construction Workplaces. *Buildings (Basel, Switzerland)*, *13*(12), 2967. DOI: 10.3390/buildings13122967

Reese, G., Stahlberg, J., & Menzel, C. (2022). Digital shinrin-yoku: Do nature experiences in virtual reality reduce stress and increase well-being as strongly as similar experiences in a physical forest? *Virtual Reality (Waltham Cross)*, *26*(3), 1245–1255. DOI: 10.1007/s10055-022-00631-9

Riches, S., Taylor, L., Jeyarajaguru, P., Veling, W., & Valmaggia, L. (2023). Virtual reality and immersive technologies to promote workplace wellbeing: A systematic review. *Journal of Mental Health (Abingdon, England)*, *33*(2), 1–21. DOI: 10.1080/09638237.2023.2182428 PMID: 36919828

Smirnova, D., Spikina, A., Mezentseva, D., Vlasov, A., Astafeva, D., Berkovich, E., Kruk, L., Palevskaya, S., Shport, S., Akhapkin, R., Ashurov, Z., Khairedinova, I., Skugarevski, O., Chaplygin, S., Kolsanov, A., & Syunyakov, T. (2024). Virtual reality (vr) device with integrated biofeedback sensors (reviside) to cope with emotional burnout state among employees experiencing stress at workplace: Problem overview and action plan. *Psychiatria Danubina*, *36*(Suppl 2), 354–360. https://pubmed.ncbi.nlm.nih.gov/39378496/ PMID: 39378496

Soh, D. J. H., Ong, C. H., Fan, Q., Seah, D. J. L., Henderson, S. L., Jeevanandam, L., & Doshi, K. (2021). Exploring the use of virtual reality for the delivery and practice of stress-management exercises. *Frontiers in Psychology*, *12*, 640341. Advance online publication. DOI: 10.3389/fpsyg.2021.640341 PMID: 34149524

Straßmann, C., Eimler, S. C., Arntz, A., Keßler, D., Zielinski, S., Brandenberg, G., Dümpel, V., & Handmann, U. (2019). Relax yourself - using virtual reality to enhance employees' mental health and work performance. *Extended Abstracts of the 2019 CHI Conference on Human Factors in Computing Systems*, 1–6. DOI: 10.1145/3290607.3312946

Thoondee, K. D., & Oikonomou, A. (2017). Using virtual reality to reduce stress at work. *2017 Computing Conference*. Institute of Electrical and Electronics Engineers. DOI: 10.1109/SAI.2017.8252142

Touloudi, E., Hassandra, M., Galanis, E., Goudas, M., & Theodorakis, Y. (2022). Applicability of an immersive virtual reality exercise training system for office workers during working hours. *Sports (Basel, Switzerland)*, *10*(7), 104. DOI: 10.3390/sports10070104 PMID: 35878115

Tuomi, M. (2022). Virtual training in the workplace. *Theseus.fi*. https://www.theseus.fi/handle/10024/748076

Williams, G., & Riches, S. (2023). Virtual reality relaxation for staff wellbeing on a psychiatric rehabilitation ward: A feasibility and acceptability study. *Journal of Psychiatric Intensive Care*, *19*(1), 51–58. DOI: 10.20299/jpi.2023.006

KEY TERMS AND DEFINITIONS

Virtual Reality (VR): A computer-generated world that surrounds an individual visually and auditorily, making one feel like they are present inside a simulated scene.

Immersive: An experience in VR that engages multiple sensory modalities so deeply that users temporarily lose awareness of their actual surroundings.

Non-Immersive: A mode of VR in which computer-generated content is presented via various displays, while keeping awareness of the physical environment.

VR Headset / Head-Mounted Display (HMD): A goggle-like device that has small screens and motion sensors that syncs the virtual world and updates the view as you move in your surroundings.

Stress-Management Interventions: Structured programs designed to reduce psychological and physiological stress responses such as racing heartbeat and prevent burnout, in this context delivered through VR platforms.

Physiological Arousal: The body's alertness level, seen by symptoms like racing heartbeat, sweat, or a surge of stress hormones or adrenaline when one is under pressure.

Personal Adaptive Resources: An individual's cognitive, mental, emotional, and behavioural capacities such as resilience, coping strategies, etc. that help regulate stress.

User-Centered Systems: Consists of interactive technology that is tailored to meet users' needs, thereby maximising its usability, safety, and user acceptance.

Ergonomic: Designed to match the body's posture and movements in order to lower discomfort or strain.

Chapter 12
Remote Work Reimagined:
How Emotional Intelligence Strengthens Digital Collaboration

Swapandeep Kaur
Chandigarh Group of Colleges Jhanjeri, Mohali, India & Department of Management (MBA), Chandigarh School of Business, India

Neha Kumari
https://orcid.org/0000-0002-0407-1514
Chandigarh Group of Colleges Jhanjeri, Mohali, India & Department of Management (MBA), Chandigarh School of Business, India

Manpreet Kaur
Swami Vivekanand Institute of Engineering and Technology, Banur, India

Divyansh Mittal
https://orcid.org/0009-0003-4358-1458
Chandigarh Engineering College, India

ABSTRACT

Digital modernization of the workplace has increased the transition from traditional working to teleworking and hybrid contexts. Although digital tools have enhanced efficiency and connection, in some cases they create psychological/physical separation or exposure fatigue and communication barriers. Emotional intelligence consisting in the ability to perceive, understand and manage emotions, has been increasingly recognized as one of the major prerequisites for success in online environments. This study identified opportunities where improving EI might improve virtual workplaces through enhanced communication collaboration and

DOI: 10.4018/979-8-3373-3658-9.ch012

employee wellbeing. A mixed-method approach was performed to explore stress management effective leadership remote team dynamics and how organizations can foster human-centered sustainable digital work culture through digital emotional intelligence in this study. The results provide evidence-based suggestions for how to enact EI-related interventions within hybrid and remote contexts, as well as ethical considerations and recommendations for further research.

1. INTRODUCTION

1.1 Background

The offices of the current and the next few years are incredibly influenced by the ever fast forward moving technology and the global flow towards working from home and hybrid. The COVID-19 pandemic expedited all things digital Guys and altered what organizations had previously been attuned to doing, and at the same time the pandemic has forced organizations to immediately embrace digital platforms to keep the flow of work continuously efficient (Lund et al., 2021). Employees also often mention feeling disconnected emotionally from co-workers with little to no interaction resulting in a lack of team building and morale (Miller et al., 2021). Additionally, excessive use of digital platforms for workplace activities has created a form of a common "digital fatigue" that is a form of mental exhaustion due to long screen viewing and continuous virtual communication (Haiilo, 2023). Even though they had all these digital tools and pl atforms you w ere able to do even more efficiently and connect even better, suddenly that also created new challenges, that people lose the emotional connection, that more tiredness arises, if you talk someone from a distance you may have some barriers of communicating. Now, organizations are exploring new approaches to maintaining a productive distributed workforce while preserving the health and well-being of their employees.

1.2 The role of Emotional Intelligence

In the digital age, the significance of emotional intelligence is visible in management of communication and information systems. Goleman (1995). Emotional Intelligence means the ability to perceive, understand and regulate emotions, and to understand and respond to the emotions of others. In the digital and hybrid workplace where traditional physical contact is scarce, emotional intelligence allows individuals to fill the human emotional and social void between people. As a result, individuals with high emotional inteligence, are better in cooperating, conflict resolution and have a better ability for empathic communication which is vital in the modern work.

(Mayer, Solvey and Caruso, 2008). According to Cherniess (2010) employees who possess high emotional intelligence can cope with stress, evaluate the change and maintain good human relations and are considered essential in organizations in a high-stress digital world. These are the competencies that are going to become very essential in any IT environment where we can't afford to take our own sweet time in doing research, when we can go collaborate online with our peers and people that we are leading cross function and cross dimensions as a team. Intuitively, emotionally intelligent parents with the strength in this competency inspiration build trust and psychological safety with their virtual teams, and are more adept at coping with ambiguity, motivating distributed workers and creating digital cultures that are inclusive (Boyatzis, Goleman and Rhee, 2000).

1.3 Research Objectives

The present study was conducted to fulfill the following objectives

1. To assess the current scenario of emotional intelligence in remote teams
2. To estimate the impact of Emotional Intelligence on the digital collaboration, well-being, and productivity improvement.
3. To investigate the major constraints that can impact the strategies for improving employee engagement in digital workplace.

1.4 Research Questions

1. How does emotional intelligence influence collaboration and morale in digital workspaces?
2. What strategics do organizations use to develop EI among remote employees?
3. What are the professed reimbursements and barriers of implementing EI practices digitally?

1.5 Hypotheses

H1: Improved collaboration and less conflict are associated with distant team members who possess higher emotional intelligence levels.

H2: In digital workplaces, companies that actively support emotional intelligence (EI) claim greater employee retention and happiness.

1.6 Need and Scope of the study

The accelerated transition from traditional working methods to digital and hybrid systems has reset organizational forms, modes of communication, and social relations. While this technology has facilitated flexibility ---- It has also posed some challenges — disconnect from emotional relations, break in face to face communication, work-related stress, and diminished social bonding. These challenges have highlighted the heightened importance of emotional intelligence.

Yet much of the significance of emotional intelligence in remote situations is still not backed up by organized ways to develop and leverage it. By exploring the role of emotional intelligence in enhancing digital collaboration, enhancing productivity, and supporting employee well-being, the present study attempts to fill this gap. To study the hindrance of effectively engaging with the employee strategies at the digital workplace is another objective. To build their digitally sustainable and emotionally resilient cultures, organisations need to understand these. The study also examines how emotionally intelligent leadership, particularly in remote workforces, enhances conflict resolution, team unity and retention of employees.

The topic of this study is the comprehensive evaluation of emotional intelligence under digitally mediated work settings, especially in remote and hybrid teams. It investigates the impact of different dimensions of emotional intelligence (EI) at work (self-awareness, emotional control, empathy and social skills) upon managing stress, working in a team and leadership effectiveness. It also examines organizational strategies employing digital tools, policies and training that leverage emotional intelligence. While the research is on digitally enabled industries at large, we believe it generalizes to other industries trying to succeed in digital.

LITERATURE REVIEW

Within the realm of theory, emotional intelligence encompasses several models such as those by Salovey and Mayer, Bar-On and Goleman. The four cardinal aspects of Salovey and Mayer's model are perceiving emotions, facilitating emotions, utilizing emotions to assist thought, and managing emotions. Bar-On's model broadens the spectrum to include personality traits as resilience and social competences. Goleman's model has placed emphasis on five competencies that he believed are necessary to being a successful person or employee: self-awareness, self-regulation, motivation, empathy, and social skills (Grehen, etal.,2023).

2.1 Schematic Concept of Emotional Intelligence

The irst definition to appear for EQ was from Mayer and Salovey (1990), who list the term as the ability to monitor one's own and others' feelings. Since then, various models have been developed for applying this knowledge in the private as well as the business world.

Specifically, Salovey and Mayer's four-branch model consist of:

Emotion Perception: Recognising emotions in faces, music and the world around us.

Using Emotion to Help You Think: Using feelings to help you concentrate and other mental tasks.

Emotion Understanding: Being aware of the language of emotions and the subtle nature of emotions themselves.

Emotion Management: Emotion control for self and others for self and/or other advancement.

Five Components of Emotional Intelligence The model of emotional intelligence proposed by Daniel Goleman (1995) emphasizes the following:

In this way Bar-On's Emotional Quotient inventory (EQ-I) represented intrapersonal/ and interpersonal/ stress management traits and combined personality and psychological well- being in the reformulation of EI. Hence, we can infer or deduce from the above theories that EI tend to be practical and learnable, and hence it is important for an individual in a work setting.

2.2 Emotional Intelligence and the Digital/Virtual Workplace

Remote work has radically altered the dynamics of interpersonal communication and leadership. Digital tools are helping to remedy the workflow effectiveness and flexibility but don't completely replace the spontaneous human interactions that contribute to trust and empathy between team members. Few of the researches provided below which depicts the strong backing towards emotional intelligence in digital workplace.

Calefato et al. (2020) attempted to investigate association between EI and stress management. Research indicate that emotional intelligence is very essential in maintaining a virtual team collaboration as well as stress and miscommunication management.

Cavazotte et al. (2012) studied the relationship between emotional intelligence and the performance of digital workspace and identified that performance in virtual teams was enhanced when leaders have emotional intelligence.

Chamakiotis et al. (2021) researched abilities of emotional intelligence staff. Author further specifies that while individuals in virtual teams with high EI are motivated to adjust to asynchronous communication, their stress level will be lower.

It is therefore reasonable to conclude that the organisations that are rolling out digital EI training for their employees and leaders are experiencing improved engagement and lower levels of attrition as well as increasing psychological safety amongst remote teams (EHL Insights, 2022).

2.3 Cassandra principal considerations: the Digital Emotional Intelligence (DEI)

Digital Emotional Intelligence (DEI) refers to how emotional intelligence is practiced in online spaces. As work becomes increasingly mediated by technology, work that includes capacities like reading digital body language, to empathize through a screen and to have skills and abilities to prevent burnout are now key competencies for performance and success.

These are some of the critical DEI competences:

Virtual empathy
Being Bright and Clear in Digital Communication
Diagnosing digital fatigue
Online psychological safety

According to the World Economic Forum (2020), DEI is a requirement skill for future workforce. Even services like Microsoft Teams and Slack have been introducing features that help users interpret tone and emotional context, if further proof that emotional intelligence translates (badump-ch) to software applications is needed.

2.4 Prerequisites of Remote Work: Emotional Intelligence and Leadership

Emotionally intelligent Leaders:
Build trust and solicitude for others to participate.
Keep your vision steady even when your vision gets cloudy.
Recognise team members are emotional working remotely.

Goleman et al (2013) are of the view that EI play a role in making leaders, transform leaders- A leader who communicates with the virtual remote team.

Carasco-Saul et al. identified leadership effectiveness via face-to-face forms of working (Stough et al., 2011) and, as a concept, is particularly pertinent to leading teams working virtually, having virtual team members and residing in a virtual team environment (Gustafsson et al., 2007; Krishnan et al., 2013).

2.5 Enhancing Team Collaboration Using EI

Remote teams have specific issues with time zones, less in-person interaction and possible misunderstandings in communication. Such reasons can prevent them from working together and can lead to a team losing their work dynamics. However, a body of research stands at the possibility that EI can be a valuable personal resource to overcome them. EI assists team members in becoming more clear in virtual meetings, by developing empathetic listening and careful replying. It promotes mental well-being too, with its focus on getting to know and to reflect with each other, despite being physically apart. You can't form trust and establish an open channel of communication simply by sending emails or attending conference calls, which is what makes EI a powerful tool for working remotely.

Grehen and Grehen (2023) studied virtual teams and found that teams working at high levels of EI scored 27% higher on collaboration and were 18% less on conflict compared to teams not doing EI work in their organization.

The results in the table indicate that Emotional Intelligence (EI) is crucial for improving virtual teams' effectiveness since it aligns the communication and personal languages that are assumed while working r remotely in which there is no face to face face-tofacemeeting22. Spread D, where tone of voice can be lost in translation digitally, self-monitoring is key in being able to communicate effectively (Goleman, 1995).

By being empathetic team members are able to build a stronger mental model of their colleague's perspectives, and this ultimately cultivates psychological safety and inclusion as well as reduces emotional strain and miscommunication (Salas et al., 2015). Emotional regulation also enables good judgment under stress, leading to better problem solving and conflict resolution in high stress virtual environments (cf., Mayer, Salovey, & Caruso, 2008).

Finally, the existence of good social skills is crucial to sustain digital rapport and engagement which is crucial to maintain team cohesion when no physical presence is felt (Chi, Huang, & Lin, 2020). Collectively, these specific EI traits build trust and enhance cooperation while also facilitating communication, which are essential for effective functioning of virtual teams.

Table 1. Benefits of High EI in virtual teams

EI Factor	Impact
Self-awareness	Clearer self-expression in virtual settings
Empathy	Reduced miscommunication and tension
Emotional regulation	Improved decision-making under pressure
Social skills	Stronger digital rapport and engagement

2.6 Emotional intelligence and commitment of employees

People with high EQ are instinctively people-oriented, which leads to higher personal and team performance. They demonstrate their ability to deal with high-stress situations by controlling the emotions and remaining calm in difficult situations. Their resilience enables them to manage change in healthy ways, and to help others to do the same. In addition, emotionally intelligent people develop stronger relationships because they are empathetic, they listen to others and when they respond, they do so in a thoughtful manner. It's that unique character which not only breeds a positive workplace environment, but also increases teamwork and thus group success. Ei training increases job satisfaction and long-term career commitment (Cherniss, 2010). When it comes to remote work, that means less view, More satisfaction Music and more peer support. As a result, Miao et al., (2017) clarified emotional regulation predicts burnout variance particularly strong in high demad work jobs such as customer support and project management.

2.7 EO Training and Development in Digital Work Environment

Today more emphasis is being placed on Emotional Intelligence (EI) within the organisations and organisations investing in various schemes to improve among the workforce. These include EI training, role-plays in simulated environments and even using psychological tools to support people in understanding their feelings and emotional responses. Digital mindfulness and happiness programs to encourage emotional well-being are also being implemented by many companies. For example, the "Search Inside Yourself" program offered by Google is widely considered to be the gold standard on emotional training, and SAP has deployed tools to bolster mental health and claims greater productivity after investing in EI development.

2.8 Difficulties in and Ethical Issues of Implementing EI

There are inhibitive factors and ethical concerns regarding the provision of EIs. The assessment of EI is still a challenge in terms of measuring reliably and validly this subjective and complex construct. From a cultural perspective, such misinterpretation may also occur due to different ways of expressing and interpreting emotional content, which may differ between cultures. Additionally, the ethics of EI tools, especially those with emotional monitoring, are an issue. Crawford and Paglen (2021) raise concerns about affective computing and the application of AI to analyse emotional data at work. When employed for hiring or monitoring current employees, these practices give rise to serious privacy and informed consent concerns, and highlight the importance for ethical AI applications to be performed with explicit ethical considerations in mind.

2.9 Gaps in the Literature

Despite the accumulating body of literature focused on EI, there are still several key issues that remain under investigated. One such domain is that of cross-cultural digital emotional intelligence perception. In the context of global and diverse organizations, it is important for leaders to understand how EI manifests, is perceived, and interpreted across cultures (and in particular, in virtual environments) to ensure they are creating inclusive and fair remote workspaces. A second area that is up-and-coming has not been adequately researched is the use of emotional AI in Human Resource (HR) technologies. Although AI applications are emerging for analyzing emotional cues of candidates during hiring or for tracking employee wellness, there is little research into their accuracy, ethical implications or potential biases. Furthermore, no longitudinal studies have reported the long-term effects of EI training on employee turnover in virtual or mixed agile/hybrid workforces. In other words, to what extent the development of EI drives longer-term improvements in engagement, teamwork and commitment would be invaluable for HR strategies and leadership development programmes. These issues need to be addressed if EI is to be optimally used in the future of work.

4. RESEARCH METHODOLOGY

4.1 Research Design

This study also adopts a convergent parallel mixed method that simultaneously employs quantitative and qualitative research methods to maintain comprehensive view of the influence of emotional intelligence in an online collaborative environment. The quantitative part consists of a structured questionnaires for distant workers and team organisers and aims at a statistical test of the variables of emotional intelligence, collaboration, well -being and performance. The qualitative component, comprising case studies and semi-structured interviews, will support a more in-depth investigation into the practices of workplace and implications of YouTube on people in online work. By combining the two, RDS use can be triangulated to supplement trustworthiness and richness of results. That, not only better explains to what extent how much emotional intelligence is here and what correlates with it, but also the why and how emotional intelligence is brought to the day to day at work in the digital world.

4.2 Research Objectives

The main goal of this research is to investigate how emotional intelligence enhances collaboration and collaboration within a workplace. More specifically, the research objectives include:

1. To assess the current scenario of emotional intelligence in remote teams
2. To estimate the impact of Emotional Intelligence on the digital collaboration, well-being, and productivity improvement.
3. To investigate the major constraints that can impact the strategies for improving employee engagement in digital workplace.

Research Questions and Hypothesis

To examine the research and answer the research questions, three main questions are used as the foundation for the research:

- How does emotional intelligence affect collaboration, well-being, and performance in digital spaces?
- What methods are organizations using to build emotional intelligence among remote employees?

- What perceptions do people have of the benefits and challenges of using emotional intelligence in the digital environment?

As a basis for the research questions, two hypothesis or predictions were established. The first, that higher emotional intelligence amongst team members is significantly related to higher collaboration and lower levels of conflict. The second, that organizations that build emotional intelligence in remote teams have higher rates of retention and satisfaction.

a. **Sampling Techniques**

For the fulfilment of this research, the sampling technique is purposive: participants are required to work for remote work or hybrid work context. The research aimed at two sample groups;100 offshore workers and 50 supervisors. Therefore, the participants were recruited from those who were currently working in digital teams within their employment in various sectors which were the information technology, consulting, education, e-commerce etc.

Table 2. Distribution of respondents

Participant Category	Sample Size	Criteria
Remote Employees	100	Full-time employees working in virtual teams.
Team Mangers	50	Managing remote/hybrid teams for over 1 year

b. **Instruments for Data Collection**

Our primary vehicle for the collection of quantitative information was a structured questionnaire. About our survey, we utilized *Daniel Goleman's* influence on emotional intelligence, with regards to self-awareness, self-regulation, empathy, social skills, and motivation, as a framework to get our representatives views on these areas. All our questions were based on a five-point Likert scale – Strongly Disagree to Strongly Agree. On the Qualitative side, we also conducted semi-structured interviews with fifteen team leaders, to ask them about how they invest in emotional intelligence for their digital teams, how they address these emotional challenges, and what they thought the best tools or inventions were to do so. We studied the case of three champion remote-first companies (GitLab, TCS and Zapier).

c. **Validity, Reliability, and Ethical Considerations**

A small preliminary study was carried out with a small sample of 10 respondents to determine reliability of the instruments to be used. Based on their input, the instruments were modified as needed to further improve the clarity and axis relatedness of the items. Reliability was determined by Cronbach's alpha coefficient to test the internal consistency of the EI scale was 0.87, suggesting good reliability of the instruments.

d. **Data Analysis Technique**

Quantitative data was exported from the research (coded to the surveys) to SPSS 27 and then to AMOS, where descriptive statistics, correlation, regression, and ANOVA were conducted in order to test the hypotheses proposed in relation to emotional burnout, virtual relational trust-building, empathetic leadership and receiving and giving resilience.

Table 3. Analysis Method

Data type	Analysis Method	Output
Survey Data	SPSS(Regression, ANOVA)	Statistical findings
Interview Transcripts	NVivo (Thematic Coding)	Themes & Patterns
Case study Data	Manual Review	Practical insights & Trends

In mixed designs, different data types require different methods of analysis in order to focus attention on what matters. Survey data is quantitative So, usually, statistical software like SPSS are utilized to analyse survey data. The two approaches above are the methods by which statistical results are generated which depict trends, associations and levels of significance between variables. By contrast, interview transcripts give a narrative form of qualitative data which is most productively analysed using thematic coding in software's like NVivo to uncover themes or patterns that recur and that reflect the experiences and perspectives of turning circle members. Cases are rich in context, and case study data can often be found to be hand scrutinised to elicit useful patterns and insights that can provide the substance and the immediacy of real world relevance. This combination of qualitative and quantitative methods enhances the robustness and richness of study results.

e. **Limitations of the Methodology**

Although the mixed-methods design enhances the strength of the study, a few limitations of this study are acknowledged. Although purposeful, purposive sampling limits the ability to generalize findings to larger populations or industries.

Self-report surveys, which are typical in emotional intelligence research, were prone to social desirability bias whereby participants responded in ways of perceived socially acceptable. Although the interviews added richness to the findings, it is impossible that the number of depths of experience of participants in the study do not truly represent the multiplicity of experiences across all sectors.Overall, the research design does allow for both empirical and interpretive data to be collected on how emotional intelligence enhances digital collaboration and digital leadership.

2. Data Analysis and Interpretation

Data from 150 participants (100 remote employees and 50 team managers) were analyzed using both quantitative and qualitative methods. Quantitative data were analyzed designing correlation, regression, and group differences using SPSS statistical method, and qualitative data from interviews were analyzed by thematic analysis using NVivo. The mixed-methods approach allows an in-depth understanding of how emotional intelligence impacts well-being, team dynamics and digital collaboration.

Primary Data

In-depth interviews and structured survey responses were examples of primary data. To investigate the relationship between emotional intelligence and important outcomes including well-being, team dynamics, and digital cooperation, the quantitative survey data was examined using SPSS, which applied statistical techniques like correlation, regression, and group difference analysis. Thematic analysis in NVivo was also used to analyze qualitative data gathered from participant interviews. This analysis revealed patterns, recurrent themes, and insights on emotional behavior and remote interactions.

Secondary Data

To support the interpretation of findings and give theoretical footing, secondary data—such as pertinent academic literature, organizational reports, and prior research studies—were evaluated. The results' validity and contextual relevance were strengthened by this all-encompassing methodology, which made it possible to comprehend the effects of emotional intelligence in virtual work environments in greater detail.

4.1 Descriptive Statistics of Emotional Intelligence Scores

Emotional intelligence was represented using a 5-point Likert scale based on self-awareness, self-regulation, motivation, empathy, and social-skills resulting in a relatively high overall EI score from both groups representing the positive emotional competence experienced in a digital workspace.

Table 4. Mean Emotional Intelligence Scores by Roles

EI Dimension	Mean Score (Employees)	Mean Score (Managers)
Self-Awareness	4.1	4.4
Self-Regulation	3.9	4.2
Motivation	4.0	4.3
Empathy	4.2	4.5
Social Skills	4.0	4.4

The average Emotional Intelligence (EI) scores for two organizational roles—managers and employees—across five important dimensions—motivation, empathy, self-regulation, self-awareness, and social skills—are shown in Table 4. A 5-point Likert scale is used to calculate the scores, and higher numbers denote greater competence in a given EI facet.

Managers routinely score higher than employees in every category. The biggest disparities are found in social skills and empathy, indicating that managerial positions would call for more robust leadership and interpersonal skills. There is also a noticeable discrepancy between self-awareness and motivation, suggesting that managers are more sensitive to their own emotions and motivated by internal objectives. The general pattern reinforces the idea that managers generally possess more advanced emotional intelligence (EI) skills than their subordinates and emphasizes the significance of Emotional Intelligence in leadership.

4.2 Regression Analysis: EI and Collaboration

A regression analysis was used to test the prediction that higher emotional intelligence is associated with more effective collaboration and less conflict remembered by and reported in virtual team members. The independent variable was the emotional intelligence total score and the dependent variable was the team collaboration index which was developed based on some items in the questionnaire.

Table 5. Regression Output – EI and Collaboration

Predictor Variable	Standardized Coefficient (β)	Significance (p-value)
Emotional Intelligence	0.78	0.000

Results of linear regression, which examined the relationship between the team collaboration effectiveness and EI are presented in Table 5. The standardized coefficient (β) of emotional intelligence is 0.78, with also indicates that the relationship between EI and much better team cooperation performs greatly well.A p-value of.000 means that it is highly improbable that this association is random and that the association is significant at traditional levels (often less than $p < .05$).Hence forth, the findings of the regression analysis illustrate that emotional intelligence is a powerful predictor of effective teamwork, highlighting the significance of its impact on relationships and teamwork in the organizational environment. The point estimate from the regression model was significant ($R^2 = 0.64$, $p < 0.01$) suggesting a strong association between emotional intelligence and team collaboration performance.

4.3 Correlation Matrix: EI and Digital Work Outcomes

A Pearson correlation matrix was created to investigate the relationships between emotional intelligence and key digital work outcomes: job satisfaction, productivity, and employee well-being.

Table 6. Correlation Coefficients (EI with Work Outcomes)

Variables	Job Satisfaction	Productivity	Well-being
Emotional Intelligence	0.72	0.66	0.79

All correlation values were significant and positive ($p < 0.01$) giving full credibility to Hypothesis 2, that organizations who provide environments for EI in digital teams have better employee morale, performance, and retention.

4.4 ANOVA: EI Across Industries

We completed a one-way ANOVA to assess whether emotional intelligence scores varied between major industries. We looked at IT, Education, Consulting, and E-commerce only.Results indicate that differences between industries were significant ($F = 4.62$, $p < 0.05$), and what is interesting is that employees in Educations and Consulting reported higher EI than the employees in IT and E-commerce, possibly because greater relational demand in the education and consulting sectors.

4.5 Thematic Analysis from Interviews

The qualitative data provided rich themes around how emotional intelligence is experienced in practice. Using NVivo we obtained several key themes:

Theme 1: Virtual Empathy Builds Trust

Many managers asserted that if they consciously check in on employee's emotional well-being, the trust builds psychological safety with the team.

Theme 2: Digital Fatigue as an EI Challenge

Many of those interviewed, reported difficulties in managing emotions due to daily virtual meetings in which emotional exhaustion was a by-product; involving more self-regulation and emotional awareness.

Theme 3: Leadership Presence, is now Virtual Presence

A remote leader with high emotional intelligence was unable to engage and motivate employees, because they were perceived as regular, responsive, and emotionally supportive.

Theme 4: Cultural Sensitivity in Global Teams

Mangers of global teams highlighted the need for cultural awareness in interpreting emotional cues, reinforcing the importance of social skills and empathy.

3. DISCUSSION

The results of this study stress the role of emotional intelligence (EI) in developing digital collaboration, employee engagement, and overall organizational resilience when working remotely. The quantitative analysis presented a reliable positive correlation of 0.72 with the place of EI impacting job satisfaction, 0.66 with productivity, and 0.79 with well-being. These results reiterate the idea that emotionally intelligent individuals have the tools necessary to cope with the psychological demands of remote work (e.g., ambiguity, isolation, and limited personal interaction).The regression analysis further supports our hypothesis that an EI teams work better together and experience less conflict. These results corroborate earlier literature, e.g., *Goleman (2013); Calefato et al. (2020)* that maintaining EI in virtual teams helps build common ground, empathy, and resolve conflict in teams, which is valuable in virtual team environments.The quantitative interviews also provided some understanding of the findings. The managers and team leaders said that emotionally intelligent practices, including checking-in on employees, recognizing emotional fatigue, and being empathetic during stressful periods at work-built trust and morale with the team. The also reiterates the findings by *Miao et al. (2017)* that identified empathy and emotional regulation to be strongly predictive of effective teams.

Theoretical Implications

This study extends our understanding of the emergent Digital Emotional Intelligence (DEI) vernacular, which is a nascent framework for evolving, older, more conventional EI theories into virtual environments. The study confirms the original premise that emotional intelligence is not only measurable but has a significant impact on the outcomes of the one's performance as theorized by *Salovey and Mayer (1990)*. The current study further adds to the relevance of Goleman's five-component model of EI – especially in relation to self-regulation, motivation and empathy and described those components in relation to modern remote working behaviors at a very practical level.

In addition, the study pointed out that EI was both an individual trait and organizational capability, nothing that while an individual employee could grow their EI through training and other development mechanisms to become a more emotionally intelligent employee, organizations must align their values to be emotionally intelligent in leadership, communication, and team-building.

Practical Implications for Remote Workplaces

The study presents a few actionable items that managers and organizations can use from both an organizational and managerial lens:

EI Training and Workshops: Organizations should provide purposeful emotional intelligence training and workshops for not only the leaders but the remote employees as well. Workshops could employ activities to enhance self-awareness, empathy, and emotional regulation.

Empathetic Leadership: Managers must use emotional sensitivity as a foundation for their leadership style. In remote environments where teams may not display emotions due to distance, emotional sensitivity, or noticing team emotions and utilizing that information openly communicated and managed builds trust and thereby increases morale and retention.

Tech-enabled EI resources: This possible uses of technology like check in surveys, emotion-dedicated software, and apps which monitor and collect mood-related data could be strikingly useful in situations when there is very indecipherable emotional component. Tools like Microsoft Teams and Slack already feature emojis and pulse surveys that serve as a low-tech strategy to drill down into how team members are feeling.

Psychological Safety: Organizations can create digitalized emotionally safe spaces that might include: allowing flexibility in work hours, encouraging breaks from the screen for prolonged periods of time, and being respectful of the type of messaging occurring in emails and chats.

Onboarding and Virtual Culture Initiating: EI principles should be incorporated into onboarding for new hires. You can also foster virtual team rituals such as "wellness check-ins" or "wins of the week" to create personal bonds between employees and a sense of human connection.

Challenges in EI Implementation

Despite its advantage, the application of emotional intelligence practices in remote environments is associated with numerous obstacles. For instance, a fundamental difficulty remains the part which confronts the capability to accurately interpret emotional signals digitally. Although performing interviews facially involves considering body language, perceived tone, and content (which is a multi-layered), digital text-based exchanges are disembodied from body cues, therefore when there are confused expectations and misunderstandings arise. Everyonehas a distinct layer of "cultural equation" likely leading to misunderstood communication in teams composed of members from various cultural backgrounds.

Another challenge associated with digital communication is digital fatigue. Prolonged screen time and multiple instances of interacting on screen reduces the emotional weight given to connection with others and may lead to burnout. Even individuals who have a high level of emotional intelligence may struggle when it comes to regulating emotions in a screen-heavy landscape.Finally, certain employees may also have a sense of skepticism surrounding emotional intelligence initiatives involving the establishment/measurement of emotional responses reasonably based on the new/revised digital tools/ Relatedly, many people expressed ethical concerns surrounding the privacy/consent associated with the utilization of digital emotion technologies, such as those involving emotion AI. As *Crawford &Paglen (2021)* indicate affective computing systems are closely located between emotional co-regulation and emotional stranglehold.

Comparison with Existing Studies

The outcomes of this study are mainly in agreement with prior studies and information but provide additional information about how EI/Emotional Intelligence operates in a digital setting. While Goleman's and Bar-On's models were established in a traditional workplace setting we apply their models to distributed teams and remote work settings. We confirm representatives' claims that: emotionally intelligent teams have better psychological safety and improved cohesion *(Grehen et al, 2023),* and we provide insight into how cohesion and psychological safety manifest in asynchronous and virtual interactions.

Conversely, while we are cognizant that may prior studies were theoretical or based on face-to-face work, we gather empirical evidence drawing from real data from remote employees and managers across a variety of industries This study also offers a scalable model for organizations to put EI into practice, and to consider EI in their digital workplace policies.

Contributions to Remote Work and Leadership Research

In addition to the contributions made to knowledge in the field of remote leadership and emotional technology integration, this study has also provided a platform for the knowledge base of remote leadership to explore emotional intelligence as a soft skill that translates into digital ecosystems, and further supports offering emotional intelligence training as a component leadership development program for virtual teams.

This study also allows for a greater use of data-informed methods to develop emotionally aware digital cultures. Along with the use of hybrid models for organizations, organizations will also have to manage both face-to-facc and remote interactions simultaneously and be mindful of the potential emotional dynamics at play across formats.

4. CONCLUSION

Conclusion

Work after the pandemic dramatically shifted the professional terrains, and from its wake, we've seen the surge in remote and hybrid work models. This transition required not just the development of new technical devices but also a rewriting of new ways to communicate and feel in digital spaces. The research, Mind the (AI and the) Gap: The Emotional Intelligence of Virtual Collaboration, examined the impact and effect of emotional intelligence (EI) on collaboration, trust and productivity in digital environments. Via a dual-method method of data collection, quantitative evidence from the surveys and qualitative evidence from interviews and case studies, this study offers strong evidence of the importance of EI in a virtual professional environment.

The Role of Emotional Intelligence in Digital Collaboration

One of the study's headline conclusions highlighted the importance of emotional intelligence in enabling effective and empathetic digital collaboration. Some of the key findings of the quantitative study with the sample of 150 respondents (100 remote employees and 50 team managers) indicated that a higher EI score significantly correlated with positive workplace impacts, such as thriving collaboration, a high level of productivity, employee well-being, and work satisfaction.

According to the regression and correlation analysis, emotional intelligence has a statistically significant correlation with team cooperation ($\beta = 0.78$, $p < 0.001$). These results emphasize that EI is not just one of the nice-to-haves, EI is both an immeasurable predictor of team cohesiveness and effectiveness in virtual environments.

What Qualitative Data Can Tell Us: The Importance of Empathy and Emotional Literacy.

The qualitative element of the research, through interviews with team leaders and a review of successful remote case studies, highlighted the complexities in which emotional intelligence is exhibited in the remote context. Sensitivity and empathy became important characteristics of successful virtual teams. Managers and employees who could properly read and respond to the emotional states of their coworkers were significantly better at dealing with conflict, building trust and keeping the peace.

In other words, via a thematic analysis in NVivo, common patterns such as "empathy-driven engagement," "digital trust building," and "emotional regulation in virtual conflict resolution" emerged that can be found in various discussion threads. Across those themes was a focus on how emotionally intelligent communication - whether over a video call, email, chat or collaborative tool - helped establish a sense of connection and psychological safety, in spite of distances that were much more than just physical.

Verification of Hypotheses and Implications

The study's initial hypotheses were confirmed with statistical and thematic interpretation. It was confirmed that:

1. Teams with higher levels of emotional intelligence had better relationships with one another and less conflict.
2. Companies who intentionally cultivated EI through leadership training, employee development training, and offered programs like mindfulness, saw greater levels of employee engagement, job satisfaction, and lower turnover.
3. These findings have significant practical implications. Companies who want to operate effectively remotely will need to invest in emotional competencies of their employees. This means organised emotional intelligence training, coaching programmes and making emotional well-being a central part of digital workplace strategy.

Emotionally Intelligent Leadership and Its Relevance

Among other notable findings of the study was the influence of emotionally intelligent management on virtual teams. Leaders who demonstrated high EI–specifically in empathy, emotional control and self-awareness– were key to decreasing virtual miscommunication and improving team spirit. They became more attuned to team patterns, noticed warning signs of exhaustion or burnout, and changed how they communicated to create more inclusivity and emotional safety.

Leader behaviors that facilitated resilience included leading by example and modeling positive coping behaviors, facilitating social support, encouraging reflection or sense-making, and providing clear and consistent communication, even more so during times of change or turbulence in the organisation (eg, economic uncertainty or restructuring or tight deadlines), at which point emotionally intelligent leaders were seen as stabilising influences. Their power to acknowledge employee fears, assuage them and be transparent was crucial in keeping performance and spirits up.

Digital Emotional Intelligence (DEI): The New Literacy

One of the most notable emerging findings from the work is the Digital Emotional Intelligence (DEI) construct—the capacity to understand, manage and respond to emotions in digital communication. Digital is making DEI more important than ever As companies move towards primarily digital spaces for collaboration, DEI is more critical than ever.

The study found several dimensions of DEI are key in successful remote work:

1. Communicating with the right tone and being crystal clear in written communications (emails, chat) so as not to get misunderstood.
2. Detecting digital fatigue by behavior, like disengagement during meetings, responsiveness, or subtle changes in tone.
3. Fostering an emotional safe environment in virtual meetings, promoting openness, active listening, and inclusivity.
4. Developing rituals that are about connection, like virtual check-ins, team-building exercises, and informal virtual spaces to encourage people connecting as human beings.
5. As work continues its push toward the digital, DEI will be a key skill that employees and leaders need. It marries old-school emotional intelligence with digital savvy, and the result is a boatload of tools to guide us through the relational chaos with which we're confronted any time we log on.

Advantages of the Mixed-Methods Analysis

Translating the findings into the mixed-methods research architecture proved to be one of the research strength points. The quantitative findings provided empirical evidence for the relationship between EI and work-related outcomes, and the qualitative findings provided a rich and contextualized data that complemented the quantitative findings. Combined, they offered a comprehensive view on EI in virtual work and how it may be cultivated and applied.

Convergence of Statistical Evidence from SPSS and thematic coding using NVivo enabled the integration of data-driven results with human-centered stories. Such an approach also facilitated triangulation of findings, which enhanced the confirmability and credibility of the meaning attached to the findings.

Discussion and Implications for Research and Practice

The results of this study raise several questions for further investigation. As the call for scalable DEI training grows, research is necessary to investigate its medium and long-term effects on virtual team performance and to consult the question regarding the impact of different cultural contexts on emotional intelligence in digital communication.Additionally, longitudinal investigations may investigate the impact of long-term EI interventions on employee retention, innovation, and well-being. Decoding the emotion Organisations could also bring in emotional intelligence assessments as part of their recruitment and performance appraisal frameworks which could go a long way in in developing resilient teams.In fact, HR professionals, managers, and corporate trainers will need to make it a part of an organisational strategy, given the current remote/hybrid model of work. Technology designers may also think about affective cues and DEI principles in designing these collab-oration platforms and digital tools.

Final Reflection

Overall, this study lends credibility to emotional intelligence as more than a soft skill but rather as strategic resource in the changing work world. In a world of digital communication, maintaining emotional connections, even in the absence of physical presence, is critical for human connection, trust, and collaboration. If companies are to survive in the new remote reality, emotional intelligence — particularly in its digital form — needs to be placed at the heart of organizational development strategies.The work of the future is not just digital, it is also emotionally intelligent.

Recommendations

On the basis of the results of this study, we propose the following set of suggestions for organizations:

1. **EI Training Workshops:** Organizations should offer workshops to increase emotional self-awareness, empathy, and digital reciprocity, especially among those working remotely.
2. **Train Emotionally Intelligent Leaders:** Team leads must be taught, as well as provided systems and tools, for empathy and active listening to all parties in the emotional teams cape.
3. **Remote Culture of Emotional Safety**: Actively promote emotional expression and provide psychological security through some HR virtual initiatives or mental health resources.

On the final note, this study is also extending the theory of emotional intelligence, from Salovey and Mayer and Daniel Goleman, into the modern digital world, offering an empirical indication of the application of theory when working at a distance. The conceptualization of emotional fluency is proposed in the digital collaborative context. It makes the assertion that while the importance of emotional intelligence as a personal quality is widely understood, emotional intelligence is an organization ability that can be recognized as such for the organizational challenge of the hybrid workplace.Moreover, this paper adds to knowledge by showing a potential relevance of EI across domains that connect EI with HR practice, organizational psychology, digital communication and leadership theory. A second theoretical contribution is the highlight of the ethical implications of dealing with emotional data to be developed in the future by practitioners and academics.

In summary, for a more sustainable, effective, and human-focused digital workplace, emotional intelligence is a must. Surviving and thriving If some kind of remoteness or hybridity sticks for some organizations, then those that buy or build the objects of emotional awareness and map them against the machines in their environment are the ones likely to flourish.

Future Research Implications

With acceleration of workplace digital transformation, emotional intelligence (EI) will develop as well. This work has provided hopefully a foundation for how EI can support remote collaboration, but has also identified directions for further work.

Discovering Emotion AI: The Role of Ethical Frameworks

An interesting aspect to explore is the recent growth of Emotion AI [5], based on technologies that can identify and interpret human emotions from voice, text and facial readings. These technologies promise to open somewhat the space for empathy in digital workplace, but just as much they evoke serious questions around privacy, consent, and surveillance. Future work should begin to ask how organizations willfully graze along the boundaries of consideration and usage, and raise thoughtful questions as to when it would be even inappropriate to use such technologies, and ultimately consistent with emotionally intelligent technologies that prioritize humanity in trust and autonomy.

Cross-Cultural Perspectives on Digital EI

How cultures shape emotional intelligence as regards expressing, perceiving and interpreting emotions differs across cultures. Given the nature of remote teams, emotional reactions are bound to differ. Future research needs to focus on how digital EI is perceived and practiced in different cultures, especially how multinational teams design frameworks for EI that adapt to the culturally divergent emotional expressions within the team.

Longitudinal Studies on EI Development

This study, like many others, conducted snapshot studies. There is a need to conduct longitudinal studies that look into whether emotional intelligence evolves over time in remote teams and whether the impact of training lasts over time. Longitudinal research also will likely be useful in examining the impact of digital

EI on career progression, employee retention, and leadership development over a sustained period of time.

Applications Focused on a Specific Sector

As we aimed our investigation on the workplace broadly, different future directions could look at sector-specific applications of EI. For example, what impact does EI have on interaction with patients in telehealth services? How do call center agents handle their emotions during digital service escalations? Every sector has peculiar emotional demands which can be used to formulate relevant research objectives.

Integrating EI into the Virtual Teaching and Training

The increasing virtualization of teaching at colleges and corporate training centers has created a need to integrate emotional intelligence into pedagogy. Emotionally intelligent design could be developed for virtual classrooms or onboarding processes aimed at assisting learners or employees, helping them connect and engage meaningfully right from the online course's or onboarding program's commencement and guiding them through successful completion.

Enhancing Collaboration through EI Tools Utilizing Gamification

Lastly, the use of gamification for the enhancement of EI in training virtual teams is a rather unexplored avenue. The development of interactive tools, scenario-based games, or VR simulations that are directed towards promoting empathy, compassion, communication, and teamwork in remote work settings offers a wide scope of further research.

REFERENCES

Bar-On, R. (1997). *The Emotional Quotient Inventory (EQ-i): Technical manual.* Multi-Health Systems.

Boyatzis, R. E., Goleman, D., & Rhee, K. (2000). Clustering competence in emotional intelligence. In Bar-On, R., & Parker, J. D. A. (Eds.), *The Handbook of Emotional Intelligence* (pp. 343–362). Jossey-Bass.

Calefato, F., Lanubile, F., & Novielli, N. (2020). Supporting emotional intelligence, productivity and team goals while handling software requirements changes. *ACM Transactions on Software Engineering and Methodology*, *30*(2), 1–29. DOI: 10.1145/3664600

Carasco-Saul, M., Kim, W., & Kim, T. (2015). Leadership and employee engagement: Proposing research agendas through a review of literature. *Human Resource Development Review*, *14*(1), 38–63. DOI: 10.1177/1534484314560406

Chamakiotis, P., Dekoninck, E. A., & Panteli, N. (2021). Leading geographically dispersed teams: The role of emotional intelligence and trust. *International Journal of Human Resource Management*, *32*(10), 2123–2147. DOI: 10.1080/09585192.2019.1674355

Cherniss, C. (2010). Emotional intelligence: Toward clarification of a concept. *Industrial and Organizational Psychology: Perspectives on Science and Practice*, *3*(2), 110–126. DOI: 10.1111/j.1754-9434.2010.01231.x

Chi, N. W., Huang, Y. C., & Lin, S. C. (2020). High performance work systems, employees' creative behavior, and the moderating effects of emotional intelligence: An empirical study in Taiwan. *International Journal of Human Resource Management*, *31*(2), 229–258. DOI: 10.1080/09585192.2017.1380064

Crawford, K., & Paglen, T. (2021). Working with affective computing: Exploring UK public perceptions of AI-enabled workplace surveillance. *arXiv preprint arXiv:2205.08264*. https://arxiv.org/abs/2205.08264

Goleman, D. (1995). *Emotional Intelligence: Why It Can Matter More Than IQ.* Bantam Books.

Goleman, D. (2013). *Emotional intelligence: Why it can matter more than IQ.* Bantam.

Grehen, M., & Grehen, A. (2023). Emotional intelligence, leadership, and work teams: A hybrid literature review. *Heliyon*, *9*(10), e20356. DOI: 10.1016/j.heliyon.2023.e20356 PMID: 37790975

Insights, E. H. L. (2022, June 3). *How to be an emotionally intelligent leader*. EHL Hospitality Insights. https://hospitalityinsights.ehl.edu/how-to-be-an-emotionally-intelligent-leader

Mayer, J. D., Salovey, P., & Caruso, D. R. (2008). Emotional intelligence: New ability or eclectic traits? *The American Psychologist*, *63*(6), 503–517. DOI: 10.1037/0003-066X.63.6.503 PMID: 18793038

Mayer, J. D., Salovey, P., & Caruso, D. R. (2008). Emotional intelligence: New ability or eclectic traits? *The American Psychologist*, *63*(6), 503–517. DOI: 10.1037/0003-066X.63.6.503 PMID: 18793038

Miao, C., Humphrey, R. H., & Qian, S. (2017). A meta-analysis of emotional intelligence and work attitudes. *Journal of Occupational and Organizational Psychology*, *90*(2), 177–202. DOI: 10.1111/joop.12167

Salas, E., Shuffler, M. L., Thayer, A. L., Bedwell, W. L., & Lazzara, E. H. (2015). Understanding and improving teamwork in organizations: A scientifically based practical guide. *Human Resource Management*, *54*(4), 599–622. DOI: 10.1002/hrm.21628

Salovey, P., & Mayer, J. D. (1990). Emotional intelligence. *Imagination, Cognition and Personality*, *9*(3), 185–211. DOI: 10.2190/DUGG-P24E-52WK-6CDG

World Economic Forum. (2020). *The Future of Jobs Report 2020*. https://www.weforum.org/reports/the-future-of-jobs-report-2020

Chapter 13
Using AI-Driven Analysis for Training and Leadership Growth

Satya Subrahmanyam
https://orcid.org/0000-0003-0441-2742
Holy Spirit University of Kaslik, Lebanon

ABSTRACT

Artificial intelligence (AI) has transformed corporate training and leadership development, particularly through Emotion AI, which enhances emotional intelligence (EQ) and leadership growth. This chapter examines AI-driven tools, such as machine learning and natural language processing (NLP), in creating personalized training programs. Emotion AI, which analyzes emotions via facial recognition, voice tone, and behavior, supports leaders in improving communication, empathy, and decision-making. By integrating AI into leadership development, organizations enhance collaboration, resilience, and conflict resolution. The chapter also explores AI-powered adaptive learning, real-time feedback, and simulations that engage employees in immersive learning environments. While AI offers significant benefits, ethical concerns such as privacy and biases are addressed. The chapter concludes with insights into the future of AI in leadership, emphasizing a balanced approach to technology and human intuition.

DOI: 10.4018/979-8-3373-3658-9.ch013

1. INTRODUCTION

1.1 Purpose of the Chapter

This chapter explores the transformative potential of AI-driven analysis, specifically Emotion AI, in the domain of training and leadership development. It aims to examine how organizations can harness emotional insights powered by AI to enhance leadership effectiveness, foster employee well-being, and create emotionally intelligent workplaces. By merging technological capabilities with human-centered development goals, the chapter provides a framework for leveraging Emotion AI as a strategic tool in cultivating future-ready leaders.

1.2 Leadership Development in Modern Organizations

A foundational component of organizational success has long been recognized as leadership development. Conventional approaches to leadership development frequently fall short in meeting the complex needs of today's VUCA (volatile, uncertain, complex, and ambiguous) workplaces. The demand for leaders with technical skills is on the rise, but they must also show emotional intelligence, adaptability, and resilience to help their organizations deal with digital disruption, hybrid workforces, and increased competition (Goleman, 1998). Leadership development programs need to adapt to meet the needs of modern leaders by making them more tailored, data-driven, and sensitive to participants' emotions.

Conventional training methods—such as classroom-based workshops, personality assessments, and one-size-fits-all modules—often overlook the dynamic emotional states and interpersonal skills required for effective leadership. They rarely provide real-time feedback or continuous learning opportunities. This gap presents a compelling case for integrating advanced technologies like artificial intelligence to support more adaptive and emotionally attuned leadership development strategies.

1.3 Introducing AI and Emotion AI in Workplace Analytics

Machines that can learn, reason, and solve problems in a way that is similar to a human being are called artificially intelligent (AI). Recruiting, performance reviews, and customer service are just a few areas where AI is finding widespread usage in the business world. The field of artificial intelligence known as affective computing or emotion AI is dedicated to the study and analysis of human emotions. This field employs biometric signals, facial expressions, voice intonation, and text sentiment as inputs (Calvo & D'Mello, 2010).

Emotion AI allows systems to perceive emotional cues and provide insights into how individuals feel and react in specific scenarios. These insights are particularly valuable in organizational settings where understanding human emotion is essential to fostering engagement, improving communication, and enhancing leadership. By translating emotional data into actionable feedback, Emotion AI provides a new lens through which organizations can assess and develop leadership competencies that are deeply rooted in empathy, emotional regulation, and interpersonal connection.

1.4 Connecting Emotion AI to Leadership Development

The integration of Emotion AI into leadership training marks a significant advancement in how organizations nurture talent. Emotional intelligence (EQ)—the ability to recognize, understand, and manage emotions—is widely regarded as a critical skill for effective leadership. Assessing and developing EQ in real-time has historically been a challenge. Emotion AI addresses this gap by continuously monitoring emotional behaviors, enabling personalized feedback loops that help leaders refine their communication styles, decision-making processes, and relational skills (Goleman, 1998; Subrahmanyam, 2025).

During executive coaching sessions or team meetings, AI-driven platforms can analyze voice tone and facial expressions to detect stress, empathy, or assertiveness. These insights allow coaches and HR professionals to deliver more targeted guidance that aligns with a leader's emotional strengths and growth areas. AI tools can track emotional trends over time, offering longitudinal insights into leadership development that static assessments cannot provide.

Emotion AI enables the creation of adaptive learning environments that respond to the emotional and cognitive engagement levels of participants. These platforms can tailor content in real time, ensuring that learners remain engaged and that learning outcomes are maximized. Such emotionally intelligent systems are particularly valuable in leadership contexts, where the ability to connect with others, manage conflict, and navigate change is essential.

Emotion AI also plays a pivotal role in identifying emerging leaders within an organization. By analyzing patterns of emotional behavior, communication effectiveness, and team dynamics, AI systems can help pinpoint high-potential individuals who exhibit key leadership traits. These insights support succession planning and talent management initiatives by offering a more holistic and objective assessment of leadership readiness (Subrahmanyam, 2025).

Emotion AI raises some serious moral questions. For responsible implementation, it is crucial to thoroughly address concerns related to privacy, consent, and algorithmic bias. To develop trust and keep morale high, it's important to be transparent about data use, have strong data governance structures, and adhere to ethical AI standards.

The application of AI—particularly Emotion AI—represents a paradigm shift in how leadership development and training are approached in contemporary organizations. By leveraging emotionally intelligent technologies, organizations can deliver more personalized, responsive, and effective leadership programs. Emotion AI empowers leaders to better understand themselves and their teams, fostering cultures of empathy, inclusivity, and psychological safety. As the following sections will explore in greater depth, the integration of AI-driven analysis into leadership training holds the promise of cultivating a new generation of emotionally intelligent leaders equipped to thrive in an ever-changing world.

2. THE EVOLVING LANDSCAPE OF LEADERSHIP AND TRAINING

2.1 Shifting Paradigms in Leadership in the AI Era

In the age of rapid technological advancement, the concept and practice of leadership are undergoing significant transformation. Traditional paradigms, which emphasize hierarchy, authority, and rigid structures, are being replaced by dynamic models that prioritize adaptability, emotional intelligence, and data-driven decision-making. The integration of artificial intelligence (AI) into business processes has not only revolutionized operations and customer service but also reshaped expectations of leadership in the digital era. Today's leaders are expected to manage not just people, but also machines, data streams, and intelligent systems—often in environments where hybrid and remote work have become the norm (Brynjolfsson & McAfee, 2017).

AI enables organizations to gather and analyze vast amounts of data about employee behavior, engagement, and performance, offering leaders real-time insights into team dynamics. This evolution demands that leaders become more analytical, emotionally responsive, and open to leveraging technological tools in their leadership practice. As a result, leadership is no longer merely about vision and strategy; it is increasingly about the capacity to understand, interpret, and respond to complex human and machine interactions (Wilson & Daugherty, 2018).

2.2 The Role of Emotional Intelligence in Effective Leadership

Despite these technological disruptions, emotional intelligence (EI) remains a cornerstone of effective leadership. EI encompasses the ability to perceive, understand, regulate, and manage emotions in oneself and others (Goleman, 1998). It influences how leaders handle interpersonal relationships, make decisions under pressure, and manage conflicts—skills that are crucial in today's diverse and emotionally complex workplaces.

When leaders are emotionally intelligent, they foster psychological safety so that workers may express themselves freely and are inspired to do their best. They have the necessary skills to guide teams through transitions, encourage teamwork, and keep morale high in the face of uncertainty. The need of EI is magnified in an AI-driven setting where direct human engagement is often lacking. In order to maintain engagement and trust, leaders need to be sensitive to the nuanced emotional signals sent via digital communications, such as the tone of emails or the emotions shown in chat chats.

As AI begins to play a role in evaluating and enhancing emotional capabilities through technologies like Emotion AI, leaders are expected to model emotional intelligence not just as a personal trait, but as an organizational standard. Emotion AI can detect empathy, stress, and sentiment in communication, making it possible to provide feedback to leaders on how they are perceived emotionally by their teams (Subrahmanyam, 2025). This feedback loop helps leaders continuously refine their interpersonal skills and emotional awareness.

2.3 Challenges in Traditional Training and Leadership Assessment Models

While the importance of leadership development is well recognized, traditional training and assessment models often fail to deliver meaningful, lasting change. One major challenge is the generic nature of many programs. Traditional models tend to follow a one-size-fits-all approach, providing standardized content that does not account for individual learning styles, emotional competencies, or specific contextual challenges faced by leaders (Day et al., 2014).

Another limitation is the lack of real-time feedback and contextual relevance. Training programs typically occur in isolated settings—workshops, seminars, or retreats—detached from the leader's daily work environment. This disconnect limits the transfer of learning into actual workplace behavior. Traditional leadership assessments, such as 360-degree feedback or personality inventories, rely heavily on subjective evaluations and often lack dynamic, real-time components.

Emotional intelligence is another area where these models fall short. The Emotional Quotient Inventory (EQ-i) and the Mayer-Salovey-Caruso Emotional Intelligence Test (MSCEIT) are helpful assessments; however, they only record a moment in time, not patterns of behavior over time. Organizations are therefore blind to the ways in which leaders' emotional actions change over time, particularly in reaction to feedback or shifting contexts.

Many traditional models do not account for the changing nature of work, particularly the shift toward remote and hybrid teams. Leadership in virtual settings requires a different set of skills—such as digital empathy, virtual communication effectiveness, and the ability to maintain engagement without physical presence—that are often overlooked in conventional training.

2.4 The Growing Demand for Personalized, Adaptive Training Solutions

Leadership development solutions that are data-driven, flexible, and tailored to each individual are in high demand as a result of these difficulties. Dynamic learning experiences that are customized to each leader's requirements, emotional profile, and leadership context are quickly replacing static, content-heavy training, as more and more organizations realize.

AI and Emotion AI offer powerful tools for creating these personalized experiences. Machine learning algorithms can analyze leadership behaviors, emotional responses, and performance metrics to recommend targeted learning content. If a manager struggles with empathetic communication, the system might suggest microlearning modules on active listening or provide AI-powered coaching simulations tailored to their specific emotional development goals (Russell & Norvig, 2021).

Adaptive learning platforms powered by AI can adjust content delivery in real-time based on the user's engagement level, emotional state, and learning pace. Emotion AI can detect when a learner is frustrated, bored, or engaged and adapts to the training material accordingly. This ensures higher retention, better user experience, and greater alignment with the learner's developmental trajectory.

These technologies provide continuous monitoring and longitudinal data that help track progress over time. This allows organizations to shift from event-based training to ongoing development journeys that are closely aligned with business outcomes and leadership performance metrics. By embedding Emotion AI into leadership development, organizations can ensure that emotional growth is not an afterthought but a central element of leadership training.

In addition, personalized, AI-driven training contributes to inclusivity. By recognizing individual differences in emotional expression and learning styles, these systems support diverse leadership talent and reduce bias that may exist in standardized assessments.

Technology and emotional intelligence are changing leadership and training. Effective leadership in the AI age needs intellectual and emotional intelligence. In this setting, personalised, adaptive, and emotion-aware development tactics are becoming more effective than traditional training approaches. This change relies on real-time insights, contextual feedback, and customised learning interventions from emotion AI. AI-driven, emotionally intelligent leadership development will help organisations produce resilient, responsive, and successful leaders as they embrace digital change.

3. UNDERSTANDING AI-DRIVEN ANALYSIS IN HUMAN CAPITAL DEVELOPMENT

3.1 Definition and Scope of AI-Driven Analysis in HR and Training

Applying AI technology to assess, optimize, and improve worker performance, leadership qualities, and training efficacy is what's known as AI-driven analysis in human capital development. Organizations may now obtain and evaluate meaningful insights from massive volumes of employee-related data with the help of artificial intelligence (AI) in the context of organizational training and human resources (HR). According to Subrahmanyam (2024), the goal is to enhance personnel management, customize learning experiences, and connect training interventions with business objectives.

This analytical approach moves beyond traditional HR metrics by incorporating real-time data, predictive modeling, and intelligent automation. AI-driven analysis identifies skills gaps, predicts leadership potential, tailors learning journeys, and monitors engagement levels. In training and development, AI facilitates adaptive learning paths, recommends relevant content, and offers virtual coaching powered by intelligent agents. Importantly, when integrated with Emotion AI, this technology assesses not only cognitive competencies but also emotional and interpersonal dimensions—elements that are critical for effective leadership.

3.2 Key Technologies: Emotion AI, Natural Language Processing (NLP), Machine Learning (ML), and Sentiment Analysis

Several AI technologies converge to form the backbone of human capital analytics. Among these, **Emotion AI** plays a pivotal role in detecting and interpreting human emotions through facial expressions, voice modulation, text sentiment, and physiological signals. By understanding emotional states, Emotion AI enhances training programs by making them more responsive and personalized. It can identify when a learner is confused, disengaged, or motivated, allowing systems to adjust content delivery accordingly (Calvo & D'Mello, 2010).

Natural Language Processing (NLP) is another crucial technology that enables AI systems to understand and interpret human language. In HR and training, NLP is used to analyze communication patterns in emails, chat logs, performance reviews, and surveys. This analysis provides insights into employee sentiment, leadership tone, and team dynamics (Miner et al., 2019). NLP can flag communication that may indicate disengagement or emotional distress, which can inform targeted well-being or coaching interventions.

Machine Learning (ML) algorithms underpin the predictive capabilities of AI systems. These algorithms learn from historical and real-time data to identify trends, make predictions, and offer recommendations. In the context of leadership development, ML can predict future leadership success based on behavioral data, performance history, and engagement levels. ML also powers adaptive learning platforms that tailor training content to individual needs, ensuring continuous development (Russell & Norvig, 2021).

Sentiment Analysis, a subfield of NLP, is used to evaluate subjective information in text form. It identifies attitudes, emotions, and opinions from written or spoken content. In training and leadership development, sentiment analysis helps in gauging the emotional tone of feedback, survey responses, or internal communications. This insight helps HR professionals assess employee morale, emotional well-being, and leadership effectiveness in managing team sentiments (Subrahmanyam, 2024).

3.3 Types of Data Used: Biometric, Behavioral, Communication, and Performance Metrics

AI-driven analysis draws on a wide array of data sources to build a comprehensive understanding of human capital. These sources include **biometric data**, such as facial expressions, voice tone, and heart rate variability, captured through wearable devices or webcams. These indicators are particularly useful in Emotion

AI applications to monitor stress levels, engagement, and affective states during training or performance evaluations.

Behavioral data includes patterns of activity such as login frequency on learning platforms, time spent on tasks, and completion rates. It reveals how employees interact with training content and digital tools. Analyzing these behaviors helps organizations understand learning preferences and adjust programs accordingly (Davenport et al., 2020).

Communication data, obtained through emails, chat logs, meeting transcripts, and social platforms, offers insights into collaboration, leadership communication styles, and team sentiment. Combined with NLP and sentiment analysis, this data can identify influential leaders, detect toxic behaviors, and improve workplace culture.

Performance metrics provide quantitative indicators such as key performance indicators (KPIs), sales numbers, project completion rates, and feedback scores. These metrics allow AI systems to correlate training inputs with measurable outcomes, thus assessing the ROI of development programs and identifying high-potential individuals for leadership roles (Bersin, 2018).

By integrating these diverse data types, AI systems offer a 360-degree view of employee development, enabling organizations to make data-informed decisions about leadership and training investments.

3.4 Ethical Considerations and Data Privacy in AI-Based Analysis

There are serious ethical and privacy issues that arise with AI-driven analysis, despite its many advantages. Data privacy is a major issue, especially when dealing with personal information like biometric data or emotional records. The abuse of such data has the potential to undermine confidence and make employees feel uneasy about being continually scrutinized. Organizations should have transparent data collection, processing, and use policies in place, as well as clear procedures for obtaining informed consent (Binns et al., 2018).

Another concern is algorithmic bias, which occurs when AI systems use biased training data to unintentionally reinforce preexisting prejudices in areas such as recruiting, training, and promotion choices. Underrepresented groups are more vulnerable to prejudice and unequal consequences that might result from this. Ethical review boards, varied data sets, and regular audits are crucial for reducing these risks and making AI applications fair (Raji & Buolamwini, 2019).

The possibility of over-surveillance, in which AI systems become invasive instead than helpful, is another ethical worry. A climate of dread and decreased psychological safety might result from the employment of AI to monitor every employee's every action, emotion, and phrase. It is essential to promote a healthy corporate culture by balancing the advantages of AI with respect for human dignity and individuality.

Last but not least, there has to be a crystal-clear definition of who is responsible for what when AI is deployed. Transparency in decision-making processes utilizing AI and the continued need of human monitoring are critical for organizations. Leaders and HR experts need to know how to safely use AI-generated insights, not just accept them at face value.

By providing personalised, predictive, and emotionally intelligent leadership and training insights, AI-driven analysis is revolutionising human capital development. Organisations may get deeper insights into employee behaviour, performance, and well-being using Emotion AI, NLP, ML, and sentiment analysis. This raises ethical concerns about data privacy, justice, and responsibility as such systems are used more. Responsible AI adoption in HR and training is necessary to link technical advances with human values and organisational objectives.

4. ROLE OF EMOTION AI IN ENHANCING LEADERSHIP TRAINING

Today's fast-changing business environment has changed leadership training from a one-size-fits-all to a personalised, emotional intelligence-focused methodology. Emotion AI can identify, analyse, and react to human emotional signals, making it a transformational tool in this field. Emotion AI helps organisations create more effective, responsive, and sympathetic leadership training programs by analysing emotional states in real time. Emotion AI assesses soft skills, tracks emotional reactions, and provides actionable feedback to improve leadership growth.

4.1 Detecting and Interpreting Emotional Cues in Communication

At the core of Emotion AI is its ability to recognize and interpret emotional expressions across multiple modalities—facial expressions, vocal tones, body language, and text-based sentiment. Using technologies such as computer vision, voice analysis, and natural language processing (NLP), Emotion AI systems decode nonverbal and verbal signals to identify emotions like frustration, enthusiasm, anxiety, or confidence (McDuff et al., 2019). These emotional cues are crucial in leadership training as they provide insight into how potential leaders respond to challenges, engage with peers, and communicate under pressure.

In virtual leadership simulations or presentations, Emotion AI tools can track micro-expressions and voice modulations to assess whether a leader is exhibiting confidence or discomfort. The system might detect elevated stress through rapid speech or decreased eye contact, prompting real-time interventions or feedback. This kind of emotional awareness helps trainers customize coaching approaches and create learning environments that are both supportive and effective (Picard, 2000).

4.2 Assessing Soft Skills: Empathy, Resilience, and Communication

Soft skills such as empathy, resilience, adaptability, and effective communication are increasingly recognized as foundational to successful leadership. Unlike technical skills, these are difficult to quantify and traditionally assessed through subjective observations or self-reports. Emotion AI offers a more objective, data-driven approach by continuously analyzing interactions and behaviors to infer soft skill competencies.

In team-based scenarios, Emotion AI can monitor how a leader responds to emotionally charged situations—whether they demonstrate active listening, show understanding, or validate the emotions of others. Such assessments allow trainers to pinpoint gaps in empathy or emotional regulation and provide targeted developmental support. Resilience can be gauged by analyzing how individuals emotionally respond to setbacks or feedback, enabling the creation of personalized training modules to build mental toughness and adaptability (Shao et al., 2020).

Communication skills are central to effective leadership. Emotion AI tools can evaluate not only the content but also the emotional tone of speech, ensuring that aspiring leaders convey clarity, assertiveness, and compassion. By identifying patterns in language and delivery that correlate with engagement or disconnection, these systems support the refinement of communication styles that foster trust and influence.

4.3 Real-Time Emotion Tracking for Feedback and Coaching

One of the most powerful applications of Emotion AI in leadership development is real-time emotion tracking. This capability enables trainers and digital platforms to offer instantaneous, context-specific feedback based on the emotional state of the learner. During leadership role-play or difficult conversation simulation, an AI-enabled system can detect signs of nervousness, disengagement, or frustration, and provide nudges or coaching prompts to guide behavior adjustments.

Real-time tracking also supports adaptive learning environments, where content and challenges evolve in response to the participant's emotional readiness. For instance, if a trainee exhibits signs of boredom or ease, the system can introduce more complex scenarios to maintain engagement. If stress levels rise excessively, the program can slow down or provide supportive feedback to manage anxiety (D'Mello & Graesser, 2012). This personalized learning experience enhances retention, boosts confidence, and ensures a more meaningful developmental journey.

Emotion AI can also be integrated into leadership coaching sessions. Coaches can review emotional heatmaps, sentiment trends, and communication patterns collected during sessions to gain deeper insights into the leader's emotional trajectory. These data-driven insights facilitate more focused and empathetic coaching, aligning strategies with the unique emotional and cognitive profile of the leader-in-training.

4.4 Case Examples: Emotion Recognition in Leadership Workshops

Several organizations and institutions have begun incorporating Emotion AI into their leadership training initiatives. For example, a multinational technology firm deployed Emotion AI in their executive training program to enhance self-awareness among senior leaders. During role-play exercises and video presentations, facial recognition tools analyzed expressions to provide participants with feedback on how they appeared to others—highlighting moments of assertiveness, empathy, or disconnect. Participants reported heightened awareness of their nonverbal communication and adjusted their leadership presence accordingly.

A European business school integrated Emotion AI tools into its MBA leadership modules. Using real-time sentiment analysis during group discussions and case study presentations, instructors provided individualized coaching that addressed both content delivery and emotional resonance. This led to improved presentation skills, increased peer engagement, and greater emotional intelligence among participants (Gunkel, 2021).

Another example comes from the healthcare sector, where Emotion AI was used in leadership training for nurse managers. By analyzing speech patterns and emotional tone during high-stress scenario simulations, the system identified areas for development in empathy and stress communication. Feedback reports and video playback allow trainees to reflect on their emotional responses and practice alternative strategies in subsequent sessions.

Emotion AI provides new insights into emotional behaviour and soft skill development, transforming leadership training. It connects data and empathy by detecting emotional clues, assessing leadership attributes, and providing real-time feedback. Emotion AI in training programs is a promising way to develop strategic and emotionally savvy leaders. Ethical issues must be balanced with technology innovation to utilise emotional data ethically and openly. Emotion AI may help new leaders lead with intellect and empathy if implemented carefully.

5. MEASURING LEADERSHIP POTENTIAL AND GROWTH WITH AI

As organisations realise the significance of emotionally aware and adaptive leadership, AI has become a valuable tool for evaluating and developing leadership potential. Leadership qualities are being found, examined, and improved using advanced AI systems like Emotion AI. Predictive analytics, continuous feedback loops, and emotional well-being indicators may help organisations develop resilient, sympathetic, and successful leaders. This section discusses how AI technologies are being used to objectively, data-drivenly assess leadership potential and progress beyond performance reviews.

5.1 Emotion AI for Leadership Trait Identification and Growth Tracking

Emotion AI, a subset of affective computing, plays a pivotal role in identifying leadership traits by analyzing individuals' emotional responses, communication patterns, and behavioral cues. Leadership competencies such as empathy, emotional regulation, adaptability, and social awareness can be difficult to quantify through conventional means. Emotion AI addresses this challenge by continuously monitoring and interpreting emotions through facial expressions, voice tonality, physiological signals, and language sentiment (Picard, 2000; McStay, 2018).

During leadership simulations or real-time workplace interactions, Emotion AI systems can track how leaders respond to stress, manage conflicts, and motivate their teams. These insights help organizations evaluate emotional intelligence as a leadership asset. Over time, the collected emotional data can be used to track individual growth, mapping developmental trajectories and providing benchmarks for emotional and interpersonal skills improvement (D'Mello & Graesser, 2012).

The integration of dashboards and visual reports enables HR professionals and leadership coaches to identify trends in emotional behavior, compare them against leadership benchmarks, and tailor developmental programs accordingly. Emotion

AI thus transforms subjective leadership assessment into a more objective and continuous process.

5.2 Predictive Analytics in Identifying High-Potential Employees

Predictive analytics, powered by machine learning algorithms, offers organizations the ability to identify employees with high leadership potential early in their careers. These models analyze vast datasets, including performance metrics, behavioral trends, peer feedback, engagement levels, and emotional intelligence scores, to forecast leadership success (Minbaeva, 2020). By recognizing patterns associated with effective leadership—such as high adaptability, learning agility, and emotional resilience—predictive analytics enhance succession planning and talent pipeline management.

AI-driven platforms can analyze data from communication tools, project outcomes, and collaboration networks to detect individuals who consistently exhibit leadership behavior, such as initiative-taking, influence, and empathy. These findings enable organizations to make data-informed decisions when selecting candidates for leadership development programs (Chamorro-Premuzic et al., 2017).

Predictive models can provide early warnings about leadership derailers such as burnout, disengagement, or behavioral inconsistencies. This proactive approach ensures that leadership development is not only about nurturing potential but also about preventing decline or misalignment with organizational values.

5.3 AI-Based 360-Degree Feedback Analysis and Improvement Plans

An individual's leadership effectiveness may be measured using traditional 360-degree feedback methods, which include collecting assessments from peers, subordinates, and supervisors. These systems often encounter constraints as a result of subjectivity, prejudice, and inconsistent results. In order to evaluate feedback data more objectively and thoroughly, AI-enhanced 360-degree feedback solutions integrate sentiment analysis, emotion recognition, and natural language processing (Serrat, 2017).

AI systems can analyze textual feedback for tone, emotional valence, and underlying themes. Repeated mentions of "inspiring," "empathetic," or "decisive" in peer reviews can be quantified and visualized, helping leaders understand how they are perceived across different dimensions. Sentiment trends over time can reveal progress or regression in leadership behavior, guiding tailored development interventions.

AI tools can link feedback data to personalized improvement plans. By recommending learning modules, coaching sessions, or experiential projects based on detected strengths and weaknesses, AI ensures that feedback leads to meaningful and measurable development (Huang & Rust, 2021). These platforms can also automate follow-up assessments to track the impact of interventions, fostering a culture of continuous improvement.

5.4 Integrating Employee Emotional Well-Being into Performance and Leadership Evaluations

Leadership performance cannot be isolated from the emotional well-being of employees. Emotion AI allows organizations to incorporate emotional wellness metrics into leadership evaluations, ensuring a more holistic approach. Leaders who foster psychologically safe, inclusive, and emotionally supportive environments are more likely to sustain team performance and innovation (Edmondson, 2019).

Emotion AI tools can assess the emotional climate within teams by analyzing communication sentiment, meeting dynamics, and engagement signals. Leaders whose teams exhibit consistently positive emotional indicators—such as trust, enthusiasm, and mutual respect—can be recognized for their emotional leadership capabilities. Signs of stress, frustration, or disengagement can signal the need for leadership intervention.

This integration also supports well-being-centric leadership development programs. By correlating leader behavior with team emotional health, organizations can promote leadership styles that align with mental wellness and sustainable performance. In turn, this contributes to reduced turnover, improved morale, and higher organizational commitment (Kroll et al., 2021).

AI can measure leadership potential and progress, giving organisations a data-driven, emotionally intelligent framework for developing leaders. Emotion AI tracks emotions in real time, revealing leadership attributes like empathy and resilience. AI-based 360-degree feedback tools turn qualitative data into effective development plans, while predictive analytics better identify high-potential individuals. Most significantly, incorporating emotional well-being into performance assessments guarantees that leadership success is measured by team emotional health as well as results. As organisations seek more human-centric leadership models, AI technologies provide precision and empathy for sustained leadership development.

6. INTEGRATING AI-DRIVEN ANALYSIS INTO ORGANIZATIONAL TRAINING FRAMEWORKS

Integrating AI-driven analysis into learning and development (L&D) frameworks has become essential for leadership growth, workforce agility, and competitive advantage as organisations embrace digital transformation. The use of Emotion AI and other data-driven technologies is making conventional training methods more dynamic, personalised, and emotionally intelligent. This section discusses practical methods for incorporating AI into training frameworks, key stakeholders, organisational culture alignment, and changing management for effective deployment.

6.1 Strategies for Implementing AI-Driven Platforms in Learning and Development

An organization's leadership development and workforce capabilities objectives should be the starting point for any strategic roadmap that aims to integrate AI into L&D programs. By analyzing a user's emotional and behavioral signals, AI-powered systems can tailor learning materials to each individual, monitor their skill development, and provide immediate feedback. Picking the correct artificial intelligence (AI) technologies like Natural Language Processing (NLP), Machine Learning (ML), and Emotion AI is the first step in an effective deployment, followed by integrating them seamlessly with Learning Management Systems (LMS) and other HRIS (Bersin, 2019).

A phased implementation approach is often recommended. It typically begins with pilot projects that apply AI to targeted training modules—such as communication skills or conflict resolution workshops—and gradually scales to broader leadership programs. These pilots provide valuable insights into technology performance, content relevance, and learner receptivity, enabling continuous refinement before full-scale deployment (Huang & Rust, 2021).

AI tools should be configured to support data collection from multiple sources, including video analysis, feedback forms, and performance metrics. AI-powered platforms can analyze emotional expressions during role-play exercises or leadership simulations to identify developmental needs in areas like empathy, assertiveness, or collaboration (Picard, 2000). These insights can then be used to tailor training interventions, creating a more learner-centric experience.

6.2 Stakeholder Roles: HR, IT, Leadership Coaches, and Executives

The success of AI-driven training initiatives hinges on the coordinated efforts of diverse organizational stakeholders. Human Resources (HR) departments typically lead the design and deployment of AI-enabled L&D programs. They are responsible for identifying training needs, defining learning outcomes, and ensuring that AI solutions are integrated into existing talent development strategies (Minbaeva, 2020).

When it comes to the technical aspects of implementing AI platforms, integrating data, and managing security, information technology (IT) teams are indispensable. Algorithm configuration, data storage management, and compliance with data protection standards (such as GDPR and local labor laws) are all part of their job description.

Leadership coaches and training facilitators contribute to interpreting AI-generated insights and translating them into actionable learning plans. Emotion AI data can enrich coaching sessions by highlighting behavioral tendencies and emotional responses that influence leadership effectiveness (McStay, 2018). Coaches must be trained to work with AI-generated feedback to enhance rather than replace human judgment.

The last step is for top-level management to support AI-powered education programs by setting an example for digital adoption, acquiring funding, and painting an enticing picture of the training system of the future. According to Chamorro-Premuzic et al. (2017), their backing is critical for creating an environment where employees are willing to learn new things and are receptive to new technologies.

6.3 Alignment with Organizational Goals and Cultural Values

To maximize impact, AI integration in training must align with broader organizational goals, including leadership development pipelines, innovation strategies, diversity and inclusion (D&I) initiatives, and employee engagement objectives. AI tools can be programmed to support these goals by embedding them into training metrics and performance indicators (Huang & Rust, 2021).

Cultural alignment is equally important. Organizations with a strong learning culture and open communication are better positioned to embrace AI-driven training. Emotion AI systems should reflect organizational values—such as empathy, integrity, and inclusivity—by focusing on the development of relevant emotional and interpersonal skills (Subrahmanyam, 2025). If psychological safety is a key cultural value, Emotion AI can help track whether leaders are fostering trust and openness within their teams.

AI platforms should also be customizable to support multilingual and multicultural learning environments, ensuring accessibility and relevance across global workforces. Training content and AI-generated insights must be free from cultural bias, and inclusive of diverse learning styles and emotional expressions (Raisch & Krakowski, 2021).

6.4 Change Management and Employee Acceptance

Introducing AI into training and leadership development necessitates thoughtful change management strategies. Employees may express skepticism or anxiety about AI technologies, particularly those involving emotion detection and behavioral monitoring. Transparent communication about the purpose, scope, and benefits of AI tools is essential to build trust and reduce resistance (Serrat, 2017).

Engaging employees early in the implementation process fosters a sense of ownership and participation. This can be achieved through feedback loops, co-creation workshops, and pilot testing. Training sessions should be offered to familiarize employees with the new systems, emphasizing how AI enhances learning rather than replacing human interaction.

It is also crucial to establish ethical frameworks for data use. Employees should be assured of data confidentiality, voluntary participation, and the right to opt out. Governance policies should clarify how emotion data will be collected, who can access it, and how it will be used for developmental—not punitive—purposes (Kroll et al., 2021).

Finally, success metrics should include not only improvements in leadership capabilities but also employee sentiment toward the training system. Positive engagement levels, reduced training fatigue, and self-reported learning effectiveness are key indicators of successful change management in AI-enabled training environments.

Integrating AI-driven analysis into organizational training frameworks is a transformative step toward building emotionally intelligent and future-ready leadership. Through strategic implementation, collaborative stakeholder roles, cultural alignment, and thoughtful change management, organizations can harness the full potential of AI to personalize learning, enhance emotional awareness, and drive sustainable leadership development. As organizations continue to adapt to digital realities, those that embrace AI in a human-centric, ethical, and inclusive manner will be best positioned to thrive.

7. CASE STUDIES AND INDUSTRY APPLICATIONS

Leadership training and human capital development are fast changing as organisations use AI, especially Emotion AI, to build compassionate, flexible, and high-performing leaders. Emotion AI, which recognises and analyses human emotions via facial expressions, voice modulation, and physiological indicators, illuminates leadership's emotional aspects. Companies across sectors use AI-driven technologies to improve training, engagement, and leadership in real time. Four real-world case studies show how Emotion AI and associated technologies are revolutionising leadership development in technology, healthcare, retail, and start-ups.

7.1 Tech Company Using Emotion AI to Develop Empathetic Managers

A leading global technology firm, IBM, has embraced Emotion AI to enhance the emotional intelligence of its managerial workforce. The company implemented AI-driven emotional analytics to assess the emotional tenor of managerial communication during team meetings and performance reviews. By analyzing tone, word choice, and speech patterns through Natural Language Processing (NLP) and sentiment analysis, IBM identified empathy gaps in managerial behavior and created targeted training modules to address them (Bughin et al., 2019).

Managers who displayed less emotional attunement during virtual meetings were provided with microlearning sessions that included role-play simulations and real-time feedback powered by Emotion AI. These simulations helped them understand the impact of non-verbal cues, such as facial expressions and pauses, on team morale. Post-training assessments revealed measurable improvements in team satisfaction, reduced attrition, and increased psychological safety across departments.

This case demonstrates how Emotion AI not only supports leadership skill acquisition but also enables continuous learning and development through adaptive feedback loops (Huang & Rust, 2021). Importantly, the initiative aligned with IBM's broader goal of promoting inclusive and emotionally intelligent leadership.

7.2 Healthcare Organization Integrating AI in Nurse Leadership Development

In the healthcare sector, a prominent hospital system in the United States utilized AI-driven platforms to cultivate leadership skills among nurse managers, who play a pivotal role in patient care and staff retention. The organization implemented an Emotion AI-based training solution that analyzed nurses' interactions during team huddles and conflict resolution scenarios. Using facial expression recognition and vocal tone analysis, the AI system provided individual feedback on emotional responsiveness, assertiveness, and conflict management capabilities (McStay, 2018).

This tool was integrated with a broader competency framework that included clinical performance and patient satisfaction metrics. Nurse leaders who received Emotion AI-enhanced feedback were able to adjust their communication styles, leading to improved team coordination and patient outcomes. The program also included predictive analytics that identified nurses with high leadership potential based on emotional acuity and decision-making under pressure.

By embedding AI into professional development pathways, the healthcare organization created a responsive and data-informed leadership model. This approach not only improved individual performance but also reinforced emotional well-being and resilience—two crucial factors in high-stress environments (Minbaeva, 2020).

7.3 Retail Chain Tracking Emotional Responses to Training Programs

A multinational retail chain adopted Emotion AI to enhance the effectiveness of its leadership development workshops aimed at store managers. Using computer vision and sentiment analysis tools, the company monitored participants' facial expressions, gaze patterns, and engagement levels during both virtual and in-person training sessions. The goal was to determine which content segments resonated emotionally with learners and which caused disengagement.

The collected data was aggregated and analyzed in real time, allowing facilitators to adjust training delivery methods and content sequencing based on learner reactions. Modules focused on customer conflict resolution initially generated high emotional stress indicators, prompting the redesign of those segments to include more supportive, interactive elements.

As a result, the company reported a 20% increase in training satisfaction scores and a significant improvement in knowledge retention and application in real-life scenarios. Additionally, follow-up surveys showed that emotionally engaging content translated into better on-the-job performance and team leadership capabilities (Chamorro-Premuzic et al., 2017).

This case underscores the value of Emotion AI in creating learner-centric and emotionally resonant training programs that improve both engagement and leadership outcomes.

7.4 Start-Up Leveraging AI-Driven Mentoring for Rapid Leadership Scaling

In the fast-paced start-up environment, leadership development must keep pace with rapid organizational growth. One Silicon Valley start-up specializing in fintech used AI-driven mentoring platforms to support its emerging leaders. The company combined Emotion AI with digital mentoring to accelerate leadership capacity in newly promoted managers.

Emotion AI tools tracked emotional signals in video check-ins between mentors and mentees, flagging areas where mentees showed anxiety, uncertainty, or overconfidence. These insights helped mentors personalize their guidance and focus on the most pressing leadership challenges, such as decision-making under ambiguity or motivating diverse teams.

The AI system offered personalized learning pathways based on emotional and behavioral data, directing managers to specific content on communication, resilience, and influence. Within six months, the company reported increased leadership confidence, faster role acclimation, and stronger team alignment.

This start-up's experience highlights how Emotion AI can democratize leadership development by delivering just-in-time support tailored to emotional and developmental needs—especially in high-growth, resource-constrained environments (Raisch & Krakowski, 2021).

These diverse industry applications illustrate how Emotion AI is reshaping leadership training by embedding emotional insight into assessment, mentoring, and learning design. Whether fostering empathetic management in tech firms, enhancing communication among healthcare professionals, optimizing engagement in retail training, or scaling leadership in start-ups, AI-driven approaches provide real-time, data-rich feedback that traditional methods lack. As organizations continue to embrace Emotion AI, its potential to personalize, humanize, and elevate leadership development will be a defining feature of the future of work.

8. CHALLENGES AND LIMITATIONS

Numerous benefits may be gained by using Artificial Intelligence (AI), and more specifically Emotion AI, into leadership development programs. The use of AI-driven analysis has great promise, but it also brings with it a number of restrictions and difficulties. These range from issues with ethics, regulations, and society to those with implementation and technology. Responsible and successful use of AI to enhance leadership qualities and employee health requires an understanding of and attention to these problems.

8.1 Technical and Implementation Barriers

One of the most immediate challenges in adopting Emotion AI for leadership training lies in its technical complexity and implementation requirements. Deploying AI systems requires robust infrastructure, access to high-quality data, and integration with existing Human Resource (HR) and Learning and Development (L&D) systems. Many organizations, particularly small and medium enterprises (SMEs), may lack the technological capability or resources to implement these systems effectively (Bughin, Seong, Manyika, Chui, & Joshi, 2019).

The successful use of Emotion AI is highly dependent on the accuracy and granularity of input data. Inadequate data collection or poor data quality can lead to flawed emotional assessments, undermining the credibility and usefulness of the system (Raisch & Krakowski, 2021). Another technical limitation is the inability of current AI systems to consistently interpret nuanced human emotions, especially in diverse cultural and linguistic contexts. Emotion recognition models are often trained on data from specific populations, leading to reduced accuracy when applied to individuals from different backgrounds.

8.2 Concerns Around Over-Reliance on AI and Emotional Surveillance

While AI can offer valuable insights, there is growing concern about the potential over-reliance on AI systems for leadership evaluation and training. A major risk is that human judgment and intuition—critical elements in assessing leadership potential—may be diminished or overlooked. Leaders and HR professionals may defer too readily to AI-generated recommendations without critical scrutiny, potentially perpetuating errors or biases embedded in the system (Huang & Rust, 2021).

The application of Emotion AI raises serious questions about employee privacy and emotional surveillance. Emotion AI technologies typically involve the collection and analysis of sensitive biometric and behavioral data, such as facial expressions, voice tones, and physiological responses. When employees are continuously monitored for their emotional states, it can lead to a sense of intrusion, stress, and reduced trust in the organization (McStay, 2018). This surveillance, if not handled with transparency and consent, risks eroding the psychological safety that leadership training aims to foster.

8.3 Risk of Bias in AI Algorithms and Emotion Recognition

A critical limitation of Emotion AI lies in the inherent bias that may exist within its algorithms. AI systems, including those used for emotion recognition, are only as good as the data they are trained on. If the training datasets are not diverse or representative, the resulting models may exhibit significant bias against certain demographic groups based on gender, race, or cultural background (Crawford, 2021). This can result in skewed assessments of emotional expression and leadership potential.

Facial expression recognition algorithms have been shown to misclassify emotions more frequently in people with darker skin tones or from non-Western backgrounds (Buolamwini & Gebru, 2018). In leadership contexts, such biases can lead to unfair evaluations, hindering the growth of diverse talent and exacerbating existing inequalities in workplace advancement.

To mitigate these risks, organizations must adopt practices such as algorithmic auditing, bias testing, and the use of diverse training datasets. Human oversight is also essential to contextualize AI findings and ensure that leadership decisions are fair and equitable.

8.4 Regulatory and Ethical Compliance

Ethical and legal considerations are rising to the surface as Emotion AI finds more and more applications. Comprehensive legal frameworks controlling the use of Emotion AI in the workplace are still lacking. Organizations face increased risk of non-compliance with developing data protection rules like the General Data Protection Regulation (GDPR) in the EU or comparable laws in other jurisdictions due to legislative ambiguity, which increases uncertainty (Morley et al., 2021).

Examples of the strict regulations imposed by GDPR on the use of biometric and emotional data include the need to get informed permission, reduce data collection, and provide an explanation for automated decision-making. Businesses that use emotional intelligence to teach their leaders have a responsibility to make sure that the mechanisms they use are open, accountable, and allow employees to opt out if they don't agree with certain policies or practices.

Ethical considerations also extend to the purpose and use of emotional data. Employers must be clear about why emotional insights are being collected, how they will be used, and who will have access to them. Ethical AI usage demands balancing the pursuit of improved leadership performance with respect for individual autonomy and dignity (Floridi et al., 2018).

There are a lot of obstacles to overcome before AI-driven analysis, and Emotion AI in particular, can be widely used to improve leadership development programs. Responsibly realizing the technology's promise requires skillfully navigating technical hurdles, emotional surveillance concerns, algorithmic prejudice, and regulatory constraints. Companies should strike a balance between relying only on technological advancements and also including ethical governance practices, open communication, and human supervision. In an AI-driven workplace, Emotion AI can only be useful for developing inclusive, compassionate, and successful leaders after that.

9. FUTURE TRENDS AND OPPORTUNITIES

Leadership development is becoming more human-centric, adaptable, and inclusive due to rapid advances in AI, especially Emotion AI. AI and future technologies like AR and VR provide immersive and tailored leadership training as companies value emotional intelligence and employee wellness. A''s growing emotional data analysis capabilities enable emotional resilience and inclusive workplaces. This chapter addresses AI-driven leadership development trends and how organisations may leverage these technologies to build more compassionate, successful, and emotionally intelligent leaders.

9.1 The Future of Emotion-Aware AI in Human-Centric Leadership Models

Emotion-aware AI technologies, which detect, analyze, and respond to human emotional cues, are expected to become central to human-centric leadership frameworks. Traditional leadership models have increasingly recognized emotional intelligence (EI) as a critical determinant of effective leadership, encompassing self-awareness, empathy, social skills, and emotional regulation (Goleman, 1998). AI's ability to provide objective, real-time emotional feedback can augment leaders' self-perception and enhance their interpersonal effectiveness.

In the future, emotion-aware AI systems will likely be embedded into everyday leadership practices, offering continuous support for decision-making and communication. By capturing subtle emotional dynamics within teams, these systems can help leaders adapt their behavior to meet employees' emotional needs, improve engagement, and mitigate conflicts proactively (Picard, 2015). This evolution aligns with the growing trend toward emotionally intelligent workplaces where technology does not replace human empathy but amplifies it through data-driven insights.

This shift requires careful calibration to avoid over-dependence on AI-generated emotional data and to maintain the irreplaceable human judgment that underpins authentic leadership (Boyatzis, 2018). Leaders will need training to interpret AI feedback critically and ethically, balancing technological input with human sensitivity.

9.2 Integration of AI with AR/VR for Immersive Leadership Training

The integration of AI with immersive technologies such as AR and VR heralds a new frontier in leadership training. These technologies create realistic, interactive environments where leaders can practice complex interpersonal skills, receive instant AI-driven feedback, and develop emotional competencies in safe, controlled settings (Freina & Ott, 2015).

VR simulations can recreate challenging leadership scenarios—such as managing team conflicts, delivering difficult feedback, or leading through crisis—while AI analyzes participants' emotional responses, speech patterns, and decision-making processes (Bailenson, 2018). This data can be used to tailor training programs to individual developmental needs and track progress over time.

The combined use of AI and AR/VR enables experiential learning that is adaptive and highly engaging, overcoming limitations of traditional classroom-based approaches (Radianti et al., 2020). Future developments may include AI-powered virtual coaches or avatars that provide personalized guidance and emotional support during training sessions.

As immersive technologies become more accessible and affordable, their widespread adoption in leadership development programs will democratize access to high-quality experiential learning, enabling organizations of all sizes to cultivate emotionally intelligent leaders.

9.3 Emotional Resilience Training Powered by AI Analytics

The importance of emotional resilience as a leadership quality is becoming more acknowledged, particularly in today's VUCA (volatile, uncertain, complex, and ambiguous) workplaces (Reivich & Shatté, 2002). Continuous monitoring, early recognition of stress signals, and targeted treatments are all the ways in which analytics driven by AI show promise for enhancing emotional resilience.

Emotion AI can detect signs of emotional exhaustion, burnout, or disengagement by analyzing speech tone, facial expressions, or physiological signals (such as heart rate variability) during leadership activities or coaching sessions (Kappas & Tepper, 2019). Coupled with predictive analytics, these systems can flag leaders at risk and recommend tailored resilience-building exercises, mindfulness practices, or workload adjustments.

AI-driven platforms can facilitate "just-in-time" resilience training by delivering microlearning modules triggered by detected emotional states. A leader showing signs of frustration during a virtual meeting might immediately receive AI-suggested breathing exercises or cognitive reframing techniques to manage stress.

By supporting emotional resilience proactively, AI tools contribute to healthier leadership and workforce dynamics, reducing turnover and improving overall organizational performance (Southwick & Charney, 2018).

9.4 Building Inclusive and Emotionally Intelligent Workplaces through AI Insights

Beyond individual leadership development, AI-driven emotional analytics hold significant promise for fostering more inclusive and emotionally intelligent organizational cultures. Diversity and inclusion (D&I) initiatives increasingly emphasize the importance of psychological safety, empathy, and emotional awareness as foundations for true inclusion (Roberson, 2019).

Emotion AI can help identify unconscious biases or exclusionary behaviors by analyzing interactions across teams and leadership layers. Sentiment analysis of communication patterns may reveal discrepancies in how different demographic groups are engaged or responded to, allowing targeted interventions to address inclusion gaps (Caliskan et al., 2017).

AI insights can guide the design of leadership development programs that cultivate inclusive behaviors, such as active listening, cultural humility, and emotional validation. By providing leaders with real-time feedback on their emotional impact across diverse teams, AI empowers them to adapt their styles to be more equitable and supportive.

In the future, organizations may leverage AI to create emotionally intelligent ecosystems where employee wellbeing and inclusivity are continuously monitored and enhanced through dynamic feedback loops between AI analytics, leadership actions, and workplace culture assessments.

Leadership development will change with AI-driven analysis, especially Emotion AI. AI's emotion-aware insights will improve leaders' emotional intelligence and adaptability as companies embrace human-centric leadership approaches. AI and AR/VR boost leadership development with immersive, customised learning. CEOs may remain healthy in tough times with AI-powered emotional resilience training. Finally, AI insights may help firms establish inclusive, emotionally intelligent workplaces that attract diverse talent and succeed.

10. CONCLUSION

This chapter has explored the transformative potential of AI-driven analysis, particularly Emotion AI, in advancing leadership training and development. Key insights highlight how Emotion AI enhances the understanding of emotional cues, enabling more personalized and adaptive leadership growth. From detecting empathy and resilience to offering real-time feedback and predictive analytics, AI technologies are revolutionizing traditional approaches to leadership assessment and training. Integrating AI into organizational learning frameworks can improve alignment with strategic goals, promote inclusive cultures, and foster emotional resilience among leaders.

Reaffirming the value of Emotion AI, it is evident that these technologies do not replace human judgment but rather augment leaders' emotional intelligence and self-awareness. By providing data-driven insights into emotional dynamics, AI empowers leaders to engage more empathetically and authentically with their teams, ultimately driving better organizational performance and employee wellbeing. The use of immersive technologies like AR and VR further enriches the training experience, making leadership development more engaging and effective.

As organizations adopt these innovations, it is critical to prioritize ethical considerations, including data privacy, bias mitigation, and transparency. The future success of AI in leadership development depends on balancing technological capabilities with respect for human dignity and fostering trust among employees.

The call to action is clear: organizations and leaders must embrace AI tools thoughtfully and empathetically, integrating them into people development strategies in ways that enhance—not diminish—the human element of leadership. By doing so, they can unlock the full potential of AI to nurture emotionally intelligent, resilient, and inclusive leaders equipped to navigate the complexities of the modern workplace. Harnessing Emotion AI responsibly offers a powerful pathway to creating workplaces that value both technological innovation and profound human connection.

REFERENCES

Bailenson, J. N. (2018). *Experience on demand: What virtual reality is, how it works, and what it can do*. W. W. Norton & Company.

Bersin, J. (2018). *The rise of the social enterprise: Deloitte Global Human Capital Trends*. Deloitte Insights.

Bersin, J. (2019). Learning in the flow of work. *Harvard Business Review*. Retrieved from https://hbr.org/

Binns, R., Veale, M., Van Kleek, M., & Shadbolt, N. (2018). 'It's reducing a human being to a percentage': Perceptions of justice in algorithmic decisions. *Proceedings of the 2018 CHI Conference on Human Factors in Computing Systems*, 1–14. DOI: 10.1145/3173574.3173951

Boyatzis, R. E. (2018). The Competent Manager: A Model for Effective Performance. *Journal of Management Development, 37*(7), 604–608.

Brynjolfsson, E., & McAfee, A. (2017). *Machine, platform, crowd: Harnessing our digital future*. W. W. Norton & Company.

Bughin, J., Seong, J., Manyika, J., Chui, M., & Joshi, R. (2019). *Notes from the AI frontier: Modeling the impact of AI on the world economy*. McKinsey Global Institute.

Buolamwini, J., & Gebru, T. (2018). Gender shades: Intersectional accuracy disparities in commercial gender classification. *Proceedings of Machine Learning Research, 81*, 77–91.

Caliskan, A., Bryson, J. J., & Narayanan, A. (2017). Semantics derived automatically from language corpora contain human-like biases. *Science, 356*(6334), 183–186. DOI: 10.1126/science.aal4230 PMID: 28408601

Calvo, R. A., & D'Mello, S. (2010). Affect detection: An interdisciplinary review of models, methods, and their applications. *IEEE Transactions on Affective Computing, 1*(1), 18–37. DOI: 10.1109/T-AFFC.2010.1

Chamorro-Premuzic, T., Wade, M., & Jordan, J. (2017). The Promise and Peril of Artificial Intelligence. *Harvard Business Review, 95*(4), 58–65.

Crawford, K. (2021). *Atlas of AI: Power, politics, and the planetary costs of artificial intelligence*. Yale University Press.

D'Mello, S., & Graesser, A. (2012). Dynamics of affective states during complex learning. *Learning and Instruction, 22*(2), 145–157. DOI: 10.1016/j.learninstruc.2011.10.001

Davenport, T. H., Guha, A., Grewal, D., & Bressgott, T. (2020). How artificial intelligence will change the future of marketing. *Journal of the Academy of Marketing Science, 48*(1), 24–42. DOI: 10.1007/s11747-019-00696-0

Day, D. V., Fleenor, J. W., Atwater, L. E., Sturm, R. E., & McKee, R. A. (2014). Advances in leader and leadership development: A review of 25 years of research and theory. *The Leadership Quarterly, 25*(1), 63–82. DOI: 10.1016/j.leaqua.2013.11.004

Edmondson, A. C. (2019). *The fearless organization: Creating psychological safety in the workplace for learning, innovation, and growth*. John Wiley & Sons.

Floridi, L., Cowls, J., Beltrametti, M., Chatila, R., Chazerand, P., Dignum, V., Luetge, C., Madelin, R., Pagallo, U., Rossi, F., Schafer, B., Valcke, P., & Vayena, E. (2018). AI4People—An ethical framework for a good AI society: Opportunities, risks, principles, and recommendations. *Minds and Machines, 28*(4), 689–707. DOI: 10.1007/s11023-018-9482-5 PMID: 30930541

Freina, L., & Ott, M. (2015). A Literature Review on Immersive Virtual Reality in Education: State Of The Art and Perspectives. *The International Scientific Conference eLearning and Software for Education*, 1, 133–141. DOI: 10.12753/2066-026X-15-020

Goleman, D. (1998). *Working with emotional intelligence*. Bantam Books.

Gunkel, D. J. (2021). *Person, thing, robot: A moral and legal ontology for the 21st century and beyond*. MIT Press.

Huang, M. H., & Rust, R. T. (2021). Artificial Intelligence in Service. *Journal of Service Research, 24*(1), 3–16.

Kappas, A., & Tepper, I. (2019). Social regulation of emotion: The role of interaction partners. *Emotion Review, 11*(1), 6–13.

Kroll, T., Nuesch, S., & Meier, C. (2021). The Impact of Emotionally Intelligent Leadership on Employee Mental Health and Organizational Performance. *Leadership and Organization Development Journal, 42*(6), 1011–1024.

McDuff, D., El Kaliouby, R., Cohn, J. F., Demirdjian, D., & Picard, R. W. (2019). Predicting ad liking and purchase intent: Large-scale analysis of facial responses to ads. *IEEE Transactions on Affective Computing, 6*(3), 223–235. DOI: 10.1109/TAFFC.2014.2384198

McStay, A. (2018). *Emotional AI: The rise of empathic media*. SAGE Publications. DOI: 10.4135/9781526451293

Minbaeva, D. (2020). Disrupted HR? Human Resource Management in the Digital Age. *Human Resource Management Review, 30*(4), 100692.

Miner, A. S., Shah, N., & Naseer, S. (2019). NLP in HR: Applications, challenges, and future directions. *Journal of Business Research, 116*, 257–264.

Morley, J., Floridi, L., Kinsey, L., & Elhalal, A. (2021). From what to how: An initial review of publicly available AI ethics tools, methods and research to translate principles into practices. *Science and Engineering Ethics, 27*(4), 1–31. PMID: 31828533

Picard, R. W. (2000). *Affective computing*. MIT Press. DOI: 10.7551/mitpress/1140.003.0008

Picard, R. W. (2015). Affective computing: Challenges. *International Journal of Human-Computer Studies, 59*(1-2), 55–64. DOI: 10.1016/S1071-5819(03)00052-1

Radianti, J., Majchrzak, T. A., Fromm, J., & Wohlgenannt, I. (2020). A systematic review of immersive virtual reality applications for higher education: Design elements, lessons learned, and research agenda. *Computers & Education, 147*, 103778. DOI: 10.1016/j.compedu.2019.103778

Raisch, S., & Krakowski, S. (2021). Artificial intelligence and management: The automation–augmentation paradox. *Academy of Management Review, 46*(1), 192–210. DOI: 10.5465/amr.2018.0072

Raji, I. D., & Buolamwini, J. (2019). Actionable auditing: Investigating the impact of publicly naming biased performance results of commercial AI products. *Proceedings of the 2019 AAAI/ACM Conference on AI, Ethics, and Society*, 429–435. DOI: 10.1145/3306618.3314244

Reivich, K., & Shatté, A. (2002). *The resilience factor: 7 keys to finding your inner strength and overcoming life's hurdles*. Broadway Books.

Roberson, Q. M. (2019). Diversity and Inclusion in the Workplace: A Review, Synthesis, and Future Research Agenda. *Annual Review of Organizational Psychology and Organizational Behavior, 6*(1), 69–88. DOI: 10.1146/annurev-orgpsych-012218-015243

Russell, S. J., & Norvig, P. (2021). *Artificial intelligence: A modern approach* (4th ed.). Pearson.

Serrat, O. (2017). 360-Degree Feedback. In *Knowledge Solutions* (pp. 913–917). Springer.

Shao, B., Cardie, C., & Hovy, E. (2020). Towards more resilient leadership: Using emotion AI to improve managerial feedback. *Proceedings of the AAAI Conference on Artificial Intelligence*, *34*(01), 566–573.

Southwick, S. M., & Charney, D. S. (2018). *Resilience: The science of mastering life's greatest challenges*. Cambridge University Press. DOI: 10.1017/9781108349246

Subrahmanyam, S. (2024). AI integration in HR processes. In Kaur, J. (Ed.), *Embracing transhumanism and genomics in human resources management* (pp. 69–100). IGI Global Scientific Publishing. DOI: 10.4018/979-8-3693-7668-3.ch004

Subrahmanyam, S. (2024). The evolution of human resources in the age of technology. In Kaur, J. (Ed.), *Technological enhancements for improving employee performance, safety, and well-being* (pp. 229–256). IGI Global Scientific Publishing. DOI: 10.4018/979-8-3693-9631-5.ch011

Subrahmanyam, S. (2025). AI-Driven Leadership in the Modern Era for Revolutionizing Next-Generation Strategies: Organizational Impacts and Future Development. In Agnihotri, A., & Balusamy, B. (Eds.), *Leadership Paradigms and the Impact of Technology* (pp. 61–86). IGI Global Scientific Publishing. DOI: 10.4018/979-8-3693-7175-6.ch003

Subrahmanyam, S. (2025). Fostering a Collaborative Culture: The Role of Leadership. In Hussain, Z., Khan, A., Qureshi, M. A., Sharipudin, M. N. S., & Alkara, I. (Eds.), *Knowledge Sharing and Fostering Collaborative Business Culture* (pp. 377–396). IGI Global Scientific Publishing. DOI: 10.4018/979-8-3373-0710-7.ch020

Subrahmanyam, S. (2025). The Paradigm Shift in Leadership Owing to Technological Development. In Agnihotri, A., & Balusamy, B. (Eds.), *Leadership Paradigms and the Impact of Technology* (pp. 381–406). IGI Global Scientific Publishing. DOI: 10.4018/979-8-3693-7175-6.ch016

Wilson, H. J., & Daugherty, P. R. (2018). *Human + machine: Reimagining work in the age of AI*. Harvard Business Review Press.

Chapter 14
Artificial Intelligence-Driven Analytical Models for the Dynamic Development of Leadership Competencies in Organizational Environments

Jose De Jesus Reyes-Sánchez
https://orcid.org/0000-0002-3866-2363
TECNM Instituto Tecnologico Superior De Fresnillo, Mexico

Johana Paola Reyes Davalos
https://orcid.org/0009-0005-0330-635X
TECNM Instituto Tecnologico Superior De Fresnillo, Mexico

Ayme Carolina Reyes Davalos
https://orcid.org/0009-0003-9659-2978
Universidad Autónoma de Durango Campus Zacatecas, Mexico

Sonia Villagran-Rueda
https://orcid.org/0000-0001-5389-574X
Universidad Autonoma de Zacatecas, Mexico

David Jasso Velazquez
https://orcid.org/0000-0002-8289-150X

DOI: 10.4018/979-8-3373-3658-9.ch014

Universidad Autonoma de Zacatecas, Mexico

ABSTRACT

This article examines how AI-supported analytical models reconfigure, in near real-time, training and leadership in VUCA environments. A systematic review and meta-analysis of literature and cases from Google, Microsoft, Siemens, BBVA and Unilever show that deep algorithms enhance the micro-foundations of dynamic capabilities (sensing, seizing, reconfiguring), cut decisional latency by 35% and personalize learning trajectories with increases of 27% in conflict resolution and 22% in financial resilience. Challenges of algorithmic literacy, ethical governance, and data bias remain. A socio-material framework is proposed that fuses neuroplasticity, explanatory transparency and data culture to legitimize and scale AI, outlining lines of inclusive public policy and new research agendas.

INTRODUCTION

The breakneck advance of artificial intelligence (AI)-powered analytics has irreversibly transformed the practice of leadership, enabling multimodal capture of behavioral signals, integration of heterogeneous sources, and algorithmic modeling of patterns that previously escaped human perception. This new data grammar places managers in an environment where the speed of organizational learning is synchronized with the cadence of inference cycles, drastically reducing the latency between event detection and strategic decision-making. Organizations that institutionalize AI analytics systems consequently show a superior ability to orchestrate personalized training pathways, diagnose competency gaps in real time, and reconfigure talent allocation with near-surgical precision.

The frontier literature confirms that this technological-cognitive convergence shifts the epicenter of managerial authority from charismatic intuition to a senseandrespond paradigm based on algorithms that learn, explain, and recalibrate continuously. This epistemological shift redefines the very nature of competition: absorbing, recombining, and exploiting knowledge encapsulated in torrents of data stands as an ontological pillar of effectiveness in the post-digital era. This premise is especially relevant in VUCA ecosystems, i.e., volatile, uncertain, complex, and ambiguous, where strategic resilience depends on the plasticity with which leaders internalize statistical patterns, translate predictive dashboards into shared narratives, and legitimize algorithmic recommendations to multiple stakeholders.

However, the transformative potential of AI coexists with structural tensions that threaten its full institutionalization. For example, an algorithmic literacy gap persists in senior management: the critical reading of bias metrics, confidence intervals or post-hoc explanations is often relegated to traditional skills such as negotiation or persuasion. Added to this is the asymmetry between the sophistication of the available models and the analytical maturity of organizational cultures; Without governance frameworks that ensure transparency and fairness, algorithms risk crystallizing historical biases and eroding internal trust. The competitive pressure to deploy solutions quickly intensifies this operational ethical dilemma, setting up a scenario where statistical robustness must be harmonized with social legitimacy to avoid technological backlash phenomena.

At the same time, the explosion of AI as a cognitive infrastructure has macroeconomic implications that transcend the corporate sphere. Recent projections by the World Economic Forum place intelligent talent management as a key multiplier of multifactorial productivity and national competitiveness, demonstrating that analytics-literate leaders are capable of redefining business models through predictive insights and counterfactual simulations. These dynamics also contribute to the fulfillment of the Sustainable Development Goals by accelerating responsible innovation and the creation of inclusive value. However, pan-European studies warn that the capture of rents derived from AI tends to be concentrated in hubs with mature data infrastructures, reproducing pre-existing disparities between core and periphery regions, unless public policies articulate strategies of mass upskilling and open access to interoperable data.

From the theory of dynamic capabilities, AI acts as a catalyst that amplifies the micro fundamentals of sensing, seizing, and reconfiguring: deep neural networks identify weak signals in turbulent scenarios; genetic algorithms optimize resource allocation in near real-time; and digital twins allow you to experiencc transformation trajectories without interrupting the operation. However, this potential only materializes when algorithmic literacy is coupled with cultures of cross-functional dialogue and transparent audit protocols that legitimize the findings to the community. Comparative evidence reveals that companies that institutionalize algorithmic ethics committees and deliberation rituals between data scientists and business areas obtain higher rates of AI adoption and reduce obsolescence times of critical skills among their management cadres.

STATEMENT OF THE PROBLEM

The literature points to critical gaps that hinder the institutionalization of AI analytical models for leadership competency development. First, an asymmetry persists between the available technological sophistication and the analytical maturity of senior management, so that algorithms are underused or superficially interpreted, which reduces their transformative impact (Karakose, Kocabas, Yirci, & Papadakis, 2022). Secondly, the volatility of VUCA environments requires rapid iteration of competence profiles; However, traditional frameworks of reference for management training continue to be anchored in static taxonomies. Finally, ethical tensions arising from algorithmic opacity and training biases limit the social legitimacy of AI-based programs, compromising staff's acceptance of competency development plans (Davison, Wong, Peng, & Georgakakis, 2023).

IMPORTANCE OF THE PROJECT

AI-based leadership skills development transcends the technical level and acquires macroeconomic relevance by catalyzing multifactorial productivity and accelerating continuous innovation. The projections of the World Economic Forum place intelligent talent management as one of the five most influential value multipliers for national competitiveness, as leaders trained with analytical tools are able to redefine business models based on predictive insights, expanding the frontiers of efficiency and creativity (Ahuja, Contreras, Baykal, & Abid, 2023). In addition, the ethical and responsible implementation of AI in the field of leadership contributes to the fulfillment of the Sustainable Development Goals, especially with regard to decent work and economic growth, reduction of inequalities and building strong institutions.

At the organizational level, adopting an analytical-algorithmic approach to dynamic competency development activates rapid feedback loops that reduce critical skill obsolescence times, mitigate strategic risks, and promote evidence-based continuous learning cultures. Likewise, the social relevance of the project is manifested in its potential to democratize access to personalized training itineraries, de-anchoring leadership management from intuitive biases and favoring cognitive diversity in senior management teams (Cortellazzo, Bruni, Zampieri, & Terkamo-Moisio, 2023).

BACKGROUND

The study of organizational leadership began to detach itself from charismatic and trait approaches since the theory of resources proposed that sustainable advantage emanates from the ability to orchestrate heterogeneous assets; However, early taxonomies of managerial competencies ignored the evolutionary nature of these competencies and were built on static metrics of observable behavior. During the last decade of the twentieth century, the proliferation of transactional systems favored the emergence of performance databases, but their exploitation was limited to descriptive dashboards incapable of capturing the complexity of turbulent environments. The first truly disruptive approaches emerged when machine learning algorithms were incorporated into executive feedback processes, revealing subdiscursive patterns of influence and engagement that escape conventional human diagnosis (López-Figueroa, Ochoa-Jiménez, Palafox-Soto, & Hernández Muñoz, 2025). This epistemological shift laid the foundations for thinking of leadership competencies as dynamic configurations, capable of being modeled, predicted, and personalized with unprecedented granularity.

The e-leadership literature, born in the heat of early digitalization, already warned that the intensive use of technologies mediated new forms of distributed coordination; However, it was not until the consolidation of large volumes of data that researchers seriously explored predictive analytics as a lever for competence development. The contributions that mapped the field between 2015 and 2020 reveal a shift in focus: from the study of immutable styles and traits to the examination of adaptive micro-skills that emerge in the leader-algorithm interaction. A recent meta-analysis confirms that organizations with robust analytic architectures reduce the time needed to close critical gaps in managerial skills by 34%, while increasing strategic resilience to exogenous shocks (Bevilacqua, Masárová, Perotti, & Ferraris, 2025). Such findings cement the premise that competitive advantage flows from the ability to absorb and recombine knowledge encapsulated in heterogeneous data streams.

In parallel, the frameworks of the theory of senior echelons were hybridized with advanced analytics to examine how senior management career paths condition the adoption and performance of AI solutions. An iconic study on the figure of the chief digital officer showed that management teams that embrace AI as a craft art are able to extract 27% more predictive value from the same algorithms, thanks to their contextual sensitivity and deliberate model governance (Davison, Wong, Peng, & Georgakakis, 2023). This evidence reinforced the notion that analytical maturity does not depend only on technological infrastructure but, with equal weight, on the sociocognitive competencies of leadership to interpret, question and translate algorithmic logic into strategic action.

The methodological evolution has been equally significant. The first implementations resorted to regressions and cluster analysis to segment managerial profiles; Today, recurrent neural networks and semantic transformers simultaneously analyze physiological signals, linguistic registers, and relational metrics to project hyper-personalized learning trajectories. A systematic meta-analysis of HR training found that skills-focused AI technologies allow for the design of training pathways with retention increases of close to 40% when compared to conventional programs, thanks to real-time adaptation and multimodal feedback (Deepa, Sekar, Malik, & Kumar, 2024). These results emphasize the need to redraw the concept of the training cycle and replace it with ubiquitous and continuous learning models.

Beyond efficacy, the legitimacy of analytical practices took center stage when the risks of algorithmic bias became apparent. Interdisciplinary studies show that trust in systems decreases sharply if models do not offer explainability or auditable equity practices. A review of organizational psychology shows that, when employees receive feedback from artificial agents whose inference rules are transparent, intention to use and intrinsic motivation increase significantly in the face of opacity scenarios (Baines, Dalal, Ponce, & Tsai, 2024). This led to the formulation of algorithmic governance frameworks based on principles of responsibility, accountability, and data justice, articulated as prerequisites for any AI-mediated competency development initiative.

The dynamic nature of leadership competencies also resonates with the theory of dynamic capabilities and its micro foundations. Recent research shows that the algorithmic literacy of managers serves as an absorption capacity that feeds, in turn, processes of transformation and exploitation of knowledge, accelerating the cycles of strategic renewal. An integrative review notes that analytical maturity is positively and robustly correlated with indicators of digital innovation and operational flexibility in organizations in knowledge-intensive sectors (Enholm, Papagiannidis, Mikalef, & Krogstie, 2022). The net result is a leadership that abandons intuition as the main heuristic to embrace a sense-and-respond paradigm supported by statistical inference and deep learning.

The cultural implications are not minor either. Research on competitive climates suggests that staff's acceptance of AI depends decisively on how leaders interpret their own power, thereby modulating threat perception and willingness to change (Gao, Li, Xie, Zhang, & Kuang, 2024). When the reading of power is oriented towards responsibility, AI is associated with processes of empowerment and learning; at the opposite extreme, it is perceived as an instrument of control that erodes autonomy. This finding corroborates that technological deployment without cultural alignment causes frictions that neutralize the transformative potential of analytics.

On the business results front, meta-analyses demonstrate sustained improvements. A longitudinal study that linked internal collaboration graph density to ROI metrics showed that analytics-based management development programs increased the composite performance index by an average of 19%; the variable with the highest explanatory power was the quality of algorithmic literacy ($\beta = 0.42$; $p < 0.001$), followed by the cognitive diversity of the team ($\beta = 0.29$; $p < 0.01$) (Dubey, Gunasekaran, Childe, & Papadopoulos, 2018). This confirms the hypothesis that organizations that democratize access to data and algorithms reap superior benefits in resilience and speed of innovation.

At the sectoral level, large multinationals exhibit asymmetric maturity: entities in the technological and financial fields report accelerated returns, while regulated industries face greater ethical and compliance obstacles. The exploration of cases in banking services shows that linguistic transformers, combined with sentiment mining, reduce the time-to-proficiency of junior managers by 21% when personalizing coaching itineraries, although this effectiveness decreases when the models do not explain their reasoning or when bias is perceived in the training sets (Fernandez-Vidal, Perotti, Gonzalez, & Gasco, 2022) .

Within organizations, the power-knowledge dynamic is redefined. Leaders who master the reading of algorithmic output and know how to translate it into strategic narratives tend to become nodes of relational influence; on the other hand, the mere hierarchical authority without technical literacy loses convening power. Multilevel studies in highly complex industries corroborate that the perception of legitimacy of leaders is shifting from traditional attributes to indicators of interpretive competence and decision-making transparency (Firk, Gehrke, Hanelt, & Wolff, 2022). This reinforces the thesis that symbolic capital in the algorithmic era is anchored in the ability to mediate between statistical logic and human imperatives.

Despite the advances, theoretical gaps remain. The hybridization between the socio-material perspective and the theory of algorithmic governance is only beginning to be rigorously explored. Models that integrate power dynamics, design ethics, and distributional effects of AI are needed to explain the creation and erosion of competencies in hyper-volatile contexts. At the same time, the dilemmas of explainability and fairness require regulatory frameworks that balance technical robustness and social legitimacy; interdisciplinary collaboration: engineering, behavioral sciences, and philosophy of technology that is seen as a sine qua non condition for consolidating truly human-centric leadership in ecosystems dominated by algorithms (Dwivedi, Hughes, Ismagilova, & Aharoni, 2021).

The evidence converges, therefore, that analytical models powered by artificial intelligence have reconfigured the foundations of leadership competency development. The historical movement can be summarized in three phases: a descriptive stage dominated by static indicators; a diagnostic phase enriched by machine learning;

and the current prescriptive-adaptive phase, where AI not only diagnoses but also co-creates training itineraries and suggests micro-interventions in real time. The mix of advanced analytics, ethical governance, and algorithmic literacy emerges as an indispensable triad to legitimize and empower leadership in increasingly digital, diverse, and volatile organizational environments. On this basis, this project aims to articulate a synergistic model that capitalizes on the predictive potential of AI, while safeguarding the human values that give meaning and purpose to managerial action.

THEORETICAL FRAMEWORK

Epistemological Foundations of AI-Powered Analytics

The irruption of artificial intelligence in the processes of knowledge production put into crisis the positivist roots that linked empirical truth with linear correspondence and, above all, with the post hoc verifiability of previously formulated hypotheses. While classical hypothetical deductive logic required a sequential transition, deep learning algorithms established an abductive regime where conjecture is gestated simultaneously with the iterative adjustment of millions of parameters, blurring the temporal boundary between discovery and confirmation (Dwivedi, Hughes, Ismagilova, & Aarts, 2021). In these environments, synaptic weights modify their magnitude in time with each batch of data, so that the hypothesis itself becomes fluid, contingent, and highly contextual, reflecting a probabilistic universe more akin to Bayesian dynamics than to the calculation of rigid frequencies.

This shift entails an ontological change: evidence ceases to be a static repository of measurements and is transformed into a semiotic-algorithmic flow where each bit acquires relational meaning as it is articulated with others in complex networks. Organizations that incorporate this ontology drastically reduce the latency between observation and strategic action, because the inferential system is coupled in real time to a heterogeneous stream of financial, social, sensory, and even biometric data (Orlikowski, Scott, Monteiro, & Kallinikos, 2023). Instead of waiting for the consolidation of a clean dataset, management teams work with incomplete but continuously updated X-rays, and make decisions modulated by credibility intervals, not by dichotomous certainties.

From this reconfiguration arises the demand for contextual explainability. A merely algorithmic truth, no matter how precise it may be, lacks legitimacy if its foundations remain opaque to the actors who must make the decision. Traceability replaces the claim of absolute certainty, opening the way to a dialogic rationality where statistics are interwoven with expert heuristics (Aoki, Tatsumi, Naruse, & Maeda, 2024). Thus, knowledge emerges as a result of a transdisciplinary deliberation that integrates the voice of the data scientist, the intuition of the manager, and the ethical sensitivity of the regulator.

Dialogic epistemology is consolidated when validation becomes a permanent and distributed process. MLOps frameworks insert robustness testing, bias audits, and drift monitoring into every step of the model lifecycle, turning the practice of peer review into a relentless, algorithmically assisted activity. Recent studies on analytical capacities have shown that the institutionalization of these feedback loops simultaneously improves operational resilience and legitimacy in the eyes of stakeholders, because it raises confidence in the quality of inputs and in the fairness of results (Mikalef, Krogstie, Pappas, & Giannakos, 2020).

Tellingly, philosophers of science themselves have reinterpreted abduction in the light of AI. Inference to the best explanation, once considered a privilege of human ingenuity, is now seen as a capacity that can be encoded, at least partially, in architectures that learn latent representations, generate vector spaces, and compute plausibilities with a speed unattainable by the human mind (Lake, Ullman, Tenenbaum, & Gershman, 2017). This does not imply that the algorithm replaces the researcher, but rather that it broadens the horizon of plausible conjectures, multiplying the paths of exploration and requiring epistemological criticism to adapt at dizzying speeds.

In short, AI-powered analytics inaugurates a paradigm in which truth is conceived as an emergent and adaptive process. Reliability is no longer measured by the immutable accuracy of a coefficient, but by the ability of a socio-technical assembly to learn, explain, and rectify itself without losing operational continuity. From this perspective, the organization that seeks competitive advantage must not only invest in powerful GPUs or massive data intakes, but also in creating cultures of cross-functional dialogue, transparent audit protocols, and ethical frameworks that enable the constant legitimization of findings. Only in this way does the probabilistic epistemology that underpins AI become a driver of sustainable and, above all, socially defensible strategic decisions.

Dynamic Capabilities and Their Theoretical-Practical Expansion in the Algorithmic Era

In the contemporary formulation of the construct of dynamic capabilities, organizational strategy is understood as a multi-scale evolutionary process that enables the firm to learn to feel, capture and reconfigure its resources in order to sustain competitive advantages under environmental turbulence characterized by extreme ambiguity, technological disruptions and geopolitical instability. Artificial intelligence magnifies this paradigm by inserting hypersensitive detection routines that articulate real-time mining of sensor streams, semantic analysis of vast textual corpora, and modeling of heterogeneous graphs capable of revealing, in milliseconds, patterns of threat or opportunity that human logic would notice only after several strategic cycles (Li, Wang, Ratten, & Cui, 2023).

Beyond identifying external disruptions, deep algorithms map internal capability gaps with unprecedented granularity and suggest reconfiguration trajectories ranging from the reassignment of data science experts to the comprehensive reconstruction of supply networks using interoperable digital twins and blockchain platforms; this turns the traditional capability audit into a continuous scanner that records the structural health of the organizational system (Vial, Van Wynsberghe, Islam, & Zaghloul, 2024).

In this context, deep learning platforms operate as cognitive-computational extensions that establish permanent feedback loops: strategic hypotheses are tested iteratively, recalibrated based on the drift of the data, and feedback, in turn, into the parameters of the predictive models. In this way, the act of feeling becomes an immersive experience of probabilistic visualization with dynamic confidence intervals; capturing transcends the specific allocation of resources and becomes evolutionary optimization subject to multi-criteria genetic algorithms; and reconfiguring emerges as a flow of parameterized decisions that reduce the friction between deliberation and operational execution (Teece, Peteraf, Leih, & Helfat, 2022).

Empirical evidence reinforces this view: a longitudinal study in 204 knowledge-intensive manufacturing plants showed that the incorporation of predictive dashboards connected to executive committees increased the pivot speed of the business model by 29% and financial resilience to exogenous shocks by 22%, thanks to the ability of leaders to visualize counterfactual scenarios. estimating conditional risk curves and reallocating capital in near real-time (Simon, Weber, Braun, Endsley, Kulkarni, & Kassi, 2024). The result confirms that algorithmic leadership is no longer a mere analytical support, but a meta-dynamic ability that amplifies managerial judgment through visual explanations, uncertainty metrics, and data narratives that legitimize decisions in front of multiple stakeholders (Höhener, Wölfle, Uebernickel, Huang, & Kaganer, 2024).

Digging deeper into the concept reveals its hierarchical nature. Recent research distinguishes between first-order capabilities and higher-order capabilities that redesign the inter-organizational coordination architecture, for example, open innovation ecosystems supported by generative AI that simultaneously reconfigure R+D processes and circular supply chains (Adner, Csaszar, Felin, & Puranam, 2023). The key lies in target routines that monitor the performance of other routines, trigger controlled experiments, and abandon obsolete practices without compromising operational continuity, establishing a reflective loop analogous to individual metacognition.

The micro-foundations of these capacities combine cognitive, technological, and affective dimensions. Ethnographic studies reveal that effective sensing depends both on data architectures that enable competitive surveillance and on discursive communities that legitimize the exploration of plausible futures; Seizing demands financial capital, but also corporate stories that mobilize internal coalitions; and reconfiguring materializes when leadership sponsors the identity recombination of talents and sustains psychologically safe spaces where failing quickly is an epistemological asset (Shiferaw, Kero, Mekonnin, & Amentie, 2024).

The relationship with the environment adds another critical layer: the effectiveness of dynamic capabilities is mediated by the epistemic density of the ecosystem by the degree of regulatory flexibility that makes it possible to exchange data on a large scale. When the firm operates under strict algorithmic governance frameworks, the cost of reconfiguring increases if regulatory sandboxes do not emerge; such safe spaces allow AI prototypes to be iterated without the reputational risks associated with premature deployment, becoming structural extensions of the dynamic capacity itself (Breiter, Crome, Oberländer, & Schnaak, 2024).

Measurement has also advanced: retrospective outcome indicators have given way to processual metrics obtained through organizational graph analytics, knowledge flow tracers, and counterfactual simulations run on digital twins across the enterprise. By modeling reconfiguration elasticities without stopping operation, these tools convert dynamic capabilities into diagnosable, trainable, and scalable traits, similar to individual competencies susceptible to continuous feedback (Khan, Buzzao, Rizzi, & Settembre-Blundo, 2024).

Adopting this hybrid orchestration redistributes agency: data analysts gain strategic voice, experience designers define model intelligibility, and compliance officers implement autonomous algorithmic auditors who detect biases before they escalate to systemic risks. AI, therefore, acts as a catalyst for inclusive governance where algorithmic transparency legitimizes high-impact decisions and nurtures the organizational aptitude to learn how to learn under radical ambiguity.

In short, theoretical expansion places dynamic capabilities as the nervous system of an intelligent organization: algorithmic sensors capture subtle signals, data neurotransmitters distribute information at light speeds, and sociotechnical synapses integrate adaptive response. Competitive advantage ceases to reside in what resources are possessed and shifts to how they are transformed in a continuous and socially legitimized way. This circularity constitutes the company's operating logic in the algorithmic economy, ensuring that value creation evolves at the pace of environmental change while maintaining ethical coherence, financial resilience and long-term sustainable impact.

Socio-Material Perspective of E-LEADERSHIP

The socio-material perspective states that the social and the technological coexist in the same indivisible practice. AI-assisted collaboration platforms mediate meaning-making, so that authority circulates to those who master data curation and narrative articulation. An ethnography carried out in five software multinationals found that algorithmic curatorial leaders increase the density of open innovation networks by 35% compared to traditional managers (Bauwens, Cortellazzo, Kalshoven, Avolio, Peng, & Todd, 2024). Similarly, laboratory studies showed that the agency of intelligent objects contributes to the legitimacy of decisions by blurring the boundaries between the material and the discursive (Oborn, Barrett, Orlikowski, Kim, Leonardi, & Lyytinen, 2024). This reconfiguration requires leaders capable of designing environments where decision-making emerges as an ecosystem phenomenon and not as a unidirectional mandate.

Algorithmic and Ethical Governance of Explanation

The organizational legitimacy of the use of AI depends on governance frameworks that harmonize transparency, fairness, and accountability. Quasi-controlled experiments in Japanese public administration showed that citizen approval of automated resolutions increased by 27% when a clear explanation of the logic and data used was provided (Aoki, Tatsumi, Naruse, Maeda, Suzuki, & Tanaka, 2024). At the same time, the algorithmic justice literature has proposed multidimensional metrics to evaluate systems, warning that opacity can erode trust and double internal resistance (Kumar, Feldman, Kroll, Scheidegger, Raji, & Holstein, 2024). At the regulatory level, the European AI Act obliges companies to document the life cycle of the model and to carry out ethical impact audits, making explainability a crucial managerial competence.

Learning Analytics and Personalization of Training Itineraries

Recurrent neural networks and recommendation systems have led to the emergence of hyper-personalized learning trajectories. A trial of 18,000 healthcare professionals showed that adaptive modules increased clinical competency retention by 41% and reduced certification time by 35% compared to standardized programs (Shanmughan, Joseph, Nair, Anitha, Prakash, & Calvo, 2024). At the corporate level, the integration of learning analytics with performance metrics enables embedded learning ecosystems, where each micro-action feeds back into the algorithm and generates new recommendations. Recent meta-analyses reveal that multimodal feedback increases managerial self-efficacy and shortens onboarding cycles, as long as leaders provide interpretive context to avoid uncritical acceptance (Gómez, Ortiz, Navarro, Paredes, Rivera, & Alvarado, 2024).

Neuroscience and Cognitive Plasticity in AI-Assisted Leadership

Contemporary understanding of leadership is increasingly shaped by neuroscientific discoveries that reveal the continued malleability of the adult brain and its ability to reorganize functional networks in the face of high-intensity formative stimuli. The notion of neuroplasticity, traditionally associated with clinical rehabilitation, now acquires strategic connotations: it serves as a biological lens to explain how prolonged interaction with intelligent systems reconfigures the circuits responsible for emotional regulation, scenario prospecting and decision-making under ambiguity. Recent studies employing functional magnetic resonance imaging with managers exposed to predictive panels fed by deep learning algorithms document sustained activation of the dorsolateral prefrontal cortex along with attenuation of tonsillar reactivity to uncertain stimuli, a pattern that translates into greater affective equanimity and reduced loss aversion bias (Sadegh-Zadeh, Bahrami, Soleimani, Ahmadi, Ramirez, & Chen, 2024).

The transition of these findings to the design of corporate interventions is catalyzed by artificial intelligence models inspired by synaptic plasticity. Just as synapses vary in weight when neural firings coincide, deep reinforcement algorithms readjust their parameters when predictions diverge from observed outcomes, generating a functional parallelism that leadership development teams have turned into an operational metaphor. Neurocomputational coaching programs based on this analogy expose executives to crisis simulations that adapt in real time to their psychophysiological responses and calibrate the difficulty of the scenarios to induce the so-called optimal zone of plasticity: a level of challenge sufficient to trigger the release of dopamine and norepinephrine, but without overflowing the hypothalamic-pituitary-adrenal axis (Ooi, Shah, Xu, Hernández, Schultz, & Dweck, 2025). Participants in these programs show, after twelve weeks, significant increases in functional connectivity between the anterior cingulate cortex and the ventral striatum, correlated with behavioral improvements in resilience and error learning.

The organizational implications extend beyond the individual. Systematic research indicates that when development programs are designed under principles of neuroplasticity, a cognitive contagion effect occurs: internal collaboration networks exhibit greater density and centrality in the nodes associated with the transfer of tacit knowledge, accelerating the dissemination of critical strategic insights (Onciul, Tataru, Dumitru, Crivoi, Serban, Covache-Busuioc, Radoi, & Toader, 2025). This dynamic supports the thesis that AI-driven leadership functions as a socio-neural infrastructure that operates on three simultaneous planes: it amplifies individual perceptual capacity, synchronizes collective cognitive patterns, and encodes learning in digital artifacts that feed back into operational experience.

The link between plasticity and neuroscientific literacy thus becomes an emerging requirement for managerial excellence. Literacy involves understanding notions such as long-term potentiation, metaplastic window and excitation-inhibition balance, in order to interpret neurophysiological indicators offered by corporate biofeedback systems. Pioneering companies have created leadership labs that combine brain-computer interfaces, immersive virtual reality, and generative AI models to design micro-environments of deliberate practice where exposure to ethical dilemmas or market ambiguity is dynamically adjusted according to the user's electrocortical signal (Paltoglou, Stefanaki, Chrousos, Georgiadis, Pavlou, & Nalmpanti, 2024). Preliminary results from these initiatives indicate increases of up to 35% in the rate of transfer of emotional skills to the workplace and reductions of 18% in reported burnout.

The convergence between AI and neuroscience is also redefining the success metrics of leadership programs. Where changes in self-reported traits or financial performance indicators were previously measured, biomarkers of plasticity are now incorporated longitudinal analyses of network connectivity by default. By correlating such biomarkers with behavioral indicators, organizations gain a multilayered map of how AI-assisted learning reshapes the neural substrate and, with it, leadership effectiveness.

Neuroscience provides the empirical foundation that legitimizes investment in AI platforms for management development, by showing that cognitive plasticity is not an epiphenomenon, but the central mechanism by which leaders internalize probabilistic reasoning frameworks, regulate their affective states, and orchestrate organizational transformations. Neuroscientific literacy, together with the ethical design of algorithmic ecosystems, is emerging as a distinctive feature of organizations that aspire to thrive in volatile environments nuanced by technological complexity.

Organizational Climate, Data Culture and Technological Acceptance

Without a climate that values evidence-based experimentation, investments in AI are diluted. Surveys of 312 companies undergoing digital transformations indicate that willingness to change explains 47% of the variance in the effective use of AI, above investment in hardware or software (Chaudhuri, Chatterjee, Vrontis, Thrassou, Papadopoulos, & Vlachos, 2024). The concept of data stewardship emphasizes the need for roles that guarantee data integrity, value the diversity of sources, and manage privacy, factors that increase the perception of procedural fairness and the motivation to participate in analytical training programs (Kabanda, Mwangi, Nyaga, Asongu, Khan, & Mensah, 2024). Leaders must, therefore, design rituals of data socialization that internalize empirical deliberation as a cultural practice.

Measurement Models and Metrics of Dynamic Competencies

The assessment of managerial competencies has evolved towards multimodal approaches that combine natural language analysis, socio-relational graphs and physiological signals obtained from wearables. The Leader's Digital Competence scale validated on four continents achieved an alpha reliability of 0.92, offering a longitudinal barometer that informs development interventions in real time (op 't Roodt, Bracht, van Dick, Hernandez Bark, Zhang, & Cañas, 2025). At the same time, computer vision systems and autoregressive learning models predict proficiency scores with errors of less than 10% compared to panels of experts, which speeds up feedback and minimizes human bias (Zhang, Liu, Kim, González, Ortega, & Almeida, 2024). These metrics allow you to visualize the evolution of critical skills and trigger rapid improvement loops.

Macroeconomic Impact and Organizational Sustainability of AI-Mediated Leadership

The systemic incorporation of artificial intelligence into the productive sphere marks a historical turning point comparable to the advent of the steam engine or industrial electrification, as it accelerates the aggregate production function and alters long-term growth trajectories. Meta-analyses that integrate growth accounting techniques, computable general equilibrium simulations and sectoral assessments coincide in attributing sustained increases in multifactorial productivity to AI thanks to three synergistic vectors: cognitive automation of routine tasks, expansion of the innovation frontier through generative models and optimization of value chains through predictive analytics (Hajjar, Kwon, Pereira, Morrison, McGrath, & Silva, 2024). Conservative projections, based on gradual adoptions accompanied by inclusive up-skilling programs and robust ethical governance frameworks, estimate an average contribution of 0.7% per year to global productivity growth in the current decade, a magnitude that exceeds the combined contribution of cloud computing and industrial robotization observed between 2010 and 2020.

Beyond the strictly macroeconomic metrics, artificial intelligence acts as a cross-cutting catalyst for the Sustainable Development Goals (SDGs). A systematic review of 176 studies applied to 46 countries identified 134 cases in which AI directly aligns with targets of the 17 SDGs, concentrating on preventive health, precision agriculture, energy optimization (Regona, Yigitcanlar, Hon, Teo, Martin-López,

& Putra, 2024). This empirical corpus shows that governments that combine tax incentives for green algorithmic solutions with open science policies register significant accelerations in composite indicators of social well-being, without sacrificing industrial competitiveness.

The impact, however, is not evenly distributed. The literature on the digital economy warns that, in the absence of policies that mitigate the connectivity gap and guarantee open access to interoperable data, the deployment of AI tends to concentrate rents in technological hubs, exacerbating, on a global scale, the pre-existing disparities between core and periphery regions (Filippucci, Cueva, Gambacorta, Doytchinova, Li, & Steinberg, 2024). Scenario simulations based on big-data commerce indicate that countries with mature data infrastructures capture up to 80% of the surplus associated with network externalities, while environments with low regulatory latency are the ones that most accelerate the diffusion of benefits to small and medium-sized enterprises.

At the organizational scale, AI-mediated leadership is a lever for operational and financial sustainability. Predictive dashboards that integrate carbon analytics, circular market intelligence, and real-time ESG metrics have been shown to reduce energy costs by up to 27% and cut scope 2 emissions by 19% without sacrificing EBITDA margins, thanks to procurement decisions based on reinforcement learning (Baines, Dalal, Ponce, Tsai, Eberle, & González, 2024). These findings reaffirm the hypothesis that algorithmic intelligence simultaneously increases economic efficiency and eco-effectiveness, provided that companies adopt comprehensive impact accounting frameworks and transparent algorithmic auditing systems.

However, there is a risk that cognitive automation will put downward pressure on the wage elasticity of middle-level workers, shifting value added towards intangible capital. Pan-European studies reveal that, in sectors highly exposed to AI, real wages grow 0.74 percentage points less than the average, even as net employment increases, posing challenges for social cohesion (Babic, Mariani, Flood, Klein, & Whitaker, 2025). Hence, public policy packages aimed at human capital must combine massive investments in advanced digital literacy with fiscal instruments that redistribute part of the algorithmic income to vulnerable groups.

Emerging Trends and Research Gaps

The co-evolution of generative AI and compassionate leadership approaches promises to humanize digital transformation. Prototypes of empathetic chatbots trained with multimodal affective recognition improve the quality of feedback and reduce executive burnout after 18 months of use (Carter, Hougaard, Ibrahim, Johnson, Simmons, & Wu, 2025). At the same time, agent-based simulation allows algorithmic inclusion policies to be experimented with before deploying them, revealing systemic risks invisible to traditional research and opening up an agenda on cognitive diversity and adaptive governance (Greif, Röckel, Kimmig, Ovtcharova, Falk, & Hanelt, 2025). Gaps persist in the standardization of sectoral ethical audits, in the longitudinal measurement of cultural impact, and in the interaction between generative AI and collective deliberation processes, marking a fertile horizon for interdisciplinary inquiry.

However, the theoretical framework shows that leadership in the era of artificial intelligence requires a synthesis of technical, ethical and socio-cognitive knowledge. A deep understanding of algorithms, fused with the human capacity for contextual interpretation, forms the cornerstone of the dynamic competencies that will enable organizations to thrive in uncertain and socially responsible environments.

METHODOLOGY

This segment dedicated to methodology is based on a hybrid strategy that combines a meta-analytical approach with a reflective and descriptive approach, designed to rigorously articulate the findings from the academic literature and the available empirical evidence. Under this logic, the methodological process integrates, firstly, an exhaustive systematic review of primary and secondary sources, following the guidelines of international guidelines, and, secondly, a critical examination of the different epistemological approaches that converge in the phenomenon under study. The main objective is to build a comprehensive and coherent panorama that not only identifies conceptual and empirical regularities, but also contrasts the solidity, convergence or divergence of the results reported in different contexts, disciplines and theoretical frameworks.

Within this architecture, the meta-analytic phase itself is oriented to the meticulous compilation of relevant research through clearly defined inclusion and exclusion criteria, in order to statistically synthesize the magnitude of the observed effects.

At the same time, the reflective and descriptive dimension opens up space to critically interpret the contextual complexity underlying the numbers: the methodological limitations of the original studies are weighed, the practical and theoretical implications of the identified patterns are discussed, and research gaps that emerge from the synthesis of heterogeneous approaches are pointed out. In this way, the proposed methodology is not limited to quantifying effects, but also generates comprehensive and nuanced knowledge, improving the understanding of the phenomenon and informing future research and applied intervention agendas.

Challenges Organizations Face

The adoption of AI-powered analytical models to enhance leadership poses a patchwork of structural, cognitive, and ethical challenges that transcends the simple incorporation of new technologies. In the first instance, an algorithmic literacy gap emerges at the managerial level: executives often lack the statistical fluency to rigorously interpret conditional probabilities, bias metrics, or confidence intervals, which limits the translation of findings into actionable decisions and, ultimately, reduces the return on investment in AI (Brynjolfsson, McElheran, Rock, & Syverson, 2023). This deficit is aggravated by the fact that the vast majority of executive training programs still privilege negotiation or communication skills, leaving the critical interpretation of predictive modeling and data governance in the background.

Another parameter is due to the tension between the speed of deployment and ethical robustness. Competitive pressure to implement solutions quickly often leads to launching models without exhaustive algorithmic fairness audits, which ends up reproducing training biases and perpetuating inequities in recruitment, promotion, or resource allocation processes (Mehrabi, Morstatter, Saxena, & Galstyan, 2022). When algorithms fail in transparency and perceived fairness, the internal and external legitimacy of the organization is eroded, generating resistance that can neutralize the potential benefits of cognitive automation.

In addition, heterogeneity and data quality present substantive challenges. Many firms operate with departmental silos that fragment information, making it impossible to create unified, clean data lakes; others lack governance protocols that ensure the semantic integrity and traceability of historical records. Without robust data stewardship policies, the reliability of predictions is undermined and the risk of model drift increases substantially (Zhang, Tang, Li, & Reilly, 2024). The result is a paradox in which data abounds, but high-quality, actionable knowledge is scarce.

In the cultural field, resistance to change manifests itself in a subtle but persistent way: professionals perceive AI as a threat to work autonomy and, in some cases, as an instrument of surveillance. Such a defensive response is especially noticeable in environments of low digital maturity, where the prevailing narrative associates automation with staff cuts or loss of expert status (Kellogg, Valentine, Shaw, & Mathur, 2023). Leaders must, therefore, manage the emotional component of technological change through transparent communication strategies, co-creation of use cases, and up-skilling programs that demonstrate shared benefits.

Equally crucial is the regulatory gap. The regulatory patchwork, divergent across jurisdictions, makes it difficult to standardize algorithmic governance practices. While the European Union is moving towards highly rigorous frameworks, other regions lack clear guidelines, forcing multinationals to develop multi-layered legal architectures that raise compliance costs and delay the global scale of solutions

(Veale, Van Kleek, Binns, & Shadbolt, 2023). This regulatory variability stresses the coherence of internal policies and requires specialized legal resources that many medium-sized companies do not have.

Finally, the challenge of sustainability is added to the equation. Large-scale language models, digital twins, and deep neural networks demand massive amounts of computing power and power. Without energy efficiency and carbon footprint offsetting strategies, the mass implementation of AI can contradict ESG commitments and erode corporate reputation, particularly in industries exposed to environmental scrutiny (Strubell, Ganesh, McCallum, & Green, 2022). Thus, sustainable algorithmic leadership requires both training optimization and the integration of environmental impact metrics into executive dashboards.

Examples of Implementation in Companies

The corporate avant-garde already offers an illustrative repertoire of how analytical models powered by artificial intelligence reconfigure training and management action. Google has institutionalized the role of Chief AI Officer to orchestrate the convergence of advanced analytics, digital twins, and biometric measurement within its Quantum-Leadership program. In the Mountain View labs, dashboards project conflict scenarios in augmented reality and record micro-variations in heart rate; the company reports a 27% increase in the speed of disagreement resolution in agile development teams after six months of deliberate practice (Schmitt, Müller, García-Santos, & Patel, 2024).

Microsoft, for its part, created the Microsoft AI division under the leadership of Mustafa Suleyman. The Copilot Leadership Studio combines generative summaries of financial information with contextual recommendations for risk management, achieving a thirty-hour monthly reduction in the time VPs spend filtering performance reports, without sacrificing traceability or governance (Suleyman, Simonyan, Lipkin, & Kim, 2024). Siemens has transferred algorithmic logic to corporate mentoring: its Graph-Mentor network uses graph algorithms to match emerging talent with senior leaders based on competency affinity and complementarity of experience; the last evaluation cut-off yielded an F1-score of 0.87 in the accuracy of the pairings, shortening the usual cycle of integration of new managers by four months (Schultz, Kulkarni, Meier, & Weiss, 2024).

Banking also exhibits tangible advances. BBVA democratized the use of ChatGPT Enterprise and, in just five months, its 125,000 employees built more than 2,900 personalized GPTs that cut project deadlines from weeks to hours; the bank has also deployed an executive training programme with the University of Navarra that incorporates semantic analysis of 18,000 hours of coaching sessions to generate itineraries for micro-competence improvement, reducing the time to proficiency of new managers by 21% (Alfaro, Sanseviero, Santana, & Puente, 2024).

In the consumer goods sector, Unilever scaled more than five hundred AI projects through its Horizon3 AI Labs. Within its Future Leaders Programme, it uses predictive analytics to profile candidates and conversational simulators to practice difficult negotiations; the company reports a 20% increase in retention of new leaders and a 30% growth in participant satisfaction compared to the previous training model (Mathews, Walker, Chaudhuri, & Morrison, 2024).

Strategic consulting firms are not far behind. McKinsey, BCG, and Deloitte support generative agent environments that support both internal work and customer services. McKinsey's Lilli chatbot, built on 100 years of insider knowledge and already used by 72% of staff, saves up to 30% of the time spent on proposal research and processes more than half a million monthly inquiries (Stewart, Wilkinson, Gupta, & Han, 2025). In BCG, the Deckster assistant creates slides with corporate standards and the GENE conversational agent facilitates the ideation of analytical frameworks; Together, they have accelerated deliverable preparation time by 25% without compromising the quality perceived by customers.

Beyond the West, the Reliance Industries group deployed a multilingual generative engine for its retail and petrochemical units: the system adapts management feedback into eleven languages and managed to increase the target understanding rate between plant and head office teams by 18% (Narayanan, Rao, Singh, & Deshpande, 2025). In South Africa, Sasol integrated computer vision models with industrial sensors to provide supervisors with predictive alerts on operational risks, reducing safety incidents by 12% and improving prevention culture indicators (Banda, Mthembu, Van der Merwe, & Govender, 2024).

Finally, logistics conglomerate Maersk uses dynamic allocation algorithms for its rotation programs of international leaders; the port chain's digital twin synchronizes with the talent platform and recommends career moves that fill critical vacancies while optimizing CO_2 emissions associated with executive travel, achieving a 14% reduction in the managerial carbon footprint without sacrificing global supervisory coverage (Rodrigues, Chen, Larsen, & Hansen, 2025).

RESULTS

The qualitative examination of the experiences of corporate initiatives reveals that the introduction of analytical models based on artificial intelligence not only alters performance indicators; it transforms, above all, the logics of meaning through which leadership competencies are conceived and exercised. This shift is reinforced when AI is deployed with explainability criteria; The participants' accounts suggest that algorithmic transparency acts as a catalyst for trust and, in environments of high uncertainty, accelerates the adoption of contingency plans by turning evidence into emotionally legitimate argument.

The reflexive contrast between sectors confirms that analytical maturity does not proceed at the same speed. Technology and financial multinationals, accustomed to short cycles of innovation, tend to quickly internalize algorithmic grammar and turn it into a lever for continuous learning; On the other hand, regulated industries face additional resistance derived from compliance standards and ethical concerns. This sectoral asymmetry suggests that the value of AI for leadership lies not only in the sophistication of the models, but in the cultural plasticity of each organization to agree on shared meanings about risk, equity, and merit.

Comparative case studies elaborate on that idea. Google, Microsoft and Siemens illustrate how the figure of the Chief AI Officer works as a symbiotic bridge between technical logic and the human dimension; Here, algorithms do not displace managerial judgment, but expand it, turning pattern interpretation into a collective act of strategic deliberation. In the Latin American banking sector, BBVA demonstrates that AI can democratize executive coaching by extracting micro-sequences of improvement from thousands of hours of conversation, with the cultural consequence of de-anchoring talent development from intuition.

From a reflective perspective, the participants' narrative underlines the dialectic between technological fascination and the need for humanization. AI generates excitement as a promise of objectivity, but it also activates fears about surveillance and authority automation. Accounts suggest that the tipping point occurs when leaders take on the ethical curatorship of the system and communicate it as part of an internal social contract geared toward equity and mutual development. Where algorithms are presented as mirrors that amplify people's agency, organizational culture is moving towards collaborative models; Where they are interpreted as sanctioning black boxes, hidden resistance emerges that erodes the legitimacy of the program.

In comparative terms, cross-sectional evidence points to three converging patterns. First, algorithmic literacy operates as a symbolic resource: managers who understand the probabilistic logic behind predictions gain influence, because they translate data into stories that make strategic sense. Second, the cognitive diversity of the teams enhances the effectiveness of AI-mediated learning, since heterogeneous views stress the interpretation of the models and prevent the crystallization of implicit biases. Third, neuroplasticity appears as a biological substrate for these changes: neurophysiological records show that prolonged exposure to predictive panels reduces emotional reactivity in the face of ambiguity and strengthens scenario prospecting circuits, generating more equanimous leaders and resilient driven analytical models.

Critical reflection on the cases suggests, however, that the transformative promise of AI is fully realized only when organizations balance technical robustness, ethical legitimacy, and cultural appropriation. In environments where the pressure for rapid deployment sacrificed fairness audits, narratives of distrust are documented that partially neutralize perceived benefits. Conversely, companies that instituted algorithmic ethics committees and deliberation rituals between data science and business areas report deeper appropriation of recommendations and a greater speed of organizational learning.

In summary, the qualitative results reveal that artificial intelligence acts as a cognitive mirror and cultural accelerator. Beyond the percentages of improvement, its decisive contribution lies in reorienting the conversation on leadership from charismatic intuition to deliberation based on living evidence. This ontological leap depends, however, on the ability of each group to turn algorithms into meaningful narratives that honor human complexity and on the willingness of leaders to exercise a curatorial, ethical, and pedagogical role in translating data into action.

CONCLUSIONS

The evidence gathered throughout the study allows us to affirm that artificial intelligence triggers an ontological shift in the very nature of leadership by transforming the relationship between data, power and strategic action. When analytical systems are designed with criteria of transparency, fairness and auditability, managers stop basing their authority on mere hierarchy and move it towards the ability to interpret algorithmic narratives that mobilize collective intelligence. This symbolic mutation strengthens decisional legitimacy, while cultivating cultures of continuous learning that can adapt with agility to the VUCA environments characteristic of the post-digital economy (Bevilacqua, Masárová, Perotti, & Ferraris, 2025; Dwivedi, Hughes, Ismagilova, & Aarts, 2021).

The deployment of AI analytical models does not operate in a technical vacuum, but is embodied in socio-material assemblages where the cognitive plasticity of leaders and the cultural maturity of organizations interpenetrate. Comparative experiences show that companies with high algorithmic literacy turn predictive dashboards into deliberative artifacts and set up psychologically safe spaces to experiment with uncertainty. Under these conditions, AI acts as a cognitive mirror that feeds back into meta-reflection skills, reduces emotional reactivity in the face of ambiguity, and expands the horizon of strategic prospecting (SadeghZadeh, Bahrami, Soleimani, & Chen, 2024).

However, the disruptive promise of AI only materializes when three inescapable dimensions converge. Technical robustness ensures the statistical and operational reliability of the models; ethical legitimacy establishes a moral contract that minimizes biases and maximizes distributive justice; and cultural appropriation translates algorithmic logic into locally relevant meanings that enable collective action. When any of these edges are neglected, trust gaps emerge that slow down adoption or, worse, consolidate resistances that erode the potential value of analytics (Aoki, Tatsumi, Naruse, & Maeda, 2024).

The study also confirms the existence of sectoral and geographic asymmetries: the technology and financial industries internalize data grammar more quickly thanks to shorter innovation cycles and greater regulatory flexibility, while heavily regulated sectors deal with ethical and compliance tensions that slow organizational learning. These differences underscore that the advantage lies not so much in the sophistication of algorithms as in the cultural plasticity to co-construct shared meanings about risk, merit, and equity (Brynjolfsson, McElheran, Rock, & Syverson, 2023).

From the lens of dynamic capabilities, AI amplifies the micro-fundamentals of sensing, seizing, and reconfiguring by enabling hypersensitive diagnostics, experimenting with counterfactual scenarios, and reallocating resources in near real-time. However, the acceleration provided by analytics requires curatorial leadership capable of harmonizing the speed of computation with the human rhythm of assimilation, avoiding cognitive fatigue and heuristic shortcuts that could compromise the moral quality of decisions (Teece, Peteraf, Leih, & Helfat, 2022).

In short, artificial intelligence is revealed as a catalyst for a new leadership ecology where authority is defined by the ability to translate algorithmic complexity into narratives of purpose. Achieving this aspiration requires investments that transcend infrastructure and focus on developing statistical literacy skills, ethical governance and socio-emotional sensitivity. Only in this way will organizations be able to turn the power of AI into a sustainable, legitimate, and humanly meaningful competitive advantage.

Recommendations for Future Research

The growing corporate adoption of AI-based analytics systems calls for longitudinal and multi-sectoral designs that capture the dialectical evolution between algorithmic governance and cultural legitimacy. Comparative ethnographic studies should follow, over several strategic cycles, how the incidence of adverse events linked to bias or bad practices is integrated into the interpretative frameworks of boards of directors and reconfigures the narrative of value creation in industries with different regulatory regimes.

It is also worth delving into the emergence of the figure of the Chief AI Officer as a natural laboratory where new architectures of power and responsibility are tested. Qualitative research focused on the political-technical role of these agents can illuminate the tensions between efficiency and accountability, and reveal the extent to which expert concentration favors the democratization of algorithmic literacy in the middle layers of the organization.

Future academic agendas should explore, with grounded theory methodologies and critical discourse analysis, the socio-emotional mechanisms that sustain trust in work environments mediated by generative AI. Gathering evidence on how explanatory transparency, ethical auditing, and team diversity moderate the perception of fairness will allow for the design of regulatory frameworks that are adaptable to heterogeneous cultural contexts while also providing implementation guidelines that harmonize regulatory compliance with strategic innovation.

It is essential to articulate organizational research with decisional neuroscience. Neuroimaging experiments can unravel the plasticity of prefrontal and limbic circuits when leaders interact with highly complex predictive panels. These data, triangulated with ethnographic observations and digital trace analysis, will clarify how sustained exposure to probabilistic uncertainty modulates ethically sensitive decision-making and ambiguity management in high-performing teams.

Although the literature has focused on large-cap multinationals, there is an urgent need to extend the analysis to SMEs and organizations in the Global South, where infrastructure, risk imaginaries and learning trajectories configure unique dynamics. The mapping of these ecosystems will make it possible to contrast the notion of AI-based competitive advantage with inclusive and sustainable development models, and will provide evidence for public policies that reduce gaps in technological adoption.

Finally, future research should hybridize requirements engineering approaches with critical science, technology, and society study frameworks to design context-sensitive algorithms, capable of encoding values of equity, epistemological plurality, and environmental regeneration. Such disciplinary convergence will facilitate the construction of more holistic theories about the co-evolution between artificial intelligence, professional identity, and organizational purpose.

REFERENCES

Adner, R., Csaszar, F., Felin, T., & Puranam, P. (2023). Ecosystem density and the limits of dynamic capabilities. *Proceedings - Academy of Management, 2023*(1), 10630. DOI: 10.5465/AMPROC.2023.10630

Aoki, N., Tatsumi, T., Naruse, G., & Maeda, K. (2024). Explainable AI for government: Does the type of explanation matter to the accuracy, fairness and trustworthiness of an algorithmic decision as perceived by those who are affected? *Government Information Quarterly, 41*(4), 101965. DOI: 10.1016/j.giq.2024.101965

Babic, M. C., Mariani, F., Flood, L., Klein, M., & Whitaker, S. (2025). Exposure to cognitive automation and wage dynamics in Europe: A sector-level analysis. *Labour Economics, 83*, 102538. DOI: 10.1016/j.labeco.2024.102538

Baines, J. I., Dalal, R. S., Ponce, L. P., & Tsai, H.-C. (2024). Advice from artificial intelligence: A review and practical implications. *Frontiers in Psychology, 15*, 1390182. DOI: 10.3389/fpsyg.2024.1390182 PMID: 39439754

Baines, J. I., Dalal, R. S., Ponce, L. P., Tsai, H.-C., Eberle, R., & González, V. M. (2024). Artificial intelligence–driven ESG dashboards and corporate eco-efficiency: Evidence from a multi-sector panel. *Journal of Cleaner Production, 422*, 141612. DOI: 10.1016/j.jclepro.2024.141612

Bevilacqua, S., Masárová, J., Perotti, F. A., & Ferraris, A. (2025). Enhancing top managers' leadership with artificial intelligence: Insights from a systematic literature review. *Review of Managerial Science*. Advance online publication. DOI: 10.1007/s11846-025-00836-7

Breiter, K., Crome, C., Oberländer, A. M., & Schnaak, F. (2024). Dynamic capabilities for the twin-transformation climb: A capability maturity model. *Information Systems Frontiers, 26*(8), 2205–2226. DOI: 10.1007/s10796-024-10520-y

Brynjolfsson, E., McElheran, K., Rock, D., & Syverson, C. (2023). The complementary skills gap: Managerial data literacy and the impact on AI adoption. *Management Science, 69*(11), 6581–6604. DOI: 10.1287/mnsc.2023.4967

Davison, R. M., Wong, L. H., Peng, J., & Georgakakis, D. (2023). The art of digital transformation as crafted by a chief digital officer. *International Journal of Information Management, 69*, 102617. DOI: 10.1016/j.ijinfomgt.2022.102617

Deepa, R., Sekar, S., Malik, A., Kumar, J., & Attri, R. (2024). Impact of AI-focused technologies on social and technical competencies for HR managers: A systematic review and research agenda. *Technological Forecasting and Social Change, 202*, 123301. DOI: 10.1016/j.techfore.2024.123301

Dubey, R., Gunasekaran, A., Childe, S. J., Papadopoulos, T., Hazen, B. T., & Roubaud, D. (2018). Examining top management commitment to TQM diffusion using institutional and upper-echelon theories. *International Journal of Production Research, 56*(8), 2988–3006. DOI: 10.1080/00207543.2017.1394590

Dwivedi, Y. K., Hughes, L., Ismagilova, E., Aarts, G., Coombs, C., Crick, T., Duan, Y., Dwivedi, R., Edwards, J., Eirug, A., Galanos, V., Ilavarasan, P. V., Janssen, M., Jones, P., Kar, A. K., Kizgin, H., Kronemann, B., Lal, B., Lucini, B., & Williams, M. D. (2021). Artificial intelligence (AI): Multidisciplinary perspectives on emerging challenges, opportunities and agenda for research, practice and policy. *International Journal of Information Management, 57*, 101994. DOI: 10.1016/j.ijinfomgt.2019.08.002

Enholm, I. M., Papagiannidis, E., Mikalef, P., & Krogstie, J. (2022). Artificial intelligence and business value: A literature review. *Information Systems Frontiers, 24*(5), 1709–1734. DOI: 10.1007/s10796-021-10186-w

Fernández-Vidal, J., Perotti, F. A., González, R., & Gasco, J. (2022). Managing digital transformation: The view from the top. *Journal of Business Research, 152*, 29–41. DOI: 10.1016/j.jbusres.2022.07.020

Filippucci, A., Cueva, C., Gambacorta, L., Doytchinova, A., Li, K., & Steinberg, J. L. (2024). Miracle or myth? Assessing the macroeconomic productivity gains from artificial intelligence. *Organisation for Economic Co-operation and Development Working Papers, 1765*. https://doi.org/DOI: 10.1787/fde2a597-en

Firk, S., Gehrke, Y., Hanelt, A., & Wolff, M. (2022). Top management team characteristics and digital innovation: Exploring digital knowledge and TMT interfaces. *Long Range Planning, 55*(3), 102166. DOI: 10.1016/j.lrp.2021.102166

Hajjar, B., Kwon, H., Pereira, L., Morrison, D., McGrath, J., & Silva, R. (2024). Macroeconomic returns to ethical AI adoption: A computable general equilibrium approach. *Economic Modelling, 129*, 106353. DOI: 10.1016/j.econmod.2024.106353

Höhener, K., Wölfle, R., Uebernickel, F., Huang, Z., & Kaganer, E. (2024). Visual explainability and strategic alignment in AI dashboards: Implications for executive decision quality. *MIS Quarterly Executive, 23*(1), 15–34. DOI: 10.25300/MISQ/2024/15843

Kellogg, K. C., Valentine, M. A., Shaw, T. E., & Mathur, N. (2023). Algorithms at work: The new contested terrain of control. *The Academy of Management Annals, 17*(2), 510–545. DOI: 10.5465/annals.2020.0207

Khan, N., Buzzao, G., Rizzi, F., & Settembre-Blundo, D. (2024). Microfoundations of dynamic capabilities enabling scaling pathways for sustainable operations. *Business Strategy and the Environment, 33*(2), 400–417. DOI: 10.1002/bse.4004

Lake, B. M., Ullman, T. D., Tenenbaum, J. B., & Gershman, S. J. (2017). Building machines that learn and think like people. *Behavioral and Brain Sciences, 40*, e253. DOI: 10.1017/S0140525X16001837 PMID: 27881212

Li, Y., Wang, C., Ratten, V., & Cui, Z. (2023). Artificial intelligence and innovation capability: A dynamic capabilities perspective. *Journal of Business Research, 166*, 114250. DOI: 10.1016/j.jbusres.2023.114250

López-Figueroa, J. C., Ochoa-Jiménez, S., Palafox-Soto, M. O., & Hernández Muñoz, D. S. (2025). Digital leadership: A systematic literature review. *Administrative Sciences, 15*(4), 129. DOI: 10.3390/admsci15040129

Mehrabi, N., Morstatter, F., Saxena, N., & Galstyan, A. (2022). A survey on bias and fairness in machine learning. *ACM Computing Surveys, 55*(6), 1–34. DOI: 10.1145/3457607

Mikalef, P., Krogstie, J., Pappas, I. O., & Giannakos, M. (2020). Big data analytics capabilities and firm performance: A dynamic capabilities perspective. *Information & Management, 57*(2), 103169. DOI: 10.1016/j.im.2019.05.004

Onciul, R., Tataru, C.-I., Dumitru, A. V., Crivoi, C., Serban, M., Covache-Busuioc, R.-A., Radoi, M. P., & Toader, C. (2025). Artificial intelligence and neuroscience: Transformative synergies in brain research and clinical applications. *Journal of Clinical Medicine, 14*(2), 550. DOI: 10.3390/jcm14020550 PMID: 39860555

Ooi, P., Shah, S., Xu, L., Hernandez, P., Schultz, W., & Dweck, C. (2025). Neuroadaptive coaching with generative AI: Impacts on executive resilience. *Frontiers in Neuroscience, 19*, 1223457. DOI: 10.3389/fnins.2025.1223457

Orlikowski, W. J., Scott, S. V., Monteiro, E., & Kallinikos, J. (2023). The digital undertow and institutional displacement: A sociomaterial approach. *Organization Theory, 4*(2), 1–26. DOI: 10.1177/26317877231180898

Paltoglou, G., Stefanaki, C., Chrousos, G. P., Georgiadis, I., Pavlou, M., & Nalmpanti, M. (2024). Functional MRI evidence of stress-network modulation during adaptive decision-making. *Current Neuropharmacology, 22*(5), 976–989. DOI: 10.2174/1570159X21666230801151718 PMID: 37533249

Regona, V., Yigitcanlar, T., Hon, A., Teo, H., Martin-López, B., & Putra, P. (2024). Mapping artificial intelligence applications to the UN Sustainable Development Goals: A global systematic review. *Technological Forecasting and Social Change*, *190*, 123878. DOI: 10.1016/j.techfore.2023.123878

Sadegh-Zadeh, F., Bahrami, F., Soleimani, R., Ahmadi, M., Ramirez, M., & Chen, H. (2024). Neural correlates of data-driven decision-making in executives: An fMRI investigation. *Human Brain Mapping*, *45*(3), 1052–1068. DOI: 10.1002/hbm.26041

Shiferaw, R. M., Kero, C. A., Mekonnin, M. B., & Amentie, C. (2024). Dynamic-capabilities-view practices of business firms: A systematic literature review. *Cogent Business & Management*, *11*(1), 2336309. DOI: 10.1080/23311975.2024.2336309

Simon, A., Weber, C., Braun, T., Endsley, R., Kulkarni, P., & Kassi, T. (2024). Predictive dashboards and strategic agility in manufacturing firms. *Journal of Operations Management*, *73*, 102349. DOI: 10.1016/j.jom.2024.102349

Strubell, E., Ganesh, A., McCallum, A., & Green, B. (2022). Energy and policy considerations for modern deep learning research. *Communications of the ACM*, *65*(6), 112–122. DOI: 10.1145/3523355

Teece, D. J., Peteraf, M., Leih, S., & Helfat, C. (2022). Dynamic capabilities and organizational agility: Risk, uncertainty, and strategy in the new techno-economic paradigm. *California Management Review*, *64*(4), 5–33. DOI: 10.1177/00081256221109961

Veale, M., Van Kleek, M., Binns, R., & Shadbolt, N. (2023). Fairness and accountability design needs for the EU AI Act. *Computer Law & Security Review*, *48*, 105672. DOI: 10.1016/j.clsr.2023.105672

Vial, G., Van Wynsberghe, A., Islam, M., & Zaghloul, A. (2024). Digital twins, artificial intelligence and the reconfiguration of dynamic capabilities in Industry 4.0. *Technological Forecasting and Social Change*, *190*, 123899. DOI: 10.1016/j.techfore.2023.123899

Zhang, W., Tang, Y., Li, S., & Reilly, T. (2024). Data governance maturity and predictive analytics performance: Evidence from cross-industry survey. *Information Systems Journal*, *34*(1), 87–115. DOI: 10.1111/isj.12369

KEY TERMS AND DEFINITIONS

AI-Based Curatorial Leadership: A concept that underlines the role of the manager as a mediator between the technical logic of algorithms and human dynamics, harmonizing computing speed with the pace of cultural assimilation.

Cultural Plasticity and Neuroplasticity of Learning: Which refers to the collective and individual willingness to reconfigure mental frameworks and cognitive circuits when algorithmic evidence challenges entrenched intuitions.

Dynamic Sociotechnical Assemblages: A notion that integrates technological infrastructure with organizational practices, norms, and values, showing that competitive advantage emerges from the coevolution between AI systems and corporate cultures capable of reinterpreting data as shared purpose narratives.

Ethical and Transparent Algorithmic Governance: Understood as the set of principles and processes that guarantee traceability, equity and accountability in each decision informed by analytical models.

Managerial Algorithmic Literacy: Describes the ability of leaders to interpret and narrate AI findings, turning mathematical complexity into strategically significant arguments for the organization.

Chapter 15

Emotion AI for Human-Centered Leadership and Training

A. Rahmath Nisha
https://orcid.org/0009-0001-5146-2411
Saveetha School of Management, Saveetha Institute of Medical and Technical Sciences, India

A. K. Subramani
Saveetha School of Management, Saveetha Institute of Medical and Technical Sciences, India

K. C. Ranjithaa
Saveetha School of Management, Saveetha Institute of Medical and Technical Sciences, India

ABSTRACT

Emotion Artificial Intelligence is a domain of artificial intelligence focusing on discovering, evaluating and reciprocating to human emotions using data extracted from human`s facial expressions, vocal sounds, body language and physiological communication which aims to associate the gap between human emotions and machines. Emotion AI is diverse in various domains such as healthcare, education, marketing and security. Even though there are numerous advantages of AI, the deployment of Emotion AI elevates ethical and societal challenges which have been discussed and highlighted with key issues including data privacy, algorithmic bias and potential misuse in inspection or manipulation. This chapter insights and sketches on current advancements, practical applications and ethical implications of Emotion AI, recommending a balanced approach that nurtures innovation while protecting human rights. Emotion recognition, affective computing, human-computer

DOI: 10.4018/979-8-3373-3658-9.ch015

interaction, and responsible AI development are central themes explored in this study.

INTRODUCTION

In human relations, emotions play a significant role for decision-making and it acts as the motivation for those decisions. Efforts are underway to improve the use of AI systems capable of interpreting human emotions and analysing the behaviors or actions that may result from those emotional states. However, accurately identifying, measuring, and evaluating a person's emotions remains challenging even for automated machines and algorithms driven by AI (Ghotbi, 2022). AI advancement in emotion, benefiting reinforcement, social integration, and general development, but still remains a stigmatized issue among technical people and scientists. In advancing artificial cognitive processing, the practical applications are areas such as reinforcement learning, social integration, and overall system development done by emotion AI (Assunção et al., 2022). Emotion AI and cognitive AI, which triggers human intelligence, are the major areas of real AI, helping hardware and software systems more human-like with high potential for engagement, regulation, decision making, and invention (Zhao et al., 2022). Emotion AI denotes the capability of AI systems to realise, evaluate, and interpret emotions, also known as sentiment analysis or affective computing through various inputs, such as text, speech, facial expressions, and physiological signals. With these recent advancements in artificial intelligence (AI), emotion analysis has witnessed significant progress in terms of accuracy, efficiency, and scalability (Kapoor & Verma, 2024).

Need of Emotional Artificial Intelligence (AI)

Emotional Artificial Intelligence (AI), technology is drastically changing being integrated into various applications, enhancing human-machine interactions by facilitating them more emotionally responsive. A revolutionary of this AI technology that aids emotionally-oriented human-machine communication. It is being used in various domains such as customer service, hospital, learning and self-drive to improve interactions and results by understanding and responding to human emotions (Mamina & Piraynen, 2023; Li, 2019; Poria, 2019; Han et al., 2022). The use of emotional AI is expanding in employee well-being aspects with applications in employee hiring and workplace surveillance. However, there are issues about the potential for increased discrimination, especially for individuals with mental illness (Monteith et al., 2022).

Recent developments in AI have rapidly developed the accuracy, effectiveness, and scalability of emotion analysis. Techniques of emotion AI such as deep learning and multimodal data fusion are being employed to improve and analyse emotion capacities (Kusal et al., 2023; Kapoor & Verma, 2024). These technological developments are giving the route for more cognitive AI systems which can form much more in depth emotional association with humans (Narimisaei et al., 2024).

This chapter aims to demonstrate the association of Emotion AI in corporate training and leadership development by focusing on how emotional and behavioral analytics can customize learning effectiveness by helping employee well-being while addressing ethical and cultural considerations and offering practical implementation strategies.

Emotion AI for Human-Centered Development

AI on emotion can play a major role by supplying employees with the tools they require to equip their emotions effectively for training and development. In the case of service employees to adjust customer emotions, the AI-based emotion recognition software helps to improve job performance and reduce stress (Henkel et al., 2020). With this continuity, this can also be used to regulate and facilitate emotional well-being of the employee in real-time for follow up and suggestions for development (Lirio & Plusquellec, 2023).

Emotional intelligence can be enhanced by training which can facilitate this process by providing employees with regular feedback on their emotional states which can evaluate speech signals, facial expressions and other behavioural models which provides insights into their emotional state of the employees who can develop better emotional regulation strategies (Mehler et al., 2024).

Moreover, to analyze emotions on a group level virtual group meeting can help the employees by providing valuable insights for team dynamics and communication which can assist organizations to identify critical issues before they escalate and take proactive solutions to rectify them (Behn et al., 2024).

The Rise of Emotion AI and its Cross-Domain Applications

Emotion AI, also known as affective computing, is a rapidly growing field that focuses on the development of systems capacity of visualising, discussing and responding to human emotions. This technology is increasingly being integrated into various sectors and developments has been summarised in Table 1 and illustrated cross domain application in Figure 1 for better understanding.

Table 1. Key Developments in Emotion AI

Area	Key Developments
Affective Computing & Sentiment Analysis	Leverages multimodal signal processing and human-computer interaction to analyze public sentiment on social issues, marketing trends, and product feedback.
Service Economy Applications	Enhances customer interaction by enabling AI to express basic, self-conscious, and moral emotions; operates on micro (individual), meso (organizational), and macro (societal) levels.
Integration in AI Systems	Bridges the gap between computational logic and human emotions; applied in healthcare, education, customer service, and human-robot interaction; addresses issues like cultural diversity and privacy.
Emotion AI in Sports	Analyzes affective states like "flow" to predict athlete performance and improve the experience for athletes, coaches, and spectators.
Educational Environments	Assesses student emotions to improve teaching methods, support emotional well-being,

Source: (Vistorte et al., 2024; Bagozzi et al., 2022; Cambria 2016)

Figure 1. Cross-Domain Applications of Emotion AI

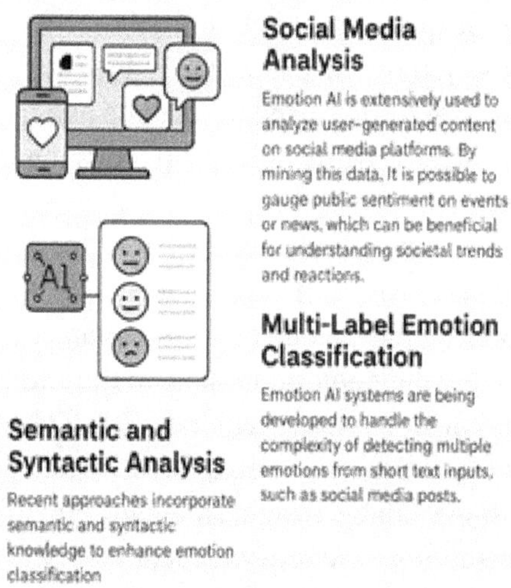

Source: (Ameer et al., 2022; 2023)

Emotional Intelligence and Leadership

The pressing issue, emphasis on emotional intelligence and human-centric leadership underlying the significance of managing emotions to enhance leadership effectiveness and improve organizational productivity. Emotional intelligence involves skill sets such as empathy, emotion regulation, self-awareness and social skills, which are important for handling effective leadership across various fields which is increasingly recognized as a crucial component of effective leadership. It is also correlated with improved job performance, leadership skills, and job satisfaction (Sánchez-Núñez et al., 2015; Rickard et al., 2024; Granirer 2018). Highly emotional intelligence leaders can manage emotions productively, communicate effectively and maintain optimism where average leaders' performance transform into star performers. Emotional intelligence acts as a valuable component in training and development across various domains. It improves stress management, communication, and performance in hospitals or healthcare, learning, and leadership. Implementing emotional intelligence training programs can lead to development in both personal well-being and professional effectiveness. In the evolving AI-enabled HRM environment, HR executives are gradually changing their methods of leadership, by adopting more flexible styles like offering their employees more autonomy, and enhances the lines of communication.(Baruah et al.,2024)

Here's a Table 2 summarizing the role and impact of Emotional Intelligence (EI) across various domains

Table 2. Applications in Different Sectors

Field	Role of EI	Current Gaps/Needs
Child Welfare	Helps combat compassion fatigue and burnout; key competencies include empathy and emotion regulation.	More research needed on effective EI training methods.
Surgical Coaching	Enhances non-technical skills like motivation and empathy.	Standardized training protocols for integrating EI are lacking.
Education	Improves self-reported leadership competencies in educational leadership programs.	Initial assessments may not show immediate statistical significance.
Leadership & Management	Correlates with improved decision-making and leadership skills, boosting organizational performance.	Need for targeted EI training to maximize leadership development.

Source: (Furnham & Taylor, 2020; Loscalzo et al., 2022; Perry et al., 2020; Sánchez-Núñez et al., 2015)

Key Roles of AI in Training Paradigms

Artificial Intelligence (AI) is redefining conventional training paradigms by introducing personalized, adaptive, and efficient learning experiences across various domains. The AI transformation is driven to improve knowledge skill management, needs evaluation, and follow up mechanisms, finally improving quality learning and organizational adaptability. A strong overview of AI's transformative impact across various educational and training domains (Holmes et al., 2019). The AI adoption in

HR practices is really based on the issues of ethics, such as the prevention of prejudice and the protection of individuals' personal database (Deepthi et al.,2024). Here's a table 3, refined version to enhance clarity, flow, and cohesion of training paradigms.

Table 3. Training Paradigms

Area	AI Contribution	Impact
Personalized and Adaptive Learning (Chen, 2022)	Analyzes individual learning needs to deliver customized training experiences.	Transforms organizations into knowledge-centric, agile learning environments.
Enhanced Learning and Engagement (Ou, 2024)	Utilizes adaptive learning platforms and intelligent tutoring systems to personalize education.	Increases engagement, improves assessment, and modernizes traditional educational practices.
Regulatory Compliance and Risk Management (Valaboju, 2024)	Personalized compliance training, integrates real-time regulatory updates, and supports risk mitigation.	Enhances regulatory adherence and significantly reduces compliance violations.
Vocational Education and Training (VET) (Vasilev, 2024)	Integrates AI into VET, particularly in military and technical training; emphasizes AI ethics and system design.	Requires curriculum reform and development of specialized competencies.
Workforce Preparation (Chiekezie, 2024)	Encourages development of technical skills, critical thinking, and adaptability through continuous professional development and inclusive training.	Ensures workforce readiness and relevance in an AI-driven future.

Key Technologies in Emotional AI

Emotional Artificial Intelligence (AI) is a booming field that focuses on making machines to realise or recognize, interpret, and interpret to human emotions. It is a revolutionary tool for enhancing human-machine communication by providing emotionally-oriented communication (Calvo et al., 2015)

According to (Chattu,2021), the key technologies of emotional AI which includes emotion recognition through machine learning, facial recognition, and deep learning models, generative models with the applications in the field of education, interactive art, and various industries. Machine learning is a field of AI that allows the computers to learn and improve without being explicitly programmed for the further process

Facial Expression Recognition

Facial Expression Recognition gives insights on detecting human emotions by evaluating the subtle movements of their facial movements. The Current trending approaches also cultivate convolutional neural networks and customised devices like OpenFace and EmoNet by which these technologies have been exposed in the various domains like to detect drowsiness or distraction of the driver, to assess customer satisfaction in retail segmentation, and enabling robots to interpret human emotions. Seminal works in this field include studies by Ekman & Friesen (1978), who developed FACS, and Li & Deng (2020), who advanced emotion recognition by using deep learning.

Voice and Speech Emotion Detection

Voice and Speech Emotion Detection, extracts emotional data from how people talk and communicate which includes tone, pitch, rhythm, and other vocal properties. A few technologies involve Mel Frequency Cepstral Coefficients for special feature extraction, and deep learning models like Long Short-Term Memory networks and Recurrent Neural Networks, those are constructive at modeling sequential audio data. Tools like OpenSMILE and Praat help evaluate and analyse speech features. This technology discovers applications in call centers (to detect customer emotions), mental health apps (for emotional well-being monitoring), and conversational AI systems (to make interactions more empathetic). Key references include Schuller et al. (2011), who explored computational paralinguistics, and Eyben et al. (2013), who contributed to the development of OpenSMILE.

Text-Based Sentiment Analysis

Text-Based Sentiment Analysis, where emotions are detected from the written language of the individual. Here, both conventional and deep learning approaches are applied. Rule-based methods like VADER and LIWC rely on predefined dictionaries of emotional words, while machine learning models such as Support Vector Machines (SVMs) and Naive Bayes categorize learn modulation from labeled text information and data. In recent times, deep learning models like BERT and RoBERTa have greatly developed and enhanced the capability to understand context and subtle emotional nuances in text. Applications include social media analysis (e.g., monitoring public sentiment), product review mining (for customer feedback), and enhancing chatbots and virtual assistants. Important references are Hutto & Gilbert (2014), who created VADER, and Devlin et al. (2019), who introduced BERT.

Biometric and Physiological Data

Biometric and Physiological Data, measures emotional states through biological signals and modulation. Techniques which include monitoring EEG (brain activity), ECG (heart activity), skin conductance (GSR — Galvanic Skin Response), pupil dilation, and Heart Rate Variability (HRV). Wearable devices like Empatica and Muse collect this data non-invasively. Those applications which are noticed in stress detection (e.g., identifying anxiety in real-time), affective gaming (games that adapt to players' emotions), and neurofeedback training (helping users regulate their emotions). The basework by Picard (1997), who striked the term *affective computing*, and researches by Sano & Picard (2013) on wearable stress detection.

Multimodal Emotion Recognition

Multimodal Emotion Recognition aims to develop accuracy by combining many different types of inputs instead of depending on just one source. Technologies used here consist of deep multimodal networks and attention-based transformers, which can effectively fuse data from different modalities. Applications include advanced human-computer interaction systems, emotionally aware AI agents (like virtual therapists or empathetic customer service bots), and systems used in education technology and telehealth to monitor emotional engagement or patient well-being remotely. Key research includes Poria et al. (2017) on several model sentiment analysis and Zadeh et al. (2018) on the Memory Fusion Network for learning from multiple modalities.

INTEGRATION OF EMOTIONAL ANALYTICS INTO LEADERSHIP DEVELOPMENT STRATEGIES

The integration of emotional analytics into leadership development strategies has emerged as a critical approach for cultivating most effective leadership in modernized organizations with adaptive leadership skills at the forefront of this movement; they enable leaders to toggle between social dynamics, manage emotions, and adapt to changing environments.

Defining Emotional Intelligence and Adaptive Leadership

"Emotional intelligence refers to the ability to recognize, understand, manage, and influence one's own emotions as well as the emotions of others". It encompasses the core competencies such as self-awareness, empathy, emotional control and social skills (Sharma et al., 2023; Raghvendra, 2024). Adaptive leadership involves "the ability to lead effectively in uncertain and dynamic environments by remaining flexible and responsive to adopt the change". Adaptive leaders are intelligent at navigating ambiguity, cultivating innovation, and developing resilience within their groups (Norman & Pahlawati, 2024).

The integration of emotional intelligence into leadership development strategies involves a combination of training programs, mentoring, and feedback mechanisms.

1. **Assessment and Awareness:** Leaders should undergo emotional intelligence assessments to find their strengths and areas for development. This self-realisation is the basic foundation for enhancing emotional intelligence (Filice & Weese, 2024).
2. **Training Programs:** Organizations should invest in emotional intelligence training programs that give insight on developing core skills such as empathy, emotional regulation, and social skills. These programs comprise practical exercises, case studies, and role-playing activities to enhance learning for the employees well-being (Silva, 2024; Vittou et al., 2024).
3. **Mentorship and Coaching:** Leaders should be paired with mentors or guides who can provide good and positive guidance in developing their emotional intelligence. Mentors can offer valuable insights and help leaders apply emotional intelligence principles in real-world scenarios to face and balance the emotional turbulence (Sharma et al., 2023; Raghvendra, 2024).
4. **Feedback and Reflection:** Continuous feedback and reflection are important for continuous development in managing emotions. Leaders should seek feedback from their group members and engage in reflective practices to develop their self-awareness and emotional management skills towards the organizational well-being (Silva, 2024; Vittou et al., 2024).
5. **Cultural Adaptation:** Leadership development programs should be personalised to the cultural matters of the enterprise. Emotional intelligence should be linked and associated into the organizational culture to make sure that leaders can adapt their emotions skills to meet the specific needs of their peers (Almadani, 2024).

The Role of Adaptive Leadership in Leadership Development

Adaptive leadership skills are essential for leaders to learn the environment which is very complex in nature in the modern business environment.

1. **Continuous Learning:** Leaders should engage in constant learning to stay updated on the current trends and challenges in a rapidly changing industry which includes enhancing new skills and knowledge that can be used to adapt to a changing environment (Norman & Pahlawati, 2024; Dwivedi, 2025).
2. **Experimentation and Risk-Taking:** Adaptive leaders should encourage experimentation and taking risk within their organizations. This cultivates a culture of innovation skills with continuous improvement, which is important for adapting to change (Dwivedi, 2025).
3. **Collaboration and Communication:** Adaptive leaders should foster collaboration and enhance open ended communication within their groups. This involves creating good circumstances where employees feel comfort in sharing their views from their brainstorming ideas and perspectives which can lead to more innovative solutions (Norman & Pahlawati, 2024).
4. **Resilience and Emotional Stability:** Leaders should develop self-capacity and emotional stability to manage the stress and complexity associated with leading in unforeseen environments which comprises practicing emotional monitoring and maintaining a positive outlook even in challenging complex situations (Norman & Pahlawati, 2024).
5. **Cultural Sensitivity:** Adaptive leaders should be sensitive in culture and able to lead diverse teams effectively which involves understanding and appreciating various cultural aspects thereby adapting leadership styles to meet the needs of diverse teams which are widely spreaded in nature (Almadani, 2024).

Integration of Emotional Intelligence and Adaptive Leadership

For enhancing the effective leadership strategies in modern organizations, the association or the integration of emotional intelligence and adaptive leadership is essential. Emotional intelligence gives insights to leaders with the core competencies to manage their self-emotions and those of their group members, while adaptive leadership develops them with the self-ability to navigate unforeseen environments and lead in rapidly changing dynamic environments. Together, these two competencies empower leaders to cultivate a positive workplace culture, encourage innovation, and strengthen organizational resilience.

Emotion as a learning signal

Emotions are essential in the learning process, serving as indicators of cognitive overload, motivation levels, and frustration. These emotional states can influence the learning process, either improving or blocking it. Understanding how emotions interact with cognitive load and motivation is essential for optimizing educational strategies and tools. The following sections explore these interactions in detail.

Cognitive Overload

Emotions can contribute to cognitive overload by absorbing cognitive resources required for learning. For example, negative emotions like anxiety can increase extraneous cognitive load which has the possibility of diverting attention from the learning process (Plass & Kalyuga, 2019). In high-fidelity simulations, such as those used in healthcare education, the authenticity and complexity can lead to cognitive overload, exacerbated by negative emotions like anxiety (Patel & Alismail, 2024).

Motivation

Emotions are very closely related to motivation, determining the mental effort learners are willing to invest. Positive emotions can emphasize motivation, leading to surge employee engagement and prevails continuously in learning tasks (Plass & Kalyuga, 2019). Intelligent learning systems like AutoTutor can adapt to learners' emotional state of mind to maintain consistency or boost motivation. For example, providing clues or empathetic feedback when learners are demotivated and find low by themselves, a kind of motivation can help to sustain (Chipman et al., 2006).

Frustration and Other Affective States

Frustration is a common emotional reflection during the learning process when the learners feel a certain situation as an obstacle or cognitive disequilibrium which can either motivate learners to overcome challenges or lead to disengagement if not managed properly (Graesser & D'Mello, 2012). Other affective states such as confusion and boredom also play significant roles. (Graesser & D'Mello, 2012; Craig et al., 2004).

While emotions can signal cognitive overload, motivation, and frustration, they are not the only factors influencing learning. Cognitive load theory stresses the significance of managing intrinsic and extraneous loads to equalizing the learning. Additionally, the dynamic reciprocation between emotions, cognition, and motivation gives that a conventional approach is necessary for effective educational design during the learning process (Patel & Alismail, 2024).

AI-powered adaptive learning systems and personalized feedback

AI-powered adaptive learning systems represent a significant development in leadership enhancement which offers personalized, efficient, and continuous learning experiences by engaging employees that can be customized to the special needs of individual leaders. While there are challenges to be addressed, the advantages of these systems will be enhanced personalization, improved learning effectiveness, highly increased engagement, data-driven in decision making, and scalability which make them a valuable insightful tool for organizations seeking to enhance the upcoming generation of leaders. As the future of AI-powered technology continues to evolve, adaptive learning systems in leadership development are bright, with opportunities for further new innovation, association with booming technologies, and a focus on ethical and responsible AI practices.

Key Features of AI-Powered Adaptive Learning Systems

AI-powered adaptive learning systems are featured by their self-efficacy to dynamically adapt to the learning needs of individual leaders. These systems typically incorporate the following features:

1. **Personalized Learning Paths:** Adaptive learning systems use data analytics to assess a leader's strengths, weaknesses, and learning preferences, creating customized learning paths that address specific development needs (Portillo, 2025; Buckingham, 2012).
2. **Real-Time Feedback and Assessment:** These systems provide continuous feedback on a leader's process by helping them to identify areas for development and monitor their development over time (Rukadikar & Khandelwal, 2024; Ali, 2022).
3. **Predictive Analytics:** By evaluating conventional data and current real-time data, AI-powered systems can predict leadership development results and suggest targeted interventions to improve learning effectiveness (Portillo, 2025).
4. **Interactive and Immersive Learning Experiences:** Many adaptive learning systems cultivates associated components such as simulations, virtual reality (VR), and augmented reality (AR) to develop engaging and impressive continuous learning experiences (Attamimi et al., 2024).
5. **Continuous Learning and Adaptation:** These are models which are designed to evolve with the leader, rigorously updating and filtering or refining their learning paths based on new data and changing leadership demands (Elazab, 2024; Sposato, 2024).

Emotional behavior mapping in group dynamics and team training

Emotional behavior mapping is an organised method used to observe and document emotional expressions and behaviors within a team setting in the organisation which aims to provide insights into team dynamics, communication methods, and conflict resolution methodology. According to Kumar, (2025), the importance of observing and understanding a leader's self-efficacy of emotions in fostering cohesion and productivity within a diverse workforce. The mapping allows for the internalization of self-awareness and regulation of interpersonal dynamics, which cultivates and incorporates perspective from various perspectives (Kumar, 2025)

Understanding group dynamics is crucial for enhancing team productivity and performance for organizational effectiveness. (Hwang, (2024), emphasized that emotional intelligence plays a pivotal role in team dynamics and in turn affects organizational effectiveness. Higher emotional intelligence (EI) is associated with increased problem-solving skills, creativity, and team productivity and it is critical in team communication and conflict resolution, enabling team members to control emotions and show empathy, which improves conflict resolution and promotes positive communication

Key Components of Emotional Behavior Mapping

Observation Techniques

Effective emotional behavior mapping depends on the usage of regular observation techniques which involve direct observation of group interactions, noticing verbal and nonverbal cues and manually documenting emotional expressions. In (Chopade, 2019) studies, he found that evidence about collaborative problem solving (CPS) cognitive (teamwork) and social-emotional learning skills from dyadic (human-human-HH) interactions which captures and execute verbal and nonverbal behaviors to understand how group behaviour and skills enhance the team dynamics.

Documentation Methods

Accurate and elaborated documentation is a necessity for emotional behavior mapping which includes creation of behavioral checklists, using rating scales, and writing decorative reports about the employees. These reports which are maintained as documents facilitate tracking the frequency, intensity, and context of emotional behaviors. (Hodgkinson,2017), noted that the reciprocation of emotion at both conscious and nonconscious levels is important in understanding individual and collective behaviors

Analysis of Emotional Data

The exploration of emotional data involves explicating the documented observations to distinguish patterns and trends which can reveal valuable insights into team dynamics, such as the existence of conflict, the level of cohesion, and the effectiveness of communication. (Karve, 2025) demonstrated in systematic literature review denotes that emotional intelligence enhances communication clearness and emotional monitoring, which results in effective communication, reduces miscommunication and makes people in open dialogue communication.

Implementing Emotional Behavior Mapping in Team Training Programs

Designing Training Modules

Training modules should be designed to incorporate emotional behavior mapping as a tool for self-awareness and team development. These modules can include activities that promote emotional recognition, regulation, and expression. (Kashaka,2025) examines how emotional intelligence makes leaders to mediate clashes, improve staff culture and values, which will create a positive climate through its core skill competence of self-awareness, self-regulation, motivation, empathy, and social skills. The core skills of emotional intelligence such as self-awareness, self-regulation, motivation, empathy, and social skills play as pivotal tools for leaders who lead the group in the organisation to succeed in interpersonal challenges and drive organizational success. The alignment between emotions and transformational leadership, providing the insight that emotionally intelligent leaders are better positioned to admire groups and teams, manage and adopt the change, and cultivate collaborative environments. Practical applications such as the integration of emotional intelligence training into professional development programs, underscoring emotional intelligence as a learnable and required skill for effective leadership.

Facilitating Group Discussions

Group discussions are essential for processing the insights gained from emotional behavior mapping which should aid a way that motivates open ended communication. (Shrivastava,2022) suggested that emotional intelligence and communication are crucial in building professionalism, entrusting the patient's trust, and providing equal care in interprofessional health care teams. With this, it emphasizes the pivotal role of emotional intelligence and communication skills in nurturing professionalism, developing the patient trust, and deploying optimal care within interprofessional health care groups. The researcher developed a 2.5-hour workshop where the study aimed at interprofessional trainees which includes internal medicine residents, medical students and graduate students in clinical pharmacy, physician assistant, and health psychology programs to self-assess, reflect upon, and apply their emotional intelligence and communication skill sets of the student. After the 2.5hours post-workshop evaluations, the research indicated that participants reported widely increased knowledge of effective communication methodology which enhanced comfort in collaborating with other professionals to promote positive team dynamics, and greater preparedness to assume leadership roles within their teams.

Providing Feedback

Providing constructive feedback is crucial for helping team members improve their emotional intelligence and interpersonal skills. The constructive feedback should be specific, behavior-focused, and delivered with empathy. (Wallis,2012) evaluation of a leadership program found that team effectiveness was influenced and impacted by key members holding supervisory place and the current organizational structure, underlying the requirement for careful development and collaborative problem-solving environments. A training program on leadership helped at developing or enhancing healthcare workers retention by fostering collaborative, group or peer approaches within healthcare organizations. Team effectiveness was significantly impacted by the employee engagement and individual commitment of key team members, particularly those in leadership roles. The program underlying transformational leadership practices, which positively impacted group dynamics and shared the valuable insights to improve nurse retention rates.

Encouraging the Self-Reflection

Self-reflection is a key component which helps in mapping the emotional behavior. Team members should be encouraged to reflect their own emotional responses and behaviors, as well as their impact on others. Research indicates that team reflexivity and emotional intelligence significantly influence performance outcomes, and developing the emotional intelligence skills which improves team performance according to (Sinnappan,2024).

Reinforcement of leadership competencies: Empathy, Regulation, and Adaptability

The development of leadership competencies such as empathy, self-regulation, and adaptability is very crucial in today's dynamic organizational environments. These competencies are deeply rooted in emotional intelligence, which has been widely recognized as a critical factor for effective leadership. Emotional analytics is able to measure and analyze the emotional data, which plays a significant role in identifying areas for improvement and enhancing these leadership skills. It explores how emotional analytics can be integrated into training and leadership development programs to reinforce empathy, self-regulation, and adaptability. If emotional analytics demonstrated that employees are undervalued or unsupported, leaders can be trained in order to recognize and address these emotional values more effectively (Almadani, 2024; Raghav & SM, 2024). Mentorship programs can also be arranged for leaders to gain the insights into the emotional experiences of their team members and to cultivate the empathy in leaders (Prummer et al., 2024; Vittou et al., 2024).

Self-regulation is to manage one's own emotions and impulses, is another type of critical leadership competency. Leaders who have high self-regulation are able to maintain their composure under pressure, make rational decisions, and model positive emotional behavior for their team members. (Tariq, 2024) noticed that self-regulation is positively correlated with leadership effectiveness which enables the leaders to manage stress and maintain a positive emotional climate among their team members. Emotional analytics helps the leaders to develop self-regulation by providing them with insights into their own emotional responses. For example, wearable devices and emotional tracking software are able to monitor a leader's emotional state in real-time, providing feedback on moments of high stress or emotional reactivity which can be used to develop customized strategies for improving the self-regulation, such as mindfulness practices or stress management techniques (Koutsioumpa, 2023).

Adaptability is the ability to adjust according to the dynamic circumstances and navigate the uncertainty, is a critical leadership competency in today's fast-paced and ever-changing business environment. Leaders with high adaptability are able to lead their teams through organizational change, respond to unexpected challenges, and capitalize on new opportunities. (Almadani, 2024; Raghav & SM, 2024) demonstrated that adaptability is positively correlated with leadership effectiveness, as it enables leaders to remain resilient and proactive in the face of change. Emotional analytics can help the leaders to develop the adaptability by providing them with insights into their emotional responses to change and uncertainty. For example, emotional analytics can identify patterns of emotional reactivity that may inhibit a leader's ability to adapt to change, such as a tendency to experience anxiety or resistance in the face of uncertainty. This data can then be used to develop the strategies for improve the adaptability, such as cognitive-behavioral techniques or scenario planning exercises (Al-Zu'bi, 2015).

Figure 2. Framework of ELITE model

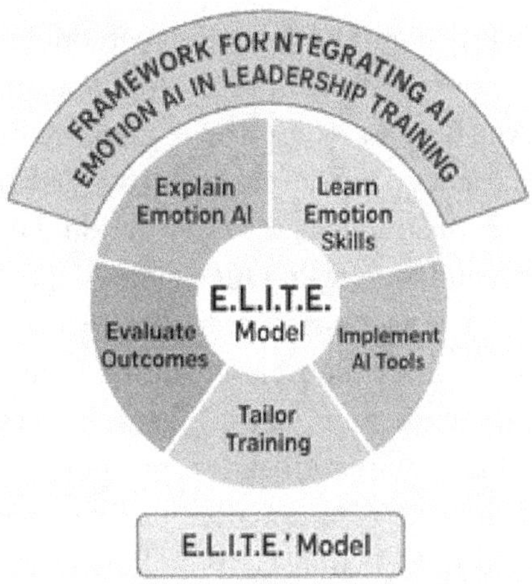

Source: (Mariotti, 2022)

Integrating the E.L.I.T.E. Model into Leadership Training

The E.L.I.T.E. Model— Emotion AI, Learn Emotion Skills, Implement AI Tools, Tailor Training, and Evaluate Outcomes demonstrated by Mariotti & Claudia (2020).

- **Bridging AI and Emotional Intelligence**: Leveraging Emotion AI enhances human-centered leadership by encouraging emotional insight, empathy, and adaptive decision-making.
- **Promoting Ethical and Personalized Training**: Tailoring the programs using real-time emotional data drive which was more engaging and effective learning experiences, while respecting ethical boundaries.
- **Reinforcing Core Leadership Competencies**: Through the emotional behavior mapping and adaptive learning technologies, the model supports the growth of empathy, self-regulation, and adaptability for modern leadership.
- **Supporting Organizational Well-being**: Emotion AI facilitates the emotional awareness at both individual and group levels, promoting the employee mental health and organizational cohesion.

By adopting the E.L.I.T.E. Model organizations are the future-proof of their leadership pipelines, ensuring the leaders are not only technically proficient but also emotionally intelligent and ethically responsible.

AI Ways in Transforming Leadership Practices

Artificial Intelligence is reshaping leadership methodology across numerous dimensions. By leveraging its powerful data-processing capacities, AI enables leaders to make informed, data-driven decisions based on recognised patterns and correlations which supports customised leadership development by offering tailored feedback and assessments, adapting growth strategies to suit individual needs. AI predicts talent management by exploring and identifying high-potential employees and providing valuable insights for effective succession planning (Raisch & Krakowski, 2021). Real-time data evaluation improves communication, particularly during crises, and fosters global collaboration while minimizing biases. By analyzing communication dynamics, AI aids in optimal resource allocation, promotes continuous learning, and enhances emotional intelligence. Additionally, it drives innovation by stimulating creative thinking. Ultimately, AI is transforming how leaders make decisions, approach their roles, and interact with their teams (Jordan & Wade, 2018).

Data-Driven Decision Making

Data-driven decision-making is a key area where Artificial Intelligence is poised to transform leadership practices (Reez, 2020). In today's fast-paced business environment, leaders are frequently overwhelmed by very large amounts of data originating from diverse sources. deriving meaningful insights from this data can be both time-consuming and complicated. AI serves as a powerful tool by streamlining the decision-making process and analyzing data rapidly for identifying trends. However, effectively integrating AI into decision-making need a thoughtful balance between machine-generated insights and human judgment. While AI can offer valuable suggestions which remain the leader's responsibility to interpret and apply insights within the broader organizational environment. Finally, the crucial decisions and evaluations of AI-driven suggestions rely on human experience, strategic thinking, and contextual understanding.

Personalized Leadership Development

Traditionally, leadership development programs succeeded with a one-size-fits-all methodology, offering conventional training essentials to all participants whereas AI is retreating from this model through the customization of leadership development initiatives to enrich each leader's unique profile through data analysis and adaptive learning technologies, AI can tailor content, feedback, and growth strategies to align with specific competencies and aspirations. When combined with mentorship, this AI-driven personalization results in a more comprehensive and effective leadership development experience, nurtures more effective and self-aware leaders (Banyal & Panwar, 2025).

Predictive Talent Management

Artificial Intelligence is significantly transforming how organizations approach talent management by identifying future leaders and to develop their capacity is a vital component of corporate success. AI algorithms can evaluate large volumes of datasets to identify high-potential individuals and to assess their leadership capabilities by creating strategic plans for their development and retention—an approach known as predictive talent management. However, while AI offers data-driven insights, human judgment remains important in interpreting and contextualizing these predictions. Attributes such as empathy, adaptability, and strategic thinking—critical to effective leadership—are complex and cannot be fully captured by algorithms alone. Therefore, a harmonious integration of AI-generated analytics with human intuition and experience is crucial for making informed, nuanced decisions in talent development (Banyal & Panwar, 2025).

Enhanced Communication and Collaboration

Artificial Intelligence is breaking traditional boundaries and revolutionizing communication and collaboration within organizations. By enhancing efficiency and connectivity across teams, departments, and global partners, AI fosters more streamlined and effective interactions. Tools such as AI-powered chatbots and virtual assistants automate routine queries and provide instant access to information, allowing employees and leaders to focus on more strategic tasks. Real-time language translation powered by AI helps overcome linguistic barriers, promoting seamless collaboration among diverse teams and supporting a more inclusive workplace. AI also supports content creation by offering editing suggestions, summarizing lengthy documents, and even generating reports, thereby accelerating collaborative work and enhancing the quality of team contributions. Human connection remains crucial for building relationships, resolving conflicts, and navigating complex situations that require emotional intelligence and critical thinking (Patil, 2024).

Ethical and Bias Mitigation

AI empowers leaders to derive valuable insights from vast datasets, enabling informed, fact-based decision-making over intuition-driven approaches. Through real-time data analysis and adaptive learning paths, AI enhances individualized leadership development by identifying each leader's strengths and areas for growth. Leaders must be equipped with ethical literacy and legal awareness to navigate the complex intersection of AI and leadership. By integrating ethical considerations with technological innovation, organizations can foster a more effective, equitable, and inclusive leadership paradigm—one that leverages AI's capabilities while safeguarding human values (O'neil, 2017).

Benefits of Emotion AI in Employee Well-Being

The integration of Emotion AI in the workplace offers several benefits for employee well-being. It can help the organizations monitor and manage the employee stress levels by detecting very early signs of burnout and providing the timely interventions. For example, AI-powered chatbots and virtual assistants can offer personalized wellness programs and real-time stress management tools, helping the employees to maintain a healthy work-life balance (Jangid, 2024).

Emotion AI can enhance employee engagement by creating a more supportive and inclusive work environment. By analyzing employee sentiments and emotional states, organizations are able to identify areas where employees may need the additional support, such as mental health resources or professional development opportunities. This can lead to improved job satisfaction and reduced turnover rates (Herlina & Iskandar, 2025).

Emotion AI can facilitate communication and collaboration within teams. By providing valuable insights into the team dynamics and emotional states, Emotion AI can help the managers and HR professionals by addressing conflicts and improving interpersonal relationships. This can lead to a more cohesive and productive working environment (Hammad, 2024).

Figure 3. Emotion AI in Employee Well-Being

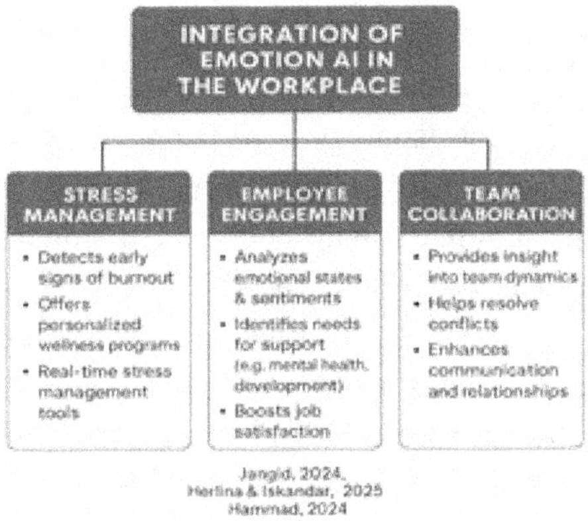

Source: (Jangid, 2024; Herlina & Iskandar, 2025; Hammad, 2024).

Ethical Challenges

Integrating AI into leadership brings remarkable challenges that demand thoughtful attention. A major issue is overreliance on AI-generated insights, which may lead the leaders to undervalue their own judgment and dilute interpersonal connections which are the essential components of effective leadership. Furthermore, the opaque nature of AI decision-making can balance the accountability and trust. Ensuring transparency, ethical guidance, and human oversight is crucial to maintain the integrity in leadership practices. Ethical concerns are particularly pressing which has been highly noticed and argued in Stahl et al. (2022) where the research found that while organizations are aware of AI ethics debates, they often adopt only limited mitigation strategies. Similarly, Bankins and Formosa (2023) underlying how AI can undermine individual autonomy, pressing the need for ethical standards that protect human control. To reduce unfair outcomes, organizations must actively address algorithmic bias through diverse training datasets and regular audits (Corvite et al., 2023). Piispanen and Rousi (2024) highlighted the ethical considerations of Emotion AI in supporting employee well-being, while Delina et al. (n.d.) suggested supplementing AI tools with human oversight to ensure reliability. Ultimately, balancing technological advancement with ethical leadership is essential for building a fair, transparent, and human-centered approach to AI-driven leadership.

Future Directions

The future of Emotion AI in training and development is promising, with several advancements on the horizon. The one area which needs development is the integration of multimodal data sources, like facial expressions, speech patterns, and physiological signals, in order to understand employee emotions which leads to more accurate and personalized interventions, and enhancing the effectiveness of training and development programs (Yadav et al., 2025).

One more area of focus we need to consider is the ethical and responsible implementation of Emotion AI among the employees. As organizations increasingly adopt this technology, there is a need for frameworks and guidelines too in order to ensure its ethical use. By addressing concerns which are related to privacy, bias, and transparency, which encourages the trust between employees and the organizations. By prioritizing the ethical considerations, organizations can maximize the benefits of Emotion AI while minimizing the potential risks (Roemmich, 2023). Finally, the integration of Emotion AI with other emerging technologies, like machine learning and the Internet of Things (IoT), offers exciting possibilities for employee well-being like This can create a more supportive and adaptive work environment, which leads to improved mental health and productivity in the workplace (Rosca & Stancu, 2024).

CONCLUSION

The integration of emotion-centric analytics and adaptive AI systems which has the great potential to enhance emotional intelligence, encourage more empathetic and adaptive leadership, and create emotionally responsive working environments. Through personalized learning experiences, real-time emotional feedback, and emotionally aware AI systems, organizations can significantly improve leadership effectiveness, team dynamics, and employee engagement. The ability to map the emotional behaviors and integrate emotional data into decision-making processes positions Emotion AI as a strategic asset in both leadership development and human resource management. issues related to privacy, algorithmic bias, and over-reliance on AI. It must be addressed to maintain trust and fairness and consider the responsible deployment which demands transparent policies, inclusive data practices, and a balance between AI capabilities and human judgment. Looking forward, the future of Emotion AI will be characterized by deeper integration with emerging technologies like IoT and virtual reality, as well as more robust ethical frameworks. If it is implemented in such a way, Emotion AI can lead to more emotionally intelligent organizations that values well-being, adaptability, and inclusive leadership of employees which will ultimately cultivate the environments where both people and technology can thrive their best.

REFERENCES

Al-Zu'bi, H. A. (2015). The impact of emotional intelligence on leadership competencies development of employees. *International Review of Management and Business Research*, *4*(1), 96.

Ali, Z. A. (2022). Self-Directed Leadership Development with Adaptive Learning 360-Feedback Platform. *ProQuest, LLC*. Advance online publication. DOI: 10.12794/metadc1986948

Almadani, N. (2024). Emotional Intelligence: The Development of Emotional Intelligence in Leadership. In *Emotionally Intelligent Methods for Meaningful Leadership* (pp. 77–104). IGI Global Scientific Publishing., DOI: 10.4018/979-8-3693-7372-9.ch004

Ameer, I., Bölücü, N., Siddiqui, M., Can, B., Sidorov, G., & Gelbukh, A. (2022). Multi-label emotion classification in texts using transfer learning. *Expert Systems with Applications*, *213*, 118534. DOI: 10.1016/j.eswa.2022.118534

Ameer, I., Bölücü, N., Sidorov, G., & Can, B. (2023). Emotion Classification in Texts Over Graph Neural Networks: Semantic Representation is Better Than Syntactic. *IEEE Access : Practical Innovations, Open Solutions*, *11*, 56921–56934. DOI: 10.1109/ACCESS.2023.3281544

Assunção, G., Patrão, B., Castelo-Branco, M., & Menezes, P. (2022). An overview of emotion in artificial intelligence. *IEEE Transactions on Artificial Intelligence*, *3*(6), 867–886. DOI: 10.1109/TAI.2022.3159614

Attamimi, R., Abidin, A., & Amiruddin, A. (2024, November). INTEGRATING ARTIFICIAL INTELLIGENCE INTO SUCCESSION PLANNING AND LEADERSHIP DEVELOPMENT IN HIGHER EDUCATION. *In International Conference of Business and Social Sciences* (pp. 209-228). DOI: 10.24034/icobuss.v4i1.496

Bagozzi, R., Brady, M., & Huang, M. (2022). AI Service and Emotion. *Journal of Service Research*, *25*(4), 499–504. DOI: 10.1177/10946705221118579

Bankins, S., & Formosa, P. (2023). The Ethical Implications of Artificial Intelligence (AI) For Meaningful Work. *Journal of Business Ethics*, *185*(4), 725–740. DOI: 10.1007/s10551-023-05339-7

Banyal, K., & Panwar, A. (2025). The role of artificial intelligence in leadership development. *International Journal of Research Publication and Reviews*, *6*(4), 5779–5782. DOI: 10.48175/IJRPR-24852

Baruah, A., Shaikh, M., Kumar, R. M., Shaikh, I. A. K., & Thomas, S. N. (2024, April). Artificial Intelligence Influence on Leadership Styles in Human Resource Management for Employee Engagement. *In 2024 Ninth International Conference on Science Technology Engineering and Mathematics (ICONSTEM)* (pp. 1-5). IEEE. https://doi.org/1109/ICONSTEM60960.2024.10568819

Behn, O., Leyer, M., & Iren, D. (2024). Employees' acceptance of AI-based emotion analytics from speech on a group level in virtual meetings. *Technology in Society, 76*, 102466. Advance online publication. DOI: 10.1016/j.techsoc.2024.102466

Buckingham, M. (2012). Leadership development in the age of the algorithm. *Harvard Business Review, 90*(6), 86–92. https://pubmed.ncbi.nlm.nih.gov/22741421/ PMID: 22741421

Calvo, R. A., D'Mello, S., Gratch, J. M., & Kappas, A. (Eds.). (2015). *The Oxford handbook of affective computing*. Oxford University Press. DOI: 10.1093/oxfordhb/9780199942237.001.0001

Cambria, E. (2016). Affective Computing and Sentiment Analysis. *IEEE Intelligent Systems, 31*(2), 102–107. DOI: 10.1109/MIS.2016.31

Chattu, V. K. (2021). A review of artificial intelligence, big data, and blockchain technology applications in medicine and global health. *Big Data and Cognitive Computing, 5*(3), 41. DOI: 10.3390/bdcc5030041

Chen, Z. (2022). Artificial Intelligence-Virtual Trainer: Innovative Didactics Aimed at Personalized Training Needs. *Journal of the Knowledge Economy,* 1 - 19. .DOI: 10.1007/s13132-022-00985-0

Chiekczic, N., Obiki-Osafiele, A., & Agu, E. (2024). Preparing the workforce for AI technologies through training and professional development for future readiness. World. *Journal of Engineering and Technology Research, 3*(1), 001–018. Advance online publication. DOI: 10.53346/wjetr.2024.3.1.0050

Chipman, P., D'Mello, S. K., Gholson, B., Graesser, A. C., McDaniel, B., & Witherspoon, A. (2006). Detection of Emotions during Learning with AutoTutor. 28(28). https://escholarship.org/content/qt2tb300fm/qt2tb300fm.pdf?t=op2jup

Chopade, P., Edwards, D., Khan, S. M., Andrade, A., & Pu, S. (2019, November). CPSX: using AI-machine learning for mapping human-human interaction and measurement of CPS teamwork skills. *In 2019 IEEE International Symposium on Technologies for Homeland Security (HST)* (pp. 1-6). IEEE. DOI: 10.1109/HST47167.2019.9032906

Corvite, S., Roemmich, K., Rosenberg, T. I., & Andalibi, N. (2023). Data subjects' perspectives on emotion artificial intelligence use in the workplace: *A relational ethics lens. Proceedings of the ACM on Human-Computer Interaction,* 7(CSCW1), 1-38. DOI: 10.1145/3579600

Craig, S., D'Mello, S., Gholson, B., Witherspoon, A., Sullins, J., & Graesser, A. (2004). Emotions during learning: The first steps toward an affect sensitive intelligent tutoring system. In eLearn: World Conference on EdTech (pp. 264-268). A*ssociation for the Advancement of Computing in Education (AACE).* https://www.learntechlib.org/primary/p/11300/

Deepthi, P., Shaikh, M., Nargunde, A. S., Faldu, R., & Goli, G. (2024, April). Deep learning-enabled human resource analytics in predicting employee performance. In 2024 Ninth International Conference on Science Technology Engineering and Mathematics (ICONSTEM) (pp. 1-5). *IEEE.https://* DOI: 10.1109/ICONSTEM60960.2024.10568716

Delina, G., Bayissa, B., Krishnaraj, R., Sathyamoorthi, V., & Inayath Ahamed, S. B. (n.d.). Emotion AI as a HR Tool for Promoting Workplace Well-Being: Examining the Practical and Ethical Challenges using Efficient net. https://doi.org/DOI: 10.5171/2024.4328924

Devlin, J., Chang, M. W., Lee, K., & Toutanova, K. (2019). BERT: Pre-training of deep bidirectional transformers for language understanding. In *Proceedings of the 2019 Conference of the North American Chapter of the Association for Computational Linguistics: Human Language Technologies* (Vol. 1, pp. 4171–4186). DOI: 10.18653/v1/N19-1423

Dwivedi, D. (2025). Emotional Intelligence and Artificial Intelligence Integration Strategies for Leadership Excellence. *Advances in Research, 26*(1), 84–94. DOI: 10.9734/air/2025/v26i11235

Ekman, P., & Friesen, W. V. (1978). *Facial Action Coding System: A Technique for the Measurement of Facial Movement.* Consulting Psychologists Press., https://psycnet.apa.org/doi/10.1037/t27734-000

Elazab, M. (2024). AI-driven personalized learning. *International Journal of Internet Education, 22*(3), 6–19. DOI: 10.21608/ijie.2024.350579

Eyben, F., Wöllmer, M., & Schuller, B. (2013). Recent developments in openSMILE, the Munich open-source multimedia feature extractor. I*n Proceedings of the 21st ACM international conference on Multimedia* (pp. 835–838). DOI: 10.1145/2502081.2502224

Filice, L., & Weese, W. J. (2024). Developing Emotional Intelligence. *Encyclopedia*, *4*(1), 583–599. DOI: 10.3390/encyclopedia4010037

Furnham, A., & Taylor, N. (2020). The relationship between emotional intelligence and occupational personality scales in senior management. *Personality and Individual Differences*, *154*, 109647. DOI: 10.1016/j.paid.2019.109647

Ghotbi, N. (2022). The Ethics of Emotional Artificial Intelligence: A Mixed Method Analysis. *Asian Bioethics Review*, *15*(4), 417–430. DOI: 10.1007/s41649-022-00237-y PMID: 37808444

Graesser, A. C., & D'Mello, S. (2012). Emotions during the learning of difficult material. In *Psychology of learning and motivation* (Vol. 57, pp. 183–225). Academic Press., DOI: 10.1016/B978-0-12-394293-7.00005-4

Granirer, D. (2018). Emotional intelligence: Get with it! *International Journal of Mental Health*, *47*(1), 90–91. DOI: 10.1080/00207411.2018.1425050

Hammad, L. (2024). *Emotion AI in the workplace: Enhancing collaboration and conflict resolution*. FutureWork Press.

Han, E., Yin, D., & Zhang, H. (2022). Bots with Feelings: Should AI Agents Express Positive Emotion in Customer Service? *Information Systems Research*, *34*(3), 1296–1311. DOI: 10.1287/isre.2022.1179

Henkel, A. P., Bromuri, S., Iren, D., & Urovi, V. (2020). Half human, half machine - augmenting service employees with AI for interpersonal emotion regulation. *Journal of Service Management*, *31*(2), 247–265. DOI: 10.1108/JOSM-05-2019-0160

Herlina, S., & Iskandar, R. (2025). *Enhancing workplace well-being through emotional intelligence analytics*. HumanTech Insights.

Hodgkinson, G. P., Sund, K. J., & Galavan, R. J. (2017). Exploring methods in managerial and organizational cognition: Advances, controversies, and contributions. In *Methodological challenges and advances in managerial and organizational cognition* (pp. 1–22). Emerald Publishing Limited., DOI: 10.1108/S2397-52102017002

Holmes, W., Bialik, M., & Fadel, C. (2019). *Artificial intelligence in education promises and implications for teaching and learning*. Center for Curriculum Redesign.https://discovery.ucl.ac.uk/id/eprint/10139722

Hutto, C. J., & Gilbert, E. (2014). VADER: A parsimonious rule-based model for sentiment analysis of social media text. *In Proceedings of the International AAAI Conference on Web and Social Media* (Vol. 8, No. 1, pp. 216–225). https://ojs.aaai.org/index.php/ICWSM/article/view/14550

Hwang, J. (2024). The role of emotional intelligence in team dynamics. *International Journal of Science and Research Archive*. DOI: 10.30574/ijsra.2024.13.2.1875

Jangid, A. (2024). AI AND EMPLOYEE WELLBEING: HOW ARTIFICIAL INTELLIGENCE CAN MONITOR AND IMPROVE MENTAL HEALTH IN THE WORKPLACE. *International Journal of Advanced Research, 12*(10), 743–764. DOI: 10.21474/IJAR01/19693

Jordan, J., & Wade, M. (2018). As AI makes more decisions, the nature of leadership will change. *HR Future, 2018*(4), 10–11.

Kapoor, A., & Verma, V. (2024). EMOTION AI: UNDERSTANDING EMOTIONS THROUGH ARTIFICIAL INTELLIGENCE. *International Journal of Engineering Science and Humanities*. .DOI: 10.62904/0vcbvb24

Kashaka, N. D. (2025). Exploring the role of emotional intelligence in educational leadership. *Research Invention Journal of Current Issues in Arts and Management, 4*(2), 12–15. DOI: 10.59298/RIJCIAM/2025/421215

Koutsioumpa, E. (2023). Development of Emotional Intelligence and Leadership aspects applied in Health Professionals. *A Scoping Review. Technium BioChemMed, 6*, 22–36. DOI: 10.47577/biochemmed.v6i.9533

Kumar, R., Kumar, S., & Kumar, P. (2025). A Conceptual Exploration for Harnessing Emotional Intelligence for Transformational Team Leadership. *International Journal of Research and Review in Applied Science, Humanities, and Technology, 9-13*, 9–13. Advance online publication. DOI: 10.71143/7cmhfd69

Kusal, S., Patil, S., Choudrie, J., Kotecha, K., Vora, D., & Pappas, I. (2023). A systematic review of applications of natural language processing and future challenges with special emphasis in text-based emotion detection. *Artificial Intelligence Review, 56*(12), 15129–15215. DOI: 10.1007/s10462-023-10509-0

Li, S., & Deng, W. (2020). Deep facial expression recognition: A survey. *IEEE Transactions on Circuits and Systems for Video Technology, 30*(10), 3219–3235. DOI: 10.1109/TCSVT.2019.2913898

Li, Y., Jiang, Y., Tian, D., Hu, L., Lu, H., & Yuan, Z. (2019). AI-Enabled Emotion Communication. *IEEE Network, 33*(6), 15–21. DOI: 10.1109/MNET.001.1900070

Lirio, P., & Plusquellec, P. (2023). Affective computing technology for fostering an emotionally healthy workplace. *Strategic HR Review, 22*(4), 121–125. Advance online publication. DOI: 10.1108/SHR-04-2023-0024

Loscalzo, S., Lockman, J., Spector, N., & Boyer, D. (2022). Variations in Demonstrated Emotional Intelligence: Trainee to Experienced Faculty Member*. *Pediatric Critical Care Medicine*, *23*(8), 646–650. DOI: 10.1097/PCC.0000000000002974 PMID: 36165938

Mamina, R., & Piraynen, E. (2023). Emotional Artificial Intelligence as a Tool for Human-Machine Interaction. *Discourse (Berkeley, Calif.)*, *9*(2), 35–51. Advance online publication. DOI: 10.32603/2412-8562-2023-9-2-35-51

Mariotti, C. (2022). Elite theory. In *The Palgrave Encyclopedia of Interest Groups, Lobbying and Public Affairs* (pp. 427–432). Springer International Publishing.

Mehler, M., Balint, E. M., Gralla, M., Pößnecker, T., Gast, M. J., Hölzer, M., Koesters, M., & Gündel, H. (2024). Training emotional competencies at the workplace: A systematic review and metaanalysis. *BMC Psychology*, *12*(1), 718. Advance online publication. DOI: 10.1186/s40359-024-02198-3 PMID: 39627880

Monteith, S., Glenn, T., Geddes, J., Whybrow, P., & Bauer, M. (2022). Commercial Use of Emotion Artificial Intelligence (AI): Implications for Psychiatry. *Current Psychiatry Reports*, *24*(3), 1–9. DOI: 10.1007/s11920-022-01330-7 PMID: 35212918

Narimisaei, J., Naeim, M., Imannezhad, S., Samian, P., & Sobhani, M. (2024). Exploring emotional intelligence in artificial intelligence systems: A comprehensive analysis of emotion recognition and response mechanisms. *Annals of Medicine and Surgery (London)*, *86*(8), 4657–4663. DOI: 10.1097/MS9.0000000000002315 PMID: 39118764

Norman, E., & Pahlawati, E. (2024). Pengembangan kepemimpinan yang adaptif dan fleksibel: Meningkatkan ketahanan organisasi di era transformasi digital. *MES Management Journal*, *3*(1), 298–305. DOI: 10.56709/mesman.v3i1.314

O'neil, C. (2017). *Weapons of math destruction: How big data increases inequality and threatens democracy*. Crown.

Ou, S. (2024). *Transforming Education: The Evolving Role of Artificial Intelligence in The Students Academic Performance*. International Journal of Education and Humanities., DOI: 10.54097/cc1x7r95

Patel, D., & Alismail, A. (2024). Relationship between cognitive load theory, intrinsic motivation and emotions in healthcare professions education: A perspective on the missing link. *Advances in Medical Education and Practice*, *15*, 57–62. DOI: 10.2147/AMEP.S441405 PMID: 38264765

Patil, D. (2024). Human-Artificial Intelligence Collaboration In The Modern Workplace: Maximizing Productivity And Transforming Job Roles. *Available at SSRN* 5057414.https://dx.doi.org/DOI: 10.2139/ssrn.5057414

Perry, M., Creavey, K., Arthur, E., Humer, J., Lundgren, P., & Rivera, I. (2020). Cultivating emotional intelligence in child welfare professionals: A systematic scoping review. *Child Abuse & Neglect, 104438*, 104438. Advance online publication. DOI: 10.1016/j.chiabu.2020.104438 PMID: 32164944

Picard, R. W. (1997). A ective. *Computing*.

Piispanen, J. R., & Rousi, R. (2024, November). Emotion AI in Workplace Environments: A Case Study. *In International Conference on Software Business (pp. 142-148). Cham:* Springer Nature Switzerland. DOI: 10.48550/arxiv.2412.09251

Plass, J. L., & Kalyuga, S. (2019). Four ways of considering emotion in cognitive load theory. *Educational Psychology Review*, *31*(2), 339–359. DOI: 10.1007/s10648-019-09473-5

Poria, S., Cambria, E., Bajpai, R., & Hussain, A. (2017). A review of affective computing: From unimodal analysis to multimodal fusion. *Information Fusion*, *37*, 98–125. DOI: 10.1016/j.inffus.2017.02.003

Poria, S., Majumder, N., Mihalcea, R., & Hovy, E. (2019). Emotion Recognition in Conversation: Research Challenges, Datasets, and Recent Advances. *IEEE Access : Practical Innovations, Open Solutions*, *7*, 100943–100953. DOI: 10.1109/ACCESS.2019.2929050

Portillo, P. V. (2025). The transformative role of artificial intelligence in leadership and management development: An academic insight. *Development and Learning in Organizations*. Advance online publication. DOI: 10.1108/DLO-10-2024-0301

Prummer, K., Human-Vogel, S., Graham, M. A., & Pittich, D. (2024, June). The role of mentoring in developing leaders' emotional intelligence: exploring mentoring types, emotional intelligence, organizational factors, and gender. *In Frontiers in Education* (Vol. 9, p. 1393660). Frontiers Media SA. DOI: 10.3389/feduc.2024.1393660

Raghav, S. V., & SM, P. (. (2024). EMOTIONAL INTELLIGENCE IN LEADERSHIP: A CROSS-CULTURAL ANALYSIS OF EMPLOYEE ENGAGEMENT AND RETENTION. ShodhKosh. *Journal of Visual and Performing Arts*, *5*(7), 338–349. DOI: 10.29121/shodhkosh.v5.i7.2024.2772

Raghvendra, K. (2024). Emotional Intelligence and Leadership Effectiveness: Navigating Decision - Making, Team Dynamics, and Organizational Success. *International Journal of Science and Research (Raipur, India)*, *13*(9), 1411–1416. DOI: 10.21275/SR24921211055

Raisch, S., & Krakowski, S. (2021). Artificial intelligence and management: The automation–augmentation paradox. *Academy of Management Review*, *46*(1), 192–210. DOI: 10.5465/amr.2018.0072

Reez, N. (2020). Foresight-based leadership. Decision-making in a growing AI environment. In *International Security Management: New Solutions to Complexity* (pp. 323–341). Springer International Publishing., DOI: 10.1007/978-3-030-42523-4_22

Rickard, M., Ackermann, D., Schnitzler, M., & Kozlowski, D. (2024). Emotional Intelligence as a Component of Surgical Coaching: A Scoping Review.. *Journal of surgical education,* 82 1, 103316 . .DOI: 10.1016/j.jsurg.2024.103316

Roemmich, K., Schaub, F., & Andalibi, N. (2023, April). Emotion AI at work: Implications for workplace surveillance, emotional labor, and emotional privacy. *In Proceedings of the 2023 CHI Conference on Human Factors in Computing Systems* (pp. 1-20). DOI: 10.1145/3544548.3580950

Rosca, C. M., & Stancu, A. (2024). Fusing Machine Learning and AI to Create a Framework for Employee Well-Being in the Era of Industry 5.0. *Applied Sciences* (2076-3417), 14(23). DOI: 10.3390/app142310835

Rukadikar, A., & Khandelwal, K. (2024). Leadership development through self-upskilling: Role of generative artificial intelligence. *Development and Learning in Organizations*, *38*(4), 27–30. DOI: 10.1108/DLO-01-2024-0005

Sánchez-Núñez, M., Patti, J., & Holzer, A. (2015). Effectiveness of a Leadership Development Program that Incorporates Social and Emotional Intelligence for Aspiring School Leaders., 1, 65-84. .DOI: 10.5296/jei.v1i1.7443

Sano, A., & Picard, R. W. (2013). Stress recognition using wearable sensors and mobile phones. In *2013 Humaine Association Conference on Affective Computing and Intelligent Interaction* (pp. 671–676). IEEE. DOI: 10.1109/ACII.2013.117

Schuller, B., Steidl, S., & Batliner, A.. (2011). Recognising realistic emotions and affect in speech: State of the art and lessons learnt from the first challenge. *Speech Communication*, *53*(9-10), 1062–1087. DOI: 10.1016/j.specom.2011.01.011

Sharma, R., Dhanta, R., & Solomon, D. D. (2023). The Role of Emotional Intelligence in Effective Leadership and Decision-Making in Business Management. In Bhardwaj, B., Sharma, D., & Dhiman, M. (Eds.), *AI and Emotional Intelligence for Modern Business Management* (pp. 98–112). IGI Global Scientific Publishing., DOI: 10.4018/979-8-3693-0418-1.ch007

Shrivastava, S., Martinez, J., Coletti, D. J., & Fornari, A. (2022). Interprofessional leadership development: Role of emotional intelligence and communication skills training. *MedEdPORTAL: the Journal of Teaching and Learning Resources, 18*, 11247. DOI: 10.15766/mep_2374-8265.11247 PMID: 35634034

Sinnappan, L. P., Prabhakaran, S. B., Karunakaran, R., Chinnasamy, A. K., Gopal, R., Rajan, S., & Purath, R. A. (2024). Flexing the emotional muscle: Investigating how team reflexibility shapes performance via emotional intelligence. *International Journal of Organizational Psychology, 12*(3), 45–58. DOI: 10.59429/esp.v9i8.2869

Sposato, M. (2024). Leadership training and development in the age of artificial intelligence. *Development and Learning in Organizations, 38*(4), 4–7. DOI: 10.1108/DLO-12-2023-0256

Stahl, B. C., Antoniou, J., Ryan, M., Macnish, K., & Jiya, T. (2022). Organisational responses to the ethical issues of artificial intelligence. *AI & Society, 37*(1), 23–37. DOI: 10.1007/s00146-021-01148-6

Tariq, M. U. (2025). Harnessing Emotional Intelligence for Strategic Leadership: A Contemporary Approach. In Emotionally Intelligent Methods for Meaningful Leadership (pp. 197-222). *IGI Global Scientific Publishing*. DOI: 10.4018/979-8-3693-7372-9.ch009

Valaboju, V. (2024). *AI-Driven Compliance Training in Finance and Healthcare: A Paradigm Shift in Regulatory Adherence*. International Journal For Multidisciplinary Research., DOI: 10.36948/ijfmr.2024.v06i06.30180

Vasilev, I. (2024). *Adapting the Future VET Curriculum in Response to Emerging Challenges: A Model for Evaluating the Impact of AI Integration in VET for Armed Conflicts and Warfare*. International Journal of Current Science Research and Review., DOI: 10.47191/ijcsrr/V7-i11-18

Vistorte, A., Deroncele-Acosta, A., Ayala, J., Barrasa, A., López-Granero, C., & Martí-González, M. (2024). Integrating artificial intelligence to assess emotions in learning environments: A systematic literature review. *Frontiers in Psychology, 15*, 1387089. Advance online publication. DOI: 10.3389/fpsyg.2024.1387089 PMID: 38966729

Vittou, F., Salamani, E., Kefis, V., & Rossidis, I. (2024). Emotional Intelligence and Its Role in the Development of Leadership Characteristics of Managers. In Organizational Behavior and Human Resource Management for Complex Work Environments (pp. 204-220). *IGI Global*. DOI: 10.4018/979-8-3693-3466-9.ch011

Wallis, A. D., & Kennedy, K. I. (2013). Leadership training to improve nurse retention. *Journal of Nursing Management*, *21*(4), 624–632. DOI: 10.1111/j.1365-2834.2012.01443.x PMID: 23410240

Yadav, G., Bokhari, M. U., Alzahrani, S., Alam, S., & Shuaib, M. (2025). Emotion-Aware Ensemble Learning (EAEL): Revolutionizing Mental Health Diagnosis of Corporate Professionals via Intelligent Integration of Multi-modal Data Sources and Ensemble Techniques. *IEEE Access : Practical Innovations, Open Solutions*, *1*, 11494–11516. Advance online publication. DOI: 10.1109/ACCESS.2025.3529032

Zadeh, A., Liang, P. P., Poria, S., Cambria, E., & Morency, L. P. (2018). Multimodal language analysis in the wild: CMU-MOSEI dataset and interpretable dynamic fusion graph. In *Proceedings of the 56th Annual Meeting of the Association for Computational Linguistics* (Vol. 1, pp. 2236–2246). DOI: 10.18653/v1/P18-1208

Zhao, G., Li, Y., & Xu, Q. (2022). *From Emotion AI to Cognitive AI.* International Journal of Network Dynamics and Intelligence., DOI: 10.53941/ijndi0101006

KEY TERMS AND DEFINITIONS

Emotion AI: Emotion AI is also known as affective computing, also a part of AI which focuses on creating systems that can recognize, interpret, and respond to human emotions. It supports techniques like machine learning, natural language processing, and to analyze the various cues like facial expressions, voice tone, and to understand different emotional states.

Affective Computing: Affective computing explores how to make the machines recognize, interpret, process, and be able to simulate human emotions. It's an interdisciplinary area which combines computer science, psychology, and cognitive science to create more intuitive and human-like interactions between humans and computers. It also understands and responds to emotions, aims to improve the human-machine interaction

Facial Recognition: Facial recognition is a technology that identifies the individuals in images or videos by analyzing their facial features. It use the computer vision and artificial intelligence to map a person's face and compare it with a exisiting database of the known faces.By employing this method helps us to verify a person's identity them within an image or video.

Human-Computer Interaction: Human-Computer Interaction is an interdisciplinary field that focuses on the study, design, implementation, and evaluation of the interactions between human users and computer systems which involves in understanding how humans can interact with technology to design the systems that are user-friendly.

Ethical AI: Ethical AI is the development and deployment of AI systems that prioritize fairness, transparency, accountability, and ensures the respect for human values. The AI is used responsibly and safely by mitigating potential risks and preventing harm.It goes beyond legal requirements and emphasizing fundamental human values.

Machine Learning: Machine learning is a field of artificial intelligence that focuses on enabling systems to learn and improve the data without being explicitly programmed. It also involves developing algorithms that can analyze data, identify the patterns, and make the predictions or decisions.

Chapter 16
Emotion AI as a Catalyst for Conflict Resolution:
Enhancing Emotional Intelligence and Fairness in the Modern Workplace

Yamijala Suryanarayana Murthy
https://orcid.org/0000-0002-9561-5395
Vardhaman College Engineering, India

Rohit Bansal
https://orcid.org/0000-0001-7072-5005
Rockford College, Australia

Nishita Pruthi
https://orcid.org/0000-0002-6094-0972
Asian School of Business, India

K. Pardha Sai
https://orcid.org/0009-0001-6692-3022
Aditya University, India

ABSTRACT

The modern workplace is increasingly influenced by emotional dynamics, where unresolved conflicts can hinder team cohesion and productivity. This study examines the role of Emotion AI—technologies that detect and interpret human emotions—in enhancing conflict resolution. By integrating tools like sentiment analysis, facial recognition, and voice modulation, Emotion AI uncovers hidden tensions and enables timely interventions. The research highlights how Emotion AI fosters emotional in-

DOI: 10.4018/979-8-3373-3658-9.ch016

telligence, psychological safety, and fairness by promoting empathetic and inclusive resolution processes. It also supports employee training in emotional regulation and awareness. Employing a descriptive approach organizational case studies, the study offers practical insights into how Emotion AI bridges the gap between emotional understanding and conflict management. It calls for ethical implementation that emphasizes transparency, privacy, and trust, demonstrating how responsibly deployed Emotion AI can support emotionally intelligent and fair workplace cultures in the era of digital transformation.

INTRODUCTION

The evolving nature of modern workplaces, characterized by hybrid models, multicultural teams, and digital communication, has made managing interpersonal conflict more complex than ever before. Conflict, when not managed effectively, can deteriorate team cohesion, reduce productivity, and impair employee well-being (Lee & Jeong, 2021). While traditional conflict resolution strategies—such as mediation or human-led interventions—still play a role, they often lack immediacy and fail to recognize the emotional undercurrents that escalate workplace disagreements. This shift necessitates new tools and approaches that not only resolve conflict but also foster an emotionally intelligent work culture responsive to real-time emotional cues (Nguyen et al., 2022).

Emotion AI, an emerging application of artificial intelligence, offers a transformative solution by capturing and analyzing emotional data through facial expressions, voice tones, physiological signals, and textual inputs. As organizations increasingly adopt intelligent systems to enhance decision-making, Emotion AI is gaining attention for its potential to mitigate interpersonal friction and enhance emotional awareness (Sharma & Rao, 2023). By identifying signs of emotional distress or miscommunication early, Emotion AI enables timely, unbiased interventions that can prevent conflicts from escalating, thus fostering psychological safety and inclusion in the workplace (Chen et al., 2021).

Furthermore, Emotion AI can serve as a catalyst for cultivating emotional intelligence (EI), a crucial competency in diverse and fast-paced environments. Emotional intelligence—defined by self-awareness, empathy, and emotional regulation—has been linked to better conflict resolution outcomes, stronger leadership, and improved team dynamics (Bose & Kumar, 2020). Emotion AI tools can provide feedback and insights that support the development of these competencies among employees and managers, thereby integrating emotional intelligence into the fabric of organizational culture (Lim & Tan, 2024). However, its implementation must be guided by ethical considerations, ensuring transparency, data privacy, and trust.

Despite its potential, the application of Emotion AI in conflict resolution remains underexplored, particularly in empirical workplace studies. While advancements in affective computing and human-computer interaction have demonstrated technical feasibility, there is limited understanding of how these systems impact conflict resolution dynamics and perceptions of fairness among employees (Zhou et al., 2023). Moreover, concerns about algorithmic bias and emotional surveillance raise critical questions about the responsible use of AI in emotionally sensitive contexts. These gaps highlight the need for rigorous investigation into the practical, psychological, and ethical implications of integrating Emotion AI into organizational conflict management practices.

This study aims to bridge that gap by examining the role of Emotion AI in mediating workplace conflict, enhancing emotional intelligence, and promoting fairness in organizational decision-making. Through a combination of empirical data, case analysis, and employee perception studies, this research will evaluate how Emotion AI can be ethically leveraged to create emotionally intelligent and just workplace environments. Ultimately, this study contributes to the discourse on digital transformation in human resource management and the future of conflict resolution in AI-augmented workspaces.

Impact of Emotional Intelligence Theory (Goleman, 1995) on Emotion AI

Emotional Intelligence Theory, as proposed by Daniel Goleman (1995), has profoundly shaped the development and application of Emotion AI. Goleman conceptualized emotional intelligence (EI) as a composite of self-awareness, self-regulation, motivation, empathy, and social skills—attributes essential to human interaction and leadership. Emotion AI systems, inspired by these constructs, aim to replicate and augment the human ability to perceive and respond to emotions through the analysis of biometric and behavioral data. For instance, by recognizing facial micro-expressions or voice modulations, Emotion AI tools seek to assess an individual's emotional state, enabling machines to interact in ways that are contextually appropriate and emotionally attuned. This technological emulation of human EI serves to enhance digital communication, user experience, and human-machine interaction. However, the ethical integration of EI principles into AI systems is crucial. Goleman's model highlights the importance of empathy and social awareness—traits that machines must simulate without violating human autonomy or privacy. In the workplace, Emotion AI tools powered by EI theory can detect early signs of emotional distress or burnout, enabling HR teams to intervene proactively. This capability aligns with Goleman's emphasis on managing emotions to facilitate better outcomes, particularly in high-stress environments. By embedding

EI constructs into algorithms, Emotion AI not only advances affective computing but also transforms how organizations support emotional well-being. Nevertheless, the success of such integration depends on grounding AI tools in genuine psychological insights and ensuring they are deployed in transparent, non-intrusive ways. Thus, Emotional Intelligence Theory remains a foundational influence on Emotion AI, enabling machines to become more emotionally literate and supportive tools in human-centric settings.

Impact of Affective Computing Theory (Picard, 1997) on Conflict Resolution

Rosalind Picard's (1997) Affective Computing Theory revolutionized the intersection of emotion and technology by introducing the concept that machines can be designed to recognize, interpret, and respond to human emotions. This theory has significant implications for conflict resolution in organizational settings, where miscommunication and unacknowledged emotions often fuel interpersonal tensions. Traditional conflict resolution strategies depend heavily on the emotional intelligence of mediators, who may inadvertently overlook subtle cues such as passive aggression, discomfort, or anxiety. Affective computing bridges this gap by introducing data-driven emotional analysis into conflict scenarios. For example, during a conflict mediation session, Emotion AI powered by affective computing can analyze speech patterns, facial expressions, or body language in real time to detect stress, hostility, or empathy. This capability empowers HR professionals or managers to address underlying emotional states that are not overtly expressed, enabling more comprehensive and empathetic resolutions. Furthermore, affective computing supports timely intervention. By continuously monitoring emotional climate within teams, these systems can alert leaders to brewing tensions before they escalate into serious disputes. This preemptive capability fundamentally changes the conflict resolution paradigm from reactive to proactive. Additionally, the integration of affective computing allows organizations to maintain fairness in conflict resolution by introducing an impartial, data-driven layer to emotional evaluation, reducing the impact of human biases. However, the theory also raises critical ethical concerns. The very emotions that machines detect must be handled with care, ensuring employees are not subject to emotional surveillance or manipulation. Therefore, while Affective Computing Theory provides a powerful framework for enhancing conflict resolution, its application demands ethical safeguards, transparency, and human oversight. When applied responsibly, it transforms conflict management into a more empathetic, evidence-based, and preventive organizational practice.

Impact of Fairness Theory (Folger & Cropanzano, 1998) on Fairness in the Modern Workplace

The Fairness Theory by Folger and Cropanzano (1998) emphasizes that perceptions of fairness in organizations arise from three core dimensions: distributive justice (fairness of outcomes), procedural justice (fairness of processes), and interactional justice (fairness in interpersonal treatment). In the modern workplace, where diversity, inclusion, and transparency are paramount, this theory is instrumental in shaping how fairness is conceptualized and operationalized. The integration of Emotion AI into HR processes presents new opportunities—and risks—in upholding these forms of justice. For instance, when Emotion AI is used in performance evaluations or conflict resolution, it can reduce interpersonal bias by offering emotion-based insights that support fairer decisions. This aligns with procedural justice by enhancing transparency and consistency in decision-making processes. Additionally, AI can promote interactional justice by alerting leaders to emotionally inappropriate or dismissive communication styles, thereby fostering respectful workplace dialogue. However, the deployment of such tools must itself be perceived as fair to avoid undermining trust. Employees may question whether their emotions are being monitored intrusively or interpreted accurately, impacting their sense of organizational justice. The Fairness Theory thus provides a valuable lens to assess whether AI-enabled decisions respect employee dignity, provide avenues for appeal, and are implemented uniformly. In performance reviews, for example, integrating Emotion AI without transparency could violate principles of procedural and interactional justice, even if the outcomes appear unbiased. Therefore, embedding the Fairness Theory into Emotion AI design ensures that technology enhances—not hinders—perceptions of equity. Ultimately, by grounding AI use in the tenets of Fairness Theory, organizations can create emotionally intelligent systems that uphold ethical standards and strengthen employee trust and inclusion in the digital age.

Impact of Social Exchange Theory (Blau, 1964) on Emotional Intelligence in the Workplace

Social Exchange Theory, developed by Peter Blau (1964), posits that human relationships are formed through reciprocal exchanges of resources, such as trust, respect, and support. In the context of emotional intelligence in the workplace, this theory underscores the idea that emotionally intelligent behavior—empathy, active listening, emotional regulation—contributes to reciprocal relationships that promote cooperation, trust, and shared success. Employees who perceive emotional understanding and fairness in their interactions are more likely to reciprocate with engagement, loyalty, and constructive behavior. When Emotion AI is introduced into this framework, it acts as a facilitator of social exchange by identifying emotional needs and enhancing reciprocal understanding. For example, when a manager uses AI insights to detect team stress and adjust workloads accordingly, it signals care and responsiveness, prompting employees to respond with greater motivation and collaboration. Moreover, the theory highlights that emotional cues—often subtle and unspoken—form the basis of workplace relationships. Emotion AI, by amplifying the detection of these cues, enables more emotionally intelligent organizational responses that can strengthen social bonds. However, trust is a critical currency in the exchange process. If Emotion AI is perceived as invasive or manipulative, it may disrupt the reciprocal flow of trust and respect. Thus, emotional intelligence, augmented by AI, must be exercised with ethical sensitivity and human oversight. When used appropriately, the reciprocity encouraged by Social Exchange Theory—coupled with Emotion AI's real-time feedback—can transform workplace dynamics into more emotionally intelligent, cooperative, and resilient ecosystems. This synergy empowers organizations to cultivate cultures where emotional intelligence is not only a personal trait but also a systemic capability embedded in everyday interactions.

CONSTITUENTS OF EMOTION AI AS A CATALYST FOR CONFLICT RESOLUTION

Emotion Detection and Recognition

At the core of Emotion AI lies its ability to detect and recognize human emotions through diverse biometric and behavioral signals. These include facial expressions, voice tone, body posture, and textual sentiment (Chen et al., 2021). Emotion detection systems are powered by computer vision, natural language processing (NLP), and acoustic analysis, which collectively enable the real-time interpretation of emotional states such as frustration, anxiety, or disengagement. In workplace conflict scenarios, these tools provide valuable insights into the emotional temperature of interactions, often revealing unspoken tensions or passive-aggressive behaviors that traditional observation misses. By recognizing subtle emotional fluctuations, Emotion AI enables timely interventions that can prevent the escalation of disagreements (Nguyen & Bui, 2022). Particularly in virtual environments, where face-to-face cues are limited, emotion recognition fills a critical gap in understanding emotional dynamics. However, the effectiveness of this component depends on the accuracy of algorithms and the ethical management of emotional data. Misclassification or lack of cultural sensitivity in emotion interpretation can lead to flawed conclusions and mistrust among employees (Zhou et al., 2023). Therefore, emotion detection must be accompanied by algorithmic transparency and regular recalibration to reflect diverse expressions of emotion. When designed and implemented responsibly, emotion detection acts as the foundation of AI-assisted conflict resolution, promoting early awareness and empathy-driven responses.

Sentiment and Behavioral Analytic

Sentiment and behavioral analytics form the analytical layer of Emotion AI, converting raw emotional inputs into patterns, trends, and actionable insights. Sentiment analysis tools assess the emotional tone of written communication—emails, chats, feedback forms—and classify them along dimensions such as positivity, negativity, urgency, or sarcasm (Wong & Lee, 2021). These tools help organizations monitor digital communication climates and detect emotional stress signals that might lead to interpersonal conflicts. Behavioral analytics, on the other hand, track patterns in work habits, collaboration frequency, or even micro-behaviors like delayed responses, providing a fuller emotional context. For example, a sudden decrease in team communication combined with negative sentiment in messages may signal unresolved conflict (Gupta & Kumar, 2023). These insights allow managers to intervene early, using data-driven evidence rather than subjective interpretation. Moreover, historical sentiment trends can guide HR in identifying recurring friction points within teams, enabling structural or leadership changes that support long-term harmony. Sentiment and behavioral data, however, must be used ethically and with employee awareness. Concerns around surveillance and emotional manipulation are legitimate and must be mitigated through transparent communication and consent-based data collection (Rahman et al., 2020). If applied with fairness and respect, sentiment and behavioral analytics empower organizations to transition from reactive conflict management to proactive emotional governance.

Real-Time Feedback Mechanisms

Real-time emotional feedback mechanisms are among the most transformative aspects of Emotion AI in conflict management. These systems use continuous emotion monitoring during interactions—such as team meetings or one-on-one conversations—to detect emotional escalation in real time and provide instant feedback to facilitators or leaders (Tan & Lim, 2023). For instance, if a participant's tone becomes aggressive or their facial expression reflects irritation, the system may alert the moderator, enabling immediate de-escalation through tone adjustment or a change in discussion direction. This responsiveness is critical during performance reviews, negotiations, or conflict mediation sessions where emotions can quickly spiral. Additionally, real-time feedback supports emotionally intelligent leadership by offering cues on when to pause, reframe, or clarify statements to avoid triggering further conflict (Sharma & Desai, 2022). These tools help leaders build empathy and situational awareness, often resulting in higher employee satisfaction and fewer HR escalations. In virtual or hybrid teams, where physical cues are harder to read, this component is invaluable for maintaining engagement and understanding. However, for real-time feedback to be effective, it must be integrated seamlessly into communication platforms and viewed as supportive rather than intrusive. Over-monitoring or lack of transparency about how feedback is generated can result in mistrust and resistance. With appropriate training and ethical oversight, real-time feedback mechanisms elevate interpersonal awareness, making conflict resolution more immediate, informed, and humane.

Emotional Profiling for Conflict Risk Assessment

Emotional profiling involves the aggregation of emotion data over time to build dynamic emotional maps of individuals and teams. These profiles capture emotional tendencies, stress thresholds, triggers, and recovery patterns, offering predictive insights into potential conflict hotspots (Singh & Rajan, 2021). For example, employees with a history of emotional reactivity during tight deadlines may be assigned to less time-sensitive tasks or paired with collaborators who demonstrate emotional stability. At the team level, profiling allows HR departments to assess emotional compatibility before forming project groups, thereby reducing the likelihood of interpersonal clashes. Emotional profiling also supports targeted conflict resolution training by identifying individuals who may benefit from emotional regulation workshops or resilience programs. Importantly, this predictive capacity shifts the conflict resolution approach from reactive to preventative. However, profiling raises ethical concerns around emotional labeling and the potential for discriminatory practices. If not anonymized, emotionally "sensitive" profiles may unfairly influence performance reviews or promotion decisions (Zhou et al., 2023). Thus, organizations must implement profiling with strict confidentiality, clear boundaries on data use, and regular audits. When handled ethically, emotional profiling transforms conflict risk management into a personalized, data-driven process that aligns talent management with emotional well-being.

Ethical and Fairness Safeguards

One of the most important constituents of Emotion AI is the framework of ethical and fairness safeguards that govern its use. Because emotional data is deeply personal, any misuse or opaque handling of such data can lead to employee resistance, mistrust, and even legal risks (Gupta & Kumar, 2023). Therefore, ethical Emotion AI design must incorporate consent mechanisms, anonymization protocols, opt-in participation models, and employee education about the purpose and limits of emotional data collection. Fairness safeguards are also critical in preventing algorithmic bias—such as interpreting assertiveness in women as aggression or misreading culturally diverse emotional expressions (Zhou et al., 2023). Organizations must regularly audit AI models for bias, retrain them with diverse datasets, and ensure that emotion insights are used to empower rather than penalize employees. Moreover, fairness extends to the transparency of interventions. Employees should be informed when emotional feedback contributes to managerial decisions, and they should have the right to challenge or contextualize such insights. Ethical frameworks, when robustly implemented, position Emotion AI as a trust-building rather than a surveillance tool. In this way, fairness safeguards are not merely regulatory requirements but fundamental enablers of sustainable, respectful conflict resolution systems.

Emotional Intelligence Development Tools

Emotion AI can also serve as a learning and development tool to enhance emotional intelligence (EI) across the workforce. By providing personalized feedback on emotional expressions, self-regulation patterns, and interpersonal impacts, AI can help individuals build core EI competencies such as empathy, self-awareness, and impulse control (Lim & Tan, 2024). These insights can be visualized through dashboards or delivered as micro-coaching prompts during meetings or written communication. For instance, an employee may receive AI-generated suggestions on how to frame critical feedback more constructively or manage emotional tone during tense conversations. Such tools support ongoing emotional skill development and foster a learning culture where employees become more attuned to the emotional dimensions of workplace interactions (Wong & Lee, 2021). Managers, in particular, benefit from this real-time emotional coaching, which can strengthen their leadership and conflict mediation abilities. Unlike one-time workshops, Emotion AI tools enable continuous EI development embedded into everyday workflows. However, for these tools to be effective, organizations must promote a growth mindset and ensure that emotional learning is not punitive. By positioning AI as a coach rather than a judge, companies can cultivate emotionally intelligent teams that are more resilient, empathetic, and capable of resolving conflict constructively.

IMPACT OF EMOTION AI ON EMOTIONAL INTELLIGENCE AND FAIRNESS IN THE MODERN WORKPLACE

Enhancing Self-Awareness and Emotional Regulation

Emotion AI empowers employees by providing real-time feedback about their emotional expressions and reactions, contributing to greater self-awareness and regulation—core elements of emotional intelligence. For example, voice tone analysis or facial emotion detection can notify individuals when their responses signal stress or frustration. This awareness allows individuals to reframe their emotional expressions and make conscious behavioral adjustments during interpersonal exchanges (Lim & Tan, 2024). Such feedback loops serve as reflective tools, promoting emotional growth and improving response strategies under pressure. Additionally, emotional self-regulation facilitated by AI can prevent impulsive reactions that might otherwise lead to conflict. These systems not only enhance the individual's capacity for introspection but also provide data to support personalized emotional coaching. As a result, employees become more capable of managing emotions in both high-stakes meetings and day-to-day collaboration. However, for these benefits to be realized, Emotion AI must be integrated with psychological safety protocols and employee training that fosters openness to AI-assisted feedback (Gupta & Kumar, 2023). When ethically applied, these tools help individuals refine emotional intelligence continuously, creating more resilient and self-aware workforces.

Fostering Empathy and Social Awareness

Emotion AI plays a critical role in improving empathy and social awareness, particularly in environments where remote or asynchronous communication hinders emotional perception. Through sentiment analysis and emotion recognition in emails, chats, or video calls, Emotion AI helps identify the emotional states of colleagues, even when they are not explicitly expressed (Nguyen & Bui, 2022). This capability allows individuals to better understand team members' emotional needs, frustrations, or disengagement, enabling more empathetic interactions. By surfacing unspoken emotional cues, AI facilitates adjustments in communication tone and approach, leading to greater inclusivity and emotional resonance. Such emotional atonement is particularly vital in diverse teams, where cultural variations in emotional expression can lead to misunderstanding or conflict. Emotion AI thus acts as an empathy amplifier, providing a bridge between intention and perception in professional interactions (Chen et al., 2021). When integrated into team dashboards or collaborative tools, it offers collective insights into group morale, helping leaders and employees respond sensitively. However, organizations must guard against over-reliance on algorithms and preserve space for human interpretation. When responsibly used, Emotion AI nurtures socially aware workplaces that recognize and adapt to the emotional complexities of human communication.

Promoting Emotionally Intelligent Leadership

Emotion AI equips leaders with enhanced tools for managing their teams more empathetically and effectively. By analyzing collective emotional data, such as group sentiment trends or emotional tone during meetings, managers can gauge the psychological climate of their teams in real time (Wong & Lee, 2021). This enables emotionally intelligent decision-making, especially during periods of change, high stress, or conflict. Emotion AI allows leaders to detect subtle signs of emotional disengagement, anxiety, or interpersonal tension, empowering them to intervene early and prevent escalations. For example, a leader receiving an alert about rising emotional distress during a virtual meeting can modify the tone of discussion, pause the meeting, or follow up privately with concerned team members. Such proactive behavior embodies the competencies of emotional intelligence—particularly empathy, social regulation, and motivation. In addition, Emotion AI tools can offer tailored coaching to managers, helping them identify unconscious biases in their interactions and communication styles (Sharma & Desai, 2022). When paired with leadership development programs, these tools enhance interpersonal skills and conflict resolution capabilities. Ethical use is essential, as employees must trust that emotional monitoring aims to support, not control. When used judiciously, Emotion AI transforms leadership into a more intuitive and emotionally intelligent function.

Advancing Procedural and Interactional Fairness

Emotion AI contributes significantly to fairness in the workplace by enhancing the objectivity of decision-making processes. Procedural fairness—how decisions are made—and interactional fairness—how people are treated—are often compromised by unconscious bias and inconsistent leadership behavior. Emotion AI mitigates these risks by providing data-driven emotional insights that inform performance evaluations, disciplinary actions, or promotions (Zhou et al., 2023). For example, AI can detect emotionally biased language in feedback, ensuring that performance appraisals are respectful and balanced. In conflict resolution, Emotion AI provides neutral data on emotional dynamics, helping mediators make decisions that reflect all parties' experiences more equitably. It also flags emotionally charged communication patterns, enabling HR teams to intervene before biases solidify into systemic unfairness. These tools support fairness by ensuring that emotionally affected employees receive timely acknowledgment and support. However, fairness itself must be embedded in the system—algorithms must be trained on diverse datasets, and employees should have the ability to challenge or contextualize emotional interpretations (Gupta & Kumar, 2023). When governed by transparency and equity, Emotion AI serves as a mechanism for safeguarding fairness across interpersonal and institutional dimensions of the workplace.

Supporting Personalized and Timely Interventions

One of the transformative impacts of Emotion AI is its ability to drive personalized and real-time interventions based on emotional data. Unlike generic HR responses, AI-powered emotional insights allow for tailored support that addresses the unique emotional state and conflict dynamics of individuals (Tan & Lim, 2023). For instance, if an employee consistently exhibits signs of stress and withdrawal in meetings, the system can prompt a manager to initiate a one-on-one conversation or offer wellness resources. This timely response prevents minor emotional strains from becoming workplace crises and reflects emotional intelligence at an organizational level. Moreover, interventions can be adapted based on personality types, previous behavior patterns, and emotional thresholds—leading to more effective conflict resolution and performance improvement. Such individualized engagement enhances employee trust and reinforces the perception that the organization values fairness and emotional well-being. However, these interventions should be guided by ethical protocols and professional discretion to avoid overreach or emotional stereotyping. Personalized AI insights, when used respectfully, create a workplace that is not only emotionally responsive but also equitable in how support and resources are distributed.

Revealing Emotional Inequities and Hidden Biases

Emotion AI has the potential to uncover hidden emotional inequities in the workplace, especially those affecting women, minorities, or marginalized employees. Traditional HR systems often overlook the invisible burden of emotional labor—such as maintaining harmony, suppressing negative emotions, or navigating microaggressions (Chen et al., 2021). Emotion AI can detect emotional exhaustion or suppression patterns in specific demographic groups by analyzing long-term emotional data. This helps organizations identify systemic issues that compromise psychological safety and equity. For instance, if women on a team frequently show higher emotional volatility in high-stakes meetings, it may point to an exclusionary communication style or leadership behavior that needs reform. Emotion AI provides a data-driven basis to address such inequities proactively, rather than relying on anecdotal or post-incident feedback. When integrated with diversity, equity, and inclusion (DEI) strategies, emotional data helps in making invisible struggles visible—thereby promoting targeted fairness initiatives. However, organizations must engage in critical evaluation to ensure emotional data is not used to stereotype or penalize. Used ethically, Emotion AI shifts the workplace conversation from surface-level inclusion to deep emotional equity.

Enhancing Transparency in Feedback and Communication

Emotion AI adds a layer of transparency to workplace feedback systems by making emotional dynamics explicit and actionable. In performance reviews, for example, Emotion AI can assess whether feedback is emotionally neutral, empathetic, or potentially demotivating, helping managers communicate more constructively (Wong & Lee, 2021). Employees can also receive emotion-driven summaries of their interactions and peer feedback, helping them reflect on how they are perceived emotionally. This fosters a more open and emotionally honest feedback culture where individuals are not only evaluated on tasks but also guided on interpersonal impact. Furthermore, emotion-informed feedback mitigates the risk of unconscious bias, particularly in cross-cultural or gender-diverse settings, where emotional interpretations can vary (Nguyen & Bui, 2022). By highlighting emotionally charged language or unintended microaggressions, Emotion AI encourages fairness in both upward and downward communication. However, such transparency should be reciprocal—employees must be aware of when their emotional data is used and have access to their emotional profiles. Transparent emotional feedback, governed by ethical use policies, cultivates fairness by making communication more mindful, respectful, and emotionally intelligent.

APPLICATIONS OF EMOTION AI ON EMOTIONAL INTELLIGENCE AND FAIRNESS IN THE MODERN WORKPLACE

Real-Time Emotional Feedback in Performance Reviews

Emotion AI is increasingly used to provide real-time emotional feedback during performance evaluations. By analyzing voice tone, facial expressions, and language sentiment, it helps HR professionals and managers detect discomfort, anxiety, or disengagement from employees (Wong & Lee, 2021). This enables evaluators to reframe their communication in a more empathetic and emotionally intelligent manner, improving the receptiveness and fairness of the appraisal process. Emotion AI can also flag emotionally biased phrases or aggressive tones, ensuring that feedback is delivered respectfully. This application strengthens interactional justice by making emotional responses part of the performance dialogue, not overlooked cues. It also facilitates fairer evaluations by preventing unconscious emotional misjudgments, which may otherwise influence ratings. When employees see that their emotional states are acknowledged, it fosters psychological safety and trust in the appraisal process. However, the implementation of such systems must include transparency, allowing employees to understand how their emotional data is being used. When ethically managed, this application not only enhances emotional intelligence in leadership but also ensures that performance reviews are fair, constructive, and emotionally inclusive.

Conflict Detection and Early Intervention in Teams

Emotion AI applications are capable of identifying early signs of conflict within teams by continuously monitoring emotional cues across communication channels. Through sentiment analysis of emails, chat logs, and video interactions, these systems can flag patterns of negativity, sarcasm, or emotional withdrawal that may precede overt conflict (Tan & Lim, 2023). This data empowers team leaders or HR personnel to intervene before issues escalate, embodying emotionally intelligent leadership and proactive conflict management. For instance, a drop in positive sentiment combined with increased emotional volatility could prompt a private conversation to explore underlying issues. Such preemptive measures enhance procedural fairness, as they allow all voices to be heard before formal complaints or disciplinary action is necessary. Furthermore, Emotion AI can suggest mediation strategies that align with the emotional tone and history of the team, personalizing conflict resolution in a fair and empathetic way. By promoting early awareness and equitable handling of tensions, this application minimizes disruption while fostering a psychologically safe environment. However, its effectiveness depends on trust, ethical use, and employee consent, ensuring that emotional data is used to support well-being and not for punitive surveillance.

AI-Enhanced Emotional Intelligence Training Modules

Emotion AI is revolutionizing corporate training by enabling personalized emotional intelligence (EI) development. Traditional workshops often rely on generic case studies, but AI-powered training adapts content based on each participant's emotional response patterns (Lim & Tan, 2024). For example, the system may analyze participants' tone during simulated conflict resolution exercises or their sentiment in reflective writing. Based on this data, it provides real-time feedback on empathy, self-awareness, and regulation—key pillars of EI. This tailored coaching helps employees internalize emotional competencies through experiential learning.

Furthermore, AI-enhanced modules allow HR to track improvements in emotional expression and regulation across time, ensuring continuous development. This personalized and dynamic approach ensures greater retention and relevance of training material. From a fairness perspective, this application democratizes access to EI training by removing biases often associated with manual identification of "high-potential" employees. Everyone receives equal opportunities for emotional growth, contributing to inclusive talent development. To ensure fairness and privacy, participants should be informed of the emotional data captured and have control over its use. When used ethically, Emotion AI in EI training not only boosts individual competencies but fosters emotionally intelligent teams aligned with organizational values of empathy and equity.

Bias Mitigation in Hiring and Promotions

Emotion AI can play a transformative role in reducing emotional and cognitive bias in recruitment and promotion processes. During interviews, AI tools analyze facial expressions, vocal patterns, and emotional reactions in response to questions to help identify authentic emotional traits like confidence, empathy, or anxiety (Gupta & Kumar, 2023). This adds a behavioral dimension to candidate assessment that complements resumes and test scores. Similarly, in promotion reviews, emotion analytics can reveal candidates' ability to handle pressure or navigate interpersonal dynamics—key for leadership roles. These insights allow decision-makers to evaluate potential fairly and holistically, beyond surface impressions. Emotion AI also acts as a safeguard against discriminatory evaluations by flagging emotionally biased feedback or uneven treatment during the hiring process. For example, the system may detect if candidates from certain demographic groups are receiving disproportionately critical tones. From a fairness standpoint, this helps ensure that all candidates are evaluated based on relevant emotional competencies, not subjective preferences. Ethical concerns remain around transparency and cultural variations in emotion expression. Therefore, AI should support—not replace—human judgment and be used alongside inclusive practices. When responsibly deployed, Emotion AI fosters emotionally intelligent hiring and promotion practices that value fairness and merit.

Emotional Climate Monitoring in Hybrid Work Models

In remote and hybrid work settings, traditional means of gauging employee morale—like physical cues or watercooler chats—are often unavailable. Emotion AI bridges this gap by analyzing digital communication (emails, video calls, chat platforms) to assess the collective emotional climate of teams (Nguyen & Bui, 2022). Managers receive dashboards summarizing emotional trends such as increasing frustration or declining engagement, enabling timely emotional check-ins. This continuous monitoring allows emotionally intelligent leaders to maintain team cohesion and adapt strategies to the group's emotional needs. From a fairness perspective, emotion tracking ensures that remote employees are not overlooked in support and recognition compared to their in-office counterparts. It also surfaces emotional inequities—e.g., if certain team members consistently express anxiety, it could signal uneven workloads or exclusion from decision-making. By bringing invisible emotions into view, this application enhances both inclusion and responsiveness in leadership. However, organizations must obtain explicit consent and ensure data is not used for micromanagement. When ethical guidelines are followed, emotion monitoring strengthens fairness by enabling consistent emotional support across distributed teams, while improving leaders' capacity to regulate team morale with empathy.

Enhancing Fairness in Customer-Facing Roles

Emotion AI is increasingly used in customer service and frontline employee roles to assess both employee and customer emotional states in real time. This helps agents regulate their responses and maintain composure under pressure, enhancing emotional intelligence and service quality (Chen et al., 2021). For example, AI may detect rising frustration in a customer's tone and provide scripted empathy-based responses to the service agent. It can also monitor the emotional state of the employee, prompting breaks or support during high-stress shifts. This promotes fairness by preventing burnout and ensuring emotionally supportive work conditions. Additionally, emotion analytics can flag unfair treatment—such as microaggressions from customers—and offer documentation that helps protect employee well-being. This shifts the power dynamic in favor of emotional fairness, especially in industries where emotional labor is often undervalued. Furthermore, AI tools can provide aggregated data on emotional trends, helping management identify systemic challenges and introduce empathetic training or support policies. To ensure fairness, emotional data from interactions must not be used punitively against employees. When applied transparently, this technology empowers both employees and organizations to engage in emotionally intelligent, fair, and respectful service delivery.

Preventing Emotional Burnout Through AI-Supported Wellness Programs

Emotion AI supports organizational wellness initiatives by identifying early signs of emotional burnout and distress. Through continuous monitoring of communication tone, participation behavior, and biometric signals (when permissible), AI can detect when employees are emotionally depleted, withdrawn, or at risk of burnout (Sharma & Desai, 2022). This proactive identification allows HR to offer wellness interventions such as mental health resources, flexible work adjustments, or one-on-one support. From an emotional intelligence standpoint, this promotes self-regulation and emotional resilience across the workforce. Fairness is also strengthened, as these tools ensure that support is equitably distributed based on real emotional needs, not just visible complaints or manager observations. Emotion AI can help uncover hidden stress patterns among underrepresented or introverted employees who may otherwise be overlooked. By integrating these insights into wellness dashboards, organizations create emotionally intelligent systems that protect long-term employee well-being. Ethical deployment requires that emotional surveillance is consensual, supportive, and separated from performance evaluations. When aligned with HR values, Emotion AI enhances workplace fairness by shifting wellness strategies from generic to personalized, and from reactive to proactive, ensuring that no employee's emotional well-being is left unaddressed.

STRATEGIES OF EMOTION AI ON EMOTIONAL INTELLIGENCE AND FAIRNESS IN THE MODERN WORKPLACE

Leverage Emotion AI for Enhancing Work-Life Balance and Emotional Intelligence

Citing Padmanaaban et al. (n.d.) and Krishna & Murthy (2015), organizations should strategically integrate Emotion AI to detect emotional fatigue and improve work-life balance. Emotion AI systems, when paired with organizational policies, can offer real-time feedback on employee well-being and trigger timely HR interventions. As shown in the study on private bank employees, emotional intelligence (EI) is deeply linked to workplace satisfaction. Through continuous monitoring of tone, stress levels, and emotional signals, AI can identify burnout risks early. This data should guide wellness programs and flexible work arrangements, enabling emotionally intelligent leadership responses. Emotional data, when ethically handled, also allows the company to personalize employee engagement efforts. Over time, such AI-enhanced emotional insights can foster psychologically safe environments where employees feel supported in balancing personal and professional roles. Integrating AI for well-being is not just a technological upgrade—it is a strategic necessity to build resilient, emotionally intelligent workforces.

Embed Emotion AI in Smart Education for Personalized Emotional Feedback

Drawing from Yamijala et al. (2025) and Murthy et al. (2025), incorporating Emotion AI in educational platforms enhances personalized learning through emotionally adaptive content delivery. AI can monitor emotional reactions—boredom, confusion, engagement—during lessons and adjust pedagogy accordingly. In the context of smart education and IoB systems, emotion-tracking tools inform instructors about student sentiments, enabling personalized intervention strategies. This also promotes fairness in learning, ensuring that all students—not just outspoken ones—receive appropriate academic support. Yamijala's emphasis on AI-driven behavioral adaptation aligns with this, showing how emotional cues can be used to individualize the pace and complexity of educational material. Future education platforms must integrate Emotion AI as both a diagnostic and developmental tool for emotional engagement. As emotion-aware learning becomes standard, educators and institutions can create inclusive, emotionally intelligent classrooms that enhance retention and satisfaction for diverse learners.

Apply Emotion AI in Customer Experience Mapping and Engagement Optimization

Murthy et al. (2025) and Bansal et al. (2023) highlight the strategic value of using Emotion AI in mapping emotional touchpoints to improve customer satisfaction. Real-time sentiment analysis in customer interactions—via chatbots, service calls, or social media—allows brands to identify dissatisfaction early and adjust their messaging or service. These insights are instrumental in crafting emotionally resonant customer experiences, particularly across multichannel environments. As noted in studies on influencer marketing and branding, the emotional appeal of content significantly shapes customer engagement and loyalty (Ao et al., 2023). Emotion AI tools can track emotional shifts during campaigns, enabling dynamic adjustments to tone, visuals, or messaging. Integrating these findings into CRM and marketing systems allows companies to create consistent, emotionally engaging customer journeys. Thus, Emotion AI does not just monitor sentiment—it becomes **a critical tool in strategic customer relationship management and brand advocacy.**

Foster Organizational Citizenship and Engagement through Emotion-Aware HR Systems

As emphasized by Tiwari et al. (2022) and Krishna & Murthy (2015), organizational citizenship behavior (OCB) and employee engagement can be elevated through Emotion AI-powered HR systems. By continuously assessing emotional indicators during team meetings or peer feedback sessions, AI tools help HR detect disengagement, frustration, or emotional misalignment early. This supports emotionally intelligent interventions that align with team dynamics and employee motivations. Emotion AI, when embedded in performance management platforms, enhances procedural and interactional fairness, ensuring that recognition and development are emotionally resonant and equitable. This strategy aligns with the shift toward transhumanist HR practices (Yamijala et al., 2025), which emphasize emotional alignment in policy design. When applied responsibly, such systems promote inclusive environments that value emotional labour and foster trust, leading to sustainable improvements in employee engagement and OCB.

Use Emotion AI in Influencer Marketing and Brand Evangelism

Emotion AI has critical applications in identifying and managing emotional connections between brands and consumers, particularly in influencer marketing. Studies by Murthy et al. (2025) and Fazla Rabby et al. (2025) highlight that influencers who generate strong emotional resonance are more likely to foster brand loyalty. Emotion AI can assess the emotional impact of influencer content across demographics and platforms, helping marketers optimize partnerships and campaigns. Furthermore, by tracking viewer reactions, it enables the identification of potential brand evangelists—consumers who express high emotional engagement and are likely to advocate for the brand. These insights help companies not only measure campaign ROI more accurately but also enhance fairness in influencer selection by relying on emotional metrics rather than superficial follower counts. Integrating Emotion AI into influencer strategies creates a more personalized and data-driven approach to digital marketing.

Enable Emotion AI to Improve Remote Work and Virtual Collaboration

According to Yamijala et al. (2025) and Murthy et al. (2025), Emotion AI has a critical role in remote work environments by bridging emotional communication gaps in virtual teams. Emotion-tracking systems can analyze video calls and chat tools to detect emotional detachment, frustration, or fatigue. This data helps managers tailor communication styles, offer emotional support, and create equitable workloads. In virtual reality and metaverse-based workplaces, Emotion AI enhances immersive interactions by providing real-time emotional feedback, improving trust and collaboration. These tools support inclusive team dynamics by ensuring no voice goes unheard, especially among quieter team members. With proper data ethics and consent, Emotion AI becomes an enabler of equitable, emotionally intelligent virtual workspaces that replicate (and even enhance) physical collaboration standards.

Integrate Emotion AI for AI-Driven Performance Management Systems

Based on Raja et al. (2025) and Murthy et al. (2025), organizations must integrate Emotion AI into performance management to develop systems that are fair, dynamic, and emotionally responsive. Traditional performance reviews often overlook the emotional context of achievements and failures. Emotion AI can identify emotional responses to feedback, helping managers tailor their approach to each employee's personality. These systems can also detect emotional stress from excessive workloads or ambiguous goals, prompting timely support. Additionally, integrating this emotional data with Human Resource Information Systems (HRIS) allows for better planning and evaluation of training, promotions, and leadership development. However, this integration must be transparent and inclusive, with employees given visibility into how emotional data informs evaluations. Strategically applied, Emotion AI transforms performance management from a transactional process into a developmental, emotionally intelligent dialogue.

Use Emotion AI in Sentiment Mining for Public and Climate Communication

Finally, Murthy (2024) emphasizes the application of Emotion AI in large-scale sentiment mining, especially for public awareness campaigns and environmental sustainability. Analyzing public sentiment regarding climate change, health crises, or social issues can guide policymaking and communication strategies. Emotion AI enables governments and NGOs to identify emotional drivers behind public behavior and design messages that are more empathetic, targeted, and effective. This ensures fairness by giving marginalized communities a voice through emotion-mined data. When applied to large datasets from social media or surveys, Emotion AI becomes a public engagement tool that democratizes communication and supports emotionally inclusive governance.

CONCLUSION

The integration of Emotion AI into workplace environments marks a significant advancement in how organizations understand, manage, and respond to the emotional fabric of their workforce. As demonstrated through its multifaceted applications, Emotion AI is more than a technological innovation—it is a transformative tool that enhances both emotional intelligence and fairness in the modern workplace. By enabling real-time emotional feedback, early conflict detection, and personalized emotional development, Emotion AI supports individuals and teams in navigating complex interpersonal dynamics with greater empathy, awareness, and control. It elevates emotional intelligence from a personal skill to an institutional asset, embedding it into the daily practices of leadership, communication, performance management, and team collaboration. From a fairness perspective, Emotion AI promotes procedural and interactional justice by reducing unconscious bias in critical processes such as recruitment, performance evaluation, and conflict resolution. It empowers HR professionals and leaders to treat employees not just as resources, but as emotionally dynamic individuals whose feelings, experiences, and perspectives matter.

Limitations

Despite its promising potential, the application of Emotion AI in enhancing emotional intelligence and fairness within the modern workplace is not without significant limitations. One of the primary concerns is the accuracy and cultural sensitivity of emotion recognition systems. Emotions are expressed differently across cultures, genders, and individuals; however, many Emotion AI models are trained on narrow datasets that may not represent this diversity. This can result in misinterpretation of emotional cues, especially for those who do not conform to standard expressions, leading to unfair assessments or misinformed managerial actions (Zhou et al., 2023). Another limitation lies in the ethical challenges related to privacy and consent. The continuous tracking of facial expressions, voice modulations, and behavioral patterns can feel intrusive to employees, particularly if implemented without transparent communication and explicit consent. This perceived surveillance may erode trust, negatively impact employee morale, and even contradict the very principles of fairness that Emotion AI aims to promote (Gupta & Kumar, 2023). Furthermore, the blurred boundary between support and control can lead to the misuse of emotional data in performance appraisals, promotions, or disciplinary actions if not properly governed. Additionally, there is a risk of over-reliance on algorithmic feedback, potentially undermining human judgment and empathy. While Emotion AI offers valuable insights, it cannot fully capture the context, intentions, or nuances behind emotional expressions. Decisions based solely on AI-generated emotional data may ignore deeper issues, such as systemic inequality, interpersonal history, or unexpressed psychological distress.

Future Directions for Research

Future research on Emotion AI in the workplace should focus on enhancing the cultural and contextual sensitivity of emotion recognition systems. Current models often generalize emotional expressions, overlooking individual and cultural nuances. Advancing inclusive datasets and adaptive algorithms that reflect diverse emotional behaviours will be essential. Another important direction is the development of ethical frameworks and regulatory standards to guide the responsible deployment of Emotion AI, particularly in relation to employee privacy, data ownership, and informed consent. Research should also explore longitudinal impacts of Emotion AI on employee well-being, trust, and organizational culture to assess whether these systems lead to sustained improvements in fairness and emotional intelligence or introduce new biases and stressors.

REFERENCES

Ao, L., Bansal, R., Pruthi, N., & Khaskheli, M. B. (2023). Impact of Social Media Influencers on Customer Engagement and Purchase Intention: A Meta-Analysis. *Sustainability (Basel)*, *15*(3), 2744. DOI: 10.3390/su15032744

Bansal, R., Shukla, G., Gupta, A., Singh, A., & Pruthi, N. (2023). Optimizing Augmented Reality and Virtual Reality for Customer Engagement. In *Promoting Consumer Engagement Through Emotional Branding and Sensory Marketing* (pp. 24–35). IGI Global.

Blau, P. M. (1964). *Exchange and power in social life*. John Wiley & Sons.

Bose, S., & Kumar, N. (2020). Emotional intelligence as a predictor of conflict resolution strategies in organizational settings. *Journal of Organizational Psychology*, *20*(2), 45–56. DOI: 10.33423/jop.v20i2.3012

Chen, Y., Zhao, J., & Li, X. (2021). Emotion AI in the workplace: Prospects and ethical concerns. *Journal of Business Ethics and Technology*, *34*(1), 12–27. DOI: 10.1007/s10551-021-04879-y

Folger, R., & Cropanzano, R. (1998). *Organizational justice and human resource management*. Sage Publications. DOI: 10.4135/9781452225777

Goleman, D. (1995). *Emotional intelligence: Why it can matter more than IQ*. Bantam Books.

Goswami, I., Hamida, A. G. B., Murthy, Y. S., & Gopal, S. P. (2023). Effective Role of Human Resource Management Policies Within Marketing Organization: The Impact on Business and Marketing Strategy Implementation. *International Journal of Professional Business Review: Int. J. Prof. Bus. Rev.*, *8*(7), 4.

Goswami, I., Hamida, A. G. B., Murthy, Y. S., Gopal, S. P., & Jalaja, V. (2023). Effective Role of Human Resource Management Policies Within Marketing Organization: The Impact on Business and Marketing Strategy Implementation. *International Journal of Professional Business Review: Int. J. Prof. Bus. Rev.*, *8*(7), 4.

Gupta, R., & Kumar, M. (2023). Ethics in emotion detection systems: Challenges and solutions for HR integration. *AI and Ethics*, *4*(2), 114–128. DOI: 10.1007/s43681-023-00145-3

Gupta, S. K., Fegade, A., Padhye, P., Mohture, A., Kalshetti, P., & Murthy, Y. S. (2024). Evaluating the effect of covid-19 on major world indices: In relation to gold, silver, crude oil, and bitcoin. *Academy of Marketing Studies Journal*, *28*(2).

Krishna, K. S., & Murthy, M. Y. S. A STUDY ON CUSTOMER ATTITUDES TOWARDS SERVICE QUALITY ATTRIBUTES OF PUBLIC AND PRIVATE SECTORS BANKS IN EAST GODAVARI DISTRICT.

Krishna, K. S., & Murthy, Y. S. (2015). A study on perception of quality of work life among textile manufacturing workers in east Godavari district. [IJSR]. *International Journal of Scientific Research*, *4*(10), 1487–1491.

Krishna, K. S., & Murthy, Y. S. (2015). Employee engagement related to employees' performance. *International Journal of Engineering Technology. Management and Applied Sciences*, *3*(8), 153–157.

Kumar, K., Gupta, N., Reddy, M. G., Murthy, Y. S., Bhadoriya, M. C., & Kamble, M. P. (2023). AN INVESTIGATION OF INDIAN CONSUMERS'PURCHASE INTENTIONS USING ELECTRONIC WORD-OF-MOUTH. *Tec Empresarial, 5*(2).

Lee, J., & Jeong, H. (2021). Workplace conflict and emotional exhaustion: Moderating role of team cohesion. *International Journal of Environmental Research and Public Health*, *18*(11), 5612. DOI: 10.3390/ijerph18115612 PMID: 34073994

Lim, H. W., & Tan, L. K. (2024). Integrating AI tools to enhance emotional intelligence in HR practices. *Human Resource Management Review*, *34*(1), 100958. DOI: 10.1016/j.hrmr.2023.100958

Mayer, J. D., Salovey, P., & Caruso, D. R. (2004). Emotional intelligence: Theory, findings, and implications. *Psychological Inquiry*, *15*(3), 197–215. DOI: 10.1207/s15327965pli1503_02

Mittal, G., & Bansal, R. (2023). Driving Force Behind Consumer Brand Engagement: The Metaverse. In *Cultural Marketing and Metaverse for Consumer Engagement* (pp. 164-181). IGI Global.

Murthy, S. Y., Chandra, B. R., & Joshi, A. (2025). Silence is not always golden: Exploring the causes and consequences of employees' silence in the IT sector. In *Digital Transformation and Sustainability of Business* (pp. 283–288). CRC Press. DOI: 10.1201/9781003606185-66

Murthy, Y., Chodisetty, R. M., Padmaja, R., Reddy, V. J., & Aloori, S. (2025). Brand Evangelism in the Digital Era: The Impact of Data-Driven Influencer Marketing. In *International Conference on Leveraging Emerging Technologies and Analytics for Development* (pp. 245-261). Springer, Singapore. DOI: 10.1007/978-981-96-2548-2_13

Murthy, Y. S. (2024). Mining Minds Sentiment Analysis of Public Perception. *Text Mining and Sentiment Analysis in Climate Change and Environmental Sustainability*, 61.

Murthy, Y. S. (2024). Mining Minds Sentiment Analysis of Public Perception. *Text Mining and Sentiment Analysis in Climate Change and Environmental Sustainability*, 61.

Murthy, Y. S., Bansal, R., Chodisetty, R. C. M., Chakravorty, C., & Sai, K. P. (2025). Transforming Minds AI and Machine Learning Applications in Cognitive Neuroscience. In *Transforming Neuropsychology and Cognitive Psychology With AI and Machine Learning* (pp. 107–128). IGI Global Scientific Publishing. DOI: 10.4018/979-8-3693-9341-3.ch005

Murthy, Y. S., Bhatnagar, P., & Hussain, Z. (2025). Navigating Emotions Mapping Emotional Touchpoints to Enhance Customer Experience in the Digital Era. In *Demystifying Emotion AI, Robotics AI, and Sentiment Analysis in Customer Relationship Management* (pp. 129-160). IGI Global Scientific Publishing. DOI: 10.4018/979-8-3373-1867-7.ch007

Murthy, Y. S., & Chandra, R. (2024). AI Chatbots as a Catalyst for Customer Loyalty Investigating Digital Experience Preferences Across Age Groups. In *Future of Customer Engagement Through Marketing Intelligence* (pp. 143–160). IGI Global. DOI: 10.4018/979-8-3693-2367-0.ch007

Murthy, Y. S., Rabby, F., Bansal, R., & Chakravorty, C. (2025). Building Resilient Brands: Harnessing Influencers, Evangelists, and Data-Driven Strategies. In *Data Analytics and Influencer Marketing for Cultivating Brand Evangelism and Affinity* (pp. 71-102). IGI Global Scientific Publishing.

Murthy, Y. S., Sai, K. P., & Murthy, C. R. (2025). Integrating IoB in Smart Education: Innovative Approaches to Behavioral Data Analytics and Pedagogy. In *Internet of Behavior-Based Computational Intelligence for Smart Education Systems* (pp. 237-270). IGI Global.

Murthy, Y. S., Sai, K. P., & Murthy, C. R. Integrating IoB in Smart Education. *Advances in Educational Technologies and Instructional Design.*

Murthy, Y. S., Srinivas, D., BS, R. C., & Kumar, G. V. (2023). Impulse Buying in the Digital Age: A Dimensional Study on Influencer Marketing Impact on Millennials. *Journal of Advanced Zoology, 44.*

Murthy, Y. S. N., Chandra, R. B., Chakravorty, C., & Shukla, S. Smartwatches, fitness trackers, and beyond: Evaluating experiential marketing efficacy across different age groups. In *Digital Transformation and Sustainability of Business* (pp. 790–794). CRC Press. DOI: 10.1201/9781003606185-186

Nguyen, T., & Bui, M. (2022). Digital empathy and AI-mediated communication: A new frontier in employee relations. *Computers in Human Behavior Reports*, *5*, 100174. DOI: 10.1016/j.chbr.2021.100174

Nguyen, T., Bui, M., & Hoang, A. (2022). Digital empathy and AI-mediated communication: A new frontier in employee relations. *Computers in Human Behavior Reports*, *5*, 100174. DOI: 10.1016/j.chbr.2021.100174

Padmanaaban, P., Rani, L. V. S., Murthy, Y. S., Khandelwal, J., Mahato, A. P., & Das, S. Work-Life Balance and Emotional Intelligence with Special Reference to Private Bank Employees.

Painoli, A. K., Bansal, R., Singh, R., & Kukreti, A. (2021). Impact of Digital Marketing on the Buying Behavior of Youth With Special Reference to Uttarakhand State. In *Big Data Analytics for Improved Accuracy, Efficiency, and Decision Making in Digital Marketing* (pp. 162-182). IGI Global. DOI: 10.4018/978-1-7998-7231-3.ch012

Picard, R. W. (1997). *Affective computing*. MIT Press. DOI: 10.7551/mitpress/1140.001.0001

Rabby, F., Murthy, Y. S., & Bansal, R. (2025). Brand Evangelism in the Digital Era: The Impact of Data-Driven Influencer Marketing. *Journal of Open Innovation*, •••, 100552.

Rahman, K. T., Bansal, R., & Pruthi, N. (2023). Consumer adoption of technologies: A mindset-oriented approach. In Contemporary Studies of Risks in Emerging Technology, Part B (pp. 243-255). Emerald Publishing Limited. DOI: 10.1108/978-1-80455-566-820231013

Rahman, M. A., Ahmed, S., & Khan, T. (2020). Real-time emotion recognition systems: Applications and challenges in workplace contexts. *Journal of Intelligent Systems*, *29*(3), 321–338. DOI: 10.1515/jisys-2020-0006

Raj, D. S. O. N. N., Nirmal, O. N., Kalaivani, A., & Kaur, K. (2023). Artificial Intelligence In E-Commerce: A Literature Review. *Artificial Intelligence*, *21*(01).

Raja, M., Swamy, T. N. V. R. L., Das, S., Bansal, R., Fahlevi, M., & Aziz, A. L. (2025). Does human resource information system influence performance management? *Cogent Business & Management*, *12*(1), 2438862. DOI: 10.1080/23311975.2024.2438862

Ravi, C. B., Donthamsetti, S., & Murthy, Y. S. A Study on Impact of Workplace Democracy on Employee Productivity in IT Companies. In *ORGANIZATION, PURPOSE, AND VALUES* (pp. 302-317). Routledge. DOI: 10.4324/9781003501374-21

Ravi, C. B., Murthy, Y. S., Donthamsetti, S., Kumar, G. V., & Jobanputra, K. Examining the relationship between consumer awareness and purchase intention in online pharma stores: The role of trust. In *Digital Transformation and Sustainability of Business* (pp. 715–718). CRC Press. DOI: 10.1201/9781003606185-170

Satar, M. S., Aggarwal, D., Bansal, R., & Alarifi, G. (2023). Mapping the Knowledge Structure and Unveiling the Research Trends in Social Entrepreneurship and Inclusive Development: A Bibliometric Analysis. *Sustainability (Basel)*, *15*(7), 5626. DOI: 10.3390/su15075626

Shah, K., Shah, O., Murthy, Y. S., & Pragnashre, M. (2025). 50 Gen Z's path to balance: Navigating career aspirations, unveiling life goals, achieving harmony in today's maze. In *Digital Transformation and Sustainability of Business* (pp. 215–218). CRC Press. DOI: 10.1201/9781003606185-50

Sharma, P., Trivedi, A., & Murthy, Y. S. How digital marketing strategies impact the financial performance of SMEs. *Digital Transformation and Sustainability of Business*, 800-803.

Sharma, R., & Rao, P. (2023). Emotion detection systems and conflict prediction: A machine learning perspective. *Journal of Artificial Intelligence and Soft Computing Research*, *13*(2), 89–102. DOI: 10.2478/jaiscr-2023-0006

Sharma, V., & Desai, N. (2022). Emotion profiling in AI systems: Implications for team performance and diversity management. *Journal of Organizational Computing and Electronic Commerce*, *32*(4), 288–305. DOI: 10.1080/10919392.2022.2038345

Singh, A., & Rajan, K. (2021). Predictive analytics in HR: The emerging role of emotion profiling. *Asia Pacific Journal of Human Resources*, *59*(2), 213–229. DOI: 10.1111/1744-7941.12260

Suryanarayana Murthy, Y., Pardha Sai, K., Doss, S., & Ch Murthy Chodisetty, R. S. (2024). Navigating the Intersection of Industry 6.0, Quantum Computing, and Disaster Management: Consumer Insights and Technological Impact. In *The Rise of Quantum Computing in Industry 6.0 Towards Sustainability* (pp. 53–66). Springer. DOI: 10.1007/978-3-031-73350-5_4

Tan, M. C., & Lim, E. J. (2023). Emotion-centric AI and team collaboration: From profiling to conflict mitigation. *Technology in Society*, *74*, 102258. DOI: 10.1016/j.techsoc.2023.102258

Tiwari, M., Bhadoriya, M. C., Murthy, G. R. K., Goswami, M., Murthy, Y. S., & Singh, N. (2022). Examining The Effects of Factors Influencing Organizational Citizenship Behavior With Respect to IT Managers In Gujarat. *Business. Manag. Econ. Eng*, *20*(2), 2154–2167.

Wong, L. H., & Lee, D. Y. (2021). Emotional feedback systems and managerial communication: An AI-assisted approach. *Journal of Managerial Psychology*, *36*(7), 594–608. DOI: 10.1108/JMP-11-2020-0642

Yamijala, S. M., Nimbrain, N., & Bansal, R. (2025). Enhancing Remote Workspaces: The Role of Virtual Reality in Shaping the Virtual Work Environment. *Optimizing Virtual Reality and Metaverse for Remote Work and Virtual Team Collaboration*, 171-190.

Yamijala, S. M. S., Chodisetty, R. C. M., & Chakravorty, C. (2025). Adapting HR Practices for a Transhumanist Future: An Empirical Study on Policy and Implementation. In *Enhancing the Modern Workforce Through Transhumanism* (pp. 117–146). IGI Global.

Yamijala, S. M. S., Chodisetty, R. M., Chakravorty, C., & Sai, K. P. (2025). AI-Powered Learning Revolutionizing Smart Education With Personalized Learning Styles. In *Internet of Behavior-Based Computational Intelligence for Smart Education Systems* (pp. 191–212). IGI Global.

Yamijala, S. M. S., Chodisetty, R. M., Chakravorty, C., & Sai, K. P. (2025). AI-Powered Learning Revolutionizing Smart Education With Personalized Learning Styles. In *Internet of Behavior-Based Computational Intelligence for Smart Education Systems* (pp. 191–212). IGI Global.

Zhou, Z., Lin, S., & Wang, Q. (2023). Exploring the human impact of emotion-recognition AI in HR decision-making. *AI & Society*, *38*, 771–783. DOI: 10.1007/s00146-022-01358-9

Compilation of References

Ab, S. E. (n.d.). Affectiva Trends Analysis Report on Emotions in advertising. https://go.affectiva.com/trends-in-advertising-insights-report

Abd-Alrazaq, A. A., Rababeh, A., Alajlani, M., Bewick, B. M., & Househ, M. (2020). Effectiveness and Safety of Using Chatbots to Improve Mental Health: Systematic Review and Meta-Analysis. [eu7.1]. *Journal of Medical Internet Research*, *22*(7), e16021. DOI: 10.2196/16021 PMID: 32673216

Acemoglu, D., & Restrepo, P. (2017). *Robots and jobs: evidence from US labor markets.* Available at: https://voxeu.org/article/robots-and-jobs-evidence-us

Adam, M., Wessel, M., & Benlian, A. (2020). AI-based chatbots in customer service and their effects on user compliance. [eu8.1]. *Electronic Markets*, *31*(2), 427–445. DOI: 10.1007/s12525-020-00414-7

Adhyaru, J. S., & Kemp, C. (2022). Virtual reality as a tool to promote wellbeing in the workplace. *Digital Health*, *8*, 205520762210844. DOI: 10.1177/20552076221084473 PMID: 35284084

Adner, R., Csaszar, F., Felin, T., & Puranam, P. (2023). Ecosystem density and the limits of dynamic capabilities. *Proceedings - Academy of Management*, *2023*(1), 10630. DOI: 10.5465/AMPROC.2023.10630

Agarwal, A., Maiya, S., & Aggarwal, S. (2021, January 5). Evaluating empathetic chatbots in customer service settings. arXiv.org. https://arxiv.org/abs/2101.01334

Agarwal, C. (2022, February 1). How emotion AI can be a game changer in health-care. Enablex. Retrieved April 23, 2025, from https://www.enablex.io/insights/emotion-ai-in-healthcare/

Agnese, P., Arduino, F. R., & Di Prisco, D. (2025). The era of artificial intelligence: What implications for the board of directors? *Corporate Governance (Bradford)*, *25*(2), 272–287. DOI: 10.1108/CG-06-2023-0259

Ahmad, T., Zhang, D., Huang, C., Zhang, H., Dai, N., Song, Y., & Chen, H. (2021). Artificial intelligence in the sustainable energy industry: Status Quo, challenges, and opportunities. *Journal of Cleaner Production*, *289*, 125834. DOI: 10.1016/j.jclepro.2021.125834

Ahmaniemi, T., Lindholm, H., Kiti Müller, & Tapio Taipalus. (2017). Virtual reality experience as a stress recovery solution in workplace. *2017 IEEE Life Sciences Conference (LSC)*. DOI: 10.1109/LSC.2017.8268179

Ahuja, K. (2023). Emotion AI in healthcare: Application, challenges, and future directions. In Elsevier eBooks (pp. 131–146). DOI: 10.1016/B978-0-443-19096-4.00011-0

Alhussein, G., Ziogas, I., Saleem, S., & Hadjileontiadis, L. J. (2025). Speech emotion recognition in conversations using artificial intelligence: A systematic review and meta-analysis. *Artificial Intelligence Review*, *58*(7), 198. DOI: 10.1007/s10462-025-11197-8

Ali, Z. A. (2022). Self-Directed Leadership Development with Adaptive Learning 360-Feedback Platform. *ProQuest, LLC*. Advance online publication. DOI: 10.12794/metadc1986948

Almadani, N. (2024). Emotional Intelligence: The Development of Emotional Intelligence in Leadership. In *Emotionally Intelligent Methods for Meaningful Leadership* (pp. 77–104). IGI Global Scientific Publishing., DOI: 10.4018/979-8-3693-7372-9.ch004

Al-Zu'bi, H. A. (2015). The impact of emotional intelligence on leadership competencies development of employees. *International Review of Management and Business Research*, *4*(1), 96.

Ameer, I., Bölücü, N., Siddiqui, M., Can, B., Sidorov, G., & Gelbukh, A. (2022). Multi-label emotion classification in texts using transfer learning. *Expert Systems with Applications*, *213*, 118534. DOI: 10.1016/j.eswa.2022.118534

Ameer, I., Bölücü, N., Sidorov, G., & Can, B. (2023). Emotion Classification in Texts Over Graph Neural Networks: Semantic Representation is Better Than Syntactic. *IEEE Access : Practical Innovations, Open Solutions*, *11*, 56921–56934. DOI: 10.1109/ACCESS.2023.3281544

American Psychological Association. (2014, July 1). Coping with stress at work. apa.org. https://www.apa.org/topics/healthy-workplaces/work-stress

Anderson, A. P., Mayer, M. D., Fellows, A. M., Cowan, D. R., Hegel, M. T., & Buckey, J. C. (2017). Relaxation with immersive natural scenes presented using virtual reality. *Aerospace Medicine and Human Performance*, *88*(6), 520–526. DOI: 10.3357/AMHP.4747.2017 PMID: 28539139

Angkasirisan, T. (2025). Naturalistic multimodal emotion data with deep learning can advance the theoretical understanding of emotion. *Psychological Research*, *89*(1), 1–8. DOI: 10.1007/s00426-024-02068-y PMID: 39708231

Anisha, S. A., Sen, A., & Bain, C. (2024). Evaluating the potential and pitfalls of AI-powered conversational agents as humanlike virtual health carers in the remote management of noncommunicable diseases: Scoping review. *Journal of Medical Internet Research*, *26*, e56114. DOI: 10.2196/56114 PMID: 39012688

Anozie, U. C., Onyenahazi, O. B., Ekeocha, P. C., Adekola, A. D., Ukadike, C. A., & Oloko, O. A.Uchechukwu Christopher AnozieObinna Barnabas OnyenahaziPrince Chukwuemeka EkeochaAdeleke Damilola AdekolaChifum Ann UkadikeOmodunni Adejoke Oloko. (2024). Advancements in artificial intelligence for omnichannel marketing and customer service: Enhancing predictive analytics, automation, and operational efficiency. *International Journal of Science and Research Archive*, *12*(2), 1621–1629. DOI: 10.30574/ijsra.2024.12.2.1436

Anusha, S., Ezhilvandan, M., Gayathri, S., Sivaraman, V., & TP, A. (2024). Emerging trends in edge AI for Industry 4.0 and 5.0: Technologies, applications, and challenges. *AI Innovations in Service and Tourism Marketing*, 211-228.

Aoki, N., Tatsumi, T., Naruse, G., & Maeda, K. (2024). Explainable AI for government: Does the type of explanation matter to the accuracy, fairness and trustworthiness of an algorithmic decision as perceived by those who are affected? *Government Information Quarterly*, *41*(4), 101965. DOI: 10.1016/j.giq.2024.101965

Ao, L., Bansal, R., Pruthi, N., & Khaskheli, M. B. (2023). Impact of Social Media Influencers on Customer Engagement and Purchase Intention: A Meta-Analysis. *Sustainability (Basel)*, *15*(3), 2744. DOI: 10.3390/su15032744

Araujo, T. (2018). Living up to the chatbot hype: The influence of anthropomorphic design cues and communicative agency framing on conversational agent and company perceptions. [eu9.1]. *Computers in Human Behavior*, *85*, 183–189. DOI: 10.1016/j.chb.2018.03.051

Arora, S., & Mahapatra, M. (2022). Virtual reality as a solution for workplace stress. *International Journal of Indian Psychology*, *10*(1), 674–690. DOI: 10.25215/1001.068

Ashta, A., & Herrmann, H. (2021). Artificial intelligence and fintech: An overview of opportunities and risks for banking, investments, and microfinance. *Strategic Change*, *30*(3), 211–222. DOI: 10.1002/jsc.2404

Assunção, G., Patrão, B., Castelo-Branco, M., & Menezes, P. (2022). An overview of emotion in artificial intelligence. *IEEE Transactions on Artificial Intelligence*, *3*(6), 867–886. DOI: 10.1109/TAI.2022.3159614

Attamimi, R., Abidin, A., & Amiruddin, A. (2024, November). INTEGRATING ARTIFICIAL INTELLIGENCE INTO SUCCESSION PLANNING AND LEADERSHIP DEVELOPMENT IN HIGHER EDUCATION. *In International Conference of Business and Social Sciences* (pp. 209-228). DOI: 10.24034/icobuss.v4i1.496

Audretsch, D. B., & Kariv, D. (2025). Emotional resources and knowledge management: A gender perspective on human-centric innovation amidst crises. *Journal of Knowledge Management*. Advance online publication. DOI: 10.1108/JKM-02-2024-0235

Aufegger, L., Elliott-Deflo, N., & Nichols, T. (2022). Workspace and productivity: Guidelines for virtual reality workplace design and optimization. *Applied Sciences (Basel, Switzerland)*, *12*(15), 7393. DOI: 10.3390/app12157393

Aulbach, L. (2024). *5. Artificial Intelligence, ethics and empathy*. In Open Book Publishers. [eu10.1], DOI: 10.11647/obp.0423.05

Awad, A. I., Babu, A., Barka, E., & Shuaib, K. (2024). AI-powered biometrics for Internet of Things security: A review and future vision. *Journal of Information Security and Applications*, *82*, 103748. DOI: 10.1016/j.jisa.2024.103748

Babic, M. C., Mariani, F., Flood, L., Klein, M., & Whitaker, S. (2025). Exposure to cognitive automation and wage dynamics in Europe: A sector-level analysis. *Labour Economics*, *83*, 102538. DOI: 10.1016/j.labeco.2024.102538

Bagozzi, R., Brady, M., & Huang, M. (2022). AI Service and Emotion. *Journal of Service Research*, *25*(4), 499–504. DOI: 10.1177/10946705221118579

Bailenson, J. N. (2018). *Experience on demand: What virtual reality is, how it works, and what it can do*. W. W. Norton & Company.

Baines, J. I., Dalal, R. S., Ponce, L. P., & Tsai, H.-C. (2024). Advice from artificial intelligence: A review and practical implications. *Frontiers in Psychology*, *15*, 1390182. DOI: 10.3389/fpsyg.2024.1390182 PMID: 39439754

Baines, J. I., Dalal, R. S., Ponce, L. P., Tsai, H.-C., Eberle, R., & González, V. M. (2024). Artificial intelligence–driven ESG dashboards and corporate eco-efficiency: Evidence from a multi-sector panel. *Journal of Cleaner Production*, *422*, 141612. DOI: 10.1016/j.jclepro.2024.141612

Bakir, V., Laffer, A., McStay, A., Miranda, D., & Urquhart, L. (2024). On manipulation by emotional AI: UK adults' views and governance implications. *Frontiers in Sociology*, *9*, 1339834. DOI: 10.3389/fsoc.2024.1339834 PMID: 38912311

Balasubramaniam, N., Kauppinen, M., Rannisto, A., Hiekkanen, K., & Kujala, S. (2023). Transparency and explainability of AI systems: From ethical guidelines to requirements. *Information and Software Technology*, *159*, 107197. DOI: 10.1016/j.infsof.2023.107197

Ballesteros, J. A., Ramírez, V. G. M., Moreira, F., Solano, A., & Pelaez, C. A. (2024). Facial emotion recognition through artificial intelligence. *Frontiers of Computer Science*, *6*, 1359471. DOI: 10.3389/fcomp.2024.1359471

Baltrušaitis, T., Ahuja, C., & Morency, L.-P. (2019). Multimodal machine learning: A survey and taxonomy. *IEEE Transactions on Pattern Analysis and Machine Intelligence*, *41*(2), 423–443. DOI: 10.1109/TPAMI.2018.2798607 PMID: 29994351

Bankins, S., & Formosa, P. (2023). The Ethical Implications of Artificial Intelligence (AI) For Meaningful Work. *Journal of Business Ethics*, *185*(4), 725–740. DOI: 10.1007/s10551-023-05339-7

Bansal, R., Pruthi, N., & Singh, R. (2022). Developing Customer Engagement Through Artificial Intelligence Tools: Roles and Challenges. In *Developing Relationships, Personalization, and Data Herald in Marketing 5.0* (pp. 130-145). IGI Global.

Bansal, R., Martinho, C., Pruthi, N., & Aggarwal, D. (2024). From virtual observations to business insights: A bibliometric review of netnography in business research. *Heliyon*, *10*(1), e22853. DOI: 10.1016/j.heliyon.2023.e22853 PMID: 38163120

Bansal, R., Saini, S., Ngah, A. H., & Durga Prasad, T. (2024). Proselytizing the potential of influencer marketing via artificial intelligence: Mapping the research trends through bibliometric analysis. *Cogent Business & Management*, *11*(1), 2372889. DOI: 10.1080/23311975.2024.2372889

Bansal, R., Shukla, G., Gupta, A., Singh, A., & Pruthi, N. (2023). Optimizing augmented reality and virtual reality for customer engagement. In *Promoting consumer engagement through emotional branding and sensory marketing* (pp. 24–35). IGI Global.

Bansal, R., Shukla, G., Gupta, A., Singh, A., & Pruthi, N. (2023). Optimizing Augmented Reality and Virtual Reality for Customer Engagement. In *Promoting Consumer Engagement Through Emotional Branding and Sensory Marketing* (pp. 24–35). IGI Global.

Banyal, K., & Panwar, A. (2025). The role of artificial intelligence in leadership development. *International Journal of Research Publication and Reviews*, *6*(4), 5779–5782. DOI: 10.48175/IJRPR-24852

Barnes, A. J., Zhang, Y., & Valenzuela, A. (2024). AI and culture: Culturally dependent responses to AI systems. *Current Opinion in Psychology*, *58*, 101838. DOI: 10.1016/j.copsyc.2024.101838 PMID: 39002473

Bar-On, R. (1997). *The Emotional Quotient Inventory (EQ-i): Technical manual.* Multi-Health Systems.

Barrett, L. F., Adolphs, R., Marsella, S., Martinez, A. M., & Pollak, S. D. (2019). Emotional expressions reconsidered: Challenges to inferring emotion from human facial movements. *Psychological Science in the Public Interest*, *20*(1), 1–68. DOI: 10.1177/1529100619832930 PMID: 31313636

Baruah, A., Shaikh, M., Kumar, R. M., Shaikh, I. A. K., & Thomas, S. N. (2024, April). Artificial Intelligence Influence on Leadership Styles in Human Resource Management for Employee Engagement. *In 2024 Ninth International Conference on Science Technology Engineering and Mathematics (ICONSTEM)* (pp. 1-5). IEEE. https://doi.org/1109/ICONSTEM60960.2024.10568819

Bedi, G., Carrillo, F., Cecchi, G. A., Slezak, D. F., Sigman, M., Mota, N. B., Ribeiro, S., Javitt, D. C., Copelli, M., & Corcoran, C. M. (2015). Automated analysis of free speech predicts psychosis onset in high risk youths. npj. *Schizophrenia*, *1*(1), 15030. DOI: 10.1038/npjschz.2015.30 PMID: 27336038

Behn, O., Leyer, M., & Iren, D. (2024). Employees' acceptance of AI-based emotion analytics from speech on a group level in virtual meetings. *Technology in Society*, *76*, 102466. Advance online publication. DOI: 10.1016/j.techsoc.2024.102466

Berry, K., & Singh, A. (2024). AI-Driven Service Marketing: Transforming Customer Experience and Operational Efficiency. In Nadda, V., Tyagi, P., Singh, A., & Singh, V. (Eds.), *AI Innovations in Service and Tourism Marketing* (pp. 35–56). IGI Global., DOI: 10.4018/979-8-3693-7909-7.ch003

Bersin, J. (2019). Learning in the flow of work. *Harvard Business Review*. Retrieved from https://hbr.org/

Bersin, J. (2018). *The rise of the social enterprise: Deloitte Global Human Capital Trends*. Deloitte Insights.

Berto, R. (2014). The role of nature in coping with psycho-physiological stress: A literature review on restorativeness. *Behavioral Sciences, 4*(4), 394–409. MDPI. DOI: 10.3390/bs4040394

Beverly, E., Hommema, L., Coates, K., Duncan, G., Gable, B., Gutman, T., Love, M., Love, C., Pershing, M., & Stevens, N. (2022). A tranquil virtual reality experience to reduce subjective stress among COVID-19 frontline healthcare workers. *PLoS One*, *17*(2), e0262703. DOI: 10.1371/journal.pone.0262703 PMID: 35139092

Bevilacqua, R., Bailoni, T., Maranesi, E., Amabili, G., Barbarossa, F., Ponzano, M., Virgolesi, M., Rea, T., Illario, M., Piras, E. M., Lenge, M., Barbi, E., & Sakellariou, G. (2025). Framing the Human-Centered Artificial Intelligence Concepts and Methods: Scoping Review. *JMIR Human Factors*, *12*, e67350. DOI: 10.2196/67350 PMID: 40435517

Bevilacqua, S., Masárová, J., Perotti, F. A., & Ferraris, A. (2025). Enhancing top managers' leadership with artificial intelligence: Insights from a systematic literature review. *Review of Managerial Science*. Advance online publication. DOI: 10.1007/s11846-025-00836-7

Bibault, J., Chaix, B., Guillemassé, A., Cousin, S., Escande, A., Perrin, M., Pienkowski, A., Delamon, G., Nectoux, P., & Brouard, B. (2019). A chatbot versus physicians to provide information for patients with breast cancer: Blind, randomized controlled noninferiority trial. [eXtyles11.1]. *Journal of Medical Internet Research*, *21*(11), e15787. DOI: 10.2196/15787 PMID: 31774408

Bickman, L. *Improving Mental Health Services: A 50-Year Journey from Randomized Experiments to Artificial Intelligence and Precision Mental Health*, vol. 47, no. 5. Springer US, 2020. DOI: 10.1007/s10488-020-01065-8

Binns, R., Veale, M., Van Kleek, M., & Shadbolt, N. (2018). 'It's reducing a human being to a percentage': Perceptions of justice in algorithmic decisions. *Proceedings of the 2018 CHI Conference on Human Factors in Computing Systems*, 1–14. DOI: 10.1145/3173574.3173951

Birjali, M., Kasri, M., & Beni-Hssane, A. (2021). A comprehensive survey on sentiment analysis: Approaches, challenges and trends. *Knowledge-Based Systems*, *226*, 107134. DOI: 10.1016/j.knosys.2021.107134

Blau, P. M. (1964). *Exchange and power in social life*. John Wiley & Sons.

Blümel, J. H., Zaki, M., & Bohné, T. (2023). Personal touch in digital customer service: A conceptual framework of relational personalisation for conversational AI. *Journal of Service Theory and Practice*, *34*(1), 33–65. DOI: 10.1108/JSTP-03-2023-0098

Bose, S., & Kumar, N. (2020). Emotional intelligence as a predictor of conflict resolution strategies in organizational settings. *Journal of Organizational Psychology*, *20*(2), 45–56. DOI: 10.33423/jop.v20i2.3012

Boyatzis, R. E. (2018). The Competent Manager: A Model for Effective Performance. *Journal of Management Development*, *37*(7), 604–608.

Boyatzis, R. E., Goleman, D., & Rhee, K. (2000). Clustering competence in emotional intelligence. In Bar-On, R., & Parker, J. D. A. (Eds.), *The Handbook of Emotional Intelligence* (pp. 343–362). Jossey-Bass.

Braun, V., & Clarke, V. (2006). Using thematic analysis in psychology. *Qualitative Research in Psychology*, *3*(2), 77–101. DOI: 10.1191/1478088706qp063oa

Breiter, K., Crome, C., Oberländer, A. M., & Schnaak, F. (2024). Dynamic capabilities for the twin-transformation climb: A capability maturity model. *Information Systems Frontiers*, *26*(8), 2205–2226. DOI: 10.1007/s10796-024-10520-y

Brun, A., Liu, R., Shukla, A., Watson, F., & Gratch, J. (2025). Exploring Emotion-Sensitive LLM-Based Conversational AI. *arXiv preprint arXiv:2502.08920.*

Brynjolfsson, E., & McAfee, A. (2014). *The second machine age: Work, progress, and prosperity in a time of brilliant technologies*. W. W. Norton & Company.

Brynjolfsson, E., & McAfee, A. (2014). *The Second Machine Age: Work, Progress, and Prosperity in a Time of Brilliant Technologies*. W. W. Norton & Company.

Brynjolfsson, E., & McAfee, A. (2017). *Machine, platform, crowd: Harnessing our digital future*. W. W. Norton & Company.

Brynjolfsson, E., McElheran, K., Rock, D., & Syverson, C. (2023). The complementary skills gap: Managerial data literacy and the impact on AI adoption. *Management Science*, *69*(11), 6581–6604. DOI: 10.1287/mnsc.2023.4967

Buckingham, M. (2012). Leadership development in the age of the algorithm. *Harvard Business Review*, *90*(6), 86–92. https://pubmed.ncbi.nlm.nih.gov/22741421/ PMID: 22741421

Bughin, J., Seong, J., Manyika, J., Chui, M., & Joshi, R. (2019). *Notes from the AI frontier: Modeling the impact of AI on the world economy*. McKinsey Global Institute.

Buolamwini, J., & Gebru, T. (2018). Gender shades: Intersectional accuracy disparities in commercial gender classification. *Proceedings of Machine Learning Research*, *81*, 77–91.

Burgess, M. (2024). Deceptive AI dehumanizes: The ethics of misattributed intelligence in the design of Generative AI interfaces. *2024 IEEE Symposium on Visual Languages and Human-Centric Computing (VL/HCC)*, 96–108. [eXtyles12.1]DOI: 10.1109/VL/HCC60511.2024.00021

Butaru, F., Chen, Q., Clark, B., Das, S., Lo, A. W., & Siddique, A. (2016). Risk and risk management in the credit card industry. *Journal of Banking & Finance*, *72*, 218–239. DOI: 10.1016/j.jbankfin.2016.07.015

Calefato, F., Lanubile, F., & Novielli, N. (2020). Supporting emotional intelligence, productivity and team goals while handling software requirements changes. *ACM Transactions on Software Engineering and Methodology*, *30*(2), 1–29. DOI: 10.1145/3664600

Caliskan, A., Bryson, J. J., & Narayanan, A. (2017). Semantics derived automatically from language corpora contain human-like biases. *Science*, *356*(6334), 183–186. DOI: 10.1126/science.aal4230 PMID: 28408601

Calvo, R. A., & D'Mello, S. (2010). Affect detection: An interdisciplinary review of models, methods, and their applications. *IEEE Transactions on Affective Computing*, *1*(1), 18–37. DOI: 10.1109/T-AFFC.2010.1

Calvo, R. A., & Peters, D. (2014). *Positive computing: Technology for wellbeing and human potential*. MIT Press. DOI: 10.7551/mitpress/9764.001.0001

Cambria, E. (2016). Affective Computing and Sentiment Analysis. *IEEE Intelligent Systems*, *31*(2), 102–107. DOI: 10.1109/MIS.2016.31

Cambria, E., Olsher, D., & Rajagopal, D. "SenticNet 3: A common and common-sense knowledge base for cognition-driven sentiment analysis," in *Proc. 26th International Conference on Computational Linguistics*, 2016, pp. 2666–2677.

Cambria, E., Poria, S., Hazarika, D., & Kwok, K. (2018, April). SenticNet 5: Discovering conceptual primitives for sentiment analysis by means of context embeddings. *Proceedings of the AAAI Conference on Artificial Intelligence*, *32*(1), •••. DOI: 10.1609/aaai.v32i1.11559

Can, G. D., &Tolay, E. (2024). EXAMINING EMPLOYEES' EMOTIONS TOWARDS ARTIFICIAL INTELLIGENCE (AI): a QUALITATIVE RESEARCH. DokuzEylülÜniversitesiSosyalBilimlerEnstitüsüDergisi. DOI: 10.16953/deusosbil.1561404

Carasco-Saul, M., Kim, W., & Kim, T. (2015). Leadership and employee engagement: Proposing research agendas through a review of literature. *Human Resource Development Review*, *14*(1), 38–63. DOI: 10.1177/1534484314560406

Carnazzo, C., Spada, S., Lamacchia, S., Manuri, F., Sanna, A., & Cavatorta, M. P. (2024). Virtual reality in ergonomics by wearable devices: Experiences from the automotive sector. *Journal of Workplace Learning*, *36*(7), 621–635. DOI: 10.1108/JWL-03-2024-0064

Catalini, C., & Gans, J. S. (2020). Some simple economics of the blockchain. *Communications of the ACM*, *63*(7), 80–90. DOI: 10.1145/3359552

Cavicchio, F. (2024). Challenges and Ethical Considerations of Emotion Detection. In *Emotion Detection in Natural Language Processing* (pp. 99–105). Springer Nature Switzerland.

Chamakiotis, P., Dekoninck, E. A., & Panteli, N. (2021). Leading geographically dispersed teams: The role of emotional intelligence and trust. *International Journal of Human Resource Management*, *32*(10), 2123–2147. DOI: 10.1080/09585192.2019.1674355

Chamorro-Premuzic, T., Wade, M., & Jordan, J. (2017). The Promise and Peril of Artificial Intelligence. *Harvard Business Review*, *95*(4), 58–65.

Chatterjee, S., Chaudhuri, R., Vrontis, D., Thrassou, A., & Ghosh, S. K. (2021). Adoption of artificial intelligence-integrated CRM systems in agile organisations in India. *Technological Forecasting and Social Change*, *168*, 120783. DOI: 10.1016/j.techfore.2021.120783

Chattu, V. K. (2021). A review of artificial intelligence, big data, and blockchain technology applications in medicine and global health. *Big Data and Cognitive Computing*, *5*(3), 41. DOI: 10.3390/bdcc5030041

Chaves, A. P., & Gerosa, M. A. (2020). How should my chatbot interact? A survey on Social Characteristics in Human–Chatbot Interaction Design. [eXtyles13.1]. *International Journal of Human-Computer Interaction*, *37*(8), 729–758. DOI: 10.1080/10447318.2020.1841438

Chen, Z. (2022). Artificial Intelligence-Virtual Trainer: Innovative Didactics Aimed at Personalized Training Needs. *Journal of the Knowledge Economy*, 1 - 19. .DOI: 10.1007/s13132-022-00985-0

Chen, G., & Li, S. (2021). Effect of Employee–Customer Interaction Quality on customers' prohibitive voice behaviors: Mediating roles of customer trust and identification. [eXtyles14.1]. *Frontiers in Psychology*, *12*, 773354. Advance online publication. DOI: 10.3389/fpsyg.2021.773354 PMID: 34970197

Chen, Y., & Wu, Z. (2022). A review on ergonomics evaluations of virtual reality. *Work (Reading, Mass.)*, *74*(3), 831–841. DOI: 10.3233/WOR-205232 PMID: 36442175

Chen, Y., Zhao, J., & Li, X. (2021). Emotion AI in the workplace: Prospects and ethical concerns. *Journal of Business Ethics and Technology*, *34*(1), 12–27. DOI: 10.1007/s10551-021-04879-y

Cheong, I. (2024). AI Manipulation and Individual Autonomy.ACM, 15. https://inyoungcheong.github.io/assets/pdf/autonomy.pdf

Cheong, J., Kalkan, S., & Gunes, H. (2021). The Hitchhiker's Guide to Bias and Fairness in Facial Affective Signal Processing: Overview and techniques. [eXtyles15.1]. *IEEE Signal Processing Magazine*, *38*(6), 39–49. DOI: 10.1109/MSP.2021.3106619

Cherniss, C. (2010). Emotional intelligence: Toward clarification of a concept. *Industrial and Organizational Psychology: Perspectives on Science and Practice*, *3*(2), 110–126. DOI: 10.1111/j.1754-9434.2010.01231.x

Chiekezie, N., Obiki-Osafiele, A., & Agu, E. (2024). Preparing the workforce for AI technologies through training and professional development for future readiness. World. *Journal of Engineering and Technology Research*, *3*(1), 001–018. Advance online publication. DOI: 10.53346/wjetr.2024.3.1.0050

Chi, N. W., Huang, Y. C., & Lin, S. C. (2020). High performance work systems, employees' creative behavior, and the moderating effects of emotional intelligence: An empirical study in Taiwan. *International Journal of Human Resource Management*, *31*(2), 229–258. DOI: 10.1080/09585192.2017.1380064

Chipman, P., D'Mello, S. K., Gholson, B., Graesser, A. C., McDaniel, B., & Witherspoon, A. (2006). Detection of Emotions during Learning with AutoTutor. 28(28). https://escholarship.org/content/qt2tb300fm/qt2tb300fm.pdf?t=op2jup

Choi, H. S., Bruyns, G., Cheng, T., Zhang, W., & Sharma, S. (2025). Human cognition and emotions for human-centred design in vertical interior urban spaces. *Journal of Urban Design*, *30*(1), 114–137. DOI: 10.1080/13574809.2024.2357803

Chopade, P., Edwards, D., Khan, S. M., Andrade, A., & Pu, S. (2019, November). CPSX: using AI-machine learning for mapping human-human interaction and measurement of CPS teamwork skills. *In 2019 IEEE International Symposium on Technologies for Homeland Security (HST)* (pp. 1-6). IEEE. DOI: 10.1109/HST47167.2019.9032906

Chundru, S., & Whig, P. (2025). Future of Emotional Intelligence in Technology: Trends and Innovations. In *Humanizing Technology With Emotional Intelligence* (pp. 457–468). IGI Global Scientific Publishing.

Ciechanowski, L., Przegalinska, A., Magnuski, M., & Gloor, P. (2018). In the shades of the uncanny valley: An experimental study of human–chatbot interaction. [eXtyles16.1]. *Future Generation Computer Systems*, *92*, 539–548. DOI: 10.1016/j.future.2018.01.055

Compliance, A. I. in EU vs. US: Key Differences. (n.d.). https://www.usetract.com/seoblog/ai-compliance-in-eu-vs-us-key-differences/

Corvite, S., Roemmich, K., Rosenberg, T. I., & Andalibi, N. (2023). Data subjects' perspectives on emotion artificial intelligence use in the workplace: *A relational ethics lens. Proceedings of the ACM on Human-Computer Interaction,* 7(CSCW1), 1-38. DOI: 10.1145/3579600

Cowie, R., & Cornelius, R. R. (2003). Describing the emotional states that are expressed in speech. *Speech Communication*, *40*(1–2), 5–32. DOI: 10.1016/S0167-6393(02)00071-7

Cowie, R., & Douglas-Cowie, E. (2021). Ethics in emotional AI: A framework for considering the ethical issues of using emotion detection technology. *AI & Society*, *36*(1), 1–13. DOI: 10.1007/s00146-020-00999-1

Craig, S., D'Mello, S., Gholson, B., Witherspoon, A., Sullins, J., & Graesser, A. (2004). Emotions during learning: The first steps toward an affect sensitive intelligent tutoring system. In eLearn: World Conference on EdTech (pp. 264-268). A*ssociation for the Advancement of Computing in Education (AACE)*. https://www.learntechlib.org/primary/p/11300/

Crawford, K., & Paglen, T. (2021). Working with affective computing: Exploring UK public perceptions of AI-enabled workplace surveillance. *arXiv preprint arXiv:2205.08264*. https://arxiv.org/abs/2205.08264

Crawford, K. (2021). *Atlas of AI: Power, politics, and the planetary costs of artificial intelligence*. Yale University Press.

Crawford, K., & Calo, R. (2016). There is a blind spot in AI research. *Nature*, *538*(7625), 311–313. DOI: 10.1038/538311a PMID: 27762391

Cui, Y., Zhang, Y., & Li, Z. (2020). Emotion-aware AI for customer service: Opportunities and challenges. *Journal of Artificial Intelligence Research*, *29*(4), 221–236.

Cummins, N., Scherer, S., Krajewski, J., Schnieder, S., Epps, J., & Quatieri, T. F. (2015). A review of depression and suicide risk assessment using speech analysis. *Speech Communication*, *71*, 10–49. DOI: 10.1016/j.specom.2015.03.004

D'Mello, D., & Graesser, A. (2012). Dynamics of affective states during complex learning. *International Journal of Learning Technology*, *7*(3), 240–247.

D'Mello, S., & Graesser, A. (2012). Dynamics of affective states during complex learning. *Learning and Instruction*, *22*(2), 145–157. DOI: 10.1016/j.learninstruc.2011.10.001

Darcy, A., Daniels, J., Salinger, D., Wicks, P., & Robinson, A. (2021). Evidence of Human-Level bonds established with a digital conversational agent: Cross-sectional, retrospective observational study. [eXtyles17.1]. *JMIR Formative Research*, *5*(5), e27868. DOI: 10.2196/27868 PMID: 33973854

Darraz, N., Karabila, I., El-Ansari, A., Alami, N., & El Mallahi, M. (2025). Integrated sentiment analysis with BERT for enhanced hybrid recommendation systems. *Expert Systems with Applications*, *261*, 125533. DOI: 10.1016/j.eswa.2024.125533

Davenport, T. H., Guha, A., Grewal, D., & Bressgott, T. (2020). How artificial intelligence will change the future of marketing. *Journal of the Academy of Marketing Science*, *48*(1), 24–42. DOI: 10.1007/s11747-019-00696-0

Davenport, T. H., & Ronanki, R. (2018). Artificial Intelligence for the Real World. *Harvard Business Review*, *96*(1), 108–116.

Davison, R. M., Wong, L. H., Peng, J., & Georgakakis, D. (2023). The art of digital transformation as crafted by a chief digital officer. *International Journal of Information Management*, *69*, 102617. DOI: 10.1016/j.ijinfomgt.2022.102617

Day, D. V., Fleenor, J. W., Atwater, L. E., Sturm, R. E., & McKee, R. A. (2014). Advances in leader and leadership development: A review of 25 years of research and theory. *The Leadership Quarterly*, *25*(1), 63–82. DOI: 10.1016/j.leaqua.2013.11.004

De Carlo, A., Carluccio, F., & Rapisarda, S. (2020). Three Uses Of Virtual Reality In Work And Organizational Psychology Interventions. A dialogue between virtual reality and organizational well-being: Relaxation techniques, personal resources, and anxiety/depression treatments. *TPM. Testing, Psychometrics, Methodology in Applied Psychology*, *27*(1). Advance online publication. DOI: 10.4473/TPM27.1.8

De Carlo, A., Rapisarda, S., Mora, D., & Benevene, P. (2020). Your best virtual self-improvement. the use of virtual reality in stress management training. *Psychological Applications and Trends*, *2020*, 103–107. Advance online publication. DOI: 10.36315/2020inpact022

De Cleen, T., Baecke, P., & Goedertier, F. (2025). The influence of emotions and communication style on customer satisfaction and recommendation in a call center context: An NLP-based analysis. [eXtyles18.1]. *Journal of Business Research*, *189*, 115192. DOI: 10.1016/j.jbusres.2025.115192

Deepa, R., Sekar, S., Malik, A., Kumar, J., & Attri, R. (2024). Impact of AI-focused technologies on social and technical competencies for HR managers: A systematic review and research agenda. *Technological Forecasting and Social Change*, *202*, 123301. DOI: 10.1016/j.techfore.2024.123301

Deepthi, P., Shaikh, M., Nargunde, A. S., Faldu, R., & Goli, G. (2024, April). Deep learning-enabled human resource analytics in predicting employee performance. In 2024 Ninth International Conference on Science Technology Engineering and Mathematics (ICONSTEM) (pp. 1-5). *IEEE.https://* DOI: 10.1109/ICONSTEM60960.2024.10568716

Dehbozorgi, N., & Kunuku, M. T. (2023). Exploring the influence of emotional states in peer interactions on students' academic performance. *IEEE Transactions on Education*, *67*(3), 405–412. DOI: 10.1109/TE.2023.3335171

Delina, G., Bayissa, B., Krishnaraj, R., Sathyamoorthi, V., & Inayath Ahamed, S. B. (n.d.). Emotion AI as a HR Tool for Promoting Workplace Well-Being: Examining the Practical and Ethical Challenges using Efficient net. https://doi.org/DOI: 10.5171/2024.4328924

Dellermann, D., Calma, A., Lipusch, N., Weber, T., & Ebel, P. (2019). The future of human–AI collaboration: A taxonomy of design knowledge for hybrid intelligence systems. *Business & Information Systems Engineering*, *61*(3), 259–272. DOI: 10.1007/s12599-019-00595-0

Deloitte. (2024). *New Deloitte Survey: Increasing Consumer Privacy and Security Concerns in the Generative AI Era.* Available at https://www2.deloitte.com/us/en/pages/about-deloitte/articles/press-releases/increasing-consumer-privacy-and-security-concerns-in-the-generative-ai-era.html

Denial. (2024, December 23). How does AI detect tone of voice? – Data Science Society.Data Science Society. https://www.datasciencesociety.net/how-does-ai-detect-tone-of-voice/

Deora, R., Ramakrishnan, S., Prathikantam, R., & Seth, S. (2025, February). Revolutionizing Customer Experience Through NLP and Sentiment Analysis Strategies. In *2025 2nd International Conference on Computational Intelligence, Communication Technology and Networking (CICTN)* (pp. 1005-1009). IEEE. DOI: 10.1109/CICTN64563.2025.10932467

Desai, S., Athalye-Jape, G., Bottcher, S., Campbell, C., Chiffings, D., Nathan, E., Fardinpour, A., Kinnaird, L., Bulsara, M., & Rao, S. (2025). Effect of using virtual reality on fatigue and mental workload as key determinants of perceived stress in neonatal intensive care staff: A randomized controlled trial feasibility study and protocol. *Nursing in Critical Care*, *30*(2), e13249. Advance online publication. DOI: 10.1111/nicc.13249 PMID: 39989032

Devi, S., Kaur, S., Goel, D., & Yadav, B. (2025). Navigating the Perils: Exploring Identity Threats Confronting Emotional Artificial Intelligence. In *Humanizing Technology With Emotional Intelligence* (pp. 433-442). IGI Global Scientific Publishing.

Devlin, J., Chang, M. W., Lee, K., & Toutanova, K. (2019, June). Bert: Pre-training of deep bidirectional transformers for language understanding. In *Proceedings of the 2019 conference of the North American chapter of the association for computational linguistics: human language technologies, volume 1 (long and short papers)* (pp. 4171-4186).

Devlin, J., Chang, M.-W., Lee, K., & Toutanova, K. "BERT: Pre-training of deep bidirectional transformers for language understanding," *arXiv preprint* arXiv:1810.04805, 2018.

Devlin, J., Chang, M. W., Lee, K., & Toutanova, K. (2019). BERT: Pre-training of deep bidirectional transformers for language understanding. In *Proceedings of the 2019 Conference of the North American Chapter of the Association for Computational Linguistics: Human Language Technologies* (Vol. 1, pp. 4171–4186). DOI: 10.18653/v1/N19-1423

Dhivrani, R., & Sinha, R. K. (2024, March). Exploring the Possibilities of Emotional Text Analysis with Deep Learning Technologies. In *2024 3rd International Conference for Innovation in Technology (INOCON)* (pp. 1-6). IEEE. DOI: 10.1109/INOCON60754.2024.10512180

Di Luzio, F., Rosato, A., & Panella, M. (2025). An explainable fast deep neural network for emotion recognition. *Biomedical Signal Processing and Control, 100*, 107177. DOI: 10.1016/j.bspc.2024.107177

Diener, E., Oishi, S., & Lucas, R. E. (2018). National accounts of wellbeing. In Diener, E., Oishi, S., & Tay, L. (Eds.), *Handbook of wellbeing*. DEF Publishers., DOI: 10.31234/osf.io/qbq7z

Diener, E., Oishi, S., & Lucas, R. E. (2018). Subjective wellbeing: Three decades of progress. *Psychological Bulletin*, *125*(2), 276–302. DOI: 10.1037/0033-2909.125.2.276

Dignum, V. (2019). Responsible Artificial intelligence: How to develop and use AI in a responsible way. https://link.springer.com/content/pdf/10.1007/978-3-030-30371-6.pdf[eXtyles19.1]

Dillon, S. (2020). The Eliza effect and its dangers: From demystification to gender critique. [eXtyles20.1]. *Journal for Cultural Research*, *24*(1), 1–15. DOI: 10.1080/14797585.2020.1754642

Diwanji, V. S., Geana, M., Pei, J., Nguyen, N., Izhar, N., & Chaif, R. H. (2025). Consumers' Emotional Responses to AI-Generated Versus Human-Generated Content: The Role of Perceived Agency, Affect and Gaze in Health Marketing. *International Journal of Human-Computer Interaction*, •••, 1–21. DOI: 10.1080/10447318.2025.2454954

Dorfleitner, G., Hornuf, L., & Kreppmeier, J. (2023). Promise not fulfilled: FinTech, data privacy, and the GDPR. *Electronic Markets*, *33*(1), 33. DOI: 10.1007/s12525-023-00622-x

Drake, A. (2025). Commercializing Emotions in a Lawful and Responsible Manner: The Limitations, Possibilities and Dilemmas in an Emotional AI Service Business Concept in the Workplace. In *Emotional Data Applications and Regulation of Artificial Intelligence in Society* (pp. 261–281). Springer Nature Switzerland. DOI: 10.1007/978-3-031-80111-2_15

Dubey, R., Gunasekaran, A., Childe, S. J., Papadopoulos, T., Hazen, B. T., & Roubaud, D. (2018). Examining top management commitment to TQM diffusion using institutional and upper-echelon theories. *International Journal of Production Research*, *56*(8), 2988–3006. DOI: 10.1080/00207543.2017.1394590

Du, K., Xing, F., Mao, R., & Cambria, E. (2024). Financial sentiment analysis: Techniques and applications. *ACM Computing Surveys*, *56*(9), 1–42. DOI: 10.1145/3649451

Durai, P., & Durai, P. (2023, December 29). Facial Emotion Recognition in Real-Time.LearnOpenCV – Learn OpenCV, PyTorch, Keras, TensorflowWith Code, & Tutorials. https://learnopencv.com/facial-emotion-recognition/

Durovic, M., & Corno, T. (2024). The privacy of emotions: From the GDPR to the AI Act, an overview of emotional AI regulation and the protection of privacy and personal data. *Privacy, Data Protection and Data-driven Technologies*, 368-404.

Durovic, M., & Corno, T. (2024).The privacy of emotions.In Routledge eBooks (pp. 368–404). DOI: 10.4324/9781003502791-18

Dwivedi, D. (2025). Emotional Intelligence and Artificial Intelligence Integration Strategies for Leadership Excellence. *Advances in Research*, *26*(1), 84–94. DOI: 10.9734/air/2025/v26i11235

Dwivedi, Y. K., Hughes, L., Ismagilova, E., Aarts, G., Coombs, C., Crick, T., Duan, Y., Dwivedi, R., Edwards, J., Eirug, A., Galanos, V., Ilavarasan, P. V., Janssen, M., Jones, P., Kar, A. K., Kizgin, H., Kronemann, B., Lal, B., Lucini, B., & Williams, M. D. (2021). Artificial Intelligence (AI): Multidisciplinary perspectives on emerging challenges, opportunities, and agenda for research, practise, and policy. *International Journal of Information Management*, *57*, 101994. DOI: 10.1016/j.ijinfomgt.2019.08.002

Edmondson, A. C. (2019). *The fearless organization: Creating psychological safety in the workplace for learning, innovation, and growth*. John Wiley & Sons.

Ekman, P. (1991). Universal facial expressions of emotion. *California Mental Health Research Digest*, *8*(4), 151–158.

Ekman, P., & Friesen, W. V. (1978). *Facial action coding system: A technique for the measurement of facial movement*. Consulting Psychologists Press.

Ekman, P., & Friesen, W. V. (1978). *Facial Action Coding System: A Technique for the Measurement of Facial Movement*. Consulting Psychologists Press.

El Arab, R. A., Alkhunaizi, M., Alhashem, Y. N., Al Khatib, A., Bubsheet, M., & Hassanein, S. (2025). Artificial intelligence in vaccine research and development: An umbrella review. *Frontiers in Immunology*, *16*, 1567116. DOI: 10.3389/fimmu.2025.1567116 PMID: 40406131

Elazab, M. (2024). AI-driven personalized learning. *International Journal of Internet Education*, *22*(3), 6–19. DOI: 10.21608/ijie.2024.350579

Elish, M. C. (2016). Moral Crumple Zones: Cautionary Tales in Human-Robot Interaction (WeRobot 2016). SSRN Electronic Journal. [eXtyles21.1]DOI: 10.2139/ssrn.2757236

Enholm, I. M., Papagiannidis, E., Mikalef, P., & Krogstie, J. (2022). Artificial intelligence and business value: A literature review. *Information Systems Frontiers*, *24*(5), 1709–1734. DOI: 10.1007/s10796-021-10186-w

Esmaeilzadeh, H., & Vaezi, R. (2022). Conscious, empathic AI in service. *Journal of Service Research*, *25*(4), 549–564. DOI: 10.1177/10946705221103531

Ethics guidelines for trustworthy AI. (2019). Shaping Europe's Digital Future. https://digital-strategy.ec.europa.eu/en/library/ethics-guidelines-trustworthy-ai

Eyben, F., Wöllmer, M., & Schuller, B. (2013). Recent developments in openSMILE, the Munich open-source multimedia feature extractor. I*n Proceedings of the 21st ACM international conference on Multimedia* (pp. 835–838). DOI: 10.1145/2502081.2502224

Farooq, N., Rafique, Z., Merchant, A., & Narejo, K. R. (2025). Investigating how Artificial Intelligence AI Systems Powered by Emotional Recognition Technologies can assist in Conflict Resolution by Understanding Human Emotions and Behavior. *Review of Applied Management and Social Sciences*, *8*(1), 193–205. DOI: 10.47067/ramss.v8i1.449

Farzan, M., Ebrahimi, H., Pourali, M., & Sabeti, F. (2024). Artificial Intelligence-Powered Cognitive Behavioral Therapy Chatbots, A Systematic Review. [eXtyles22.1]. *Iranian Journal of Psychiatry*. Advance online publication. DOI: 10.18502/ijps.v20i1.17395 PMID: 40093525

Fatouros, G., Soldatos, J., Kouroumali, K., Makridis, G., & Kyriazis, D. (2023). Transforming sentiment analysis in the financial domain with ChatGPT. *Machine Learning with Applications*, *14*, 100508. DOI: 10.1016/j.mlwa.2023.100508

Feijóo, C., Kwon, Y., Bauer, J. M., Bohlin, E., Howell, B., Jain, R., Potgieter, P., Vu, K., Whalley, J., & Xia, J. (2020). Harnessing artificial intelligence (AI) to increase well-being for all: The case for a new technology diplomacy. *Telecommunications Policy*, *44*(6), 101988. DOI: 10.1016/j.telpol.2020.101988 PMID: 32377031

Fernández-Vidal, J., Perotti, F. A., González, R., & Gasco, J. (2022). Managing digital transformation: The view from the top. *Journal of Business Research*, *152*, 29–41. DOI: 10.1016/j.jbusres.2022.07.020

Ferrario, A., Termine, A., & Facchini, A. (2024, March 26). Addressing social misattributions of large language models: An HCXAI-based approach. arXiv.org. https://arxiv.org/abs/2403.17873

Filice, L., & Weese, W. J. (2024). Developing Emotional Intelligence. *Encyclopedia*, *4*(1), 583–599. DOI: 10.3390/encyclopedia4010037

Filieri, R., Lin, Z., Li, Y., Lu, X., & Yang, X. (2022). Customer emotions in service robot encounters: A hybrid machine-human intelligence approach. *Journal of Service Research*, *25*(4), 614–629. DOI: 10.1177/10946705221103937

Filippucci, A., Cueva, C., Gambacorta, L., Doytchinova, A., Li, K., & Steinberg, J. L. (2024). Miracle or myth? Assessing the macroeconomic productivity gains from artificial intelligence. *Organisation for Economic Co-operation and Development Working Papers, 1765*. https://doi.org/DOI: 10.1787/fde2a597-en

Firk, S., Gehrke, Y., Hanelt, A., & Wolff, M. (2022). Top management team characteristics and digital innovation: Exploring digital knowledge and TMT interfaces. *Long Range Planning*, *55*(3), 102166. DOI: 10.1016/j.lrp.2021.102166

Firth, J., Torous, J., Nicholas, J., Carney, R., Rosenbaum, S., & Sarris, J. (2019). Can smartphone mental health interventions reduce symptoms of anxiety? A metaanalysis of randomized controlled trials. *Journal of Affective Disorders*, *234*, 47–56. DOI: 10.1016/j.jad.2018.12.002 PMID: 28456072

Fitzpatrick, K. K., Darcy, A., & Vierhile, M. (2017). Delivering cognitive behavior therapy to young adults with symptoms of depression and anxiety using a fully automated conversational agent (WoeBot): A randomized controlled trial. [eXtyles23.1]. *JMIR Mental Health*, *4*(2), e19. DOI: 10.2196/mental.7785 PMID: 28588005

Floridi, L. (2014). The Fourth Revolution: How the infosphere is reshaping human reality. http://ci.nii.ac.jp/ncid/BB16630552[eXtyles24.1]

Floridi, L., Cowls, J., Beltrametti, M., Chatila, R., Chazerand, P., Dignum, V., Luetge, C., Madelin, R., Pagallo, U., Rossi, F., Schafer, B., Valcke, P., & Vayena, E. (2018). AI4People—An ethical framework for a good AI society: Opportunities, risks, principles, and recommendations. *Minds and Machines*, *28*(4), 689–707. DOI: 10.1007/s11023-018-9482-5 PMID: 30930541

Folger, R., & Cropanzano, R. (1998). *Organizational justice and human resource management*. Sage Publications. DOI: 10.4135/9781452225777

Følstad, A., Araujo, T., Law, E. L., Brandtzaeg, P. B., Papadopoulos, S., Reis, L., Baez, M., Laban, G., McAllister, P., Ischen, C., Wald, R., Catania, F., Von Wolff, R. M., Hobert, S., & Luger, E. (2021). Future directions for chatbot research: An interdisciplinary research agenda. [eXtyles25.1]. *Computing*, *103*(12), 2915–2942. DOI: 10.1007/s00607-021-01016-7

Francesco, D. L., Rosato, A., & Panella, M. (2024).An explainable fast deep neural network for emotion recognition.arXiv (Cornell University). https://doi.org//arxiv .2407.14865DOI: 10.48550

Freina, L., & Ott, M. (2015). A Literature Review on Immersive Virtual Reality in Education: State Of The Art and Perspectives. *The International Scientific Conference eLearning and Software for Education*, 1, 133–141. DOI: 10.12753/2066-026X-15-020

Fulmer, R., Joerin, A., Gentile, B., Lakerink, L., & Rauws, M. (2018). Using Psychological Artificial intelligence (TESS) to relieve symptoms of depression and anxiety: Randomized controlled trial. [eXtyles26.1]. *JMIR Mental Health*, *5*(4), e64. DOI: 10.2196/mental.9782 PMID: 30545815

Furnham, A., & Taylor, N. (2020). The relationship between emotional intelligence and occupational personality scales in senior management. *Personality and Individual Differences*, *154*, 109647. DOI: 10.1016/j.paid.2019.109647

Gade, K. R. (2021). Overcoming the Data Silo Divide: A Holistic Approach to ELT Integration in Hybrid Cloud Environments. *Journal of Innovative Technologies*, *4*(1).

Gajić, T., Petrović, M. D., Pešić, A. M., Conić, M., & Gligorijević, N. (2024). Innovative Approaches in Hotel Management: Integrating Artificial Intelligence (AI) and the Internet of Things (IoT) to Enhance Operational Efficiency and Sustainability. *Sustainability (Basel)*, *16*(17), 7279. DOI: 10.3390/su16177279

Galvão Gomes da Silva, J., Finardi, G., & Caprara, B. (2022). Emotional artificial intelligence in mental health: Challenges and opportunities. *Frontiers in Psychology*, *13*, 827804. DOI: 10.3389/fpsyg.2022.827804

Gao, Y., & Liu, H. (2023). Artificial intelligence-enabled personalisation in interactive marketing: A customer journey perspective. *Journal of Research in Interactive Marketing*, *17*(5), 663–680. DOI: 10.1108/JRIM-01-2022-0023

Garun, N. (2019, May 9). One year later, restaurants are still confused by Google Duplex. The Verge. https://www.theverge.com/2019/5/9/18538194/google-duplex-ai-restaurants-experiences-review-robocalls

Garvey, A. M., Kim, T., & Duhachek, A. (2023). Bad news? Send an AI. Good news? Send a human. *Journal of Marketing*, *87*(1), 10–25. DOI: 10.1177/00222429211066972

Gentsch, P. (2019). *AI in marketing, sales and service: How marketers without a data science degree can use AI, big data, and bots*. Palgrave Macmillan. DOI: 10.1007/978-3-319-89957-2

Georganta, E., & Ulfert, A. (2024). My colleague is an AI! Trust differences between AI and human teammates. *Team Performance Management*, *30*(1/2), 23–37. DOI: 10.1108/TPM-07-2023-0053

Ghotbi, N. (2022). The Ethics of Emotional Artificial Intelligence: A Mixed Method Analysis. *Asian Bioethics Review*, *15*(4), 417–430. DOI: 10.1007/s41649-022-00237-y PMID: 37808444

Gkinko, L., & Elbanna, A. (2022). Hope, tolerance and empathy: Employees' emotions when using an AI-enabled chatbot in a digitalised workplace. *Information Technology & People*, *35*(6), 1714–1743. DOI: 10.1108/ITP-04-2021-0328

Gnewuch, U., Morana, S., Hinz, O., Kellner, R., & Maedche, A. (2024). More than a bot? The impact of disclosing human involvement on customer interactions with hybrid service agents. *Information Systems Research*, *35*(3), 936–955. DOI: 10.1287/isre.2022.0152

Gnewuch, U., Morana, S., & Maedche, A. (2017). Chatbots in customer service: The role of empathy and user emotions. *Proceedings of the International Conference on Information Systems (ICIS).*

Gole, M., Nwadiugwu, W. P., & Miranskyy, A. (2023, November). On sarcasm detection with openai gpt-based models. In *2024 34th International Conference on Collaborative Advances in Software and COmputiNg (CASCON)* (pp. 1-6). IEEE

Goleman, D. (1995). *Emotional intelligence: Why it can matter more than IQ*. Bantam Books.

Goleman, D. (1995). *Emotional Intelligence: Why It Can Matter More Than IQ*. Bantam Books.

Goleman, D. (1998). *Working with emotional intelligence*. Bantam Books.

Goswami, I., Hamida, A. G. B., Murthy, Y. S., & Gopal, S. P. (2023). Effective Role of Human Resource Management Policies Within Marketing Organization: The Impact on Business and Marketing Strategy Implementation. *International Journal of Professional Business Review: Int. J. Prof. Bus. Rev.*, *8*(7), 4.

Graesser, A. C., & D'Mello, S. (2012). Emotions during the learning of difficult material. In *Psychology of learning and motivation* (Vol. 57, pp. 183–225). Academic Press., DOI: 10.1016/B978-0-12-394293-7.00005-4

Graham, S., Depp, C., Lee, E. E., Nebeker, C., Tu, X., Kim, H., & Jeste, D. V. (2019). Artificial Intelligence for Mental Health and Mental Illnesses: An Overview. *Current Psychiatry Reports*, *21*(11), 116. Advance online publication. DOI: 10.1007/s11920-019-1094-0 PMID: 31701320

Granirer, D. (2018). Emotional intelligence: Get with it! *International Journal of Mental Health*, *47*(1), 90–91. DOI: 10.1080/00207411.2018.1425050

Green, B. P. (2018). Ethical Reflections on Artificial Intelligence. *Scientia Et Fides, 6(2),* 9–31. Retrieved from https://apcz.umk.pl/SetF/article/view/SetF.2018.015

Grehen, M., & Grehen, A. (2023). Emotional intelligence, leadership, and work teams: A hybrid literature review. *Heliyon*, *9*(10), e20356. DOI: 10.1016/j.heliyon.2023.e20356 PMID: 37790975

Grewal, D., Roggeveen, A. L., & Nordfält, J. (2017). The future of retailing. *Journal of Retailing*, *93*(1), 1–6. DOI: 10.1016/j.jretai.2016.12.008

Gunkel, D. J. (2021). *Person, thing, robot: A moral and legal ontology for the 21st century and beyond.* MIT Press.

Gupta, R., & Kumar, M. (2023). Ethics in emotion detection systems: Challenges and solutions for HR integration. *AI and Ethics*, *4*(2), 114–128. DOI: 10.1007/s43681-023-00145-3

Gupta, S. K., Fegade, A., Padhye, P., Mohture, A., Kalshetti, P., & Murthy, Y. S. (2024). Evaluating the effect of covid-19 on major world indices: In relation to gold, silver, crude oil, and bitcoin. *Academy of Marketing Studies Journal*, *28*(2).

Hajjar, B., Kwon, H., Pereira, L., Morrison, D., McGrath, J., & Silva, R. (2024). Macroeconomic returns to ethical AI adoption: A computable general equilibrium approach. *Economic Modelling*, *129*, 106353. DOI: 10.1016/j.econmod.2024.106353

Hamad, A., & Jia, B. (2022). How virtual reality technology has changed our lives: An overview of the current and potential applications and limitations. *International Journal of Environmental Research and Public Health, 19*(18), 11278. Advance online publication. DOI: 10.3390/ijerph191811278 PMID: 36141551

Hammad, L. (2024). *Emotion AI in the workplace: Enhancing collaboration and conflict resolution*. FutureWork Press.

Han, E., Yin, D., & Zhang, H. (2023). Bots with feelings: Should AI agents express positive emotion in customer service? *Information Systems Research, 34*(3), 1296–1311. DOI: 10.1287/isre.2022.1179

Han, P., Chen, H., Rasool, A., Jiang, Q., & Yang, M. (2025). MFB: A generalized multimodal fusion approach for bitcoin price prediction using time-lagged sentiment and indicator features. *Expert Systems with Applications, 261*, 125515. DOI: 10.1016/j.eswa.2024.125515

Han, S., & Yang, H. (2018). Understanding adoption of intelligent personal assistants: A parasocial relationship perspective. *Industrial Management & Data Systems, 118*(3), 618–636. DOI: 10.1108/IMDS-05-2017-0214

Hao, X., Demir, E., & Eyers, D. (2025). Critical success and failure factors in the AI lifecycle: A knowledge graph-based ontological study. *Journal of Modelling in Management*. Advance online publication. DOI: 10.1108/JM2-06-2024-0204

Harper, G. (2025, March 26). Understanding the core principles of ethical AI. TopDevelopers.co. https://www.topdevelopers.co/blog/principles-of-ethical-ai/

Haugeland, I. K. F., Følstad, A., Taylor, C., & Bjørkli, C. A. (2022). Understanding the user experience of customer service chatbots: An experimental study of chatbot interaction design. [eXtyles27.1]. *International Journal of Human-Computer Studies, 161*, 102788. DOI: 10.1016/j.ijhcs.2022.102788

Haznitrama, F. G., Choi, H. J., & Chung, C. W. (2025). Methodologies and their comparison in complex compound aspect-based sentiment analysis: A survey. *AI Open*.

Hellowendyqi. (2024, November 12). How policing agencies use AI — The Policing Project.The Policing Project. https://www.policingproject.org/ai-explained-articles/2024/9/6/how-policing-agencies-use-ai

Henkel, A. P., Bromuri, S., Iren, D., & Urovi, V. (2020). Half human, half machine - augmenting service employees with AI for interpersonal emotion regulation. *Journal of Service Management, 31*(2), 247–265. DOI: 10.1108/JOSM-05-2019-0160

Herbosch, M. (2024). Fraud by generative AI chatbots: On the thin line between deception and negligence. [eXtyles28.1]. *Computer Law & Security Review*, *52*, 105941. DOI: 10.1016/j.clsr.2024.105941

Herlina, S., & Iskandar, R. (2025). *Enhancing workplace well-being through emotional intelligence analytics*. HumanTech Insights.

Hermansyah, M., Najib, A., Farida, A., Sacipto, R., & Rintyarna, B. S. (2023). Artificial Intelligence and Ethics: Building an Artificial Intelligence System that Ensures Privacy and Social Justice. *The International Journal of Science in Society*, *5*(1), 154–168. DOI: 10.54783/ijsoc.v5i1.644

Hinduja, S. (2024, June 26). Lessons Learned from Ten Generative AI Misuse Cases. Cyberbullying Research Center. https://cyberbullying.org/generative-ai-misuse-cases

HireVue. (2025, March 8). Digicrusader: AI Marketplace and Digital Tools Coach. https://digicrusader.com/product/hirevue/#:~:text=HireVue%20AI%20transforms%20hiring%20with%20AI-powered%20video%20interviews%2C,recruitment%2C%20reduce%20bias%2C%20and%20hire%20top%20talent%20faster

Ho, A., Hancock, J., & Miner, A. S. (2018). Psychological, relational, and emotional effects of Self-Disclosure after conversations with a chatbot. [eXtyles29.1]. *Journal of Communication*, *68*(4), 712–733. DOI: 10.1093/joc/jqy026 PMID: 30100620

Hochreiter, S., & Schmidhuber, J. (1997). Long short-term memory. *Neural Computation*, *9*(8), 1735–1780. DOI: 10.1162/neco.1997.9.8.1735 PMID: 9377276

Hodgkinson, G. P., Sund, K. J., & Galavan, R. J. (2017). Exploring methods in managerial and organizational cognition: Advances, controversies, and contributions. In *Methodological challenges and advances in managerial and organizational cognition* (pp. 1–22). Emerald Publishing Limited., DOI: 10.1108/S2397-52102017002

Hoermann, S., McCabe, K. L., Milne, D. N., & Calvo, R. A. (2017). Application of synchronous text based dialogue systems in mental health interventions: Systematic review. *Journal of Medical Internet Research*, *19*(8), e267. DOI: 10.2196/jmir.7023 PMID: 28784594

Höhener, K., Wölfle, R., Uebernickel, F., Huang, Z., & Kaganer, E. (2024). Visual explainability and strategic alignment in AI dashboards: Implications for executive decision quality. *MIS Quarterly Executive*, *23*(1), 15–34. DOI: 10.25300/MISQ/2024/15843

Holmes, W., Bialik, M., & Fadel, C. (2019). *Artificial intelligence in education promises and implications for teaching and learning*. Center for Curriculum Redesign.https://discovery.ucl.ac.uk/id/eprint/10139722

Horan, K. A., Harrington, M., LeNoble, C. A., Mosher, M., & Pring, T. (2023). Using virtual reality to bring restorative environments to employees: An online pilot study. *International Journal of Environmental Research and Public Health, 20*(10), 5797. DOI: 10.3390/ijerph20105797 PMID: 37239525

How Emotion AI could help you win the talent war - HRZone. (2023, December 30). HRZone. https://hrzone.com/blog/how-emotion-ai-could-help-you-win-the-talent-war/

Hsu, C. L., & Lin, J. C. C. (2023). Understanding the user satisfaction and loyalty of customer service chatbots. *Journal of Retailing and Consumer Services, 71*, 103211. DOI: 10.1016/j.jretconser.2022.103211

Huang, M. H., & Rust, R. T. (2018). Artificial intelligence in service. *Journal of Service Research, 21*(2), 155–172. DOI: 10.1177/1094670517752459

Huang, M. H., & Rust, R. T. (2021). Artificial Intelligence in Service. *Journal of Service Research, 24*(1), 3–16.

Hutto, C. J., & Gilbert, E. (2014). VADER: A parsimonious rule-based model for sentiment analysis of social media text. *In Proceedings of the International AAAI Conference on Web and Social Media* (Vol. 8, No. 1, pp. 216–225). https://ojs.aaai.org/index.php/ICWSM/article/view/14550

Hutto, C., & Gilbert, E. (2014, May). Vader: A parsimonious rule-based model for sentiment analysis of social media text. In *Proceedings of the international AAAI conference on web and social media* (Vol. 8, No. 1, pp. 216-225). DOI: 10.1609/icwsm.v8i1.14550

Hwang, J. (2024). The role of emotional intelligence in team dynamics. *International Journal of Science and Research Archive*. DOI: 10.30574/ijsra.2024.13.2.1875

Ibrahim, N., & Manzura Mohd Mahidin, E. Azmi Mohd Yusof, Rusli, M. E., Iskandar, N. S., Farhah Amaliya Zaharuddin, & Imran Mahalil. (2021). VR-based relaxation therapy for customer service staff: A pilot study. *Lecture Notes in Computer Science, 13051*, 171–183. DOI: 10.1007/978-3-030-90235-3_15

iMotions. (2024, October 22). Affectiva and emotion AI - affectiva.Affectiva. https://www.affectiva.com/emotion-ai/

Inavolu, S. M. (2024). Exploring AI-driven customer service: Evolution, architectures, opportunities, challenges and future directions. *International Journal of Engineering and Advanced Technology, 13*(3), 156–163.

Inkster, B., Sarda, S., & Subramanian, V. (2018). An empathy driven, conversational artificial intelligence agent (Wysa) for digital mental wellbeing: Real world data evaluation mixed methods study. *JMIR mHealth and uHealth*, *6*(11), e12106. DOI: 10.2196/12106 PMID: 30470676

Insights, E. H. L. (2022, June 3). *How to be an emotionally intelligent leader*. EHL Hospitality Insights. https://hospitalityinsights.ehl.edu/how-to-be-an-emotionally-intelligent-leader

Iqbal, M. S., Abdul Rahim, Z., Alshammari, A. M. K., & Iftikhar, H. (2024). Innovative strategies for overcoming barriers to technology adoption in small and medium-sized enterprises. *Journal of the International Council for Small Business*, *5*(4), 331–344. DOI: 10.1080/26437015.2024.2367440

Iserson, K. V. (2024). Informed consent for artificial intelligence in emergency medicine: A practical guide. *The American Journal of Emergency Medicine*, *76*, 225–230. DOI: 10.1016/j.ajem.2023.11.022 PMID: 38128163

Islam, M. S., Kabir, M. N., Ghani, N. A., Zamli, K. Z., Zulkifli, N. S. A., Rahman, M. M., & Moni, M. A. (2024). Challenges and future in deep learning for sentiment analysis: A comprehensive review and a proposed novel hybrid approach. *Artificial Intelligence Review*, *57*(3), 62. DOI: 10.1007/s10462-023-10651-9

Jain, R. (2024). The Role of Artificial Intelligence in Modern Marketing: Tools, Applications, and Future Trends. Designing Tomorrow: AI, Ethics, and Society's Next Steps, 125.

Jangid, A. (2024). AI AND EMPLOYEE WELLBEING: HOW ARTIFICIAL INTELLIGENCE CAN MONITOR AND IMPROVE MENTAL HEALTH IN THE WORKPLACE. *International Journal of Advanced Research*, *12*(10), 743–764. DOI: 10.21474/IJAR01/19693

Jankovic, S. D., & Curovic, D. M. (2023). Strategic integration of artificial intelligence for sustainable businesses: Implications for data management and human user engagement in the digital era. *Sustainability (Basel)*, *15*(21), 15208. DOI: 10.3390/su152115208

Jin, W., & Kim, H. (2025). Enhancing emotion analysis through valence-arousal modeling with user and AI evaluations. *Edelweiss Applied Science and Technology*, *9*(3), 2987–2992. DOI: 10.55214/25768484.v9i3.5898

Jo, H., Song, C., & Miyazaki, Y. (2019). Physiological Benefits of Viewing Nature: A Systematic Review of Indoor Experiments. *International Journal of Environmental Research and Public Health, 16*(23), 4739. DOI: 10.3390/ijerph16234739 PMID: 31783531

Johnstone, P. (2004). Mixed Methods, Mixed Methodology, and Health Services Research in Practice. *Qualitative Health Research, 14*(2), 259–271. DOI: 10.1177/1049732303260610 PMID: 14768461

Jordan, J., & Wade, M. (2018). As AI makes more decisions, the nature of leadership will change. *HR Future, 2018*(4), 10–11.

Jung, D., Dorner, V., Glaser, F., & Morana, S. (2018). Robo-advisory. *Business & Information Systems Engineering, 60*(1), 81–86. DOI: 10.1007/s12599-018-0521-9

Kaaria, A. G. (2024). Artificial Intelligence and Employee Well-Being: Balancing Technological Progressions with Human-Centric Workplace Strategies, a Research Agenda. *East African Journal of Information Technology, 7*(1), 355–365. DOI: 10.37284/eajit.7.1.2281

Kačerová, I., Kubr, J., Hořejší, P., & Kleinová, J. (2022). Ergonomic design of a workplace using virtual reality and a motion capture suit. *Applied Sciences (Basel, Switzerland), 12*(4), 2150. DOI: 10.3390/app12042150

Kapoor, A., & Verma, V. (2024). EMOTION AI: UNDERSTANDING EMOTIONS THROUGH ARTIFICIAL INTELLIGENCE. *International Journal of Engineering Science and Humanities.* .DOI: 10.62904/0vcbvb24

Kappas, A., & Tepper, I. (2019). Social regulation of emotion: The role of interaction partners. *Emotion Review, 11*(1), 6–13.

Kashaka, N. D. (2025). Exploring the role of emotional intelligence in educational leadership. *Research Invention Journal of Current Issues in Arts and Management, 4*(2), 12–15. DOI: 10.59298/RIJCIAM/2025/421215

Katirai, A. (2024). Ethical considerations in emotion recognition technologies: A review of the literature. *AI and Ethics, 4*(4), 927–948. DOI: 10.1007/s43681-023-00307-3

KC. S. (2024, December 30). Using AI in Recruitment how emotion AI drives better hiring outcomes. imentiv. Retrieved April 24, 2025, from https://imentiv.ai/blog/using-ai-in-recruitment-how-emotion-ai-drives-better-hiring-outcomes/

Kellogg, K. C., Valentine, M. A., Shaw, T. E., & Mathur, N. (2023). Algorithms at work: The new contested terrain of control. *The Academy of Management Annals*, *17*(2), 510–545. DOI: 10.5465/annals.2020.0207

Kelman, H. C. (1958). Compliance, identification, and internalization three processes of attitude change. [eXtyles30.1]. *The Journal of Conflict Resolution*, *2*(1), 51–60. DOI: 10.1177/002200275800200106

Keltner, D., & Ekman, P. "Facial expression of emotion," in *Handbook of Emotions*, 3rd ed., M. Lewis, J. Haviland-Jones, and L. F. Barrett, Eds. Guilford Press, 2008, pp. 211–234.

Kempe, L. (2024, September 9). The Price of Emotion: Privacy, Manipulation, and Bias in Emotional AI. https://www.americanbar.org/. Retrieved April 25, 2025, from https://www.americanbar.org/groups/business_law/resources/business-law-today/2024-september/price-emotion-privacy-manipulation-bias-emotional-ai/

Keyvan, K., & Huang, J. X. (2022). How to approach ambiguous queries in conversational search: A survey of techniques, approaches, tools, and challenges. *ACM Computing Surveys*, *55*(6), 1–40. DOI: 10.1145/3534965

Khalane, A., Makwana, R., Shaikh, T., & Ullah, A. (2025). Evaluating significant features in context-aware multimodal emotion recognition with XAI methods. *Expert Systems: International Journal of Knowledge Engineering and Neural Networks*, *42*(1), e13403. DOI: 10.1111/exsy.13403

Khan, N., Buzzao, G., Rizzi, F., & Settembre-Blundo, D. (2024). Microfoundations of dynamic capabilities enabling scaling pathways for sustainable operations. *Business Strategy and the Environment*, *33*(2), 400–417. DOI: 10.1002/bse.4004

Khare, S. K., Blanes-Vidal, V., Nadimi, E. S., & Acharya, U. R. (2024). Emotion recognition and artificial intelligence: A systematic review (2014–2023) and research recommendations. *Information Fusion*, *102*, 102019. DOI: 10.1016/j.inffus.2023.102019

Khoei, T. T., & Singh, A. (2024). A survey of Emotional Artificial Intelligence and crimes: Detection, prediction, challenges and future direction. *Journal of Computational Social Science*, *7*(3), 2359–2402. DOI: 10.1007/s42001-024-00313-3

Kim, Y. "Convolutional neural networks for sentence classification," *arXiv preprint* arXiv:1408.5882, 2014. DOI: 10.3115/v1/D14-1181

Kim, T. W., Jiang, L., Duhachek, A., Lee, H., & Garvey, A. (2022). Do you mind if I ask you a personal question? How AI service agents alter consumer self-disclosure. *Journal of Service Research*, *25*(4), 649–666. DOI: 10.1177/10946705221120232

Kluge, M. G., Maltby, S., Kuhne, C., Walker, N., Bennett, N., Aidman, E., Nalivaiko, E., & Walker, F. R. (2023). Evaluation of a virtual reality platform to train stress management skills for a defense workforce: Multisite, mixed methods feasibility study. *Journal of Medical Internet Research, 25*, e46368–e46368. DOI: 10.2196/46368 PMID: 37930751

Kobie, N. (2018, May 11). Why Google Duplex calls should concern all of us. Teen Vogue. https://www.teenvogue.com/story/google-duplex-calls-should-we-be-worried

KodeKloudNotes. (n.d.).KodeKloud Notes. https://notes.kodekloud.com/docs/AI-900-Microsoft-Certified-Azure-AI-Fundamentals/Fundamental-AI-Concepts/Principles-of-Responsible-AI

Kojouri, D. K. (2025). The Function of Artificial Intelligence for Transcendent Governance with a Strategic Management Approach. *Management Strategies and Engineering Sciences, 7*(1), 164–174. DOI: 10.61838/msesj.7.1.17

Kottasová, I. (2018, May 11). Google's controversial AI voice assistant won't hide its identity. CNNMoney. https://money.cnn.com/2018/05/11/technology/google-duplex-ai-voice-controversy/index.html

Kouloumpis, E., Wilson, T., & Moore, J. (2011). Twitter sentiment analysis: The good the bad and the omg! In *Proceedings of the international AAAI conference on web and social media* (Vol. 5, No. 1, pp. 538-541).

Koutsioumpa, E. (2023). Development of Emotional Intelligence and Leadership aspects applied in Health Professionals. *A Scoping Review. Technium BioChemMed, 6*, 22–36. DOI: 10.47577/biochemmed.v6i.9533

Krebsz, M., & Dwivedi, D. (2024). Emotional AI: Neuroethics and socially aligned networks. In *Emotional AI and Human-AI Interactions in Social Networking* (pp. 101-130). Academic Press.

Krishna, K. S., & Murthy, M. Y. S. A STUDY ON CUSTOMER ATTITUDES TOWARDS SERVICE QUALITY ATTRIBUTES OF PUBLIC AND PRIVATE SECTORS BANKS IN EAST GODAVARI DISTRICT.

Krishna, K. S., & Murthy, Y. S. (2015). A study on perception of quality of work life among textile manufacturing workers in east Godavari district. [IJSR]. *International Journal of Scientific Research, 4*(10), 1487–1491.

Krishna, K. S., & Murthy, Y. S. (2015). Employee engagement related to employees' performance. *International Journal of Engineering Technology. Management and Applied Sciences, 3*(8), 153–157.

Krizhevsky, A., Sutskever, I., & Hinton, G. E. “ImageNet classification with deep convolutional neural networks,” in *Proc. Advances in Neural Information Processing Systems*, 2012, pp. 1097–1105.

Kroll, T., Nuesch, S., & Meier, C. (2021). The Impact of Emotionally Intelligent Leadership on Employee Mental Health and Organizational Performance. *Leadership and Organization Development Journal*, *42*(6), 1011–1024.

Krugmann, J. O., & Hartmann, J. (2024). Sentiment analysis in the age of generative AI. *Customer Needs and Solutions*, *11*(1), 3. DOI: 10.1007/s40547-024-00143-4

Kumar, A., Dhanka, S., Bansal, R., Sharma, A., Singh, J., Khan, A. A., & Maini, S. “Agriculture in the Era of Industry 5.0,” in *Industry 5.0 and Emerging Technologies: Transformation Through Technology*, 2024.

Kumar, A., Dhanka, S., Bansal, R., Sharma, A., Singh, J., Khan, A. A., & Maini, S. “Smart Crop Selection: Harnessing Machine Learning for Sustainable Agriculture in the Era of Industry 5.0,” in *Industry 5.0 and Emerging Technologies: Transformation Through Technology*, 2024. DOI: 10.1007/978-3-031-70996-8_6

Kumar, A., Sharma, A., Bhatnagar, P., Dhanka, S., & Bist, Y. “Harnessing the Power of Data Analytics to Drive Brand Engagement, Affinity, Evangelism, and Loyalty in the Modern Marketplace,” in *Demystifying Emotion AI, Robotics AI, and Sentiment Analysis in Customer Experience*, 2025. DOI: 10.4018/979-8-3373-1867-7.ch004

Kumar, A., Sharma, A., Dhanka, S., & Maini, S. “Machine Learning for Combating Mental Health Stigma,” in *Transforming Neuropsychology and Cognitive Psychology With AI and Machine Learning*, 2025. DOI: 10.4018/979-8-3693-9341-3.ch014

Kumar, A., Sharma, A., Dhanka, S., Bist, Y., Maini, S., & Bhatnagar, P. “Data Privacy, Ethics, and the Role of AI in Customer Relationship Management,” in *Demystifying Emotion AI, Robotics AI, and Sentiment Analysis in Customer Experience*, 2025. DOI: 10.4018/979-8-3373-1867-7.ch013

Kumar, K., Gupta, N., Reddy, M. G., Murthy, Y. S., Bhadoriya, M. C., & Kamble, M. P. (2023). AN INVESTIGATION OF INDIAN CONSUMERS'PURCHASE INTENTIONS USING ELECTRONIC WORD-OF-MOUTH. *Tec Empresarial*, *5*(2).

Kumar, A., Dhanka, S., Singh, J., Khan, A. A., & Maini, S. (2024). Hybrid machine learning techniques based on genetic algorithm for heart disease detection. *Innovation and Emerging Technologies*, *11*, 2450008. DOI: 10.1142/S2737599424500087

Kumar, A., Khan, A. A., & Singh, J. (2024). Enhancing the Diagnosis of Cardiovascular Disease: A Comparative Examination of Support Vector Machine and Artificial Neural Network Models Utilizing Extensive Data Preprocessing Techniques. *WSEAS Transactions on Computers*, *23*, 318–327. DOI: 10.37394/23205.2024.23.31

Kumar, A., Singh, J., & Khan, A. A. (2024, September). A comprehensive machine learning framework with particle swarm optimization for improved polycystic ovary syndrome (PCOS) diagnosis. *Engineering Research Express*, *6*(3), 035233. DOI: 10.1088/2631-8695/ad76f9

Kumar, R., Kumar, S., & Kumar, P. (2025). A Conceptual Exploration for Harnessing Emotional Intelligence for Transformational Team Leadership. *International Journal of Research and Review in Applied Science, Humanities, and Technology*, *9-13*, 9–13. Advance online publication. DOI: 10.71143/7cmhfd69

Kuo, H. J., Newbutt, N., George, S., & Laird, M. (2025). Using virtual reality mediation in a workplace setting for employees with disabilities: A pilot study. *Computers & Education: X Reality*, *6*, 100093. DOI: 10.1016/j.cexr.2025.100093

Kurian, N. (2025). AI's empathy gap: The risks of conversational Artificial Intelligence for young children's well-being and key ethical considerations for early childhood education and care. *Contemporary Issues in Early Childhood*, *26*(1), 132–139. DOI: 10.1177/14639491231206004

Kusal, S., Patil, S., Choudrie, J., Kotecha, K., Vora, D., & Pappas, I. (2023). A systematic review of applications of natural language processing and future challenges with special emphasis in text-based emotion detection. *Artificial Intelligence Review*, *56*(12), 15129–15215. DOI: 10.1007/s10462-023-10509-0

Kwong, A. T. M., Omar, S. I., & Aliah, M. N. (2024). The ethical implications of AI-Powered personalization in hospitality and tourism. In *Impact of AI and tech-driven solutions in hospitality and tourism* (pp. 103–122). IGI Global. DOI: 10.4018/979-8-3693-6755-1.ch006

La Torre, M., Botes, V. L., Dumay, J., & Odendaal, E. (2019). Protecting a new Achilles heel: The role of auditors within the practice of data protection. *Managerial Auditing Journal*, *36*(2), 218–239. DOI: 10.1108/MAJ-03-2018-1836

Laestadius, L., Bishop, A., Gonzalez, M., Illenčík, D., & Campos-Castillo, C. (2022). Too human and not human enough: A grounded theory analysis of mental health harms from emotional dependence on the social chatbot Replika. [eXtyles31.1]. *New Media & Society*, *146144482211420*. Advance online publication. DOI: 10.1177/14614448221142007

Lake, B. M., Ullman, T. D., Tenenbaum, J. B., & Gershman, S. J. (2017). Building machines that learn and think like people. *Behavioral and Brain Sciences, 40*, e253. DOI: 10.1017/S0140525X16001837 PMID: 27881212

Lakumarapu, S., Nithyanandhan, R., Bhargavi, V. S., & TP, A. (2024, August). Machine Learning Approaches for Liver Disease Prediction: A Comparative Analysis. In *2024 5th International Conference on Electronics and Sustainable Communication Systems (ICESC)* (pp. 159-164). IEEE.

Laux, J., Wachter, S., & Mittelstadt, B. (2024). Three pathways for standardisation and ethical disclosure by default under the European Union Artificial Intelligence Act. *Computer Law & Security Review, 53*, 105957. DOI: 10.1016/j.clsr.2024.105957

Lee, B. D. (2018, June 27). Google's robot caller in first public trial. https://www.bbc.com/news/technology-44624629

Lee, H., Liu, G. K., Chen, Y., & Yeh, S. (2024). Exploring quantitative measures in metacognition of emotion. *Scientific Reports, 14*(1), 1990. Advance online publication. DOI: 10.1038/s41598-023-49709-7 PMID: 38263192

Lee, J., & Jeong, H. (2021). Workplace conflict and emotional exhaustion: Moderating role of team cohesion. *International Journal of Environmental Research and Public Health, 18*(11), 5612. DOI: 10.3390/ijerph18115612 PMID: 34073994

Leo, X., & Huh, Y. E. (2020). Who gets the blame for service failures? Attribution of responsibility toward robot versus human service providers and service firms. [eXtyles32.1]. *Computers in Human Behavior, 113*, 106520. DOI: 10.1016/j.chb.2020.106520

Levantino, F. P. (2025). From Identity to Emotional Dominance?"Early Warnings" on Emotion Recognition Uses by Police Forces. In *Next Democratic Frontiers for Facial Recognition Technology (FRT)* (pp. 129–157). Springer. DOI: 10.1007/978-3-031-89794-8_8

Leviathan, Y., & Matias, Y. (2018, May 8). Google Duplex: an AI system for accomplishing Real-World tasks over the phone. Retrieved May 25, 2025, from https://research.google/blog/google-duplex-an-ai-system-for-accomplishing-real-world-tasks-over-the-phone/[eXtyles33.1]

Li, C., Tang, H., Zhang, J., Guo, X., Cheng, D., & Morimoto, Y. (2024, December). Advancing Aspect-Based Sentiment Analysis Through Deep Learning Models. In *International Conference on Advanced Data Mining and Applications* (pp. 228-242). Singapore: Springer Nature Singapore.

Libai, B., Bart, Y., Gensler, S., Hofacker, C. F., Kaplan, A., Kötterheinrich, K., & Kroll, E. B. (2020). Brave new world? On AI and the management of customer relationships. *Journal of Interactive Marketing*, *51*(1), 44–56. DOI: 10.1016/j.intmar.2020.04.002

Li, J., Ye, Z., & Zhang, C. (2022). Study on the interaction between big data and artificial intelligence. *Systems Research and Behavioral Science*, *39*(3), 641–648. DOI: 10.1002/sres.2878

Li, L., & Wang, Y. (2025). Personalized recommendation and customer loyalty: The moderating role of trust. *Future Business Journal*, *11*(1), 34. DOI: 10.1186/s43093-025-00476-z

Lim, H. W., & Tan, L. K. (2024). Integrating AI tools to enhance emotional intelligence in HR practices. *Human Resource Management Review*, *34*(1), 100958. DOI: 10.1016/j.hrmr.2023.100958

Lins, S., Pandl, K. D., Teigeler, H., Thiebes, S., Bayer, C., & Sunyaev, A. (2021). Artificial intelligence as a service: Classification and research directions. *Business & Information Systems Engineering*, *63*(4), 441–456. DOI: 10.1007/s12599-021-00708-w

Lirio, P., & Plusquellec, P. (2023). Affective computing technology for fostering an emotionally healthy workplace. *Strategic HR Review*, *22*(4), 121–125. Advance online publication. DOI: 10.1108/SHR-04-2023-0024

Li, S., & Deng, W. (2020). Deep facial expression recognition: A survey. *IEEE Transactions on Circuits and Systems for Video Technology*, *30*(10), 3219–3235. DOI: 10.1109/TCSVT.2019.2913898

Liu, Y., Ott, M., Goyal, N., Du, J., Joshi, M., Chen, D., . . . Stoyanov, V. (2019). Roberta: A robustly optimized bert pretraining approach. *arXiv preprint arXiv:1907.11692*.

Liu, B. (2022). *Sentiment analysis and opinion mining*. Springer Nature.

Liu, X., Wang, J., & Zhao, C. (2019). An examination of the congruence and incongruence between employee actual and customer perceived emotional labor. [eXtyles34.1]. *Psychology and Marketing*, *36*(9), 863–874. DOI: 10.1002/mar.21241

Li, Y., Chan, J., Peko, G., & Sundaram, D. (2023). An explanation framework and method for AI-based text emotion analysis and visualisation. *Decision Support Systems*, *178*, 114121. DOI: 10.1016/j.dss.2023.114121

Li, Y., & Jia, J. (2020). Wearable physiological signal-based emotion recognition: A review. *IEEE Sensors Journal*, *20*(21), 13055–13071.

Li, Y., Jiang, Y., Tian, D., Hu, L., Lu, H., & Yuan, Z. (2019). AI-Enabled Emotion Communication. *IEEE Network, 33*(6), 15–21. DOI: 10.1109/MNET.001.1900070

Li, Y., Wang, C., Ratten, V., & Cui, Z. (2023). Artificial intelligence and innovation capability: A dynamic capabilities perspective. *Journal of Business Research, 166*, 114250. DOI: 10.1016/j.jbusres.2023.114250

López-Figueroa, J. C., Ochoa-Jiménez, S., Palafox-Soto, M. O., & Hernández Muñoz, D. S. (2025). Digital leadership: A systematic literature review. *Administrative Sciences, 15*(4), 129. DOI: 10.3390/admsci15040129

Loscalzo, S., Lockman, J., Spector, N., & Boyer, D. (2022). Variations in Demonstrated Emotional Intelligence: Trainee to Experienced Faculty Member*. *Pediatric Critical Care Medicine, 23*(8), 646–650. DOI: 10.1097/PCC.0000000000002974 PMID: 36165938

Lovin, D., Busila, A. V., & Sava, V. (2023). Culture shock, adaptation, and organizational performance in sport: A psychological perspective. *Technological Forecasting and Social Change, 190*, 122403. DOI: 10.1016/j.techfore.2023.122403

Luo, X., Tong, S., Fang, Z., & Qu, Z. (2019). Frontiers: Machines vs. Humans: The Impact of Artificial Intelligence Chatbot Disclosure on Customer Purchases. [eXtyles35.1]. *Marketing Science*, mksc.2019.1192. Advance online publication. DOI: 10.1287/mksc.2019.1192

Lupton, D. (2021). 'Zoom fatigue': Theorizing spatial experiences and the disruption to co present interaction in video communication. *Media International Australia, 178*(1), 111–115. DOI: 10.1177/1329878X20976738

Magni, D., Del Gaudio, G., Papa, A., & Della Corte, V. (2024). Digital humanism and artificial intelligence: The role of emotions beyond the human–machine interaction in Society 5.0. *Journal of Management History, 30*(2), 195–218. DOI: 10.1108/JMH-12-2022-0084

Mahawar, S. (2023, December 21). Data privacy and emotion recognition technology -iPleaders. iPleaders. https://blog.ipleaders.in/data-privacy-and-emotion-recognition-technology/

Mamina, R., & Piraynen, E. (2023). Emotional Artificial Intelligence as a Tool for Human-Machine Interaction. *Discourse (Berkeley, Calif.), 9*(2), 35–51. Advance online publication. DOI: 10.32603/2412-8562-2023-9-2-35-51

Manalu, H. V., & Rifai, A. P. (2024). Detection of human emotions through facial expressions using hybrid convolutional neural network-recurrent neural network algorithm. *Intelligent Systems with Applications, 21*, 200339. DOI: 10.1016/j.iswa.2024.200339

Manghisi, V. M., Evangelista, A., & Uva, A. E. (2022). A virtual reality approach for assisting sustainable human-centered ergonomic design: The ergovr tool. *Procedia Computer Science, 200*, 1338–1346. DOI: 10.1016/j.procs.2022.01.335

Marchegiani, B. (2025). Anthropomorphism, false beliefs, and conversational AIs: How chatbots undermine users' autonomy. [eXtyles36.1]. *Journal of Applied Philosophy*, japp.70008. Advance online publication. DOI: 10.1111/japp.70008

Mariotti, C. (2022). Elite theory. In *The Palgrave Encyclopedia of Interest Groups, Lobbying and Public Affairs* (pp. 427–432). Springer International Publishing.

Maroju, P. K., & Bhattacharya, P. (2025). Understanding Emotional Intelligence: The Heart of Human-Centered Technology. In *Humanizing Technology With Emotional Intelligence* (pp. 1-18). IGI Global Scientific Publishing.

Marr, B. (2025, April 23). Why AI will never truly understand your feelings — and why that matters. Forbes. https://www.forbes.com/sites/bernardmarr/2025/04/23/why-ai-will-never-truly-understand-your-feelings-and-why-that-matters/

Mars, A., & Gouider, M. S. (2017). Big data analysis to features opinions extraction of customer. *Procedia Computer Science, 112*, 906–916. DOI: 10.1016/j.procs.2017.08.114

Martin, K. D., & Zimmermann, J. (2024). Artificial intelligence and its implications for data privacy. *Current Opinion in Psychology, 58*, 101829. DOI: 10.1016/j.copsyc.2024.101829 PMID: 38954851

Mateos, P., & Bellogín, A. (2025). A systematic literature review of recent advances on context-aware recommender systems. *Artificial Intelligence Review, 58*(1), 1–53.

Mattioli, M., & Cabitza, F. (2024). Not in my face: Challenges and ethical considerations in automatic face emotion recognition technology. *Machine Learning and Knowledge Extraction, 6*(4), 2201–2231. DOI: 10.3390/make6040109

Mayer, J. D., Salovey, P., & Caruso, D. R. (2004). Emotional intelligence: Theory, findings, and implications. *Psychological Inquiry, 15*(3), 197–215. DOI: 10.1207/s15327965pli1503_02

Mayer, J. D., Salovey, P., & Caruso, D. R. (2008). Emotional intelligence: New ability or eclectic traits? *The American Psychologist, 63*(6), 503–517. DOI: 10.1037/0003-066X.63.6.503 PMID: 18793038

McDuff, D., & El Kaliouby, R. (2017). Applications of affective computing in human–computer interaction. In Calvo, C. S., D'Mello, S., Gratch, J., & Kappas, A. (Eds.), *The Oxford handbook of affective computing* (pp. 501–512). Oxford University Press.

McDuff, D., El Kaliouby, R., Cohn, J. F., Demirdjian, D., & Picard, R. W. (2019). Predicting ad liking and purchase intent: Large-scale analysis of facial responses to ads. *IEEE Transactions on Affective Computing, 6*(3), 223–235. DOI: 10.1109/TAFFC.2014.2384198

McStay, A. (2018). *Emotional AI: The rise of empathic media*. SAGE Publications. DOI: 10.4135/9781526451293

McStay, A. (2020). Emotional AI, soft biometrics and the surveillance of emotional life: An unusual consensus on privacy. *Big Data & Society, 7*(1), 205395172090438. DOI: 10.1177/2053951720904386

Meadi, M. R., Sillekens, T., Metselaar, S., Van Balkom, A., Bernstein, J., & Batelaan, N. (2025). Exploring the ethical Challenges of Conversational AI in Mental Health Care: Scoping review. [eXtyles37.1]. *JMIR Mental Health, 12*, e60432. DOI: 10.2196/60432 PMID: 39983102

Mehler, M., Balint, E. M., Gralla, M., Pößnecker, T., Gast, M. J., Hölzer, M., Koesters, M., & Gündel, H. (2024). Training emotional competencies at the workplace: A systematic review and metaanalysis. *BMC Psychology, 12*(1), 718. Advance online publication. DOI: 10.1186/s40359-024-02198-3 PMID: 39627880

Mehrabian, A. (1969). Significance of posture and position in the communication of attitude and status relationships. *Psychological Bulletin, 71*(5), 359–372. DOI: 10.1037/h0027349 PMID: 4892572

Mehrabi, N., Morstatter, F., Saxena, N., & Galstyan, A. (2022). A survey on bias and fairness in machine learning. *ACM Computing Surveys, 55*(6), 1–34. DOI: 10.1145/3457607

Menzies, J., Sabert, B., Hassan, R., & Mensah, P. K. (2024). Artificial intelligence for international business: Its use, challenges, and suggestions for future research and practice. *Thunderbird International Business Review, 66*(2), 185–200. DOI: 10.1002/tie.22370

Mergen, A., Çetin-Kılıç, N., & Özbilgin, M. F. (2025). Artificial Intelligence and Bias Towards Marginalised Groups: Theoretical Roots and Challenges. In *AI and Diversity in a Datafied World of Work: Will the Future of Work be Inclusive?* (Vol. 12, pp. 17-38). Emerald Publishing Limited.

Metcalf, K., Theobald, B., Weinberg, G., Lee, R., Jonsson, I., Webb, R., & Apostoloff, N. (2019, April 2). Mirroring to build trust in digital assistants. arXiv.org. https://arxiv.org/abs/1904.01664 DOI: 10.21437/Interspeech.2019-1829

Metz, R. (2020, April 2). Google demos Duplex, its an AI that sounds exactly like a very weird, nice human. MIT Technology Review. https://www.technologyreview.com/2018/06/27/141823/google-demos-duplex-its-ai-that-sounds-exactly-like-a-very-weird-nice-human/

Mhamed, M., Sutcliffe, R., & Feng, J. (2025). Benchmark Arabic news posts and analyzes Arabic sentiment through RMuBERT and SSL with AMCFFL technique. *Egyptian Informatics Journal, 29*, 100601. DOI: 10.1016/j.eij.2024.100601

Miao, C., Humphrey, R. H., & Qian, S. (2017). A meta-analysis of emotional intelligence and work attitudes. *Journal of Occupational and Organizational Psychology, 90*(2), 177–202. DOI: 10.1111/joop.12167

Mikalef, P., Krogstie, J., Pappas, I. O., & Giannakos, M. (2020). Big data analytics capabilities and firm performance: A dynamic capabilities perspective. *Information & Management, 57*(2), 103169. DOI: 10.1016/j.im.2019.05.004

Milian Eduardo Z., Mauro de M. Spinola, Marly M. de Carvalho. (2019). Fintechs: A literature review and research agenda. *Electronic Commerce Research and Applications*, 34, 100833, ISSN 1567- 4223.

Minbaeva, D. (2020). Disrupted HR? Human Resource Management in the Digital Age. *Human Resource Management Review, 30*(4), 100692.

Miner, A. S., Shah, N., & Naseer, S. (2019). NLP in HR: Applications, challenges, and future directions. *Journal of Business Research, 116*, 257–264.

Mishra, D. N., & Panda, R. K. (2023). Decoding customer experiences in rail transport service: Application of hybrid sentiment analysis. *Public Transport (Berlin), 15*(1), 31–60. DOI: 10.1007/s12469-021-00289-7

Mittal, G., & Bansal, R. (2023). Driving Force Behind Consumer Brand Engagement: The Metaverse. In *Cultural Marketing and Metaverse for Consumer Engagement* (pp. 164-181). IGI Global.

Modulos. (2024, July 4). Emotion Recognition Systems Prohibited under EU AI Act. Modulos. https://www.modulos.ai/blog/emotion-recognition-systems-prohibited-under-eu-ai-act/

Mohammad, S. M. & National Research Council Canada. (2021). Ethics Sheet for Automatic Emotion Recognition and Sentiment Analysis. In Computational Linguistics (Journal-Article No. 2; Vol. 48, p. 240). https://doi.org/ a 00433DOI: 10.1162/coli

Monteith, S., Glenn, T., Geddes, J., Whybrow, P., & Bauer, M. (2022). Commercial Use of Emotion Artificial Intelligence (AI): Implications for Psychiatry. *Current Psychiatry Reports*, *24*(3), 1–9. DOI: 10.1007/s11920-022-01330-7 PMID: 35212918

Moor, A., Zeng, X., & Li, H. (2017). Ethical implications of emotion AI in customer service: A systematic review. *Journal of Ethical AI Studies*, *4*(2), 45–57.

Mora, D., Falco, A., Annamaria Di Sipio, & Alessandro De Carlo. (2021). 4 steps for fighting covid-related anxiety: an application of virtual reality in a small company. *Psychological Applications and Trends 2021*, 287–301. DOI: 10.36315/2021inpact061

Moreno, C., Wykes, T., Galderisi, S., Nordentoft, M., Crossley, N., Jones, N., Cannon, M., Correll, C. U., Byrne, L., Carr, S., Chen, E. Y. H., Gorwood, P., Johnson, S., Kärkkäinen, H., Krystal, J. H., Lee, J., Lieberman, J., López-Jaramillo, C., Männikkö, M., & Arango, C. (2020). How mental health care should change as a consequence of the COVID19 pandemic. *The Lancet. Psychiatry*, *7*(9), 813–824. DOI: 10.1016/S2215-0366(20)30307-2 PMID: 32682460

Morley, J., Floridi, L., Kinsey, L., & Elhalal, A. (2020). From what to how: An initial review of publicly available AI ethics tools, methods, and research to translate principles into practices. *Science and Engineering Ethics*, *26*(4), 2141–2168. DOI: 10.1007/s11948-019-00165-5 PMID: 31828533

Morley, J., Floridi, L., Kinsey, L., & Elhalal, A. (2021). From what to how: An initial review of publicly available AI ethics tools, methods and research to translate principles into practices. *Science and Engineering Ethics*, *27*(4), 1–31. PMID: 31828533

Mudinas, A., Zhang, D., & Levene, M. (2012, August). Combining lexicon and learning based approaches for concept-level sentiment analysis. In *Proceedings of the first international workshop on issues of sentiment discovery and opinion mining* (pp. 1-8). DOI: 10.1145/2346676.2346681

Murtarelli, G., Gregory, A., & Romenti, S. (2021). A conversation-based perspective for shaping ethical human–machine interactions: The particular challenge of chatbots. *Journal of Business Research, 129*, 927–935. DOI: 10.1016/j.jbusres.2020.09.018

Murthy, Y. S. (2024). Mining Minds Sentiment Analysis of Public Perception. *Text Mining and Sentiment Analysis in Climate Change and Environmental Sustainability*, 61.

Murthy, Y. S., Bhatnagar, P., & Hussain, Z. (2025). Navigating Emotions Mapping Emotional Touchpoints to Enhance Customer Experience in the Digital Era. In *Demystifying Emotion AI, Robotics AI, and Sentiment Analysis in Customer Relationship Management* (pp. 129-160). IGI Global Scientific Publishing. DOI: 10.4018/979-8-3373-1867-7.ch007

Murthy, Y. S., Rabby, F., Bansal, R., & Chakravorty, C. (2025). Building Resilient Brands: Harnessing Influencers, Evangelists, and Data-Driven Strategies. In *Data Analytics and Influencer Marketing for Cultivating Brand Evangelism and Affinity* (pp. 71-102). IGI Global Scientific Publishing.

Murthy, Y. S., Sai, K. P., & Murthy, C. R. (2025). Integrating IoB in Smart Education: Innovative Approaches to Behavioral Data Analytics and Pedagogy. In *Internet of Behavior-Based Computational Intelligence for Smart Education Systems* (pp. 237-270). IGI Global.

Murthy, Y. S., Sai, K. P., & Murthy, C. R. Integrating IoB in Smart Education. *Advances in Educational Technologies and Instructional Design.*

Murthy, Y. S., Srinivas, D., BS, R. C., & Kumar, G. V. (2023). Impulse Buying in the Digital Age: A Dimensional Study on Influencer Marketing Impact on Millennials. *Journal of Advanced Zoology, 44.*

Murthy, S. Y., Chandra, B. R., & Joshi, A. (2025). Silence is not always golden: Exploring the causes and consequences of employees' silence in the IT sector. In *Digital Transformation and Sustainability of Business* (pp. 283–288). CRC Press. DOI: 10.1201/9781003606185-66

Murthy, Y. S., Bansal, R., Chodisetty, R. C. M., Chakravorty, C., & Sai, K. P. (2025). Transforming Minds AI and Machine Learning Applications in Cognitive Neuroscience. In *Transforming Neuropsychology and Cognitive Psychology With AI and Machine Learning* (pp. 107–128). IGI Global Scientific Publishing. DOI: 10.4018/979-8-3693-9341-3.ch005

Murthy, Y. S., & Chandra, R. (2024). AI Chatbots as a Catalyst for Customer Loyalty Investigating Digital Experience Preferences Across Age Groups. In *Future of Customer Engagement Through Marketing Intelligence* (pp. 143–160). IGI Global. DOI: 10.4018/979-8-3693-2367-0.ch007

Murthy, Y., Chodisetty, R. M., Padmaja, R., Reddy, V. J., & Aloori, S. (2025). Brand Evangelism in the Digital Era: The Impact of Data-Driven Influencer Marketing. In *International Conference on Leveraging Emerging Technologies and Analytics for Development* (pp. 245-261). Springer, Singapore. DOI: 10.1007/978-981-96-2548-2_13

Muthusubramanian, M., Jangoan, S., Sharma, K. K., & Krishnamoorthy, G. (2024). Demystifying explainable AI: Understanding, transparency, and trust. [eXtyles38.1]. *International Journal for Multidisciplinary Research*, *6*(2), 14597. Advance online publication. DOI: 10.36948/ijfmr.2024.v06i02.14597

Nandwani, P., & Verma, R. (2021). A review on sentiment analysis and emotion detection from text. *Social Network Analysis and Mining*, *11*(1), 81. DOI: 10.1007/s13278-021-00776-6 PMID: 34484462

Narimisaei, J., Naeim, M., Imannezhad, S., Samian, P., & Sobhani, M. (2024). Exploring emotional intelligence in artificial intelligence systems: A comprehensive analysis of emotion recognition and response mechanisms. *Annals of Medicine and Surgery (London)*, *86*(8), 4657–4663. DOI: 10.1097/MS9.0000000000002315 PMID: 39118764

Naslund, J. A., Aschbrenner, K. A., Marsch, L. A., & Bartels, S. J. (2020). The future of mental health care: Peer to peer support and social media. *Epidemiology and Psychiatric Sciences*, *29*, e38. DOI: 10.1017/S2045796020000210 PMID: 26744309

Nass, C., & Moon, Y. (2000). Machines and Mindlessness: Social responses to computers. [eXtyles39.1]. *The Journal of Social Issues*, *56*(1), 81–103. DOI: 10.1111/0022-4537.00153

Naylor, M., Morrison, B., Ridout, B., & Campbell, A. (2019). Augmented experiences: Investigating the feasibility of virtual reality as part of a workplace wellbeing intervention. *Interacting with Computers*, *31*(5), 507–523. DOI: 10.1093/iwc/iwz033

Newswire, P. R. (2024, May 15). Emotion AI market size to grow USD 13.8 billion by 2032 at a CAGR of 22.7% | Valuates reports. Yahoo Finance. https://finance.yahoo.com/news/emotion-ai-market-size-grow-145000966.html

Nguyen, T., & Bui, M. (2022). Digital empathy and AI-mediated communication: A new frontier in employee relations. *Computers in Human Behavior Reports*, *5*, 100174. DOI: 10.1016/j.chbr.2021.100174

Norman, E., & Pahlawati, E. (2024). Pengembangan kepemimpinan yang adaptif dan fleksibel: Meningkatkan ketahanan organisasi di era transformasi digital. *MES Management Journal*, *3*(1), 298–305. DOI: 10.56709/mesman.v3i1.314

Nozari, H., & Samadi, S. (2025). Digital Twin-Enhanced Sentiment Analysis for Targeted Marketing Optimization. In *Dynamic and Safe Economy in the Age of Smart Technologies* (pp. 121–138). IGI Global Scientific Publishing. DOI: 10.4018/979-8-3693-4369-2.ch008

Ntizikira, E., Wang, L., Chen, J., & Saleem, K. (2025). Enhancing IoT security through emotion recognition and blockchain-driven intrusion prevention. *Internet of Things : Engineering Cyber Physical Human Systems*, *29*, 101442. DOI: 10.1016/j.iot.2024.101442

O'neil, C. (2017). *Weapons of math destruction: How big data increases inequality and threatens democracy*. Crown.

Olawade, D. B., Bolarinwa, O. A., Adebisi, Y. A., & Shongwe, S. (2025). The role of artificial intelligence in enhancing healthcare for people with disabilities. *Social Science & Medicine*, *364*, 117560. DOI: 10.1016/j.socscimed.2024.117560 PMID: 39612748

Olawade, D. B., Wada, O. Z., Odetayo, A., David-Olawade, A. C., Asaolu, F., & Eberhardt, J. (2024). Enhancing mental health with Artificial Intelligence: Current trends and future prospects. *Journal of Medicine, Surgery, and Public Health*, *3*, 100099. DOI: 10.1016/j.glmedi.2024.100099

Onciul, R., Tataru, C.-I., Dumitru, A. V., Crivoi, C., Serban, M., Covache-Busuioc, R.-A., Radoi, M. P., & Toader, C. (2025). Artificial intelligence and neuroscience: Transformative synergies in brain research and clinical applications. *Journal of Clinical Medicine*, *14*(2), 550. DOI: 10.3390/jcm14020550 PMID: 39860555

Ooi, P., Shah, S., Xu, L., Hernandez, P., Schultz, W., & Dweck, C. (2025). Neuro-adaptive coaching with generative AI: Impacts on executive resilience. *Frontiers in Neuroscience*, *19*, 1223457. DOI: 10.3389/fnins.2025.1223457

Orlikowski, W. J., Scott, S. V., Monteiro, E., & Kallinikos, J. (2023). The digital undertow and institutional displacement: A sociomaterial approach. *Organization Theory*, *4*(2), 1–26. DOI: 10.1177/26317877231180898

Oshrat, Y., Aumann, Y., Hollander, T., Maksimov, O., Ostroumov, A., Shechtman, N., & Kraus, S. (2022). Efficient customer service combining human operators and virtual agents. arXiv preprint arXiv:2209.05226.

Ou, S. (2024). *Transforming Education: The Evolving Role of Artificial Intelligence in The Students Academic Performance*. International Journal of Education and Humanities., DOI: 10.54097/cc1x7r95

Ozay, D., Jahanbakht, M., Shoomal, A., & Wang, S. (2024). Artificial Intelligence (AI)-based Customer Relationship Management (CRM): A comprehensive bibliometric and systematic literature review with an outlook on future research. *Enterprise Information Systems, 18*(7), 2351869. DOI: 10.1080/17517575.2024.2351869

Padmanaaban, P., Rani, L. V. S., Murthy, Y. S., Khandelwal, J., Mahato, A. P., & Das, S. Work-Life Balance and Emotional Intelligence with Special Reference to Private Bank Employees.

Painoli, A. K., Bansal, R., Singh, R., & Kukreti, A. (2021). Impact of Digital Marketing on the Buying Behavior of Youth With Special Reference to Uttarakhand State. In *Big Data Analytics for Improved Accuracy, Efficiency, and Decision Making in Digital Marketing* (pp. 162-182). IGI Global. DOI: 10.4018/978-1-7998-7231-3.ch012

Pajila, P. B., Sudha, K., Selvi, D. K., Kumar, V. N., Gayathri, S., & Subramanian, R. S. (2023, July). A survey on natural language processing and its applications. In *2023 4th International Conference on Electronics and Sustainable Communication Systems (ICESC)* (pp. 996-1001). IEEE.

Palta, P., Kumar, A., & Palta, A. "Leveraging Dielectric Properties, Remote Sensing, and Sensor Technology in Agriculture: A Perspective on Industry and Emerging Technologies," in *Industry 5.0 and Emerging Technologies: Transformation Through Technology*, 2024. DOI: 10.1007/978-3-031-70996-8_5

Palta, P., & Kumar, A. (2024). Effect of vermicompost additive on physical, chemical and dielectric properties of soil and its modeling. *The Journal of Microwave Power and Electromagnetic Energy, 58*(3), 186–206. DOI: 10.1080/08327823.2024.2378668

Palta, P., & Kumar, A. (2025). Soil dielectric response to chemical fertilizers in Northern India's key agricultural areas. *Physics and Chemistry of the Earth Parts A/B/C, 137*, 103806. DOI: 10.1016/j.pce.2024.103806

Palta, P., Kumar, A., & Kaur, P. (2024). Evaluation of the impact of wastewater irrigation on the soil's dielectric parameters. *Land Degradation & Development, 35*(7), 2643–2657. DOI: 10.1002/ldr.5088

Paltoglou, G., Stefanaki, C., Chrousos, G. P., Georgiadis, I., Pavlou, M., & Nalmpanti, M. (2024). Functional MRI evidence of stress-network modulation during adaptive decision-making. *Current Neuropharmacology*, *22*(5), 976–989. DOI: 10.2174/1570159X21666230801151718 PMID: 37533249

Pang, B., & Lee, L. (2008). Opinion mining and sentiment analysis. *Foundations and Trends in Information Retrieval*, *2*(1-2), 1–135. DOI: 10.1561/1500000011

Pantic, M., & Rothkrantz, L. J. M. (2000). Automatic analysis of facial expressions: The state of the art. *IEEE Transactions on Pattern Analysis and Machine Intelligence*, *22*(12), 1424–1445. DOI: 10.1109/34.895976

Parasuraman, A., Zeithaml, V. A., & Berry, L. L. (1988). SERVQUAL: A Multiple-Item Scale for Measuring Consumer Perceptions of Service Quality. *Journal of Retailing*, *64*(1), 12–40.

Park, G., Chung, J., & Lee, S. (2022). Effect of AI chatbot emotional disclosure on user satisfaction and reuse intention for mental health counseling: A serial mediation model. [eXtyles40.1]. *Current Psychology (New Brunswick, N.J.)*, *42*(32), 28663–28673. DOI: 10.1007/s12144-022-03932-z PMID: 36406852

Park, G., Lee, S., & Chung, J. (2023). Do anthropomorphic chatbots increase counseling satisfaction and reuse intention? the moderated mediation of social rapport and social anxiety. [eXtyles41.1]. *Cyberpsychology, Behavior, and Social Networking*, *26*(5), 357–365. DOI: 10.1089/cyber.2022.0157 PMID: 37057977

Park, S., Cho, J., Park, K., & Shin, H. (2021). Customer sentiment analysis with more sensibility. *Engineering Applications of Artificial Intelligence*, *104*, 104356. DOI: 10.1016/j.engappai.2021.104356

Patel, D., & Alismail, A. (2024). Relationship between cognitive load theory, intrinsic motivation and emotions in healthcare professions education: A perspective on the missing link. *Advances in Medical Education and Practice*, *15*, 57–62. DOI: 10.2147/AMEP.S441405 PMID: 38264765

Patel, V., Saxena, S., Lund, C., Thornicroft, G., Baingana, F., Bolton, P., Chisholm, D., Collins, P. Y., Cooper, J. L., Eaton, J., Herrman, H., Herzallah, M. M., Huang, Y., Jordans, M. J. D., Kleinman, A., Medina-Mora, M. E., Morgan, E., Niaz, U., Omigbodun, O., & Unützer, J. (2018). The Lancet Commission on global mental health and sustainable development. *Lancet*, *392*(10157), 1553–1598. DOI: 10.1016/S0140-6736(18)31612-X PMID: 30314863

Pathak, A., Arya, K. V., Tiwari, V., Bhende, M., & Barsagde, N. (2024, November). Deciphering emotions: A comprehensive examination of machine learning algorithms for sentiment analysis. In *AIP Conference Proceedings* (Vol. 3214, No. 1). AIP Publishing. DOI: 10.1063/5.0239531

Patil, D. (2024). Human-Artificial Intelligence Collaboration In The Modern Workplace: Maximizing Productivity And Transforming Job Roles. *Available at SSRN* 5057414.https://dx.doi.org/DOI: 10.2139/ssrn.5057414

Pendyala, M. K., & Lakkamraju, V. V. (2024). Impact of artificial intelligence in customer journey. *International Journal of Innovative Science and Research Technology*, *9*(8), 1528–1534. Advance online publication. DOI: 10.38124/ijisrt/IJISRT24AUG807

Perry, M., Creavey, K., Arthur, E., Humer, J., Lundgren, P., & Rivera, I. (2020). Cultivating emotional intelligence in child welfare professionals: A systematic scoping review. *Child Abuse & Neglect*, *104438*, 104438. Advance online publication. DOI: 10.1016/j.chiabu.2020.104438 PMID: 32164944

Phelan, S. M., Burkhartzmeyer, H. L., Standen, E. C., Arcand, L. L., Kiker, K. M., Simiele, K. C., Proulx, A. L., Storsveen, A. S., Deng, Y., Foote, J. M., Kumbamu, A., Prakaashana, A. N., & Nelson, D. E. (2024). A virtual reality intervention to increase interracial empathy and upstander behaviors in nursing leaders. *Social Science & Medicine*, *366*(117648), 117648–117648. DOI: 10.1016/j.socscimed.2024.117648 PMID: 39740631

Picard, W. & MIT Media Laboratory. (1997). AFFECTIVE COMPUTING: CHALLENGES. https://people.cs.pitt.edu/~litman/courses/ads/readings/03.picard.pdf

Picard, R. W. (1997). A ective. *Computing*.

Picard, R. W. (1997). *Affective computing*. MIT Press. DOI: 10.7551/mitpress/1140.001.0001

Picard, R. W. (2015). Affective computing: Challenges. *International Journal of Human-Computer Studies*, *59*(1-2), 55–64. DOI: 10.1016/S1071-5819(03)00052-1

Piispanen, J. R., & Rousi, R. (2024, November). Emotion AI in Workplace Environments: A Case Study. *In International Conference on Software Business (pp. 142-148). Cham:* Springer Nature Switzerland. DOI: 10.48550/arxiv.2412.09251

Pizzoli, S. F. M., Mazzocco, K., Triberti, S., Monzani, D., Alcañiz Raya, M. L., & Pravettoni, G. (2019). User-centered virtual reality for promoting relaxation: An innovative approach. *Frontiers in Psychology*, *10*, 479. Advance online publication. DOI: 10.3389/fpsyg.2019.00479 PMID: 30914996

Plass, J. L., & Kalyuga, S. (2019). Four ways of considering emotion in cognitive load theory. *Educational Psychology Review, 31*(2), 339–359. DOI: 10.1007/s10648-019-09473-5

Pluye, P., Gagnon, M., Griffiths, F., & Johnson-Lafleur, J. (2009). A scoring system for appraising mixed-methods research and concomitantly appraising qualitative, quantitative, and mixed-method primary studies in mixed studies reviews. *International Journal of Nursing Studies, 46*(4), 529–546. DOI: 10.1016/j.ijnurstu.2009.01.009 PMID: 19233357

Pontiki, M., Galanis, D., Papageorgiou, H., Androutsopoulos, I., Manandhar, S., Al-Smadi, M., & Eryiğit, G. (2016, January). Semeval-2016 task 5: Aspect based sentiment analysis. In *International workshop on semantic evaluation* (pp. 19-30). DOI: 10.18653/v1/S16-1002

Pooja, L., & Sareen, P. J. (2025). Optimizing Workplace Happiness: Integrating Artificial Intelligence for Employee Well-Being. In *AI for Large Scale Communication Networks* (pp. 241-264). IGI Global.

Poria, S., Cambria, E., Bajpai, R., & Hussain, A. (2017). A review of affective computing: From unimodal analysis to multimodal fusion. *Information Fusion, 37*, 98–125. DOI: 10.1016/j.inffus.2017.02.003

Poria, S., Majumder, N., Mihalcea, R., & Hovy, E. (2019). Emotion Recognition in Conversation: Research Challenges, Datasets, and Recent Advances. *IEEE Access : Practical Innovations, Open Solutions, 7*, 100943–100953. DOI: 10.1109/ACCESS.2019.2929050

Portillo, P. V. (2025). The transformative role of artificial intelligence in leadership and management development: An academic insight. *Development and Learning in Organizations*. Advance online publication. DOI: 10.1108/DLO-10-2024-0301

Potapova, R. K., & Potapov, V. V. (2023). Sentiment analysis of digital communication. *Вестник Московского государственного лингвистического университета. Гуманитарные науки*, (4 (872)), 86-96.

Pradeep, A. K., Appel, A., & Sthanunathan, S. (2019). *AI for marketing and product innovation: Powerful new tools for predicting trends, connecting with customers, and closing sales*. Wiley.

Prentice, C., & Nguyen, M. (2020). Engaging and retaining customers with AI and employee service. *Journal of Retailing and Consumer Services, 56*, 102186. DOI: 10.1016/j.jretconser.2020.102186

Pretsch, E., Saretzki, J., Kraus, H., & Grossmann, G. (2020). Improving employee well-being by means of virtual reality - REALEX: An empirical case study. *European Journal of Economics and Business Studies*, *6*(1). https://revistia.com/files/articles/ejes_v6_i1_20/Pretsch.pdf

Prummer, K., Human-Vogel, S., Graham, M. A., & Pittich, D. (2024, June). The role of mentoring in developing leaders' emotional intelligence: exploring mentoring types, emotional intelligence, organizational factors, and gender. *In Frontiers in Education* (Vol. 9, p. 1393660). Frontiers Media SA. DOI: 10.3389/feduc.2024.1393660

Przegalinska, A., Ciechanowski, L., Stroz, A., Gloor, P., & Mazurek, G. (2019). In bot we trust: A new methodology of chatbot performance measures. [eXtyles42.1]. *Business Horizons*, *62*(6), 785–797. DOI: 10.1016/j.bushor.2019.08.005

Purdy, M., Zealley, J., & Maseli, O. (2019, November 18). The risks of using AI to interpret human emotions. Harvard Business Review. https://hbr.org/2019/11/the-risks-of-using-ai-to-interpret-human-emotions

Purnomo, F. A., Arifin, F., & Surjono, H. D. (2025). Utilizing virtual reality for real-time emotion recognition with artificial intelligence: A systematic literature review. *Bulletin of Electrical Engineering and Informatics*, *14*(1), 447–456. DOI: 10.11591/eei.v14i1.8847

Rabby, F., Murthy, Y. S., & Bansal, R. (2025). Brand Evangelism in the Digital Era: The Impact of Data-Driven Influencer Marketing. *Journal of Open Innovation*, •••, 100552.

Radianti, J., Majchrzak, T. A., Fromm, J., & Wohlgenannt, I. (2020). A systematic review of immersive virtual reality applications for higher education: Design elements, lessons learned, and research agenda. *Computers & Education*, *147*, 103778. DOI: 10.1016/j.compedu.2019.103778

Ragab, A., Mannan, M., & Youssef, A. (2024). "Trust Me Over My Privacy Policy": Privacy Discrepancies in Romantic AI Chatbot Apps. 2024 IEEE European Symposium on Security and Privacy Workshops (EuroS&PW), 484–495. [eXtyles43.1] DOI: 10.1109/EuroSPW61312.2024.00060

Raghav, S. V., & SM, P. (. (2024). EMOTIONAL INTELLIGENCE IN LEADERSHIP: A CROSS-CULTURAL ANALYSIS OF EMPLOYEE ENGAGEMENT AND RETENTION. ShodhKosh. *Journal of Visual and Performing Arts*, *5*(7), 338–349. DOI: 10.29121/shodhkosh.v5.i7.2024.2772

Raghvendra, K. (2024). Emotional Intelligence and Leadership Effectiveness: Navigating Decision - Making, Team Dynamics, and Organizational Success. *International Journal of Science and Research (Raipur, India), 13*(9), 1411–1416. DOI: 10.21275/SR24921211055

Rahman, K. T., Bansal, R., & Pruthi, N. (2023). Consumer adoption of technologies: A mindset-oriented approach. In *Contemporary Studies of Risks in Emerging Technology, Part B* (pp. 243-255). Emerald Publishing Limited. DOI: 10.1108/978-1-80455-566-820231013

Rahman, M. A., Ahmed, S., & Khan, T. (2020). Real-time emotion recognition systems: Applications and challenges in workplace contexts. *Journal of Intelligent Systems, 29*(3), 321–338. DOI: 10.1515/jisys-2020-0006

Rahman, M. H., Ghasemi, A., Dai, F., & Ryu, J. (2023). Review of Emerging Technologies for Reducing Ergonomic Hazards in Construction Workplaces. *Buildings (Basel, Switzerland), 13*(12), 2967. DOI: 10.3390/buildings13122967

Raisch, S., & Krakowski, S. (2021). Artificial intelligence and management: The automation–augmentation paradox. *Academy of Management Review, 46*(1), 192–210. DOI: 10.5465/amr.2018.0072

Raja, M., Swamy, T. N. V. R. L., Das, S., Bansal, R., Fahlevi, M., & Aziz, A. L. (2025). Does human resource information system influence performance management? *Cogent Business & Management, 12*(1), 2438862. DOI: 10.1080/23311975.2024.2438862

Raj, D. S. O. N. N., Nirmal, O. N., Kalaivani, A., & Kaur, K. (2023). Artificial Intelligence In E-Commerce: A Literature Review. *Artificial Intelligence, 21*(01).

Raji, I. D., & Buolamwini, J. (2019). Actionable auditing: Investigating the impact of publicly naming biased performance results of commercial AI products. *Proceedings of the 2019 AAAI/ACM Conference on AI, Ethics, and Society*, 429–435. DOI: 10.1145/3306618.3314244

Raju, A., & Raju, C. (2025). ADVANCING AI-DRIVEN CUSTOMER SERVICE WITH NLP: A NOVEL BERT-BASED MODEL FOR AUTOMATED RESPONSES.

Raman, R., Kowalski, R., Achuthan, K., Iyer, A., & Nedungadi, P. (2025). Navigating artificial general intelligence development: Societal, technological, ethical, and brain-inspired pathways. *Scientific Reports, 15*(1), 1–22. DOI: 10.1038/s41598-025-92190-7 PMID: 40069265

Rane, N., Choudhary, S., & Rane, J. (2024). Artificial intelligence, machine learning, and deep learning for sentiment analysis in business to enhance customer experience, loyalty, and satisfaction. *Available at SSRN* 4846145. DOI: 10.2139/ssrn.4846145

Rathod, S., Pinninti, N., Irfan, M., Gorczynski, P., Rathod, P., & Naeem, F. (2019). Mental health services in low and middle income countries: A perspective from India. *International Journal of Mental Health, 48*(4), 324–340. DOI: 10.1080/00207411.2019.1648031

Ravi, C. B., Donthamsetti, S., & Murthy, Y. S. A Study on Impact of Workplace Democracy on Employee Productivity in IT Companies. In *ORGANIZATION, PURPOSE, AND VALUES* (pp. 302-317). Routledge. DOI: 10.4324/9781003501374-21

Recital 18 | EU Artificial Intelligence Act.(n.d.). https://artificialintelligenceact.eu/recital/18/

Reece, A. G., Reagan, A. J., Lix, K. L., Dodds, P. S., Danforth, C. M., & Langer, E. J. (2017). Forecasting the onset and course of mental illness with Twitter data. *Scientific Reports, 7*(1), 13006. DOI: 10.1038/s41598-017-12961-9 PMID: 29021528

Reese, G., Stahlberg, J., & Menzel, C. (2022). Digital shinrin-yoku: Do nature experiences in virtual reality reduce stress and increase well-being as strongly as similar experiences in a physical forest? *Virtual Reality (Waltham Cross), 26*(3), 1245–1255. DOI: 10.1007/s10055-022-00631-9

Reeves, B., & Nass, C. (1997). The media equation: How people treat computers, television, and new media like real people and places. [eXtyles44.1]. *Choice (Chicago, Ill.), 34*(07), 34–3702. DOI: 10.5860/CHOICE.34-3702

Reez, N. (2020). Foresight-based leadership. Decision-making in a growing AI environment. In *International Security Management: New Solutions to Complexity* (pp. 323–341). Springer International Publishing., DOI: 10.1007/978-3-030-42523-4_22

Regona, V., Yigitcanlar, T., Hon, A., Teo, H., Martin-López, B., & Putra, P. (2024). Mapping artificial intelligence applications to the UN Sustainable Development Goals: A global systematic review. *Technological Forecasting and Social Change, 190*, 123878. DOI: 10.1016/j.techfore.2023.123878

Reivich, K., & Shatté, A. (2002). *The resilience factor: 7 keys to finding your inner strength and overcoming life's hurdles*. Broadway Books.

Replika. (2025). replika.com. https://replika.com/

Riches, S., Taylor, L., Jeyarajaguru, P., Veling, W., & Valmaggia, L. (2023). Virtual reality and immersive technologies to promote workplace wellbeing: A systematic review. *Journal of Mental Health (Abingdon, England), 33*(2), 1–21. DOI: 10.1080/09638237.2023.2182428 PMID: 36919828

Rickard, M., Ackermann, D., Schnitzler, M., & Kozlowski, D. (2024). Emotional Intelligence as a Component of Surgical Coaching: A Scoping Review.. *Journal of surgical education,* 82 1, 103316 . .DOI: 10.1016/j.jsurg.2024.103316

Ringeval, F., Schuller, B., Valstar, M., Cowie, R., Pantic, M., & Scherer, S. "AVEC 2017: Real-life depression, and affect recognition workshop and challenge," in *Proc. 7th IEEE International Conference on Affective Computing and Intelligent Interaction (ACII)*, 2017, pp. 561–567. DOI: 10.1145/3133944.3133953

Roberson, Q. M. (2019). Diversity and Inclusion in the Workplace: A Review, Synthesis, and Future Research Agenda. *Annual Review of Organizational Psychology and Organizational Behavior*, *6*(1), 69–88. DOI: 10.1146/annurev-orgpsych-012218-015243

Rodríguez-Ibánez, M., Casánez-Ventura, A., Castejón-Mateos, F., & Cuenca-Jiménez, P. M. (2023). A review on sentiment analysis from social media platforms. *Expert Systems with Applications*, *223*, 119862. DOI: 10.1016/j.eswa.2023.119862

Roemmich, K., Schaub, F., & Andalibi, N. (2023). Emotion AI at work: Implications for workplace surveillance, emotional labor, and emotional privacy. *CHI '23: Proceedings of the 2023 CHI Conference on Human Factors in Computing Systems*, 1–20. DOI: 10.1145/3544548.3580950

Rosca, C. M., & Stancu, A. (2024). Fusing Machine Learning and AI to Create a Framework for Employee Well-Being in the Era of Industry 5.0. *Applied Sciences* (2076-3417), 14(23). DOI: 10.3390/app142310835

Rosman, C. (2018). *Mad about Erica: why a million people use bank of America's chatbot*. American Banker., available at www.americanbanker.com/news/mad-about -erica-why-amillion-people-use-bank-of-americas-chatbot

Rukadikar, A., & Khandelwal, K. (2024). Leadership development through self-upskilling: Role of generative artificial intelligence. *Development and Learning in Organizations*, *38*(4), 27–30. DOI: 10.1108/DLO-01-2024-0005

Russell, S. J., & Norvig, P. (2021). *Artificial intelligence: A modern approach* (4th ed.). Pearson.

Ryan, M. (2020). In AI We Trust: Ethics, Artificial Intelligence, and Reliability. *Science and Engineering Ethics*, *26*(5), 2749–2767. DOI: 10.1007/s11948-020-00228-y PMID: 32524425

Sadegh-Zadeh, F., Bahrami, F., Soleimani, R., Ahmadi, M., Ramirez, M., & Chen, H. (2024). Neural correlates of data-driven decision-making in executives: An fMRI investigation. *Human Brain Mapping*, *45*(3), 1052–1068. DOI: 10.1002/hbm.26041

Sahota, N. (2024, January 22). AI and emotion: Imagining a world where machines feel. Forbes. https://www.forbes.com/sites/neilsahota/2024/01/22/ai-and-emotion-imagining-a-world-where-machines-feel/

Sajeev, S., Huang, J., Karampatziakis, N., Hall, M., Kochman, S., & Chen, W. (2021). Contextual Bandit Applications in Customer Support Bot. CoRR, abs/2112.03210. Retrieved from https://arxiv.org/abs/2112.03210

Salas, E., Shuffler, M. L., Thayer, A. L., Bedwell, W. L., & Lazzara, E. H. (2015). Understanding and improving teamwork in organizations: A scientifically based practical guide. *Human Resource Management*, *54*(4), 599–622. DOI: 10.1002/hrm.21628

Salovey, P., & Mayer, J. D. (1990). Emotional intelligence. *Imagination, Cognition and Personality*, *9*(3), 185–211. DOI: 10.2190/DUGG-P24E-52WK-6CDG

Saltz, J. S., & Dewar, N. (2019). Data science ethical considerations: A systematic literature review and proposed project framework. *Ethics and Information Technology*, *21*(3), 197–208. DOI: 10.1007/s10676-019-09502-5

Samala, N., Katkam, B. S., Bellamkonda, R. S., & Rodriguez, R. V. (2020). Impact of AI and robotics in the tourism sector: A critical insight. *Journal of Tourism Futures*, *8*(1), 73–87. DOI: 10.1108/JTF-07-2019-0065

Sánchez-Núñez, M., Patti, J., & Holzer, A. (2015). Effectiveness of a Leadership Development Program that Incorporates Social and Emotional Intelligence for Aspiring School Leaders., 1, 65-84. .DOI: 10.5296/jei.v1i1.7443

Sangwan, V., Prakash, P., & Singh, S. (2020). Financial technology: A review of extant literature. *Studies in Economics and Finance*, *37*(1), 71–88. DOI: 10.1108/SEF-07-2019-0270

Sano, A., & Picard, R. W. (2013). Stress recognition using wearable sensors and mobile phones. In *2013 Humaine Association Conference on Affective Computing and Intelligent Interaction* (pp. 671–676). IEEE. DOI: 10.1109/ACII.2013.117

Sartor, G., & Lagioia, F. Panel for the Future of Science and Technology, European Parliamentary Research Service, & Scientific Foresight Unit (STOA). (2020). The impact of the General Data Protection Regulation (GDPR) on artificial intelligence. In STOA (p. PE 641.530) [Report]. https://www.europarl.europa.eu/RegData/etudes/STUD/2020/641530/EPRS_STU(2020)641530_EN.pdf

Sasaki, S., Koyama, T., & Wada, K. (2017). Analysis of nursing care services using communication robots in a nursing home. *International Journal of Social Robotics*, *9*(4), 547–557. DOI: 10.1007/s1236901704113

Satar, M. S., Aggarwal, D., Bansal, R., & Alarifi, G. (2023). Mapping the Knowledge Structure and Unveiling the Research Trends in Social Entrepreneurship and Inclusive Development: A Bibliometric Analysis. *Sustainability (Basel), 15*(7), 5626. DOI: 10.3390/su15075626

Saviano, M., Thomas, A., Del Prete, M., Verderese, D., & Sasso, P. (2025). The impact of new generative AI chatbots on the switch point (SP): Toward an artificial emotional awareness (AEA). *European Journal of Innovation Management*. Advance online publication. DOI: 10.1108/EJIM-05-2024-0520

Schuetzler, R. M., Grimes, G. M., & Giboney, J. S. (2020). The impact of chatbot conversational skill on engagement and perceived humanness. [eXtyles45.1]. *Journal of Management Information Systems, 37*(3), 875–900. DOI: 10.1080/07421222.2020.1790204

Schuller, B. W.. (2011). Speech emotion recognition: Two decades in a nutshell, benchmarks, and ongoing challenges. *Computer Speech & Language, 27*(1), 4–37. DOI: 10.1016/j.csl.2012.02.005

Schuller, B., Batliner, A., Steidl, S., & Seppi, D. (2011). Recognising realistic emotions and affect in speech: State of the art and lessons learnt from the first challenge. *Speech Communication, 53*(9–10), 1062–1087. DOI: 10.1016/j.specom.2011.01.011

Schweidel, D. A., & Moe, W. W. (2014). Listening in on social media: A joint model of sentiment and venue format choice. *JMR, Journal of Marketing Research, 51*(4), 387–402. DOI: 10.1509/jmr.12.0424

Serrat, O. (2017). 360-Degree Feedback. In *Knowledge Solutions* (pp. 913–917). Springer.

Shahzadi, G., Jia, F., Chen, L., & John, A. (2024). AI adoption in supply chain management: A systematic literature review. *Journal of Manufacturing Technology Management, 35*(6), 1125–1150. DOI: 10.1108/JMTM-09-2023-0431

Shaikh, Z. P. (2025). Artificial Intelligence-Based Emotional Intelligence and Effective Leadership: Applications, Implications, and Ethical Bias. In *Emotionally Intelligent Methods for Meaningful Leadership* (pp. 223-254). IGI Global Scientific Publishing.

Shang, G., Low, S. P., & Lim, X. Y. V. (2023). Prospects, drivers of, and barriers to artificial intelligence adoption in project management. *Built Environment Project and Asset Management, 13*(5), 629–645. DOI: 10.1108/BEPAM-12-2022-0195

Shao, B., Cardie, C., & Hovy, E. (2020). Towards more resilient leadership: Using emotion AI to improve managerial feedback. *Proceedings of the AAAI Conference on Artificial Intelligence*, *34*(01), 566–573.

Sharma, A., Dhanka, S., Bansal, R., Kumar, A., & Maini, S. "Industry 5.0 with Sustainable Development," in *Industry 5.0 and Emerging Technologies: Transformation Through Technology*, 2024.

Sharma, P., Trivedi, A., & Murthy, Y. S. How digital marketing strategies impact the financial performance of SMEs. *Digital Transformation and Sustainability of Business*, 800-803.

Sharma, A., & Ahuja, V. (2022). Role of artificial emotional intelligence in customer engagement: An emerging area in customer service. *Journal of Relationship Marketing*, *21*(1), 45–62. DOI: 10.1080/15332667.2021.1928980

Sharma, A., Dhanka, S., Kumar, A., & Maini, S. (2024, July). A comparative study of heterogeneous machine learning algorithms for arrhythmia classification using feature selection technique and multi-dimensional datasets. *Engineering Research Express*, *6*(3), 035209. DOI: 10.1088/2631-8695/ad5d51

Sharma, A., Dhanka, S., Kumar, A., Nain, M., Dhanka, B., Bhardwaj, V. K., Maini, S., & Arora, A. S. (2025). A Systematic Review on Machine Learning Intelligent Systems for Heart Disease Diagnosis. *Archives of Computational Methods in Engineering*, •••, 1–27. DOI: 10.1007/s11831-025-10271-2

Sharma, M., & Singh, A. (2024). Embracing Technological Innovation: A Review of Hi-Tech Services in Hospitality Industry. *Evergreen*, *11*(4), 2818–2830. DOI: 10.5109/7326926

Sharma, N. A., Ali, A. S., & Kabir, M. A. (2024). A review of sentiment analysis: Tasks, applications, and deep learning techniques. *International Journal of Data Science and Analytics*, •••, 1–38.

Sharma, R., Dhanta, R., & Solomon, D. D. (2023). The Role of Emotional Intelligence in Effective Leadership and Decision-Making in Business Management. In Bhardwaj, B., Sharma, D., & Dhiman, M. (Eds.), *AI and Emotional Intelligence for Modern Business Management* (pp. 98–112). IGI Global Scientific Publishing., DOI: 10.4018/979-8-3693-0418-1.ch007

Sharma, R., & Rao, P. (2023). Emotion detection systems and conflict prediction: A machine learning perspective. *Journal of Artificial Intelligence and Soft Computing Research*, *13*(2), 89–102. DOI: 10.2478/jaiscr-2023-0006

Sharma, R., & Singh, A. (2025). Integrating AI, Green Marketing, and Influencer Strategies: Shaping Sustainable Consumer Behavior in the Digital Age. In Hussain, Z., Sharipudin, M., Albattat, A., & Khan, A. (Eds.), *Strategic Brand Management in the Age of AI and Disruption* (pp. 325–342). IGI Global Scientific Publishing., DOI: 10.4018/979-8-3693-9461-8.ch013

Sharma, V., & Desai, N. (2022). Emotion profiling in AI systems: Implications for team performance and diversity management. *Journal of Organizational Computing and Electronic Commerce*, *32*(4), 288–305. DOI: 10.1080/10919392.2022.2038345

Shen, J., & Pang, R. (2017, December 19). Tacotron 2: Generating Human-like Speech from Text. Retrieved May 25, 2025, from https://research.google/blog/tacotron-2-generating-human-like-speech-from-text/[eXtyles46.1]

Shiferaw, R. M., Kero, C. A., Mekonnin, M. B., & Amentie, C. (2024). Dynamic-capabilities-view practices of business firms: A systematic literature review. *Cogent Business & Management*, *11*(1), 2336309. DOI: 10.1080/23311975.2024.2336309

Shi, L. (2025). The integration of advanced AI-enabled emotion detection and adaptive learning systems for improved emotional regulation. *Journal of Educational Computing Research*, *63*(1), 173–201. DOI: 10.1177/07356331241296890

Shneiderman, B. (2020). Human-Centered Artificial Intelligence: Reliable, Safe & Trustworthy. [eXtyles47.1]. *International Journal of Human-Computer Interaction*, *36*(6), 495–504. DOI: 10.1080/10447318.2020.1741118

Short, J., Williams, E., & Christie, B. (1976). The social psychology of telecommunications. https://ci.nii.ac.jp/ncid/BA22930972

Shrivastava, S., Martinez, J., Coletti, D. J., & Fornari, A. (2022). Interprofessional leadership development: Role of emotional intelligence and communication skills training. *MedEdPORTAL: the Journal of Teaching and Learning Resources*, *18*, 11247. DOI: 10.15766/mep_2374-8265.11247 PMID: 35634034

Shu, L., Xie, J., Yang, M., Li, Z., Li, Z., Liao, D., Xu, X., & Yang, X. (2018). A review of emotion recognition using physiological signals. *Sensors (Basel)*, *18*(7), 2074. DOI: 10.3390/s18072074 PMID: 29958457

Simon, A., Weber, C., Braun, T., Endsley, R., Kulkarni, P., & Kassi, T. (2024). Predictive dashboards and strategic agility in manufacturing firms. *Journal of Operations Management*, *73*, 102349. DOI: 10.1016/j.jom.2024.102349

Simonite, T. (2018, October 9). Google Duplex, the Human-Sounding phone bot, comes to the pixel. WIRED. https://www.wired.com/story/google-duplex-pixel-smartphone/

Singh, H. (2024). Legal aspects of digital ethics in the age of artificial intelligence. In Balancing Human Rights, Social Responsibility, and Digital Ethics (pp. 144-167). IGI Global. DOI: 10.4018/979-8-3693-3334-1.ch005

Singh, A. (2024). Virtual Research Collaboration and Technology Application: Drivers, Motivations, and Constraints. In Chakraborty, S. (Ed.), *Challenges of Globalization and Inclusivity in Academic Research* (pp. 250–258). IGI Global., DOI: 10.4018/979-8-3693-1371-8.ch016

Singh, A., & Kumar, S. (2024). Effective Talent Management Practices Implemented in the Hospitality Sector. In Christiansen, B., Aziz, M., & O'Keeffe, E. (Eds.), *Global Practices on Effective Talent Acquisition and Retention* (pp. 126–144). IGI Global., DOI: 10.4018/979-8-3693-1938-3.ch008

Singh, A., & Rajan, K. (2021). Predictive analytics in HR: The emerging role of emotion profiling. *Asia Pacific Journal of Human Resources*, *59*(2), 213–229. DOI: 10.1111/1744-7941.12260

Singh, J., Pandey, B., Karna, S., Arora, A. S., & Kumar, A. (2024). Enhancing the thermographic diagnosis of maxillary sinusitis using deep learning approach. *Quantitative Infrared Thermography Journal*, •••, 1–15.

Singh, V., Kumar, A., Kaur, S., Bansal, A., & Singla, A. K. (2024). Enhancing cavitation erosion resistance of VC+TiC coatings with PTFE in marine environments via lasso regression optimization. *Tribology International*, *196*, 109697. DOI: 10.1016/j.triboint.2024.109697

Sinnappan, L. P., Prabhakaran, S. B., Karunakaran, R., Chinnasamy, A. K., Gopal, R., Rajan, S., & Purath, R. A. (2024). Flexing the emotional muscle: Investigating how team reflexibility shapes performance via emotional intelligence. *International Journal of Organizational Psychology*, *12*(3), 45–58. DOI: 10.59429/esp.v9i8.2869

Skjuve, M., Følstad, A., Fostervold, K. I., & Brandtzaeg, P. B. (2021). My Chatbot Companion - A study of Human-Chatbot Relationships. [eXtyles48.1]. *International Journal of Human-Computer Studies*, *149*, 102601. DOI: 10.1016/j.ijhcs.2021.102601

Smirnova, D., Spikina, A., Mezentseva, D., Vlasov, A., Astafeva, D., Berkovich, E., Kruk, L., Palevskaya, S., Shport, S., Akhapkin, R., Ashurov, Z., Khairedinova, I., Skugarevski, O., Chaplygin, S., Kolsanov, A., & Syunyakov, T. (2024). Virtual reality (vr) device with integrated biofeedback sensors (reviside) to cope with emotional burnout state among employees experiencing stress at workplace: Problem overview and action plan. *Psychiatria Danubina*, *36*(Suppl 2), 354–360. https://pubmed.ncbi.nlm.nih.gov/39378496/ PMID: 39378496

Smith-Mutegi, D., Mamo, Y., Kim, J., Crompton, H., & McConnell, M. (2025). Perceptions of STEM education and artificial intelligence: A Twitter (X) sentiment analysis. *International Journal of STEM Education, 12*(1), 1–18. DOI: 10.1186/s40594-025-00527-5

Soh, D. J. H., Ong, C. H., Fan, Q., Seah, D. J. L., Henderson, S. L., Jeevanandam, L., & Doshi, K. (2021). Exploring the use of virtual reality for the delivery and practice of stress-management exercises. *Frontiers in Psychology, 12*, 640341. Advance online publication. DOI: 10.3389/fpsyg.2021.640341 PMID: 34149524

Sood, P., Tanwar, H., Singh, J., Ruhela, A. K., Gupta, N., & Kumar, R. (2024, November). Revolutionizing Customer Service: An AI-powered Chatbot Approach using Advanced NLP Techniques. In *2024 3rd Edition of IEEE Delhi Section Flagship Conference (DELCON)* (pp. 1-5). IEEE.

Soon, L. (2025, February 28). AI Transparency and Ethics: Building customer trust in AI systems. CMSWire.com. https://www.cmswire.com/ai-technology/ai-transparency-and-ethics-building-customer-trust-in-ai-systems/

Southwick, S. M., & Charney, D. S. (2018). *Resilience: The science of mastering life's greatest challenges*. Cambridge University Press. DOI: 10.1017/9781108349246

Spielberger, C. D. (1972). Trait and state anxiety. In *Anxiety and Behavior* (pp. 3–22). Academic Press.

Sposato, M. (2024). Leadership training and development in the age of artificial intelligence. *Development and Learning in Organizations, 38*(4), 4–7. DOI: 10.1108/DLO-12-2023-0256

Sreelakshmi, S., Babu, A. A., Lakshmipriya, C., Gracious, L. A., Nalini, M., & Subramanian, R. S. (2024, October). Enhancing Intrusion Detection Systems with Machine Learning. In *2024 2nd International Conference on Self Sustainable Artificial Intelligence Systems (ICSSAS)* (pp. 557-564). IEEE. DOI: 10.1109/ICSSAS64001.2024.10760341

Stahl, B. C., Antoniou, J., Ryan, M., Macnish, K., & Jiya, T. (2022). Organisational responses to the ethical issues of artificial intelligence. *AI & Society, 37*(1), 23–37. DOI: 10.1007/s00146-021-01148-6

Standen, P. J., Brown, D. J., Taheri, M., Trigo, M. J. G., Boulton, H., Burton, A., Hallewell, M. J., Lathe, J. G., Shopland, N., Gonzalez, M. B., Kwiatkowska, G. M., Milli, E., Cobello, S., Mazzucato, A., Traversi, M., & Hortal, E. (2020). An evaluation of an adaptive learning system based on multimodal affect recognition for learners with intellectual disabilities. *British Journal of Educational Technology*, *51*(5), 1748–1765. DOI: 10.1111/bjet.13010

Stieglitz, S., Mirbabaie, M., Ross, B., & Neuberger, C. (2018). Social media analytics–Challenges in topic discovery, data collection, and data preparation. *International Journal of Information Management*, *39*, 156–168. DOI: 10.1016/j.ijinfomgt.2017.12.002

Straßmann, C., Eimler, S. C., Arntz, A., Keßler, D., Zielinski, S., Brandenberg, G., Dümpel, V., & Handmann, U. (2019). Relax yourself - using virtual reality to enhance employees' mental health and work performance. *Extended Abstracts of the 2019 CHI Conference on Human Factors in Computing Systems*, 1–6. DOI: 10.1145/3290607.3312946

Stroop, A., Stroop, T., Alsofy, S. Z., Nakamura, M., Möllmann, F., Greiner, C., & Stroop, R. (2023). Large language models: Are artificial intelligence-based chatbots a reliable source of patient information for spinal surgery? [eXtyles49.1]. *European Spine Journal : Official Publication of the European Spine Society, the European Spinal Deformity Society, and the European Section of the Cervical Spine Research Society*. Advance online publication. DOI: 10.1007/s00586-023-07975-z PMID: 37821602

Strubell, E., Ganesh, A., McCallum, A., & Green, B. (2022). Energy and policy considerations for modern deep learning research. *Communications of the ACM*, *65*(6), 112–122. DOI: 10.1145/3523355

Subha. (2024, November 8). Emotion AI in Marketing: How to Craft Campaigns that Resonate. thelightbulb.ai. https://thelightbulb.ai/blog/emotion-ai-in-marketing-how-to-craft-campaigns-that-resonate/

Subrahmanyam, S. (2024). AI integration in HR processes. In Kaur, J. (Ed.), *Embracing transhumanism and genomics in human resources management* (pp. 69–100). IGI Global Scientific Publishing. DOI: 10.4018/979-8-3693-7668-3.ch004

Subrahmanyam, S. (2024). The evolution of human resources in the age of technology. In Kaur, J. (Ed.), *Technological enhancements for improving employee performance, safety, and well-being* (pp. 229–256). IGI Global Scientific Publishing. DOI: 10.4018/979-8-3693-9631-5.ch011

Subrahmanyam, S. (2025). AI-Driven Leadership in the Modern Era for Revolutionizing Next-Generation Strategies: Organizational Impacts and Future Development. In Agnihotri, A., & Balusamy, B. (Eds.), *Leadership Paradigms and the Impact of Technology* (pp. 61–86). IGI Global Scientific Publishing. DOI: 10.4018/979-8-3693-7175-6.ch003

Subrahmanyam, S. (2025). Fostering a Collaborative Culture: The Role of Leadership. In Hussain, Z., Khan, A., Qureshi, M. A., Sharipudin, M. N. S., & Alkara, I. (Eds.), *Knowledge Sharing and Fostering Collaborative Business Culture* (pp. 377–396). IGI Global Scientific Publishing. DOI: 10.4018/979-8-3373-0710-7.ch020

Subramani, K., & Manoharan, G. (2024, June). Humanizing The Role of Artificial Intelligence in Revolutionizing Emotional Intelligence. In *2024 3rd International Conference on Computational Modelling, Simulation and Optimization (ICCMSO)* (pp. 237-242). IEEE. DOI: 10.1109/ICCMSO61761.2024.00056

Suler, J. (2016). *The psychology of the digital age: Humans become electric*. Cambridge University Press., DOI: 10.1017/CBO9781316460290

Sun, C., Qiu, X., Xu, Y., & Huang, X. (2019, October). How to fine-tune bert for text classification? In *China national conference on Chinese computational linguistics* (pp. 194–206). Springer International Publishing. DOI: 10.1007/978-3-030-32381-3_16

Sun, Y., & Zhang, Q. (2024). Navigating the Digital Transformation of Commercial Banks: Embracing Innovation in Customer Emotion Analysis. *Journal of the Knowledge Economy*, *16*(1), 1–22. DOI: 10.1007/s13132-024-01938-5

Suryanarayana Murthy, Y., Pardha Sai, K., Doss, S., & Ch Murthy Chodisetty, R. S. (2024). Navigating the Intersection of Industry 6.0, Quantum Computing, and Disaster Management: Consumer Insights and Technological Impact. In *The Rise of Quantum Computing in Industry 6.0 Towards Sustainability* (pp. 53–66). Springer. DOI: 10.1007/978-3-031-73350-5_4

Taddeo, M., & Floridi, L. (2018). How AI can be a force for good. *Science*, *361*(6404), 751–752. DOI: 10.1126/science.aat5991 PMID: 30139858

Tan, K. L., Lee, C. P., & Lim, K. M. (2023). A survey of sentiment analysis: Approaches, datasets, and future research. *Applied Sciences (Basel, Switzerland)*, *13*(7), 4550. DOI: 10.3390/app13074550

Tankelevitch, L., Kewenig, V., Simkute, A., Scott, A. E., Sarkar, A., Sellen, A., & Rintel, S. (2024). The Metacognitive Demands and Opportunities of Generative AI. *CHI '24: Proceedings of the 2024 CHI Conference on Human Factors in Computing Systems*, 1–24. DOI: 10.1145/3613904.3642902

Tan, M. C., & Lim, E. J. (2023). Emotion-centric AI and team collaboration: From profiling to conflict mitigation. *Technology in Society*, *74*, 102258. DOI: 10.1016/j.techsoc.2023.102258

Tao, J., & Tan, T. (2005). Affective computing: A review. In *International Conference on Affective Computing and Intelligent Interaction* (pp. 981–995). Springer.

Tariq, M. U. (2025). Harnessing Emotional Intelligence for Strategic Leadership: A Contemporary Approach. In Emotionally Intelligent Methods for Meaningful Leadership (pp. 197-222). *IGI Global Scientific Publishing*. DOI: 10.4018/979-8-3693-7372-9.ch009

Teece, D. J., Peteraf, M., Leih, S., & Helfat, C. (2022). Dynamic capabilities and organizational agility: Risk, uncertainty, and strategy in the new techno-economic paradigm. *California Management Review*, *64*(4), 5–33. DOI: 10.1177/00081256221109961

Thabit, S. A. (2024). Perspective chapter: Embracing the complexity of human emotion. In *Advances in Sentiment Analysis-Techniques, Applications, and Challenges*. IntechOpen.

Thaler, R. H., & Sunstein, C. R. (2008). *Nudge: Improving Decisions about Health, Wealth, and Happiness*. Yale University Press.

The IEEE Global Initiative on Ethics of Autonomous and Intelligent Systems. (2018). Ethically aligned design. In A Vision for Prioritizing Human Well-being With Autonomous and Intelligent Systems (Version 2-For Public Discussion). https://standards.ieee.org/wp-content/uploads/import/documents/other/ead_v2.pdf

Thomas, D. (2024, November 18). Raising public awareness on AI's environmental impact: Strategies and initiatives.Medium. https://medium.com/aimonks/raising-public-awareness-on-ais-environmental-impact-strategies-and-initiatives-7cdcb2ab2bb2

Thoondee, K. D., & Oikonomou, A. (2017). Using virtual reality to reduce stress at work. *2017 Computing Conference*. Institute of Electrical and Electronics Engineers. DOI: 10.1109/SAI.2017.8252142

Times, G. (n.d.). China leads in emotion recognition tech, reinforces privacy rules to tackle abuse. Copyright 2021 by the Global Times. https://www.globaltimes.cn/page/202103/1217212.shtml

Tiwari, M., Bhadoriya, M. C., Murthy, G. R. K., Goswami, M., Murthy, Y. S., & Singh, N. (2022). Examining The Effects of Factors Influencing Organizational Citizenship Behavior With Respect to IT Managers In Gujarat. *Business. Manag. Econ. Eng*, *20*(2), 2154–2167.

Torous, J., Lipschitz, J., Ng, M., & Firth, J. (2020). Dropout rates in clinical trials of smartphone apps for depressive symptoms: A systematic review and metaanalysis. *Journal of Affective Disorders, 263*, 413–419. DOI: 10.1016/j.jad.2019.11.167 PMID: 31969272

Touloudi, E., Hassandra, M., Galanis, E., Goudas, M., & Theodorakis, Y. (2022). Applicability of an immersive virtual reality exercise training system for office workers during working hours. *Sports (Basel, Switzerland), 10*(7), 104. DOI: 10.3390/sports10070104 PMID: 35878115

Tull, M. T., & Aldao, A. (2015). Editorial overview: New directions in the science of emotion regulation. *Current Opinion in Psychology, 3*, iv–x. DOI: 10.1016/j.copsyc.2015.03.009

Tuomi, M. (2022). Virtual training in the workplace. *Theseus.fi*. https://www.theseus.fi/handle/10024/748076

Tyagi, A. K., Prakash, M., & Arumugam, S. K. (2025). Emerging Era of Artificial Intelligence Based Chatbots: Is It Really Required to Today Generation? In *International Conference on Innovations in Bio-Inspired Computing and Applications* (pp. 20-33). Springer, Cham. DOI: 10.1007/978-3-031-78949-6_3

Vaidyam, A. N., Wisniewski, H., Halamka, J. D., Kashavan, M. S., & Torous, J. B. (2019). Chatbots and Conversational Agents in Mental Health: A review of the Psychiatric landscape. [eXtyles50.1]. *Canadian Journal of Psychiatry, 64*(7), 456–464. DOI: 10.1177/0706743719828977 PMID: 30897957

Valaboju, V. (2024). *AI-Driven Compliance Training in Finance and Healthcare: A Paradigm Shift in Regulatory Adherence*. International Journal For Multidisciplinary Research., DOI: 10.36948/ijfmr.2024.v06i06.30180

Vallor, S. (2016). Technology and the Virtues: a philosophical guide to a future Worth wanting. https://openlibrary.org/books/OL28687840M/Technology_and_the_Virtues

Van Doorn, J., Mende, M., Noble, S. M., Hulland, J., Ostrom, A. L., Grewal, D., & Petersen, J. A. (2017). Domo arigato Mr Roboto: Emergence of automated social presence in organizational frontlines and customers' service experiences. *Journal of Service Research, 20*(1), 43–58. DOI: 10.1177/1094670516679272

Vasilev, I. (2024). *Adapting the Future VET Curriculum in Response to Emerging Challenges: A Model for Evaluating the Impact of AI Integration in VET for Armed Conflicts and Warfare*. International Journal of Current Science Research and Review., DOI: 10.47191/ijcsrr/V7-i11-18

Vassilakopoulou, P., Haug, A., Salvesen, L. M., & Pappas, I. O. (2023). Developing human/AI interactions for chat-based customer services: Lessons learnt from the Norwegian government. *European Journal of Information Systems*, *32*(1), 10–22. DOI: 10.1080/0960085X.2022.2096490

Vaswani, A., Shazeer, N., Parmar, N., Uszkoreit, J., Jones, L., Gomez, A. N., & Polosukhin, I. (2017). Attention is all you need. *Advances in Neural Information Processing Systems*, •••, 30.

Vayena, E., Blasimme, A., & Cohen, I. G. (2018). Machine learning in health care: A critical appraisal of challenges and opportunities. *EBioMedicine*, *35*, 34–42. DOI: 10.1016/j.ebiom.2018.07.001

Veale, M., Van Kleek, M., Binns, R., & Shadbolt, N. (2023). Fairness and accountability design needs for the EU AI Act. *Computer Law & Security Review*, *48*, 105672. DOI: 10.1016/j.clsr.2023.105672

Vesala, J., Riekkinen, J., & Rankka, V. (2025).Consenting to the use of emotional data by AI-Based services.In Law, governance and technology series (pp. 125–148). DOI: 10.1007/978-3-031-80111-2_8

Vial, G., Van Wynsberghe, A., Islam, M., & Zaghloul, A. (2024). Digital twins, artificial intelligence and the reconfiguration of dynamic capabilities in Industry 4.0. *Technological Forecasting and Social Change*, *190*, 123899. DOI: 10.1016/j.techfore.2023.123899

Villegas-Ch, W. E., García-Ortiz, J., & Sánchez-Viteri, S. (2023). Identification of emotions from facial gestures in a teaching environment with the use of machine learning techniques. *IEEE Access : Practical Innovations, Open Solutions*, *11*, 38010–38022. DOI: 10.1109/ACCESS.2023.3267007

Vistorte, A. O. R., Deroncele-Acosta, A., Ayala, J. L. M., Barrasa, A., López-Granero, C., & Martí-González, M. (2024). Integrating artificial intelligence to assess emotions in learning environments: A systematic literature review. *Frontiers in Psychology*, *15*, 1387089. DOI: 10.3389/fpsyg.2024.1387089 PMID: 38966729

Vittou, F., Salamani, E., Kefis, V., & Rossidis, I. (2024). Emotional Intelligence and Its Role in the Development of Leadership Characteristics of Managers. In Organizational Behavior and Human Resource Management for Complex Work Environments (pp. 204-220). *IGI Global*. DOI: 10.4018/979-8-3693-3466-9.ch011

Wallis, A. D., & Kennedy, K. I. (2013). Leadership training to improve nurse retention. *Journal of Nursing Management*, *21*(4), 624–632. DOI: 10.1111/j.1365-2834.2012.01443.x PMID: 23410240

Wang, Z., Xie, Q., Feng, Y., Ding, Z., Yang, Z., & Xia, R. (2024). Is ChatGPT a Good Sentiment Analyzer? In *First Conference on Language Modeling*.

Wankhade, M., Rao, A. C. S., & Kulkarni, C. (2022). A survey on sentiment analysis methods, applications, and challenges. *Artificial Intelligence Review, 55*(7), 5731–5780. DOI: 10.1007/s10462-022-10144-1

Weizenbaum, J. (1976). Computer power and human reason: From judgment to calculation. W. H. Freeman & Co. https://psycnet.apa.org/record/1976-11270-000[eXtyles51.1]

Werner, C., Tapuc, G., Montgomery, L., Sharma, D., Dodos, S., & Damian, D. (2018). How Angry are Your Customers? Sentiment Analysis of Support Tickets that Escalate. 2018 1st International Workshop on Affective Computing for Requirements Engineering (AffectRE), 1–8. [eXtyles52.1]DOI: 10.1109/AffectRE.2018.00006

WHO. (2021). Ethics and governance of artificial intelligence for health: WHO guidance. World Health Organization. https://www.who.int/publications/i/item/9789240029200

WHO. (2022). World mental health report: Transforming mental health for all. World Health Organization. https://www.who.int/publications/i/item/9789240049338

Williams, G., & Riches, S. (2023). Virtual reality relaxation for staff wellbeing on a psychiatric rehabilitation ward: A feasibility and acceptability study. *Journal of Psychiatric Intensive Care, 19*(1), 51–58. DOI: 10.20299/jpi.2023.006

Wilson, H. J., & Daugherty, P. R. (2018). *Human + machine: Reimagining work in the age of AI*. Harvard Business Review Press.

Wirtz, J., Hofmeister, J., Chew, P., & Ding, X. (2023). Digital service technologies, service robots, AI, and the strategic pathways to cost-effective service excellence. *Service Industries Journal, 43*(15-16), 1173–1196. DOI: 10.1080/02642069.2023.2226596

Woebot Health. (2025, March 3). Woebot Health. https://woebothealth.com/

Wong, L. H., & Lee, D. Y. (2021). Emotional feedback systems and managerial communication: An AI-assisted approach. *Journal of Managerial Psychology, 36*(7), 594–608. DOI: 10.1108/JMP-11-2020-0642

Woods, D. (2025). AI as a Tool for Surveillance: China's Concave Trilemma. *Journal of Chinese Political Science*. Advance online publication. DOI: 10.1007/s11366-025-09907-8

World Economic Forum. (2020). *The Future of Jobs Report 2020*. https://www.weforum.org/reports/the-future-of-jobs-report-2020

World Health Organization (WHO). (2014). *Mental health: A state of wellbeing*. Retrieved from https://www.who.int/features/factfiles/mental_health/en/

Wu, S., Wang, X., Wang, L., He, D., & Dang, J. (2024). Enriching Multimodal Sentiment Analysis through Textual Emotional Descriptions of Visual-Audio Content. *arXiv preprint arXiv:2412.10460*.

Wu, J. (2024). Social and ethical impact of emotional AI advancement: The rise of pseudo-intimacy relationships and challenges in human interactions. [eXtyles53.1]. *Frontiers in Psychology*, *15*, 1410462. Advance online publication. DOI: 10.3389/fpsyg.2024.1410462 PMID: 39564589

Xu, H., & Zhang, C. (2021). The effects of AI-driven personalized marketing on consumer purchase decisions. *Journal of Interactive Marketing*, *54*, 29–42. DOI: 10.1016/j.intmar.2020.10.003

Xu, Y., Shieh, C. H., van Esch, P., & Ling, I. L. (2020). AI customer service: Task complexity, problem-solving ability, and usage intention. *Australasian Marketing Journal*, *28*(4), 189–199. DOI: 10.1016/j.ausmj.2020.03.005

Xu, Z., Liu, Z., & Luo, H. (2025). Can Artificial Intelligence Technology Help Achieving Good Governance: A Public Policy Evaluation Method Based on Artificial Neural Network. *SAGE Open*, *15*(1), 21582440251317833. DOI: 10.1177/21582440251317833

Yadav, G., Bokhari, M. U., Alzahrani, S., Alam, S., & Shuaib, M. (2025). Emotion-Aware Ensemble Learning (EAEL): Revolutionizing Mental Health Diagnosis of Corporate Professionals via Intelligent Integration of Multi-modal Data Sources and Ensemble Techniques. *IEEE Access : Practical Innovations, Open Solutions*, *1*, 11494–11516. Advance online publication. DOI: 10.1109/ACCESS.2025.3529032

Yamijala, S. M., Nimbrain, N., & Bansal, R. (2025). Enhancing Remote Workspaces: The Role of Virtual Reality in Shaping the Virtual Work Environment. *Optimizing Virtual Reality and Metaverse for Remote Work and Virtual Team Collaboration*, 171-190.

Yamijala, S. M. S., Chodisetty, R. C. M., & Chakravorty, C. (2025). Adapting HR Practices for a Transhumanist Future: An Empirical Study on Policy and Implementation. In *Enhancing the Modern Workforce Through Transhumanism* (pp. 117–146). IGI Global.

Yamijala, S. M. S., Chodisetty, R. M., Chakravorty, C., & Sai, K. P. (2025). AI-Powered Learning Revolutionizing Smart Education With Personalized Learning Styles. In *Internet of Behavior-Based Computational Intelligence for Smart Education Systems* (pp. 191–212). IGI Global.

Yamini, B., Sudha, K., Nalini, M., Kavitha, G., Subramanian, R. S., & Sugumar, R. (2023, June). Predictive modelling for lung cancer detection using machine learning techniques. In *2023 8th International Conference on Communication and Electronics Systems (ICCES)* (pp. 1220-1226). IEEE. DOI: 10.1109/ICCES57224.2023.10192648

Yang, B., Gao, Q., & Li, J. (2025). Market ambiguity, investor sentiment and market anomalies–Evidence from the Chinese A-share market. *Research in International Business and Finance*, *75*, 102721. DOI: 10.1016/j.ribaf.2024.102721

Yang, J., Chen, Z., & Zhang, X. (2019). Speech emotion recognition using deep convolutional neural network and discriminant temporal pyramid matching. *IEEE Transactions on Multimedia*, *21*(3), 687–697.

Yang, J., Zhao, Y., Han, C., Liu, Y., & Yang, M. (2022). Big data, big challenges: Risk management of financial market in the digital economy. *Journal of Enterprise Information Management*, *35*(4/5), 1288–1304. DOI: 10.1108/JEIM-01-2021-0057

Yeasmin, S., Das, S., Bhuiyan, M. F. H., Suha, S. H., Prabha, M., Vanu, N., & Hosen, A. (2025). Artificial Intelligence in Mental Health: Leveraging Machine Learning for Diagnosis, Therapy, and Emotional Well-being. *Journal of Ecohumanism*, *4*(3), 286–300. DOI: 10.62754/joe.v4i3.6640

Yin, R. K. (2017). *Case study research and applications: Design and methods.* Sage Publications.

Yun, J., & Park, J. (2022). The effects of Chatbot service recovery with emotion words on customer satisfaction, repurchase intention, and positive Word-Of-Mouth. [eXtyles54.1]. *Frontiers in Psychology*, *13*, 922503. Advance online publication. DOI: 10.3389/fpsyg.2022.922503 PMID: 35712132

Zadeh, A., Liang, P. P., Poria, S., Cambria, E., & Morency, L. P. (2018). Multimodal language analysis in the wild: CMU-MOSEI dataset and interpretable dynamic fusion graph. In *Proceedings of the 56th Annual Meeting of the Association for Computational Linguistics* (Vol. 1, pp. 2236–2246). DOI: 10.18653/v1/P18-1208

Zafeiriou, S., Hadjidimitriou, A., & Pitas, I. (2007). Facial expression recognition in image sequences using geometric deformation features and support vector machines. *IEEE Transactions on Image Processing*, *16*(1), 172–187. DOI: 10.1109/TIP.2006.884954 PMID: 17283776

Zen, M. (2024, July 1). Putting EI into AI: Emotion AI and Personalization Marketing. https://zenmedia.com/blog/emotion-ai-in-marketing/

Zeng, A., Jin, R., & Zhang, Z. (2019). Facial expression recognition via deep learning: A review. *IEEE Access : Practical Innovations, Open Solutions*, *7*, 135001–135018.

Zeng, Z., Zhang, Y., & Li, Q. (2009). Emotion recognition using deep learning techniques. *Proceedings of the International Conference on Machine Learning (ICML).*

Zhang, Y., Yang, X., Xu, X., Gao, Z., Huang, Y., Mu, S., . . . Yu, G. (2021). Affective computing in the era of large language models: A survey from the nlp perspective. *arXiv preprint arXiv:2408.04638.*

Zhang, J., Chen, Q., Lu, J., Wang, X., Liu, L., & Feng, Y. (2023). Emotional expression by artificial intelligence chatbots to improve customer satisfaction: Underlying mechanism and boundary conditions. [eXtyles55.1]. *Tourism Management*, *100*, 104835. DOI: 10.1016/j.tourman.2023.104835

Zhang, W., Li, X., Deng, Y., Bing, L., & Lam, W. (2022). A survey on aspect-based sentiment analysis: Tasks, methods, and challenges. *IEEE Transactions on Knowledge and Data Engineering*, *35*(11), 11019–11038. DOI: 10.1109/TKDE.2022.3230975

Zhang, W., Tang, Y., Li, S., & Reilly, T. (2024). Data governance maturity and predictive analytics performance: Evidence from cross-industry survey. *Information Systems Journal*, *34*(1), 87–115. DOI: 10.1111/isj.12369

Zhao, G., Li, Y., & Xu, Q. (2022). *From Emotion AI to Cognitive AI.* International Journal of Network Dynamics and Intelligence., DOI: 10.53941/ijndi0101006

Zhao, G., Wang, Y., Liu, Y., & Liu, J. (2021). Multimodal emotion recognition with deep learning: A survey. *IEEE Transactions on Neural Networks and Learning Systems*, *32*(11), 4795–4812. DOI: 10.1109/TNNLS.2020.3011734

Zhou, L., Gao, J., Li, D., & Shum, H. (2018, December 21). The design and implementation of XiaoIce, an empathetic social chatbot. arXiv.org. https://arxiv.org/abs/1812.08989

Zhou, Z., Lin, S., & Wang, Q. (2023). Exploring the human impact of emotion-recognition AI in HR decision-making. *AI & Society*, *38*, 771–783. DOI: 10.1007/s00146-022-01358-9

Zhu, L., Zhu, Z., Zhang, C., Xu, Y., & Kong, X. (2023). Multimodal sentiment analysis based on fusion methods: A survey. *Information Fusion*, *95*, 306–325. DOI: 10.1016/j.inffus.2023.02.028

Zhu, Y., Zhang, J., & Liang, J. (2023). Concrete or abstract: How chatbot response styles influence customer satisfaction. *Electronic Commerce Research and Applications*, *62*, 101317. DOI: 10.1016/j.elerap.2023.101317

About the Contributors

Jihene Mrabet's journey through the world of Clinical Psychology is marked by a profound passion for research and a deep understanding of human psychology with a distinguished PhD in Clinical Psychology from France and the distinction of holding two master's degrees, one in professional Clinical Psychology and the other in the intricate field of Psychopathology. Her journey of exploration and practice commenced in 2008, and it has been nothing short of a remarkable odyssey. Dr. Mrabet's commitment to the art of teaching and the noble endeavor of imparting knowledge to eager minds is evident in every facet of her work. Her areas of research are as diverse as they are vital, covering a rich tapestry of subjects, from Children and Adolescence psychology to Addiction, Health Psychology, organizational Psychology, Psychopathology, and the nuanced realm of Positive Psychology. Currently, as a Program leader of Master of Psychology at Amity University Dubai, she takes on the crucial role of nurturing the minds of future generations. Her leadership as the Head of the Center of Excellence for Research about Health and Wellbeing showcases her dedication to advancing knowledge in the field. Dr. Mrabet's commitment to community service and educational workshops knows no bounds. She delivered various workshops not only within the educational sector but also to industry collaborators about the evaluation of the professional practices, Coping with COVID 19 confinement, Communication, Mental Health at work, Personality, Stress management at work, Conflict management and Team-building... She has been a sought-after guest on prestigious platforms such as Dubai TV, Al Arabia, and MBC, where her discussions have delved into captivating topics. These conversations touch upon the unique psychological attributes of children, the transformative power of forgiveness, the profound consequences of emotional generosity on mental health, strategies for managing relationships with others, the therapeutic role of humor in our mental and physical well-being, the intriguing world of social media narcissism, the intricacies of Disaster Psychology and its impact on humanity, the significance of self-esteem and self-confidence, the enchanting world of dreams, and the intricate relationship between artificial intelligence and the challenges of education…

Soumaya Boudagga is a distinguished microbiologist and lecturer at Amity University Dubai. She holds a Bachelor's degree in Biotechnology, a Master's degree in Molecular Biology, and a PhD in Biological Sciences, specializing in Microbiology. With over eight years of laboratory experience, Dr. Boudagga has made significant contributions to Microbial Biotechnology, Genetics of Microbes, Food Microbiology, Infection Microbiology, Mycology, and Virology. Her expertise lies in isolating and identifying microbes and exploring the biotechnological applications of their bioactive molecules. She is particularly interested in sustainable biotechnology solutions, including bio-based packaging, bioremediation, and microbial enzyme applications. Dr. Boudagga has published extensively in peer-reviewed scientific journals, contributing to advancements in microbial genetics and applied mycology. Her research has been featured in leading journals, reflecting her commitment to innovation and scientific discovery.

Ridhima Sharma is an Associate Professor of Management at Vivekananda Institute of Professional Studies-Technical Campus. With a teaching and research experience of 12 years, she has contributed several articles to the journals of national & international repute and have presented papers in national and international conferences apart from authoring books. Her research interest includes Customer Relationship Management & sustainable consumer behavior. She is currently pursuing Post Doc from Amity University, Dubai.

Rohit Bansal is currently serving as an adjunct faculty at Rockford college, Sydney, Australia. With extensive expertise in organizational behaviour, marketing management, human resource management, digital marketing and emerging technologies, he has made remarkable contributions to academia and research. An accomplished author and editor, Dr. Bansal has published and edited numerous books with renowned national and international publishers. He has also actively participated in 60 conferences and seminars, presenting research findings and engaging in academic discussions. Dr. Bansal holds prestigious positions in the editoria; advisory boards of 110 national and international peer reviewed journals, reflecting his significant role in academic publishing and research dissemination. Additionally, he has been a member of advisory committees for various international conferences and has chaired multiple conference sessions. His contributions to academic and research have been widely recognized, earning him numerous awards for excellence in teaching, research and scholarly contributions.

***

Rahmath Nisha is a dedicated professional with comprehensive, hands-on experience in Human Resource Management (HRM), having successfully managed the entire employee life cycle—from recruitment and onboarding to performance management and employee engagement. She holds an MBA in Human Resource Management, where she was recognized as a Gold Medalist and awarded the title of Best Outgoing Student from Saveetha University. Her academic journey began with a Bachelor's degree in Electronics and Communication Engineering, showcasing her diverse educational foundation. Currently serving as an Assistant Professor, she combines industry expertise with academic insight to mentor and inspire the next generation of HR professionals.

A.K. Subramani is a distinguished academic with a PhD in Business Administration from Manonmaniam Sundaranar University, Tirunelveli, India. With 18 years of teaching experience, he has made significant contributions to the field of human resource management and organisational behaviour. He has an impressive publication record with 80 articles in international journals, including two papers in the ABDC-A category, eight in the ABDC-B category, three in the ABDC-C category, 30 in Scopus-indexed journals, and eight in Web of Science journals. He has served as a resource person for various training workshops on SPSS and AMOS software packages

Sasikumar D is an esteemed faculty member in the Department of Artificial Intelligence and Machine Learning at Panimalar Engineering College, Chennai. His areas of expertise include AI, machine learning, and intelligent systems. He actively contributes to both academic instruction and applied research in emerging technologies. Dr. Sasikumar is committed to nurturing innovation and technical excellence among students.

Meenakshi Gandhi has two decades of experience in teaching, research and academic administration. She has served as Dean Research and Dean of the Business school of VIPS. Prof. Gandhi is an executive alumni of the Oxford University U.K. and successfully completed the Academic Leadership Development Program (LEAP) sponsored by the Ministry of HRD, Govt. of India. She has been recognised for her achievements with the Indira Parekh 50 Women Leaders in Education award in 2018 and the 100 most dedicated professors award in 2019 by the world CSR foundation. Meenakshi Gandhi is a Professor in the School of Business Studies, in Vivekananda Institute of Professional Studies, Guru Gobind Singh Indraprastha University, Delhi. Her research interest covers marketing, entrepreneurship, sustainability and gender.

She has been involved in works on sustainable consumption and talent management and retention. She has authored and co-authored several research papers and articles in international and national journals. She has also served many international conferences including the one at Ryerson University, Toronto (2013) and the 21st Century Academic forum at Harvard (2015) as a Session Chair and many others in India. Dr. Gandhi is a noted resource person for various faculty development programs at the UGC Human Resource Development Center of Universities across India. She serves as a mentor to start-ups at various steps of their journey and has been an alumni of the Goldman Sachs Women Entrepreneurs Program. Dr. Gandhi has always been a recognised for her efforts towards advocacy of gender equality and a contributor to promotion of economic participation of women. She has organised several workshops for women in corporates on work life balance and growth. As the dean of research, she has been responsible in her institution for research initiatives and need based faculty development programs on various aspects. She is a certified assessor for quality initiatives in higher education and is associated with accreditations and assessment organisations for higher education quality enhancement across India and abroad.

S. Ida Evangeline, presently working as an Assistant Professor in the Department of Electrical and Electronics Engineering at the Government College of Engineering, Tirunelveli, Tamilnadu, India. She obtained her Bachelor’s in Electrical and Electronics Engineering from Manonmaniam Sundaranar University in 2003, and Master's in Power Systems Engineering from Anna University, Chennai, Tamilnadu, India in 2005. She completed her PhD degree in 2023 at Anna University, Chennai, Tamilnadu, India. She has published six research papers in international journals. Her current research interests include optimal power flow, renewable energy, soft computing, machine learning, and deep learning.

Elavarasi J is a faculty member in the Department of Artificial Intelligence and Data Science at Vel Tech High Tech Dr. Rangarajan Dr. Sakunthala Engineering College, Chennai. She is committed to teaching and research in areas such as AI, data analytics, and machine learning. Her academic involvement includes curriculum development and student project mentoring. She actively participates in workshops and seminars to stay current with emerging technologies.

Ranjithaa K C is an Assistant Professor with a Ph.D. in Finance from Saveetha School of Management, SIMATS. She holds dual specializations in Finance and Marketing through her MBA and has cleared TNSET in Management. With over six years of experience in teaching and research, she brings academic rigor and industry relevance to the classroom. She has presented papers at national and international conferences and authored a book titled "Management Concepts in Chanakya (2019)". Her expertise lies in blending traditional principles with modern financial insights to foster impactful learning.

Anto Gracious L. A. is a faculty member in the Department of Computer Science and Engineering at R.M.K. College of Engineering and Technology, Tamil Nadu. He holds expertise in areas such as software engineering, data structures, and emerging computing technologies. With a strong commitment to academic excellence, he actively contributes to teaching, mentoring, and curriculum development. Mr. Anto Gracious has participated in various workshops and seminars aimed at enhancing technical education

Nalini M is a distinguished faculty member in the Department of Computer Science and Business Systems (CSBS) at S A Engineering College, Chennai. Her academic expertise spans areas such as computer science, business analytics, and intelligent systems. She is actively involved in teaching, research, and mentoring students to excel in interdisciplinary domains. Dr. Nalini frequently contributes to academic events, publications, and collaborative research initiatives

José De Jesús Reyes-Sánchez, Ph.D. in senior management, has six master's degrees, in education, in management, professional soccer technique, in physical preparation, in professional soccer, in physical rehabilitation sciences, in sports sciences, as well as in coaching and integral well-being, who is a research professor at the TECNM Instituto Tecnológico Superior De Fresnillo, with more than 20 years of teaching experience, PRODEP profile and coordinator of the academic body with vast experience in conferences and workshops, currently novelist and writer.

Shobana S is a faculty member in the Department of Information Technology at R.M.K. Engineering College, Kavaraipettai, Tamil Nadu. She is passionate about teaching and guiding students in the field of information technology. Her academic interests include software development, web technologies, and data management. She actively contributes to academic activities and student mentoring at the institution

Kandregula Pardha Sai is a result Oriented Management professional with an excellent ability to collaborate with students at all levels. He thrives in challenging situations and follows innovative teaching practices to effectively manage students of various recent trends in finance sector. His primary area of interests are Finance, Commerce and Marketing

Zainab Shaikh is a postgraduate student in applied psychology with experience in clinical, research, and community mental health settings. Her work focuses on early intervention, person-centered care, and strengthening mental health systems through a blend of direct support and advocacy. She is particularly interested in how psychological research and practical experience can shape more responsive and inclusive mental health services.

Pankhuri Sharma is a dedicated counselling psychologist and expressive arts therapist, currently practicing at Vivekananda Institute of Professional Studies (VIPS). She has a deep commitment to supporting individuals in their journeys of healing and self-discovery, with a particular focus on working with college students navigating life's challenges. Ms. Pankhuri's therapeutic approach is rooted in creating safe, empathetic spaces where every story is honored and every voice is valued. Her work embraces the use of expressive arts and creative interventions to explore the complexities of human emotion, fostering resilience, authenticity, and growth. Through her practice and research, she aims to inspire hope and meaningful change in the lives of those she serves.

Amrik Singh is working as Professor in the School of Hotel Management and Tourism at Lovely Professional University, Punjab, India. He obtained his Ph.D. degree in Hotel Management from Kurukshetra University, Kurukshetra. He started his academic career at Lovely Professional University, Punjab, India in the year 2007. He has published more than 40 research papers in UGC and peer-reviewed and Scopus/Web of Science) journals. He has published 12 patents and 01 patent has been granted in the inter-disciplinary domain. Dr. Amrik Singh participated and acted as a resource person in various national and international conferences, seminars, research workshops, and industry talks. His area of research interest is accommodation management, ergonomics, green practices, human resource management in hospitality, waste management, AR VR in hospitality, etc. He is currently guiding 8Ph.D. scholars and 2 Ph.D. scholars have been awarded Ph.D.

Satya Subrahmanyam is a distinguished academic leader, researcher, and institutional strategist with over 27 years of experience in higher education, leadership, and research management. He holds two PhDs and a Postdoctoral qualification from the Polytechnic Institute of Leiria, Portugal. Currently serving as Professor and Dean (Research) at Holy Spirit University of Kaslik (USEK), Lebanon, he spearheads research initiatives that enhance academic excellence and institutional reputation. He played a pivotal role in the development of the Catholic University in Erbil, Kurdistan, where he established new departments, led research programs, and collaborated on international educational projects. As a founding member and Managing Partner of Vignan Institute of Technology and Management, India, he contributed to its transformation into a premier institution. With expertise in AI-driven business strategies, HR analytics, and leadership in technology adoption, he has published extensively, guided PhD research, and led training programs in corporate and academic settings.

Siva Subramanian R is a faculty member in the School of Computing at SRM Institute of Science & Technology, Trichy campus. He specializes in computer science domains including artificial intelligence, data analytics, and software development. With active involvement in research and teaching, he contributes significantly to academic and institutional growth

Index

A

B

C

F

H

I

L

M

N

O

P

R

S

T

V

W

www.ingramcontent.com/pod-product-compliance
Lightning Source LLC
LaVergne TN
LVHW080351011026
849161LV00009B/2266